T0183102

Lecture Notes in Computer Science 9428

Commenced Publication in 1973
Founding and Former Series Editors:
Gerhard Goos, Juris Hartmanis, and Jan van Leeuwen

More information about this series at http://www.springer.com/series/7412

Jinfeng Yang · Jucheng Yang
Zhenan Sun · Shiguang Shan
Weishi Zheng · Jianjiang Feng (Eds.)

Biometric Recognition

10th Chinese Conference, CCBR 2015
Tianjin, China, November 13–15, 2015
Proceedings

 Springer

Editors
Jinfeng Yang
Civil Aviation University of China
Tianjin
China

Jucheng Yang
Tianjin University of Science
    and Technology
Tianjin
China

Zhenan Sun
Chinese Academy of Sciences
Beijing
China

Shiguang Shan
Chinese Academy of Sciences
Beijing
China

Weishi Zheng
Sun Yat-sen University
Guangzhou
China

Jianjiang Feng
Tsinghua University
Beijing
China

ISSN 0302-9743   ISSN 1611-3349   (electronic)
Lecture Notes in Computer Science
ISBN 978-3-319-25416-6   ISBN 978-3-319-25417-3   (eBook)
DOI 10.1007/978-3-319-25417-3

Library of Congress Control Number: 2015950918

LNCS Sublibrary: SL6 – Image Processing, Computer Vision, Pattern Recognition, and Graphics

Printed on acid-free paper

Springer International Publishing AG Switzerland is part of Springer Science+Business Media
(www.springer.com)

Preface

Today, the development of hardware in information acquisition and transmission has led to information security being firmly tied up with person authentication. So far, the most reliable and convenient solution is biometric identification technology. In China, biometrics has been highlighted in many social and economic activities. For example, the high mobility of large populations has created a big demand for accurate person identification in China, and the "Internet Plus" strategy of the Chinese government has given strong impetus to biometric technology in the Internet environment. Biometrics will be integrated with the mobile Internet, cloud computing, and big data to improve information security. Certainly, it has already shown its outstanding performance in many other traditional applications. However, it cannot be denied that many biometric-based solutions also have their limitations in real situations owing to the variability of user environments.

In China, there are several scholars who have been concentrating on biometric technology, and significant contributions have recently been made in this domain. Therefore, organizing an annual conference has become a sustaining platform to bring together these talented biometric researchers and designers to share their outstanding work in this field. This helps to promote the development of the theory and application of biometrics. The Chinese Conference on Biometric Recognition (CCBR) has been successfully held in Beijing, Hangzhou, Xi'an, Guangzhou, Jinan, and Shenyang nine times since 2000. The 10th Chinese Conference on Biometric Recognition (CCBR 2015) was held in Tianjin, during November 13–15, 2015. This volume of conference proceedings contains 85 papers selected from among 120 submissions; all papers were carefully reviewed by three reviewers on average in a double-blind manner. The papers address the following topics: problems in face, fingerprint and palmprint, vein, iris, and ocular biometrics, behavioral biometrics, applications and systems of biometrics, multi-biometrics and information fusion, and other biometric recognition and processing issues.

We would like to express our sincere gratitude to all the contributors, reviewers, and Program Committee and Organizing Committee members. They made this conference a success. We also wish to acknowledge the support of the Chinese Association for Artificial Intelligence, Springer, the Civil Aviation University of China, Tianjin University of Science and Technology, and CASIA Institute of Intelligent Recognition in Tianjin for sponsoring this conference. Special thanks are due to Jianzheng Liu, Guimin Jia, Chuanlei Zhang, Yarui Zhang, Xi Zhao, Ruimin Li, and Weibing Liu for their hard work in organizing the conference.

November 2015

Jinfeng Yang
Jucheng Yang
Zhenan Sun
Shiguang Shan
Weishi Zheng
Jianjiang Feng

Organization

Advisors

Tieniu Tan	Institute of Automation, Chinese Academy of Sciences, China
David Zhang	Hong Kong Polytechnic University, SAR China
Jingyu Yang	Nanjing University of Science and Technology, China
Xilin Chen	Institute of Computing Technology, Chinese Academy of Sciences, China
Jianhuang Lai	Sun Yat-sen University, China

General Chairs

Jie Zhou	Tsinghua University, China
Yunhong Wang	Beijing University of Aeronautics and Astronautics, China
Zhenan Sun	Institute of Automation, Chinese Academy of Sciences, China
Jucheng Yang	Tianjin University of Science and Technology, China

Program Chairs

Jinfeng Yang	Civil Aviation University of China, China
Shiguang Shan	Institute of Computing Technology, Chinese Academy of Sciences, China
Weishi Zheng	Sun Yat-sen University, China
Jianjiang Feng	Tsinghua University, China

Program Committee

Caikou Chen	Yangzhou University, China
Fanglin Chen	National University of Defense Technology, China
Wensheng Chen	Shenzhen University, China
Xi Chen	Kunming University of Science and Technology, China
Zhen Cui	Huaqiao University, China
Weihong Deng	Beijing University of Posts and Telecommunications, China
Fuqing Duan	Beijing Normal University, China
Yuchun Fang	Shanghai University, China
Jufu Feng	Peking University, China
Yuqing He	Beijing Institute of Technology, China

Ran He	Institute of Automation, Chinese Academy of Sciences, China
Qingyang Hong	Xiamen University, China
Dewen Hu	National University of Defense Technology, China
Haifeng Hu	Sun Yat-sen University, China
Di Huang	Beijing University of Aeronautics and Astronautics, China
Mingxing Jia	Northeastern University, China
Wei Jia	Institute of Nuclear Energy Safety Technology, Chinese Academy of Sciences, China
Changlong Jin	Shandong University (Weihai), China
Zhong Jin	Nanjing University of Science and Technology, China
Xiaoyuan Jing	Nanjing University of Posts and Telecommunications, China
Wenxiong Kang	South China University of Technology, China
Peihua Li	Dalian University of Technology, China
Wei Li	Fudan University, China
Stan. Li	Institute of Automation, Chinese Academy of Sciences, China
Heng Liu	Hisense Multimedia R&D Center, China
Qingshan Liu	Nanjing University of Information Science and Technology, China
Yuanning Liu	Jilin University, China
Zhi Liu	Shandong University, China
Chaoyang Lu	Xidian University, China
Yuan Mei	Nanjing University of Information Science and Technology, China
Zhichun Mu	Beijing University of Science and Technology, China
Gang Pan	Zhejiang University, China
Hong Pan	Southeast university, China
Haifeng Sang	Shenyang University of Technology, China
Linlin Shen	Shenzhen University, China
Dongmei Sun	Beijing Jiaotong University, China
Taizhe Tan	Guangdong University of Technology, China
Ying Tan	Peking University, China
Zengfu Wang	Institute of Intelligent Machines, Chinese Academy of Sciences, China
Kejun Wang	Harbin Engineering University, China
Yiding Wang	North China University of Technology, China
Xiangqian Wu	Harbin Institute of Technology, China
Lifang Wu	Beijing University of Technology, China
Xiaohua Xie	Shenzhen Institutes of Advanced Technology, Chinese Academy of Sciences, China
Yuli Xue	Beijing University of Aeronautics and Astronautics, China
Gongping Yang	Shandong University, China
Wankou Yang	Southeast University, China

Xin Yang	Institute of Automation, Chinese Academy of Sciences, China
Yingchun Yang	Zhejiang University, China
Yilong Yin	Shandong University, China
Shiqi Yu	Shenzhen University, China
Weiqi Yuan	Shenyang University of Technology, China
Shu Zhan	Hefei University of Technology, China
Baochang Zhang	Beijing University of Aeronautics and Astronautics, China
Lei Zhang	Hong Kong Polytechnic University, SAR China
Yongliang Zhang	Zhejiang University of Technology, China
Zhaoxiang Zhang	Institute of Automation, Chinese Academy of Sciences, China
Cairong Zhao	Tongji University, China
Qijun Zhao	Sichuan University, China
Hong Zhen	Wuhan University, China
Huicheng Zheng	Sun Yat-sen University, China
Dexing Zhong	Xi'an Jiaotong University, China
En Zhu	National University of Defense Technology, China

Organizing Committee Chairs

Jianzheng Liu	Tianjin University of Science and Technology, China
Guimin Jia	Civil Aviation University of China, China

Organizing Committee

Chuanlei Zhang	Tianjin University of Science and Technology, China
Yarui Chen	Tianjin University of Science and Technology, China
Xi Zhao	Tianjin University of Science and Technology, China
Ruimei Li	Civil Aviation University of China, China
Weibing Lu	Civil Aviation University of China, China

Contents

Face

Fingerprint and Palmprint

Vein Biometrics

Iris and Ocular Biometrics

Behavioral Biometrics

Face

Adaptive Quotient Image with 3D Generic Elastic Models for Pose and Illumination Invariant Face Recognition

Zhongjun Wu and Weihong Deng[⊠]

School of Information and Communication Engineering, Beijing University of Posts and Telecommunications, Beijing, China
wuzhongjun1992@126.com, whdeng@bupt.edu.cn

Abstract. Large pose and illumination variations are very challenging for face recognition. In this paper, we address this challenge by combining an Adaptive Quotient Image method with 3D Generic Elastic Models (AQI-GEM). Frontal, neutral light face is re-rendered virtually under varying illumination conditions by AQI. Nearly accurate 3D models are constructed from each re-rendered image by GEM so as to virtually synthesize images under varying poses and illumination conditions. Pose-specific metrics are learnt for recognition. Experiments on Multi-PIE demonstrate that it outperforms state-of-the-art face recognition methods, with much simpler parameter tuning, and much less training data.

Keywords: Face recognition · Pose and illumination · Face re-rendering · 3D face construction

1 Introduction

Face recognition techniques have made great progress under active research these years. However, under uncontrolled circumstance, the performance of face recognition system may drop significantly affected by pose, illumination and expression variations. Pose and illumination problems are two main challenges that unconstrained face recognition encounters.

Recently, 3D Generic Elastic Models (3D GEM) [1] was proposed as a low computational but efficient 3D face modeling method which constructs near accurate 3D model from a single frontal image. GEM-based method [2][3][4] get satisfactory performance toward pose-invariant face recognition while no relevant extension about illumination problem has been made on GEM.

Quotient Image Method (QI) [5] is a classical work of frontal face re-rendering. Inspired by the ability of QI, in this paper, we combine an Adaptive Quotient Image Method (AQI) with 3D GEM (called AQI-GEM) to address the challenge of pose and illumination variations in face recognition. We modify the alignment process in QI to achieve better face re-rendering results, which we called AQI.

© Springer International Publishing Switzerland 2015
J. Yang et al. (Eds.): CCBR 2015, LNCS 9428, pp. 3–10, 2015.
DOI: 10.1007/978-3-319-25417-3_1

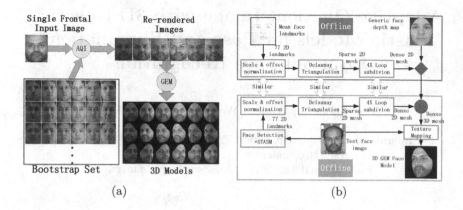

Fig. 1. (a)Visual illustration of overall off-line process. The 3D Models generated by GEM are relatively rendered at yaw $0°, -30°, +30°$ from top to bottom. (b)3D GEM face construction from a frontal face image.

The off-line process can be summarized as: Given a frontal, neutral light face image, re-render it by AQI, virtually under various illumination conditions. Construct 3D models from the re-rendered frontal images by GEM. Rotate them under different pose in order to simulate face under different poses and illumination conditions (see Fig. 1(a)). In on-line recognition, pose of probe face is estimated and an pose-specific metric learning is proposed for recognition.

This work makes three major contributions: (1)We combine Adaptive Quotient Image method with 3D GEM with to simulate faces under different poses and illumination conditions. (2)Uncertainty of illumination at the target pose can be removed by our proposed metric learning method. (3)Large-scale experiments on MultiPIE database [6] show that our AQI-GEM could outperform state-of-the-art methods on pose and illumination invariant face recognition.

2   Adaptive Quotient Image

In this section, we first review the face re-rendering part of Quotient Image method [5] and proposed our Adaptive Quotient Image.

2.1   Quotient Image

As a class of object, face can be considered as Lambertian surface with a reflectance function: $\rho(x, y)n(x, y)^T s$, $0 \leq \rho(x, y) \leq 1$ is the surface reflectance (gray-level) and $n(x, y)$ is the surface normal direction (associated with point (x, y)) in the image, and s is the point light source direction whose magnitude is light source intensity [5].

Face (frontal) is then treated in [5] as an *Ideal Class of Object*, i.e., the objects that have same shape but differ in the surface albedo. Under this

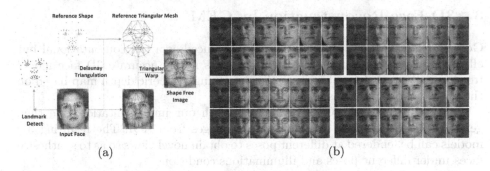

Fig. 2. (a)Visual illustration of "shape free" process in AQI. (b)Example results of re-rendered faces. First row: Ground truth images captured under specific illuminations; Second row: Corresponding re-rendered results by AQI; The result images of AQI are close to the ground truth images (close to nature).

assumption, the *Quotient Image* $Q_y(u,v)$ of object y against object a is defined: $Q_y(u,v) = \frac{\rho_y(u,v)}{\rho_a(u,v)}$, where u, v range over the image. Thus, the image Q_y depends only on the relative surface texture information and is independent of illumination. A bootstrap set containing N faces under three independent illumination (totally $3N$ images) is employed. Q_y of a input image $Y(u,v)$ can be calculated as $Q_y(u,v) = \frac{Y(u,v)}{\sum_j \bar{A}_j(u,v)x_j}$, where $\bar{A}_j(u,v)$ is the average of images under illumination j in the bootstrap set and x_j can be determined by the bootstrap set images and the input image $Y(u,v)$. The image space created by the input object y, under varying illumination, is spanned by the product of images Q_y and $\sum_j \bar{A}_j z_j$ for all choices of z_j.

2.2 Adaptive Quotient Image

The definition of *Ideal Class of Object* in QI can not be well satisfied in by the "roughly" alignment way in [5] (the center of mass was aligned and scale was corrected manually). Therefore, we modify the face alignment process to almost entirely meet the *Ideal Class of Objects* definition, as is described below.

(1) "Shape Free": 77 corresponding 2D facial landmarks (detected by STASM [7]) of all the bootstrap set images and input image are aligned to the same positions, that is to say, the distinct shapes of different faces are transformed to a reference shape (see Fig. 2(a) for detail). Quotient Image method is then applied on the "shape free" images for face re-rendering.

(2) "Reference Shape" back to "Distinct Shape": The re-rendered images have to be transformed to the original shape of that object. This procedure is in inverse process of "shape free", transforming the reference mesh to the distinct mesh of the input object.

Fig. 2(b) shows example results of faces re-rendered by AQI . Ground truth images refer to frontal images captured under specific illumination conditions. The result images of AQI are close to ground truth images.

3   3D Face Reconstruction by GEM

Generic Elastic Models (GEM) [1] was introduced as a low computational but efficient 3D modeling method which generates nearly accurate 3D face model from a single frontal face by elastically deforming a generic depth map based on the (x, y) spatial positions of the input face.

Fig. 1(b) shows the GEM framework with our implementation. We then generate 3D GEMs from the re-rendered images from AQI. The resulting 3D models can be rendered at different poses to obtain novel views so as to synthesize faces under different poses and illuminations conditions.

Why the face image under specific illumination at non-frontal view point can be synthesized by the 3D models that is constructed from the frontal faces (same object) under corresponding illumination, rendered at the same pose?

As is mentioned, face can be represented as Lambertian surface with the function: $\rho(x, y)n(x, y)^T s$. No variable in this formula will be affected by altering the view point. That is to say, under the specific illumination condition, the intensity of a certain vertex on a face will not change when altering the view point. Therefore, the constructed 3D models under different illuminations virtually can be rendered at different poses to synthesize faces under different poses and various illumination conditions.

4   Face Recognition via Pose-Specific Metric

The recognition task requires us to match a non-frontal input image under unknown illumination to the corresponding identity in the database. The galleries are 3D models virtually under different illuminations constructed from the frontal, neutral light face images of all identities by AQI-GEM.

4.1   Pose Estimation and Alignment

Given an input non-frontal face, five facial fiducial landmarks are automatically located by using SDM [8], including two eyes center, tip of the nose, two corners of the mouth. A linear regression framework, enlightened by the face 3D Alignment process in [9], is employed to make pose estimation based on the five landmarks. This method provides a weak pose estimation. However, experimental results shows that it still assures reasonable recognition rates.

Each 3D model in the database is rendered at the estimated pose and 2D images are synthesized after 2D projection. The virtually rendered images and probe image are aligned by a affine transformation, in order to compensate for scaling and in-plane rotation, using two eyes and midpoint of two mouth corners. Specifically, faces are aligned to 65×75 pixels with eyes position of $(15, 20)$ and $(50, 20)$ and midpoint of mouth corners position of $(32.5, 60)$ (see Fig. 3(a)).

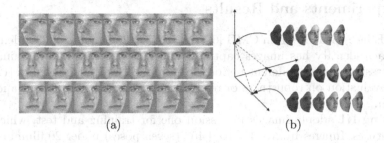

(a)   (b)

Fig. 3. (a)Aligned faces of quantized poses (yaw $-50°$ to $+50°$ in step of $5°$) (b)The geometric interpretation of a metric space at the yaw $45°$ pose. Three groups of rendered images with varying lightings are mapped to $[1; 0; 0]^T$,$[0; 1; 0]^T$,$[0; 0; 1]^T$ respectively.

4.2 Recognition via Pose-Specific Metric

The 3D continuous pose space can be divided into limited number of quantized poses. For example, one could be sampled along the yaw with a range of ±90 degrees at steps of 5 degrees (see Fig. 3(a)). At each quantized poses, we render the 3D models with virtually varying illumination of each gallery subject as the training set, and learn a transformation matrix W_p by which the illumination subspace of each subject (at this pose) is mapped to the corresponding class indicator vector. Fig. 3(b) illustrates a geometric interpretation of this mapping at the yaw pose of $45°$. The purpose of this mapping is to eliminate the illumination uncertainty at this pose by mapping the illumination subspace to a single point. At the same time, this mapping could enhance the discrimination between similar faces by mapping them to equidistant targets.

This method is termed "Linear Regression of an Indicator Matrix" in [10], and optimal mapping matrices are readily computed by the least-square regression. Specifically, to minimize the sum of square error, the optimal transformation matrix can be computed as: $W_p = Y X_p^\dagger$, derived from the mapping equation: $Y = W_p X_p$, where $X^\dagger$ denotes the generalized inverse of X, X is the stacked feature vectors of all rendered images at the pose p, Y is the corresponding stacked class indictor vectors.

For automatic recognition, we estimate the pose of the probe image using head pose estimator, index the nearest quantized pose p, and recognize the image using the corresponding Pose-Specific Metric (called **pose quantization strategy**). The response vector y is derived by a linear transformation: $y = W_p x$, where x is the feature vector of probe face, and the recognition result is determined by the largest component of the response vector y. Also, another strategy called **pose quantization plus search range** can be defined as using the corresponding Pose-Specific Metrics of the most two nearest quantized pose to determine the recognition result.

5   Experiments and Results

MultiPIE face database from CMU [6] contains 754,204 images of 337 identities, where each identity has images captured under 15 poses and 20 illuminations in four sessions during different periods. **Setting-III** was introduced in [11][12], for the evaluation on robustness of recognition algorithms across pose and illumination.

Setting-III adopts images in session one for training and test, which has 249 identities. Images from $-45°$ to $+45°$ (seven poses) under 20 illuminations (marked as ID 00-19) are used. Images of first 100 identities are for training, and the images of the remaining 149 identities for test. During test, one frontal image of each identity in the test set is selected in the gallery. The remaining images from $-45°$ to $+45°$ except $0°$ are selected as probes. All images that we selected were converted to gray scale.

For AQI-GEM, the frontal image under illumination marked as ID 07 of each identity in the test set is chosen in the gallery (the input image of our AQI method). We empirically select frontal images of 12 identities from the first 100 identities (id 001, 002, 007, 008, 011, 012, 016, 019, 025, 026, 042, 047), under illuminations marked as ID 00-19 except 07, as the bootstrap set in AQI. Such small size bootstrap set is sufficient to achieve reasonable re-rendering results. The feature that we extract from the rendered images and probe image is LBP.

Our experiments compare the AQI-GEM to three existing state-of-the-art pose and illumination invariant methods. (1)Li [11] represents a test face as a linear combination of training images, and utilizes the regularized linear regression coefficients as features for face recognition. (2)**RL+LDA** [12] first reconstructs the frontal-view face images using FIP features extracted from an image under any pose and illumination, and then applies LDA to further enhance class separation. (3)**CPF** [13] is a recent work which can rotate an arbitrary pose and illumination image to a target-pose face image by multi-task deep neural network.

We have tested three pose strategies: (1)Matching against true pose (assuming that true pose is pre-known); (2)Matching by **pose quantization** strategy; (3)Matching by **pose quantization plus search range** strategy.

5.1   Results

Table. 1 and Table. 2 report results of **Setting III**. The recognition rate under a pose is the averaged result over all the possible illuminations (marked as id 00-19, 07 excluded). Similarly, the recognition rate under one illumination condition is the averaged result of all possible poses ($-45° \sim +45°$, $0°$ excluded).

The overall recognition rate of PS ♯2 is just 0.3% lower than that of PS ♯1, indicating that our pose estimator is reliable and performance won't be affected significantly by the slight error between true pose and estimated pose.

PS ♯1 achieves best performance under $-15°$, $+15°$, $+30°$, indicating that, under small angles (deviating from frontal), using the true pose gets best performance. It is noticed that PS ♯3 boost the performance of PS ♯1 under $45°$ by

Table 1. Average Recognition Rate (Percent) on Different Poses under **Setting-III**. The Best Performance Are in **Bold**. Pose Strategy is as **PS** for simplification.

Methods	$-45°$	$-30°$	$-15°$	$+15°$	$+30°$	$+45°$	Avg.
Li [11]	63.5	69.3	79.7	75.6	71.6	54.6	69.3
RL [12]+LDA	67.1	74.6	86.1	83.3	75.3	61.8	74.7
CPF [13]	73.0	81.7	89.4	89.5	80.4	70.3	80.7
AQI-GEM (PS ♮1)	76.5	88.3	**98.5**	**99.2**	95.4	84.3	90.4
AQI-GEM (PS ♮2)	76.3	89.5	97.0	98.3	94.1	85.1	90.1
AQI-GEM (PS ♮3)	**79.0**	**90.3**	97.0	98.3	94.7	**87.4**	**91.1**

Table 2. Average Recognition Rate (Percent) on Different Illuminations conditions under **Setting-III**. The Best Performance Are in **Bold**. Pose Strategy is as **PS** for simplification.

Methods	00	01	02	03	04	05	06	08	09	10
Li [11]	51.5	49.2	55.7	62.7	79.5	88.3	97.5	97.7	91.0	79.0
RL [12]+LDA	72.8	75.8	75.8	75.7	75.7	75.7	75.7	75.7	75.7	75.7
CPF [13]	59.7	70.6	76.3	79.1	85.1	89.4	91.3	92.3	90.6	86.5
AQI-GEM (PS ♮1)	85.7	**78.0**	82.3	**87.8**	92.5	96.0	98.7	99.0	97.4	95.1
AQI-GEM (PS ♮2)	85.8	75.1	81.3	87.1	93.0	96.7	99.1	99.0	**98.0**	95.0
AQI-GEM (PS ♮3)	**87.4**	76.4	**82.7**	87.7	**94.7**	**97.1**	**99.4**	**99.6**	98.0	**95.5**
	11	12	13	14	15	16	17	18	19	Avg.
Li [11]	64.8	54.3	47.7	67.3	67.7	75.5	69.5	67.3	50.8	69.3
RL [12]+LDA	75.7	75.7	75.7	73.4	73.4	73.4	73.4	72.9	72.9	74.7
CPF [13]	81.2	77.5	72.8	82.3	84.2	86.5	85.9	82.9	59.2	80.7
AQI-GEM (PS ♮1)	89.0	83.0	75.3	**93.3**	94.7	95.6	95.3	92.7	85.2	90.4
AQI-GEM (PS ♮2)	88.6	81.3	76.5	92.0	94.7	95.2	94.7	93.0	85.1	90.1
AQI-GEM (PS ♮3)	**89.8**	**84.1**	**77.7**	92.7	**95.3**	**96.9**	**95.9**	**94.9**	85.8	91.1

an average margin of 2.8%, showing that strategy of **pose quantization plus search range** works well under large angles.

The overall performance of AQI-GEM PS ♮3, 91.1%, is around 10% better than that of the state-of-the-art [13], which clearly validates the superiority of AQI-GEM, for the reason that frontal, neutral light images are re-rendered by AQI realistically, faces under different poses and illumination conditions virtually can be synthesized, and illumination uncertainty is removed at the target pose.

6 Conclusion

Identifying subjects with variations caused by different poses and illumination conditions is an extremely challenging problem in face recognition, since the appearance and texture difference caused by poses and illumination conditions is difficult to model. In this paper, we make adaption on Quotient Image method (called Adaptive Quotient Image, AQI) to achieve more natural results on face re-rendering. We combine AQI with GEMs in order to virtually synthesize images under different poses and illumination conditions. A pose-specific metric learning method is also proposed to remove illumination uncertainty at the target pose. Experiments on MultiPIE database show that our AQI-GEM achieves state-of-the-art recognition rates, with extremely simple parameter tuning and few training data, compared to other methods.

Acknowledgments. The authors would like to thank the anonymous reviewers for their thoughtful and constructive remarks that are helpful to improve the quality of this paper. This work was partially sponsored by supported by the Fundamental Research Funds for the Central Universities under Grant No. 2014ZD03-01, NSFC (National Natural Science Foundation of China) under Grant No. 61375031, No. 61471048, and No.61273217. This work was also supported by the Beijing Higher Education Young Elite Teacher Program, and the Program for New Century Excellent Talents in University.

References

1. Heo, J.: Generic Elastic Models for 2D Pose Synthesis and Face Recognition. Ph.D thesis, Department of Electrical and Computer Engineering, Carnegie Mellon University (2009)
2. Prabhu, U., Heo, J., Savvides, M.: Unconstrained pose-invariant face recognition using 3d generic elastic models. J. IEEE Transactions on PAMI **33**(10), 1952–1961 (2011)
3. Heo, J., Savvides, M.: Gender and ethnicity specific generic elastic models from a single 2d image for novel 2d pose face synthesis and recognition. J. IEEE Transactions on PAMI **34**(12), 2341–2350 (2012)
4. Moeini, A., Moeini, H.: Real-World and Rapid Face Recognition Toward Pose and Expression Variations via Feature Library Matrix. J. Information Forensics and Security **10**(5), 969–984 (2015)
5. Shashua, A., Riklin-Raviv, T.: The quotient image: Class-based re-rendering and recognition with varying illuminations. J. IEEE Transactions on PAMI **23**(2), 129–139 (2001)
6. Gross, R., Matthews, I., Cohn, J., et al.: Multi-pie. J. Image and Vision Computing **28**(5), 807–813 (2010). Elsevier
7. Milborrow, S., Nicolls, F.: Active shape models with sift descriptors and MARS. J. VISAPP **1**(2), 5 (2014)
8. Xiong, X. De la Torre, F.: Supervised descent method and its applications to face alignment. In: IEEE Conference on Computer Vision and Pattern Recognition (CVPR), pp. 532–539 (2013)
9. Taigman, Y., Yang, M., Ranzato, M.A., et al.: Deepface: Closing the gap to human-level performance in face verification. In: 2014 IEEE Conference on Computer Vision and Pattern Recognition (CVPR), pp. 1701–1708 (2014)
10. Hastie, T., Tibshirani, R., Friedman, J., et al.: The elements of statistical learning. Springer, New York (2009)
11. Li, A., Shan, S., Gao, W.: Coupled bias-variance tradeoff for cross-pose face recognition. J. Image Processing **21**(1), 305–315 (2012)
12. Zhu, Z., Luo, P., Wang, X., et al.: Deep learning identity-preserving face space. In: 2013 IEEE International Conference on Computer Vision (ICCV), pp. 113–120 (2013)
13. Jung, J.Y.H., Yoo, B.I., Choi, C., et al.: Rotating Your Face Using Multi-task Deep Neural Network (2015)

Low Rank Analysis of Eye Image Sequence – A Novel Basis for Face Liveness Detection

Chengyan Lin, Yuwu Lu, Jian Wu, and Yong Xu[✉]

Bio-computing Research Center, Shenzhen Graduate School,
Harbin Institute of Technology, Shenzhen, People's Republic of China
CYLin2011@gmail.com, {yuwulu2008,wujianhitsz}@163.com,
laterfall@hitsz.edu.cn

Abstract. The security of the face recognition technology has attracted more and more attention because of the wide applications of this technology. A lot of studies on face liveness detection have been performed. In this paper, we cast the face liveness detection problem as a classification problem to distinguish the images of true faces and photo samples based on the rank analysis of sample matrices. We assume that the rank of the true face sample matrix is much higher than that of the photo sample matrix under an ideal situation. If we denoise the real world samples and convert them into pure samples, we can find a well boundary, that is, a basis for liveness detection. Experiments are conducted on the NUAA imposter database to verify the efficiency of the proposed method.

Keywords: Face liveness · Eye sequence · Low rank · Classification basis

1 Introduction

The face recognition technology is one of the most popular biometrics technologies in pattern recognition field [1-3]. More and more attentions have been paid to the safety of the face recognition system. Face liveness detection has become an important means to identify the cheating behaviors to the face recognition system. The ways of cheating 2D face recognition systems include using the photo and the short video of an authorized user to spoof the system [4]. The photo attack seems to be the easiest and cheapest cheating approach because facial images of users are easily available.

Many methods to resist the photo attack have been proposed. These methods can be classified from different perspectives. Some methods perform the face liveness detection using only one single facial image. Most of such methods detect photo attacks by analyzing the texture features of the captured facial images. The most widely used texture feature is the local binary pattern (LBP) [5]. Määttä J et al. [6] used the multi-scale LBP of one single facial image for face liveness detection. The individual histograms produced by the multi-scale LBP were combined into a concatenated feature histogram. Finally, the obtained feature histogram was used for classification by a nonlinear SVM classifier. LBP can also combine with other features such as frequency [7] and local shape [8]. However, LBP has its inherent weaknesses: noise-sensitive and weak performance in flat regions [9]. Such drawbacks would be

© Springer International Publishing Switzerland 2015
J. Yang et al. (Eds.): CCBR 2015, LNCS 9428, pp. 11–18, 2015.
DOI: 10.1007/978-3-319-25417-3_2

amplified when the attacking photo with high quality. For example, the light reflection on a high resolution photo will not generate obvious reflective stripe which can be captured by frequency or texture analysis.

Other methods make a decision by analyzing a continuous image sequence of one's face or some facial parts. The optical flow field based methods differentiate liveness and photo by analyzing four types of optical flow field generated by 2D and 3D objects. There are some existing optical flow algorithms [10, 11]. In the facial part analysis methods, eye area is the most popular area that has been discussed because of eye-blink. In [12], the authors adopted a motion magnification operation before liveness detection to improve the facial expressions from one's video sequence. LBP is still an important technique for the algorithm in [12]. In [13], the authors constructed a Conditional Random Field (CRF) framework to model eye-blink behaviors. In addition, they used a discriminative measure of eye states to improve the classification performance. The complexity of the image sequences based methods is higher than that of the one single image based methods.

Face liveness detection plays an important role to ensure the security of a face recognition system during the recognition stage. Considering the safety of the whole recognition process and the computation and preprocessing cost, the eye image sequence is a good target for liveness detection research.

In this paper, we cast the face liveness detection problem as a problem of classification for matrices. We argue that the matrices ranks of the liveness and photo samples are different. The rank of the liveness sample matrix is much higher than that of the photo sample matrix under an ideal situation. If we denoise the real world samples and revert them to pure samples, we can find a well boundary, that is, a basis for liveness detection. We conduct a series of experiments to verify the classification performance of the obtained basis.

2   Motivations

One sample is consisted by an eye image sequence. Assume that there is a dataset $X=\{X_1, X_2, ..., X_c\}$ which contains c samples from the same class. X_i $(0<i\leqslant c)$ includes γ_i eye images. Each eye image in X_i is resized into a vector, and stack these vectors as columns of a matrix

$$X_i = [x_1, x_2, ..., x_{\gamma_i}], \gamma_i > 0 \tag{1}$$

where x_i represents the ith frame of X_i, and the length of X_i, that is, the number of frames in X_i.

In the face liveness detection task, there are two kinds of samples: photo and liveness. In the ideal situation, frames in a photo sample are with little differences, which produces a low-rank of the photo sample matrix. Besides, the rank of a liveness sample matrix is much higher because of the facial movements (such as blink). Fig. 1 takes several images of the liveness and photo samples from the NUAA database for example to explain the motivation visually.

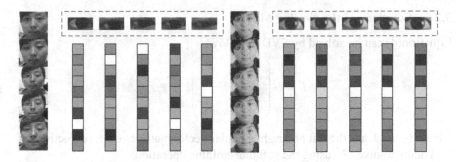

Fig. 1. An example of the representation of liveness and photo samples.

We can obtain the conclusion that there exist a threshold or a boundary θ_1 about rank to differentiate liveness samples from photo samples. Let ω_1 be the set of liveness samples and ω_0 the set of photo samples. The classification rules can be defined as follow:

$$\Phi(X) = \begin{cases} X \in \omega_1, & rank(X) \geq \theta_1 \\ X \in \omega_0, & rank(X) < \theta_1 \end{cases}.$$ (2)

If the rank of X_i satisfies the condition that $rank(X_i) \geq \theta_1$, we consider X_i as a liveness sample and vice versa. If the lengths of the samples are different, we should divide the rank of each sample by its length for equalization. In this case, $rank(X_i)$ can be rewritten as $rank(X_i) / Y_i$.

3   Proposed Method

3.1   Sample Noising Model

We assume that the photo sample matrix has a low rank. However, most of the samples we obtained in reality are not of low rank. Thus, we consider that there exist noises which increase some small eigenvalues to the matrices of the real samples. Suppose that the sample noising model is

$$A = L + N,$$ (3)

where A denotes the real world sample matrix, L is a low-rank sample matrix, and N is an additive Gaussian white noise with standard deviation σ. The smaller the norm of N is, the closer A gets to L, which means that the outcome fits the ideal situation.

According to (3), there exists an optimal solution of L. We adopt a matrix denoising scheme to solve the optimal solution of L:

$$L^* = \arg\min_L \frac{1}{2}\|A - L\|_F^2 + \lambda \|L\|_*,$$ (4)

where $\|L\|_*$ denotes the nuclear norm of a matrix, i.e., sum of singular values. λ is a hyper-parameter to balance the square loss function and the regulation function.

3.2   Solutions of the Noising Model

Equation(4) can be solved by SVD as follow:

$$L^* = U \begin{pmatrix} \lambda_1^* & & \\ & \ddots & \\ & & \lambda_n^* \end{pmatrix} V^T \tag{5}$$

where U and V are the left and right singular vector matrices of A, respectively.

Then we solve λ_i^* using the soft thresholding operation:

$$\lambda_i^* = \max(|\lambda_i| - \lambda, 0)sign(\lambda_i), \tag{6}$$

where λ_i is the singular value of A, and λ is the hyper-parameter mentioned in (4). Since λ_i is always positive, Eq.(6) can be simplified as

$$\lambda_i^* = \max(|\lambda_i| - \lambda, 0). \tag{7}$$

After the thresholding operation, $rank(L^*)$ is just the number of non-zero singular values λ_i^*.

The physical interpretation of λ is the standard deviation of the noise σ. To estimate λ, we adopt the following adaptive strategy

$$\lambda = \theta_1 \sum_{i=1}^{r} \lambda_i, \tag{8}$$

or

$$\lambda = \theta_1 \|A\|_* . \tag{9}$$

As the energy weight of the noise in the noisy data, θ_1 can be learned or trained by minimizing the training error.

3.3   Basis for Classification

Once θ_1 is given, the distributions of ranks of two classes of samples are available. Then a classification boundary θ_2 (or decision surface) can be set by either Bayes rule or k-means clustering. Fig. 2 simulates the distribution of two classes and their classification boundary with a given θ_1.

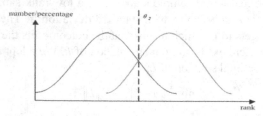

Fig. 2. A simulation of the distribution of two classes and their classification boundary with a given θ_1. The blue bell curve represents the photo samples and the red one the liveness samples. Assume that the samples from one single class form a normal distribution.

A Bayesian minimal error rate can be solved, that is, $ER(\theta_1)$ is essentially dependent on θ_1. Thus, θ_1 can be determined by:

$$\theta_1 = \arg\min_{\theta} ER(\theta) \tag{10}$$

The solution of (10) can be solved by enumerating.

3.4   The Proposed Algorithm

Given an image set of the liveness or photo samples, there are two part of searching for the classification basis. The first part is to preprocess the sample set and obtain the relative data about its singular values which to be used in the second part. The second part is to enumerate an optimal boundary between two types of data with a given θ_1.

The preprocess of a sample set:

- Given a set of one type of sample sequences $A=\{A_1, A_2, \ldots, A_c\}$
- For each $A_i \in A$
  1) Transfer a sequence into a matrix
  $$A_i = [a_1, a_2, \ldots, a_{\gamma_i}], \gamma_i > 0$$
  2) Do SVD to A_i, and obtain its singular values $\{\lambda_1, \lambda_2, \ldots, \lambda_r\}$
  3) Sum the singular values of A_i using $s_{A_i} = \sum_{j=1}^{r} \lambda_j$
- Obtain a data set about class A, $S_A = \{s_{A_1}, s_{A_2}, \ldots, s_{A_c}\}$

The process of training a classification basis between two sample classes with a given $(0 < \theta_1 < 1)$:

- Given two preprocessed data set of different classes
  $$S_A = \{s_{A_1}, s_{A_2}, \ldots, s_{A_c}\} \text{ and } S_B = \{s_{B_1}, s_{B_2}, \ldots, s_{B_d}\}$$
- Estimate the λ of every sample, then we have $E_A = \theta_1 S_A$ and $E_B = \theta_1 S_B$
- Enumerate an optimal boundary between E_A and E_B: θ_2

Within the range of θ_1, we are able to find an optimal value. The θ_2 connected with the optimal θ_1 value produces a minimum Bayesian minimal error rate. The specific θ_1 and the corresponding θ_2 form a basis for classification of face liveness detection.

4   Experiments

In order to verify the feasibility of our method, we did experiments on the NUAA imposter database [13]. The target of our experiments is the eye areas of the pictures of the database. We detected the eye areas of the pictures in the same size of 32×16. Due to the symmetry of eyes in a face, we just need to consider the left-eye image sequences.

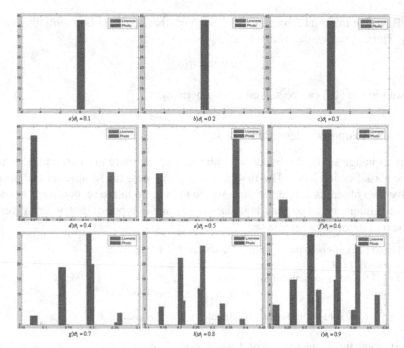

Fig. 3. Histograms of E_A and E_B with the increase of θ_1 when the length of samples is 15. The histograms in red are from liveness samples, while those in blue are from photo samples.

The NUAA imposter database includes 15 subjects. The images of this database are collected in three sessions. The first session is the only session which involves all the subjects. This session contains no special location and light conditions which needs extra preprocess such as image alignments. Moreover, our experiments focus on the feasibility of the classification basis in general cases. Thus, we paid most of our attention to the first session in the experiments.

There are 9 subjects involved in the first session of the database. The length of each sequence from a subject in a certain session is about 100 or more. In our tests, we observed the effect of θ_1 under a fixed length of samples. In the experiments, θ_1 is increased by 0.1 from 0.1 to 0.9 under a fixed length.

Let E_A and E_B be the super-parameter set of liveness and photo samples, respectively. Fig. 3 is the histograms of E_A and E_B when the length of the samples is 15. With the increase of θ_1, the difference between liveness and photo samples is becoming more and more apparent. Especially, Fig. 3(i) fits Fig. 2 very well. When the samples of liveness and photo can be well divided, most of the values in E_A is larger than those in E_B.

Due to the Frames per Second (FPS) of the general web camera is 15 at least and 60 at most, we can fix the length of image sequence between 15 and 60 in practice.

Table 1. The error rate for different sequence length (θ_1=0.90).

Sequence length	10	15	20	25	30	35	40	45	50	55	60	65
Error rate	0.28	0.22	0.23	0.16	0.16	0.12	0.11	0.10	0.11	0.12	0.13	0.13

Table. 1 shows the error rate for different sequence length. Given a fixed θ_1, the change of the error rates obtained with different lengths of the samples is steady. When the length of the samples is above 30, the error rate would fluctuate around some value. Thus, we can make a conclusion that the performance of our method is independent with the length of the samples. When the length of a sample is too short, the dimension of the sample matrix is not enough to produces a comparable rank.

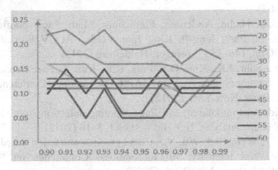

Fig. 4. The error rate for different sequence length when the range of θ_1 is from 0.90 to 0.99.

We narrow the range of θ_1 from 0.9 to 0.99 according to the conclusion of Fig. 3. The error rates for different sequence lengths are shown in Fig. 4. When the length of sequences is small, the error rate drops obviously with the increase of θ_1. The overall error rates tend to be smaller with the increase of θ_1.

5   Conclusion

In this paper, we analyzed the differences between liveness and photo sample matrices, and argued that the matrices ranks of the liveness and photo samples can be used to distinguish the images of true faces and photo samples. We found a boundary which can be seen as a basis for liveness detection during the process of denoising the real world samples. Such a novel basis is related to the matrices ranks of the samples. Through the experiments, we verified that the obtained basis is able to classify liveness and photo samples.

Acknowledgments. This work was supported in part by the National Natural Science Foundation of China uder Grant 61370163, and the Shenzhen Municipal Science and Technology Innovation Council under Grant JCYJ20130329151843309, Grant JCYJ20140904154630436 and Grant CXZZ20140904154910774.

References

1. Wright, J., Yang, A., Ganesh, A., Sastry, S., Ma, Y.: Robust face recognition via sparse representation. IEEE Trans. Pattern. Anal. Mach. Intell. **31**, 210–227 (2009)
2. Zhang, Z., Xu, Y., Yang, J., Li, X.L., Zhang, D.: A survey of sparse representation: algorithms and applications. IEEE Access **3**, 490–530 (2015)
3. Xu, Y., Zhang, D., Yang, J., Yang, J.Y.: A two-phase test sample sparse representation method for use with face recognition. IEEE Trans. Circ. Syst. Video Technol. **21**, 1255–1262 (2011)
4. Nixon, K.A., Aimale, V., Rowe, R.K.: Spoof detection schemes. In: Jain, A.K., Flynn, P., Ross, A.A. (eds.) Handbook of biometrics, pp. 403–423. Springer, US (2008)
5. Ojala, T., Pietikäinen, M., Mäenpää, T.: Multiresolution gray-scale and rotation invariant texture classification with local binary patterns. IEEE Trans. Pattern. Anal. Mach. Intell. **24**, 971–987 (2002)
6. Komulainen, Jukka, Hadid, Abdenour, Pietikäinen, Matti: Face spoofing detection using dynamic texture. In: Park, Jong-Il, Kim, Junmo (eds.) ACCV Workshops 2012, Part I. LNCS, vol. 7728, pp. 146–157. Springer, Heidelberg (2013)
7. Kim, G., Eum, S., Suhr, J.K., Kim, D.I., Park, K.R., Kim, J.: Face liveness detection based on texture and frequency analyses. In: IAPR International Conference on Biometrics, pp. 67–72. IEEE Press, New York (2012)
8. Maatta, J., Hadid, A., Pietikäinen, M.: Face spoofing detection from single images using texture and local shape analysis. IET Biometrics **1**, 3–10 (2012)
9. Xu, J., Ding, X.Q., Wang, S.J, Wu, Y.S.: Background subtraction based on a combination of texture, color and intensity. In: International Conference on Signal Processing, pp. 1400–1405. IEEE Press, New York (2008)
10. Barron, J., Fleet, D., Beauchemin, S.: Performance of optical flow techniques. Int. J. Comput. Vis. **12**, 43–77 (1994)
11. Fleet, D., Jepson, A.: Computation of component image velocity from local phase information. Int. J. Comput. Vis. **5**, 77–104 (1990)
12. Bharadwaj, S., Dhamecha, T.I., Vatsa, M., Richa, S.: Computationally efficient face spoofing detection with motion magnification. In: Proceedings of IEEE Conference on Computer Vision and Pattern Recognition Workshops, pp. 105–110. IEEE Press, New York (2013)
13. Pan, G., Sun, L., Wu, Z.H., Lao, S.H.: Eyeblink-based anti-spoofing in face recognition from a generic webcamera. In: Proceedings of the 11th IEEE International Conference on Computer Vision, pp. 1–8 IEEE Press, New York (2007)

Non-negative Compatible Kernel Construction for Face Recognition

Yang Zhao, Wensheng Chen, Binbin Pan$^{(\boxtimes)}$, and Bo Chen

College of Mathematics and Statistics, Shenzhen Key Laboratory of Media Security,
Shenzhen University, Shenzhen 518060, China
{chenws,pbb,chenbo}@szu.edu.cn

Abstract. The existing Kernel Nonnegative Matrix Factorization (KNMF) cannot ensure the non-negativity of the mapped data in the kernel feature space. This is called the nonnegative in-compatible problem of KNMF. To tackle this problem, this paper presents a new methodology to construct Nonnegative Compatible Kernel (NC-Kernel) for face recognition. We obtain a Nonnegative Nonlinear Mapping (NN-Mapping) by using the techniques of symmetric NMF and nonnegative interpolation strategy. The symmetric function generated by the NN-Mapping is proven to be a nonnegative compatible Mercer kernel function. We apply the NC-Kernel to the Kernel Principle Component Analysis (KPCA) and KNMF for face recognition. The ORL and Pain Expression face databases are selected for evaluations. Experimental results indicate our NC-Kernel based methods outperform some RBF or polynomial kernel based algorithms.

Keywords: Kernel Nonnegative Matrix Factorization · Nonnegative nonlinear mapping · Face recognition

1 Introduction

Face recognition technologies have been extensively developed in the past decades. One of the challenges for face recognition is the extraction of robust facial features. PCA [1] and NMF [2–5] are the classical methods for feature extraction. PCA aims to reduce the dimensionality of sample by extracting the principal component. It projects the sample along the directions where the variance is largest. NMF aims to express the facial images using the nonnegative linear combination of part-based images. It decomposes the sample matrix into two nonnegative matrices, that is the basis matrix and coefficient matrix. The non-negativity of NMF is natural to reflect the intuition of combining the parts to form a whole.

PCA and NMF are linear methods. However, the facial images are always nonlinearly distributed due to complicated variations such as illumination, facial expression, pose and occlusion. The linear methods cannot discover the nonlinear structure of the facial images. In order to extract nonlinear facial features,

© Springer International Publishing Switzerland 2015
J. Yang et al. (Eds.): CCBR 2015, LNCS 9428, pp. 19–26, 2015.
DOI: 10.1007/978-3-319-25417-3_3

the kernel methods are widely used. The idea of kernel methods is to map the samples into a high dimensional space $\mathcal{F}$ via a nonlinear mapping φ firstly, then the classical linear methods are used in $\mathcal{F}$. The dimensionality of $\mathcal{F}$ could be very large, even infinite. A kernel function can be used to characterize the inner product in $\mathcal{F}$, which could potentially reduce the computational costs. The common kernel functions are radial basis function (RBF) and polynomial kernel function. Recently, several KNMF algorithms have been developed [6–8,13] and successfully applied to face recognition. They aim to represent the mapped facial images as nonnegative linear combinations of basis in $\mathcal{F}$. Nevertheless, these KNMF methods cannot guarantee that the images of the implicit nonlinear mappings are nonnegative in $\mathcal{F}$. For example, [13] can only ensure the non-negativity of the pre-images and coefficients. So, the kernel functions are in-compatible under nonnegative constraints.

To address the nonnegative compatible problem of KNMF methods, this paper proposes a novel methodology to construct a Nonnegative Compatible Kernel (NC-Kernel) for face recognition. At first, a kernel matrix K is generated upon the training samples. Then K is decomposed by Symmetric NMF (SNMF) [9] to obtain a nonlinear mapping, which is nonnegative and well-defined on the training samples. The interpolation strategy is utilized to non-negatively extend the nonnegative nonlinear mapping to the whole sample space. The constructed NC-kernel function is proven to be a valid Mercer kernel based on the kernel theory [10,11] and successfully applied to some kernel based algorithms for face recognition. Experimental results indicate the high performance of the proposed NC-kernel function.

The rest of the paper is organized as follows: Section 2 proposes our nonnegative compatible kernel. In section 3, the proposed nonnegative compatible kernel is applied to face recognition. Section 4 draws the conclusions.

2   Nonnegative Compatible Kernel Construction

This section proposes a method to construct a nonnegative compatible kernel using SNMF and interpolation. The training sample set $\mathcal{X} = \{x_1, \cdots, x_n\}$. The dimension of the training sample is m. And the training sample matrix is denoted as $X = [x_1, x_2, \cdots, x_n] \in \mathbb{R}_+^{m \times n}$, where $\mathbb{R}_+$ denotes the set of nonnegative real numbers.

2.1   Symmetric NMF

This subsection will briefly introduce symmetric NMF algorithm. Details can be found in literature [9]. Given a nonnegative symmetric and positive semi-definite matrix $K \in \mathbb{R}_+^{n \times n}$, SNMF finds a nonnegative matrix $P \in \mathbb{R}_+^{n \times r}$ such that

$$K \approx PP^T.$$

The beta divergence is selected to measure the errors between K and $\hat{K}$

$$D_\beta(\hat{K}\|K) = \sum_{ij}[\hat{K}_{ij}\frac{\hat{K}_{ij}^\beta - K_{ij}^\beta}{\beta(\beta+1)} + K_{ij}^\beta\frac{K_{ij} - \hat{K}_{ij}}{\beta+1}]$$

$$= \sum_{ij}[\frac{\hat{K}_{ij}^{\beta+1}}{\beta+1} - \frac{K_{ij}^\beta}{\beta}\hat{K}_{ij} + \frac{\hat{K}_{ij}^{\beta+1}}{\beta(\beta+1)}]$$

The optimization problem becomes:

$$\min_{P\geq 0} D_\beta(PP^T\|K) \tag{1}$$

The update rules of P can be obtained by coordinate descent method:

$$P_{nk} \leftarrow P_{nk} \sqrt[2\beta+1]{\frac{(K^\beta P_{nk})}{[(PP^T)^\beta P]_{nk}}}, \tag{2}$$

where $K^\beta \triangleq (K_{ij}^\beta)_{N\times N}$, $(PP^T)^\beta \triangleq [(PP^T)_{ij}^\beta]_{N\times N}$.

2.2   Nonnegative Interpolatory Basis Function Construction

We construct n nonnegative interpolatory basis functions $L_i(x)$ as follows

$$L_i(x) = \frac{\gamma_i(x)}{\sum_j \gamma_j(x)} \tag{3}$$

where $\gamma_i(x) = \prod_{p\neq i}\|x - x_p\|, p = 1, 2, \cdots, n, x \in R^m$. It can be easily seen that $\gamma_i(x)$ has the following property:

$$\gamma_i(x) = \begin{cases} \prod_{p\neq i}\|x_i - x_p\|, & x = x_i \\ 0, & x \in X\backslash\{x_i\}. \end{cases}$$

Thus, the interpolatory basis function $L_i(x)$ satisfies that:

$$L_i(x_p) = \begin{cases} 1, p = i \\ 0, p \neq i \end{cases}, \text{ for all } x_p \in X.$$

From (3), we see that basis function $L_i(x)$ is bounded and its range is in the internal $[0, 1]$. For convenience, we denote a interpolatory basis vector function $L(x)$ as follow:

$$L(x) = [L_1(x), L_2(x), \cdots, L_n(x)]^T. \tag{4}$$

2.3   Nonnegative Compatible Kernel Construction

The kernel matrix K is computed by the RBF kernel upon the training sample set $\mathcal{X}$:

$$K_{ij} = k_{RBF}(x_i, x_j) = \exp(\frac{-\|x_i - x_j\|^2}{t}), \tag{5}$$

where $t > 0$. The matrix K is a symmetric and positive semi-definite matrix. By performing SNMF on K, we have $K \approx PP^T \in \mathbb{R}_+^{n \times n}$, where

$$P^T = [p_1, p_2, \cdots, p_n]. \tag{6}$$

A nonlinear mapping φ is defined on the training sample set $\mathcal{X}$ by

$$\varphi(x_i) = p_i, i = 1, 2, \cdots, n.$$

To extend the nonnegative nonlinear mapping to the whole sample space $\mathbb{R}^m$, we use the interpolatory technique. In details, we denote the nonnegative nonlinear mapping φ as follows:

$$\varphi(x) = P^T \cdot L(x), \quad x \in \mathbb{R}^m \tag{7}$$

where $L(x)$ is the nonnegative interpolatory basis vector function defined by (4) and matrix P is computed by (6). Then, the function $k(x, y)$ is denoted by:

$$k(x, y) = \langle \varphi(x), \varphi(y) \rangle,$$

where $\langle \varphi(x), \varphi(y) \rangle$ is the inner product of $\varphi(x)$ and $\varphi(y)$. It can be directly got that

$$k(x, y) = L^T(x) K L(y). \tag{8}$$

In order to show that the function $k(x, y)$ is a Mercer kernel which is defined by (8), the following lemma is used.

Lemma 1. *[10] If $k(x, y)$ is a symmetric function defined on $\mathbb{R}^m \times \mathbb{R}^m$, and for any finite data set, it always yields a symmetric and positive semi-definite matrix $K = (K_{ij})_{n \times n}$, where $K_{ij} = k(y_i, y_j), i, j = 1, 2, \cdots, n$, then function $k(x, y)$ is a Mercer kernel function.*

Theorem 1. *The function $k(x, y) = L^T(x) K L(y)$, $x \in \mathbb{R}^m$, $y \in \mathbb{R}^m$, is a Mercer kernel function, where $L(\cdot)$ and K are defined by (4) and (5) respectively.*

Proof. It is obvious that function $k(x, y)$ is apparently a symmetric function. So it is only to show that the Gram matrix G which is yielded by $k(x, y)$ on any finite training data is a positive semi-definite matrix. For any finite training sample set $\{y_l | l = 1, 2, \cdots, N\} \subset \mathbb{R}^m$, the Gram matrix G can be computed as $G = [k(y_l, y_s)]_{N \times N}$. If we denote matrix L_N by $L_N = [L(y_1), L(y_2), \cdots, L(y_N)]_{n \times N}$, then Gram matrix G can be rewritten as $G = L_N^T K L_N$. For any column vector $\alpha \in R^n$, we have

$$\alpha^T G \alpha = (L_N \alpha)^T K (L_N \alpha) \geq 0,$$

using the fact that K is a positive semi-definite matrix. So we can infer that the matrix G is a symmetric and positive semi-definite matrix. The theorem is concluded from Lemma 1 immediately.

We see that the nonlinear mapping defined in (7) is nonnegative. So the proposed kernel in (8) is nonnegative compatible.

3   Experimental Results

In this section, the proposed method will be performed in two face databases. Our nonnegative nonlinear mapping will be used in KPCA [12] and KNMF, named NCKPCA and NCKNMF, respectively. The compared algorithms are KPCA (RBF kernel) and PNMF (polynomial kernel). In KPCA and NCKPCA, we keep the eigenvectors whose eigenvalues are large than 0.001. In PNMF and NCKNMF, the maximal number of iteration is 800. The parameters in SNMF are set as $\beta = 1$, and the maximal number of iteration is 500. The degree of the polynomial kernel is set as $d = 0.5$ in KNMF-based methods. In KPCA-based methods, the parameters of RBF kernel function is set as $t = 5 \times 10^3$. The whole database is randomly divided into training set and test set. The accuracy is computed using nearest neighbor classifier. The experiments are repeated 10 times and the average accuracies are recorded.

3.1   Experiments on ORL Database

In the ORL database, there are 400 gray images with 40 persons. Each person has 10 images with different poses and expressions. Images from one person are shown in Figure 1. The size of each image is 112×92. So the dimensionality of the sample is 10304. We use the wavelet transformation to reduce the dimensionality of the image from 10304 to 750. The dimensionality of the extracted feature in NMF-based methods is 350. We randomly select n ($n = 2, 3, \cdots, 9$) images from each person for training, while the rest $(10 - n)$ images of each individual are for testing.

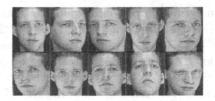

Fig. 1. Images of one person from ORL database.

The results are shown in Table 1 and Figure 2. It is noted that NCKPCA is superior to KPCA and NCKNMF outperforms PNMF. This indicates that the nonnegative compatible kernel is more suitable for face recognition.

3.2   Experiments on Pain Expression Database

This database is a subset of Psychological Image Collection at Stirling (PICS). There are 84 gray images with 12 women. Each woman has 7 images with different expressions such as happy, sad, surprised and doubtful. The images have

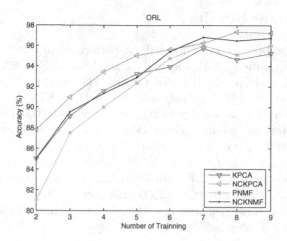

Fig. 2. Recognition rate on ORL face database.

Table 1. Mean accuracy (%) versus Training Number (TN) on ORL database.

TN	2	3	4	5	6	7	8	9
KPCA	85.00	89.14	91.58	93.25	93.94	95.75	94.63	95.25
PNMF	81.00	87.50	90.00	92.35	94.75	96.00	95.13	96.00
NCKPCA	**87.81**	**90.96**	**93.42**	**95.05**	**95.63**	96.25	**97.38**	**97.25**
NCKNMF	85.03	89.54	91.33	92.90	95.44	**96.83**	96.50	96.75

variations in open/close eyes and open/close mouths. Images from two persons are shown in Figure 3. The size of the original image is 181×241. Thus the dimensionality of each image is 43621. The dimensionality of each image is reduced to 2914 after the wavelet transformation. In NMF-based methods, the dimensionality of the extracted feature is 350. We arbitrarily select n ($n = 2, 3, \cdots, 6$) images from each individual for training, while the rest $(7 - n)$ images of each individual are for testing.

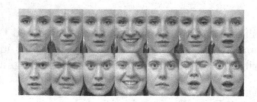

Fig. 3. Images of two persons from pain expression database.

The results are reported in Table 2 and Figure 4. It can be seen that NCK-PCA is superior to KPCA and NCKNMF outperforms PNMF. The recognition rate of NCKPCA increases from 83.00% with training number 2 to 94.17% with training number 6, and the recognition rate of NCKNMF increases from 85.83% with training number 2 to 94.17% with training number 6 respectively. The methods with nonnegative compatible kernel still perform better than other methods.

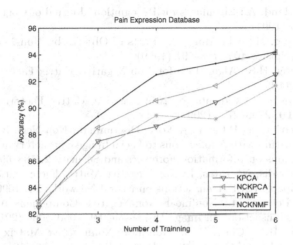

Fig. 4. Recognition rate on pain expression face database.

Table 2. Mean accuracy (%) and standard deviation versus Training Number (TN) on pain expression database.

TN	2	3	4	5	6
KPCA	82.50	87.50	88.61	90.42	92.50
PNMF	82.83	86.67	89.44	89.17	91.67
NCKPCA	83.00	88.54	90.56	91.67	**94.17**
NCKNMF	**85.83**	**89.37**	**92.50**	**93.33**	**94.17**

4   Conclusions

In this paper, we propose a methodology to construct nonnegative compatible kernel. It is generated by making use of the SNMF and interpolation strategy. We also obtain the explicit expression of the nonlinear mapping which ensures the non-negativity of the mapped samples. The nonnegative compatible kernel is used to KPCA and KNMF. Experimental results on ORL and pain expression databases demonstrate the superiority of our methods.

Acknowledgments. This paper is partially supported by NSF of China (61272252, 61472257) and Science & Technology Planning Project of Shenzhen City (JCYJ2013 0326111024546) and the Special Fund of the Central Finance for the Development of Local Universities (000022070152). We would like to thank Olivetti Research Laboratory and University of Stirling (pics.stir.ac.uk) for providing the face image databases.

References

1. Turk, M., Pentland, A.: Eigenfaces for Recognition. Journal of Cognitive Neuroscience **3**, 71–86 (1991)
2. Lee, D.D., Seung, H.S.: Learning the Parts of Objects by Non-Negative Matrix Factorization. Nature **401**, 788–791 (1999)
3. Lee, D.D., Seung, H.S.: Algorithms for Non-Negative Matrix Factorization. NIPS **13**, 556–562 (2001)
4. Lin, C.J.: Projected Gradients for Non-Negative Matrix Factorization. Neural Computation **19**, 2756–2779 (2007)
5. Kotsia, I., Zafeiriou, S., Pitas, I.: A Novel Discriminant Non-Negative Matrix Factorization Algorithm with Applications to Facial Image Characterization Problems. IEEE Transactions on Information Forensics and Security **2**, 588–595 (2007)
6. Buciu, I., Nikolaidis, N., Pitas, I.: Non-Negative Matrix Factorization in Polynomial Feature Space. IEEE Transactions on Neural Networks **19**, 1090–1100 (2007)
7. Zafeiriou, S., Petrou, M.: Nonlinear Non-Negative Component Analysis Algorithms. IEEE Transactions on Image Processing **19**, 1050–1066 (2010)
8. Pan, B.B., Lai, H.L., Chen, W.S.: Nonlinear Nonnegative Matrix Factorization Based on Mercer Kernel Construction. Pattern Recognition **44**(10–11), 2800–2810 (2011)
9. Shi, M., Yi, Q., Lv, J.: Symmetric Nonnegative Matrix Factorization with Beta-Divergences. IEEE Signal Processing Letters **19**, 539–542 (2012)
10. Schölkopf, B., Smola, A.J.: Learning with Kernels-Support Vector Machine, Regularization, Optimization, and Beyond. The MIT Press, Cambridge, MA (2002)
11. Shawe-Taylor, J., Cristianini, N.: Kernel Methods for Pattern Analysis. Cambridge University Press, Cambridge (2004)
12. Schölkopf, B., Smola, A., Müller, K.R.: Nonlinear Component Analysis as a Kernel Eigenvalue Problem. Neural Computation **10**, 1299–1319 (1998)
13. Zhu, F., Honeine, P., Kallas, M.: Kernel Nonnegative Matrix Factorization without the Curse of the Pre-Image. arXiv preprint, arXiv:1407.4420 (2014)

3D Face Recognition Using Local Features Matching on Sphere Depth Representation

Hanchao Wang, Zhichun Mu$^{(\boxtimes)}$, Hui Zeng, and Mingming Huang

School of Automation and Electrical Engineering,
University of Science and Technology Beijing, Beijing 100083, China
{wanghanchao314,hzeng,mmhuang1205}@163.com, mu@ies.ustb.edu.cn

Abstract. This paper proposes a 3D face recognition approach using sphere depth image, which is robust to pose variations in unconstrained environments. The input 3D face point clouds is first transformed into sphere depth images, and then represented as a 3DLBP image to enhance the distinctiveness of smooth and similar facial depth images. An improved SIFT algorithm is applied in the following matching process. The improved SIFT algorithm employs the learning to rank approach to select the keypoints with higher stability and repeatability instead of manually rule-based method used by the original SIFT algorithm. The proposed face recognition method is evaluated on CASIA 3D face database. And the experimental results show our approach has superior performance than many existing methods for 3D face recognition and handles pose variations quite well.

Keywords: 3D face recognition · Sphere depth image · Local binary patterns · Learning to rank

1 Introduction

The face has its own advantages over other biometrics for human recognition, since it is natural, nonintrusive, and contactless. Using 3D face scans has been proposed as an alternative solution to conventional 2D face recognition approaches, which is more robust to pose and lighting variations. However, there are still questions worth studying in 3D face recognition in real world application. In this paper, we propose a method of dealing with 3D face recognition in unconstrained scene.

1.1 Related Work

The task of recognizing 3D face scans has been approached in many ways, leading to varying levels of successes [1]. Global-based recognition uses the entire face region to compute similarity. E.g., PCA [2], LDA [3] and ICP-based matching [4]. Facial surface shape descriptors can be used in the face recognition, too. Such as curvature [5], point signature [6], Extended Gaussian Image (EGI) [7] signed shape-difference map [8] and eLBP [9] etc. These holistic methods usually need an accurate normalization step with respect to pose and scale changes.

© Springer International Publishing Switzerland 2015
J. Yang et al. (Eds.): CCBR 2015, LNCS 9428, pp. 27–34, 2015.
DOI: 10.1007/978-3-319-25417-3_4

To improve the face recognition performances of various post changes in unconstraint scenes, some studies using multiple multi-view images to identify human faces [10]. Liu et al [11] use the spherical fitting point cloud data to convert 3D data to 2D depth image. This conversion keeps complete three-dimensional structural information, transforming the post changes to rotation changes.

1.2   Motivation and Approach Overview

In a conventional face recognition experiment, both the probe and gallery scans are acquired cooperatively in a controlled environment so as to precisely capture and represent the whole face [12]. Differently, in semi-cooperative or uncooperative scenarios, probe scans are acquired under unconstrained conditions that may result in face scans with post variations or partial data, thus demanding for methods capable of performing recognition in unconstraint condition.

In this paper, we first establish the spherical representation of the 3D human face using a sphere fitting algorithm. 3D face shape is then represented as sphere depth image. Using 3DLBP Depth Face [9] generated on depth image, we apply SIFT [13] descriptors to the sphere 3DLBP image for the detection of keypoints. In order to extract keypoints with more repeatability and robustness, learning to rank [14] algorithm is adopted to the keypoints extraction. Proposed method is tolerant of face pose variations and gains higher recognition rates when compared with other 3D face recognition methods. The general framework is illustrated in Fig. 1.

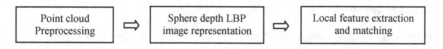

Fig. 1. General framework of proposed method

The paper can be summarized as follows: Section 2 describes the point cloud preprocessing and the sphere depth image generation. In section 3, we introduce the local features matching on sphere LBP depth image utilizing learning to rank strategy. The experimental results are provided in section 4. Section 5 concludes the paper.

2   Generation of Sphere Depth Image

The basic assumption is that the shape of human head can be viewed as a ball. Sphere depth image of 3D face shape is an object-centered shape representation using data-fitting Algorithm. This object-centered representation is uncorrelated with pose variation which is very appropriate in uncooperative scenarios.

A 3D face shape is fitted on a sphere through a linear least square method [11] to get the optimal solution of sphere parameters. After the sphere center and radius is acquired, the sphere depth r is defined as the distance between the point and the sphere surface. Then the Cartesian coordinates of input point clouds can be transformed to spherical coordinates $[r, \theta, \rho]$ .The points in spherical coordinates then can construct a sphere depth image using interpolation on θ and ρ.

This sphere representation completely displays the 3D face shape without any information loss. This representation is invariant of scale, pose, and illumination, which is essential to the face recognition without face-alignment.

3   Local Feature Extraction on Sphere Depth Image

There are some local features remain invariant compared to the corresponding 3D facial scan in the gallery set. Once located and characterized accurately, these local features can be utilized to identify 3D faces.

The 3DLBP [15] on depth images extracts the absolute depth value difference between the central pixel and its neighbors, which is better describe local shapes than origin depth image. Multiple layers of 3DLBP depth images are further used in local features matching process. Combining these local features on multiple layers of LBP depth images can improve the final accuracy.

3.1   Problem in Keypoints Selection

SIFT features [13] is widely used to calculate a similarity score between two object images in the subsequent matching process. However, Faces are non-rigid, round and smooth objects. The depth changes in face images are gradual and slow, the blob and corner structures are not significantly different from their neighboring pixels. In the keypoint detection of SIFT, The candidate keypoints need to be selected by experiential thresholds.

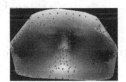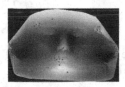

Fig. 2. Keypoints detected in a face image: (a) The initial keypoints; (b) The keypoints remain after removal keypoints with low contrast; (c) The keypoints remain after applying a threshold with high edge responses.

Fig. 2 shows the deficiencies of unreliable keypoints removal algorithm in the SIFT approach; (a) shows the full extracted keypoints; (b) illustrates the keypoints remain after applying a threshold γ_1 on the minimum contrast of each candidate keypoint; (c) shows the final keypoints remain after further removing keypoints with high edge responses γ_2. The keypoints marked with ellipse are eliminated by the removal strategies. But these keypoints can represent distinctive structures, and are in the area of high repeatability with the pose changes.

Therefore, the keypoint removal scheme in the SIFT framework will eliminate some useful features when applied to face images.

3.2   Ranking Keypoints in Keypoints Selection

To overcome the problem above, we adopt a supervised approach to select the key-points rather than using thresholds. Keypoint repeatability $R(x_i)$ is defined as the times that the same keypoints appear in a sequence of same person's face images. It is a significant measure of the keypoint robustness and stability. We can select keypoints according to their repeatability.

We use the learning to rank algorithm [14] to train a ranking model to rank key-points according to their stability. The features utilized in the ranking model are asso-ciated with the steps in keypoints extraction and removal, including the first/second derivatives of the depth image, the eigenvalues (λ_1, λ_2), determinant Det (H), and the eigenvalue ratio *Trac* $(H)^2/Det(H)$ of the Hessian matrix H. Suppose x_i, x_j are two key-points in train images, if $R(x_i) > R(x_j)$, we obtain a pair $< x_i > x_j >$.The Rank-SVM train these pairs to find the optimal classification function ,which is also the optimal rank function to rank these keypoints. However, the original Rank-SVM treats the keypoint ranking scores equally, and the original Rank-SVM treats the difference in the pairs equally, which ignores the fact that points with higher repeatability and pairs with more disparity is more concerning in the keypoint matching.

Therefore, we set a weight $Q(x_i, x_j)$ for different pair distinguish their contribution to the rank. The $Q(x_i, x_j) = |R(x_j) - R(x_j)|*[R(x_i) + R(x_j)]$. $|R(x_i) - R(x_j)|$ is the difference of two points' repeatability in pair. $[R(x_i) + R(x_j)]$ denotes the signi-ficance of keypoints location in rank list. The larger the $Q(x_i, x_j)$ is, the more crucial the pair is.

We construct a SVM model to solving this Quadratic Optimization problem:

$$\min_{\omega,\xi_{ij}} \frac{1}{2} \| \omega \|^2 + C \sum Q(x_i, x_j) \xi_{ij}$$

$$s.t <\omega x_i - x_j > 1 - \xi_{ij}; \forall x_i > x_j, \xi_{ij} \geq 0 \tag{1}$$

We utilize the weight of SVM function ω to form a ranking function for ranking keypoints.

$$f_{\vec{w}}(\vec{x}) = \langle \vec{w}, \vec{x} \rangle \tag{2}$$

In the following features matching steps, we can use the ranking function to select original keypoints with high repeatability rather than using the threshold to choose keypoints manually.

4   Experiment Analysis

To examine the performance on pose changes and partially occluded 3D facial scans, we compared our method with existing methods using the CASIA 3D face database. This database covers 123 subjects and contains complex variations in pose that are challenging for any algorithm. Fig. 3 shows some example of the database with pose variations. We select front faces of 80 people as the gallery set, and the multi-pose images of these people as the test set.

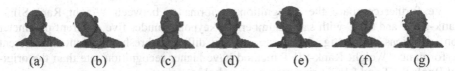

(a)　　(b)　　(c)　　(d)　　(e)　　(f)　　(g)

Fig. 3. Example of CASIA 3D face: (a) Up 20°-30°. (b) Tilt left 20°-30°. (c) Left 20°-30°. (d) Front (e) Right 20°-30°. (f) Tilt right 20°-30°. (g) Down 20°-30°.

The raw 3D face scans consist not only human heads but also shoulders, necks as well as noise points. We use median filter to smooth the human face surface. The face and non-face area can be separated using thresholding technique. These extracted point clouds of face region then are converted to sphere depth images and sphere LBP images using the method mentioned in section3. Fig. 4 illustrates some sphere depth images and different layers of LBP images.

We apply SIFT to each layer of LBP images and fuse the features in the hybrid matching process, making use of the original weight calculation as proposed in [16] to dynamically determine corresponding weights of each layers. The overall numbers of matching pairs calculated above then are used as the similarity to identify the test image in the gallery.

Sphere depth image　　3DLBP-L1　　3DLBP-L2　　3DLBP L3

Fig. 4. Sphere depth images and different layers of 3DLBP images

We establish the ranking model in keypoint extraction and matching, a training set is constructed by calculating repeatability of candidate keypoints appearing in an image sequence of different poses as ranking scores, including Left Right, Tilt left, Tilt right, Up and Down. We adopt the ranking model shown in section 3.2.

4.1　Experiment on Ranking Model

To validate the effectiveness of ranking model, we then compare the repeatability of the same number of interest points both extracted by SIFT and improved SIFT algorithm Weight Rank-SIFT. Original SIFT use the standard threshold $\gamma_1=0.03$, $\gamma_2=10$, while the top ranked interest points obtained by Rank-SIFT and Weight Rank-SIFT methods are kept. As shown in Table 1, the Weight Rank-SIFT algorithm selects keypoints has higher repeatability than the other two methods.

Table 1. Keypoints repeatability in different images with pose changes.

Repeatability	Left 30°	Right 30°	Tilt Left 30°	Tilt Left 30°	Up 30°	Down 30°
SIFT	0.421	0.413	0.476	0.462	0.436	0.418
Rank-SIFT	0.476	0.466	0.512	0.485	0.471	0.462
Weight Rank-SIFT	0.493	0.477	0.541	0.533	0.486	0.467

We further compare the recognition performance between Weight Rank-SIFT, Rank-SIFT and SIFT with same numbers of keypoints under five different parameter configurations. From Fig. 5, we can see that different thresholds result in different performance. Weight Rank-SIFT method have higher recognition rate than the original Rank-SIFT and SIFT using manual threshold to select keypoints.

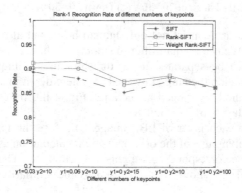

Fig. 5. Rank-1 recognition rate of different numbers of keypoints

4.2   Experiment on Pose Change 3D Faces Images

We compare our approach with some existing methods. We divide the test set into Small Pose Variation (SPV): including views of front, left/right 20–30°, up/down 20–30°and tilt left/right 20–30°. Large Pose Variation (LPV): including views of left/right 50–60°. Table 2 and Fig. 6 shows that our method preserves the stable local features in post invariant spherical representation has better performance in Rank-1 recognition rate even the objects have large pose changes. Although Mesh-SIFT [19] have better performance than our method, it costs more time to process on 3D mesh directly, while our method based on depth image is rapid in real world application. To sum up, the experimental results prove that with selecting repeatable local features from spherical representation, our method can deal with pose changes and even partial missing data in 3D face recognition.

Table 2. Recongnition rate on CASIA pose change testset

Approach	SPV	LPV	Overall
ICP	74.2%	64.7%	67.1%
3DLBP	89.2%	68.4%	82.1%
Depth + Intensity [17]	89.2%	70%	85.2%
RBGR [18]	93.2%	82%	89.6%
SIFT on Sphere 3DLBP	91.4%	84.5%	88.4%
Extended-LBP [9]	N/A	N/A	90.4%
V-LBP[20]	N/A	N/A	90.4%
Mesh SIFT	N/A	N/A	92.1%
Weight Rank-SIFT	93.4%	85.6%	91.4%

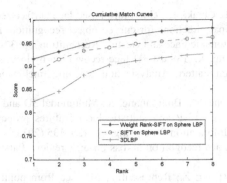

Fig. 6. CMC curves on pose change test set

5   Conclusion

Our method has been proposed to address a challenging topic, 3D face recognition in uncontrolled environments, in which pose variations is a big obstacles. We have presented an effective approach to solve the problem using sphere depth image and 3DLBP representation. This pose-invariant representation allows for accurate and fast description of local shape variations, thus enhancing the distinctiveness of 3D faces. An improved SIFT algorithm Weight Rank-SIFT is then used to select more stable and repeatable keypoints on face image to the following local features matching process. The promising recognition performance shows its potential to deal with the 3D face recognition in unconstraint scene.

Acknowledgements. This paper was supported by (1) National Natural Science Foundation of China under the Grant No. 61472031; (2) Portions of the research in this paper use the CASIA-3D FaceV1 collected by the Chinese Academy of Sciences' Institute of Automation (CASIA).

References

1. Bowyer, K., Chang, K., Flynn, P.: A Survey of Approaches and Challenges in 3D and Multi-Modal 3D + 2D Face Recognition. Computer Vision and Image Understanding **101**(1), 1–15 (2006)
2. Turk, M., Pentland, A.: Eigenfaces for recognition. Journal of Cognitive Neuroscience **3**(1), 71–86 (1991)
3. Belhumeur, P., Hespanha, J., Kriegman, J.: Eigenfaces vs. fisherfaces: Recognition using class specific linear projection. IEEE Transactions on Pattern Analysis and Machine Intelligence **19**(7), 711–720 (1997)
4. Lu, X., Jain, A., Colbry, D.: Matching 2.5D face scans to 3D models. IEEE Transactions on Pattern Analysis and Machine Intelligence **28**(1), 31–43 (2006)
5. Gordon, G.: Face recognition based on depth and curvature features. In: Proceeding of IEEE Conference Computer Vision and Pattern Recognition, pp. 808–810 (1992)
6. Chua, C., Han, F., Ho, F.: 3D human face recognition using point signature. In: Proceeding International Conference Automatic Face and Gesture Recognition, pp. 233–238 (2000)

7. Tanaka, H., Ikeda, M., Chiaki, H.: Curvature-based face surface recognition using spherical correlation–Principal directions for curved object recognition. In: Proceeding International Conference Automatic Face and Gesture Recognition, pp. 372–377 (1998)
8. Wang, Y., Liu, J., Tang, X.: Robust 3D face recognition by local shape difference boosting. IEEE Transaction Pattern Analysis and Machine Intelligence **32**(10), 1858–1870 (2010)
9. Ouamane, A., Belahcene, M., Bourennane, S.: Multimodal 3D and 2D face authentication approach using extended LBP and statistic local features proposed. In: 4th European Workshop on Visual Information Processing, pp. 130–135 (2013)
10. Zhang, X., Gao, Y.: Face recognition across pose: A review. Pattern Recognition **42**(11), 2876–2896 (2009)
11. Liu, P., Wang, Y., Zhang, Z.: Representing 3D face from point cloud to face-aligned spherical depth map. International Journal of Pattern Recognition and Artificial Intelligence 26(01) (2012)
12. Phillips, P., Flynn, P., Scruggs, T., Bowyer, K., Chang, J., Hoffman, K., Marques, J., Min, J., Worek, W.: Overview of the face recognition grand challenge. In: IEEE Workshop on Face Recognition Grand Challenge Experiments, pp. 947–954 (2005)
13. Lowe, D.: Distinctive image features from scale-invariant keypoints. International Journal of Computer and Vision **60**(4), 91–110 (2004)
14. Li, B., Xiao, R., Li, Z.: Rank-SIFT: Learning to rank repeatable local interest points. In: IEEE International Conference on Computer Vision and Pattern Recognition, pp. 1737–1744 (2011)
15. Huang, Y., Wang, Y., Tan, T.: Combining Statistics of Geometrical and Correlative Features for 3D Face Recognition. In: British Machine Vision Conference, pp. 879–888 (2006)
16. Mian, A., Bennamoun, M.: Keypoint detection and local feature matching for textured 3D face recognition. International Journal of Computer and Vision **79**(1), 1–12 (2008)
17. Xu, C., Li, S., Tan, T.: Automatic 3D face recognition from depth and intensity Gabor features. Pattern Recognition **42**(9), 1895–1905 (2009)
18. Ming, Y.: Robust regional bounding spherical descriptor for 3D face recognition and emotion analysis. Image and Vision Computing **35**, 14–22 (2015)
19. Smeets, D., Keustermans, J., Vandermeulen, D.: meshSIFT: Local surface features for 3D face recognition under expression variations and partial data. Computer Vision and Image Understanding **117**(2), 158–169 (2013)
20. Tang, H., Yin, B., Sun, Y.: 3D face recognition using local binary patterns. Signal Processing **93**(8), 2190–2198 (2013)

Face Recognition Using Local PCA Filters

Yida Wang, Shasha Li, Jiani Hu, and Weihong Deng[✉]

Beijing University of Posts and Telecommunications, Beijing, China
{wangyida1,lishasha,jnhu,whdeng}@bupt.edu.cn

Abstract. We propose an efficient feature extraction architecture based on PCANet. Our method performs far better than many traditional artificial feature extraction methods with the help of standalone filter learning and multiscale local feature combination. Such structure cascaded by both linear layers with convolution filters and non-linear layers in binarization process shows better adaptability in different databases. With the help of parallel computing, training time is much shorter than PCANet and also more fixed compared to convolutional neural network. Experiment in LFW and FERET shows that such a data oriented structure shows good performance both on stability and accuracy in various environments.

Keywords: Feature extraction · PCANet · Filter learning · Standalone training · Multiscale · Binarization

1 Introduction

Face recognition shows more and more values in machine learning research with typical databases and is also widely used in real life applications. As alignment of face based on key points being more accurate, feature description plays a determining factor on face recognition. Different classical hand-crafted features aiming at ad hoc recognition goals behave well. Some unsupervised features like LBP and Gabor capture discriminant feature while getting rid of ill effects caused by different lightings, occlusion, corruption and solving problems related to rotation and displacemen because unlike holistic methed such as Eigenface and Fisherface. They are local feature based descriptors which can eliminate some intra person interference. But such methods are still powerless towards some difficulties like flexible deformation impacts. Within-class variance components could make a huge misleading to the classifier result. Shallow layer based methods like Gabor, LBP, SIFT and Shallow Neural Networks share some common ground which all extracting feature with just one hidden layer. By increasing the number of layers, DNN is advanced in liberating multifarious works of structure matching process regarding to distinct recognition condition with the help of back propagation algorithm. Cascaded layers in CNN [2] make parameters more suitable for sophisticated condition compared to shallow networks. PCANet [1] which consists of concatenated layers stacked one by one behave well in field of face recognition. Its filter learning process is driven by local image patches

© Springer International Publishing Switzerland 2015
J. Yang et al. (Eds.): CCBR 2015, LNCS 9428, pp. 35–42, 2015.
DOI: 10.1007/978-3-319-25417-3_5

for just once and brings advantages in speeding up in contrast with convolution kernels learning in CNN by using eigenvalue decomposition on the output of previous layer. The convolution output of the bottom layer directly passed to the next convolution layer. Such simplified structure reduces the computation and abates the uncertainty of time for convergence. PCANet also have greater ability in task immigration with fixed structure along with higher accuracy in comparison with LBP and Gabor. Novel improved descriptors derived from this architecture has been proposed recently, such as in [3]. We further modifies this architecture to achieve higher recognition accuracy and adaptability in different missions. Our improved approach which is also based on such structure shows better performance than the original one.

Our structure fully exploits the information by constructing filter banks directly from data which are complementary with each other. It could satisfy the expectation without optimization through iterations. There are two main modifications about filters learning based on PCANet. Filter banks solved by eigenvalue decomposition is driven by the previous layer's output separately. Outputs from different convolutional kernels differ much in texture because of their orthogonalization relations, we train every few filters from exact one part of the output of former layer. We could fully exploit the discriminative information in previous layers and enhance the robustness for feature extraction. We select a group of continuous size for filter training and feature extraction. Training result shows that smaller filters is not just an approximation to any sub region in bigger filters. So training PCA filters in such manner is guaranteed on a more adequate feature representation, discriminant statistic pattern extracted from different filters might lie in various position of the same structure of network. Some experiments prefer to mix different features together by adding up similarity scores calculated by normalized feature rather than concatenate all features together for purpose of saving memory. Separately trained structure with form of cascaded network and mutiscale feature combination extracts richer information which is robust and discriminative. Experiment on Feret and LFW data base shows that there are about 2% recognition accuracy improvement in difficult classification environments while the feature dimension keeps unchanged. There are even better improvement in accuracy which achieves up to 2.6% in further experiments with key point alignment and affine transformation applied on the image.

2   Method

2.1   Filter Learning

The 1st Stage Training. Like the 1st stage training in PCANet, given N training samples $\{I_i\}_{i=1}^{N}$ with the same size of $m \times n$. The patch size doesn't change in a certain cascading queue, so multiscale filter banks is trained separately.

Overlapping patches in a particular size of images are collected for training a filter bank using SVD(Singular Value Decomposition). Patches are combined of adjacent pixels. As for the pixels on the edge of a image, we use zero padding to make it still useful. Patch mean is subtracted from each patch before SVD. Then the whole resource for filter training is represented as $X = [\bar{X}_1, \bar{X}_2, ..., \bar{X}_N] \in R^{k_1 k_2 * Nmn}$ where the image size of all N samples is $m \times n$ and the patch size is $k_1 \times k_2$. A single patch feature matrix $\bar{X}_1$ extracted from an image is formed by a set of vectors as $[\bar{x}_{i,1}, \bar{x}_{i,2}, ..., \bar{x}_{i,mn}]$ where $\bar{x}_{i,j}$ denotes the jth vectorized patches in the ith image.

The meaning of PCA is projecting the original data to another orthogonal space which uses as less basis as possible maximizing the variance of data, so basis in such orthogonal space is selected follows constraint: $\max_{V \in R^{k_1 k_2 \times S_1}} ||V^T X||_F^2$ while $V^T V = I_{S_1}$ it is solved by eigenvalue decomposition of XX^T, so the convolution kernel could be expressed as

$$W_l^1 = mat_{k_1, k_2}(q_l(XX^T)) \in R^{k_1 \times k_2}, l = 1, 2, ..., S_1 \tag{1}$$

where S_1 means the number of the set of principle eigenvectors in the 1st layer, $mat_{k_1, k_2}(v)$ is a reshaping function aims to transform v to the size of $k_1 \times k_2$ and function $q_l(XX^T)$ denotes the lth principal eigenvector of XX^T or the lth left singular vector of X.

Such goal is equivalent to minimize the reconstruction error with a set of eigenvectors as shown below where I_{S_1} is identity matrix with the size of $L_1 \times L_2$:

$$\min_{V \in R^{k_1 k_2 \times S_1}} ||X - VV^T X||_F^2, s.t : V^T V = I_{S_1} \tag{2}$$

Concatenated Filter Learning. We optimize the concatenated structure to extract efficient feature by taking full advantage of textures in images and rearranging them properly. For the aim of enriching discriminative features and exploiting benefits from the detachment of the back propagation process, we train the cascaded layers only using the output of the particular convolution kernel. Feature extraction is also formed as a tree-like structure. No input-output pairs uses the same filter banks between two layers. As shown in Figure 2, this feature extraction process is a 'tree' like concatenated structure rather than a 'chain' like one of traditional PCANet. The number of filters in higher stages will be no smaller than previous stage, number of filters will only keep as the same when the remaining dimension of SVD is fixed as always 1 except for the 1st stage.

Assuming that layer t contains S_t filter sets where each set contains l_t filters which could be represented as $l_t = \prod_{L=1}^{t} S_L/S_t$ and such tree-like concatenate structure has $l_{total} = \prod_{L=1}^{n} S_L$ outputs for one sample in all where n is the number of layers used. In such a feature enriched network, benefit comes with the cost for the increasing of convolution kernels, which is $F = \sum_{t=1}^{n} S_t l_t$ in total; Filters in stage t is trained separately one by one from a single group of outputs of previous layer where the lth filter output of the $(t - 1)$th stage is $I_i^l = I_i * W_l^{t-1}$ while $i = 1, 2, ..., N$. One set of filters in such standalone training process only uses reconstructed samples from one filter in previous stage as source data, so different filters in previous layer would produce distinguishing learning resource where $*$ denotes 2D convolution and N is always equal to the number of input images due to the standalone training process. Overlapping patches are collected as the same manner as the 1st layer. Patch means are removed from each patch as $\bar{Y}_i = [\bar{y}_{i,l,1}, \bar{y}_{i,l,2}, ..., \bar{y}_{i,l,mn}]$ where $\bar{y}_{i,l,j}$ is the jth mean-subtracted patch in I_i^l. A single filter bank is then obtained from eigenvalue decomposition of $Y^l = [\bar{Y}_1^l, \bar{Y}_2^l, ..., \bar{Y}_N^l] \in R^{k_1 k_2 \times Nmn}$. To make images in different layers having the same size, zeros padding is applied before 2D convolution. Filter is solved as: $W_{l_t}^l = mat_{k_1,k_2}(ql(YY^T)) \in R^{k_1 \times k_2}$ while $l_t = 1, 2, ..., S_l$. As filters is learned standalone, which means that the training data in previous stage is much fewer than PCANet. This means that data would be much fewer the original one for a single branch of filter learning, so less time will be cost on convolution with filter of previous stage. With the help of parallel computing, separate branches of current stage will be computed at the same time. Much training time will be saved. Feature extracted by multiscale filters is beneficial to recognition. Here we just choose continuous odd numbers for filter scales k_1 and k_2. Convolution kernels are squares matrix for most of our experiment which means that $k_1 = k_2$.

Fig. 1. Multi scale Filters(odd-numbered rows) learned in the $1st$ layer and modulus of their FFT represented by 10 based log function(even-numbered rows).

2.2 Feature Coding

Number of output images in the last layer equals to the amount of convolution filters, we represent discriminant features by regrouping and combining sets of outputs. All pixels in output images are converted to binaries with unit step function $S(.)$ whose output is 1 for positive input and 0 otherwise. A single threshold makes it possible for convolution results combining with each other properly and forming a more robust feature. Decimal number representing a single pixel is formed by concatenated binaries in the same position which are converted from convolutional output corresponding to a particular convolution kernel in the penultimate layer. Such reconstructed integer-valued (in range of $[0, 1, ..., 2^{S_n}-1]$) image could be expressed as $\mathcal{O}^l = \sum_{s=1}^{S_n} 2^{s-1} S(\mathcal{I}^l * W_s^n)$ where s is the id of sets, $\mathcal{I}^l$ and $\mathcal{O}^l$ are a pair of input and output image in the last layer corresponding to the lth filter in the penultimate layer.

Every output image for a single scale of filter bank are partitioned into B blocks for precisely statistics in histogram for images in normal view. Block histograms each with the same length of 2^{S_n} in an image are concatenated in a vector afterwards. In the next step, all vectors deriving from the same input image at the beginning are concatenated together in the same sequence to form the feature f based on the filter scale K_i which are all set as odd numbers.

$$f_k = [[Hist(\mathscr{I}_1^1), ..., Hist(\mathscr{I}_B^1)], ..., [Hist(\mathscr{I}_1^{l_{n-1}}), ..., Hist(\mathscr{I}_B^{l_{n-1}})]] \qquad (3)$$

All features extracted from filters in several proper scales are concatenated to represent the feature of a sample $\mathscr{F} = [f_{K_1}, f_{K_2}, ..., f_{K_n}]$. Based on the fact that the likelihood of concatenated features equals to the form represented as cosine distance computed by normalized feature vectors: $\sum_{k=K_1}^{K_n} <$ $Norm(f_k^i), Norm(f_k^j) >$ equals to $< \mathscr{F}^i, \mathscr{F}^j >$ where $<, >$ denotes the matrix inner product, $\mathscr{F} = [Norm(f_{K_1}), Norm(f_{K_2}), ..., Norm(f_{K_n})]$, we carried out our experiment on such manner instead of concatenating all discriminant sub-feature together for the sake of saving memory in some databases. Such process could also be carried out after feature projection using classifiers as a mean of similarity fusion.

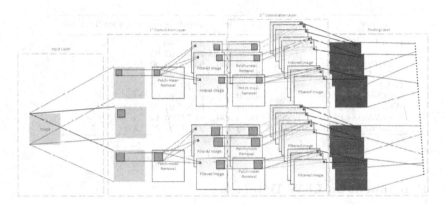

Fig. 2. Architecture of Enriched Feature Network

3 Experiment

3.1 Experiment on Feret Database

FERET tests employed frontal images gathered between 1993 and 1996. All tests are based on a single gallery containing 1196 images for training. test data with name of fb, fc and dup1, dup2 represents that expression, illumination and aging effect is the main changes from gallery data separately. Experiments of original PCANet [1] shows that Feret database has weaker environmental disturbance compared to LFW database so accuracy on Feret is better and filters trained on FERET database show greater advantage to randomly initialized filters. LDA used in LFW database is not applied because samples of each individual aren't enough for intraclass variance rebuilding. Inner products between features in four separate test sets and pseudo inverse matrix of gallery feature are regarded as the similarity for classification. Testes are carried on structure with two convolution layers which each contains 8 filters which suit for the 8 threads of CPU for parallel computing. Output images in the last layer are partitioned into 10*10 blocks for histogram statistic. Multiscale similarities calculated from scale 7 and 9 are summarized together for experiment aiming at improving performance on accuracy and stability. Performance of such a two stage network and its variances are also compared with other local pattern feature extracting algorithms such as DFD [4]using the same classifier and others such as DT-LBP [5] copied from the original paper.

From experiments of parameter adjustment, we found that 2 stage is enough in such structure, the number of filters in the first stage should be the multiples of 2 for parallel computing.

Table 1. Accuracy on FERET, Multiscale means that we are using joint similarity for classification

Structure	fb	fc	dup-1	dup-2	Time for Training
DT-LBP [5]	99	100	84	80	*
DFD [4]	99.25	94.33	79.36	67.95	*
G-LQP [6]	99.90	100	93.20	91.00	*
sPOEM+POD [7]	99.70	100	94.90	94.00	*
GOM [8]	99.90	100	95.70	93.10	*
PCANet [1]	99.50	100	94.18	93.59	240s
Whitened PCA	99.58	100	94.88	94.02	253s
Standalone+PCA	99.58	100	94.74	94.44	73s
Standalone+Multiscale+PCA	99.75	100	95.57	95.30	123s

3.2 Experiment on LFW Database

LFW [9] data set contains 13233 images of faces collected from the web detected by the Viola-Jones face detector. 1680 of all 5749 individuals have two or more distinct photos in the data set which make it possible training LDA classifier used for projecting the high dimensional feature on low-dim spaces. Most of the experiments were carried on this database because all photos are not captured in restricted condition. All extracted features are projected with supervised matrix learning after dimension reduction using PCA. We mainly tested our method on LFW-a database and another database processed with affine transformation by using three manually annotated key points of the two apple of eyes and the center of corners of mouth for precisely histogram statistic.

Training uses photos not included in 10 test folds. LDA matrix is learned from labeled data in the rest 9 folds. Similarity between two feature of samples is defined as cosine distance between two low-dim features got by projection with LDA matrix after firstly projected by a PCA to form a low rank matrix.

Our experiments are mainly carried on a 2 stages network which each contains 8 sets of filters separately for convenience of parallel computing. All images are cropped to 150*80 and the histogram block is set to 25*20, resulting in a

Table 2. Accuracy on LFW Database; Standalone represent a standalone training precess; Multiscale represent concatenating multiscale features

Structure	LFW(aligned)	LFW(affine transformed)	Time for Training
MRF-MLBP [10]	79.08	*	*
SFRD [11]	84.81	*	*
I-LQP [12]	86.20	*	*
OCLBP [13]	86.66	*	*
Fisher vector faces [14]	87.47	*	*
Eigen-PEP [15]	88.97	*	*
PCANet [1]	88.95	89.58	639s
Standalone+PCA	89.05	90.15	185s
Standalone+Whitened PCA	89.08	90.18	192s
Standalone+Multiscale+PCA	91	92.21	696s

dimension of 81920 in most experiments of Table 1 for convenience of comparison. The dimension of PCA matrix for rank-reducing for LDA is 700 and the dimension of LDA matrix is selected between 40 and 300 in trial. We select 7, 9, 11, 13 as side length of filters in multiscale filter experiment. The similarity score is the summation of ones computed in each scale. The accuracy is defined as the average of verification rates and true negative rate $Accuracy = (TP + TN)/2$ LFW database are aligned with a commercial face alignment software and is applied with affine transformation based on 3 key points annotated by hand. Results show that the enriched feature did improves the performance. Experiment results is the average performance of each method and * denotes that there are no comparable result which could be found. As shown in the table, experiment on our structure and PCANet both using Matlab for training on a 4 core Intel i7 4770 CPU, with the help of parallel computing, the training time of standalone training is just one-third of PCANet with the same filter numbers. Though the using of multiscale feature mixtrue, its only takes a bit more time than PCANet and get a more perfect prediction result. The standalone training saves much time for training, we also observed that using filters learned from FERET database only reduce around 2 percent of accuracy.

4 Conclusion

Experiments show that such an unsupervised feature extraction architecture may do well in different classification issues. The concatenated network achieves better performance with the help of reconstruction in convolution kernels and joint similarity. Visualization of trained filters and their 2D FFT indicates that filters learned from image patches extract low frequency textures which are complementary with each others. This solver has certain ability to do the same job carried by back propagation process in traditional convolutional neural network.

Acknowledgements. The authors would like to thank the anonymous reviewers for their thoughtful and constructive remarks that are helpful to improve the quality of this paper. This work was partially sponsored by supported by the Fundamental Research Funds for the Central Universities under Grant No. 2014ZD03-01, NSFC (National Natural Science Foundation of China) under Grant No. 61375031, No. 61471048, and No.61273217. This work was also supported by the Beijing Higher Education Young Elite Teacher Program, and the Program for New Century Excellent Talents in University.

References

1. Chan, T., Jia, K., Gao, S., Lu, J., Zeng, Z., Ma, Y.: PCANet: A Simple Deep Learning Baseline for Image Classification? arXiv preprint, arXiv:1404.3606 (2014)
2. Krizhevsky, A., Sutskever, I., Hinton, G.E.: ImageNet classification with deep convolutional neural networks. In: Advances in Neural Information Processing Systems, vol. 25, pp. 1097–1105. Curran Associates, Inc. (2012)
3. Zeng, R., Wu, J., Shao, Z., Senhadji, L., Shu, H.: Multilinear Principal Component Analysis Network for Tensor Object Classification. Eprint Arxiv (2014)
4. Lei, Z., Pietikainen, M., Li, S.Z.: Learning Discriminant Face Descriptor. IEEE Transactions on PAMI 36(2), 289–302 (2014)
5. Maturana, D., Mery, D., Soto, A.: Face recognition with decision tree-based local binary patterns. In: Kimmel, R., Klette, R., Sugimoto, A. (eds.) ACCV 2010, Part IV. LNCS, vol. 6495, pp. 618–629. Springer, Heidelberg (2011)
6. Hussain, S.U., Napoleon, T., Jurie, F.: Face recognition using local quantized patterns. In: BMVC, Guildford, United Kingdom (2012)
7. Vu, N.S.: Exploring Patterns of Gradient Orientations and Magnitudes for Face Recognition. IEEE Transactions on Information Forensics and Security 8(2), 295–304 (2013)
8. Chai, Z., Sun, Z., Mendez-Vazquez, H., He, R., Tan, T.: Gabor Ordinal Measures for Face Recognition. IEEE Transactions on Information Forensics and Security 9(1), 14–26 (2014)
9. Huang, G.B., Ramesh, M., Berg, T., Learned-Miller, E.: Labeled Faces in the Wild: A Database for Studying Face Recognition in Unconstrained Environments. Technical Report, pp. 07–49, University of Massachusetts, Amherst (2007)
10. Arashloo, S.R., Kittler, J.: Efficient processing of mrfs for unconstrained-pose face recognition. In: 2013 IEEE Sixth International Conference on BTAS, pp. 1–8 (2013)
11. Cui, Z., Li, W., Xu, D., Shan, S., Chen, X.: Fusing robust face region descriptors via multiple metric learning for face recognition in the wild. In: 2013 IEEE Conference on CVPR, pp. 3554–3561 (2013)
12. Hussain, S., Triggs, B.: Visual recognition using local quantized patterns. In: Fitzgibbon, A., Lazebnik, S., Perona, P., Sato, Y., Schmid, C. (eds.) ECCV 2012, Part II. LNCS, vol. 7573, pp. 716–729. Springer, Heidelberg (2012)
13. Barkan, O., Weill, J., Wolf, L., Aronowitz, H.: Fast high dimensional vector multiplication face recognition. In: 2013 IEEE International Conference on Computer Vision (ICCV), pp. 1960–1967 (2013)
14. Simonyan, K., Parkhi, O.M., Vedaldi, A., Zisserman, A.: Fisher vector faces in the wild. In: BMVC (2013)
15. Li, H., Hua, G., Shen, X., Lin, Z., Brandt, J.: Eigen-PEP for video face recognition. In: Cremers, D., Reid, I., Saito, H., Yang, M.-H. (eds.) ACCV 2014. LNCS, vol. 9005, pp. 17–33. Springer, Heidelberg (2015)

Block Statistical Features-based Face Verification on Second Generation Identity Card

Hegui Zhu, Yang Wang, Xiuping Mao, and Xiangde Zhang[✉]

College of Sciences, Northeastern University, Shenyang 110819, China
{zhuhegui,wangy_neu,maoxiuping426324,zhangxdneu}@163.com

Abstract. Face verification has been extensively studied in recent decades. Nevertheless, face verification for identity card has subject to relatively little attention. This paper proposes a block statistical features(BSF) learning method combining with local Gabor binary pattern(LGBP) for face verification in both second generation identity card(2nd ID card) and video set, which show many differences in biometric caused by age gap and image acquisition conditions. To alleviate computation complexity of Gabor transformation, we exploit energy check Gabor filters to speed up calculation. Specially, the verification rate of our approach on NEU-ID database achieves 97.71 %. It has a comparable performance with lower computation complexity.

Keywords: Face verification · 2nd ID card · BSF · LGBP

1 Introduction

Face verification is an important problem in compute vision due to its widely practical applications. As the most representative identity certification, identity card is being widely used in economy, business, and security [1]. The task of face verification for 2nd ID card is extremely challengeable for its complexity. While a large number of face verification methods have been proposed in the literature [2-4], face verification for 2nd ID card has subject to relatively little attention. Most of these methods cannot work well in real environment [5-6]. This is exacerbated when there is a gap of age and resolution between face images in identity card and video. Su et al. propose a 2nd ID card face verification method based on multi-model parts and PCA [7]. In [8], LGBP has been proved to be effective for face verification on 2nd ID card. However, Gabor feature extraction is time consuming with multi-scale and multi-orientation. In this paper, we propose a block statistical features(BSF) learning method combining with LGBP for 2nd ID card face verification, which shows strong robustness to variations. Furthermore, to reduce computation complexity, we propose a fast Gabor computation method based on energy check. Our approach achieves high verification rate(97.71%) on our NEU-ID database.

The rest of the paper is organized as follows: Section 2 describes LGBP operator. Section 3 introduces the computation of the proposed BSF face representation in detail as well as some analysis on the fast Gabor computation

© Springer International Publishing Switzerland 2015
J. Yang et al. (Eds.): CCBR 2015, LNCS 9428, pp. 43–50, 2015.
DOI: 10.1007/978-3-319-25417-3_6

method. The experimental part comparing with other approaches is presented in section 4. And some conclusions and discussions of our paper are drawn in section 5.

2   Face Representation Based on LGBP

As indicated in [9], 2-D Gabor filters are highly joint in spatial location, orientation and frequency, thus can offer sufficient information. To enlarge differences, Guo et al. in [10] used LBP to further encode the Gabor maps. Generally, multi-orientation and multi-scale Gabor filters are used to dispose face images [10-12]. The Gabor filter is formulated as follows:

$$\psi_{u,v} = \frac{\|k_{u,v}\|^2}{\sigma^2} e^{-\frac{\|k_{u,v}\|^2 \|z\|^2}{2\sigma^2}} \left[e^{ik_{u,v}} - e^{-\frac{\sigma^2}{2}} \right] \tag{1}$$

where $k_{u,v} = k_v e^{i\phi_u}$, $k_v = \frac{k_{max}}{f^v}$ define the scale of Gabor and $\phi_u = \frac{u\pi}{8} \in [0, \pi]$ defines the orientation. Gabor features can be derived by convoluting the face image $f(x, y)$ with the Gabor filter $\psi_{u,v}$. That is,

$$G(x, y, u, v) = f(x, y) * \psi_{u,v} \tag{2}$$

The values in Gabor maps come from points in a square neighbourhood, so the values change slowly with displacement. In order to enlarge the differences between central pixel and its surroundings in a local patch, LBP is used to encode the Gabor values [10-11]. LBP operator encodes an image by comparing central value with its neighbourhoods' and generating a binary code. That is,

$$S(f_p - f_c) = \begin{cases} 1, & f_p > f_c \\ 0, & f_p \le f_c \end{cases} \tag{3}$$

where f_p, f_c denote the neighbourhood and central values respectively. Then, the LBP value of each pixel is equal to a decimal number formulated as followed:

$$LBP = \sum_{p=1}^{l^2} S(f_p - f_c) 2^p \tag{4}$$

Actually, LGBP maps are derived by applying LBP operator on Gabor maps.

$$LGBP\ maps = LBP\{Gabor\{f\}\} \tag{5}$$

where $LBP\{\cdot\}$ and $Gabor\{\cdot\}$ represent the LBP and Gabor operators respectively.

3   The Proposed Algorithm

The overall framework of the proposed algorithm based on BSF is shown in Fig. 1. In our approach, we firstly extract a histogram from a face image through the use of BSF by the following steps: (1) An input face image is normalized by similarity transform followed by illumination preprocess. (2) Apply Gabor and LBP operators to normalized face images to obtain LGBP maps. (3) Each LGBP map is further used to extract BSF histogram and all histograms are concatenated to represent a face image. After histograms extracting, we adopt Cosine distance to compute similarity between face images for face verification. The following sub-sections will discuss the procedure in detail.

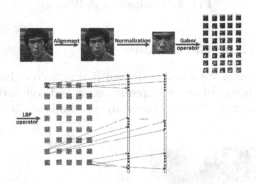

Fig. 1. The framework of the proposed algorithm.

3.1   Face Presentation Based on BSF

In this section, we described BSF learning method combining with LGBP. Different from Gabor magnitude statistical features used in [8, 10], we exploit to use real and imaginary parts of Gabor maps to construct block statistical features. For histogram extracting, LGBP maps are firstly partitioned into $M_r \times M_r$ non-overlapping regions, and then each region is further divided into $M_s \times M_s$ non-overlapping sub-regions. The histogram of $r-th$ region of the specific LGBP map is computed by

$$H_{u,v,r} = \left(h_{u,v,1}^{real}, h_{u,v,1}^{imag}, \cdots, h_{u,v,i}^{real}, h_{u,v,i}^{imag}, \cdots, h_{u,v,M_s \times M_s}^{real}, h_{u,v,M_s \times M_s}^{imag} \right) \quad (6)$$

where $h_{u,v,i}^{real}, h_{u,v,i}^{imag}$ are the real and imaginary part histograms of $i-th$ sub-region for (u, v)-LGBP map.

Then, the histograms of $r - th$ region in 5-scale and 8-orientation LGBP maps are concatenated to form the corresponding face part presentation. That is,

$$R_r = (H_{0,0,r}, H_{0,1,r}, \cdots, H_{u,v,r}, \cdots, H_{4,7,r}) \quad (7)$$

For feature combination, we use PCA followed by LDA to project histogram feature of each region into a latent discriminative subspace [2]. The architecture of BSF is shown in Fig. 2.

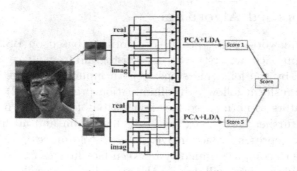

Fig. 2. Architecture of BSF.

3.2   Energy Check on Gabor Filter

In the proposed scheme, we use 5-scale and 8-orientation Gabor filters, which are high time consuming. In order to reduce noise and computation complexity, we propose a method called energy check to speed up calculation.

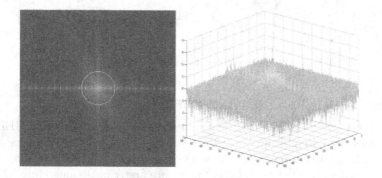

Fig. 3. Energy of specific Gabor filter.

As shown in Fig. 3, Gabor filter's energy is mostly focused in the centre. And the energy around edge is too low to extract effective face features. Instead, it enlarge noise of face features. Considering this, we propose a method to decrease the size of filters but preserve adequate energy. The energy of a filter is equal to summing energy at each point. We select those points from centre to sides, until the energy of them is beyond the given threshold. The energy of a specific Gabor filter is formulated as follows:

$$E_{filter_{u_0,v_0}} = \sum_{-\lfloor \frac{M}{2} \rfloor}^{\lfloor \frac{M}{2} \rfloor} \sum_{-\lfloor \frac{N}{2} \rfloor}^{\lfloor \frac{N}{2} \rfloor} e_{ij}^{u_0,v_0} \qquad (8)$$

where, $e_{ij}^{u_0,v_0}$ denotes the energy at the point (i,j) in the specific Gabor filter $filter_{u_0,v_0}$, and M, N present the height and width of the filter perspectively. Note that,the origin point is set at the center of the filter.

Then, our purpose is to get the size (M', N') of filter to renew the original one by using the given threshold.That is,

$$arg\min_{M',N'} \parallel \sum_{-\lfloor\frac{M'}{2}\rfloor}^{\lfloor\frac{M'}{2}\rfloor} \sum_{-\lfloor\frac{N'}{2}\rfloor}^{\lfloor\frac{N'}{2}\rfloor} e_{ij}^{u_0,v_0} - \alpha \sum_{-\lfloor\frac{M}{2}\rfloor}^{\lfloor\frac{M}{2}\rfloor} \sum_{-\lfloor\frac{N}{2}\rfloor}^{\lfloor\frac{N}{2}\rfloor} e_{ij}^{u_0,v_0} \parallel^2 \tag{9}$$

where α defines the percentage threshold of filter's energy. For instance, if we set $\alpha = 95\%$, it turns out to choose elements whose energy beyonds $0.95\% \times E_{filter}$.

For Gabor filter renewing, we directly extract the new filter from the original one by equation (10).

$$filter_{new} = filter_{origional}\left(-\lfloor\frac{M'}{2}\rfloor : \lfloor\frac{M'}{2}\rfloor, \ -\lfloor\frac{N'}{2}\rfloor : \lfloor\frac{N'}{2}\rfloor\right) \tag{10}$$

3.3 Face Verification Based on BSF

Many similarity measurement methods have been proposed for histogram matching [11]. In this paper, we use Cosine distance $d\left(H^1, H^2\right)$ to measure the similarity of two histograms [8]:

$$d\left(H^1, H^2\right) = \frac{\langle H^1, H^2\rangle}{\|H^1\|\|H^2\|} \tag{11}$$

Through this measurement, the similarity of two faces f^1, f^2 based on BSF representation is computed by

$$S\left(f^1, f^2\right) = \sum_{r=1}^{M_r \times M_r} d\left(R_r^1, R_r^2\right) \tag{12}$$

where

$$R_r^1 = \left(H_{0,0,r}^1, H_{u,v,r}^1, \cdots, H_{4,7,r}^1\right)$$
$$R_r^2 = \left(H_{0,0,r}^2, H_{u,v,r}^2, \cdots, H_{4,7,r}^2\right)$$

4   Experiments

4.1   Experimental Settings

For lacking of benchmark of face verification for identity card, we collect our own 2nd ID card database named NEU-ID database. The NEU-ID database contains 10877 facial images from 481 people with each identity one 2nd ID card image and several video images. Fig. 4 shows some samples in our NEU-ID database.

Fig. 4. Image samples in NEU-ID database.

The image stored in the second generation identity card is 102×126 pixels with low quality and obvious serrated edge. And video images are obtained under uncontrolled environment with several variations in expression, pose, and illumination. In our experiment, images are first aligned by eyes' coordinates through the use of ESR in [11] and cropped into 150×130 followed by illumination preprocess in [14]. We set $M_r = 7, M_s = 2$ and use uniform LBP, so the dimension of each image is 925120. For face verification, we exploit PCA+LDA to reduce feature dimension. To learn the projection matrix, we randomly choose 400 identities including its corresponding 2nd ID card and video images as the training set, and the remaining 81 identities for testing.

4.2 Experiment with NEU-ID Database

To verify the effectiveness of combining Gabor features' real and imaginary part, we do experiments on NEU-ID database with Gabor magnitude, Gabor real part, Gabor imaginary part and Gabor real & imagianry parts respectively. All experiments are carried out in MATLAB R2013b environment running on a desktop with CPU Intel Core i5 3.10GHz and 4 GB RAM.

Table 1. Comparisons among different features. (FAR=0.1)

Features (Gabor)	Magnitude	Real	Imaginary	Real & Imaginary
Accuracy	84.69%	67.34%	68.66%	97.71%

Table 1 is the feature comparisons, the result shows that our approach of combining real and imaginary apart to construct BSF can achieve the highest performance. We evaluate the performance of our approach by comparing with EBGM, SVM and MBC on NEU-ID database. Fig. 5 shows the ROC curves of the four methods. It is clearly that our method significantly outperforms all other compared methods.

To explain more detailly, we list the verification rates on NEU-ID database of the above four methods in table 2. As we can see, our method achieves a high accuracy 97.71%, which is 13.33% higher than the second best.

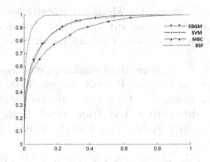

Fig. 5. The ROC curves on NEU-ID database. Our method achieves the best performance.

Table 2. Evaluation of performance of four methods. (FAR=0.1)

Method	LGBP+BSF	LGBP+SVM	MBC	EBGM
Accuracy	97.71%	74.38%	76.10%	66.79%

5 Conclusion and Discussion

This paper proposes an approach for face verification on the 2nd ID card, experiment on our NEU-ID database shows that our method achieve high accuracy (97.71%). Specially, with our proposed BSF, which is a statistical based learning, we are able to learn discriminative features. Again, we show the effectiveness of LGBP, to solve the problem of computation complexity, we exploit the filter energy check, which could achieve comparable verification rate but with significantly lower time. Further effort will be focused on learning efficient face image preprocess method, which can reduce gaps between ID images and video images.

Acknowledgments. This work is supported by the National Natural Science Foundation of China (*GrantNO*.61402097); And the Fundamental Research Funds for the Central Universities of China (*GrantNo.N*140503004).

References

1. Jain, A.K., Li, S.Z.: Handbook of Face Recognition. Springer, New York (2005)
2. Yang, M., Zhang, L., Shiu, S.K.: Monogenic binary coding: an efficient local feature extraction approach to face recognition. IEEE Trans. Inf. Forens. Sec. **7**, 1738–1751 (2012)
3. Chopra, S., Hadsell, R., LeCun, Y.: Learning a similarity metric discriminatively, with application to face verification. In: IEEE Computer Society Conference on Computer Vision and Pattern Recognition, pp. 539–546. IEEE Press, New York (2005)
4. Xie, S., Shan, S., Chen, X., Chen, J.: Fusing local patterns of gabor magnitude and phase for face recognition. IEEE Trans. Image Process. **19**, 1349–1361 (2010)

5. Sungatullina, D., Lu, J., Wang, G., Moulin, P.: Multiview discriminative learning for age-invariant face recognition. In: 10th IEEE International Conference and Workshops on Automatic Face and Gesture Recognition, pp. 1–6. IEEE Press, China (2013)

6. Jun, B., Lee, J., Kim, D.: A novel illumination-robust face recognition using statistical and non-statistical method. Pattern Recogn. Lett. **32**, 329–336 (2011)

7. Ren, X.L., Su, G.D., Xiang, Y.: Face authentication system using the Chinese second generation identity card. CAAI Trans. Intell. Syst. **4**, 213–217 (2009)

8. Feng, T.C.: Face recognition system based on the second generation identity card. Inf. surv. **1**, 6–10 (2013)

9. Felsberg, M., Sommer, G.: The monogenic signal. IEEE Trans. Signal Process. **49**, 3136–3144 (2001)

10. Guo, Z., Zhang, D.: A completed modeling of local binary pattern operator for texture classification. IEEE Trans. Image Process. **19**, 1657–1663 (2010)

11. Zhang, W., Shan, S., Gao, W., Chen, X., Zhang, H.: Local Gabor binary pattern histogram sequence(LGBPHS): a novel non-statistical model for face representation and recognition. In: 10th IEEE International Conference on Computer Vision, pp. 786–791. IEEE Press, China (2005)

12. Liu, C., Wechsler, H.: Gabor feature based classification using the enhanced Fisher linear discriminant model for face recognition. IEEE Trans. Image Process. **11**, 467–476 (2002)

13. Xiong, X., De la Torre, F.: Supervised descent method and its applications to face alignment. In: 2013 IEEE Conference on Computer Vision and Pattern Recognition, pp. 532–539. IEEE Press, Portland (2013)

14. Tan, X., Triggs, B.: Enhanced local texture feature sets for face recognition under difficult lighting conditions. IEEE Trans. Image Process. **19**, 1635–1650 (2010)

Towards Practical Face Recognition: A Local Binary Pattern Non Frontal Faces Filtering Approach

Yikui Zhai, Xiaolin Wang, Junying Gan, and Ying Xu[✉]

School of Information Engineering, Wuyi University, Jiangmen, China
{yikuizhai,xiaolinwang2,junyinggan,xuying117}@163.com

Abstract. In dynamic real-time face detection and recognition system, the non frontal faces with different tilt and deflection pose has great influence on the recognition accuracy, in order to solve these problems, we propose non frontal faces filter's method via support vector machine(SVM) and local binary patterns(LBP). By this method the images with large pose deflection will be filtered. Firstly, we apply the AdaBoost algorithm into real-time face detection and join the nose detection to further filter non face images. Then we extract texture feature from the detected face images by LBP feature operator. Finally, SVM is used to classify frontal and non frontal faces. Experimental results show that the proposed method has good classification capability for face images with varying pose. It contribute to eliminate the impact of pose variation in dynamic face recognition system.

Keywords: Face recognition · LBP · Pose classification · SVM

1 Introduction

After nearly three decades of research and development, automatic face recognition system has made great progress in recent years [1]. Performance of the face recognition system has reached a high recognition rate and accuracy rate in the conditions where the ideal image condition and the user likes to cooperate, but these research results are ideal in the laboratory environment, and mostly are positive face images [2]. If we want to apply face recognition technology to practical face recognition system, it is necessary to overcome the illumination [3], pose variation [4] due to non-ideal collect conditions or the user does not fit. In the practical application, the face and the camera can't always keep the perfect and ideal pose, and users do not cooperate in the face detection process will lead to false detection and missing detection, more practical, we cannot require users to deliberately coordinate the identification system to complete collection in face detection process, even if the user actively cooperate with the collection, it is not likely to require the user has been always keep a pose, there must be a lot of side faces in the process of the collection. So the face database which doped with this side face of pose variation, it is bound to cause serious interference for subsequent recognition result. To solve the above problems, this paper proposes a face images classifier based on local binary patterns(LBP) and support vector machine(SVM).

© Springer International Publishing Switzerland 2015
J. Yang et al. (Eds.): CCBR 2015, LNCS 9428, pp. 51–59, 2015.
DOI: 10.1007/978-3-319-25417-3_7

The method proposed in this paper can classify positive face and side face, and then filter out non frontal face, then screening database of face pose will to be more standard, if the re-use of this face pose database to recognition, the recognition rate will be greatly improved.

The difference between our method in this paper and pose correction is the latter use side face image synthesis of a positive face image, some loss information are added by side face symmetry ideas [5]. However, the information added by some algorithms, the actual situation may not be so. So the added information may be noise, it might interfere with recognition results. The purpose of this paper is to classify positive face and side face, thus we can know whether the picture of collection can meet experimental requirements. The idea of this paper is to give a face pose image database added with some mechanism: a nose filter to further determine whether exists a face, an eye filter can further judge the pose, and the side face filter can further filter out non positive face pose. So the processed face image database is more standard, and subsequent recognition rate will be improved.

2   Overall Design Framework

First, compared with several mainstream face detection algorithm, we choose Ada-Boost algorithm as face detection method. AdaBoost method is one of the most advanced technique in face detections. It has strong real-time properties, we combine the traditional face detection method with nose detection for secondary screening, and a dual detection method is obtained. Secondly, the LBP feature of images is extracted. LBP feature operator has strong robustness to illumination. Finally according to pattern recognition theory, the training data collected in the actual environment are classified by SVM. The main idea is to learn some inherent rules after feature processing for the labeled training data, then using these rules to predict unknown data.

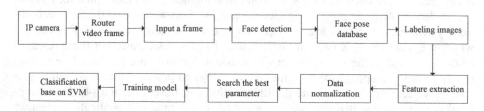

Fig. 1. Overall Design Flowchart

2.1   Face Detection

Compared with several mainstream face detection algorithm, we choose AdaBoost[6] algorithm as face detection method. Combining traditional method of face detection with nose detection, we get a double detection method. The testing process is shown in Fig.2. We input a frame image of YV12 format and transform it into the format of RGB24, which can be processed by OpenCV. Then we load the face detection classifier provided by OpenCV to complete the human face detection. If the collection is empty, it means that there exists no face and the next video frame is loaded. Otherwise, we begin the next step of detecting the nose which has the same process of face detection. If the nose can be tested from the detected face image, we save the image.

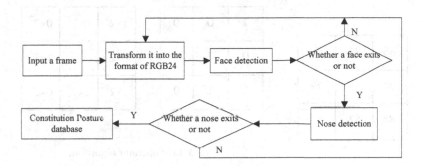

Fig. 2. Detection Processing

2.2   LBP Feature Extraction

Local binary pattern (LBP) operator was first mentioned by Harwood et al.[9] and then introduced to image texture description by Ojala et al.[10] for texture analysis. LBP[8] is non-parametric operator which is a description of the local spatial structure. LBP operator is defined as a kind of gray scale invariant texture operator and the basic idea is: regard the center pixel gray value as a threshold, and get the binary code which describe the local texture feature by comparing with its neighborhood. Its main advantages are the following: (1) The gray scale of LBP operator does not vary with any single transformation, so the gray scale has good robustness under the condition of lighting. (2) The calculation speed is fast. It can be obtained by comparison operations in a small neighborhood, which makes it possible to analyze image under the condition of complex real-time. (3) LBP operator is a kind of method without parameters (Non Parametric), so it don not need to make hypothesis in advance in the process of the application.

LBP algorithm is generally defined as the window of 3×3, which regard gray value of the center pixel of window as a threshold to get binaryzation of other pixels, and then obtained LBP values of the window according to weighted sum of the different position of pixels. Figure 3 shows an example of the LBP operator, the gray value of middle pixel is 45 and its surrounding eight points gray value are 65, 21, 43, 79, 32, 57, 88, 24, etc. LBP binary =01101001, LBP code= 1 + 8+ 32 + 64 = 105. LBP feature extraction algorithm is as follows:

$$LBP(x_c, y_c) = \sum_{r=0}^{8} 2^r sign(P_r - P_c) \tag{1}$$

where (x_c, y_c) is the coordinates of the center pixel and the gray value is P_c, P_r is the gray value of neighborhood. *sign* is a symbolic function, and its define such that:

$$sign(x) = \begin{cases} 1 & if\ x > 0 \\ 0 & otherwise \end{cases} \qquad (2)$$

1	0	0
0		1
1	1	0

1×2^0	0×2^1	0×2^2
0×2^7		1×2^3
1×2^6	1×2^5	0×2^4

65	21	43
24	45	79
88	57	32

Fig. 3. LBP operator algorithm

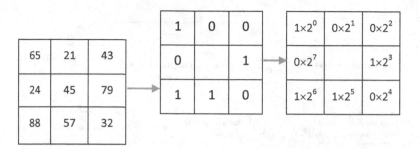

A Original image   B LBP image

Fig. 4. LBP feature extraction

3   Experiment

3.1   Establish Facial Pose Database

Here we create a face pose database, the face database is get by HIK DS-2CD3212D-I5 IP camera in a real environment, and has a total of 2022 face images. The database is collected at different times, by different cameras, in different illumination conditions, and the training set is a consisting of 991 positive images, 931 negative samples face images, and 100 test sample images. The database is collected in three phases, the first phase collects 200~250 images of 12 people in the same time, including positive face, right side of the face and left side of the face. The second stage is the freedom to collect, collecting method is to put a camera at the door of the laboratory, and to capture and save as long as there is a face in two weeks in a row, this phase includes the different light, different time. The third stage is to capture 25 individuals of 100 images in the same period. And then three stages are merged to get face pose database as shown in Fig.5, which show part of the training and test data.

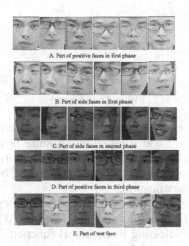

A. Part of positive faces in first phase

B. Part of side faces in first phase

C. Part of side faces in second phase

D. Part of positive faces in third phase

E. Part of test face

Fig. 5. Test and train database show

3.2   Experimental Procedure and Results

The experimental hardware environment is Intel Core i7 CPU, 3.40 GHz, 8 GB of memory, VS2010. This paper is mainly based on the source function libsvm provided, and by rewriting linear kernel function whose equation is $k(u,v)=u^\mathrm{T}v$, and the radial basis kernel function whose equation is $k(u,v)=e^{-g\|u-v\|}$. The concrete steps is as follows: at first reads the image data, and conducts features processing by using LBP, and then according to the scaling rules as shown in equation (3) to get normalization of data, the reason for the normalized processing is to prevent a feature too big or too small which plays a role in training imbalance, another reason is that it would use the inner product operations or exp operations in the nuclear calculation, imbalanced data may cause difficulty of calculation, and the data are normalized to between -1 and 1, can also be normalized to between 0 and 1.

$$y'_{nem} = lower + (upper - lower) * \frac{y'_{origina} - \min^i}{\max^i - \min^i} \qquad (3)$$

$$y'_{nem} = lower \qquad (4)$$

where $y'_{original}$ is the data before the resized, y'_{new} is the data after the resized. The *lower* is the data lower specified in a parameter and *upper* is upper bound specified in the parameters. min^i is the minimum of ith characteristic values in all of the training data, max^i is the maximum of ith characteristic values in all the training data. As is shown in figure 6, there are three samples, each sample has 256 features, the min^1 shows a minimum in the first column, the value is 5. The min^2 shows the minimum value in the second column, the value is 10, so and so on. Equation (4) is used to process data when $min^i = max^i$.

Label	Indel1: value1	Indel2:value2	......	Indel256: value256
1	1:5	2:10	......	256:90
1	1:9	2:20	......	256:78
-1	1:6	2:17	......	256:100

Fig. 6. Data Format

We can find out the optimal parameters c and g through cross validation, c represents penalty coefficient and g represents gamma factor in radial basis kernel function. What we need to be aware of is that the method finding out the parameters through cross validation isn't the best to classify the data, but it provides an approximate range of the data's classification.

The next step is to calculate the kernel function, and this paper is mainly using the linear kernel function and radial basis kernel function. When choosing the kernel function, our experience is selecting linear kernel function. While radial basis kernel function can map the data into high-dimensional space nonlinearly and can process the feature data and non-linear relationship between their properties, radial basis kernel function is not universal especially their feature data is very large, thus the linear kernel function is more practical.

The third step is choosing parameters to train model by utilizing the solvesmo() function. The final step is to predict the results by using svm_predict() function. The experimental results is shown in Table 1,2,3,4.

The experimental results show that we should normalize the collected images to the same size according to data's characteristic. We can see that the size of the picture has a great influence for classification rate, for our pose face image database size is in the range of $48\times60 \sim 70\times80$, and normalize the image into the size of 32×40 can get the best result, and the image inappropriate normalization will also affect the classification result, for example, when the size is 58×70, the classification rate only has 86.31%.

Table 1. Comparison of Classification Rate on Different Image Resolution

Dim	kernel function	parameter c	Classification rate	time(ms)
24×30	Linear	1	90%	78.6
32×40	Linear	1	95%	136.2
50×60	Linear	1	92%	312.6
58×70	Linear	1	88%	420.7

The experimental results of Table 2 compared with Table 1, we found that when using a linear kernel function and radial basis function kernel function, the classification rate is also 94.73%, but former less 26 milliseconds, so radial basis function is not a panacea. When the value of the characteristic is relatively large, the linear kernel function to be more practical and less with time, especially for real-time face recognition systems, real-time is pursued all long. Table 2 also shows that the importance of the parameters selection, after testing we found that the time of procedure will increase with parameter g increases, meanwhile we can find under the same parameters the test results will vary a lot when the image size is different, when c=10, g=0.001, the image size is 32×40 more than 50×60 higher by 2.1%, at the same time program running time is less for small size.

Table 2. Comparison of Classification Rate on Different Image Size and Parameter Choice

Dim	Kernel function	Parameter c	Parameter g	Classification rate	Time(ms)
32×40	RBF	1	0.008	90%	191.7
32×40	RBF	1	0.006	91%	185.5
32×40	RBF	10	0.001	95%	163.8
32×40	RBF	10	0.002	94%	167.7
32×40	RBF	9	0.001	94%	170.0
32×40	RBF	8	0.002	94%	168.1
50×60	RBF	10	0.001	91%	401.4
50×60	RBF	10	0.002	90%	427.4
50×60	RBF	9	0.001	91%	401.9

Experimental results in Table 3 show that the method of LBP outperforms LPQ using not only linear kernel function but also RBF kernel function, and LBP is robust to illumination.

Table 3. Comparison of Classification Rate on Different Feature Choice

Method	Linear kernel function	RBF kernel function
LBP+SVM	95%	95%
LPQ+SVM	87%	85%

Which portion of picture made a great difference to pose's variation, is it up of the nose or down of nose? The main idea is that a real-time face recognition system have high requirement on speed, if we know which part of picture made a great difference to pose's variation, then we can segment image in order to save primary information, remove minor information, and reduce the amount of data stored on the one hand, and on the other hand to accelerate the speed of classification and improve efficiency. Here, the image is divided into upper and lower portions. We regarded the left bottom of the picture as origin. Segmenting image in one-third, one-quarter, one-half, two-third, three-quarter respectively, as Fig.7 shows. The results in Table 4 show that the below of nose, especially mouth portion has a strong influence on pose's variation. Experimental result with including mouth portion is much better than without mouth portion, for example, lower's results is better than upper's but image is segmented into three-quarter, because images contain mouth at this moment. So mouth portion do make great contributions to pose classification. Therefore, in the subsequent real-time face recognition system we can add more information about mouth part, and remove information of non-mouth portion so that improve the classification speed.

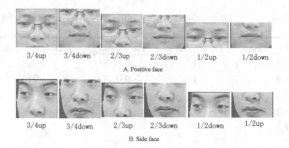

3/4up   3/4down   2/3up   2/3down   1/2up   1/2down

A. Positive face

3/4up   3/4down   2/3up   2/3down   1/2down   1/2up

B. Side face

Fig. 7. Local Image Segmentation

Table 4. Comparison of Classification Rate on Different Local Feature

image segmentation		Dim	kernel function	Classification rate	time(ms)
upper	1/2	20×32	RBF	76 %	84.4
		20×32	Linear	74%	71.8
	2/3	26×32	RBF	82%	106.2
		26×32	Linear	77%	90.9
	3/4	30×32	RBF	83%	121.7
		30×32	Linear	84%	103.7
lower	1/2	20×32	RBF	82%	85.5
		20×32	Linear	83%	70.0
	2/3	26×32	RBF	85%	108.0
		26×32	Linear	88%	91.2
	3/4	30×32	RBF	82%	124.0
		30×32	Linear	84%	204.3

For dynamic face recognition system, many weak classifier mechanisms could be added to improve recognition rate, a nose filter to further determine whether exists a face, an eye filter can further judge the pose, a speed filter to further determine whether user is willing to recognition, the side face filter can further filter out non positive face pose and so on. So many mechanisms are added will have an influence on real-time. Compare with real-time, we may need a week filter to filter non frontal face. So the method of segmentation images to save mouth portion information not only can meet needs of real-time but also can filter non frontal face. The shortest time when classification rate reach to maximum is 131.0 milliseconds for global image, while the shortest time when classification rate reach to maximum is 91.0 milliseconds for local image, the latter is less 40 milliseconds than former.

4   Summary and Prospect

In this paper, we introduce a novel mechanism to dynamic face recognition system, which can filter non frontal face via SVM and LBP. Experimental results indicate that this method can not only correct filter side face but also have high speed. We can apply this method to practical face recognition systems and maintain real-time performance at the same time. We also find that mouth portion make a great contribution to pose's classification. In the future work, we will apply the filter to the real-time face recognition system, and filter tilted larger images to improve recognition rate.

Acknowledgments. This work is supported by NNSF (No.61072127, No. 6137219, No. 61070167), NSF of Guangdong Province, P.R.C. (No.S2013010013311, No.1015290200100002, NO.S2011010001085, NO.S2011040004211), Higher Education Outstanding Young Teachers Foundation of Guangdong Province under Grant (NO.SYQ2014001) and youth foundation of Wuyi University (No.2013zk07).

References

1. Harmon, L.D., Khan, M.K., Lasch, R., Ramig, P.F.: Machine identification of human faces. Pattern Recognition **13**, 97–110 (1981)
2. Phillips, P.J., Moon, H., Rizvi, S., Rauss, P.J.: The FERET evaluation methodology for face-recognition algorithms. IEEE Transactions on Pattern Analysis and Machine Intelligence **22**, 1090–1104 (2000)
3. Phillips, P.J., Wechsler, H., Huang, J., Rauss, P.J.: The FERET database and evaluation procedure for face-recognition algorithms. Image and Vision Computing **16**, 295–306 (1998)
4. Blanz, V., Romdhani, S., Vetter, T.: Face identification across different poses and illuminations with a 3d morphable model. In: 5th IEEE International Conference on Automatic Face and Gesture Recognition, pp. 192–197. IEEE Press, New York (2002)
5. Chai, X., Shan, S., Chen, X., Gao, W.: Locally linear regression for pose-invariant face recognition. IEEE Transactions on Image Processing **16**, 1716–1725 (2007)
6. Viola, P., Jones, M.: Rapid object detection using a boosted cascade of simple features. In: Proceedings of the 2001 IEEE Computer Society Conference on Computer Vision and Pattern Recognition, vol. 1, pp. 504–511. IEEE Press, New York (2001)
7. Chang, C.C., Lin, C.J.: LIBSVM: A library for support vector machines. ACM Transactions on Intelligent Systems and Technology **2**, 27–33 (2011)
8. Ojala, T., Pietikäinen, M., Mäenpää, T.: Multiresolution gray-scale and rotation invariant texture classification with local binary patterns. IEEE Transactions on Pattern Analysis and Machine Intelligence **24**, 971–987 (2002)
9. Tan, X., Triggs, B.: Enhanced local texture feature sets for face recognition under difficult lighting conditions. IEEE Transactions on Image Processing **19**, 1635–1650 (2010)
10. Hwang, W., Wang, H., Kim, H., Kee, S.C., Kim, J.: Face recognition system using multiple face model of hybrid fourier feature under uncontrolled illumination variation. IEEE Transactions on Image Processing **20**, 1152–1165 (2011)

Metric Learning Based False Positives Filtering for Face Detection

Nanhai Zhang[✉], Jiajie Han, Jiani Hu, and Weihong Deng

Beijing University of Posts and Telecommunications, Beijing, China
{nhzhang,dxs,jnhu,whdeng}@bupt.edu.cn

Abstract. Face detection in the wild is a challenging task within the field of computer vision. Many face detectors fail to distinguish face images and non-face images because intra-class variations surpass inter-class variations. To overcome it, we propose a metric learning based false positives filtering for face detection. With 8 average faces as standard face, we apply metric learning to seek a linear transformation to reduce the distance between face images and standard faces while enlarge the distance between non-face images and standard faces. To solve our defining objective function for metric learning, we adopt a batch-stochastic gradient descent scheme, with which we can get stable solution fast. The results on FDDB and our self-collected dataset show a good performance of our method for improving Viola-Jones face detectors.

Keywords: Metric learning · False positives filtering · Batch-stochastic

1 Introduction

Face detection is a challenging task within the field of computer vision. Great success have been made over past years, especially in constrained environments. However, it is still a challenge to detect face in wild environments, due to lighting, illumination, expression and occlusion.

The main challenge comes from that intra-class variations (between faces and faces) caused by lighting, expression, pose, etc may be larger than inter-class variations (between faces and complex background). Fig. 1 shows the situation. To deal with this problem, diverse approaches have been proposed. For the feature-based methods, researchers try to extract robust features, e.g. SURF[1] and learned feature with CNN[2]. For the model-based methods, researchers try to model large variations with deformable part-based model[3]. Nevertheless, most of these approaches are time consuming or computation expensively.

The fundamental principle of most improvement work is to reduce the large variations of face appearances into a controllable limit, which shares the same principle with metric learning. Motivated by this idea, we propose an universal false positives filtering process for face detection based on metric learning, which can efficiently improve the results of classical Viola-Jones detector[4]. With well trained linear mapping matrix, we can map the feature into a new data space

© Springer International Publishing Switzerland 2015
J. Yang et al. (Eds.): CCBR 2015, LNCS 9428, pp. 60–67, 2015.
DOI: 10.1007/978-3-319-25417-3_8

Fig. 1. Example illustrates the situation where intra-class variations surpass inter-class variations. *Left* is a face image, *middle* is an average face and *right* is a non-face image. The cosine similarity between face image and average face is 0.37 which is lower than 0.62 that is the cosine similarity between non-face image and average face.

where the inter-class differences surpass the intra-class differences. And then the existence of face can be easily predicated by a thresholding process. This process is quite fast and efficient.

In summary, the contributions of this paper are threefold:

1) We propose a new framework of false positives filtering process for face detection based on metric learning. With this approach, non-face images can be filtered quickly and robustly.
2) We refer average faces(Fig. 2) as standard faces, because they are baseline shape of human face free from kinds of variations. And we propose a batch-stochastic gradient descent scheme to learn the linear transformation of metric learning fast and robustly.
3) To evaluate our approach, we collect an unconstrained face detection dataset from real world. On this dataset, our approach shows efficient improvement. To be more persuasion, we also test it on the challenge FDDB[5] and achieve significant improvement of Viola-Jones detector .

2   Related Work

Face Detection: As a fundamental task in computer vision, face detection attracts lots of researchers. The seminal work by Viola and Jones[4] has become a standard paradigm for face detection. Since that, most improvements follow the paradigm. Recently, Chen et al.[6] propose a unified framework for cascade face detection and alignment with simple shape indexed feature. Different from the boosted cascade framework, deformable part-based models also achieve state-of-the-art result[3]. Besides, Shen et al.[7] propose a more different framework. In their work they first present a novel exemplar-based face detector and it is improved by Li et al.[8]. While as far as we know, few papers discuss the post process for face detection except Chen et al.[6]. To prove using facial point based features can improve face detector, they introduce a simple SVM classifier in the post process. Different from that, our false positives filtering process is more universe and fast and can significantly improve face detector without the help of face landmarks.

Metric Learning: Since the pioneering work of Xing et al.[9], many metric learning algorithms have been proposed. Most classic metric learning

(a)   (b)   (c)   (d)

Fig. 2. Illustration of 8 average faces, which are compounded by experimental psychologists[1]. Four groups of average faces respectively stands for four country's average faces:(a) China, (b) Japan, (c) Korea and (d) India

methods utilize the Mahalanobis distance form including LMNN[10], ITML[11], OASIS[12]. For non-linear metrics, many works try to capture the non-linear structure with kernel tricks to linear models[13]. Besides, neural network, due to its powerful representative ability, is also used to map data into non-linear space where the squared L2 distances can be directly used to metric similarity[14]. Our approach benefits from these works especially the DDML[14]. Based on this work, we propose the batch-stochastic gradient descent scheme to optimize the cost function.

3   Proposed Approach

Given a set of N training samples $X = [x_1, x_2, \cdots, x_N] \in \mathbb{R}^{d \times N}$, where $x_i \in \mathbb{R}^d$ denotes the ith training sample, and a prototype set of K standard faces $Y = [y_1, y_2, \cdots, y_K] \in \mathbb{R}^{d \times K}$, where $y_i \in \mathbb{R}^d$ denotes the ith prototype face. Our approach adopts the Mahalanobis distance form. So the distance between a sample from X and a sample from Y can be computed as:

$$d_M(x_i, y_j) = \sqrt{(x_i - y_j)^T M (x_i - y_j)} = \sqrt{(x_i - y_j)^T W^T W (x_i - y_j)} = \|W x_i - W y_j\|_2 \tag{1}$$

where M is some symmetric and positive semi-definite matrix which parameterizes the squared Mahalanobis distance. Since the property of positive semidefinite, M can be factorized as $M = W^T W$.

From Eq.(1), we find that with parameter W the data points are mapped into a new space where the distance between two data point can be computed with squared L2 distances. Consequently our goal is to seek a linear transformation matrix that reduces the distance between face images and standard faces while enlarges the distance between non-face images and standard faces. We define another two sets which can be constructed by set X an Y. $S = \{(x_i, y_j) \mid x_i \ is \ face \ image \ from \ X, \ y_j \in Y\}$, $D = \{(x_i, y_j) \mid x_i \ is \ nonface \ image \ from \ X, y_j \in Y\}$, where S denotes the face pairs and D denotes the face and non-face pairs.

The goal of metric learning is to minimize the distance of pairs from S and maximize the distance of pairs from D. Different from some metric learning methods based on large margin, we believe it is enough to discriminate face and

---

[1] http://faceresearch.org/

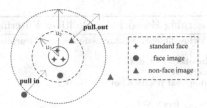

Fig. 3. Schematic illustration of our method. In the origin data space, there is one sample of non-face being close to the space formed by standard faces and one sample being far away. The goal of metric learning is to pull the outside face sample into threshold u_1 and pull the inside non-face sample out to the threshold u_2.

non-face image if distance of intra-class is below a threshold and distance of inter-class is above a threshold. Then our approach can be formulated as:

$$\min_{W} \|W\|_F^2$$
$$s.t.\ d_M^2(x_i, y_j) \leq u_1\ \forall (i,j) \in S \tag{2}$$
$$d_M^2(x_i, y_j) \geq u_2\ \forall (i,j) \in D$$

where $\|\cdot\|_F$ denotes Frobenius norm, u_1 and u_2 denote the pre-specified threshold and they obey $u_2 \geq u_1$. Choosing $\|W\|_F^2$ as objective function because we follow the experience that simple W contributes to stronger generalization ability.

Fig. 3 intuitively illustrate the proposed method. To reduce the parameters, we adopt the trick of [14]. The relationship between hyperparameter u_1 and u_2 just ensure a safe margin between intra-class difference and inter-class difference, so that we can simply set $u_1 = \delta - 1$ and $u_2 = \delta + 1$. For the constraints, we can encode them with hinge loss:

$$(d_M^2(x_i, y_j) - \delta + 1)_+\ ,\ \forall (i,j) \in S$$
$$(\delta + 1 - d_M^2(x_i, y_j))_+\ ,\ \forall (i,j) \in D \tag{3}$$

where $(z)_+$ denotes the hinge loss function $max(0, z)$. Then the final form of the optimization is formulated as:

$$\min_{W} \mathcal{L}(W) = \sum_i^N \sum_j^K (1 - l_{ij}(\delta - d_M^2(x_i, y_j)))_+ + \gamma \|W\|_F^2 \tag{4}$$

where l_{ij} is the label of image pair (x_i, y_j), $l_{ij} = 1$ for $(x_i, y_j) \in S$ and $l_{ij} = -1$ for $(x_i, y_j) \in D$. The γ term is a trade-off between the regularization term and the hinge loss. The cost function $\mathcal{L}(W)$ is to minimise the hinge loss of all over N training samples while keep parameter W simple.

For minimising the cost function $\mathcal{L}(W)$, we utilize a batch-stochastic gradient descent scheme to solve it. Since the hinge loss $(z)_+$ is not differentiable at point $z = 0$, we use a generalized logistic loss function $h_\beta(z)$ to smoothly approximate the hinge loss[15], where $h_\beta(z) = \frac{1}{\beta} log(1 + exp(\beta z))$ and β is a sharpness parameter. $h_\beta(z) - (z)_+$ converges to zero as the sharpness

Algorithm 1. Metric Learning Based False Positives Filtering

Input: Training set X and Y, threshold δ, regularization term γ, learning rate ν, convergence error ε, test set T

Output: parameter W and labels of test data

    Step 1 (training the parameter W):

    Initialization W with 1 at diagonal position, otherwise 0

    for $iter = 1, 2, 3, \dots$ **do**

        Randomly select a sample x_i from X

        Compute batch-stochastic gradient according to Eq.(5)

        Update W with $W = W - \nu \dfrac{\partial \mathcal{L}}{\partial W}$

        if $|\mathcal{L}(W)_{iter} - \mathcal{L}(W)_{iter-1}| < \varepsilon$ **then**

            break

        end if

    end for

    Step 2 (predication):

    for each test data t_m in T **do**

        label for t_m is predicated by $l(m) = \underset{j \in [1, K]}{mean}(d_M^2(t_m, y_j)) < \delta$

    end for

    return parameter W and labels l

---

parameter β increases. Then we can compute the batch-stochastic gradient of the cost function:

$$\frac{\partial \mathcal{L}}{\partial W} = \frac{2}{K} \sum_j^K (h'(z_j) l_{ij} (W x_i - W y_j) x_i^T + h'(z_j) l_{ij} (W y_j - W x_i) y_j^T) + 2\gamma W \qquad (5)$$

where

$$z_j = 1 - l_{ij}(\delta - d_M^2(x_i, y_j)) \qquad (6)$$

From Eq.(5) we can see that the batch in our batch-stochastic gradient descent scheme means a batch of K standard face from dataset Y and the stochastic means randomly select a sample from dataset X. Then parameter W can be updated by the batch-stochastic gradient multiplying a learning rate.

The main procedure of our method is shown as **Algorithm 1**. Besides, to achieve a advance performance of false positives filtering, we combine the results of our method and Viola-Jones detector. Since the Viola-Jones detector adopt the number of neighbors for filtering false face, we propose to use following formulation to combine the two method:

$$Socre = num\_neighbors \times \exp(-\underset{j \in [1, K]}{mean}(d_M^2(t_m, y_j))) \qquad (7)$$

4   Experiments

To evaluate our proposed approach, we test it on the challenge FDDB and our own dataset. And we compare our approach with some state-of-art metric learning methods. Following detailedly describe it.

4.1   Implementation Details

The training set for metric learning is collected as following: we firstly collect a large set of images containing face. Then we use the Viola-Jones detector[4] to detect faces within these images. Due to limited performance of Viola-Jones detector, the detected results contain many non-face images. Lastly, we annotate these detected results and get the training set which consists of about 20000 face images and 10000 non-face images.

For the feature, we extract two kinds of features: HOG and LBP. Before that we align all images with face alignment algorithm SDM[16]. For LBP feature, we divide each image into 10×10 non-overlapping blocks with size 10×10. For each block we extract a 59-dimensional uniform pattern LBP feature. Lastly we apply LDA to project the 5900-dimensional feature into a 100-dimensional feature. For HOG feature, we divide each image like LBP. For each block, we choose the cell size as 5×5 and 18 directions. We also apply LDA to project the HOG feature into a 100-dimensional feature. Finally we get a 200-dimensional feature each image and we apply WPCA to the feature before training. For the parameters of metric learning, we set threshold $\delta = 2$, regularization term $\gamma = 0.01$ and learning rate $\nu = 0.001$.

4.2   Experiments on Our Wild Dataset

We collect an unconstrained face detection dataset to evaluate our approach. Different from FDDB, our self-collected face dataset is collected from people's daily life, which contains many pose pictures, scenery pictures and group pictures. It altogether contains 225 images with a total of 630 faces. We follow the evaluation protocols as FDDB that we use the discrete setting which counts the correct detections according to intersection ratio. We compare our method with original Viola-Jones detector[4], the cosine similarity and two other classic metric learning based false positives filtering. From Fig. 4(a), we can see that our approach slightly outperforms ITML[11] and OASIS[12] while significantly outperforms the cosine similarity. Besides, all of these metric learning based methods show efficient improvement to original Viola-Jones detector. Fig. 4(c) shows some results of two detectors. We can see that some easily misclassified images are misclassified by Viola-Jones detector but can be well classified by our approach on our dataset.

4.3   Experiments on FDDB

The FDDB is a challenge dataset for evaluating the performance of face detector[5]. It contains 2845 images with a total of 5171 faces. For the evaluation protocols, we also use the discrete setting. From Fig. 4(b), we can see that our result outperforms the cosine similarity significantly while achieves competitive result comparing with ITML[11] and OASIS[12]. Comparing with Viola-Jones detector, single model of metric learning sightly outperforms it while the combining method outperforms two single models and get the best result. Fig. 4(d) shows some results of two detectors. And we can see that some easily misclassified images are misclassified by Viola-Jones detector but can be well classified by our approach on FDDB.

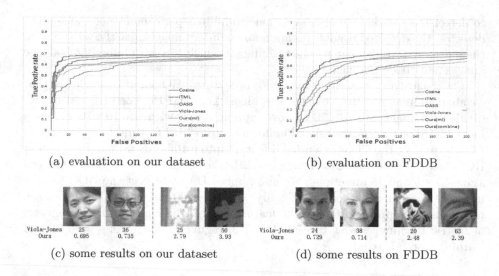

(a) evaluation on our dataset   (b) evaluation on FDDB

(c) some results on our dataset   (d) some results on FDDB

Fig. 4. (a)Evaluation on our dataset (Discontinuous score), (b)Evaluation on FDDB (Discontinuous score), (c)(d)some results of two detectors on two datasets, below is the score of two model, for Viola-Jones detector, the greater number means the greater probability of face, converse for our method

5 Conclusion

In this article, we propose a new false positives filtering process based on metric learning for face detection. Our approach shows significant improvements for Viola-Jones detector on challenge FDDB and our self-collected dataset. As metric learning is a unified method to enhance the given feature, our approach can be also used to improve some other face detectors. How to learn some representative prototype faces as the standard faces will be our future work.

Acknowledgments. The authors would like to thank the anonymous reviewers for their thoughtful and constructive remarks that are helpful to improve the quality of this paper. This work was partially sponsored by supported by the Fundamental Research Funds for the Central Universities under Grant No. 2014ZD03-01, NSFC (National Natural Science Foundation of China) under Grant No. 61375031, No. 61471048, and No.61273217. This work was also supported by the Beijing Higher Education Young Elite Teacher Program, and the Program for New Century Excellent Talents in University.

References

1. Li, J., Wang, T., Zhang, Y.: Face detection using SURF cascade. In: IEEE International Conference on Computer Vision Workshops, ICCV 2011 Workshops, November 6–13, 2011, pp. 2183–2190. IEEE, Barcelona (2011)

2. Li, H., Lin, Z., Shen, X., Brandt, J., Hua, G.: A convolutional neural network cascade for face detection. In: Proceedings of the IEEE Conference on Computer Vision and Pattern Recognition, pp. 5325–5334 (2015)

3. Zhu, X., Ramanan, D.: Face detection, pose estimation, and landmark localization in the wild. In: 2012 IEEE Conference on Computer Vision and Pattern Recognition, June 16–21, 2012, pp. 2879–2886. IEEE Computer Society, Providence (2012)

4. Viola, P.A., Jones, M.J.: Rapid object detection using a boosted cascade of simple features. In: 2001 IEEE Computer Society Conference on Computer Vision and Pattern Recognition (CVPR 2001), with CD-ROM, December 8–14, 2001, pp. 511–518. IEEE Computer Society, Kauai (2001)

5. Jain, V., Learned-Miller, E.G.: FDDB: A benchmark for face detection in unconstrained settings (2010)

6. Chen, D., Ren, S., Wei, Y., Cao, X., Sun, J.: Joint cascade face detection and alignment. In: Fleet, D., Pajdla, T., Schiele, B., Tuytelaars, T. (eds.) ECCV 2014, Part VI. LNCS, vol. 8694, pp. 109–122. Springer, Heidelberg (2014)

7. Shen, X., Lin, Z., Brandt, J., Wu, Y.: Detecting and aligning faces by image retrieval. In: 2013 IEEE Conference on Computer Vision and Pattern Recognition, June 23–28, 2013, pp. 3460–3467. IEEE, Portland (2013)

8. Li, H., Lin, Z., Brandt, J., Shen, X., Hua, G.: Efficient boosted exemplar-based face detection. In: 2014 IEEE Conference on Computer Vision and Pattern Recognition, CVPR 2014, June 23–28, 2014, pp. 1843–1850. IEEE, Columbus (2014)

9. Xing, E.P., Ng, A.Y., Jordan, M.I., Russell, S.J.: Distance metric learning with application to clustering with side-information. In: Becker, S., Thrun, S., Obermayer, K. (eds.) Advances in Neural Information Processing Systems, vol. 15 [Neural Information Processing Systems, NIPS 2002, December 9–14, 2002, Vancouver, British Columbia, Canada], pp. 505–512. MIT Press (2002)

10. Weinberger, K.Q., Saul, L.K.: Distance metric learning for large margin nearest neighbor classification. Journal of Machine Learning Research 10, 207–244 (2009)

11. Pardowitz, M., Zöllner, R., Dillmann, R.: Incremental learning of task sequences with information-theoretic metrics. In: Christensen, H.I. (ed.) First European Robotics Symposium 2006, EUROS 2006, Palermo, Italy. Springer Tracts in Advanced Robotics, vol. 22, pp. 51–63. Springer (2006)

12. Chechik, G., Sharma, V., Shalit, U., Bengio, S.: Large scale online learning of image similarity through ranking. Journal of Machine Learning Research 11, 1109–1135 (2010)

13. Xu, Z.E., Weinberger, K.Q., Chapelle, O.: Distance metric learning for kernel machines (2012). CoRR abs/1208.3422

14. Hu, J., Lu, J., Tan, Y.: Discriminative deep metric learning for face verification in the wild. In: 2014 IEEE Conference on Computer Vision and Pattern Recognition, CVPR 2014, June 23–28, 2014, pp. 1875–1882. IEEE, Columbus (2014)

15. Mignon, A., Jurie, F.: PCCA: A new approach for distance learning from sparse pairwise constraints. In: 2012 IEEE Conference on Computer Vision and Pattern Recognition, June 16–21, 2012, pp. 2666–2672. IEEE Computer Society, Providence (2012)

16. Xiong, X., la Torre, F.D.: Supervised descent method and its applications to face alignment. In: 2013 IEEE Conference on Computer Vision and Pattern Recognition, June 23–28, 2013, pp. 532–539. IEEE, Portland (2013)

Face Recognition via Compact Fisher Vector

Hongjun Wang$^{(\boxtimes)}$ and Weihong Deng

Beijing University of Posts and Telecommunication,
No 10, Xitucheng Road, Haidian District, Beijing, People's Republic of China
surlogics@gmail.com, whdeng@bupt.edu.cn

Abstract. Efficient encoding of facial descriptors remains to be a major topic for face recognition. Among various methods, Fisher vector (FV) representations have shown satisfying performance on most benchmark datasets. However, its representation is huge. In this paper, we present a novel approach to make Fisher vector compact and improves its performance. We utilize handcrafted low-level descriptors as FV do. However, we retain only 1st order statistics of FV, introduce Gaussian block to sparsify FV, alter its formulation, and normalize properly. We evaluate our method on LFW and FERET dataset, and result shows our method effectively compresses Fisher vector and achieves satisfying result at the same time.

Keywords: Fisher vector · Face recognition · Compact descriptor · Discriminant descriptor

1 Introduction

The pursuit of automatic and precise recognition of face has motivated researchers in a range of fields, and related works have been applied to public security, human-computer interaction, etc. However, face representation and recognition is still an open problem due to high variability such as in illumination, scales, rotation, pose, and occlusion. Two main kinds of face recognition tasks are: face identification, which is to identify an unknown person given a gallery set; and face verification, which is to decide whether two images are of the same person. We address both the verification task and identification task.

The last decade has witnessed the flourish of Bag-of-Features (BoF) model for object recognition. The approach is inspired by the bag-of-words (BoW) model, where a bag of words is a histogram of local image features. The BoF model benefits from the power of local feature descriptors as well as machine learning techniques to extract discriminative ones and to form a global representation. A standard pipeline of the BoF model consists of: local descriptors extraction; codebook generation; local feature encoding and classification [4, 5]. Meanwhile, majority of efforts have been focused on generating codebooks and encoding features with them. Huang [4] introduced a taxonomy based on motivation. They categorized popular coding strategies into voting-based, Fisher coding-based, reconstruction-based (sparse coding, local coordinate coding, local-constraint linear coding), local tangent-based (local tangent

© Springer International Publishing Switzerland 2015
J. Yang et al. (Eds.): CCBR 2015, LNCS 9428, pp. 68–77, 2015.
DOI: 10.1007/978-3-319-25417-3_9

coding, super vector coding), saliency-based (salient coding, group salient coding). Our method is based on Fisher coding.

Fisher coding is inspired by the technique of Fisher kernel, which represents visual words by means of a Gaussian Mixture Model (GMM). Fisher coding describes a signal with a gradient vector derived from its probability density function. Fisher coding has achieved satisfying performances in various image categorization tasks [18]. However, it comes at the expense of high memory usage and computational complexity. A Fisher encoding of a set of local descriptors $x_1, ..., x_r \in R^D$ with K Gaussian components has a final representation size of $K(2D+1)$. In [7], Fisher representation of ILSVRC 2010 dataset (1.4 million images) with 512K dimensions per image, using a 4 byte floating-point representation, requires almost 3TB. This makes Fisher encoding impractical in large-scale image representation. Binarization[1] and product quantization [7] are suggested to cope up with its high storage price.

Vector of Locally Aggregated Descriptors (VLAD) introduced by Jegou et al. [8] is a compact state-of-the-art encoding method. VLAD is similar in spirit to Fisher coding, as both captures deviations of the distribution of local descriptors assigned to a cluster center. Different from Fisher coding where the data is modeled by GMM, in VLAD the codebook is learned using K-means, with each local descriptor x_i associated to its nearest visual word in the codebook. VLAD can be seen as a simplified non-probabilistic version of Fisher encoding [9,10]. VLAD has a final representation size of KD, with K the number of cluster centers. Arandjelovic [17] show that intra-normalization (L2 normalization within each cluster) significantly improves performance. Inspired by [6], we regard Fisher coding may also be regarded as a Gaussian kernel codebook with uncertainty and plausibility integrated, whereas VLAD is represented by traditional codebook with constant weight and hard-voting.

In this paper, we devise a simple approach to compress Fisher vector to the size of VLAD under same condition. We seek methods to sparsify Fisher encoding, alternate its representation and apply proper normalization method. We zero out features that has low posteriors, forming Gaussian blocks. We show that performing intra-normalization for each Gaussian block could cause the loss of information regarding its norm, thus we suggests a function mapping to preserve important information about the distribution of local descriptors around each codewords. Our approach achieves better performance on the LFW benchmark than Fisher encoding, with memory usage halved. Figure 1 describes our pipeline, details have been elaborated in section 3.

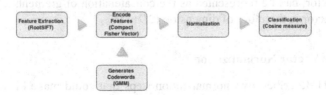

Fig. 1. Pipeline of our approach

2   Fisher Vector and Related Encoding Strategies

2.1   Fisher Kernel and Fisher Vector

Fisher coding derives from Fisher kernel, which describes a feature by a gradient vector derived from its probability density function – GMM. Let θ denote the parameter of the GMM, where $\theta = \{w_k, \mu_k, \Sigma_k, i=1...K\}$ denote prior, mean vector and covariance matrix of the k-th Gaussian respectively; $X = \{x_1, ..., x_\tau\}$ denotes the set of local feature vectors extracted from the image. One can characterize X with the gradient vector $\nabla_\theta \log p(X|\theta)$. Suppose all features are independent, the log-likelihood of the extracted features are:

$$L(X \mid \theta) = \sum_{t=1}^{\tau} \log p(x_t \mid \theta) \tag{1}$$

The likelihood that x_t was generated by the GMM is $P(x_t|\theta) = \sum_{k=1}^{K} w_k\, p_k(x_t|\theta)$, with $\sum_{k=1}^{K} w_k = 1$ and $p_k(x_t|\theta) = \exp\{-(x-\mu_\gamma)'\Sigma_k^{-1}(x-\mu_\gamma)/2\}/\{(2\pi)^{\sigma 2}|\Sigma_k|^{1/2}\}$. Assume that the covariance matrices are diagonal.

Let $\gamma_t(k)$ be the soft assignment of x_t to Gaussian k, i.e. the probability for feature x_t to have been generated by the k-th Gaussian. We have $\gamma_t(k) = w_k p_k(x_t|\theta)/\{\sum_{j=1}^{N}\log w_j p_j(x_t|\theta)\}$.

The gradients of feature x_t with respect to GMM parameters can be calculated. To normalize input vectors, Fisher information matrix is suggested. Thus gradients with respect to GMM parameters are:

$$\varsigma_{w_k}^{X} = \frac{1}{\sqrt{w_k}}\sum_{t}(\gamma_t(k) - w_k) \tag{2}$$

$$\varsigma_{\mu k}^{X} = \frac{1}{\sqrt{w_k}}\sum_{t}\gamma_t(k)\frac{x_t - \mu_k}{\sigma_k} \tag{3}$$

$$\varsigma_{\sigma k}^{X} = \frac{1}{\sqrt{2w_k}}\sum_{t}\gamma_t(k)[\frac{(x_t - \mu_k)^2}{\sigma_k^2} - 1] \tag{4}$$

where ς_{wv}^{X} is a scalar of 0th order statistics, and $\varsigma_{\mu v}^{X}$, $\varsigma_{\sigma v}^{X}$ are vectors of D dimensions of 1st and 2nd order statistics respectively. The final coding vector of a feature, i.e. the Fisher vector, can be represented as the concatenation of gradients ς_{wv}^{X}, $\varsigma_{\mu v}^{X}$, $\varsigma_{\sigma v}^{X}$. The Fisher vector is therefore of dimension $(2D+1)K$.

2.2   Fisher Vector Normalization

Perronnin [11] described two normalization steps that could make Fisher vector obtain competitive results when combine with a linear classifier: L2 normalization and power normalization. We apply power-normalization first and then L2 normalization.

Sanchez [7] provides two justifications on L2 normalization. Firstly, L2 normalization cancels out the effects of the amounts of background information. Without it, images that contain same object at different scales could have different signatures as they contain different amounts of background information that hamper representation. Secondly, for high-dimensional vectors, L2-normalization is valid to maximize information as long as similarity is measured using dot-products.

Power normalization is performed to each dimension of the FV, which takes the form $z \leftarrow \text{sign}(z)|z|^\rho$, $0 < \rho \leq 1$. A reasonable value of ρ could be $1/2$ and the transformation is referred to as 'signed square-rooting'. This operation can be views as data comparison using Hellinger measures. Power normalization basically has the same form as RootSIFT [23]. Power normalization avoids peakiness effects, which is the influence of descriptors frequently seen within images. It unsparsifies the resulting representation as well.

2.3 Integrating Spatial Information

The BoF model encode local features via their appearance patterns in features space and ignores its spatial information in image space. However, without taking spatial structure into account, we may lose important information, as similar local descriptor may signify distinct features under diverse background and therefore function differently if perceived at different locations.

Spatial pyramid representation is a popular spatial model introduced in [12] to capture spatial layout of an image. It subdivide an image iteratively into finer scales, encode features over these regions respectively and concatenate them to form the final representation. Krapac [13] introduced an extension of BoF by representing spatial layout using GMM. In [14] had proposed an image layout model without partitioning it. Modeling the joint distribution of local descriptors and patch locations can be done by simply augmenting the local feature with their spatial coordinates. We follow the notation in [15], define the augmented feature vector $x_t = [x_i; x/w\text{-}1/2; y/k\text{-}1/2] \in R^{D+2}$, where w and h represents the image height and width, respectively. The augmented features reflect not only descriptors in feature space, but also location in image space.

2.4 VLAD and Intra-Normalization

VLAD encoding [10] can be regarded as a simplified version of Fisher vector encoding. Firstly, through K-means clustering, we first learn a codebook of visual words. With x_t and μ_k denoting local descriptor and visual words respectively, the residual vector is calculated by:

$$\varsigma_k = x_t - \mu_k \tag{5}$$

VLAD inherits ambiguity problems like BoW model as the k-means clustering algorithm can be viewed as a non-probabilistic version of GMM clustering.

In [17], intra-normalization is proposed to tackle burstiness, where in Fisher vector we address the problem by power normalization. It was found in [17] that intra-normalization is more effective than power normalization, and it can simply be done by independently L2 normalize the sum of residuals within each VLAD cluster. In [18], intra-normalization is applied to Fisher vector for each Gaussian.

3   Compact Fisher Vector Representation

3.1   Sparsifying Fisher Vector

In section 2.1, the posterior probability of x_t of the k-th Gaussian is $\gamma_t(k) = w_\gamma p_\gamma(x_t |\theta)/\{\sum_{j=1}^{N} \log w_j p_j(x_t |\theta)\}$. In practice, this probability is small for most cases. In [19], the author obtained a sparse image representation by picking k out of the K Gaussian components and set the rest $K-k$ Gaussian posteriors to zero.

To get a proper block size for each cluster so that we could apply intra-normalization effectively. We zero out posteriors that gone below a certain threshold. This approach could also abate negative impacts of Gaussian visual words located faraway from local descriptors.

Finally, to ensure our Gaussian posteriors of the K Gaussians sum to one for each data, we update posterior by normalization: $\gamma_t(k) = \gamma_t(k)/\sum_j \gamma_t(j)$.

3.2   Fisher Vector with First Order Statistically Only

In [7], it is argued that the 0th order statistics does not help improving results. Besides this, we argue that with proper normalization, 2nd order statistics could be ignored without much hindering classification accuracy. We focus on the deviation of the local features from the Gaussian visual words, whose location in feature space can be described by its mean μ_k. Thus, we simply retain one of the three features in Fisher vector.

3.3   Residual Normalization

In [20], VLAD performance was improved by L2 normalize residuals that sum up in VLAD representation. Normalize residuals results in all descriptors contribute equally at the stage of summation. This strategy is beneficial when combined with approaches to handle burstiness, like power normalization. We experiment this with Fisher vector, i.e. we normalize the difference $(x_t-\mu_k)/\sigma_k$.

3.4   Tweaking Fisher Vector Representation

In [1], the division of the square root of Gaussian prior probability $\sqrt{w_k}$ is believed to have discounted burstiness [21] and act in a similar way to tf-idf. However, we exclude it as the extra gain it brings is rather minor, as shown in [22].

As we represent the learned features by deviations from Gaussians, and as we mentioned in Section 3.1, the posteriors are normalized for each data. However, for each Gaussian visual word, posteriors of which local features assigned to it may be impacted by another Gaussian. To gain robust representation, we consider replacing the original $\sqrt{w_i}$ in the denominator with the sum of posteriors assigned to a certain Gaussian, so our final representation is:

$$\varsigma_{\mu k}^{x} = \frac{1}{\sum_{t} \gamma_{t}(k)} \sum_{t} \gamma_{t}(k) \frac{x_{t} - \mu_{k}}{\sigma_{k}} \qquad (6)$$

3.5   Normalization

The application cosine measure between two residuals is a comparison of angle. Given two feature sets and a Gaussian block, these features may be near to each other but their distance may be large if they lie close to the center of the block. Figure 2 illustrate this scenario.

Fig. 2. Two different scenario where angle between feature sets are identical

We consider a function mapping that could reflect actual distance between features compared. For each Gaussian block, our Fisher vector represent the residual between features and the Gaussian visual word. We consider adding information about the norm of the residual when doing intra-normalization. We hope that residual could vanish when its norm is small. One example of this normalization procedure is:

$$\varsigma_{\mu k}^{x} \leftarrow \frac{\log(1 + \| \varsigma_{vk}^{x} \|)}{\sqrt{\| \varsigma_{vk}^{x} \|}} \varsigma_{\mu k}^{x} \qquad (7)$$

4   Experiments

4.1   FERET

The FERET database is composed of 14051 facial images. It contains a set of 1196 people, and testing set with variations on lighting, facial expressions, pose, and age.

The images are horizontally cropped to 3 overlapping sub-images, with size 65×130, 70×130, 60×130 respectively. Dense SIFT features are extracted via VLFeat [3] with 2-pixel spacing. Then perform RootSIFT transformation, and do principle component analysis (PCA) to reduce the dimension of the features to 64, and append location information to the descriptor as [15] do. Then train GMM model independently for each sub-images and each scale, and each GMM has 256 Gaussians. Our final compact Fisher vector are of 50688 dimension for each image.

We perform WPCA to the final descriptor to reduce its dimension to 500, 600, 700, 800, 900, 1000, and evaluate accuracy via cosine measure. We denote Fisher vector as FV, and Super vector as SV. From the Table 1, our method is on par with Fisher vector. Note that Fisher vector is approximately 2 times large compared to our representation, so we gain accuracy with less feature dimension.

Table 1. Comparison of accuracy of different encoding methods

Test set	fafc	fafb	dup1	dup2
FV	**1.0000**	0.9992	0.9335	0.9444
SV[4] (s=2)	**1.0000**	0.9992	0.9252	0.9444
SV[4] (s=1)	**1.0000**	**1.0000**	0.9321	0.9402
SV[4] (s=0.5)	**1.0000**	**1.0000**	0.9321	0.9402
Ours	0.9948	0.9983	**0.9377**	**0.9573**

4.2   Labeled Faces in the Wild (LFW)

We experiment on the challenging dataset, Labeled Face in the Wild (LFW). The set contains 13233 training images of 5749 people and is considered as a standard benchmark for face verification. The evaluation procedure is to divide predefined image pairs into 10 folds and for each fold verify whether the image pair is of the same person.

In our experiments, images are firstly cropped and centered to 150×80 pixels. We crop the image horizontally to 3 sub-images, each of which of size 65×80, 35×80 and 50×80. Multiscale Dense SIFT features are extracted via VLFeat [3] with 2-pixel spacing and the sliding windows are 16×16 and 24×24 pixels respectively. Then, in light of [2], we evaluate the power (L2 norm) of the patch extracted and retain only 60% of the most prominent features extracted to build a more robust dictionary. After that, we L1 normalize the feature, do RootSIFT transformation, and do principle component analysis (PCA) to reduce the dimension of the features to 64. We append location information to the resulting descriptor as [15] do. We train GMM model independently for each sub-images and each scale, and each GMM has 128 Gaussians. In the encoding stage, we zero out posteriors which are below 5×10^{-5}. We perform normalization according to Section 3.5 for each Gaussian block, and do L2 normalization for the final representation. Our final compact Fisher vector are of 50688 dimension for each image.

We do principle component analysis (PCA) and linear discriminant analysis (LDA) to reduce the dimension of our compact Fisher vector and verify each pair of face by cosine measure. We iterate with various PCA and LDA dimensions and choose the best LDA dimension for each PCA setting. Our verification accuracy compared with original Fisher vector (FV) and Super vector with $s=1$ (SV) are shown in Figure 3. In the figure, we compare different normalization approaches and its effects on final result as well. Normalization approaches in consideration are: component-wise square rooting (CSR), power normalization (PN), residual normalization (RN). We can see that our method outperforms Fisher vector and super vector, and other normalization process do not further improve the recognition accuracy.

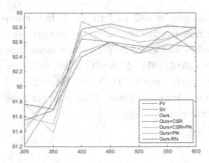

Fig. 3. Comparison of accuracy of different encoding methods under various PCA dimensions

As shown in Table 2, our results in the unrestricted LFW outperforms the state-of-the-art by a considerable margin, thus confirm that the proposed face descriptor is effective and robust.

Table 2. Comparison of accuracy with state-of-the-art methods in the unrestricted LFW

Methods	Accuracy(%)
CMD ensemble metric learning[24]	91.70
SLBP ensemble metric learning[24]	90.00
Combined PLDA[25]	90.07
High dimensional SIFT[26]	91.77
High dimensional HOG[26]	91.10
High dimensional Gabor[26]	90.97
LDML-MkNN[27]	87.50
Joint Bayesian[28]	90.90
2-Stage ConvNet[29]	85.39
ConvNet-RBM[30]	91.75
Ours	**92.88**

5   Conclusion

The Fisher vector is still a powerful representation framework for facial images, though its power comes at a computational and storage cost. In this paper, we proposed a compact Fisher vector representation framework for face verification and identification. We retain only the most discriminative part of the Fisher vector, then we sparsify them in the feature space. Next, we alter the discriminative descriptor to gain robustness. Finally, we apply a novel normalization scheme to represent relative spatial information in the feature space. Experiment results on FERET and LFW dataset showed superior performances over state-of-the-art Fisher vector representation with less storage and computational price. Comparison of accuracy with other methods in LFW database has also proved the merit of our approach.

Acknowledgements. The authors would like to thank the anonymous reviewers for their thoughtful and constructive remarks that are helpful to improve the quality of this paper. This work was partially sponsored by supported by the Fundamental Research Funds for the Central Universities under Grant No.2014ZD03-01, NSFC (National Natural Science Foundation of China) under Grant No.61375031, No. 61471048, and No.61273217. This work was also supported by the Beijing Higher Education Young Elite Teacher Program, and the Program for New Century Excellent Talents in University.

References

1. Perronnin, F., Liu, Y., Sánchez, J., Poirier, H.: Large-scale Image Retrieval with Compressed Fisher Vectors. In: Conference on Computer Vision and Pattern Recognition (CVPR), pp. 3384–3391. IEEE (2010)
2. Everts, I., van Gemert, J., Mensink, T., Gevers, T.: Robustifying Descriptor Instability Using Fisher Vectors. Transaction on Image Processing (TIP) 23(12), 5698–5706 (2014). IEEE
3. Vedaldi, A., Fulkerson, B.: VLFeat: An Open and Portable Library of Computer Vision Algorithms. In: Proceedings of the International Conference on Multimedia, pp. 1469–1472. ACM (2010)
4. Chatfield, K., Lempitsky, V., Vedaldi, A., Zisserman, A.: The Devil is in the Details: an Evaluation of Recent Feature Encoding Methods. In: British Machine Vision Conference (2011)
5. Huang, Y., Wu, Z., Wang, L., Tan, T.: Feature Coding in Image Classification: a Comprehensive Study. IEEE Transactions on Pattern Analysis and Machine Intelligence 36(3), 493–506 (2014). IEEE
6. Van Gemert, J.C., Veenman, C.J., Smeulders, A.W., Geusebroek, J.M.: Visual Word Ambiguity. IEEE Transactions on Pattern Analysis and Machine Intelligence 32(7), 1271–1283 (2010). IEEE
7. Sánchez, J., Perronnin, F., Mensink, T., Verbeek, J.: Image Classification with the Fisher Vector: Theory and Practice. International Journal of Computer Vision 105(3), 222–245 (2013). ACM
8. Jégou, H., Douze, M., Schmid, C., Pérez, P.: Aggregating Local Descriptors into a Compact Image Representation. In: IEEE Conference on Computer Vision and Pattern Recognition (CVPR), pp. 3304–3311. IEEE (2010)
9. Jégou, H., Perronnin, F., Douze, M., Sánchez, J., Pérez, P., Schmid, C.: Aggregating Local Image Descriptors into Compact Codes. IEEE Transactions on Pattern Analysis and Machine Intelligence 34(9), 1704–1716 (2012). IEEE
10. Jegou, H., Douze, M., Schmid, C.: Product Quantization for Nearest Neighbor Search. IEEE Transactions on Pattern Analysis and Machine Intelligence 33(1), 117–128 (2011). IEEE
11. Perronnin, F., Sánchez, J., Mensink, T.: Improving the fisher kernel for large-scale image classification. In: Daniilidis, K., Maragos, P., Paragios, N. (eds.) ECCV 2010, Part IV. LNCS, vol. 6314, pp. 143–156. Springer, Heidelberg (2010)
12. Lazebnik, S., Schmid, C., Ponce, J.: Beyond Bags of Features: Spatial Pyramid Matching for Recognizing Natural Scene Categories. In: IEEE Computer Society Conference on Computer Vision and Pattern Recognition, pp. 2169–2178. IEEE (2006)
13. Krapac, J., Verbeek, J., Jurie, F.: Modeling Spatial Layout with Fisher Vectors for Image Categorization. In: IEEE International Conference on Computer Vision (ICCV), pp. 1487–1494. IEEE (2011)
14. Sánchez, J., Perronnin, F., De Campos, T.: Modeling the Spatial Layout of Images Beyond Spatial Pyramids. Pattern Recognition Letters 33(16), 2216–2223 (2012). Elsevier

15. Simonyan, K., Parkhi, O.M.: Fisher Vector Faces in the Wild. In: British Machine Vision Conference (2013)
16. Li, H., Hua, G., Lin, Z., Brandt, J., Yang, J.: Probabilistic Elastic Matching for Pose Variant Face Verification. In: IEEE Conference on Computer Vision and Pattern Recognition (CVPR), pp. 3499–3506. IEEE (2013)
17. Arandjelovic, R., Zisserman, A.: All about VLAD. In: IEEE Conference on Computer Vision and Pattern Recognition (CVPR), pp. 1578–1585. IEEE (2013)
18. Chatfield, K., Simonyan, K., Vedaldi, A., Zisserman, A.: Return of the Devil in the Details: Delving Deep into Convolutional Nets. In: British Machine Vision Conference (2014)
19. Garg, V., Chandra, S., Jawahar, C.V.: Sparse Discriminative Fisher Vectors in Visual Classification. In: Proceedings of the Eighth Indian Conference on Computer Vision, Graphics and Image Processing, p. 55. ACM (2012)
20. Delhumeau, J., Gosselin, P.H., Jégou, H., Pérez, P.: Revisiting the VLAD Image Representation. In: Proceedings of the 21st ACM International Conference on Multimedia, pp. 653–656. ACM (2013)
21. Jégou, H., Douze, M., Schmid, C.: On the Burstiness of Visual Elements. In: IEEE Conference on Computer Vision and Pattern Recognition (CVPR), pp. 1169–1176. IEEE (2009)
22. Wu, Y.H., Ku, W.L., Peng, W.H., Chou, H.C.: Global Image Representation using Locality-constrained Linear Coding for Large-scale Image Retrieval. In: 2014 IEEE International Symposium on Circuits and Systems (ISCAS), pp. 766–769. IEEE (2014)
23. Arandjelovic, R., Zisserman, A.: Three Things Everyone Should Know to Improve Object Retrieval. In: IEEE Conference on Computer Vision and Pattern Recognition (CVPR), pp. 2911–2918. IEEE (2012)
24. Huang, C.: Large Scale Strongly Supervised Ensemble Metric Learning, with Applications to Face Verification and Retrieval. In: CoRR (2012). http://arxiv.org/abs/1212.6094
25. Prince, S., Li, P.: Probabilistic Models for Inference about Identity. IEEE Transactions on Pattern Analysis and Machine Intelligence 34(1), 144–157 (2012). IEEE
26. Chen, D., Cao, X., Wen, F., Sun, J.: Blessing of Dimensionality: High-dimensional Feature and its Efficient Compression for Face Verification. In: IEEE Conference on Computer Vision and Pattern Recognition (CVPR), pp. 3025–3032. IEEE (2013)
27. Guillaumin, M., Verbeek, J.J., Schmid, C.: Is That You? Metric Learning Approaches for Face Identification. In: IEEE International Conference on Computer Vision (ICCV), pp. 498–505. IEEE (2009)
28. Chen, D., Cao, X., Wang, L., Wen, F., Sun, J.: Bayesian face revisited: a joint formulation. In: Fitzgibbon, A., Lazebnik, S., Perona, P., Sato, Y., Schmid, C. (eds.) ECCV 2012, Part III. LNCS, vol. 7574, pp. 566–579. Springer, Heidelberg (2012)
29. Dai, X.: A Convolutional Neural Network Approach for Face Identification. In: Proceedings of the 30th International Conference on Machine Learning, pp. 98–113. IEEE (2013)
30. Sun, Y., Wang, X., Tang, X.: Hybrid Deep Learning for Face Verification. In: IEEE International Conference on Computer Vision (ICCV), pp. 1489–1496. IEEE (2013)

Nonlinear Metric Learning with Deep Convolutional Neural Network for Face Verification

Rongbing Huang[1,2]([✉]), Fangnian Lang[1], and Changming Shu[1]

[1] Key Laboratory of Pattern Recognition and Intelligent Information Processing of Sichuan, Chengdu University, Sichuan 610106, China
{Langfn,shuchangm}@cdu.edu.cn
[2] Department of Computer Science, State University of NewYork, Binghamton, NY, USA
huangrb@126.com, huangrb@binghamton.edu

Abstract. Face verification is a very challenge problem, due to large variations in expression, background, pose, and occlusion. It involves two crucial problems, one is face representation and the other is the similarity computation of face vectors. Addressing the two problem, this paper proposes a method for simultaneously learning features and a corresponding similarity metric for a real world face verification, which apply novel regularization to learn a nonlinear metric learning with deep convolution neural network. Experimental results on the widely used LFW dataset are presented to show the effectiveness of the proposed method.

Keywords: Deep learning · Face verification · Distance metric learning · Convolutional neural network

1 Introduction

Over the last twenty years, a large number of face recognition approaches have been proposed in the literature[1], and most of them have improved the face recognition performance under controlled environments. However, their performance drops heavily when face images are captured in the wild scenario as the camera pose changes, non-rigid deformations or different lighting conditions and large intra-class variations usually occur by varying expression and occlusion. Therefore, we can assume that the unconstrained images distribute on a nonlinear manifold. Of course, recently, there have been many methods proposed to improve the face verification performance in unconstrained environments[2],[3],[4]. Yet most current face verification methods use handcrafted features. Typical feature descriptors include SIFT[5], LBP [6], Gabor[7], and fisher vector faces[8]. Factually, face recognition technologies based on shallow features are far reaching the social and cultural implications gap between machines and the human visual system. Then a variety of methods based on deep learning, such as Boltzmann machine[4], deep neural net[11],[12] have been

© Springer International Publishing Switzerland 2015
J. Yang et al. (Eds.): CCBR 2015, LNCS 9428, pp. 78–87, 2015.
DOI: 10.1007/978-3-319-25417-3_10

proposed to apply to face recognition. Face recognition can be divided into identification and verification. This paper mainly addresses in the latter.

In this paper, we propose a nonlinear metric leaning with deep convolution neural network(DConvNet). As DConvNet has many advantage properties, which can learn optimal shift-invariant local feature detectors and build representations that are robust to geometric distortions of the input images. Our system architecture is similar to that of Hu[13], but we apply the Deep ConvNet and novel regularization to learn similarity for unrestricted face images. Hu only used the Euclidean distance and traditional BP networks or analogue to convolutional structure. We implement experiments on the Labeled Faces in the Wild (LFW) [10] dataset, a standard testbed for unconstrained face verification. The results show the proposed method achieves 89.6% in the unrestricted setting, which outperforms the current best result 87.83% in[13].

The paper is organized as follows. Section 2 discusses the related work and Section 3 presents the proposed model. Experimental results are reported in Section 4. Section 5 concludes the paper.

2   Related Work

In this section, we first briefly review the conventional similarity distance metric learning, and deep convolution neural network.

2.1   Similarity Distance Metric Learning

Let $X = [x_1, x_2, \cdots, x_N] \in R^{d \times N}$ be the training set, where $x_i \in R^d$ is the ith training sample and N is the total number of training samples. The conventional Mahalanobis distance metric learning aims to seek a square matrix $M \in R^{d \times d}$ which can be computed as:

$$d_M(x_i, x_j) = \sqrt{(x_i - x_j)^T M (x_i - x_j)} \tag{1}$$

where is symmetric and positive semi-definite. Another popular similarity learning is bilinear similarity function defined by $S_M(x, t) = x^T M t$ or called cosine similarity $CS_M(x, t) = x^T M t / \sqrt{x^T M x} \sqrt{t^T M t}$.

2.2   Deep Learning and Convolutional Neural Network

Recent several years, deep learning has received wide research and many deep learning methods have been proposed, especially deep convolutional nerual network(DConvNet) has been widely applied to image classification[14] and computer vision. The overall architecture of DConvNet is shown in Fig. 1.

Deep learning models also have been used for face verification or identification. Huang et al.[4] generatively learned features with convolutional deep belief networks, then used information-theoretic metric learning and linear SVM for face verfication. Cai et al.[15] learned deep metrics under the Siamese network,

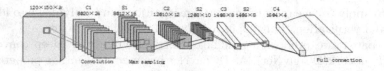

Fig. 1. The architecture of Deep convolutional neural networks.

but used a two-level independent subsapce anslysis network as the sub-networks instead. Sun et al.[16] used multiple deep ConvNets to lean high-level faces similarity features and trained classification restricted Boltzmann machine(RBM) for face verification. They [17] further proposed to take the last hidden layer neuron activations of deep ConvNets as DeepID features and used the Joint Bayesian technique for face verification. Taigman et al.[21] proposed deepface for face representation from a nine-layer deep convolutional neural netwok to proceed face verification, which also showed that the Deepface closed the majority of the remaining gap in the most popular benchmark in unconstrained face recognition and was at the brink of human level accuracy. Hu et al.[13] proposed a discriminative deep metric learning (DDML) approach to train a deep neural network which learned a set of hierarchical nonlinear transfromations for face verification.

3   Proposed Method

In this section, we present the proposed method of learning a nonlinear similarity metric with ConvNets for face verification, which will be described as follows.

3.1   Nonlinear Metric Learning with Deep ConvNet

Currently, deep models such as ConvNets have been proved effective for extracting high-level visual features and are used for face verification[4]. The similarity distance metric learning has also received widely studies by researchers[1]. Combining these studies, we proposes a nonlinear metric learning method embedding deep ConvNets for face verification which is illustrated in Fig. 2.

Let x_1 and x_2 be a pair of images shown to the input of proposed method. Let y_{ij} be a binary label of the pair, $y_{ij} = 1$ if the x_1 and x_2 images are from the same subject,i.e. the same person and $y_{ij} = -1$ otherwise. Then, we construct a deep convolutional neural network to computate the representations of one face pair by passing them to multiple layer of nonliear transformations. In our proposed systems, the deep ConvNets adopt the similar structure to [17] which contains four convolutional layers($C1 \backsim C4$)(with max-pooling) followed by the fully-connected layer, but deletes the softmax output layer. The input is $80 \times 150 \times k$, where k denotes channes, $k = 3$ for color images and $k = 1$ for gray images.

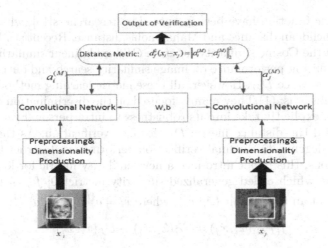

Fig. 2. The flowchart of proposed method for face verification.

The convolution operation is expressed as

$$y^h = \max(0, b^h + \sum_i k^{ih} * x^i) \tag{2}$$

where x_i and y^h are the i-th input map and the h-th ouput map, respectively. $k^t h$ is the convolutional kernel between the i-th input map and the h-th output map. $*$ denotes convolution. b is the bias of the h-th output map. We use ReLU nonlicarity $((y = \max(o, x))$ for hidden neurons, which is shown to have better fitting abilites than sigmoid function. Max-pooling is formulated as

$$y^i_{h,k} = \max_{0 \le m,n < s} \{x^i_{h \cdot s+m, k \cdot s+n}\} \tag{3}$$

where each neuron in the i-th output map y^i pools over an $s \times s$ non-overlapping local region in the i-th input map x^i.

The last layer, i.e. output layer is fully connected to fourth convolutional layer (after max-pooling) such that it sees multi-scale property[17] and it takes the following ReLU non-linearity function

$$a^{(M)}_i = \max(0, \sum_i a^4_i \cdot w^4_{i,p} + b_p) \tag{4}$$

3.2 Discrimination Similarity Distance Metric with Deep ConvNets

To obtain a good similarity metric function to measure the similarity between face images, we formulate the learning objective by considering both the robustness to the large intra-personal variations and the discrimination for separating similar image-paris from dissimilar image-pairs. In past years, many similarity distance metric function have been proposed by researchers[18], which includes traditional Euclidean distance and Mahalanobis distance. Recent studies[10],[19] observed that the Cosine similarity function CS_M or bilinear similarity function S_M has a promising performance on image similarity search and outperform the Mahalanobis distance D_M. However, all these metric learning methods have the same two limitations: (1) They mainly focused on the discrimination of the metric and do not explicitly take into its robustness to intra-personal variations; (2) They only used the distance metric D_M for face verification. As the two limitations could degenerate the final verification performance. In order to outcome these limitations, this paper introduce a new similarity metric for learning similarity metrics, which called generalized similarity metric[20] $f_{(T,G)}$ to measure the similarity of an image pair $(\tilde{x}_i, \tilde{x}_j)$, where $\tilde{x}_i = a_i^{(M)}, \tilde{x}_j = a_j^{(M)}$:

$$f_{(T,G)}(\tilde{x}_i, \tilde{x}_j) = S_G(\tilde{x}_i, \tilde{x}_j) - D_T(\tilde{x}_i, \tilde{x}_j) \tag{5}$$

Let $P = S \bigcup D$ denotes the index set of all pairwise constraints. If image $\tilde{x}_i$ and $\tilde{x}_j$ are from the same subject, then the label $y_{ij} = 1$ and -1 otherwise. In order to better discriminate similar image-pairs from dissimilar image-pairs, we also need to learn T and G from the available data. In this paper, we adopt the empirical discrimination formulation using the hinge loss:

$$\epsilon_{emp}(T, G) = \sum_{(i,j)\in P} (1 - y_{ij} f_{(T,G)}(\tilde{x}_i, \tilde{x}_j)) \tag{6}$$

Minimizing the above empirical error will encourage the discrimination of similar image-pairs from dissimilar ones.

By applying the above formulation, we can obtain our optimization problem:

$$arg \min_{f(T,G)} J = \epsilon_{emp}(T, G) + \frac{\lambda}{2} \Sigma_{l=1}^{M} (\| W^{(l)} \|_F^2 + \| b^{(l)} \|^2) \tag{7}$$

where $\| W \|_F$ denotes the Frobenius norm of the matrix W, and λ is regularization parameter.

To solve Eq(7), we use the stochastic gradient descent scheme to obtain the parameters $\{W^{(l)}, b^{(l)}\}$, where $l = 1, 2, \cdots, M$. The gradient of the object function J with the parameters $W^{(l)}, b^{(l)}$ can be computed as follows:

$$\Delta_{i,j}^{(l)} = ((W^{(l)} \Delta_{i,j}^{(l+1)}) \odot g'(z_i^{(l)}), \quad l = 1, 2, \cdots, M-1 \tag{8}$$

$$\Delta_{j,i}^{(l)} = ((W^{(l)} \Delta_{j,i}^{(l+1)}) \odot g'(z_j^{(l)}), \quad l = 1, 2, \cdots, M-1 \tag{9}$$

$$\Delta_{i,j}^{(M)} = s'(\Im) y_i j (a_i^{(M)} - a_j^{(M)}) \odot g'(z_i^{(M)}) \tag{10}$$

$$\Delta_{j,i}^{(M)} = s'(\Im) y_i j (a_j^{(M)} - a_i^{(M)}) \odot g'(z_j^{(M)}) \tag{11}$$

where $\Delta^{(l)}$ denotes the error for the l-th layer in the network, and the mark $\odot$ denotes the element-wise multiplication; $\Im$ and $z_k^{(\nu)}$ are defined as follows:

$$\Im \equiv \Sigma_{(i,j)\in P}(1 - y_{ij} f_{(T,G)}(a_i^{(M)}, a_j^{(M)})) \tag{12}$$

$$z_k^{(\nu)} = W^{(\nu)} a_k^{(\nu-1)} + b^{(\nu)} \tag{13}$$

Then the gradients are:

$$\nabla_{W^{(l)}} J(W, b; x_i, x_j, y_{(i,j)}) = \Sigma_{(i,j)}(\Delta_{(i,j)}^{(l+1)}(a_i^{(l)})^T + \Delta_{(j,i)}^{(l+1)}(a_j^{(l)})^T) + \lambda W^{(l)} \tag{14}$$

$$\nabla_{b^{(l)}} J(W, b; x_i, x_j, y_{(i,j)}) = \Sigma_{(i,j)}(\Delta_{(i,j)}^{(l+1)} + \Delta_{(j,i)}^{(l+1)}) + \lambda b^{(l)} \tag{15}$$

where $y_{(i,j)}$ is the label. Then, $W^{(l)}$ and $b^{(l)}$ can be updated by using the following gradient descent algorithm:

$$W^{(l)} = W^{(l)} - \alpha \nabla_{W^{(l)}} J(W, b; x_i, x_j, y_{(i,j)}) \tag{16}$$

$$b^{(l)} = b^{(l)} - \alpha \nabla_{b^{(l)}} J(W, b; x_i, x_j, y_{(i,j)}) \tag{17}$$

where α is the learning rate. If the l-th layer is a convolutional and subsampling layer then the error is propagated through as

$$\Delta_k^{(l)} = upsample((W_k^{(l)})^T \Delta_k^{(l+1)}) \odot g'(z_k^{(l)}) \tag{18}$$

3.3 Implementation Details

In this subsection, we talk about the nonlinear activation functions and the initializations of $W^{(l)}$ and $b^{(l)}, l = 1, 2, \cdots, M$. For the nonlinear activation function choice, although there are many nonlinear activation functions, in our proposed method, we use the ReLU non-linearity defined as $f(x) = \max(0, x)$, where x is the input to a neuron. This function has been argued to be more biologically plausible thant logistic sigmoid and hyperbolic tangent function, and our experiment has demonstrate its better performance. For the initializations of $W^{(l)}$ and $b^{(l)}$, we utilize the denoising autoencoder (DAE)[22] method.

4 Preliminary Experiment

In this section, to evaluate the effectiveness of our proposed NMLDConvNets method, we perform unconstrained face verification experiments on the Labeled Faces in the Wild(LFW)[9]. The following settings describe the details of the experiments and results.

4.1 Datasets and Experimental Settings

The LFW dataset contains 13233 face images of 5749 people, and 1680 of them appear in more than two images. It is commonly regarded to be a challenging dataset for face verification since the faces were detected from images taken from Yahoo! News and show large variations in pose, expression, lighting, and etc. There are two training paradigms for supervised learning on this dataset: the restricted and unrestricted setting. Under the restricted setting, the identity information of each face is not given. The only available information is a pair of input images which are labeled as the similar or dissimilar pair. Under the unrestricted setting, the identity information of each image is available. In our experiments, we use the image unrestricted setting which can allows us to generate more image pairs for training, and performance is measured by ten-fold cross-validation. Each fold consists of 200 matched (positive) pairs and 200 mispatched (negative) pairs.

All face images are cropped into 120×150 pixels to remove the background information. For each cropped image, we apply Whitened PCA(WPCA) to project the combined feature descriptors into a 600-dimensional feature vector to remove the redundancy.

For our proposed method, we train the Deep Convnets with four convolutional layers and one full-connected layer ($l = 5$), and the learning rate and regularization parameter λ are empirically set as 0.004, 0.01 for all experiments, respectively.

4.2   Comparison with Existing Deep Metric Learning Methods

In this subsection, we compare our proposed approach with several recently proposed deep learning based face verification methods: CDBN[4], DNLML-ISA[15] and DDML[13]. Table 1 shows the performance of these deep learning methods. From this table, we can see that our NMLDeepConvnet method outperforms the other deep learning methods, especially DDML which is the latest deep metric learning approach in terms of the mean verification rate. The reason is that our methods combined the deep convolutional neural network with generally discriminative similarity metric which overcome the limitation that DDML method only focused on the discrimination of the metric and did not explicitly take into account its robustness. Comparing with the CDBN and DSML, our method is a supervised deep metric learning method and adopts deep convolutional network which can learn optimal sift-invariant local feature detectors and explore better hierarchical information that are robust to geometric distortions of the input face images.

Table 1. Performance comparison of the mean verification rate(standard error)with different deep learning methods.

Method	Accuracy
CDBN[4]	86.88 ± 0.62
DNLML-ISA[15]	88.50 ± 0.40
DDML[13]	87.83 ± 0.93
Our method	*89.60 ± 0.35*

4.3   Comparison with State-of-the-Art Methods

In order to fairly compare with the state-of-the-art methods on the LFW datasets, we also extract three types of feature for the cropped images: SIFT[5], LBP[6], and POEM. For each feature, we still use the square root feature of three types of feature. We compare our method with PCCA[23], Sub-SML[20], and DML-eig[24]. Table 2 lists the verification rate with standard error and Fig. 3 shows the ROC curves of these methods on this dataset, respectively. From the table 2 and Fig. 3, we clearly see that our method has better performance than the state-of-the-art methods in terms of the mean verification rate.

Table 2. Performance comparison of the mean verification rate (standard error) with the state-of-the-art methods.

Method	Accuracy
PCCA[23]	83.80 ± 0.40
Sub-SML[20]	89.73 ± 0.38
DML-eig[24]	80.55 ± 0.17
Our method	*91.34 ± 0.40*

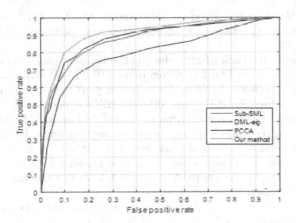

Fig. 3. Comparisons of ROC curves between our method and the state-of-the-art methods for face verification on the LFW dataset.

5   Conclusion

As DConvNet can learn optimal shift-invariant local feature detectors and build representations that are robust to geometric distortions of the input images, in this paper, we have proposed a nonlinear metric learning embedding Deep

Convolutional neural network for face verification in the wild. Comparing the state-of-the-art methods, our method achieves the very competitive verification performance on the widely used LFW datasets.

Acknowledgments. This paper is partially supported by the research grant for the Natural Science Foundation from Sichuan Provincial Department of Education (13ZB0336) and China Scholarship Council (CSC).

References

1. Lu, J., Tan, Y.-P., Wang, G.: Discriminative multimanifold analysis for face recognition from a single training sample per person. IEEE TPAMI **35**(1), 39–51 (2013)
2. Cui, Z., Li, W., Xu, D., Shan, S., Chen, X.: Fusing robust face region descriptors via multiple metric learning for face recognition in the wild. In: CVPR, pp. 3554–3561. IEEE Press, Portland (2013)
3. Wolf, L., Hassner, T., Maoz, I.: Face recognition in unconstrained videos with matched background similarity. In: CVPR, pp. 529–534 (2011)
4. Huang, G.B., Lee, H., Learned-Miller, E.: Learning hierarchical representations for face verification with convolutional deep belief networks. In: CVPR, pp. 2518–2525. IEEE Press, Washington (2012)
5. Lowe, D.G.: Distinctive image features from scale-invariant keypoints. IJCV **60**(2), 91–110 (2004)
6. Ahonen, T., Member, S., Hadid, A., Pietikanen, M., Member, S.: Face description with local binary patterns: application to face recognition. IEEE TPAMI **28**, 2037–2041 (2006)
7. Liu, C., Wechsler, H.: Gabor feature based classification using the enhanced fisher linear discriminant model for face recognition. TIP **11**, 467–476 (2002)
8. Guillaumin, M., Verbeek, J., Schmid, C.: Is that you? metric learning approaches for face identification. In: ICCV, pp. 498–505. IEEE Press, Kyoto (2009)
9. Gary, B.H, Manu, R., Tamara, B., Erik, L.-M.: Labeled faces in the wild: a database for studying face recognition in unconstrained environments. University of Massachusetts, Amherst, Technical Report, pp. 07–49 (2007)
10. Nguyen, H.V., Bai, L.: Cosine similarity metric learning for face verification. In: Kimmel, R., Klette, R., Sugimoto, A. (eds.) ACCV 2010, Part II. LNCS, vol. 6493, pp. 709–720. Springer, Heidelberg (2011)
11. Luo, P., Wang, X., Tang, X.: A deep sum-product architecture for robust facial attributes analysis. In: ICCV, pp. 2864–2871 (2013)
12. Sun, Y., Chen, Y., Wang, X., Tang, X.: Deep learning face representation by joint identification-verification. In: NIPS, pp. 1988–1996 (2014)
13. Hu, J., Lu, J., Tan, Y.-P.: Discriminative deep metric learning for face verification in the wild. In: CVPR, pp. 1875–1882 (2014)
14. Krizhevsky, A., Ilya, S., Geoffrey, E.H.: ImageNet classification with deep convolutional neural networks. In: NIPS, pp. 1106–1114 (2012)
15. Cai, X., Wang, C., Xiao, B., Chen, X., Zhou, J.: Deep nonlinear metric learning with independent subspace analysis for face verification. In: ACM Multimedia, pp. 749–752. ACM press, NewYork (2012)
16. Sun, Y., Wang, X., Tang, X.: Hybrid deep learning for face verification. In: ICCV, pp. 1489–1496. IEEE press, Washington (2013)

17. Sun, Y., Wang, X.G., Tang, X.: Deep learning face representation from predicting 10,000 classes. In: CVPR, pp. 1891–1898 (2014)
18. Yang, L., Jin, R.: Distance metric learning: a comprehensive survey. In: Technical report, Michigan State University (2007)
19. Chechik, G., Sharma, V., Shalit, U., Bengio, S.: Large scale online learning of image similarity through ranking. J. Mach. Learn. Res. **11**, 1109–1135 (2010)
20. Cao, Q., Ying, Y., Li, P.: Similarity metric learning for face recognition. In: ICCV, pp. 2408–2415 (2013)
21. Yaniv, T., Yang, M., MarcAurelio, R., Wolf, L.: DeepFace: closing the gap to human-level performance in face verification. In: CVPR, pp. 1701–1708 (2014)
22. Vincent, P., Larochelle, H., Bengio, Y., Manzagol, P.-A.: Extracting and composing robust features with denoising autoencoders. In: ICML, pp. 1096–1103 (2008)
23. Mignon, A., Jurie, F.: Pcca: a new approach for distance learning from sparse pairwise constraints. In: CVPR, pp. 2666–2672 (2012)
24. Ying, Y., Li, P.: Distance metric learning with eigenvalue optimization. JMLR **13**, 1–26 (2012)

Locally Collaborative Representation in Similar Subspace for Face Recognition

Riqiang Gao[1,2], Wenming Yang[1(✉)], Xiang Sun[1], Hong Li[2], and Qingmin Liao[1]

[1] Shenzhen Key Laboratory of Information Science & Tech/Engineering
Laboratory of IS & DRM, Department of E.E./Graduate School at Shenzhen,
Tsinghua University, Beijing, China
yangelwm@163.com
[2] School of Information Science and Engineering, Central South University, Changsha, China

Abstract. Sparse representation and collaborative representation have been widely used in face recognition (FR). Collaborative Representation based Classification (CRC) is superior to Sparse Representation based Classification (SRC) in both accuracy and complexity. It is the collaborative representation (CR) mechanism rather than l_1-minimization improves recognition rate in FR. In this paper, based on K-nearest neighbor (KNN), we find K most similar images as the projective subspace for testing sample. Then we propose a new algorithm named Locally Collaborative Representation based Classification in Similar Subspace (LCRC_SS), which changes the projective space from global space to local similarity subspace. The main advantages lie in LCRC_SS are making full use of "similar" resources and discarding the redundant "dissimilar" images in CR. Extensive experiments show that LCRC_SS has better recognition rate than CRC.

Keywords: Collaborative representation · KNN · Locally similar subspace · LCRC_SS

1   Introduction

The design of classifier is a key point of face recognition (FR). There are some classical classifiers, such as Nearest Neighbor (NN) [1] and Nearest Subspace (NS) [2], but they didn't get a satisfactory recognition rate. Sparse representation [3] is more robust to occlusion and corruption compare with NN and NS.

With the development of l_0-minimization and l_1-minimization regularization theory [5], sparse coding is widely used in image restoration applications [6]. In [3], Wright *et al.* consider the problem of face recognition as a multiple linear regression modules and propose the Sparse Representation based Classification (SRC). Zhang *et al.* [4] propose a simpler face classification method named Collaborative Representation based Classification (CRC), which indicates that it is the collaborative representation rather than the l_1-minimization making the representation more powerful. Afterwards, improved SRC is used for Face Recognition with Single Sample per Person [10, 11].

In sparse representation [3, 14], we assume that every class has enough training samples so that the dictionary X_i is over-complete, where X_i is the dictionary which

© Springer International Publishing Switzerland 2015
J. Yang et al. (Eds.): CCBR 2015, LNCS 9428, pp. 88–95, 2015.
DOI: 10.1007/978-3-319-25417-3_11

composed of class i. However, X_i is usually under-complete in practice. If we use under-complete dictionary to represent a testing sample, the representation accuracy decreases. Fortunately, the images of different classes have some similarities, the samples from class j may be helpful to represent testing sample from class i. It is the CR, but not the l_1-minimization, that plays the essential role for classification [4].

However, does it really need to represent testing sample in a global collaboration covering all samples? Can we just find a smaller but more rational subspace for collaborative representation? In this paper, we propose a new method named Locally Collaborative Representation based Classification in Similar Subspace (LCRC_SS) to improve collaborative representation: representing the testing sample on a locally similar subspace. Thus, the faces in obtained subspace are highly similar with the testing sample, making full use of "similar" resources and abandoning the redundant "dissimilar" images in collaborative representation. Experiments show that it makes the classification more effective.

The rest of this paper is organized as follows. We briefly recall sparse representation and collaborative representation in Section 2. The proposed LCRC method is in Section 3. At last, we conduct extensive experiments to test LCRC in Section 4 and summarize the paper in Section 5.

2   Sparse Representation and Collaborative Representation

2.1   Sparse Representation Based Classification (SRC)

In the theory of SRC, a signal y is coded over an over-complete dictionary A such as $y=A\alpha$, the coefficient α is usually calculated by l_0-minimization [7] [8]. With the development of sparse representation and compressed sensing [9-11], we know that if the coefficient α is sparse enough, the l_0-minimization problem is equal to l_1-minimization. That is

$$\left(\alpha_i\right)=\arg\min_{\alpha}\left\{\left\|y-A\alpha\right\|_2^2+\lambda\left\|\alpha\right\|_1\right\} \tag{1}$$

where A is the dictionary. We call eq.(1) Sparse Representation based Classification (SRC), and problem could be solved by many efficient methods such as Homotopy [12] and l1_ls [13].

2.2   Collaborative Representation Based Classification (CRC)

In [4], Zhang *et al.* put a query in SRC. They demonstrate that the key to the success of SRC is the collaborative representation rather than the sparseness of coefficient. They change the method from l_1-minimization to regularized least square in classification and propose the CRC.

Similar with SRC, the method of CRC could be generally described as

$$\left(\hat{\rho}\right)=\arg\min_{\rho}\left\{\left\|y-A\rho\right\|_2^2+\lambda\left\|\rho\right\|_2^2\right\} \tag{2}$$

We also call Eq.(2) Collaborative Representation based Classification with Regularized Least Square (CRC_RLS). The solution of Eq.(2) can be expressed as $\hat{\rho}=Py$,where $P=\left(A^T A+\lambda I\right)^{-1} A^T$. The projection matrix P could be pre-calculated, which makes CRC very fast. The algorithm is showed in Table 1.

Table 1. The CRC_RLS Algorithm

Input: train samples A , testing samples y.

1. Normalize the columns of A ;

2. Solve the problem $\hat{\rho}=Py$, where $P=\left(A^T A+\lambda I\right)^{-1} A^T$.

3. Compute the residuals

$$e_i(y)=\left\|y-A_i\hat{\rho}_i\right\|_2$$

Where $\hat{\rho}_i$ is the coding coefficient vector achieved in Step 2.

Output: Identity of testing sample y achieved by the rule as

$$identity(y)=\arg\min(e_i)$$

---

3 Locally Collaborative Representation Based Classification

In [4], Zhang *et al.* put forward that face images of different classes share similarities. Different classes show different degrees of similarity. We did experiments on several databases, and the result shows that more similar images do greater contribution to the recognition.

In order to make full use of "similar" resources and abandoning the redundant "dissimilar" images in CR, we change the projective space from global training space to locally similar subspace.

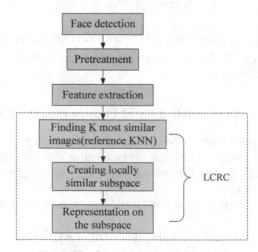

Fig. 1. The flow chart of the LCRC_SS

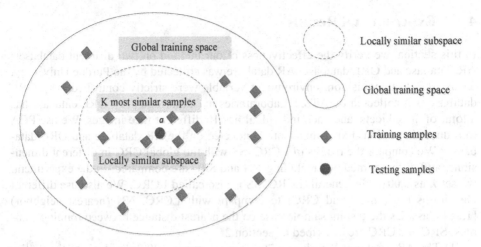

Fig. 2. The schematic of locally similar subspace

Based on K-nearest neighbor (KNN) algorithm [16, 17], we find K most similar images for testing sample. We use this K images as a new projective space, then we collaboratively represent testing sample in this new space. We call this method Locally Collaborative Representation based Classification in Similar Subspace (LCRC_SS). Fig.1 shows the flow of LCRC_SS and Fig.2 show the schematic of locally similar subspace. The general idea of LCRC_SS is summarized in Table 2.

Table 2. The LCRC_SS Algorithm

Input: train samples A, testing samples y.

    1. Normalize the columns of A;

    2. Use KNN as reference, find the most K similar images;

    3. Treat this K images as the local subspace A';

    4. Code testing sample y over A' by $\hat{\rho} = Py$

$$P = \left(A'^{T} A' + \lambda I \right)^{-1} A'^{T}$$

    5. Compute the residuals

$$e_i(y) = \left\| y - A'_i \hat{\rho}_i \right\|_2$$

Output: Identity of testing sample y achieved by the rule as

$$identity(y) = \arg\min(e_i)$$

---

4   Experimental Results

In this section, we verify the effectiveness of our method on two different databases: AR database and ORL database. AR database was collected by the Purdue University, during the data acquisition, environment variable were strictly controlled [18]. ORL database was collected by AT&T Laboratories in Cambridge [19], ORL database has a total of 40 subjects, and each individual has 10 different face images. We use PCA to reduce dimension. Experiments are conducted on the AR database and ORL database. We compare the results of LCRC_SS with the global CRC in different dimensions, and different methods including NN and SRC are compared. In the experiment, we set λ as 0.001. In general, LCRC_SS is also called LCRC. We also use different algorithms (NN, SRC and CRC) to compare with LCRC. NN (nearest neighbor) [1,20] classifies the testing sample base on the nearest distance between training samples. SRC and CRC are described in Section 2.

(1) The AR database: We choose 700 face images of 100 individuals as the dictionary, each individual has 7 images. These 100 individuals contain 50 male subjects and 50 female subjects. We choose different K value for experiments, and we set up three values (30, 50 and 100) as dimensions after feature extraction, they are showed in Table 3 and Figure 3.

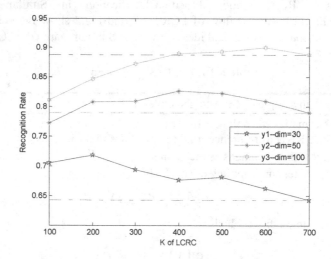

Fig. 3. Recognition rate of LCRC on AR database

Table 3. Recognition rate of LCRC on AR database (%)

K	100	200	300	400	500	600	CRC
dim=30	70.5	71.8	69.4	67.7	68.1	66.2	64.2
dim=50	77.3	80.8	81.0	82.7	82.3	81.0	79.0
dim=100	81.1	84.7	87.3	89.0	89.3	90.0	88.8

Table 4 shows the recognition rates of LCRC compared with different algorithms in different dimension.

Table 4. Recognition rate of different algorithms on AR database

dim	30	50	100
NN	52.4	56.7	57.8
SRC	73.2	81.1	88.8
CRC	64.2	79.0	88.8
LCRC	71.8	82.7	90.0

From the above forms and image, we can find that when the K value is chosen achieved appropriately, the LCRC act better than the CRC. Moreover, the results show that the lower the dimension is, the better results would be achieved in LCRC in AR database.

(2) The ORL database: We use the first 5 face images of each individual as the dictionary, and the rest as testing samples.

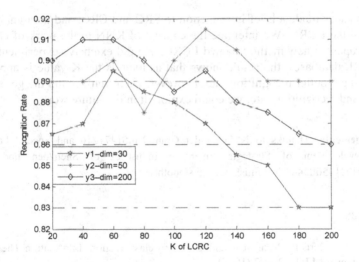

Fig. 4. Recognition rate of LCRC in ORL database

Table 5. Recognition rate of LCRC in ORL(%)

K	40	60	80	100	120	140	160	180	CRC
dim=30	87.0	89.5	88.5	88.0	87.0	85.5	85.0	83.0	83.0
dim=50	89.0	90.0	87.5	90.0	91.5	90.5	89.0	89.0	89.0
dim=200	91.0	91.0	90.0	88.5	89.5	88.0	87.5	86.5	86.0

Table 5 and Figure 4 show the comparison of LCRC and CRC with different K values in three dimensions.

Table 6 show the results of LCRC compared with NN, SRC and CRC, and LCRC has better recognition rate.

Table 6. Recognition rate of different algorithms in ORL(%)

dim	30	50	200
NN	68.0	69.0	69.0
SRC	85.5	88.5	86.0
CRC	83.0	89.0	86.0
LCRC	89.5	91.5	91.0

From Table 5-6 and Figure 4 we can learn that no matter the dimension is high or low, we could find a suitable K value to obtain the competitive results. Moreover, in the dimension of 30 and 200, the result of the LCRC has always been better than that of CRC.

5   Conclusion and Discussion

Firstly, this paper made a brief introduction to SRC and CRC, and then analyzed the feasibility of the LCRC. We integrate the concept of KNN to the work of classification, and propose a new method named LCRC. We did extensive experiments on the AR and ORL databases, the result shows that as long as the K value is appropriate, LCRC could get better recognition rate. However, we haven't found the general rules between K and recognition rate, we could explore it in the future work.

Acknowledgements. Thamks to NSFC under Grant No.61471216 and Special Foundation for the Development of Strategic Emerging Industries of Shenzhen under Grant No.YJ20130402145002441, we finish our job smoothly.

References

1. Cover, T.M., Hart, P.: Nearest neighbor pattern classification. Information Theory IEEE Transactions on **13**(1), 21–27 (1967)
2. Zhou, Z., Ganesh, A., Wright, J., et al..: Nearest-Subspace Patch Matching for face recognition under varying pose and illumination. IEEE International Conference on Automatic Face & Gesture Recognition, FG (2008)
3. Wright, J., Yang, A.Y., Ganesh, A., et al.: Robust face recognition via sparse representation. IEEE Trans Pattern Anal Mach Intell **31**(2), 210–227 (2008)
4. Zhang, D., Yang, M., Feng, X.: Sparse representation or collaborative representation: Which helps face recognition? In: 2011 IEEE International Conference on Computer Vision (ICCV), IEEE, 471–478 (2011)
5. Tropp, J.A., Wright, S.J.: Computational methods for sparse solution of linear inverse problems. Proceedings of IEEE, Special Issue on Applications of Compressive Sensing & Sparse Representation **98**(6), 948–958 (2010)

6. Aharon, M., Elad, M., Bruckstein, A.M.: The K-SVD: An algorithm for designing of over-complete dictionaries for sparse representation. IEEE SP **54**(11), 4311–4322 (2006)
7. Donoho, D.: For most large underdetermined systems of linear equations the minimal l1-norm solution is also the sparsest solution. Comm. On Pure and Applied Math **59**(6), 797–829 (2006)
8. Candès, E., Romberg, J., Tao, T.: Stable signal recovery from incomplete and inaccurate measurements. Comm. On Pure and Applied Math **59**(8), 1207–1223 (2006)
9. Zhu, P., Yang, M., Zhang, L., Lee, I.-Y.: Local generic representation for face recognition with single sample per person. In: Cremers, D., Reid, I., Saito, H., Yang, M.-H. (eds.) ACCV 2014. LNCS, vol. 9005, pp. 34–50. Springer, Heidelberg (2015)
10. Zhao, P., Yu, B.: On Model Selection Consistency of Lasso. J. Machine Learning Research, no. 7, pp. 2541–2567 (2006)
11. Gao, S., Jia, K., Zhuang, L., et al.: Neither Global Nor Local: Regularized Patch-Based Representation for Single Sample Per Person Face Recognition. International Journal of Computer Vision **111**(3), 365–383 (2014)
12. Malioutove, D., Cetin, M., Willsky, A.: Homotopy continuation for sparse signal representation. In: ICASSP (2005)
13. Kim, S.J., Koh, K., Lustig, M., Boyd, S.D.: Gorinevsky. A interior-point method for large-scale l1-regularized least squares. IEEE Journal on Selected Topics in Signal Processing **1**(4), 606–617 (2007)
14. Tang, X., Feng, G., Cai, J.: Weighted group sparse representation for under sampled face recognition. Neuro computing **145**(18), 402–415 (2014)
15. Wright, J., Ganesh, A., Yang, A., Zhou, Z.H., Ma, Y.: Sparsity and Robustness in Face Recognition (2011). arXiv:1111.1014v1
16. Hastie, T., Tibshirani, R., Friedman, J.: The Elements of Statistical Learning: Data Mining, Inference, and Prediction (2001)
17. Bulut, F., Amasyali, M.F.: Locally adaptive k parameter selection for nearest neighbor classifier: one nearest cluster. Pattern Analysis and Application (2015)
18. Martmhnez, A.M.: The AR-Face database. Cvc Technical Report (1998)
19. Samaria, F., Harter, A.: Parametrisation of a stochastic model dor human face identification. Proc IEEE Workshop on Applications of Computer Vision (1994)
20. Tutz, G., Koch, D.: Improved nearest neighbor classifiers by weighting and selection of predictors. Statistics and Computing (2015)

A DCNN and SDM Based Face Alignment Algorithm

Qingsong Tang, Qinqin Zhang, Xiaomeng Zhang,
Zhenlin Cai, and Xiangde Zhang(✉)

School of Sciences, Northeastern University, Shenyang, China
zhangxdneu@163.com

Abstract. We present a coarsely locating little points and finely locating many points approach for face alignment. This cascade structure replies to 2 problems existing all the time in face alignment: the initialization and great accuracy difference between inner points and outline points. First, we adopt DCNN to coarsely localize 5 points: two pupils, nose and two mouth corners. Second, based on shape initialization of coarse location, using SDM with extracting simplified SIFT features, we finely localizes 49 inner points and 17 outline points. Experiments on CAS-PEAL-R1 and FERET database show that our approach is accurate and robust. The proposed method achieves 99.23% localization accuracy of eyes on CAS-PEAL-R1.

Keywords: Face alignment · Deep Convolution Neural Network · SIFT · SDM

1 Introduction

Building a convenient, private, non-touch, user-friendly face recognition system has aroused general interest in Computer Vision. Face alignment plays an important role in face recognition. Due to factors such as lighting, partial occlusions, various expressions and extreme poses, face alignment is still confronted with many challenges.

This critical problem has been studied extensively recent years, many existing face alignment methods could be boiled down to regression. Model such as Active Appearance Model (AAM) [1] is very iconic to solve linear regression, but it is prone to get stuck in local optima. Since 2013, Deep Convolution Neural Networks (DCNN) [2, 3] and Supervised Descent Method (SDM) [4] which can be considered as regression methods were proposed. DCNN fits any nonlinear functions by deep connection. Under the premise of achieving high accuracy, DCCN shows high complexity of structure and time. SDM embarks from the theory and proposes an approximately linear regression model, which provides the optimal solution to non-linear least squares problem in computer vision.

In order to overcome the shortage of above algorithms, we present a cascade algorithm based on DCNN and SDM. Firstly, we locate a few points coarsely based on DCNN model, and then we locate a lot inner points and outline points finely based on SDM. To our knowledge, it is the first time to introduce a cascade of DCNN and SDM. This cascade algorithm has some advantages: (1) It can provide a good initialization for

J. Yang et al. (Eds.): CCBR 2015, LNCS 9428, pp. 96–102, 2015.
DOI: 10.1007/978-3-319-25417-3_12

SDM which is not prone to trap into local optima. (2) Coarsely locating little points by DCNN and finely locating many points by SDM can reduce the complexity of [2, 3] without losing much accuracy and make good use of SDM's efficiency.

2   Coarsely Localize 5 Landmarks Based on DCNN

In the study of face landmark localization, initializations of facial shape have a great impact on result. A good initialization can avoid locating getting stuck in local optimum, which is one of our motivations.

DCNN is often used to classify, and it can also be used in face landmark localization. But all of them take the cascade strategy and take batches with different scales and different locations as inputs. To a great extent, these operations increase space and time complexity. From a practical point of view, DCNN is not so good.

However there is one advantage of DCNN: unlike most of traditional methods, we don't have to initialize shape locations. Thus, we can avoid getting stuck in local optima for the sake of poor shape initialization. Based on this, we adopt one level DCNN to locate 5 landmarks (two pupils, nose tip, two mouth corners) coarsely, which is convenient for follow-up initialization in finely locating. Considering real time performance, we use one-level DCNN here. As shown in Figure 1.

Set x_j^l as j^{th} feature map of lth layer. As the shape of sample image and kernel is both square, we only define one parameter here to denote size. Set h_i as size of lth feature map, and c_l, d_l as size of convolution kernel and pooling factor. Set w_l as the number of lth feature map corresponding to input map x_1^l, $h_l=60$, $w_l=l$. Let k_{ij} denotes convolution kernel between i^{th} feature map in previous layer and j^{th} feature map in current layer, i.e., globally shared weights.

For convolution layers,

$$x_j^l = f(\sum_{i \in M_j} x_i^{l-1} * k_{ij}^l + b_j^l). \tag{1}$$

For activation functions,

$$x_{uvj}^l = \tanh(\sum_{x=1}^{c_l} \sum_{y=1}^{c_l} \sum_{i=1}^{w_{l-1}} x_{u-x,v-y,i}^{l-1} * k_{x,y,i,j}^l + b_j^l), j = 1,...,w_l. \tag{2}$$

$$x_j^l = f(\sum_{i \in M_j} x_i^{l-1} * k_{ij}^l + b_j^l).$$

For pooling layers,

$$x_{uvj}^l = \max_{1 \le x \le d_l, 1 \le y \le d_l} (x_{(u-1)*d_l+x,(v-1)*d_l+y,j}^{l-1}), j = 1,...,w_l. \tag{3}$$

For output layer, since the property that features in deeper layer are more abstract, we map feature to landmark coordinates directly.

We adopt square errors as loss function in training DCNN model. After that, controlling the loss descending in a suitable interval that achieves the optimal solution meanwhile avoid over-fitting.

We remark that we don't aim to concentrate on learning a good feature through DCNN, but a better initial shape for following procedures with SDM algorithm.

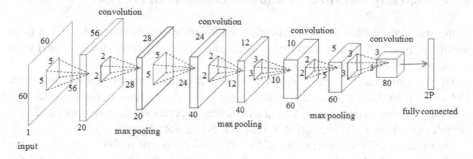

Fig. 1. Structure of DCNN

3   Finely Localize 68 Landmarks Based on SDM

3.1   Initialization

There are 3 mean shapes in finely locating procedure: 5-points mean shape, inner-points mean shape and outline-points mean shape. We get 5 points coordinates as DCNN outputs, and then align 5-points mean shape to these coordinates by affine transform. We complete aligning mean shape of inner-points and outline-points to corresponding initial shapes with obtained transform parameters. The coordinate obtained after aligning is seen as initial shape x0 in SDM algorithm. Thank to the 5-points shape, the output of DCNN, providing better initializations, our algorithm avoids getting stuck in local optimum.

3.2   Finetune Landmarks

For a given train sample, note $\{d^i\}, \{x_*^i\}$ is ground truth coordinates of ith sample image labeled manually, x_0^i is initial coordinates of ith training sample. Minimizing:

$$\arg\min_{R_k, b_k} \sum_{d^i} \sum_{x_k^i} \left\| \Delta x_*^{ki} - R_k \phi_k^i - b_k \right\|^2 \tag{4}$$

where $\Delta x^i = x_*^i - x_0^i$, $\phi_0^i = h(d^i(x_0^i))$ is the extracted feature.

Feature Extraction. This paper adopts Scale Invariant Feature Transform (SIFT) [5, 6] feature as model features. Commonly, calculating SIFT takes a bit long time, which is difficult to achieve real-time locating. In this paper, we simplify SIFT with only choosing one scale. With amount of experiments, we find that there is no direct relation between high complexity of multiple scale SIFT and accuracy of location.

The solution of Linear Least Squares. Formula (4) is a typical least squares problem. There exists analytical solution. But commonly, matrix may be singular in real application scene. Thus we solve to get R_k and b_k with Batch Gradient Descent instead of analytical solution.

Locating Strategy. The alignment algorithm of this paper is mainly based on gray information of source image. Gray distribution varies severely for different location of landmark. For example, an eye image with iris, sclera and pupil, its gray value changes greatly even in neighbor area, but gray distribution changes gently in part of cheek. Thus it isn't reasonable to deal with each landmark with same model. In order to achieve good results, we trained inter points and outline points separately.

4   Experiments and Analysis

This paper adopts evaluation criteria formula (5) that is more strict than criteria adopted in [2]:

$$err = \frac{\frac{1}{M}\sum_{j=1}^{M}\|p_j - g_j\|}{\|C_l - C_r\|}, \tag{5}$$

where M is the number of landmark points. p_j, g_j are estimated value and ground truth value of jth landmark point, C_l and C_r represent real distance of bi-ocular. Because of the difference of inner points and outline points, we set threshold of inner point 0.05, and outline point 0.10. Our training data is totally more than 5000 images, containing part of images from LFPW, few non-HD images of Helen, part of images from Cohn-Kanade datasets, and the others are downloaded from Internet.

Table 1. Location results on a subset of the CAS-PEAL-R1 database in this paper

Name	Ace	Age	Back	Dist	Exp	Glass	Nom
#test	2236	66	651	324	1881	812	1040
eyes	98.70%	100%	98.31%	100%	99.68%	99.01%	100%
in	98.70%	100%	97.85%	99.38%	99.47%	99.01%	100%
out	97.81%	96.97%	96.62%	95.68%	99.04%	99.01%	99.52%

CAS-PEAL-R1. We choose 6 sub-databases for test: Accessory, Aging, Back- ground, Distance, Expression and Normal. The result of testing shows in Table 1. Results in Table 1 illustrate that, our alignment algorithm performs robustly to face gestures, ages, decorations, backgrounds and distances change. However, alignment accuracy of outline decrease obviously as the test face image is low revolution or affected by some noise factors. It turns out that it's necessary to locate inner point and outline points separately.

FERET. FERET includes images covering gesture changes, illuminate changes and ages changes face image etc. The alignment accuracy on FERET of our algorithm is shown in Table 2. The localization accuracy is lower than CAS-PEAL-R1's. The reason may be the majority of training data is Asian samples, but the majority of FERET is Western and testing images with different sources of light. But the result can still illustrate the validity of our algorithm. Some results in LFPW and Helen are shown in Figure 2.

Table 2. Location results on a subset of the FERET database in this paper

Name	dup1	dup2	fb	fc	gallery	total
#test	719	234	1189	194	1193	3529
eyes	97.91%	96.15%	98.99%	99.48%	98.19%	98.44%
inner	97.64%	96.15%	98.74%	99.48%	97.74%	98.04%

Fig. 2. Part of location images of validation set which are accurate

Comparison with other Methods. Our training data involve images of LFPW, thus we select BioID database [10] as test set for fairness. BioID includes 23 people, 1521 front face gray images size of 384*286. Each image sample was taken from different camera angle, distance, environment illumination and object in mutative gesture and posture. Locating on BioID is more difficulty than on CAS-PEAL-R1 and FERET. Figure 3 illustrates the comparative results among our algorithms, Component based Discriminative Search (CBDS) [7], Boosted Regression with Markov Network (BoRMaN) [9], and a newer commercial software (Microsoft Research Face SDK [8]). The results are shown in Figure 3. It illustrates our method outperforms others.

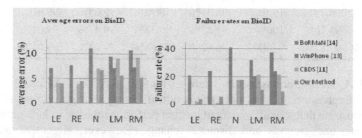

Fig. 3. Comparison of average errors and failure rates testing on BioID

Experiments with Distinct Structure. It's just one small step to present cascade algorithm, suitable structure and parameters need to be searched and examined through lots of experiments. Restricted by article space, we just show 2 groups of representative experiments results with different structures and parameters. Results are shown as Figure 4.

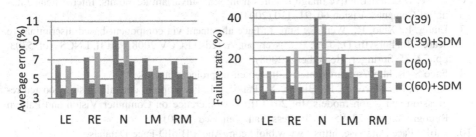

Fig. 4. Comparison of mean errors testing on BioID with different parameters

In figure 4, C(39) represents the size of input layer of DCNN is 39×39, C(60) means the size of input layer of DCNN is 60×60. +SDM indicates algorithm cascaded with SDM. The results in figure 4 indicate that, structure of C(60)+SDM performs better, particularly in robustness. Comparasion C(39) with C(39)+SDM, C(60) with C(60)+SDM illustrate that cascade algorithm performs better than single DCNN. Comparison C(39) with C(60) illustrates C(60) achieves better localization accuracy than C(39), i.e., C(60) provides a better initial value than C(39). Furthermore, C(60)+SDM performs better than any other groups, indicates that SDM achieve higher accuracy with better initial values.

5   Conclusion

We present a "from little to lot, from coarse to fine" cascade face alignment approach. Experiments on different databases show our method can accurately locate plenty of keypoints with good generalization and robustness. The strategy of separately locating inner points and outline points relieves the problem of low localization accuracy issues from different types of points which also gives a chance to parallel.

References

1. Cootes, T.F., Edwards, G.J., Taylor, C.J.: Active appearance models. In: Burkhardt, H., Neumann, B. (eds.) ECCV 1998. LNCS, vol. 1407, pp. 484–498. Springer, Heidelberg (1998)
2. Sun, Y., Wang, X., Tang, X.: Deep convolutional network cascade for facial point detection. In: 2013 IEEE Conference on Computer Vision and Pattern Recognition, pp. 3476–3483. IEEE Press, Portland (2013)
3. Zhou, E., Fan, H., Cao, Z., Jiang, Y., Yin, Q.: Extensive facial landmark localization with coarse-to-fine convolutional network cascade. In: 2013 IEEE International Conference on Computer Vision Workshops, pp. 386–391. IEEE Press, Sydney (2013)
4. Xiong, X.H., Fernando, D.F.: Supervised descent method and its applications to face alignment. In: 2013 IEEE Conference on Computer Vision and Pattern Recognition, pp. 532–539. IEEE Press, Portland (2013)
5. Lowe, D.G.: Object recognition from local scale-invariant features. In: 10th IEEE International Conference on Computer vision, pp. 1150–1157. IEEE Press, Kerkyra (1999)

6. Lowe, D.G.: Distinctive image features from scale-invariant keypoints. International Journal of Computer Vision **60**, 91–110 (2004)
7. Liang, L., Xiao, R., Wen, F., Sun, J.: Face alignment via component-based discriminative search. In: Forsyth, D., Torr, P., Zisserman, A. (eds.) ECCV 2008, Part II. LNCS, vol. 5303, pp. 72–85. Springer, Heidelberg (2008)
8. Face SDK. http://research.microsoft.com/en-us/projects/facesdk
9. Valstar, M., Martinez, B., Binefa, X., Pantic, M.: Facial point detection using boosted regression and graph models. In: 2010 IEEE Conference on Computer Vision and Pattern Recognition, pp. 72–85. IEEE Press, San Francisco (2010)
10. BioID Face Database. https://www.bioid.com/About/BioID-Face-Database

Robust Face Detection Based on Enhanced Local Sensitive Support Vector Machine

Xiaohong Li[✉], Qinqin Tao, Jingjing Zhao, Yiming Mao, and Shu Zhan

School of Computer & Information, Hefei University of Technology, Hefei, China
jsjlxh@hfut.edu.cn

Abstract. In recent years, local classifiers have obtained great success in classification task due to its powerful discriminating ability on local regions. Based on it, we employ a locality-sensitive SVM (LSSVM) to build a local model on each local region to solve the problem of large intra-class variances between different face images. On the other hand, the use of SVM with local kernels was presented. Compared with the conventional global kernel, it's more robust since it can utilize the local features which are influenced only specific parts under partial occlusion. So in order to detect face effectively, we want to utilize the global and local features of face comprehensively. Thus we combine the global and local kernels and apply the combination kernel to the LSSVM algorithm, proposing a robust face detection algorithm. Extensive experiments on the widely used CMU+MIT dataset and FDDB dataset demonstrate the robustness and validity of our algorithm.

Keywords: Kernel combination · Face detection · Local classifier · Support vector machine

1   Introduction

Face detection is the foundation of computer vision and pattern recognition technology. It has an important role in face related topics [1-2].

Because of the viewpoint, illumination, facial expression, occlusion and other reasons, the difference between the face images may be large, and the difference between the background and face image may be fuzzy. Hence a single classifier globally constructed over the whole space may be inadequate to capture all the variants of feature representations. On the contrary, it is promising to divide the whole space into a set of locality-sensitive regions, on each of which a local classifier is learned for face detection. For example, Cheng et al. [3] partitioned the training examples into clusters and built a separate linear SVM model for each cluster. Based on it, Qi et al. [4] proposed a locality sensitive support vector machine (LSSVM) algorithm. It imposed a global regularizer across local regions so that the local classifiers can be smoothly glued together to form a regularized overall classifier. However, the LSSVM algorithm did not study the kernel function which is very important for objection detection.

© Springer International Publishing Switzerland 2015
J. Yang et al. (Eds.): CCBR 2015, LNCS 9428, pp. 103–111, 2015.
DOI: 10.1007/978-3-319-25417-3_13

In general, a kernel function in SVM is applied to global features extracted from a sample. However, global features are influenced easily by noise or occlusion, so conventional methods are not robust to occlusion. In recent years, SVM with local kernels has been proposed for better use of local features since partial occlusion affects only specific local features [5-7]. For example, Kazuhiro Hotta [6] arranged local kernels at all local regions of recognition target and used in SVM to realize robust face recognition under partial occlusion.

In this paper, we combine the global and local kernels and apply the combination kernel to the LSSVM algorithm, putting forward an improved local sensitive support vector machine using kernel combination. Our model has the characteristics of LSSVM model: build the local classifiers for each cluster, which making the classification more easily. At the same time, our model can utilize the global and local feature of face image comprehensively through the combination of global and local kernels used in SVM, thereby making the algorithm more robust.

2   Background: LSSVM

In this section, we present a brief review of LSSVM which forms the basis of the proposed algorithm in this paper.

Give a set of training examples $S = \{(x_i, y_i)|\ i=1,...,N\}$. The whole training examples are clustered into several clusters by clustering, and then a local classifier $f_i = w_i x: X_L \in R$, $i=1,..., L$ is built for each cluster. Denote the classifier for region X_l by f_l, then for an arbitrary sample $x \in X$ the classifier is

$$f(x) = \sum_{l=1}^{L} f_l(x) \, \mathrm{I}(x \in X_l) \tag{1}$$

here $\mathrm{I}(E)$ is the indicator function taking value 1 if the event E occurs or 0 otherwise. This is the overall classifier described in literature [3].

Since individual local learner is limited on local region, the overall classifier (1) combining these local learners cannot guarantee the regularity on the whole space even though local learners have regularization performance on their own regions. So, literature [4] modeled the correlation in each local region, and added this correlation to the regularization term. Denote the following regularization term on each local region X_l as

$$\begin{aligned}\Omega(w, w_l) &= (w - w_l)^T X_l X_l^T (w - w_l) \\ &= (w - w_l)^T S_l (w - w_l)\end{aligned} \tag{2}$$

where X_l is the matrix with x_{jL}, $j=1,...,N_l$ as its columns, x_{jL} is the jth example in the lth region. N_l is the number of training examples on the lth region. With the above regularizer on each region, the learning problem for locality-sensitive classifier can be formulated as

$$\min_{w, w_l} \frac{1}{2} \lambda \| w \|_2^2 + \frac{1}{2} \sum_{l=1}^{L} (w - w_l)^T S_l (w - w_l) + C \sum_{l=1}^{L} \sum_{j=1}^{N_l} \zeta_{jl} \tag{3}$$

s. t. , $y_{jl}.w_l^T S_l x_{jl} \geq 1 - \zeta_{jl}, \zeta_{jl} \geq 0, j = 1,..., N_l,\ l = 1,..., L$.

2.1   Discussion

According to (3), we can acquire the overall classifier that is smooth enough on the whole feature space as well as best approximates the local learners on each local region. Thus, it can keep the sensitivity to the local region, making the classification easier. Nevertheless, in the literature [4], it does not consider the selection of kernel function which is a very effective method for object detection.

As we know, face detection in real-world situation is still challenging, with obstacles such as occlusion, illumination changes and pose changes to be overcome. With such obstacles, the global feature of face maybe destroyed. However, local feature is more robust compared with global feature since partial occlusion affects only specific local feature. So in this paper, we combine the global and local kernels to utilize the global and local feature of face comprehensively, and then apply the combination kernel to LSSVM. In particular, the global kernel is applied to the whole feature extracted from face, and the local kernel is applied to the local region of the feature. The use of local kernels in SVM requires local kernel integration. The summation of local kernels is used as the integration method in this paper.

3   Proposed Method

In this paper, we train a background filter in order to filter away the simple backgrounds as soon as possible. For this purpose, Adaboost algorithm is used since it is very effective and real time since Viola and Jones' [9] work. The flow chart of the proposed method is as shown in Fig. 1.

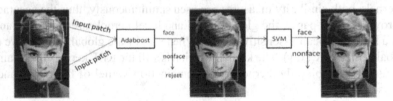

Fig. 1. Flow chart of face detection

3.1   The Adaboost Based Background Filter

The boosting cascade framework by Viola and Jones [9] is a great breakthrough in the field of face detection. So we adopt the detector as our background filter in the first stage to filter out those obvious backgrounds, which ensuring the detection rate and increasing the speed of system at the same time.

It is important to set the threshold of the Adaboost appropriately. Setting the threshold too high may cause too many positive examples be rejected, reducing the overall detection rate, and setting it too low may lead to too many pass-through patches that needs to be classified further by the SVM, slowing down the overall detection speed. So a minimum detection rate of 99.8% and a maximum false positive rate of 50% were set as the training parameters.

3.2   Locality-Sensitive SVM Using Kernel Combination

We choose the most common RBF kernel as the basic kernel function. In the proposed method, local kernels are arranged at all positions on the face. Then the outputs of all the local kernels are integrated and used for detection. The summation of local kernels is considered as the integration method which satisfies Mercer's theorem and is more robust to occlusion compared with the product integration [6]. The local RBF kernel at position p is defined by

$$K_P(x(p), y(p)) = \exp\left(-\|x(p) - y(p)\|^2 / \sigma_P^2\right) \tag{4}$$

where p is the label of position, and $x(p)$ and $y(p)$ are the local features centered at position p. σ_p is the local variance at position p.

Specific, the face we processed is 28×28. So we can divide the face image into 4×4 patches, each size is 7×7 pixels. Every patch is a local region of face. We extract the features of the local region and apply one local kernel to the region. Thus, there are total 16 local kernels within a face image. So the summation of local kernel's output is defined as

$$K_l(x, y) = \frac{1}{N_p} \sum_{p=1}^{N_p} K_P(x(p), y(p)) = \frac{1}{N_p} \sum_{p=1}^{N_p} \exp\left(-\|x(p) - y(p)\|^2 / \sigma_P^2\right) \tag{5}$$

where N_p is the number of local kernels. x and y are the global feature of the whole face.

Local kernel measures detailed similarity and global kernel measures rough similarity. Therefore, there is the case where a local features-based method misclassifies samples which are classified easily by global features. By combining the global and local kernels, both similarity measures are used simultaneously, thus the accuracy will be improved. In this paper, the global kernel and local kernels are combined and then used as a kernel in locality-sensitive SVM. When x and y are global features, we denote the global kernel as $K_g(x, y)$. The kernel function is still the RBF kernel. The summation is also used to combine the kernels. The combination kernel of the global and local kernels is defined as

$$K_{com}(x, y) = K_g(x, y) + K_l(x, y) \tag{6}$$

This kernel also satisfies Mercer's theorem [6], the proof does not repeat here. After the derivation above, we get the form of the combination kernel. Then we will introduce how to apply the kernel to locality-sensitive SVM.

First, we use the combination kernel to measure the similarity between examples, including detailed and rough similarity, and get a correlation matrix K_t.

$$K_t = [K_{com}(x_i, x_j)]_{N \times N} \tag{7}$$

where x_i and x_j denote the ith and jth sample in the feature space respectively. N is the number of training examples. The category is not considered here.

Then we calculate the kernel matrix K across the whole feature space through the correlation matrix K_t.

$$K(X_l, X_m) = K_t(X_l, X_l) \times K_t(X_l, X_m) \times K_t(X_m, X_m) + \delta_{lm} \times K_t(X_l, X_m) \times K_t(X_m, X_m) \quad (8)$$

where δ_{lm} taking the value 1 if $l = m$ or 0 otherwise. X_l and X_m are the example matrixes in the lth and mth regions.

Therefore the final object function can be rewritten as:

$$\max_{\partial_{jl}} \sum_{l=1}^{L} \sum_{j=1}^{Nl} \partial_{jl} - \frac{1}{2} \sum_{l=1}^{L} \sum_{m=1}^{L} \sum_{j=1}^{Nl} \sum_{i=1}^{Nm} \partial_{jl} \partial_{im} . K(X_l, X_m) \quad (9)$$

So, give a test example x, we first calculate the distance between the test example and the cluster center of the training examples, and determine which cluster it belongs to. Then we calculate the correlation matrix K_t between the test example and training examples.

$$K_t(x, x_i) = [K_{com}(x, x_i)]_{1 \times N} \quad (10)$$

where x is the test example and x_i is the ith training example. N is the number of training examples.

Similarity, we calculate the kernel matrix between the test example and training examples $K(x, Xtr_m)$ using the correlation matrix K_t.

$$K(x, Xtr_m) = K_t(x, Xtr_l) \times K_t(Xtr_m, Xtr_l) \times K_t(Xtr_m, Xtr_m)$$
$$+ \delta_{lm \times} K_t(x, Xtr_l) \times K_t(Xtr_m, Xtr_m) \quad (11)$$

where δ_{lm} taking the value 1 if $l = m$ or 0 otherwise. Xtr_m and Xtr_l are the training examples in the mth and lth region respectively. x is the test sample that belongs to the lth region.

Finally, when the coefficient ∂_{jl} are solved, the local classifiers are given as

$$f_l(x) = \sum_{l=1}^{L} \sum_{j=1}^{Nl} \partial_{jl} K(x, Xtr_m) \quad (12)$$

4   Experiments

In this paper, the performance of the proposed detector is evaluated on the CMU+MIT [8] data set and FDDB [14] data set.

For training and testing, a set of 1500 frontal face images were collected from various sources. All face images were scaled to a base resolution of 28×28 pixels, and then histogram equalization and intensity normalization were performed. Additionally 4500 non-face images were collected as negative examples. The same pretreatment was performed to these examples.

Firstly, we train the Adaboost background filter, setting the minhitrate as 0.998, maxfalsealarm as 0.5, stage as 3, so Adaboost classifier can quickly remove more than 80% backgrounds. Secondly, in order to use local kernels effectively, we want to use local appearance features. For this purpose, we use LBP features which give good performance in objection detection and recognition. Since LBP features extracted from an example are 28×28 dimensional features, local kernels can be applied to a 7×7 region without overlap. Thus, there are total 16 local kernels applied to the LBP features. Besides, the global kernel is applied to the whole LBP features. At last, we use the LBP features and the kernel matrix calculated by ourselves to train the SVM classifier. Training SVM need to set many parameters, the most important two parameters are -c and –g. In order to seek the optimal parameters, we employ the PSO algorithm for SVM parameters optimization during our experiment process.

4.1   Evaluation on CMU+MIT Dataset

The CMU+MIT data set contains test sets A, B, C (test, test-low, new-test) and rotated test set. We use the three test sets (test A, B, C), without the rotated ones, containing 130 images with 511 faces.

We first show some detection results by our detector on the CMU+MIT data set.

Fig. 2. Examples of detecting results in CMU+MIT dataset.

The faces in CMU+MIT data set have different sizes, poses, expressions, and lighting conditions, but the proposed method can handle them well. For example, Fig. 2 (a)-(b) show some examples of detecting rotated faces. It proves that our method can detect not only frontal faces, but also some rotated faces. The low quality faces and hand-drawn faces can also be successfully detected as shown in Fig. 2 (c)-(d) and Fig. 2(g)-(h). For those faces under the dim light, we can also detect them effectively, as shown in Fig. 2(e)-(f). However, when the illumination is too dark, both the global features and local features are not obvious, the detector may fail to detect those faces. In Fig. 2(f) there are two very dark faces are missed by the proposed method.

To illustrate the robustness to occlusion of our detector, we conduct a set of occlusion experiments and compare the detection results with the famous Viola and Jones' detector [9]. In particular, we select several face images from CMU+MIT data set and manually occlude them. As showing in Fig. 3, our detector can successfully detect these faces under partial occlusion. However Viola and Jones' detector is failed for all of them. This is because we apply the local kernels to the local regions of the features extracted from face. So even though the face is occluded, only partial features are influenced, our method that using global and local kernels simultaneously can still work.

Fig. 3. Examples of detect occluded face images from CMU+MIT dataset.

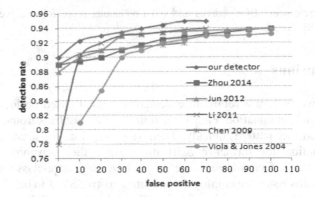

Fig. 4. ROC curves of different algorithms on CMU+MIT dataset.

Finally, we compare our work with other several popular face detection algorithms on CMU+MIT frontal face dataset. Fig. 4 plots the Receiver Operating Characteristics (ROC) curves of our method as well as other popular face detection algorithms including Viola and Jones [9], Li et al. [10], Jun et al. [11], Zhou et al. [12], Chen et al. [13]. As shown in fig. 4, our detector is more efficient than other algorithms. Especially for cases at low false positive, our detector can still achieve good results.

4.2   Evaluation on FDDB Dataset

To study the performance of proposed face detector on natural images encountered in real-life, we evaluate the face detector on a famous face annotated database "FDDB [14]: Face Detection Data Set and Benchmark" which consists of annotated face images collected from news photographs. It contains 2845 images with a total of 5771 faces under a wide range of conditions. Fig. 5 show the discrete score and continuous score ROC curve generated by our detector in comparison to available results on the benchmark [9, 15-18].

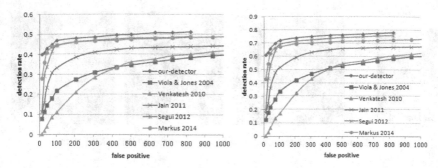

Fig. 5. (a) Discrete score ROC curves and (b) Continuous score ROC curves for different methods on FDDB dataset.

5   Conclusions

In this paper, we present a robust face detection method based on locality-sensitive SVM using kernel combination. Firstly, we train an Adaboost background filter to filter away simple non-face patterns quickly. Then we employ locality-sensitive SVM using kernel combination for further classification. Since the viewpoint, illumination, occlusion and other effect, different face images have large intra-class variances. So in order to handle this issue, we employ the locality-sensitive SVM to build a local model on each local region, which making the classification task on each local region simple. On the other hand, we assemble the global and local kernels to utilize the global and local features of face simultaneously, and then apply the combination kernel to locality-sensitive SVM, solving the problem of occlusion further. The experiment on the dataset also proves the validity of our method.

Acknowledgments. This work is supported by National Natural Science Foundation of China (61371156 and 61371155).

References

1. Chen, W.S., Dai, X.L., Pan, B.B.: A novel discriminant criterion based on feature fusion strategy for face recognition. Neurocomputing **159**, 67–77 (2015)
2. Sun, Y., Wang, X.G., Tang, X.O.: Deep convolutional network cascade for facial point detection. In: CVPR, pp. 3476–3483. IEEE Press, Portland (2013)
3. Cheng, H., Tan, P.N., Jin, R.: Localized support vector machine and its efficient algorithm. In: SIAM Conference on Data Mining, pp. 461–466. SIAM Press, Minneapolis (2007)
4. Qi, G.J., Tian, Q., Huang, T.: Locality-sensitive support vector machine by exploring local correlation and global regularization. In: CVPR, pp. 841–848. IEEE Press, Providence (2011)
5. Hotta, K.: Local normalized linear summation kernel for fast and robust recognition. Pattern Recognition **43**, 906–913 (2010)

6. Hotta, K.: Robust face recognition under partial occlusion based on support vector machine with local Gaussian summation kernel. Image and Vision Computing **26**, 1490–1498 (2008)
7. Hotta, K.: View independent face detection based on horizontal rectangular features and accuracy improvement using combination kernel of various sizes. Pattern Recognition **42**, 437–444 (2009)
8. Rowley, H.A., Baluja, S., Kanade, T.: Neural network-based face detection. PAMI **20**, 23–38 (1998)
9. Viola, P., Jones, M.: Robust real-time face detection. International Journal of Computer Vision **57**, 137–154 (2004)
10. Li, J., Wang, T., Zhang, Y.: Face detection using SURF cascade. In: ICCV Workshops, pp. 2183–2190. IEEE Press, Barcelona (2011)
11. Jun, B., Kim, D.: Robust face detection using local gradient patterns and evidence accumulation. Pattern Recognition **45**, 3304–3316 (2012)
12. Zhou, S., Yin, J.: Face Detection using Multi-block Local Gradient Patterns and Support Vector Machine. Journal of Computational Information Systems **10**, 1767–1776 (2014)
13. Chen, Y., Han, C.: A CNN-Based Face Detector with a Simple Feature Map and a Coarse-to-fine Classifier. PAMI **99**, 1–13 (2009)
14. Jain, V., Learned-Miller, E.: FDDB: A benchmark for face detection in unconstrained settings. Technical Report UM-CS-2010-009, University of Massachusetts, Amherst (2010)
15. Venkatesh, B.S., Marcel, S.: Fast bounding box estimation based face detection. In: ECCV Workshops on Face Detection. Springer Press, Crete (2010)
16. Jain, V., Learned-Miller, E.: Online domain adaptation of a pre-trained cascade of classifiers. In: CVPR, pp. 577–584. IEEE Press, Providence (2011)
17. Segui, S., Drozdzal, M., Radeva, P., et al.: An integrated approach to contextual face detection. In: ICPPAM, pp. 90–97. Springer Press, Vilamoura (2012)
18. Markus, N., Frljak, M., Pandzic, I.: A method for object detection based on pixel intensity comparisons organized in decision trees, arXiv preprint arXiv:1305.4537 (2013)

An Efficient Non-negative Matrix Factorization with Its Application to Face Recognition

Yugao Li, Wensheng Chen$^{(\boxtimes)}$, Binbin Pan, Yang Zhao, and Bo Chen

College of Mathematics and Statistics, Shenzhen University, Shenzhen 518060, China
chenws@szu.edu.cn

Abstract. This paper attempts to develop a novel Non-negative Matrix Factorization (NMF) algorithm to improve traditional NMF approach. Based on gradient descent method, we appropriately choose a larger step-length than that of traditional NMF and obtain efficient NMF update rules with fast convergence rate and high performance. The step-length is determined by solving some inequalities, which are established according to the requirements on step-length and non-negativity constraints. The proposed algorithm is successfully applied to face recognition. The rates of both convergence and recognition are utilized to evaluate the effectiveness of our method. Compared with traditional NMF algorithm on ORL and FERET databases, experimental results demonstrate that the proposed NMF method has superior performance.

Keywords: Non-negative matrix factorization · Multiplicative update method · Face recognition

1 Introduction

In recent decades, face recognition has become one of the most promising research areas, and various approaches for face recognition have been developed. The face recognition algorithms can be clarified into two main categories, namely global feature extraction and local feature extraction. Typical approaches for local feature extraction are Locality Preserving Projection (LPP) [1] and Unsupervised Discriminant Projection (UDP) [2]. They are able to uncover the manifold structure on which the facial images reside. The classical methods for global feature extraction, such as Principal Component Analysis (PCA) [3] and Linear Discriminant Analysis (LDA) [4], aim to model the structure of Euclidean distance and rely on global facial features to form a whole face. Different from above mentioned approaches, NMF [5]-[10], also as a local feature extraction method, does not allow subtraction operation when it is performed. NMF exploits multiplicative update method to approximately factorize a nonnegative matrix into two matrices with nonnegative entries.

In detail, for a given $n \times m$ non-negative data matrix X whose each column vector represents an image, and a constant r which is generally chosen to satisfy $(n + m)r < nm$ or $r < n$ (or m), the task of NMF is to seek an $n \times r$ matrix

© Springer International Publishing Switzerland 2015
J. Yang et al. (Eds.): CCBR 2015, LNCS 9428, pp. 112–119, 2015.
DOI: 10.1007/978-3-319-25417-3_14

W ($W_{ij} \geq 0$) and an $r \times m$ matrix H ($H_{ij} \geq 0$) such that $X \approx WH$, where W and H are called the basis image matrix and the coefficient matrix, respectively. Each column vector of W represents a basis image and each column vector of H is called encoding [5] including r coefficients. NMF can be applied to facial image data because of nonnegative pixels. The nonnegative facial features learnt by NMF contains the information of the shape and location of facial components (such as eyes, eyebrows, nose, mouth), and they are able to be non-negatively combined to reconstruct a whole facial image. Another motivation of NMF comes from biological indications [5]. For example, the firing rates in visual perception neurons are non-negative and synaptic strengths do not change sign.

The main technique of traditional NMF [6] is to develop multiplicative update formulae using gradient descent method. Although its multiplicative update rules can be easily implemented, NMF could be further enhanced in aspects of both convergence rate and performance. To this end, this paper proposes a novel efficient NMF method, which is also based on the gradient descent method. The proposed method properly selects the step-length which is controlled to be larger than that of traditional NMF. The task of finding step-length is to solve some inequalities derived from the requirements of a longer step-length and non-negativity constraints. The obtained nonnegative update formulae are simply expressed as quadratic forms. Our algorithm is tested on two aspects, namely convergence rate and recognition accuracy. Experimental results show that our method not only has faster convergence rate than traditional NMF, but also achieves superior performance on face recognition.

The rest of the paper is organized as follows. Section 2 briefly takes a review of the related work. In section 3, the proposed method is presented in details. The experimental results are reported in section 4. Finally, the conclusions are drawn in section 5.

2 Traditional NMF

This section will briefly introduce the traditional NMF algorithm. Details can be found in [6]. For a given data matrix $X_{n \times m}$ ($X_{ij} \geq 0$) of total m training samples, NMF aims to find two non-negative matrices, namely basis image matrix $W_{n \times r}$ and coefficient matrix $H_{r \times m}$, such that $X \approx WH$. Euclidean distance is employed to measure the quality of approximation between X and WH. Therefore, NMF is equivalent to the following optimization problem

$$\min_{W,H} F(W, H) = \frac{1}{2} \|X - WH\|_F^2, \tag{1}$$

subject to $\quad W_{ij} \geq 0$ and $H_{ij} \geq 0, \quad \sum_{a=1}^{n} W_{ab} = 1, \quad \forall i, j, a, b.$

It can be easily derived two gradient formulae of the cost function $F(W, H)$ as follows,

$$\nabla_H F(W, H) = W^T W H - W^T X \text{ and } \nabla_W F(W, H) = WHH^T - XH^T,$$

which are partial derivatives to elements in W and H, respectively. According to the gradient descent method, NMF has the following iterative equation,

$$H^{k+1} = H^k - \rho_k \odot \nabla_H F(W^k, H^k), \tag{2}$$

where $\odot$ denotes Hadamard product of two matrices and ρ_k is a matrix whose elements denote step-size in gradient descent direction. The non-negativity on H^{k+1} can be guaranteed by setting that

$$H^k - \rho_k \odot (W^k)^T W^k H^k = 0. \tag{3}$$

Therefore, it yields from equation (3) that the step-length matrix ρ_k satisfies

$$\rho_k = \frac{H^k}{(W^k)^T W^k H^k}, \tag{4}$$

where notation $\frac{A}{B}$ means the component-wise quotient of two matrices. Substituting (4) into (2), we have

$$H^{k+1} = \frac{H^k \odot W^k X}{(W^k)^T W^k H^k}.$$

The update rule on W^{k+1} can be obtained if the similar procedure is performed on W. Finally, the iterative formulae of traditional NMF are as below,

$$H^{k+1} = \frac{H^k \odot (W^k)^T X}{(W^k)^T W^k H^k}, W^{k+1} = \frac{W^k \odot X(H^{k+1})^T}{W^k H^{k+1}(H^{k+1})^T}, W_{ij}^{k+1} \leftarrow \frac{W_{ij}^{k+1}}{\sum_{a=1}^m W_{aj}}. \tag{5}$$

3   The Proposed NMF

This section will develop a novel NMF algorithm with fast convergence rate and high performance. Based on the gradient descent method, our NMF could be achieved by properly choosing the step-length $\widetilde{\rho}_k$ which is constrained to be greater than that of traditional NMF. The nonnegative update formulae of the proposed NMF have quadratic forms and are expressed as follows,

$$H^{k+1} = H^k \odot \left[(1 - \epsilon_k)Q_H^k + \epsilon_k(Q_H^k)^2\right], \tag{6}$$

$$W^{k+1} = W^k \odot \left[(1 - \epsilon_k)Q_W^k + \epsilon_k(Q_W^k)^2\right], \tag{7}$$

$$W_{ij}^{k+1} \leftarrow \frac{W_{ij}^{k+1}}{\sum_{a=1}^m W_{aj}} \tag{8}$$

where

$$Q_H^k = \frac{(W^k)^T X}{(W^k)^T W^k H^k}, \quad Q_W^k = \frac{X(H^{k+1})^T}{W^k H^{k+1}(H^{k+1})^T},$$

notation A^2 denotes $A \odot A$ and ϵ_k is a parameter which is in $[0, 1]$.

The motivation of the proposed method is to improve the traditional NMF. For this purpose, we attempt to appropriately adjust the step-length $\tilde{\rho}_k$ via reconstructing the equation (3). In the process of determining step-size, the following two conditions must be satisfied: 1) $\tilde{\rho}_k \geq \rho_k$; 2) preserve non-negativity constraints. Details are as follows.

We first rewrite the equation (2) as follows,

$$H^{k+1} = \alpha_k \odot H^k + (1 - \alpha_k) \odot H^k - \tilde{\rho}_k \odot (W^k)^T W^k H^k$$
$$+ \tilde{\rho}_k \odot (1 - \beta_k) \odot (W^k)^T X + \tilde{\rho}_k \odot \beta_k \odot (W^k)^T X, \qquad (9)$$

where α_k and β_k are two parameter matrices whose elements range in $[0, 1]$. Here $\mathbf{1}$ is a $r \times m$ matrix with all entries equal to 1. To reconstruct the equation (3), we need that

$$\alpha_k \odot H^k - \tilde{\rho}_k \odot (W^k)^T W^k H^k + \tilde{\rho}_k \odot \beta_k \odot (W^k)^T X = 0, \qquad (10)$$

and then

$$H^{k+1} = (1 - \alpha_k) \odot H^k + \tilde{\rho}_k \odot (1 - \beta_k) \odot (W^k)^T X. \qquad (11)$$

By direct computation, it can be calculated from equation (10) that,

$$\tilde{\rho}_k = \frac{\alpha_k \odot H^k}{(W^k)^T W^k H^k - \beta_k \odot (W^k)^T X}. \qquad (12)$$

In the proposed method, the first condition imposed on step-length $\tilde{\rho}_k$ requires that

$$\tilde{\rho}_k \geq \rho_k, \qquad (13)$$

where the sign $\geq$ denotes the component-wise comparison. The second is that the non-negativity constraint on $\tilde{\rho}_k$. This indicates that the following inequality must be held,

$$(W^k)^T W^k H^k - \beta_k \odot (W^k)^T X \geq 0. \qquad (14)$$

Combining (13) and (14), we have got the following inequalities that α_k, β_k should satisfy,

$$\min \left\{ \frac{(W^k)^T W^k H^k}{(W^k)^T X}, 1 \right\} \geq \beta_k \geq \frac{(1 - \alpha_k) \odot (W^k)^T W^k H^k}{(W^k)^T X}. \qquad (15)$$

Considering the inequality in the left side of (15), it is natural to set

$$\beta_k = \frac{(W^k)^T W^k H^k}{(W^k)^T W^k H^k + (W^k)^T X}. \qquad (16)$$

Combining (16) and the inequality in the right side of (15), we obtain

$$\alpha_k = \frac{(W^k)^T W^k H^k + \epsilon_k (W^k)^T X}{(W^k)^T W^k H^k + (W^k)^T X}, \qquad (17)$$

where ϵ_k is a parameter $\in [0, 1]$. By substituting (16) and (17) into (12), it yields that

$$\widetilde{\rho}_k = \frac{H^k}{(W^k)^T W^k H^k} + \epsilon_k \frac{(W^k)^T X \odot H^k}{((W^k)^T W^k H^k)^2}$$

$$= \rho_k + \epsilon_k \frac{(W^k)^T X \odot H^k}{((W^k)^T W^k H^k)^2}. \tag{18}$$

Hence, the iterative formula (6) is obtained via substituting expressions (16)-(18) into (11). The update formula (7) can be derived out in a similar way and expression (8) is a normalization step which let the sum of each column of W^{k+1} equal to 1. Especially, it can be seen from (18) that $\widetilde{\rho}_k$ is larger than ρ_k. This implies that our NMF has faster convergence rate than that of traditional NMF.

4   Experimental Results

In this section, we will evaluate the convergence rate of proposed NMF (Prop NMF) via comparing with traditional NMF (Trad NMF), and the performance of proposed method on face recognition. For our method, the parameter ϵ_k is set to

$$\epsilon_k = \begin{cases} 1 - \frac{1}{k}, \ 1 \leq k \leq 10 \\ 0.9, \qquad \text{else} \end{cases},$$

where k is the number of iteration.

4.1   Comparisons on Convergence

In order to take account of the convergence of each approach, two nonnegative matrices, namely a small matrix $X_{100 \times 50}$ and a large matrix $X_{1000 \times 500}$ with their elements uniformly distributed in $(0, 1)$, will be selected for evaluations. We randomly initialized two factor matrices $W_{m \times r}$ and $H_{r \times n}$ whose entries are also distributed uniformly in $(0, 1)$. For the small matrix $X_{100 \times 50}$, the number of basis images r and the maximum iteration number I_{max} are set to $r = 30$ and $I_{max} = 500$ respectively. While for the large matrix $X_{1000 \times 500}$, we let $r = 300$ and $I_{max} = 2000$. Each algorithm, including Prop NMF and Trad NMF, is repeatedly run for ten times. The average error cost $E(k) = \|X - W_k H_k\|_F$ against the number of iteration k are calculated and plotted in Fig. 1. Because low error cost at each iteration means high convergence rate, it can be seen from Fig. 1 that Prod NMF surpasses Trad NMF on the convergence.

We would also like to see the detailed convergence rate on the time cost of each method. The curve of the mean time cost against the mean error cost is plotted in Fig. 2. It shows that the convergence rate of our method is faster than that of the traditional NMF as well.

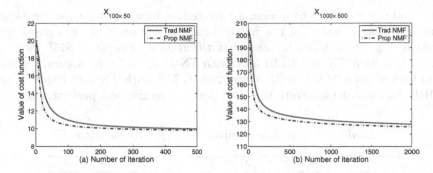

Fig. 1. The mean costs versus the number of iteration on small matrix $X_{100 \times 50}$ (Left) and large matrix $X_{1000 \times 500}$ (Right)

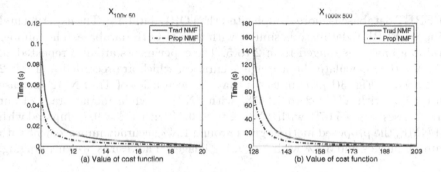

Fig. 2. The value of cost function versus computational time on small matrix $X_{100 \times 50}$ (Left) and large matrix $X_{1000 \times 500}$ (Right)

4.2   Comparisons on Performance

This subsection will choose two face databases, namely ORL database and FERET database, to evaluate the performance of our NMF. ORL database includes 400 face images of 40 persons and each person consists of 10 images with different facial expressions (open and closed eyes , smiling or not smiling), small variations in scales and orientations. The resolution of each image is 112×92, and with 256 gray levels per pixel. On FERET database, we select 120 people, 6 images from each person. The resolution of each image is also 112×92. Six images of each person are taken from four different sets, namely Fa, Fb, Fc and duplicate. The images from Fa and Fb are taken with the same camera on the same day and are different from facial expressions. Images from Fc are take from different camera on the same day. In duplicate set and images from duplicate are taken about $6 - 12$ months after the day where Fa and Fb was set up.

In the experiments, the number of iteration k and the basis number r are respectively set to that $k = 30$ and $r = 150$. TN denotes the training number per class. We randomly selected n $(n = 2, \ldots, 9)$ training images from each person and the rest $(10 - n)$ images are for testing images. The experiments are repeated 10 times, and then the mean accuracies are recorded in Table 1 and plotted in Fig. 3(a). It can be seen that the accuracies of Trad NMF increase from 78.19% with TN = 2 to 94.50% with TN = 9, while the accuracy of our method arises from 79.63% with TN = 2 to 95.75% with TN = 9. Experiments on ORL database demonstrate that our method has the best performance.

Table 1. Recognition accuracies (%) on ORL database

TN	2	3	4	5	6	7	8	9
Trad NMF	78.19	84.89	86.75	90.05	91.69	93.83	94.38	94.50
Prop NMF	**79.63**	**85.61**	**87.79**	**91.50**	**92.50**	**94.83**	**95.38**	**95.75**

FERET database is more complicated than ORL database. The experimental setting on FERET database is similar with that of ORL database. The number of training images is ranged from 2 to 5. The experiments are also repeated 10 times. We then calculate the average accuracies, which are recorded in Table 2 and plotted in Fig. 3(b). It indicates that the accuracies of Trad NMF increase from 63.88% with TN = 2 to 78.67% with TN = 9, while the accuracy of our method arises from 65.67% with TN = 2 to 82.00% with TN = 9. Compared with Trad NMF, the proposed method gives around 1.8% accuracy improvement with 2 training images and 3.3% with 5 training images. The results are encouraging.

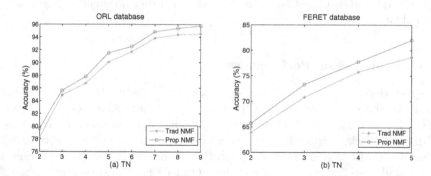

Fig. 3. Performance comparisons on ORL database (Left) and FERET database (Right)

Table 2. Recognition accuracies (%) on FERET database

TN	2	3	4	5
Trad NMF	63.88	70.78	75.75	78.67
Prop NMF	**65.67**	**73.28**	**77.71**	**82.00**

5 Conclusions

In this paper, we proposed a novel improved NMF approach, which is based on gradient descent method and developed via solving some inequalities derived from the requirements of a large step-length and non-negativity constraints. Compared with traditional NMF method, experimental results have shown that our approach not only has the faster convergence rate, but also gives the best performance on face recognition.

Acknowledgments. This paper is partially supported by NSF of PR China (61272252, 61472257), NSF of Guangdong Province (2015A030313544), Science and Technology Planning Project of Shenzhen City (JCYJ20130326111024546), the Special Fund of the Central Finance for the Development of Local Universities (000022070152), and the HD Video R & D Platform for Intelligent Analysis and Processing in Guangdong Engineering Technology Research Centre of Colleges and Universities (no. GCZX-A1409). We would like to thank Olivetti Research Laboratory and Amy Research Laboratory for providing the face image databases.

References

1. He, X.F., Niyogi, P.: Locality preserving projections. In: Thrun, S., Saul, L.K., Schölkopf, B. (eds.) NIPS, vol. 16, pp. 153–160. MIT Press, Cambridge (2004)
2. Yang, J., Zhang, D., Yang, J.Y., Niu, B.: Globally Maximizing, Locally Minimizing: Unsupervised Discriminant Projection with Applications to Face and Palm Biometrics. IEEE Transactions on Pattern Analysis and Machine Intelligence **29**(4), 650–664 (2007)
3. Turk, M., Pentland, A.: Eigenfaces for Recognition. J. Cogn. Neurosci. **3**(1), 71–86 (1991)
4. Belhumeur, P.N., Hespanha, J.P., Kriegman, D.J.: Eigenfaces vs. Fisherfaces: Recognition Using Class Specific Linear Projection. IEEE Transactions on Pattern Analysis and Machine Intelligence **19**(7), 711–720 (1997)
5. Lee, D.D., Seung, H.S.: Learning the Parts of Objects by Non-negative Matrix Factorization. Nature **401**, 788–791 (1999)
6. Lee, D.D., Seung, H.S.: Algorithms for non-negative matrix factorization. In: Leen, T.K., Dietterich, T.G., Tresp, V. (eds.) NIPS, vol. 13, pp. 556–562. MIT Press, Cambridge (2000)
7. Li, L.X., Wu, L., Zhang, H.S.: Nonnegative Matrix Factorization: A Comprehensive Review. IEEE Transactions on Neural Networks and Learning Systems **25**(6), 1336–1353 (2013)
8. Wang, Y.X., Zhang, Y.J., Wu, F.X.: A Fast Algorithm for Nonnegative Matrix Factorization and Its Convergence. IEEE Transactions on Knowledge and Data Engineering **25**(10), 1855–1863 (2014)
9. Korattikara, A., Boyles, L., Welling, M., Kim, J., Park, H.: Statistical optimization of non-negative matrix factorization. In: 14th International Conference on Artificial Intelligence and Statistics, pp. 128–136. Microtome Publishing, Brookline (2011)
10. Mizutani, T.: Ellipsoidal Rounding for Nonnegative Matrix Factorization Under Noisy Separability. Journal of Machine Learning Research **15**, 1011–1039 (2014)

Patch-based Sparse Dictionary Representation for Face Recognition with Single Sample per Person

Jianquan Gu[1], Le Liu[2], and Haifeng Hu[1(✉)]

[1] School of Information Science and Technology, Sun Yat-sen University, Guangzhou, China
578987072@qq.com, huhaif@mail.sysu.edu.cn
[2] Supercomputer Office, Sun Yat-sen University, Guangzhou, China
liule2@mail.sysu.edu.cn

Abstract. In this paper, we solve the problem of robust face recognition (FR) with single sample per person (SSPP). FR with SSPP is a very challenging task due to in such a scenario lacking of information to predict the variations of the query sample. We propose a novel method patch-based sparse dictionary representation (PSDR) to tackle the problem of various variations e.g. expressions, illuminations, corruption, occlusion and disguises in FR with SSPP. The key idea of our scheme is to combine a local sparse representation and a patch-based generic variation dictionary learning to predict the possible facial variations of query image and classification. To extract more feature information in classification, we adopt a patch-based method. Our experiments on Extended Yale B and AR databases show that our method outperforms the state-of-art approaches.

Keywords: Local sparse representation · Patch-based generic variation dictionary

1 Introduction

Face recognition has been an active research topic in computer vision and pattern recognition community. Recently, Wright et al. have demonstrated that a query face can be represented by a sparse linear combination of training samples from all classes. The promising result is supported by the experimental results in SRC [1]. However, SRC requires a lot of training images of each subject to compensate the facial variations [10]. In real-world applications, e.g. e-passport, driving license, or ID card identification, only offer single sample per subject to recognize [9], and the traditional FR methods [12][13] can't provide a good performance. To alleviate this problem, researchers have proposed to learn the facial variations from external data [2][3][4] to compensate the lack of training samples in FR. The Extended SRC (ESRC) [2] computes an intra-class variation dictionary and cast the recognition problem as finding a sparse representation of the query image in terms of the training set and the intra-class variation dictionary. The sparse variation dictionary learning (SVDL) [5] method joint learning a projection to connect the generic training set with the gallery set. Patch-based methods [6][7] partition all face images into several patches, and then perform feature extraction and classification on them.

© Springer International Publishing Switzerland 2015
J. Yang et al. (Eds.): CCBR 2015, LNCS 9428, pp. 120–126, 2015.
DOI: 10.1007/978-3-319-25417-3_15

In this paper, we propose a novel method patch-based sparse dictionary representation (PSDR) by using a local sparse representation and a patch-based generic variation dictionary learning to tackle the problem of FR with SSPP. First, we adopt a local sparse representation approach by partitioning the gallery set and a generic training set into several patches. Then we construct a local gallery dictionary to extract the feature information of the adjacent patches from the gallery dataset, and build a patch-based generic variation dictionary by using an external dataset to predict the possible facial variations. Considering different importance of different patches in FR, the face classification is reached via calculating the weight of each patch. Each patch of the query image is represented by the patches of gallery dictionary and the generic variation dictionary at the corresponding position. The feature-based local face recognition approaches can extract more feature information to address local variations, such as illumination, expression and occlusion better. Learning a patch-based generic variation dictionary can effectively integrate the external data into the framework of sparse representation based classification to handle the problems of various variations in face recognition. Our method aims to minimize the total representation residual of all patches.

2 Related Work

SRC and Extended SRC. In SRC, a query image is sparsely represented over all training images, and then find the class that leads to the minimal reconstruction error to obtain the classification result. Given a query image y, SRC represents y as a sparse linear combination of dictionary $A = [A_1, A_2,..., A_n]$, where A_i denotes the training images associated with class i. Then SRC get the coding vector x of y by solving the L1-minimization problem:

$$\min_{x} \| y - Ax \|_2^2 + \lambda \| x \|_1 \tag{1}$$

After obtaining the coding vector x, the query image y is recognized as class l^* if it satisfies:

$$l^* = \arg\min_{l} \| y - A\delta_l(x) \|_2 \tag{2}$$

where $\delta_l(x)$ is a vector whose only nonzero entries are the entries in x that are associated with class l. That means the query image y is assigned to the class with the minimum reconstruction error. The Eq. (1) shows that a query sample y can be represented by the gallery set dictionary D as:

$$y = Dx + e \tag{3}$$

where e is the representation residual. However, SRC assume that it collect a large amount of training data as the over-complete dictionary D. Therefore, for FR with SSPP, Eq. (3), the y cannot be well represented by the single sample in D. To address this problem, ESRC [2] proposed that the query sample y can be represented by the gallery set dictionary D and the generic intra-class variation dictionary A simultaneously:

$$y = Dx_d + Ax_a + e \tag{4}$$

where x_d and x_a are the representation vectors of y over D and A respectively, and e is the representation residual.

3 Our Proposed Method

We now present our classification scheme for FR with SSPP. Taking the facts that different parts of human faces have different discrimination in classification into account, we present a patch-based sparse dictionary representation scheme. Considering the fact that face variations for different subjects share much similarity, a generic variation dataset which is constructed by external data could bring useful information to predict the variation of query image. Therefore, we employ a generic training set to extract variant discrimination information for our proposed scheme.

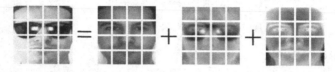

Fig. 1. Patch-based sparse dictionary representation. The first image is the patches of the query image, and the second image is recovered by the training set, and the third is recovered by the external data, and the last is the residual error.

As shown in Fig. 1, we partition the query image y into B (overlapped) patches, and denote these patches as $\{y_1, y_2,..., y_B\}$. We also partition the gallery dictionary D and the generic variation dictionary A as $\{D_1, D_2,..., D_B\}$ and $\{A_1, A_2,..., A_B\}$ respectively. For each local patch y_i, $i=1,2,...,B$, its associated local gallery dictionary and local generic variation dictionary are D_i and A_i respectively. We represent each local patch yi as:

$$y_i = D_i x_{id} + A_i x_{ia} + e_i, i = 1, 2, ..., B \tag{5}$$

where x_{id} and x_{ia} are the sparse representation vectors of the patch y_i over the corresponding patchs D_i and A_i respectively, and e_i is the representation residual.

For the generic variation dictionary, ESRC directly applies external data as generic intra-class variation dictionary A, which can be noisy. We suggest extracting representative information from external data via dictionary learning, and [11] has shown that the dictionary learning from data outperforms approaches using predefined ones. These learned dictionaries can guarantee the recognition performance for the subjects of interest. Dictionary learning is suitable for image denoising. The PSDR learned a generic variation dictionary by jointing the relationships between the gallery set and the external generic set, and has shown promising results in recent literatures of dictionary learning in robust face recognition [5]. Therefore, we adopt the PSDR model for our patch-based external generic variation dictionary learning. For each patch i, we individually learn the generic variation dictionary A_i by using the SVDL in the corresponding patches of the training images and the external images.

In order to get the optimal solutions of vectors x_{id} and x_{ia}, we consider the following minimization problem:

$$\min_x \sum_{i=1}^{B} (\| y_i - Dx_{id} - Ax_{ia} \|_2^2) + \lambda \| x \|_F^2 \tag{6}$$

where $x = \{x_1, x_2, ..., x_B\}$ with $x_i = [x_{id}; x_{ia}]$. The Eq. (6) is a least square regression problem, and we get the closed-form solution of each $x_i = [x_{id}; x_{ia}]$:

$$[x_{id}; x_{ia}] = ([D_i, A_i]^T [D_i, A_i] + \lambda I)^{-1} [x_i, D_i]^T y_i \tag{7}$$

After obtaining all coding vectors $\{\tilde{x}_i\}_{i=1}^{B}$, we calculate the weight of each patch by its residual error :

$$w_i = (1 + \exp(-e_i / 2\delta^2))^{-1} \tag{8}$$

where $e_i = \| y_i - Dx_{id} - A_{ia} \|_2^2$ and $\delta = \sum_{i=1}^{i=B} e_i / 2$.

4   Classification

After obtaining the optimal solutions of x and w, an PSDR based classification scheme is proposed to determine the class of query image y. Our classification principle is to find the smallest reconstruction error of all classes over all patches.

$$IDENTITY(y) = \arg\min_i \sum_{i=1}^{B} w_i \| y_i - D_i^j x_{id}^j - A_i x_{ia} \|_2^2 / \| x_{id}^j; x_{ia} \|_2^2 \tag{9}$$

where x_{id}^j is a vector that only nonzero entry are the entry in x_{id} that are associated with class j. The query image y is classified to the class which has the minimal weighted representation residual over all patches.

5   Experiment

We performed the experiments on Extended Yale B database and AR database. In all our experiments, we fix the parameter as $\lambda = 0.013$, and the face images are resized to 80×80. For each patches, the size is fixed as 20×20, and the overlapped margin is 10 pixels.

Fig. 2. The left is the gallery image, and the right is some variations of one person in Extended Yale B database

Fig. 3. The left is the gallery image, and the right is some variations of one person in AR database

For the Extended Yale B database, we select the first 32 subjects from the database to be recognized, and the remaining 6 subjects are considered as external data for patch-based generic variation dictionary learning. For the 32 subjects of interest, we select the only image in the illumination condition: A+000E+00 as the gallery set, and the remaining 63 images for testing. Some examples of Extended Yale B database are shown in Fig. 2. Table 1 provides the excellent performance of our proposed method to other competing methods. Fig. 4 shows the performance of our proposed scheme which is effected by the number of dictionary atoms on the Extended Yale B database. By exploiting the feature information in each patch and the variation information from the patch-based generic variation dictionary, the proposed PSDR achieves the highest recognition rate.

For the AR database, the first 80 subjects in Session 1 and Session 2 are selected: the single neutral image of each subject for training, and all the other images for testing. The remaining 20 subjects are considered as external data to construct patch-based generic variation dictionary. Some examples of AR database are shown in Fig. 3. Fig. 5 shows the performance of our proposed scheme which is effected by the number of dictionary atoms on the AR database. It can be seen that as the number of generic variation dictionary atoms increases, the recognition rate of PSDR also increases. Table 2 presents the recognition rates of FR with SSPP on the AR database using query images from Session 1 and 2 respectively. By taking the advantages of both local representation and patch-based generic variation dictionary learning, the proposed PSDR method outperforms the state-of-art approaches.

Table 1. Performance comparisons with single sample per person on the Extended Yale B database

Method	RSC[8]	SVDL	LGR[3]	PSDR
Extend Yale B	30.01	60.96	84.23	**92.46**

Table 2. Performance comparisons with single sample per person on the AR database (session 1 and session 2)

Method	RSC	SVDL	LGR	PSDR
AR1	76.49	80.00	97.81	**98.12**
AR2	57.19	59.72	90.00	**91.04**

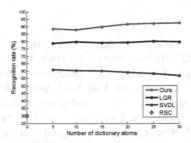

Fig. 4. Performance comparisons on the Extend Yale B database with different number of generic variation dictionary atoms.

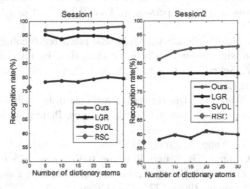

Fig. 5. Performance comparisons on the AR database with different number of generic variation dictionary atoms. The left and right figures show the recognition rates using query images from Session 1 and 2 respectively.

6   Conclusion

We propose a patch-based sparse dictionary representation scheme for face recognition with single sample per person that takes the advantages of both local representation and patch-based generic variation dictionary learning. Our proposed scheme were demonstrated that can solve the problem of various variations e.g. expressions, illuminations, corruption, occlusion and disguises in FR with SSPP. The results of the experiment on the Extended Yale B database and AR face database show that PSDR outperforms the state-of-the-art SSPP methods.

Acknowledgments. This work is supported by the National Science Foundation of China (60802069 and 61273270), the Fundamental Research Funds for the Central Universities of China, the Natural Science Foundation of Guangdong Province (2014A030313173), the Science and Technology Program of Guangzhou (2014Y2-00165, 2014J4100114 and 2014J4100095).

References

1. Wright, J., Yang, A.Y., Ganesh, A., Sastry, S.S., Ma, Y.: Robust face recognition via sparse representation. IEEE Trans. Pattern Anal. Mach. Intell. **31**(2), 210–227 (2009)
2. Deng, W., Hu, J., Guo, J.: Extended SRC: Undersampled face recognition via intraclass variant dictionary. IEEE Trans. Pattern Anal. Mach. Intell. **34**(9), 1864–1870 (2012)
3. Zhu, P., Yang, M., Zhang, L., Lee, I.-Y.: Local generic representation for face recognition with single sample per person. In: Cremers, D., Reid, I., Saito, H., Yang, M.-H. (eds.) ACCV 2014. LNCS, vol. 9005, pp. 34–50. Springer, Heidelberg (2015)
4. Wei, C.P., Frank, W.Y.C.: Undersampled Face Recognition via Robust Auxiliary Dictionary Learning, Image Processing. IEEE Trans. Image Processing **24**(6), 1722–1734 (2015)
5. Yang, M., Van, L.G., Zhang, L.: Sparse variation dictionary learning for face recognition with a single training sample per person. In: Proc. IEEE Int. Conf. Comput. Vis. (ICCV), pp. 689–696 (2013)
6. Zhu, P., Zhang, L., Hu, Q., Shiu, S.C.: Multi-scale patch based collaborative representation for face recognition with margin distribution optimization. In: Fitzgibbon, A., Lazebnik, S., Perona, P., Sato, Y., Schmid, C. (eds.) ECCV 2012, Part I. LNCS, vol. 7572, pp. 822–835. Springer, Heidelberg (2012)
7. Lu, J., Tan, Y.P., Wang, G.: Discriminative multimanifold analysis for face recognition from a single training sample per person. IEEE Trans. Pattern Anal. Mach. Intell. **35**(1), 39–51 (2013)
8. Yang, M., Zhang, L., Yang, J., Zhang, D.: Robust sparse coding for face recognition. In: Proc. IEEE Conf. Comput. Vis. Pattern Recognit. (CVPR), pp. 625–632 (2011)
9. Tan, X., Chen, S., Zhou, Z.H., Zhang, F.: Face recognition from a single image per person: A survey. Pattern Recognit. **39**(9), 1725–1745 (2006)
10. Wagner, A., Wright, J., Ganesh, A., Zhou, Z., Ma,Y.: Towards a Practical Face Recognition System: Robust Registration and Illumination by Sparse Representation. In: proc. IEEE Conf. Computer Vision and Pattern Recognition, pp. 597–604 (2009)
11. Rubinstein, R., Bruckstein, A., Elad, M.: Dictionary learning for sparse representation modeling. Proceeding of the IEEE **98**(6), 1045–1057 (2010)
12. Turk, M., Pentland, A.: Eigenfaces for recognition. J. Cognit. Neurosci. **3**(1), 71–86 (1991)
13. He, X., Yan, S., Hu, Y., Niyogi, P., Zhang, H.J.: Face recognition using Laplacianfaces. IEEE Trans. Pattern Anal. Mach. Intell. **27**(3), 328–340 (2005)

Non-negative Sparsity Preserving Projections Algorithm Based Face Recognition

Yuan Li[✉] and Zhiyan Li

University of Science & Technology Beijing, Beijing, China
lyuan@ustb.edu.cn

Abstract. In this paper, we propose a Non-negative Sparsity Preserving Projections (NSPP) algorithm and apply the proposed algorithm to face recognition. We propose a more reasonable method of constructing the weight matrix and the coefficients of the weight matrix are all non-negative. This method is more consistent with the biological modeling of visual data and often produces much better results for data representation. Experimental results have shown that NSPP algorithm outperforms Locality Preserving Projections and Sparsity Preserving Projections on both ORL and FERET face database. The weight matrix is non-negative and posses more sparsity, which can enhance recognition performance in the projected low-dimensional subspace.

Keywords: NSPP · Face recognition · The weight matrix

1 Introduction

Face recognition has been one of the hot-spots of biometric recognition and computer vision in recent years. The face image feature extraction plays a crucial role in face recognition. Due to the high dimensionality of face images, it becomes quite necessary to project the face images from the high-dimensional space onto a low-dimensional subspace and then make classification. Local Preserving Projections (LPP) algorithm [1] is a local manifold learning algorithm based on the same variational principle that gives rise to the Laplacian Eigenmap. The main idea of the algorithm is to make the points which are close to each other in the original space still be closer in the subspace after dimensionality reduction, and it can preserve the local structure of the original data. So it can be widely applied to pattern recognition and computer vision like PCA and LDA. It provides a linear subspace technology for biometric recognition, and it is used for feature extraction in face recognition, image retrieval and many other fields. LPP [2] needs to encounter model parameters such as the neighborhood size and heat kernel width, which are generally difficult to set in practice. Although cross-validation technique can be used in these cases, it is very time-consuming and tends to waste the limited training data.

For excavating the high-dimensional nonlinear structure of the face image, Cai proposed a graph embedding model to encode the discriminating and geometrical structure in terms of data affinity [3]. With the embedding results, a set of sparse basis can be

© Springer International Publishing Switzerland 2015
J. Yang et al. (Eds.): CCBR 2015, LNCS 9428, pp. 127–134, 2015.
DOI: 10.1007/978-3-319-25417-3_16

learnt by using regularized regression. Qiao proposed Sparsity Preserving Projections[2] for face recognition to preserve the sparse reconstructive relationship of the face data by minimizing a L1 regularization-related objective function. The projections of SPP are sought such that the sparse reconstructive weights can be best preserved.

Because the weight matrix constructed by the above algorithms all contains negative elements and the study of biologists represents that non-negativity is more consistent with the biological modeling of visual data, so we propose Non-negative Sparsity Preserving Projections algorithm in this paper.

2   Algorithm Overview

2.1   Locality Preserving Projections

Local Preserving Projections (LPP) [1] is a linear approximation of nonlinear Laplacian Eigenmap. The algorithm considers the points close to each other in the high-dimensional space should remain close when they are mapped to a low-dimensional space. Based on this point, when the sample points are very close we can use a positive weight to show the relationship between the two. The weight $S = (S_{ij})_{n \times n}$ is defined as follows:

$$\begin{cases} s_{ij} = 1 & i = j \\ s_{ij} = \exp(-\|x_i - x_j\|^2 / \sigma^2) & i \neq j \end{cases} \tag{1}$$

The objective function of LPP is:

$$\begin{aligned} a_{opt} &= \sum_{ij} (y_i - y_j)^2 S_{ij} = \sum_{ij} (a^T x_i - a^T x_j)^2 S_{ij} \\ &= 2a^T X(D-S)X^T = 2a^T XLX^T a \end{aligned} \tag{2}$$

where a is a transformation vector and $y_i = a^T x_i$, $i=1,2,...,n$. L is the Laplacian matrix: $L=D\text{-}S$. D is a diagonal matrix: $D_{ii} = \sum_j S_{ij}$. By imposing a constraint: $a^T XDX^T a = 1$, the minimization problem reduces to finding:

$$\arg\min_a a^T XLX^T a \quad \text{s.t.} \quad a^T XDX^T a = 1 \tag{3}$$

The transformation vector a that minimizes the objective function is given by the minimum eigenvalue solution to the generalized eigenvalue problem:

$$XLX^T a = \lambda XDX^T a \tag{4}$$

2.2   Non-negative Sparsity Preserving Projections

As can be seen from the above, the weight matrix plays a vital role in dimensionality reduction and identification. The sparse coding coefficients of sparse representation will decide the final classification performance. But the weight matrix constructed by SPP may comprise both positive and negative coefficients. The negativity of the coding coefficients allows the data to "cancel each other out" by subtraction, which lacks physical interpretation for visual data [4]. In fact, non-negativity is more consistent with the biological modeling of visual data and often produces much better results for data representation. In view of this, we propose a Non-negative Sparsity Preserving Projections (NSPP) algorithm which constructs the weight matrix S using non-negative sparse representation. NSPP chooses its neighborhood automatically and the weights are all positive.

Since $X = [x_1, x_2,..., x_n] \in R^{m \times n}$ is the data matrix, and its columns are training samples $\{x_i\}_{i=1}^n$, where $x_i \in R^m$. We need to use as few samples as possible to reconstruct each face image. Then firstly we find a sparse reconstructive weight vector for each sample through the following modified l_1 minimization problem:

$$\min_{s_i} \|s_i\|_1 \quad s.t. \quad x_i = Xs_i, \ 1 = 1^T s_i, \ \forall i, j : s_i \geq 0 \tag{5}$$

where si = $[s_{i1},..., s_{i,i-1}, 0, s_{i,i+1},..., s_{in}]^T$, and in order to make x_i removed from X, we make the i-th element equal to zero. The elements $s_{ij}, j \neq i$ denote the contribution of each x_j to reconstruct x_i; $1 \in R^n$ is a vector of all ones [2]. And the sparse reconstructive weight matrix $S = (\tilde{s}_{ij})_{n \times n}$ is defined as follows:

$$S = (\tilde{s}_1, \tilde{s}_2,..., \tilde{s}_n)^T \tag{6}$$

where $\tilde{s}_i$ is the optimal solution of equation (5), which can be obtained by the minimum of the following model:

$$O_F(X, s_i) = \frac{1}{2}\|x_i - Xs_i\| + \lambda \sum_j s_{ij} \quad s.t. \ \forall i, j : X_{ij} \geq 0, s_{ij} \geq 0 \tag{7}$$

In which the parameter λ is used to adjust the balance between reconstruction error and the sparsity of coding coefficients [4].

Appropriate dictionary design plays an important role in the framework of non-negative sparse representation model [4] in equation (7). In this paper, we propose to use Gabor features extracted from all the training face images as the dictionary based non-negative sparse preserving projection model. We use Gaussian function as Gabor kernel function. It is defined as follows [5]:

$$\Psi_{u,v}(z) = \frac{\|k_{u,v}\|^2}{\sigma^2} e^{(-\|k_{u,v}\|^2 \|z\|^2 / 2\sigma^2)} \left[e^{ik_{u,v}z} - e^{-\sigma^2/2} \right] \tag{8}$$

where $\|.\|$ represents the norm operation. The wave vector is defined as $k_{u,v} = k_v e^{i\varphi}{}_u$, and $\varphi_u = \pi u/4$, $k_v = k_{max}/f^v$; k_{max} is the maximum sampling frequency and f is the sampling step of the frequency. In the paper, $u \in \{0,..., 7\}$, $v \in \{0,..., 4\}$; $f = \sqrt{2}$, $k_{max} = \pi/2$, $\sigma = 2\pi$. The Gabor feature of the face image can be defined as follows:

$$G_{u,v}(z) = I(z) * \psi_{u,v}(z) \tag{9}$$

and * denotes the convolution operation. It can also be represented as

$$G_{u,v}(z) = M_{u,v}(z) \cdot \exp(i\theta_{u,v}(z)) \tag{10}$$

where $M_{u,v}$ is the magnitude and $\theta_{u,v}$ is the phase. Figure 1 shows the Gabor features of an input face image.

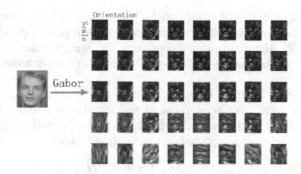

Fig. 1. The Gabor features of an face image

The equation(7) can be solved by an efficient non-negative sparse representation model algorithm, which is proposed by Baoqing Zhang [6] and extremely simple to implement. An iterative formula can be got by solving the Lagrange function of the objective function, and on solving the iterative equation we can get the non-negative coefficient vector s_i and then get the weight matrix S.

For the reason that we expect the desirable characteristics in the original high-dimensional space can be preserved in the low-dimensional embedding subspace, we define the following objective function to seek the projections which best preserve the optimal weight vector $\widetilde{s}_i$.

$$\min_a \sum_{i=1}^n \left\| a^T x_i - a^T X \widetilde{s}_i \right\|^2 \tag{11}$$

Through some algebraic formulation and simplification which can refer to [2], the optimal a' is constructed by the eigenvectors corresponding to the largest d eigenvalues of the following generalized eigenvalue problem [2]:

$$XS_\beta X^T a = \eta XX^T a \tag{22}$$

where $S_\beta = S + S^T - S^T S$. To sum up, the steps of Non-negative Sparsity Preserving Projections can be described as follows:

(1) Solve equation (5) to get non-negative weight matrix S;

(2) Solve equation (12) to get the projection, and then obtain the optimal subspace spanned by the eigenvectors corresponding to the largest d eigenvalues.

3   Experiments

3.1   Experiments on ORL Face Database

The database used for this experiment is ORL face database [7]. It is created by AT & T Laboratories Cambridge. It contains 400 grayscale images of 40 distinct subjects with lighting, facial expressions and facial details variations. The size of the face image is 112×92. Thus, each image can be represented by a 10304-dimensional vector. Example images of the ORL face database are shown in Figure 2.

Fig. 2. Examples of the ORL face database

For each individual, five images are taken to form the training set. The rest of the database are considered to be the testing set. The training samples are used to construct the weight matrix S and get the optimal subspace. The testing samples are then projected onto the low-dimension subspace. Recognition is performed using the nearest neighbor classifier.

(1) Comparison of the weight matrix S between SPP and NSPP

In the experiment on ORL face database, we respectively construct the weight matrix S using SPP and our proposed NSPP algorithm. Some parameters are set as follows: The Gabor kernel's width and height are both 31; The Gabor kernel's energy preserving ratio is 0.9; The Gabor kernel's number is 40; The λ is 0.001.

For a given training sample, the sparse coefficients got from SPP and NSPP are distributed as shown in Fig. 3 and Fig. 4. By comparing Fig. 3 and Fig. 4 we can see that: the weight matrix constructed by NSPP not only has no negative coefficients, but also gets better sparsity. Fig. 5 shows the weight relationship between the sample image and its related training images. We can see that the top 4 closet samples to the given training sample all came from the same class as the given training sample, and the given training sample is less correlated or irrelevant to the other training samples.

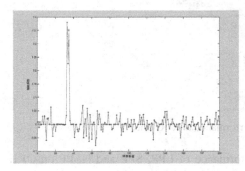
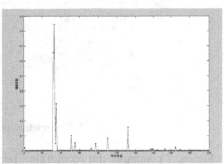

Fig. 3. The sparse coefficients of SPP   **Fig.4.** The sparse coefficients of NSPP

(2) Recognition performance comparison between SPP and NSPP

In order to verify the effectiveness of the new algorithm in face recognition, we display the projection of test samples on subspace manifold in a two-dimensional diagram. The images of faces are mapped into the 2-dimensional plane described by the first two coordinates of the SPP and NSPP. Figure 6 shows the clustering results. We can see that NSPP algorithm has better divisibility and more manifolds compared to SPP algorithm.

Fig. 5. The relationship of the sample image and the other training images

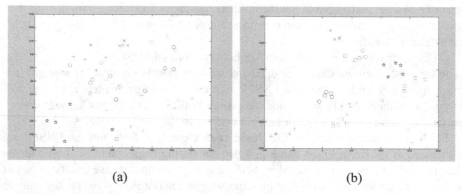

(a)   (b)

Fig. 6. The clustering situation of testing samples projected onto subspace: (a) SPP, (b) NSPP

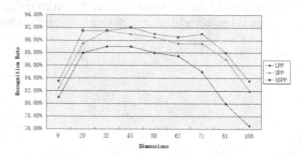

Fig. 7. Recognition performance on ORL face

Figure 7 compares the recognition performance of LPP, SPP and NSPP on ORL face database. As can be seen, NSPP outperforms both SPP and LPP.

3.2   Experiments on FERET Face Database

In this experiment, we choose FERET face database [8]. There are 200 subjects, and seven images are taken per subject with pose, lighting and facial expressions variations. The size of the face image is 128×128. Thus, it can be represented by a 16384-dimensional vector. Some sample images of FERET face database are shown in Figure 8.

Fig. 8. Example images of FERET face

For each subject, four images are taken to form the training set. The rest of the database are considered to be the testing set. The recognition rate of LPP, SPP and NSPP algorithm on FERET face database are shown in Figure 9.

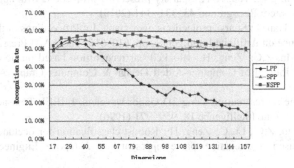

Fig. 9. Recognition comparison on FERET face

3.3   Experimental Analysis

From Figure 7 and Figure 9 we can find that: compared with LPP and SPP, our proposed Non-negative Sparsity Preserving Projections algorithm improves the recognition rate to some extent on both ORL and FERET face database. Besides, the recognition rate is relatively stable when the sub-space dimensions change. In the experiment, it shows that NSPP can also improve the recognition efficiency.

Compared to LPP, NSPP has the following advantages:

(1) the weight matrix constructed by NSPP is positive, and it has better sparsity and divisibility, so it certainly can raise the recognition rate;

(2) the NSPP algorithm not only can improve the recognition efficiency when there are too many samples, but also has better robustness;

(3) the NSPP model has no parameters such as the neighborhood size and heat kernel width incurred in LPP, which makes it quite simple to use in practice.

4   Conclusions

In this paper, motivated by non-negative sparse representation, we propose a new algorithm called Non-negative Sparsity Preserving Projections for unsupervised dimensionality reduction. The projections of NSPP are sought such that the sparse reconstructive weights can be best preserved. NSPP is shown to outperform LPP and SPP on ORL and FERET face database, and it is very simple to perform like PCA by avoiding the difficulty of parameter selection as in LPP.

Acknowledgments. This paper is supported by the National Natural Science Foundation of China (Grant no. 61300075).

References

1. He, X., Niyogi, P.: Advances in Neural Information Processing Systems: Locality Preserving Projections. The MIT Press, Cambridge (2004)
2. Qiao, L.S., Chen, S.C., Tan, X.Y.: Sparsity preserving projections with applications to face recognition. J. Pattern Recognition **43**, 331–341 (2010)
3. Cai, D., He, X., Han, J.: Sparse projections over graph. In: Proceedings of the Twenty-Third AAAI Conference on Artificial Intelligence, pp. 610–615. The AAAI Press, Chicago (2008)
4. Zhang, B.Q., Mu, Z.C., Zeng, H.: Blocked ear recognition based on non-negative sparse representation. Journal of Computer-Aided Design & Computer Graphics. 26, 1339–1345 (2014)
5. Lee, T.S.: Image representation using 2D Gabor wavelets. J. IEEE Transactions on Pattern Analysis and Machine Intelligence **18**, 959–971 (1996)
6. Zhang, B.Q., Mu, Z.C., Li, C., Zeng, H.: Robust classification for occluded ear via Gabor scale feature-based non-negative sparse representation. J. Optical Engineering **53**, 061702 (2014)
7. The Database of Faces. http://www.cl.cam.ac.uk/research/dtg/attarchive/facedatabase.html
8. The FERET Database. http://www.itl.nist.gov/iad/humanid/feret/feret_master.html

WLD-TOP Based Algorithm against Face Spoofing Attacks

Ling Mei[1,2], Dakun Yang[1,2], Zhanxiang Feng[1,2], and Jianhuang Lai[1,2]($\boxtimes$)

[1] School of Information Science and Technology, Sun-Yat-Sen University,
Guangzhou, China
[2] Guangdong Key Laboratory of Information Security Technology, Sun Yat-sen
University, Guangzhou, China
meil3@mail2.sysu.edu.cn, stsljh@mail.sysu.edu.cn

Abstract. Face liveness detection is more and more important in face
recognition systems, which are vulnerable to spoof attacks made by non-
real faces. Recent work has revealed that some algorithms based on image
descriptors are applied to face liveness detection against face spoofing
attacks, such as LBP and LBP-TOP. However, these image descriptors
are not robust to spoofing attacks. In this paper, we propose a robust
and powerful local descriptor, called WLD-TOP. It combines temporal
and spatial information into a single descriptor with a multiresolution
strategy. Extensive experiments on CASIA and our new SYSU-MFSD
database demonstrate that the descriptor can achieve a better liveness
detection performance in both intra and cross-databases compared to
the state-of-the-art techniques based on descriptors.

Keywords: WLD-TOP · Spoofing attack · Local descriptor · Dynamic
texture

1 Introduction

Biometric systems are more and more often used for authentication in various
security applications. Face recognition has developed rapidly in recent years
and is more convenient compared to other biometric methods. However, face
recognition systems are vulnerable to spoof attacks made by non-real faces. A
spoofing attack occurs when a person tries to masquerade as someone else. In
order to guard against such spoofing, a secure face system of liveness detection
[1] is needed.

A large number of methods have been proposed in recent years to combat
spoofing for face liveness detection. Among these methods, the micro-textures
approaches [2] exploit the surface texture of the skin for face anti-spoofing, such
as LBP [3], WLD [4], LBP-TOP [5], DoG [6], etc. These methods are non-
intrusive methods without extra devices, and they could be easily integrated
into an existing face recognition system, where usually only a generic webcam is
equipped.

© Springer International Publishing Switzerland 2015
J. Yang et al. (Eds.): CCBR 2015, LNCS 9428, pp. 135–142, 2015.
DOI: 10.1007/978-3-319-25417-3_17

In this paper, we propose a novel descriptor which considers three orthogonal planes based on WLD against face spoofing, called WLD-TOP. The main contributions in our work are summarized as: Firstly, our approach uses a multiresolution strategy based on WLD-TOP against face spoofing. Secondly, We improve and simplify the calculation for orientation of WLD in [4]. Thirdly, we also collect a face spoof database, SYSU Mobile Face Spoofing Database (SYSU-MFSD), using two mobile devices (iphone 5c and ipad Air2) with three different spoofing scenes which consider illumination variation. Experiments conducted on the CASIA [6] and SYSU-MFSD databases indicate that our approach has a better performance in detecting face spoofing attacks using photographs and videos than state-of-the-art techniques.

The remainder of the paper is organized as follows: Section 2 presents a brief review of the relevant literature. The proposed WLD-TOP for face liveness detection is described in Section 3. Our experimental set-up and results on the two databases, CASIA and SYSU-MFSD, are discussed in Section 4. Finally, we summarize the work and draw conclusions in Section 5.

2   Related Work

In this section, we review anti-spoofing related work for face based on the texture and our focus in this paper.

Recently, researchers are devoted to come up with more generalized and discriminative features based on the analysis of textures for face anti-spoofing. Among the texture approaches, some techniques are based on the Local Binary Patterns (LBP), a descriptor first proposed in 2002 [3] for texture classification. We expand the detected face to holistic-face (H-Face) [7]. The method proposed in [8] divides the images in blocks, and eventually concatenated by different LBP operators, which outperformed previous methods on the NUAA Photograph Imposter Database [9]. Furthermore, its efficiency on the REPLAY-ATTACK database was presented in [10].

Since dynamic textures can encompass the class of video sequences that exhibit some stationary properties in time,the micro-texture-based analysis for spoofing detection was extended in the spatiotemporal domain. In [5], Pereira et al. used a spatio-temporal texture feature called Local Binary Patterns from Three Orthogonal Planes (LBP-TOP), which combines spatial and temporal information based on LBP approach. This method has shown to be very effective in describing the horizontal and vertical motion patterns in addition to appearance. According to the experimental results on the REPLAY-ATTACK database, it outperformed the LBP-based method in [5].

Recently, Chen. J [4] et al. proposed WLD based on Weber's Law. The WLD is built starting from two dense fields of features, orientation and differential excitation. WLD histogram is used for human face detection. With regard to the LBP descriptor, it represents an input image by building statistics on the local micropattern variations, but WLD computes and builds statistics on salient patterns which is more sensitive to dynamic textures in liveness face detection.

3   WLD from Three Orthogonal Planes (WLD-TOP) for Image Representation

3.1   Modified WLD

In this section, we simply introduce the modified WLD. It consists of two components: differential excitation denoted by ξ and orientation denoted by θ. WLD is inspired by Weber's Law expressed as

$$\frac{\Delta I}{I} = k. \tag{1}$$

where ΔI represents the increment threshold of the initial stimulus intensity I. Then k signifies the proportion of (1) which remains constant. Since the change of the central pixel reflects the intensity differences between current pixel x_c and its adjacent pixels, the differential excitation of the current pixel $\xi(x_c)$ can be computed as

$$\xi(x_c) = \arctan\left\{\sum_{i=0}^{p-1}(\frac{x_i - x_c}{x_c})\right\} \tag{2}$$

where x_i is the neighbors of x_c as illustrated in Fig. 1.

x_0	x_1	x_2
x_7	x_c	x_3
x_6	x_5	x_4

Fig. 1. The 3×3 neighbors of the current pixel x_c

The orientation part of WLD is the gradient orientation, which reflects the distribution feature of different gradient information. Firstly, the gradient is calculated as

$$\theta(x_c) = \arctan\left[\frac{x_7 - x_3}{x_5 - x_1}\right] = \arctan\left(\frac{v_2}{v_1}\right) \tag{3}$$

Then, we modify the method in [4] that map θ to θ' as (4), where $\theta' \in [0, 2\pi)$.

$$\theta' = \begin{cases} \theta & v_1 > 0 \text{ and } v_2 > 0 \\ \pi + \theta & v_1 < 0 \\ 2\pi + \theta & v_1 > 0 \text{ and } v_2 < 0 \\ 0 & v_1 = 0 \end{cases} \tag{4}$$

Finally, θ' is quantified to G dominant orientations which is calculated more simplified than [4] as follows

$$\Phi_t = \lfloor \frac{\theta'}{2\pi/G} \rfloor, \Phi_t = 0, 1, \cdots, G-1 \tag{5}$$

By combining the two components of WLD feature per pixel, WLD represents an input image with a histogram. We simplify the calculation method on the basis of preserving the original WLD features.

3.2 WLD-TOP

Motivated by LBP-TOP, the method of TOP extracts descriptor code from XY, XT and YT plane, which supplement temporal information into the descriptor. We propose a simplified WLD-TOP descriptor by concatenating WLD on three orthogonal planes: XY, XT and YT, as it can be seen in Fig. 2. Since WLD can obtain a NG dimensional vector, where N is the dimension of ξ which normalized to integers. We define $f(x, y, t)$ as WLD code of the central pixel $x_c(x, y, t)$ as

$$f(x, y, t) = N\Phi_t + \xi(x_c). \tag{6}$$

in which x, y, t are the coordinates of XY, XT and YT planes, respectively. Then a histogram of the ith planes(i=1:XY, 2:XT and 3:YT) can be defined as

$$h_{i,j} = \sum_{x,y,t} M\{f(x, y, t) = j\}, j = 0, 1, \cdots, NG-1, \tag{7}$$

where $M(A)$ is defined as

$$M(A) = \begin{cases} 0 & \text{if } A \text{ is false} \\ 1 & \text{if } A \text{ is true.} \end{cases} \tag{8}$$

We transfer $h_{i,j}$ to a row vector h_i, and concatenate them orderly to a new row vector denoted by $H = [h_1 \; h_2 \; h_3]$, which is the WLD-TOP feature vector. With this method, the 3D histogram $\{WLD(\xi_j, \Phi_t, i)\}, i = 1, 2, 3, j = 0, 1, \cdots, N - 1, t = 0, 1, \cdots, G-1$, is encoded into a 1D histogram H of WLD-TOP.

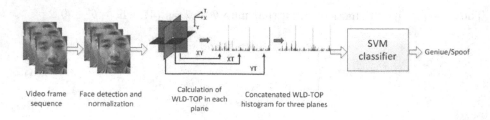

| Video frame sequence | Face detection and normalization | Calculation of WLD-TOP in each plane | Concatenated WLD-TOP histogram for three planes |

Fig. 2. Block diagram of liveness face detection using WLD-TOP descriptor

Fig. 3. Face detection method for $R_t=1$

Table 1. Results on the Intra-database of CASIA and SYSU-MFSD.

Method	Train ID	Test ID	Accuracy(%)	Train ID	Test ID	Accuracy(%)
WLD-TOP	**C1-C20**	**C21-C50**	**90.78**	**C21-C50**	**C1-C20**	**88.02**
LBP-TOP	C1-C20	C21-C50	79.06	C21-C50	C1-C20	78.75
WLD	C1-C20	C21-C50	87.08	C21-C50	C1-C20	85.61
LBP	C1-C20	C21-C50	78.35	C21-C50	C1-C20	76.50
WLD-TOP	**S1-S20**	**S21-S29**	**93.44**	**S21-S29**	**S1-S20**	**92.25**
LBP-TOP	S1-S20	S21-S29	83.12	S21-S29	S1-S20	79.85
WLD	S1-S20	S21-S29	87.05	S21-S29	S1-S20	84.70
LBP	S1-S20	S21-S29	81.51	S21-S29	S1-S20	77.05

Fig. 3 shows that R_t is the radii in axes T around selected bounding box, which displays the region of selected continuous video frames. To build a multiresolution WLD-TOP, the histograms in time domain(XT and YT) are combined for different values of R_t. For example, $R_t=3$ means that WLD-TOP operator will be computed for $R_t=1$, $R_t=2$ and $R_t=3$ and all resultant histograms will be concatenated. As R_t increases, WLD-TOP can obtain more spatial feature which can be useful for distinguish spoof faces from genuine faces.

4   Experiments

This section evaluates four different types of spoof detection feature vectors: WLD-TOP, LBP-TOP, WLD and LBP. We have done experiments on both intra-database and cross-database with $R_t=1$.

4.1   Data Set

In our experiments, we build a database named SYSU Mobile Face Spoofing Database. This database is recorded by iphone and ipad, it includes 29 subjects, which are split into the training set (containing 20 subjects, ID:S1-S20) and the testing set (containing 9 subjects, ID:S21-S29). Two kinds of fake face attacks by iphone and ipad are implemented, and each attack way has three different shooting scenes which consider illumination and other environmental variations, so there are 87 fake face video clips recorded by iphone and ipad respectively. In contrast, the genuine videos are shot by ipad, every subject has also three shooting scenes, so there are 87 genuine face video clips in total. The CASIA face anti-spoofing database [6] consists of 50 genuine subjects, Specifically, the database is divided into 20 training subjects (ID:C1-C20) and 30 testing subjects (ID:C21-C50).

4.2   Results on the Intra-database

In the CASIA and SYSU-MFSD database, we test LBP [3], LBP-TOP [5] and WLD [4] on its training and testing set. For classification, We use LibSVM library [11] to obtain the discrimination accuracy. We present the corresponding accuracy for the test scenarios with these descriptors on two kinds of intra-databases in Table 1. The ROC curve of WLD-TOP compared with some state-of-the-art anti-spoofing methods like [6,8] on overall CASIA test are shown in Fig. 4. Since WLD-TOP has added spatial information, it can find the salient difference of dynamic video frames between genuine and spoof faces better than other methods. All the results indicate that our proposed descriptor outperforms the other descriptors on the intra-database scenarios.

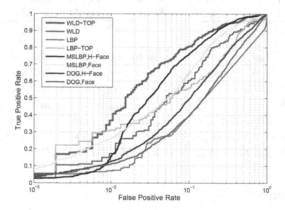

Fig. 4. ROC curves of some previous methods for Overall CASIA database

4.3   Results on the Cross-Database

Besides the intra-database performance, we are more interested in the cross-database generalization ability of different face spoof detection descriptors. All cross-database results are shown in Table 2. Compared with WLD, the proposed WLD-TOP features which is more robust to dynamic textures in the videos combine spatial and temporal information . Compared with LBP-TOP, the proposed method has the additional gradient orientation feature which is stable to illumination and other environmental variation, so WLD-TOP is expected to have better cross-database performance than other features. the results indicate that our proposed descriptor achieves a perfect cross-database performance.

Table 2. Results on the Cross-database of CASIA and SYSU-MFSD.

Method	Train ID	Test ID	Accuracy(%)
WLD-TOP	**C1-C50**	**S1-S29**	**74.62**
LBP-TOP	C1-C50	S1-S29	59.30
WLD	C1-C50	S1-S29	64.81
LBP	C1-C50	S1-S29	53.96
WLD-TOP	**S1-S29**	**C1-C50**	**73.61**
LBP-TOP	S1-S29	C1-C50	69.04
WLD	S1-S29	C1-C50	58.77
LBP	S1-S29	C1-C50	53.85

4.4 Effectiveness of Each WLD-TOP Plane

Firstly, we analyse the performance of each plane and then combinations. After that, we increase the multiresolution area (R_t), and use LibSVM as the classification. Fig. 5 shows the evolution of HTER considering individual and combined histograms of WLD-TOP planes on CASIA database's test set. According to the results, by combing the two time planes(XT and YT), the HTER is decreased. This suggests that temporal information is a necessary component. The integration of the three planes have obtained the best results which manifest that both spatial and temporal component are useful to classify real and fake faces. It also can be seen that, the results are improved when the (R_t) is increased, which have more temporal component but increase the computational complexity.

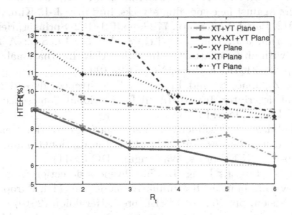

Fig. 5. Evaluation of HTER(%) in eath plane when the multiresolution area(R_t) is increased with WLD-TOP and SVM classifier

5   Conclusion

We have introduced an algorithm against face spoofing attacks using the WLD-TOP descriptor. By combining WLD and TOP, the most important temporal component in videos is considered, which obtain more dynamic features that traditional methods lacked. Experiments on different planes presented the combination of the three planes obtained the best result. We have built a new anti-spoofing database for the experiment, the results on both intra and cross-database show that WLD-TOP descriptor has a great performance against different kinds of face spoof scenarios, outperforming the state of art descriptor.

Acknowledgments. This project was supported by National Science & Technology Pillar Program (No. 2012BAK16B06) and GuangZhou Program (2014J41 00114, 2014Y2-00165).

References

1. Sun, L., Huang, W.B., Wu, M.H.: TIR/VIS correlation for liveness detection in face recognition. In: Real, P., Diaz-Pernil, D., Molina-Abril, H., Berciano, A., Kropatsch, W. (eds.) CAIP 2011, Part II. LNCS, vol. 6855, pp. 114–121. Springer, Heidelberg (2011)
2. Chakraborty, S., Das, D.: An overview of face liveness detection. arXiv preprint arXiv. 1405, 2227 (2014)
3. Ojala, T., Pietikäinen, M., Mäenpää, T.: Multiresolution gray-scale and rotation invariant texture classification with local binary patterns. IEEE Trans. PAMI. **24**(7), 971–987 (2002)
4. Chen, J., Shan, S., He, C., Zhao, G., Pietikäinen, M., Chen, X., Gao, W.: WLD: A robust local image descriptor. IEEE Trans. PAMI. **32**(9), 1705–1720 (2010)
5. de Freitas Pereira, T., Anjos, A., De Martino, J.M., Marcel, S.: *LBP − TOP* based countermeasure against face spoofing attacks. In: Park, J.-I., Kim, J. (eds.) ACCV Workshops 2012, Part I. LNCS, vol. 7728, pp. 121–132. Springer, Heidelberg (2013)
6. Zhang, Z.W., Yan, J.J., Liu, S.F., Lei, Z., Yi, D., Li, S.Z.: A face antispoofing database with diverse attacks. In: 5th IAPR International Conference on Biometrics, pp. 26–31. IEEE Press, New Delhi (2012)
7. Yang, J., Lei, Z., Liao, S. and Li, S. Z.: Face liveness detection with component dependent descriptor. In: 6th IAPR International Conference on Biometrics, pp. 1–6. IEEE Press, Madrid (2013)
8. Määttä, J., Hadid, A., Pietikäinen, M.: Face spoofing detection from single images using micro-texture analysis. In: 2011 IEEE International Joint Conference on Biometrics, pp. 1–7. IEEE press, Washington, DC (2011)
9. Tan, X.Y., Li, Y., Liu, J., Jiang, L.: Face liveness detection from a single image with sparse low rank bilinear discriminative model. In: 11th European Conference on Computer Vision, pp. 504–517. IEEE press, Heraklion (2010)
10. Chingovska, I., Anjos, A., Marcel, S.: On the effectiveness of local binary patterns in face anti-spoofing. In: International Conference of Biometrics Special Interest Group, pp. 1–7. IEEE press, Darmstadt (2012)
11. Chang, C., Lin, C.: LIBSVM: a library for support vector machines. ACM Transactions on Intelligent Systems and Technology **2**(3), 27 (2011)

Heterogeneous Face Recognition
Based on Super Resolution Reconstruction
by Adaptive Multi-dictionary Learning

Jingjing Zhao[1], Yiming Mao[1], Qi Fang[1], Zhicheng Liang[1], Fumeng Yang[2],
and Shu Zhan[1(✉)]

[1] School of Computer and Information, HeFei University of Technology, Hefei, China
shu_zhan@hfut.edu.cn
[2] Sanjiang University, Nanjing, China

Abstract. The heterogeneous face recognition algorithm is based on super resolution reconstruction and two-dimensional marginal fisher analysis. In this paper, a super resolution reconstruction algorithm by adaptive multi-dictionary
learning is adopted. Compared with the traditional global dictionary learning,
this algorithm spends less time on dictionary training and image reconstruction
to a great extent. Firstly, a sketch is transformed to a photo by eigenface algorithm. Secondly, super resolution reconstruction by improved adaptive multi-
dictionary learning is used to reconstruct the synthesized photo, which is able to
enhance the quality of synthesized photo effectively. Finally, the synthesized
photo is recognized by two-dimensional marginal fisher analysis. We demonstrate these ideas in practice and show how they lead to faster operation speed
and ideal recognition rate.

Keywords: Adaptive multi-dictionary learning · Two-dimensional marginal
fisher analysis · Super resolution reconstruction · Face recognition

1 Introduction

Recently, there is a growing demand of sketch face recognition in the areas such as
law enforcement, video monitoring and bank security, which helps the police narrow
down potential suspects quickly. Sketch face belongs to the category of heterogeneous face, which has become an advanced research hotspot in the field of criminal
investigation.

In the last several years, many papers have shown that they can deliver outstanding
performance on this challenging task. Silva [1] proposed a sketch-photo recognition
algorithm based on the local feature-based discriminant analysis. Galoogahi [2] proposed the local radon binary pattern to match face photos and sketches directly. Liu
[3] proposed a face photo-sketch recognition method using joint dictionary learning.

The biggest difference between a sketch image and a photo image is that the sketch
image tends to exaggerate some details so that the traditional face recognition algorithm can't be applied to sketch face recognition directly. In order to overcome such a

© Springer International Publishing Switzerland 2015
J. Yang et al. (Eds.): CCBR 2015, LNCS 9428, pp. 143–150, 2015.
DOI: 10.1007/978-3-319-25417-3_18

weakness, we first transform a sketch into a photo using eigenface algorithm. Then super resolution reconstruction based on adaptive multi dictionary learning is executed on synthesized photo, which can describe the details of the faces better for the further criminal investigation. Finally, two-dimensional marginal fisher analysis is used to perform classification and recognition.

2   Sketch-to-Photo Transformation

Eigenface algorithm is a traditional method and has been widely used in face recognition [4-5]. Though eigenface method is sensitive to illumination, expression, and rotation changes, this is presumably not a first-order concern given that our analysis focuses on law enforcement where standard frontal face images are generally used.

For each sketch, remove the mean sketch first and we can get $S_i = Q_i - m_s$, The sketch training set can be written as $A_s = [S_1, S_2, ..., S_M]$. Hence, the covariance matrix of sketch training set is computed as $W = A_s A_s^T$ and the orthonormal eigenvector matrix of W is

$$U_s = A_s V_s \Lambda_s^{-\frac{1}{2}}. \tag{1}$$

Here, V_s is the eigenvector matrix and Λ_s is the diagonal eigenvalue matrix. Map a testing sketch S_k into the eigensketch space then we can get a vector $b_s = U_s^T S_k$. It is a viable strategy to synthesize a sketch S_r when the eigensketch space and b_s are known.

$$\vec{S}_r = U_s \vec{b}_s = A_s V_s \Lambda_s^{-\frac{1}{2}} \vec{b}_s. \tag{2}$$

For each training sketch image, there is a corresponding training photo image $\vec{P}_i$. Replacing each $\vec{S}_i$ in the equation (2) with $\vec{P}_i$, we can get

$$\vec{P}_r = A_p V_s \Lambda_s^{-\frac{1}{2}} \vec{b}_s. \tag{3}$$

Because of the structural similarity between the sketch and the photo, it's a reasonable assumption that the synthesized sketch resembles the real photo. In the process of transforming, a sample photo $\vec{P}_i$ contributes more weight to the synthesized photo if its corresponding sample sketch $\vec{S}_i$ contributes more weight to the synthesis. It is conceivable that if two sketches are alike, their corresponding photos should be alike.

3   Super-Resolution of Synthesized Photos

Super resolution reconstruction can improve image's resolution and the visual effect effectively without the need of additional equipment. Now super resolution reconstruction algorithm can be divided into two categories, one category is based on reconstruction, while the other is on the basis of learning. The latter introduce the prior knowledge and recovery the image details better.

Normally, the details in the synthesized photo have the vague details and low resolution. We need to introduce super resolution reconstruction to improve the visual effect of synthesized photo.

In 2010, Yang et al. [6] first proposed sparse representation in super resolution. Research on image statistics suggest that image patches can be well-represented as a sparse linear combination of elements from an appropriately chosen over-complete dictionary. Through this algorithm, sufficient additional information can be obtained, but there are still two weaknesses, one is the high time-consuming of dictionary training, while the other is the insufficient representation of different morphological structures of the image via global dictionary. To overcome these problems, a super resolution reconstruction by adaptive multi dictionary learning is employed. Image patches in the training set are clustered into several groups first and adaptive multi-dictionary learning is used to learn corresponding dictionaries for different groups. Compared with the global dictionary learning, this algorithm can greatly reduce the samples of each group, which avoids the high-dimensional data calculation and improves the efficiency of dictionary training.

3.1   Super Resolution Reconstruction Based on Sparse Representation

X and Y represent high resolution image and low resolution image respectively. The relationship between the two can be expressed by

$$Y = SHX + v. \tag{4}$$

Here, S, H, v represent a down sampling operator, a blurring filter and additive noise respectively. The essence of the dictionary training is a kind of optimization, just like the following equation (5).

$$\min_{\Psi, A} \{ \| S - \Psi A \|_F^2 \}, s.t. \ \forall i, \| \alpha_i \|_0 < T_0 \tag{5}$$

Here, S, Ψ, A and T_0 represent samples, an over-complete dictionary, the sparse matrix and the sparse degree respectively. According to the equation (5), Ψ_l and Ψ_h can be trained by low image patches and high image ones.

According to the theory of sparse representation of images, as for the image patch x the most sparse coefficient α can be calculated in the over-complete dictionary Ψ trained by high resolution images.

$$\min \| \alpha \|_0 \ s.t. \ x = \Psi \alpha. \tag{6}$$

According to equation (6) it is necessary to calculate the sparse coefficient α of the low resolution image patches under the Ψ_l first and then reconstruct the high image patches using α and Ψ_h.

3.2   Adaptive Multi-dictionary Learning

According to the learning method, dictionary learning can be divided into the global dictionary learning and the adaptive dictionary learning. What's more, based on the number of dictionaries, dictionary learning can be classified into single dictionary learning and multi dictionary learning. The adaptive dictionary learning can choose an optional dictionary for each image patch during the reconstruction process, which can describe the details of the images well. And the multi-dictionary learning can contribute to the higher degree of similarity between the training samples because of the introduction of pre-clustering.

3.3   Training Samples Clustering

K-means algorithm is a classical clustering algorithm based on distance and the shorter distance between two objects the greater similarity between them. This algorithm possesses the advantages of high efficiency, scalability, hence it has been used in large scale data mining.

Let x_i be the patches of the training images and z_i be the corresponding high frequency of x_i. We can get K clusters $C_k = [z_1^k,..., z_{qi}^k]$ by K-means algorithm. The center of the kth cluster can be computed by $\mu_k = (\sum_{i=1}^{q_k} z_i^k)/q_k$. When performing the clustering operation, compute the distance d_i^k between z_i and μ_k.

$$d_i^k = \|z_i - \mu_k\|, k = 1,..., K \tag{7}$$

If the minimum d_j^{ki} of dj^k satisfy $d_j^{ki} < \varepsilon$, z_i should be classified into kth cluster. Here ε is a parameter that controls the degree of similarity between the image patches and the cluster centers.

3.4   Multi-dictionary Learning

After training samples clustering, the image patches of low and high samples have been respectively clustered into K groups. For each group, it is necessary to construct the corresponding dictionary Ψ_k.

$$\min_{\Psi_k, A_k} \{\|S_k - \Psi_k A_k\|_F^2\}, \ s.t. \ \|\alpha_i^k\|_0 \leq T_k, i = 1,..., s_k \tag{8}$$

3.5   Super Resolution Reconstruction Model

Due to the employment of super resolution based on adaptive multi-dictionary, it is necessary to determine the optional dictionary for each image patch of low resolution image before reconstruction. The selection of the optimal dictionary is determined by calculating the Euclidean distance between the image patch and the cluster center:

$$k_i = \arg\min_k \|y - \mu_k\|_2^2 \tag{9}$$

Computing the upper formulation can select the optional dictionary for the image patch of the inputting low resolution image. To super resolution reconstruct the image patch y, we should calculate the sparse coefficient α under the dictionary trained by low resolution images:

$$\alpha = \arg\min \left\| \Psi_{l_k} \alpha - y \right\|_2^2 + \lambda \left\| \alpha \right\|_1 \tag{10}$$

here, λ is a parameter to balance the certain sparse degree. High resolution image patch can be obtained by $y = \Psi_{hk}\alpha$.

4   Face Recognition Based on 2DMFA

Face recognition is a biometric technology, which attracts more and more researchers' interest and attention. Linear Discriminant Analysis (LDA) and Principal Components Analysis (PCA) are two classic algorithms which have been widely used in extensive face recognition technology. In 2007 Yan et al. [7] proposed Marginal Fisher Analysis (MFA) which overcomes the limitation of the data distribution hypothesis of the traditional LDA algorithm effectively. Later, Wan et al. [8] proposed 2DMFA on the basis of MFA which maintains the intrinsic structure of two-dimensional image better.

4.1   Marginal Fisher Analysis

In the MFA algorithm, there are two graphs, intrinsic graph and penalty graph. Intrinsic graph can depict the intra-class compactness and connects each data point with its neighboring points in the same class. However, penalty graph shows the separation degree of multi-class and connects the marginal points.

Compared with the LDA algorithm, MFA is a more general method of discriminant analysis, which has more available projection direction, and can better describe the separation between different classes.

4.2   Two-Dimensional Marginal Fisher Analysis

The dimension reduction method of features in most face recognition algorithm is based on one dimension vector, that is, when processing data, people usually transform the data into a row vector or a column vector first. However, when input is an image, it may lose the intrinsic structure. In 2011, Wan et al. proposed the 2DMFA which solve this problem well.

Similar to MFA algorithm, intrinsic graph $\tilde{S}_w$ and penalty graph $\tilde{S}_b$ are constructed to describe the intra-class compactness and the separation degree of multi-class. And we can calculate the projected direction w by the two-dimensional margin fisher Criterion

$$\tilde{w} = \arg\min \frac{w^T X^w w}{w^T X^b w}. \tag{11}$$

The optimal projected direction can be calculated by Lagrange operator. Project the training images and testing images on w respectively and then we get the projected matrix $y^{2dmfa} = w^T x$. At last, the nearest neighbor classifier is used for recognition.

5   Experiments

In order to demonstrate the effectiveness of the new algorithm, we conduct a set of experiments on two public face databases. CIS face database contains 11 faces and every person has 7 different expression photos and Yale database contains 15 faces and each person has 11 different expression photos. Fig. 1 and Fig. 2 show the sketch-to-photo transformation examples on the two databases respectively.

Fig. 1. Sketch-to-photo transformation examples on CIS database (rows from top to bottom) sketches; synthesized photos; original photos

Fig. 2. Sketch-to-photo transformation examples on Yale database (rows from top to bottom) sketches; synthesized photos; original photos

We construct the synthesized photos by super resolution based on adaptive multi dictionary learning. Fig. 3 performs the super resolution experiment results by adaptive multi dictionary learning algorithm. The edges of the reconstructed image are not jagged or fuzzy and solve the small size of original images. What's more, because of the introduction of prior knowledge reconstructed photo performs better in details for the further observation of criminal investigation.

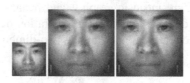

Fig. 3. Super resolution experiment results (from left to right): original image; bicubic interpolation and adaptive multi dictionary learning.

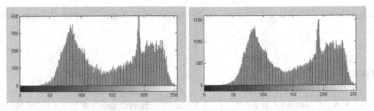

Fig. 4. Image gray histograms before (left) super resolution and after (right)

Fig. 4 performs the gray histograms of the image before and after the reconstruction. It can be seen from the figure that the gray histogram of image after super resolution becomes smoother and the gray information increased significantly. The super resolution based on adaptive multi-dictionary learning provides higher speed than algorithm based on global dictionary. Tab.1 records the running time respectively when the setting of parameters is the same.

Table 1. Running time in different algorithms

	dictionary training	photo reconstructing
ScSR	25395.13	44.35
This paper	236.46	25.07

Table 2. Recognition rate with different number of eigenvalues on CIS and Yale databases

Number of eigen-values	1	2	3	4	5	6	7	8	9
CIS Recognition rate(%)	65.91	79.55	86.36	90.91	90.91	90.91	90.91	90.91	90.91
Yale Recognition rate(%)	70.45	90.91	88.64	88.64	88.64	88.64	90.91	88.64	88.64

Tab. 2 shows the recognition rate on CIS database and Yale database respectively. As is shown in the table above, when the number of eigenvalues is no more than 8, the recognition rates can reach their maximum and stable at 90.91% and 88.64% respectively.

6   Conclusion

There are two weaknesses in photo transformed by sketch, vague details and low resolution. To solve the problems and for the further observation of criminal investigation, a heterogeneous face recognition based on super resolution reconstruction by adaptive multi-dictionary learning is proposed. Adaptive multi-dictionary learning has higher speed than traditional global dictionary learning. The results of experiment which is done on two international public databases show that this method can create an ideal effect on sketch face recognition.

Acknowledgments. This work is supported by National Natural Science Foundation of China (61371156).

References

1. Silva, M.A.A., C'amara-Ch'avez, G.C.: Face sketch recognition from local features. 27th SIBGRAPI Conference on Graphics. Patterns and Images, pp. 58–64. IEEE Press, Rio de Janeiro (2014)
2. Galoogahi, H.K., Sim, T.C.: Face sketch recognition by local radon binary pattern: LRBP. In: 19th IEEE International Conference on Image Processing, pp. 1837–1840. IEEE Press, Coronado Springs (2012)
3. Liu, J.X., Bae, S., Park, H., Li, L., Yoon, S., Yi, J.C.: Face photo-sketch recognition based on joint dictionary learning. 14th IAPR International Conference on Machine Vision Applications. MVA Orgnization, pp. 77–80. IEEE Press, Tokyo (2015)
4. Tang, X., Wang, X.: Face Sketch Recognition. J. IEEE Transactions on Circuits and Systems for Video Technology **14**, 50–57 (2004)
5. Wang, X.G., Tang, X.O.: Face Photo-Sketch Synthesis and Recognition. J IEEE Transactions on Pattern Analysis and Machine Intelligence **31**, 1955–1967 (2009)
6. Yang, J., Wright, J., Huang, T., et al.: Image super-resolution via sparse representation. J. IEEE Transactions on Image Processing. **19**, 2861–2873 (2010)
7. Yan, S., Xu, D., Zhang, B., Zhang, H., Yang, Q., Lin, S.: Graph Embedding and Extensions: A General Framework for Dimensionality Reduction. J. IEEE Transactions on Pattern Analysis and Machine Intelligence **29**, 40–51 (2007)
8. Wan, M., Lai, Z., Shao, J., et al.: Two-dimensional local graph embedding discriminant analysis (2DLGEDA) with its application to face and palm biometrics. J. Neurocomputing **73**, 197–203 (2009)
9. Freeman, T., Jones, T.R., Pasztor, E.: Example based superresolution. J. IEEE Computer Graphics and Applications **22**, 56–65 (2002)
10. Smith, L.N., Elad, M.: Improving Dictionary Learning: Multiple Dictionary Updates and Coefficient Reuse. J. IEEE Signal Processing Letters **20**, 79–82 (2013)
11. Pan, Z.X., Yu, J., Xiao, C.B., Sun, W.D.: Single Image Super Resolution Based on Adaptive Multi-Dictionary Learning (in Chinese). J. Acta Electronica Sinica **43**, 209–216 (2015)
12. Tang, X., Wang, X.C.: Face photo recognition using sketch. In: 2002 International Conference on Image Processing, pp. 257–260. IEEE Press, New York (2002)

3D Face Recognition Fusing Spherical Depth Map and Spherical Texture Map

Shuai Liu[1], Zhichun Mu[1(✉)], and Hongbo Huang[2]

[1] School of Automation and Electrical Engineering,
University of Science and Technology Beijing, Beijing 100083, China
ustbliu2013@163.com, mu@ies.ustb.edu.cn
[2] Computing Center, Beijing Information Science
and Technology University, Beijing 100192, China
hauck@sohu.cn

Abstract. Face recognition in unconstrained environments is often influenced by pose variations. And the problem is basically the identification that uses partial data. In this paper, a method fusing structure and texture information is proposed to solve the problem. In the register phase, the approximate 180 degree information of face is acquired, and the data used to identify individual is obtained from a random single view. Pure face is extracted from 3D data first, then convert the original data to the form of spherical depth map (SDM) and spherical texture map (STM), which are invariant to out-plane rotation, subsequently facilitating the successive alignment-free identification that is robust to pose variations. We make identification through sparse representation for its well performance with the two maps. Experiments show that our proposed method gets a high recognition rate with pose and expression variations.

Keywords: Face recognition · Spherical Depth Map · Spherical Texture Map · Sparse representation

1 Introduction

In modern society, person identification is very helpful, especially in some important roles of public information and security. In practical application, face recognition has received much attention in the distance and uncontrolled scene for its friendly and non-intrusive [1]. Although great advances have been made in 2D face recognition, it is still a challenging task to overcome the effect of light and pose [2]. Research has begun to focus on 3D data recent years with the development of 3D scanner. Compared with 2D data, 3D point cloud preserves the structure information. However, it still has limits in occlusion and data missing.

In fact, person identification in unconstrained environments is basically the identification that uses partial data. But, registration is possible under controlled environments, able to acquire data contained the approximate 180 degree information of face. Build a library, including the complete individual information, could help us use the partial data obtained from a random single view to identify individual. As we all

© Springer International Publishing Switzerland 2015
J. Yang et al. (Eds.): CCBR 2015, LNCS 9428, pp. 151–159, 2015.
DOI: 10.1007/978-3-319-25417-3_19

know, ear recognition has become an effective identification method because it is a rigid body, containing rich structure features [3]. And ear data acquisition is similar to face data, both can realize non-intrusive acquisition. In addition, ear has unique physical location, when face to the side, ear is in positive. All the reasons make ear be a useful supplement to face recognition. Some researchers get a panoramic 2D image by stitching multiple angle views of head for face recognition. Liu [4] used a statistical model for face image alignment, and introduced a recognition method by projecting images to the surface of a 3D ellipsoid. Singh [5] proposed a hierarchical registration algorithm to align different view faces and they had experiments on three databases. Fan [6] built a simple acquisition system composed of 5 standard cameras which, together, could take simultaneously 5 views of a face at different angles. Then they chose an easily hardware-achievable algorithm, consisting of successive linear transformations, to compose a panoramic face. At last, recognition experiments based on principal component method was conducted. Rama [7] presented a method for the automatic creation of 180° aligned cylindrical projected face images using nine different views. The alignment was done by applying first a global 2D affine transformation of the image, and afterward a local transformation of the desired face features using a triangle mesh. This local alignment allows a closer look to the feature properties and not the differences. Finally, these aligned face images were used for training a pose invariant face recognition approach.

But, most 3D face recognition is based on structure information only, and texture features are used for 2D face recognition [8, 9]. However, texture and structure infor-mation are two different description forms, which have a certain complementarity [10].

In this paper, we propose a method fusing 3D depth data and 2D texture data. Pure head is extracted first because point cloud obtained through 3D scanner contains not only face and ear, but also includes a shoulder and other redundant information. Then, a sphere is fitted to the 3D data, based on the fact that human head looks like a ball. 2D spherical depth map (SDM) is generated by expanding the fitting sphere and the pixel value on the map is the distance of point cloud to the center of the fitting sphere. Meanwhile, according to the correspondence between the original texture and depth information, texture is mapped to the fitting sphere and we expand the sphere like before to generate the spherical texture map (STM). At last, we make identification through sparse representation using the two maps.

The rest of this paper is organized as follows: Section 2 presents a method to extract pure face from 3D point cloud by detecting nose tip and central profile. In Section 3, the recognition method using spherical depth map and spherical texture map is illustrated in detail. The experiments and results are provided in Section 4. Finally, some concluding remarks are given in Section 5.

2   Pure Face Extraction

Point cloud obtained through 3D scanner contains not only face and ear, but also includes a shoulder and other redundant information. It will have a significant impact later whether we get rid of the redundant information accurately. Considering the fact that nose tip and central profile are usually easy to detect in a random single view within the scope of 180 degree of face, we extract pure face from 3D point cloud by detecting the obvious part.

About nose tip detection, one simple method is to assume that it is the point closest to the camera, but it will fail under non-frontal pose. However, the tip still has the maximum depth value as long as the original coordinate rotating to the right direction, shown in Fig. 1.

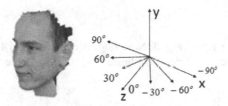

Fig. 1. Rotated Coordinate

So, nose tip will have the largest local polar radius after cylindrical coordinate transformation. Let θ and R denote the rotated angle and polar radius in cylindrical coordinate system respectively, and y is the point cloud vertical coordinate with the same meaning as in Cartesian coordinates.

We first assume that every point may be nose tip. For a point P, search its neighboring points P_i within the distance of 10. If one polar radius of P_i is larger than that of P, we no longer believe P is a nose tip. Certainly, this method has a large computational load on localizing the neighboring points. Considering the actual situation, we don't consider the points with their y too large or too small, and the points whose polar radius less than 40% of the largest polar radius are also ignored. The rest points are calculated by KD-Tree algorithm. The final candidate nose tip points are marked in Fig. 2.

For further conform, we calculate the Shape Index of every candidate point and some points around it. The calculation is in original point cloud data. The Shape Index was put forward by Dorai [11], computed as:

$$ShapeIndex(s) = \frac{1}{2} - \frac{1}{\pi} \tan^{-1} \frac{k_1(s) + k_2(s)}{k_1(s) - k_2(s)}. \tag{1}$$

where $k_1(s)$ and $k_2(s)$ represent the maximum and minimum principal curvature respectively. In our experiments, the Shape Index is set to 0.7-1.

After nose tip P was confirmed, take out all the points in the box, which width is 30 and height is 25, shown in Fig. 3. And y-coordinate of the points in the box is quantized to an integer. Let F_i be the set $f = (f.\theta, f.y, f.R)$ such that $|f.y| = i$, the point with the largest polar radius of F_i belongs to nose ridge. The θ and y belong to nose ridge is denoted by a matrix $A_{m \times 2}$ and the θ and y of all pure face points is denoted by a matrix $A'_{m \times 2}$, where m is the points number of nose ridge and n is the points number of pure face. PCA is used to A, able to get two feature vectors $v1$, $v2$ and two characteristic values $r1$, $r2$ ($r1 > r2$). Let $\theta' = A \times v2$, the points in pure face whose θ' is equal to θ'_P are the points belong to central profile, shown in Fig. 4. Where θ'_P is the θ' of nose tip P.

Central profile bottom could be confirmed because nose tip is almost the midpoint of the central profile, and pure face is extracted by getting rid of the points below the bottom point.

  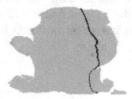

Fig. 2. Candidate nose tips in cylindrical coordinate

Fig. 3. Nose ridge in cylindrical coordinate

Fig. 4. Central profile in Cartesian coordinate

3   Recognition Process

3.1   Spherical Depth Map and Spherical Texture Map

A sphere is fitted to 3D face point cloud since the shape of human head can be approximated by a sphere. The spherical equation in 3D Cartesian coordinates is:

$$(x-x_0)^2 + (y-y_0)^2 + (z-z_0)^2 = r^2. \tag{2}$$

The Spherical Depth Map (SDM) was first introduced in [12]. In [12], a linear least square method is used to solve the fitting problem. Fig. 5 shows the fitting result.

(1) complete data   (2) partial data

Fig. 5. Sphere fitting

After moving the original coordinate to the center of fitting sphere, Cartesian coordinate is translated to spherical coordinate. The theta and phi which are inclination angle and azimuth angle in spherical coordinate, make up the coordinates of spherical depth map. Fig. 6 (1), (2) shows the panoramic SDM and partial SDM generated by holistic data and partial data. The pixel on the map is the distance of point cloud to the center of fitting sphere. Because point cloud is discrete, linear interpolation is needed.

Texture information is mapped to the fitting sphere as the original texture information has correspondence with the original depth information. Then spherical texture map (STM) can be obtained like spherical depth map, shown in Fig. 6 (3), (4).

Panoramic SDM and STM can be obtained in the register phase, holistic structural and textural information are made available, which is definitely helpful to alleviate the problems induced by pose variations and facial expression. Partial SDM and STM produced by test data acquired from a random single view. These spherical maps, in addition, are invariant to out-plane rotation, subsequently facilitating the successive alignment-free identification that is robust to pose variations. Meanwhile, the way of data presenting of the maps in 2D form reduces the cost of data storage and the load of computation involved in recognition process.

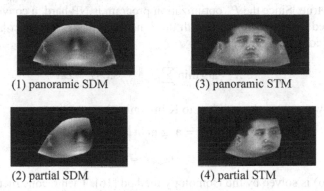

(1) panoramic SDM   (3) panoramic STM

(2) partial SDM   (4) partial STM

Fig. 6. SDM and STM

3.2   Sparse Representation

Person identification in unconstrained environments is basically the identification that uses partial data of the 180 degree face. So we can't use classification method based on global features for identification due to the different feature numbers among the partial images. Sparse representation classification method is applied to image classification and recognition widely because its state-of-the-art performance for image block or data missing [13]. Liao [14] developed an alignment-free face representation method based on Multi-Keypoint Descriptors (MKD), where the descriptor size of a face is determined by the actual content of the image. In that way, any probe face image, holistic or partial, can be sparsely represented by a large dictionary of gallery descriptors. In this paper, we investigate the depth image and texture image with multi-task sparse representation classification method respectively, the feature used for the two maps is Affine Sift [15].

Assume we have m features for each holistic spherical image i, corresponding descriptors are $D_i=[d_{i1}, d_{i2}, ..., d_{im}]$, and denote by D the collection of n images:

$$D = (D[1], D[2], \cdots, D[n]).$$ (3)

where D is a dictionary containing $m = \sum_{i=1}^{n} m_i$ descriptors.

Given a test example $Y=(d_{y1}, d_{y2}, ..., d_{yK})$, which belongs to one of the n classes, our goal is to find the class to which the test example belongs. We are interested in solving the following optimization:

$$X = \arg\min_X \sum_{k=1}^{K} \|x_k\|_0 , \quad \text{s.t. } Y = DX . \tag{4}$$

where $X=[x_1, x_2, ..., x_K]$ are sparse coefficient and $\|\cdot\|_0$ denotes the l_0 semi-norm indicating the number of nonzero elements of the given vector, that is $\|x\|_0 = \sum_k I(x_k \neq 0)$, where $I = 1$ is true. Since the P_{l0} optimization program is NP-hard, a convex relaxation of it is obtained by replacing the l_0 with the l_1 norm, which is $\|x\|_1 = \sum_k |x_k|$, and solving the following convex program:

$$X = \arg\min_X \sum_{k=1}^{K} \|x_k\|_1 , \quad \text{s.t. } Y = DX . \tag{5}$$

In this paper, we convert the problem to K minimization problems:

$$\hat{x}_k = \arg\min_{x_k} \|x_k\|_1 , $$
$$s.t. \ \ y_k = Dx_k, k = 1, 2, \cdots, K \tag{6}$$

And the Eq. (6) is solved by the Homotopy method [16]. Then reconstruction error for every class is calculated:

$$r_i(Y) = \frac{1}{K} \sum_{k=1}^{K} \|y_k - D[i]\hat{x}_k[i]\|_2^2 . \tag{7}$$

where $x[i]$ denotes that we select coefficients related with class i only, and others are set to 0. Besides, the negative coefficients are also set to 0 for the non-negativity is more consistent with the biological modeling of visual data [17]. The test example Y belongs to the class with the smallest $r(Y)$.

4   Experiments

4.1   Database

Since there is no existing public library containing the complete data, a small set containing 50 people is built for our experiments. The complete individual data is obtained though the multiple perspectives and we fuse the data by ICP algorithm [18]. Meanwhile, the test data is obtained from a random single view and part of the test data contained expression varieties. Every single view is taken two times, and 1700 images in total. Fig. 7 shows the schematic diagram of data acquired for registration and test.

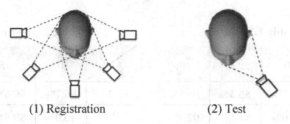

(1) Registration   (2) Test

Fig. 7. Data acquisition for registration and test

4.2   Recognition

Features are extracted from spherical depth map and spherical texture map respectively, using Affine Sift. And the parameter transition tills defined in Affine Sift is set to 3. The data used in our experiments are acquired under different posture, containing the rotation of three axes. We first identify individuals through sparse representation using SDM and STM respectively, and the results are shown in Table 1, 2. The match features are shown in Fig. 8.

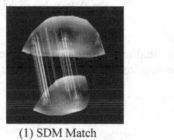
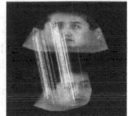

(1) SDM Match   (2) STM Match

Fig. 8. Match features

And then make identification fusing the two maps. We assume Eq. (8) the probability of the test sample belongs to class i, $r(i)$ denotes the reconstruction error. According to Bayesian decision, the test sample belongs to the class with maximal probability P, which is the product of P' calculated by SDM and STM. And the results are shown in Table 3.

$$P' = \frac{1/r_i^2}{\sum_{j=1}^n 1/r_j^2} \cdot \tag{8}$$

Table 1. SDM

β⟋α	0	±45	±90
0	93.3%	86.5%	93.5%
30	91.0%	84.5%	92.5%
-30	88.0%	85.0%	94.0%

Table 2. SDM + STM

β⟋α	0	±45	±90
0	96.7%	90.0%	95.5%
30	96.0%	89.5%	94.5%
-30	94.0%	91.5%	95.0%

Table 3. STM

β⟋α	0	±45	±90
0	95.3%	88.5%	92.0%
30	93.0%	85.5%	89.5%
-30	90.0%	83.0%	90.5%

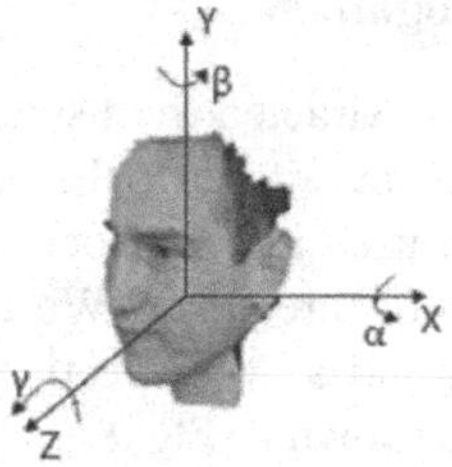

Fig. 9. Rotation of three axes

As can be seen, we can identify individual using the information acquired from a random single view. And if we fuse the texture and structure information together, a better result can be obtained.

5   Conclusion

In this paper, we propose a 3D face recognition method fusing spherical depth map and spherical texture map. The 3D data of pure face is converted to 2D data, and at the same time we save the structure information and texture information completely. After panoramic registration in the case of controlled circumstances, we can recognize individual using the partial data acquired from a random single view. This will have a high application value for person identification in unconstrained environments.

Acknowledgments. This paper is supported by (1) National Natural Science Foundation of China under the Grant No. 61472031; (2) National Natural Science Foundation of China under the Grant No. 61170116.

References

1. Jain, A.K., Flynn, P., Ross, A.A. (eds.).: Handbook of biometrics, Springer, US (2007)
2. Zhang, H., Zhang, Y., Huang, T.S.: Pose-robust face recognition via sparse representation. Pattern Recognition **46**(5), 1511–1521 (2013)

3. Nixon, M.S., Bouchrika, I., Arbab-Zavar, B., Carter, J.N.: On use of biometrics in forensics: Gait and ear. In: European Signal Processing Conference (2010)
4. Liu, X., Chen, T.: Pose-robust face recognition using geometry assisted probabilistic modeling. In: IEEE Computer Society Conference on Computer Vision and Pattern Recognition, pp. 1:502–509. IEEE (2005)
5. Singh, R., Vatsa, M., Ross, A.: A mosaicking scheme for pose-invariant face recognition. IEEE Transactions Systems, Man, and Cybernetics, Part B: Cybernetics 37(5), 1212–1225 (2007)
6. Yang, F., Paindavoine, M., Abdi, H., Monopoli, A.: Development of a fast panoramic face mosaicking and recognition system. Optical Engineering, 44(8) (2005)
7. Rama, A., Tarres, F., Rurainsky, J.: Aligned texture map creation for pose invariant face recognition. Multimedia Tools and Applications 49(3), 545–565 (2010)
8. Lei, Y., Bennamoun, M., El-Sallam, A.A.: An efficient 3D face recognition approach based on the fusion of novel local low-level features. Pattern Recognition 46(1), 24–37 (2013)
9. Mohammadzade, H., Hatzinakos, D.: Iterative Closest Normal Point for 3D Face Recognition. IEEE Transactions on Pattern Analysis and Machine Intelligence 35(2), 381–397 (2013)
10. Huang, D., Ardabiliab, M., Wang, Y., Chen, L.: Asymmetric 3D/2D face recognition based on LBP facial representation and canonical correlation analysis. In: 16th IEEE International Conference on Image Processing (ICIP), pp.3325–3328. IEEE (2009)
11. Dorai, C., Jain, A.K.: COSMOS-A representation scheme for 3d free-form objects. IEEE Transactions on Pattern Analysis and Machine Intelligence 19(10), 1115–1130 (1997)
12. Liu, P., Wang, Y., Zhang, Z.: Representing 3D face from point cloud to face-aligned spherical depth map. International Journal of Pattern Recognition and Artificial Intelligence, 26(1) (2012)
13. Wright, J., Yang, A.Y., Ganesh, A., Sastry, S.S.: Robust face recognition via sparse representation. IEEE Transactions on Pattern Analysis and Machine Intelligence 31(2), 210–227 (2009)
14. Liao, S., Jain, A.K., Li, S.Z.: Partial face recognition: Alignment-free approach. IEEE Transactions on Pattern Analysis and Machine Intelligence 35(5), 1193–1205 (2013)
15. Yu, G., Morel, J.M.: ASIFT: An Algorithm for Fully Affine Invariant Comparison, Image Processing On Line. 1 (2011)
16. Donoho, D.L., Tsaig, Y.: Fast Solution of L1-Norm Minimization Problems When the Solution May be Sparse. IEEE Transactions on Information Theory 54(11), 4789–4812 (2008)
17. Zhang, B., Mu, Z., Li, C., Zeng, H.: Robust classification for occluded ear via Gabor scale feature-based non-negative sparse representation. Optical Engineering, 53(6) (2014)
18. Besl, P.J., Mckay, N.D.: A method for registration of 3-D shape. IEEE Transaction on Pattern Analysis and Machine Intelligence 14(2), 239–256 (1992)

Privacy Preserving Face Identification
in the Cloud through Sparse Representation

Xin Jin[1,2](✉), Yan Liu[1,2,3], Xiaodong Li[1,2], Geng Zhao[1,2], Yingya Chen[1,2],
and Kui Guo[1,2]

[1] Beijing Electronic Science and Technology Institute, Beijing 100070, China
{jinxins,lxd}@besti.edu.cn
[2] GOCPCCC Key Laboratory of Information Security, Beijing 100070, China
[3] Xidian University, Xi'an 710071, China

Abstract. Nowadays, with tremendous visual media stored and even processed in the cloud, the privacy of visual media is also exposed to the cloud. In this paper we propose a private face identification method based on *sparse representation*. The identification is done in a secure way which protects both the privacy of the subjects and the confidentiality of the database. The face identification server in the cloud contains a list of registered faces. The surveillance client captures a face image and require the server to identify if the client face matches one of the suspects, but otherwise reveals no information to neither of the two parties. This is the first work that introduces sparse representation to the secure protocol of private face identification, which reduces the dimension of the face representation vector and avoid the patch based attack of a previous work. Besides, we introduce a secure Euclidean distance algorithm for the secure protocol. The experimental results reveal that the cloud server can return the identification results to the surveillance client without knowing anything about the client face image.

Keywords: Privacy preserving · Face identification · Private computing · Sparse representation · Cloud computing

1 Introduction

Face recognition has played an important role in surveillance and security. Nowadays, cloud computing has changed the way of traditional face recognition system. The big data of face images or videos and powerful face recognition program have been stored and running in the cloud server, which supports large scale video surveillance applications such as face tracking, suspect searching.

However, tremendous surveillance cameras have distributed everywhere. The privacy of people in the surveillance videos from the public places is being violated. The suspect searching applications can be misused to track the wanted person of criminals. Once the face recognition system is linked to a universal database such as ID cards, civilians could be tracked as someone's wishes.

© Springer International Publishing Switzerland 2015
J. Yang et al. (Eds.): CCBR 2015, LNCS 9428, pp. 160–167, 2015.
DOI: 10.1007/978-3-319-25417-3_20

On the other hand, the suspect list could be released to public, which may cause more crimes.

In this work, as show in Fig. 1, our scenario is set as that the surveillance client captures a face image and send to the cloud server which contains a list of suspects. The server compares the client face to each suspect in the list. The match or not match results are returned to the client. Using current face recognition methods, the contents of client face image are completely known to the server. Meanwhile, the client can guess out who are in the suspect list through several times of face identification.

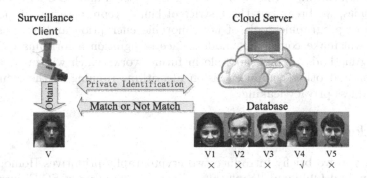

Fig. 1. The application scenario. The surveillance client capture a face image from public places such as airport, railway station. The face image is identified through our privacy preserving method with the suspect face data in the cloud server. After that, the client only learns the matching results. The cloud server learns nothing.

To protect the privacy of both the face captured by the client and the suspects in the cloud server, we propose a privacy preserving face identification method based on sparse representation and several cryptography tools. The client only knows the matching result. The cloud server knows nothing.

Recently, a system called Secure Computation of Face Identification (SCiFI) [1] was developed. This system use two cryptography tools (homomorphic encryption and oblivious transfer) to implement a privacy preserving computation of the Hamming distance between two binary vectors. Each of the face in both the client and the server is represented as a binary vector using a local image patch based method with the assistant of a third party face database.

The SCiFI system [1] has two main drawbacks: (1) the dimension of the face representation vector is large because of the binary representation, which reduce the running efficiency of the system, (2) the local patch based representation could be attracted by reconstructing a fragmented face [2]. Recently, Luong et al. [2] has proposed a method of reconstructing a fragmented face to attack the SCiFI system and reconstruct faces from the secure identification protocol.

We employ sparse representation to reduce the dimension of the face representation vector of [1] and avoid the patch based attack. As the classical sparse representation method does, a dictionary is learned from the list of suspects in the server. However, one can recover faces in the server easily using the learned dictionary. Thus we also add a third party face database and learn the dictionary form it. Then we use the sparse parameters as the representation vector of a face. After that, a privacy preserving computing method of Euclidean distance between two sparse parameter vectors is proposed. We extent the privacy preserving hamming distance of [1] to privacy preserving Euclidean distance. Experimental results reveal that our method can achieve comparable correction rate of identification to the local patch based method and need less computing time. Besides, we break out the restrict of binary representation of face when using the cryptographic tools of homomorphic encryption and obvious transfer. This will make converting modern face recognition algorithms to privacy preserving methods become possible in future work, which will make the face recognition and other computer vision algorithms running in the cloud more secure and less privacy leaking.

2 Background

In this section we briefly introduce two cryptography primitives(Homomorphic Encryption and Oblivious Transfer) and some basic parts of SCiFI system [1], just as what have been discussed in [2].

2.1 Cryptography Primitives

Homomorphic Encryption. The Paillier cryptosystem [3] [4], named after and invented by Pascal Paillier in 1999, is a probabilistic asymmetric algorithm for public key cryptography. The problem of computing n-th residue classes is believed to be computationally difficult. The decisional composite residuosity assumption is the intractability hypothesis upon which this cryptosystem is based. The scheme is an additive homomorphic cryptosystem; this means that, given only the public-key and the encryption of m_1 and m_2, one can compute the encryption of $m_1 + m_2$. The two properties of Paillier system are described as:

$$\mathrm{E}(m_1) \equiv g^{m_1} \cdot x_1^N (mod\ N^2)$$
$$\mathrm{E}(m_2) \equiv g^{m_2} \cdot x_2^N (mod\ N^2)$$
$$\mathrm{E}(m_1) \cdot \mathrm{E}(m_2) \equiv g^{m_1} \cdot x_1^N \cdot g^{m_2} \cdot x_2^N mod\ N^2 \tag{1}$$
$$\equiv g^{m_1+m_2}(x_1 \cdot x_2)^N mod\ N^2$$
$$\equiv \mathrm{E}(m_1 + m_2)$$

$$\mathrm{E}(km_1) = \mathrm{E}(m_1)^k \tag{2}$$

where m_1 and m_2 are 2 plan texts. $E(\cdot)$ is the encryption function. $N = p \cdot q$, p and q are two large prime numbers. $N \in Z$. The plan text $m \in Z_N$. x is a random number. $x \in Z_N^*$. $\gcd(L(g^e \bmod N^2), N) = 1$. e is the encryption key. Z, Z_N^*, e and $L(\cdot)$ are defined as:

$$Z_N = \{x | x \in Z, 0 \le x < N\},$$
$$Z_N^* = \{x | x \in Z, 0 \le x < N, \gcd(x, N) = 1\},$$
$$e = \text{lcm}(p - 1, q - 1),$$
$$S = \{x < N^2 | x = 1 \bmod N\},$$
$$\forall x \in S, L(x) = \frac{x - 1}{N} \tag{3}$$

where lcm means Least Common Multiple. gcd means Greatest Common Divisor.

Obvious Transfer. In cryptography, an oblivious transfer protocol (often abbreviated OT) is a type of protocol in which a sender transfers one of potentially many pieces of information to a receiver, but remains oblivious as to what piece (if any) has been transferred. The first form of oblivious transfer was introduced in 1981 by Michael O. Rabin. In this form, the sender sends a message to the receiver with probability 1/2, while the sender remains oblivious as to whether or not the receiver received the message. Rabin's oblivious transfer scheme is based on the RSA cryptosystem. A more useful form of oblivious transfer called 1-2 oblivious transfer or "1 out of 2 oblivious transfer," was developed later by Shimon Even, Oded Goldreich, and Abraham Lempel , in order to build protocols for secure multiparty computation. It is generalized to "1 out of n oblivious transfer" where the user gets exactly one database element without the server getting to know which element was queried, and without the user knowing anything about the other elements that were not retrieved. The latter notion of oblivious transfer is a strengthening of private information retrieval, in which the database is not kept private [5].

2.2   SCiFI Overview

The SCiFI system proposes a face representation method to represent a face image as a n dimensions binary vector $\mathbf{w} = [w_0, w_2, ..., w_{n-1}]$ using a public face database. The cloud server contains a list of M face binary vectors $\{\mathbf{w}_1, \mathbf{w}_2, ..., \mathbf{w}_M\}$ and thresholds $\{t_1, t_2, ...t_M\}$. The output of the protocol is R:

$$R = \begin{cases} \text{match, if } H(\mathbf{w}, \mathbf{w}_i) < t_i \\ \text{not match, if otherwise} \end{cases}, \tag{4}$$

where $H(\cdot)$ is the Hamming distance of two binary vectors.

The client uses the Paillier cryptosystem [3] to share the public key with the server and keeps the private key to itself. Through an oblivious transfer protocol, the client learns only if the Hamming distance between any pair of their vectors exceeds a threshold. The cloud server learns nothing. See [1] for implementation details [2].

3   Privacy Preserving Face Identification

An overview of our method is shown in Fig. 2. In this section, we first introduce the modified spares represent based face identification. Then the private face identification protocol using our modified sparse representation is described.

Algorithm 1. Private Face Identification

Input:

The client's input is a face vector $\mathbf{s} = (s_0, s_1, ..., s_{l-1})$. In our application $l = 200$. The server's input is a list of Q face vectors $\{s^1, s^2, ..., s^Q\}$. The server has additional inputs $\{t_1, t_2, ..., t_Q\}$ for each s^i. The two parties both know an upper bound d_{max}, in our application we set
$d_{max} \leq 1 \times 10^6$.

Output:

The client learns the indices i for which $ED(s, s^i) \leq t_i$. The server learns nothing.

1: The client uses Paillier to encrypt and send face vector $s = (s_0, s_1, ..., s_{l-1})$ item by item and the square of each item $(s)^2 = ((s_0)^2, (s_1)^2, ..., (s_{l-1})^2)$. The cloud server receives the encryption results of each item $(E_{pk}(s_0), E_{pk}(s_1), ..., E_{pk}(s_{l-1}))$ and $(E_{pk}((s_0)^2), E_{pk}((s_1)^2), ..., E_{pk}((s_{l-1})^2))$. For each face in the list of suspects of the server, the following steps are repeated.

2: For ith face in the server and for jth parameter in the face vector, the cloud server computes $E_{pk}(v_j)$, where $v_j = (s_j - s_j^i)^2$.

$$
\begin{aligned}
E_{pk}((s_j - s_j^i)^2) &= E_{pk}((s_j)^2 - 2s_j s_j^i + (s_j^i)^2) \\
&= E_{pk}((s_j)^2) \cdot E_{pk}(s_j)^{-2s_j^i} \cdot E_{pk}((s_j^i)^2)
\end{aligned}
\tag{5}
$$

The s_j^i is known to the server.

3: According to the properties of homomorphic encryption, the cloud server can compute the encrypted $d_E = (ED(s, s^i))^2$ by $E_{pk}(d_E) = \sum_{j=0}^{l-1} E_{pk}(v_j)$, $d_E \in [0, d_{max}]$. Then the server chooses a random number r_i for each face vector, and computes $E_{pk}((ED(s, s^i))^2 + r_i)$. This number is sent to the client.

4: The client receives the $E_{pk}((ED(s, s^i))^2 + r_i)$ and decrypts it.

5: The two parties use $OT_1^{\frac{d_{max}}{4000}}$ protocol to judge if $(d_E)^i < t_i$ securely. The result R_i computed in the client is:

$$
R_i = \begin{cases} 1 \text{ if } ((d_E)^i + r_i) \ mod \ (d_{max} + r_i) \leq t_i + r_i \\ 0 \text{ if otherwise} \end{cases}
\tag{6}
$$

6: **return** R_i.

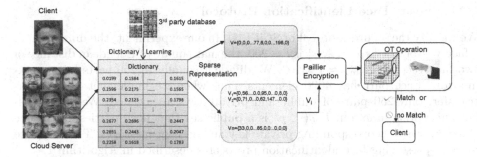

Fig. 2. The overview of our method. A third party face database is used to learn a dictionary. The face captured by the client and the faces in the list of the cloud server are represented sparse parameter vector. The Euclidean distance of the client face vector and each of the face vector in the server is computed in a privacy preserving way. The matching result is only known by the client. The cloud server learns nothing.

3.1 Modified Sparse Representation Based Face Identification

The local image patch based face representation of SCiFI [1] is attacked by [2]. Besides, the dimension of binary face vector is 3000 (we have 100 face images in the 3rd database), which reduces the computing efficiency using cryptographic tools. Thus we introduce sparse representation into the secure protocol of SCiFI to reduce the dimension of face vector through sparse parameters and avoid fragment attack proposed by [2].

However, introducing the sparse representation to the secure protocol is a non-trivial work. If the dictionary is learned from the list of faces in the cloud server, the contents of the suspect list will be leaked to public. Besides, solving the linear system in the secure protocol based on Paillier system and oblivious transfer is too complicated and time consuming. Thus, we modify the classical sparse representation based face identification [6] from two aspects. (1) We add a third party face database to learn the dictionary. (2) We directly use the sparse parameter vector as the representation of a face image. The Euclidean distance is considered as the similarity criteria between two faces. Thus, we can compute the square of Euclidean distance in the secure protocol, which is less time consuming than solving a linear system.

We denote the face vector of our sparse parameter as $s = \{s_1, s_2, ...s_l\}$. The square of Euclidean distance between face vector s^1 and s^2 is $ED(s^1, s^2) = \sum_{i=1}^{l}(s_i^1 - s_i^2)^2$. If the square of Euclidean distance is below a threshold, we consider that s^1 and s^2 belong to the same face. Learning individual thresholds is a hard task because these thresholds depend on variations in different images of the same face.

We learn the individual threshold for each face in the cloud server by the set difference for each person that will discriminate him/her from an ensemble of people. The threshold for the ith face is based on the smallest set difference between him and the rest of people in the ensemble [1].

3.2   Private Face Identification Protocol

We modify the secure protocol of SCiFI [1]. In our experiment, the dimension of a face vector $\mathbf{s} = \{s_1, s_2, ...s_l\}$ is $l = 200$. the max square of Euclidean distance of two face vector is $d_{max} = 1 \times 10^6$. We divide it equally to 250 parts for approximation. Each part has 4000 elements Thus when we implement the obvious transfer, only 250 pairs of public and private keys are needed. We use a Paillier encryption function, $E_{pk}(\cdot)$. pk is a public key that both parties know. The client knows the corresponding private key and decrypt messages. The complete privacy preserving face identification protocol is described in Algorithm 1.

4   Experimental Results

We test our method and compare the performance with SCiFI [1] in the faces94 dataset [7]. The server has totally 100 facial images of 20 persons. Each person has 5 different facial images. The third face database also contains 100 facial image of 20 different persons to the server. The $3rd$ face database contains 100 facial images randomly selected from the faces94 dataset. The average top one matching rate of our method is 91.55% which is a little less than 95.5% of the local image patch based method of [1]. However, we use only 200 dimension vector comparing with 3000 dimension vector of [1]. Furthermore, the fragment reconstruction based attack method by [2] cannot attack our method any more, because we do not use any fragment of facial images.

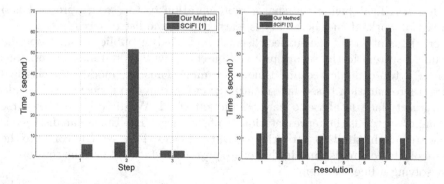

Fig. 3. The computing time of each main step. $step1$ for face vector generation, $step2$ for the Paillier encryption, $step3$ for the oblivious transfer. The computing times of face vector generation and the Paillier encryption of our method are less than those of SCiFI [1]. The resolutions tested are $138 * 168, 230 * 280, 276 * 336, 322 * 392, 38 * 448, 414 * 504, 460 * 560$.

In addition, the sparse representation make our face vector much shorter than that of SCiFI [1], which reduces the computing time using time-consuming cryptography algorithm. The Paillier encryption is called each item of the face vector.

We test the computing time of each main step. In *step*1 the sparse face vector is computed. In *step*2 the Paillier encryption is called. In *step*3 the oblivious transfer is executed. To avoid network delay, we set the client and server in the same PC (Windows 32, 2.92GHz Intel Core2 Duo CPU, 3GB RAM). As shown in Fig. 3, the computing times of face vector generation and the Paillier encryption of our method are less than those of SCiFI [1]. All the time in this experiment is the average time of 10 facial images.

The computing times in different resolutions are also compared with those of SCiFI [1]. The total computing times of each resolutions are shown in Fig. 3. Our method is obvious faster than the method of SCiFI [1].

5 Conclusion and Discussion

In this paper we propose a private face identification method based on sparse representation. The identification is done in a secure way which protects both the privacy of the subjects and the confidentiality of the database. This is the first work that introduces sparse representation to the secure protocol of private face identification, which reduces the dimension of the face representation vector and avoid the patch based attack of a previous work.

Acknowledgments. This work is partially supported by the National Natural Science Foundation of China (No.61402021, No.61402023, No.61170037), the Fundamental Research Funds for the Central Universities (No.2014XSYJ01, No.2015XSYJ25), and the Science and Technology Project of the State Archives Administrator. (No.2015-B-10).

References

1. Osadchy, M., Pinkas, B., Jarrous, A., et al.: SCiFI - a system for secure face identification. In: IEEE Symposium on Security and Privacy (S&P), pp. 239–254. IEEE (2010)
2. Luong, A., Gerbush, M., Waters, B., Grauman, K.: Reconstructing a fragmented face from a cryptographic identification protocol. In: IEEE Workshop on Applications of Computer Vision (WACV), pp. 238–245. IEEE (2013)
3. Paillier, P.: Public-key cryptosystems based on composite degree residuosity classes. In: Stern, J. (ed.) EUROCRYPT 1999. LNCS, vol. 1592, pp. 223–238. Springer, Heidelberg (1999)
4. Paillier Cryptosystem. https://en.wikipedia.org/wiki/Paillier_cryptosystem
5. Oblivious Transfer. https://en.wikipedia.org/wiki/Oblivious_transfer
6. Wright, J., Ganesh, A., et al.: Robust Face Recognition via Sparse Representation. IEEE Trans. Pattern. Anal. Mach. Intell. **31**(2), 210–227 (2008). IEEE
7. Collection of Facial Images: Faces94. http://cswww.essex.ac.uk/mv/allfaces/faces94.html

Infrared Face Recognition Based on ODP
of Local Binary Patterns

Zhihua Xie[✉] and Ying Xiong

Key Lab of Optic-Electronic and Communication,
Jiangxi Sciences and Technology Normal University, Nanchang, Jiangxi Province, China
xie_zhihua68@aliyun.com

Abstract. Local binary pattern (LBP) is an effective local feature descriptor for infrared face representation. To extract discriminative subset in LBP patterns, infrared face recognition based on optimized discriminative patterns (ODP) is proposed in this paper. Firstly, LBP operator is applied to infrared face for the extraction of texture information. Secondly, based on the two-class discriminative ability, for each subject, we adaptively select the optimized discriminative patterns from LBP features. Then, dissimilarity metrics base on chi-square distance is computed for each two-classifier. Finally, the final recognition algorithm is built on all two-classifiers using voting mechanism. The experimental results show the ODP can extract compact and discriminative features for infrared face feature extraction, which outperform the existing LBP uniform and discriminative patterns.

Keywords: Local Binary Pattern · Optimized Discriminative Patterns · Personalized subset · Dimensionality reduction · Infrared face recognition

1   Introduction

Automatic face recognition is an area with immense practical potential which includes a wide range of commercial and law enforcement applications [1]. Visual face recognition systems have achieved high performance under controlled environments, but they are still challenged by variations in illumination, facial expression, and pose [2]. Work on alternative imaging modalities attracts much interest recently [1, 3]. A solution to high performance face recognition is to acquire face images beyond the visible spectrum [1]. Infrared imagery is a modality which has attracted particular attention, in large part due to its invariance to the changes in illumination by visible light [2].

The infrared spectrum typically is separated into two categories: reflected infrared band (0.77-2.4um) and thermal infrared band (2.4um-14mm) [4, 5]. Near infrared spectra is geared to the reflected infrared category, it can be reflected by a body, so it usually is used for an active illumination source. On the other hand, Thermal infrared imagery for face recognition has the three advantages: thermal infrared imagery collects the heat energy emitted by an object instead the light; it can work even in the situation of complete darkness; human skin has a high emissivity in 8-12um presenting a discriminative signature. Therefore, thermal infrared face recognition has

© Springer International Publishing Switzerland 2015
J. Yang et al. (Eds.): CCBR 2015, LNCS 9428, pp. 168–175, 2015.
DOI: 10.1007/978-3-319-25417-3_21

received the most attention in recent years [3]. In this paper, thermal infrared imagery is only considered for infrared face recognition.

As for face recognition, the discriminative feature extraction is the key for robust infrared face recognition. The main drawbacks of thermal infrared face recognition are ambient temperature and low resolutions of thermal sensors. Therefore, feature extraction methods using global statistical information can not be applied in infrared face recognition research, which are popular in visible face recognition. To cope with those issues, the local feature extraction methods are more appreciated than the traditional methods based on global appearance. In a series of influential works, Li et al were the first to use local binary patterns (LBP) features extraction from infrared images [4], which got a better performance than appearance based methods such as principle component analysis (PCA), linear discriminant analysis (LDA) and independence component analysis (ICA) [4]. To reduce the dimensionality of traditional LBP features, far infrared face recognition using discriminative patterns from LBP was proposed by Xie et al [5], which got the same bins label of LBP patterns for different infrared face subjects. Furthermore, Xie et al, focused on the feature selection in LBP histogram for far infrared face recognition, which was based on the statistical character in the whole training samples [5]. However, those feature selection algorithms are based on the fixed subset for all subjects and can not emphasize the hard subjects [6]. Therefore, the features selection method in LBP histogram space still is an important issue for high performance infrared face recognition.

With regarding to infrared face recognition, a personalized features extraction from LBP patterns still is a big challenging problem [7]. To address this issue, the optimized discriminative patterns (ODP) are introduced to represent useful information in different infrared face images. Based on the ODP, we perform the classification task based on all two-classifiers using voting mechanism [8].

2   Discriminative Patterns Based on Local Binary Patterns

Local binary pattern (LBP) operator was introduced by Ojala et al as an excellent texture retrieval method [9]. Furthermore, it also has shown excellent performance in biometrics studies, in terms of speed and discriminative performance. In its simplest form, LBP describes a central pixel by threshold the values of its 3×3 neighborhoods and encoded the feature using a binary number [10].

The binary encoding idea of this approach is demonstrated in Fig 1. LBP numberfor the center pixel g_c can be obtained by equation (1).

$$LBP_{P,R}(g_c) = \sum_{i=0}^{P-1} 2^i \times S(g_i - g_c)$$ (1)

$$S(g_i - g_c) = \begin{cases} 1, g_i - g_c \geq 0 \\ 0, g_i - g_c < 0 \end{cases}$$ (2)

where g_c is the gray value of the central pixel, g_i is the value of its neighbors, P is the total number of involved neighbors and R is the radius of the neighborhood. The parameter (P, R) can be (8, 1), (8, 2) and (16, 2) etc.

For LBP based infrared face feature extraction, original infrared face can be split into non-overlapping regions [11]. In each region, LBP patterns occurrence histogram is computed by:

$$H(r) = \sum_{x_c=2}^{N-1} \sum_{y_c=2}^{M-1} f(LBP_{P,R}(x,y),r) \tag{3}$$

$$f(LBP_{P,R}(x,y),r) = \begin{cases} 1, LBP_{P,R}(x,y)=r \\ 0, \text{otherwise} \end{cases} \tag{4}$$

where N is the length of region, M is the width of region, r is the pattern label, (x, y) is the coordinate of a pixel in one region. The dimensionality of histogram from LBP is 2^P. All the histograms of all local regions are concatenated into one feature vector to build the final infrared face features [12].

The main drawback of LBP histogram representation is large dimensionality, which may contain some useless information [13, 14]. To reduce the dimensionality of LBP representation for infrared faces, the discriminative patterns (DP) are introduced by Xie et al [5]. Assuming there are "C" classes in all samples and S training samples for each class, Separability discriminant (SD) is defined by:

$$SD(i) = \frac{D_b(i)}{D_w(i)} \tag{5}$$

$$D_w(i) = \sum_{c=1}^{C} \frac{1}{C} \sum_{s=1}^{S} \frac{1}{S} (H_i(s,c) - \bar{H}_i^c)^2 \tag{6}$$

$$D_b(i) = \sum_{c=1}^{C} \frac{1}{C} \sum_{s=1}^{S} \frac{1}{S} (H_i(s,c) - \bar{H}_i^c)^2 \tag{7}$$

where $\bar{H}_i^c$ is each coefficient mean of the c th class, $\bar{H}_i$ is the each coefficient mean of the all samples. The selected patterns are based on the values of SD. Therefore, the discriminative patterns, which are based on LDA, select the fixed patterns for all   subjects in training database.

3   Optimized Discriminative Patterns (ODP) of LBP

Although the discriminative LBP patterns can capture the useful information of infrared face representation, it is possibly problematic for different infrared face classes [5]. The reason is that discriminative LBP patterns have the same subset bins for different infrared faces from different people, which can not make full use of discriminative information in those objects [7]. As we know, different subjects should have different local features which are distinguished from another subject [8]. To extract compact and personalized features from different subjects, optimized discriminative patterns (ODP) are proposed to adaptively select the useful patterns for different subjects. The key of optimized discriminative patterns (ODP) is the discriminative ability description based on two-class classifier by fisher discrimination analysis.

With the successful experiences of multiple two-class problems for a multi-class problem, this paper proposes the discriminative ability (DA) by two-class problem.

Assuming there are two class subjects, their class labels are A and B. DA is defined by the discriminative criterion in pattern recognition theory [6].

$$DA(i) = [\mu_A(i) - \mu_B(i)]^2 \Big/ [\delta_A^2(i) + \delta_B^2(i)] \qquad (8)$$

where $\mu_A(i)$, $\mu_B(i)$ is the mean of $H(i)$ (the i th pattern) from class A and class B respectively. $\delta_A(i)$, $\delta_B(i)$ is the variance of $H(i)$ from class A and class B respectively. In this way, we can adaptively select the patterns for the two-class classifier based on the value of DA. In other words, we retain n patterns whose DA are the top n. In this paper, n is determined on the condition that the occurrences of patterns reserved equals to 80 percents of the sum occurrences from all patterns.

4   The Multi-classifier Based on Voting Mechanism

The flow chart of the multi-classifier using voting mechanism is shown in Fig1. If there are w people in training stage, the $w(w-1)/2$ classifiers need to be constructed. Each two-class classifier corresponds to the optimized discriminative subset from LBP patterns. In this paper, the two-classifier is base on traditional chi-square distance [15, 16].

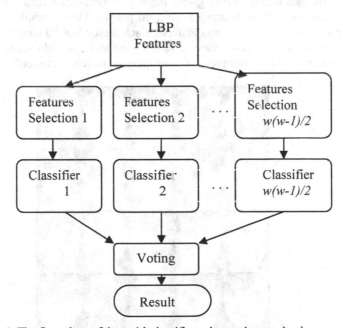

Fig. 1. The flow chart of the multi-classifier using voting mechanism

In test stage, for a certain probe u, the final recognition result can be obtained by all two-class classifier using voting mechanism. For instance, if A/B classifier gets the result A, the label A gets one vote and the label B gains no vote. The final recognition result can be determined by the label with the most votes [7].

$$u \in i, if \quad c(i,u) = \max_{j=1,2,\dots,w} p(j,u) \tag{9}$$

$$p(j,u) = \sum_{\eta=1}^{w(w-1)/2} c(\eta,j,u) \tag{10}$$

$$c(\eta,j,u) = \begin{cases} 1, & if \quad \eta(u) = j \\ 0, & else \end{cases} \tag{11}$$

where $\eta(u)$ is the classification result of u by the classifier η.

Finally, the final recognition algorithm is built on all two-classifiers using voting mechanism.

5   Experiment Results

To verify the effectiveness of our method and other ones, all experiments are done under an infrared face database built by ourselves with a ThermoVisionA40 infrared camera supplied by FLIR Systems Inc [3, 5]. The training database contains 400 samples from 40 individuals. Those thermal infrared face images were carefully captured on November 17, 2006 and under the same environmental temperature controlled by air conditioner. The test database is divided into two groups: one group belongs to same-session data and the other group belongs to time-lapse data. The same-session group includes 400 thermal images from 40 people. Those samples are collected in the same situation to the training database. Each person has 10 templates: 2 in frontal-view, 2 in up-view, 2 in down-view, 2 in left-view and 2 in right-view. The time-lapse group consists of 165 samples of one person which were collected indifferent

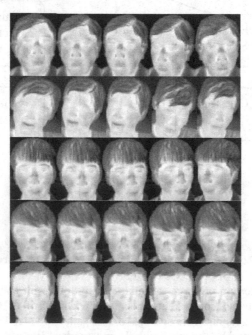

Fig. 2. Infrared Face Samples from Training Data

situation from the training data. The original resolution of each image is 240×320. The resolution of infrared face image turns to be 80×60 after face detection and geometric normalization, as demonstrated in Fig 2.

In this paper, the parameter (P, R) LBP code is (8, 1) for all experiments. To show the contribution of our adaptive pattern labels, Five modes of partitioning are used: 1 is non-partitioning, 2 is 2×2, 3 is 4×2, 4 is 2×4, and 5 is 4×4. To verify the effectiveness of the proposed ODP from LBP for infrared face recognition, the two other LBP-based infrared face recognition methods are used for comparisons analysis including LBP uniform patterns [10], LBP discriminative patterns [5]. These recognition results are shown in Fig 3.

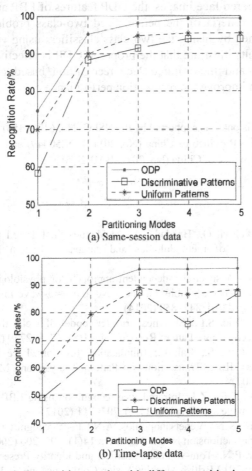

Fig. 3. Recognition results with different partitioning modes

It can be seen from the Fig 3 that recognition rates based on optimized discriminative patterns (ODP) and discriminative uniforms are higher than ones based on uniform patterns. This means that uniform patterns is not suitable for infrared face representation. From Fig 3 one can see: The robustness performance of ODP outperforms the performance of discriminative patterns with both same-session data and time-lapse data. Especially for elapse-time database, compared with discriminative patterns, the best recognition rate of ODP patterns has a significant lift (from 88.2% to 95.8%). The main reason is that the ODP patterns can extract optimal discriminative features by means of personalized two-class classifier.

6   Conclusions

Infrared face representation based on conventional LBP uniform or discriminative pattern, has the fixed pattern labels for different people. To extract the optimal subset features of LBP in infrared face images, the ODP features of LBP are proposed based on the discriminative criteria of the personalized two-class problem. Infrared face recognition is performed by fusing the two-class classifiers using voting mechanism. The experimental results illustrate that the proposed ODP is effective in extraction of personalized features and the infrared face recognition based on multi-classifier voting mechanism can improve the recognition performance.

Acknowledgements. This paper is supported by the NSFC (No. 61201456), the key technology R &D Program of Jiangxi Province of China (No. 20112BDE50049) and the Natural Science Foundation of Jiangxi Province of China (No. 20142BAB 207029).

References

1. Ghiass, R.S., Arandjelovi, O., Bendada, A., Maldague, X.: Infrared face recognition: A comprehensive review of methodologies and databases. Pattern Recognition **47**(9), 2807–2824 (2014)
2. Osia, N., Bourlai, T.: A spectral independent approach for physiological and geometric based face recognition in the visible, middle-wave and long-wave infrared bands. Image and Vision Computing **32**(6), 847–859 (2014)
3. Wu, S.Q., Li, W.S., Xie, S.L.: Skin heat transfer model of facial thermograms and its application in face recognition. Pattern Recognition **41**(8), 2718–2729 (2008)
4. Stan, Z., Li, R.F., Chu, S., Cai, L.: Illumination Invariant Face Recognition Using Near-Infrared Images. IEEE Transactions on Pattern Analysis and Machine Intelligence **29**(12), 627–639 (2007)
5. Xie, Z.H., Wu, S.Q., Fang, Z.J.: Infrared face recognition using LBP and discrimination patterns. Journal of Image and Graphics **17**(6), 707–711 (2012)
6. Lu, J.W., Plataniotis, K.N., Venetsanopoulos, A.N.: Face recognition using LDA-based algorithms. IEEE Transactions on Neural Networks **14**(1), 195–200 (2003)
7. Berg, T., Belhumeur, P.N.: Tom-vs-Pete Classifiers and Identity-Preserving Alignment for Face Verification. In: 2012 British Machine Vision Conference, pp. 1–11 (2012)
8. Ekenel, H.K, Stiefelhagen, R.: Two-class linear discriminant analysis for face recognition. In: 15th Signal Processing and Communications Applications, pp. 1–4 (2007)
9. Ojala, T., Pietikäinen, M.: Multi-resolution, Gray-Scale and Rotation Invariant Texture Classification with Local Binary Patterns. IEEE Transaction on Pattern Analysis and Machine Intelligence **24**(7), 971–987 (2002)

10. Ahonen, T., Hadid, A., Pietikäinen, M.: Face description with local binary patterns: application to face recognition. IEEE Transactions Pattern Analysis and Machine Intelligence **18**(12), 2037–2041 (2006)
11. Zhang, B.C., Shan, S.G., Gao, W.: Histogram of Gabor Phase Patterns (HGPP): A Novel Object Representation Approach for Face Recognition. IEEE Trans on Image Processing **16**(1), 57–68 (2007)
12. Liao, S., Chung, A.C.S.: Face Recognition with Salient Local Gradient Orientation Binary Pattern. In: 2009 IEEE International Conference on Image Processing, pp. 3317–3320 (2009)
13. Tan, X.Y., Triggs, B.: Enhanced Local Texture Feature Sets for Face Recognition under Difficult Lighting Conditions. IEEE Transactions on Image Processing **19**(6), 1635–1650 (2010)
14. Nanni, L., Brahnam, S., Lumini, A.: A simple method for improving local binary patterns by considering non-uniform patterns. Pattern Recognition **45**(10), 3844–3852 (2012)
15. Bianconi, F., Fernández, A.: On the Occurrence Probability of Local Binary Patterns: A Theoretical Study. Journal of Mathematical Imaging and Vision **40**(3), 259–268 (2011)
16. Liao, S., Law, M., Chung, C.S.: Dominant local binary patterns for texture. IEEE Transactions on Image Processing **18**(5), 1107–1118 (2009)

Image Classification Based on Discriminative Dictionary Pair Learning

Shuai Yuan, Huicheng Zheng$^{(\boxtimes)}$, and Dajun Lin

School of Information Science and Technology, Sun Yat-sen University,
135 West Xingang Road, Guangzhou 510275, China
zhenghch@mail.sysu.edu.cn

Abstract. Dictionary learning plays an increasingly important role in image classification in recent years. Most of existing dictionary learning methods aim to enhance discrimination of the learned dictionaries. Recently, learning a pair of dictionaries shows effectiveness and efficiency in image classification. Such a pair consists of a synthesis dictionary and a projective analysis dictionary. Different from traditional sparse representation, such a model enforces group sparsity based on structured representation of the pair of dictionaries, which consists with the objective of classification. In this paper, we propose to enhance the discrimination of coding coefficients to further improve the structure of the dictionary pair. More specifically, a regularization term on the coding coefficients is introduced to push pattern representations of the same class closer and those of different classes further away. At the classification stage, we use the learned dictionaries to improve image classification. The experimental results on several representative benchmark image databases demonstrate the effectiveness of the proposed method.

Keywords: Image classification · Dictionary learning · Sparse representation

1 Introduction

Recently, sparse representation has been successfully applied in image restoration [1-3], compressed sensing [4-5], and image classification [6-7]. It generally utilizes a linear combination of a few items sparsely selected from an over-complete dictionary to represent a query signal. Sparse representation based classification (SRC) [8] has achieved competitive performance on face recognition [8-11], handwritten digit recognition [12-15], and human action recognition [16-17], etc.

The performance of SRC depends on an appropriate dictionary. Generally, a discriminative dictionary can be learned from training samples to improve representation of query samples. At present, many methods for dictionary learning have been proposed. Broadly, the strategies adopted by existing methods can be classified into the following two categories.

© Springer International Publishing Switzerland 2015
J. Yang et al. (Eds.): CCBR 2015, LNCS 9428, pp. 176–185, 2015.
DOI: 10.1007/978-3-319-25417-3_22

The first strategy focuses on improving the structure of the dictionary. Instead of learning a shared dictionary for all classes, these methods learn class-specific structured dictionaries [13, 15, 18]. Ramirez *et al.* [13] proposed an incoherence promoting term to improve the pattern classification performance. Gu *et al.* [17] proposed dictionary pair learning (DPL), which can not only achieve competitive performance, but also greatly reduce the time complexity by introducing an extra projective analysis dictionary.

Another strategy concentrates on enhancing the discrimination of the coding coefficients. Zhang *et al.* [10] proposed D-KSVD, which incorporates the classification error into the objective function. Jiang *et al.* [19] proposed a modified KSVD algorithm named LC-KSVD, which includes label-consistent regularization to enforce the discrimination of coding vectors. Yang *et al.* [15] proposed Fisher discrimination dictionary learning (FDDL), where a discriminative coefficient term based on Fisher discrimination criterion is introduced to learn a structured dictionary. Cai *et al.* [16] proposed a support vector guided dictionary learning (SVGDL) model, which could adaptively assign different weights to different pairs of coding coefficients.

In this paper, we adopt the dictionary pair learning framework due to the efficient linear projective coding and consistence of group sparsity with class-specific discrimination. A pair of structured dictionaries, namely, the analysis dictionary and synthesis dictionary is implemented to represent the query sample. Inspired by Fisher discriminative criterion, we further introduce a discriminative coefficient term to enhance discrimination of the learned dictionaries and the coding coefficients. We show that the structure of the dictionary will be improved and therefore more suitable for image classification. In the classification stage, we use both the pair of dictionaries and the coding coefficients to improve the classification accuracy. Extensive experiments on image classification are carried out to demonstrate the effectiveness of the proposed method.

The rest of this paper is organized as follows. Section 2 introduces the proposed discriminative dictionary pair learning. Section 3 describes the optimization procedure of our model and summarizes the overall algorithm. Section 4 presents the classification scheme. Experimental results are reported in Section 5. Finally, this paper is concluded by Section 6.

2 Discriminative Dictionary Pair Learning

Let $X = [X_1, ..., X_k, ..., X_K]$ be the set of p-dimensional training samples, where K is the number of classes and X_k the subset of n training samples from class k. Denote the learned dictionary by D. Let A be the coding coefficient matrix of X over D. A general discriminative dictionary learning model [15, 16, 19] can be formulated under the following framework:

$$\{D^*, A^*\} = \arg \min_{D, A} \|X - DA\|_F^2 + \lambda_1 \|A\|_p + \lambda_2 \Psi(A) \qquad (1)$$

where λ_1 and λ_2 are parameters introduced to balance various terms in the objective function. $\|X - DA\|_F^2$ is the reconstruction term, $\|A\|_p$ is the l_p -norm regularization term, and $\Psi(A)$ denotes the discrimination term for A.

It is known that the l_0-norm or l_1-norm is effective for discrimination of the representation coefficients. However, the related optimization often leads to heavy computation. Besides, the role of sparse coding is still an open problem in classification. For classification, we would like that representations of the same class be close together, while those of different classes be far away. This coincides with group sparsity, where data items within the same class are expected to share the same sparsity pattern in their latent representation. In [17], group sparsity was realized through DPL, where a pair of structured dictionaries is implemented to enhance discrimination between different classes. Instead of solving a l_0-norm or l_1-norm optimization problem, DPL uses linear projection to obtain the coding coefficients efficiently. More specifically, an analysis dictionary (or projective matrix) P is introduced to approximate the coding coefficients A, i.e., $A \approx PX$. Considering the structured representation, the following minimization is implemented:

$$\min_{P,A} \sum_{k=1}^{K} \|P_k X_k - A_k\|_F^2 \tag{2}$$

The traditional reconstruction error is also included:

$$\min_{A,D} \sum_{k=1}^{K} \|X_k - D_k A_k\|_F^2 \tag{3}$$

where $\{D_k \in \Re^{p \times m}, P_k \in \Re^{m \times p}\}$ is a sub-dictionary pair corresponding to the k-th class, m is the number of atoms in the sub-dictionary for each class.

In DPL, the projective dictionary P_k is designed such that samples corresponding to the same class k can be well represented. That is, the energy of $P_k X_k$ will be much larger than $P_k X_i$, $\forall k \neq i$. Though DPL shows effectiveness in pattern classification, discrimination of coding coefficients is still not fully exploited. To further improve the structure of the learned dictionary pair, we propose to enhance discrimination of the coding coefficients of X_k over D_k. Inspired by Fisher discrimination criterion [15], we require that coding coefficients of the same class be close together, while those of different classes be far away. Since A is approximated by PX, the discriminative coefficient term is defined as:

$$f_k(P_k X_k) = \|P_k X_k - M_k\|_F^2 - \|m_k - m\|_2^2 \tag{4}$$

where m_k is the mean vector of all the column vectors of A_k (associated with $P_k X_k$), m is the mean vector of all class, and M_k is a matrix with all the columns being m_k.

Based on previous analysis, the overall objective function is defined as follows:

$$\{P^*, A^*, D^*\} = \arg \min_{P,A,D} \sum_{k=1}^{K} \|X_k - D_k A_k\|_F^2 + \tau \|P_k X_k - A_k\|_F^2 + \lambda \|P_k \tilde{X}_k\|_F^2$$

$$+ \omega(\|P_k X_k - M_k\|_F^2 - \|m_k - m\|_2^2) \quad s.t. \quad \|d_i\|_2^2 \leq 1 \tag{5}$$

where λ, ω, τ are scalar constants, $\widetilde{\boldsymbol{X}}_k$ denotes the samples in the whole training set $\boldsymbol{X}$ excluding $\boldsymbol{X}_k$, and $\boldsymbol{d}_i$ denotes the i-th atom of $\boldsymbol{D}$. The constraints $\|\boldsymbol{d}_i\|_2^2 \leq 1$ is introduced to avoid the trivial solution as in [17].

To appreciate the improved discrimination, we show the reconstruction errors $\|\boldsymbol{y} - \boldsymbol{D}_k^* \boldsymbol{P}_k^* \boldsymbol{y}\|_2^2$ on the Extended YaleB dataset with DPL and the proposed method, respectively, in Fig. 1. As expected, only the query samples which have the same class labels as $\boldsymbol{P}_k^*$ have small residuals. With the proposed method, query samples with class labels different from the sub-dictionaries have larger residuals than those with DPL. This is further confirmed in Fig. 2. The error ratio is defined as in (6). The proposed method significantly improves the discrimination of the learned dictionary pair.

$$Error\ ratio = \frac{\|\boldsymbol{y} - \boldsymbol{D}_k \boldsymbol{P}_k \boldsymbol{y}\|_2^2}{\sum_{i \neq k}^{K} \|\boldsymbol{y} - \boldsymbol{D}_i \boldsymbol{P}_i \boldsymbol{y}\|_2^2} \tag{6}$$

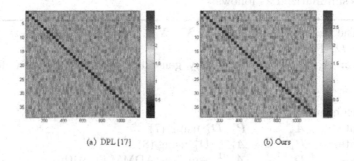

(a) DPL [17]   (b) Ours

Fig. 1. Reconstruction errors on Extended Yale B. The row and column numbers indicate the class indices and the test samples, respectively.

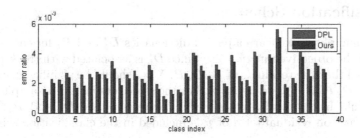

Fig. 2. Error ratio on Extended Yale B.

3 Optimization

To optimize (5), we adopt an alternative minimization approach for updating A and $\{D, P\}$. When $\{D, P\}$ are fixed, the minimization of A is a standard least squares problem. When A is fixed, the minimization of P is also a standard least squares problem. We can obtain their closed-form solutions as follows:

$$A_k^* = [D_k^T D_k + (\tau + \omega)I - \omega(\frac{1}{n} - \frac{2}{nK} + \frac{1}{nK^2})I]^{-1}$$

$$\cdot [D_k^T D_k + \tau P_k X_k + \frac{\omega}{n} P_k X_k \cdot 1 \cdot 1^T + \omega(\frac{1}{nK^2} - \frac{1}{nK}) \sum_{i=1}^{K} m_i \cdot 1^T] \tag{7}$$

$$P_k^* = (\tau A_k X_k^T + \omega M_k X_k^T)[(\tau + \omega)X_k X_k^T + \lambda \widetilde{X}_k \widetilde{X}_k^T]^{-1} \tag{8}$$

where $m_k = A_k \cdot 1/n$, $1 \in \Re^{n \times 1}$; $m = \sum_{k=1}^{K} m_i/K$; $M_k = m_k \cdot 1^T$. After updating P and A, we use the ADMM algorithm [17] to optimize D. The overall algorithm is summarized as follows:

---

1. Input: The training samples $X = [X_1, X_2, ..., X_K]$ and parameters: τ, λ, ω.
2. Output: D, P
3. Initialize: A, D, P are randomly generated with unit l_2-norm for each column.
4. repeat
5.   **for** each class **do**
6.   update $A_k^{i+1} \longleftarrow P_k^i, D_k^i$ using (7)
7.   update $P_k^{i+1} \longleftarrow A_k^{i+1}, D_k^i$ using (8)
8.   update $D_k^{i+1} \longleftarrow A_k^{i+1}$ using the ADMM algorithm
9.   **end for**
10. until converge
11. return D, P

---

4 Classification Scheme

In the training phase, we learn a pair of dictionaries D_k^* and P_k^* for each class by minimizing the objective function (5). Since D_k^* is associated with the k-th class, it is expected that the residual $\|X_k - D_k^* P_k^* X_k\|_F$ should be significantly smaller than $\|X_i - D_k^* P_k^* X_i\|_F$, where $i \neq k$. For the same reason, a test sample y from class k should have trivial residuals when represented by D_k^* and P_k^*. Hence, the reconstruction residual term of y is included in the classification scheme:

$$e_{1,i} = \|y - D_i^* P_i^* y\|_2 \tag{9}$$

As in [15], we further exploit traditional sparse coding coefficients to improve the classification performance:

$$\hat{a} = \arg\min_a \|y - Da\|_2^2 + \lambda_1 \|a\|_1 \tag{10}$$

where λ_1 is a constant. The solution is denoted by $\hat{a} = [\hat{a}_1; \hat{a}_2; \ldots; \hat{a}_K]$, where $\hat{a}_i$ is the coefficient sub-vector associated with class i. Define coding vectors $a_i = [0; \ldots; \hat{a}_i; \ldots; 0]$. Considering the global characteristics of P, we expect that for the query sample y from the i-th class, Py should be close to the sparse coding vector a_i. Therefore, the following term is included in the classification scheme,

$$e_{2,i} = \|Py - a_i\|_2 \tag{11}$$

During the process of solving coding vectors in (10), the choice of the dictionary D is important. As in [15], when the number of training samples is small, we should use the full D to faithfully represent the query sample. When each sub-dictionary D_i has considerable size, D_i will be used directly in (10) to obtain $\hat{a}_i$.

The final classification scheme is defined as follows:

$$identity(y) = \arg\min_i \{e_i\} \tag{12}$$

Where $e_i = e_{1,i} + \beta e_{2,i}$, β is a constant to balance the relative contributions of the two terms for classification.

5   Experiments

To validate the performance of our method, we carry out experiments on three databases, including Extended YaleB [20], AR [21], and MNIST [22]. We compare the proposed approach to SVM, FDDL [15], SVGDL [16], and DPL [17]. All experiments are run on a desktop PC with 3.4GHz Intel Core i7-3770 CPU and 8 GB memory.

5.1   Face Recognition

The experimental settings in this part are the same as those in [19]. Random faces [8] are used as feature descriptors. Each face image is projected onto a p-dimensional feature vector with a randomly generated matrix from a zero-mean normal distribution. Each row of the matrix is l_2 normalized. The random-face feature dimension is 504 for Extended YaleB and 540 for AR face. We use the whole D to obtain coding vectors. The parameters are set as: $\tau = 0.5$, $\omega = 0.5$, $\lambda = 0.001$, $\lambda_1 = 0.5$, $\beta = 10^2$.

1). *Extended Yale B:* This database consists of 2,414 frontal-face images from 38 individuals. It has large variations in illumination and expressions, as illustrated in Fig. 3. For each subject, we randomly select half of the images for training and the remaining images for testing. The results of different competing algorithms are listed in Table 1. It can be seen that our method has a significant improvement over the other methods. In the testing phase, when only using $e_{1,i}$ term, the accuracy has slight promotion. When only using $e_{2,i}$ term, it achieves a recognition rate of over 98.67%, 1.17% higher than that of PDL. The combination of $e_{1,i}$ and $e_{2,i}$ shows the overall best performance.

Fig. 3. Sample images in the Extended Yale B database.

Table 1. The recognition rates on the Extended Yale B database.

Algorithms	SVM	FDDL	SVGDL	DPL	$e_{1,i}$	$e_{2,i}$	$e_{1,i} + e_{2,i}$
Accuracy rate	95.60%	96.70%	97.20%	97.50%	97.66%	98.67%	**98.84%**

2). AR: This database contains over 4,000 frontal face images correspond-ing to 126 individuals with different expressions (neutral, smile, anger, scream), illumination conditions (left light on, right light on, all side lights on), and occlu-sions (sun glasses and scarf), as illustrated in Fig. 4. For each subject, 26 pictures were taken in two sessions. We choose a subset consisting of 50 males and 50 females. For each subject, we select randomly 20 images for training and the other 6 images for testing. We carry out two experiments with different training samples.

Fig. 4. Sample images in the AR database.

Experiment 1. For each subject, we select 20 images containing at least one with the scream expression for training. The results are listed in Table 2. With only the $e_{1,i}$ term, the results are comparable to those of DPL. The $e_{2,i}$ term shows significant advantage. Finally, the combination of $e_{1,i}$ and $e_{2,i}$ achieves the best results among all the competing methods.

Experiment 2. The scream expression only exists in the testing set, but not in the training set. The results are listed in Table 3. It can be seen that the recognition rates of all methods deteriorate significantly. Our method achieves

Table 2. The recognition rates on AR database in Experiment 1.

Algorithms	SVM	FDDL	SVGDL	DPL	$e_{1,i}$	$e_{2,i}$	$e_{1,i} + e_{2,i}$
Accuracy	96.50%	97.52%	97.43%	98.83%	98.30%	99.17%	**99.21%**

Table 3. The recognition rates on AR database in Experiment 2.

Algorithms	SVM	FDDL	SVGDL	DPL	**Ours** $(e_{1,i} + e_{2,i})$
Accuracy	88.67%	89.12%	88.69%	88.74%	**91.77%**

the best performance with a 2.65% improvement of accuracy over the second best result. The experiment verified the robustness of our method.

5.2 Handwritten Digit Recognition

We further evaluate our method for handwritten digit recognition on the MNIST database. The MNIST database contains a training set of 60000 images, and a test set of 10000 images. The digits have been size-normalized and centered in a fixes-size image of 28×28 pixels, as illustrated in Fig. 5. In the experiment, for each digit, we randomly select a number of images from the training set for training. The whole test set is used for testing. HOG features of different dimensions are implemented in the experiments. We use the sub-dictionary D_i to obtain coding vectors. The parameters are set as: $\tau = 0.003$, $\omega = 0.0001$, $\lambda = 0.00002$, $\lambda_1 = 50$, $\beta = 10$.

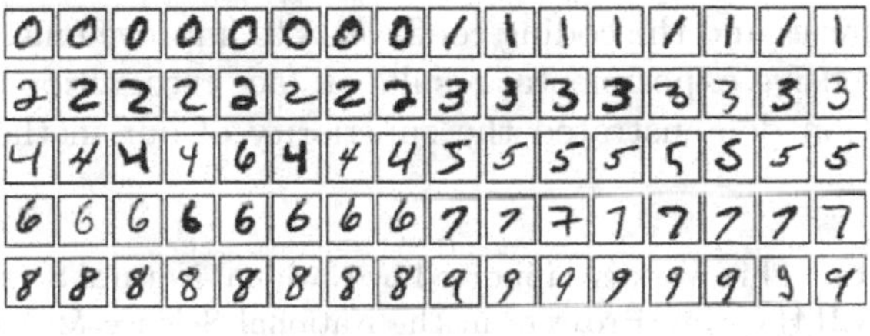

Fig. 5. Sample images in MNIST.

Experiment 1. We select 50 training samples for each digit with features of different dimensions. The results of different competing algorithms are listed in Table 4. Our method has slight improvement compared to other methods. The accuracy increases with the increasing dimension.

Experiment 2. We use 1984-dimensional features with different numbers of training samples. The results are recorded in Table 5. We can see that the accuracy increases with the increasing number of samples. But when the number of samples is large enough, the accuracy only increases slightly.

Table 4. The recognition rates on the MNIST database with features of different dimensions.

Dimension	SVM	FDDL	SVGDL	DPL	Ours
755	94.10%	94.42%	93.38%	94.63%	**94.88%**
1116	94.61%	94.62%	93.77%	95.28%	**95.40%**
1984	94.88%	95.36%	94.25%	95.60%	**95.96%**

Table 5. The recognition rates on the MNIST database with different numbers of training samples.

TrainNum	SVM	FDDL	SVGDL	DPL	Ours (D)	Ours (D_i)
50	94.88%	95.36%	94.25%	95.60%	95.69%	**95.96%**
100	96.29%	96.34%	95.58%	96.95%	97.24%	**97.39%**
200	96.96%	96.96%	96.08%	97.71%	97.84%	**97.96%**
500	97.91%	98.01%	97.00%	98.19%	98.17%	**98.28%**
1000	98.04%	98.09%	97.50%	98.39%	98.36%	**98.40%**
1500	98.15%	98.18%	97.80%	98.55%	98.57%	**98.57%**
2000	98.33%	98.33%	98.10%	98.59%	98.64%	**98.78%**

6   Conclusion

In this paper, we propose a discriminative dictionary pair learning approach for image classification. The classical dictionary pair learning learns an analysis dictionary to express the coding coefficients and a synthesis dictionary to reconstruct query samples. We introduce a discriminative coefficient term to enhance discrimination of the learned dictionaries. During classification, we utilize both the pair of dictionaries and the coding coefficients to improve image classification performance. Extensive experimental results on face recognition and handwritten digit recognition demonstrated the superiority of our method to state-of-the-art methods.

Acknowledgments. This work is supported by National Natural Science Foundation of China (No. 61172141), Key Projects in the National Science & Technology Pillar Program during the 12th Five-Year Plan Period (No. 2012BAK16B06), and Major Projects for the Innovation of Industry and Research of Guangzhou.

References

1. Mairal, J., Elad, M., Sapiro, G.: Sparse representation for color image restoration. IEEE Trans. Image Processing **17**(1), 53–69 (2008)
2. Yang, J., Wright, J., Huang, T.S., Ma, Y.: Image super-resolution via sparse representation. IEEE Trans. Image Processing **19**(11), 2861–2873 (2010)
3. Mairal, J., Bach, F., Ponce, J., Sapiro, G.: Online learning for matrix factorization and sparse coding. J. Machine Learning Research **11**, 19–60 (2010)
4. Baraniuk, R.: Compressive sensing. IEEE Signal Processing Magazine **24**(4), 118–121 (2007)

5. Candes, E.: Compressive sampling. Int. Congress of Mathematics **3**, 1433–1452 (2006)
6. Yang, J., Yu, K., Gong, Y., Huang, T.: Linear spatial pyramid matching using sparse coding for image classification. In: CVPR, pp. 1794–1801 (2009)
7. Shabou, A., LeBorgne, H.: Locality-constrained and spatially regularized coding for scene categorization. In: CVPR, pp. 3618–3625 (2012)
8. Wright, J., Yang, A.Y., Ganesh, A., Sastry, S.S., Ma, Y.: Robust face recognition via sparse representation. IEEE Trans. PAMI **31**(2), 210–227 (2009)
9. Yang, M., Zhang, L.: Gabor feature based sparse representation for face recognition with Gabor occlusion dictionary. In: Daniilidis, K., Maragos, P., Paragios, N. (eds.) ECCV 2010, Part VI. LNCS, vol. 6316, pp. 448–461. Springer, Heidelberg (2010)
10. Zhang, Q., Li, B.X.: Discriminative K-SVD for dictionary learning in face recognition. In: CVPR, pp. 2691–2698 (2010)
11. Yang, M., Zhang, L., Yang, J., Zhang, D.: Robust sparse coding for face recognition. In: CVPR, pp. 625–632 (2011)
12. Mairal, J., Bach, F., Ponce, J., Sapiro, G., Zisserman, A.: Supervised dictionary learning. In: NIPS (2009)
13. Ramirez, I., Sprechmann, P., Sapiro, G.: Classification and clustering via dictionary learning with structured incoherence and shared features. In: CVPR, pp. 3501–3508 (2010)
14. Yang, J.C., Yu, K., Huang, T.: Supervised translation-invariant sparse coding. In: CVPR, pp. 3517–3524 (2010)
15. Yang, M., Zhang, L., Feng, X., Zhang, D.: Fisher discrimination dictionary learning for sparse representation. In: ICCV, pp. 543–550 (2011)
16. Cai, S., Zuo, W., Zhang, L., Feng, X., Wang, P.: Support vector guided dictionary learning. In: Fleet, D., Pajdla, T., Schiele, B., Tuytelaars, T. (eds.) ECCV 2014, Part IV. LNCS, vol. 8692, pp. 624–639. Springer, Heidelberg (2014)
17. Gu, S.H., Zhang, L., Zuo, W.M., Feng, X.C.: Projective dictionary pair learning for pattern classification. In: NIPS (2014)
18. Gao, S., Tsang, I., Ma, Y.: Learning category-specific dictionary and shared dictionary for fine-grained image categorization. IEEE Trans. Image Processing **23**(2), 623–634 (2013)
19. Jiang, Z., Lin, Z., Davis, L.: Label consistent K-SVD: learning a discriminative dictionary for recognition. IEEE Trans. PAMI **35**(11), 2651–2664 (2013)
20. Georghiades, A., Belhumeur, P., Kriegman, D.: From few to many: Illumination cone models for face recognition under variable lighting and pose. IEEE Trans. PAMI **23**(6), 643–660 (2001)
21. Martinez, A., Benavente., R.: The AR face database. CVC Technical Report (1998)
22. LeCun, Y., Bottou, L., Bengio, Y., Haffner, P.: Gradient-based learning applied to document recognition. Proceedings of the IEEE **86**(11), 2278–2324 (1998)

Weber Local Gradient Pattern (WLGP) Method for Face Recognition

Shanshan Fang, Jucheng Yang$^{(\boxtimes)}$, Na Liu, and Yarui Chen

College of Computer Science and Information Engineering,
Tianjin University of Science and Technology, Tianjin, China
jcyang@tust.edu.cn

Abstract. Robust and discriminative feature extraction without any controlled light intensity condition is vital for a real-time face recognition system. The Weber Local Descriptor (WLD) is an effective and robust face representation algorithm. However, WLD actually exploits the contrast information, which can still be sensitive to illumination changes. To overcome this problem, in this article, we take gradients into account and propose a novel operator, called Weber Local Gradient Descriptor (WLGD).This method produces the fusion characteristic and describes the facial texture through the computation of horizontal and diagonal gradients respectively. Experimental results on the ORL face database and infrared face database demonstrate that the proposed WLGD algorithm outperforms some state-of-art methods.

Keywords: Feature extraction · Face representation · Weber local descriptor · Weber local gradient descriptor · ORL · Infrared face database

1   Introduction

As one of the most important biometric technologies (fingerprint, palmprint, voice, iris), the facial expression contains luxuriant information about human behavior, and automatic face recognition has been adopted to the fields of the social security, entrance guard system, electronic commerce, law enforcement and surveillance [1], due to its universality, uniqueness, stability and collectability.

Facial expression recognition system composes of expression image collecting and preprocessing, face detection, expression feature extraction as well as expression classification. As an important part of the facial expression recognition system, expression feature extraction is also a pivotal step to improve the expression classification accuracy. In recent years, a range of face recognition methods have been presented to overcome the variations among illumination, shelter and posture. In general, they can be divided into two categories: global approaches and local approaches.

The global approaches usually extract features from the whole face image. For instance, Principal Components Analysis (PCA) [2] method is popular in face recognition. The Fisherfaces [3] method tried to construct a subspace, which could maximize the between-class differences and minimize the intra-class differences. Whereas, these global methods are sensitive to variations in expressions, occlusions poses and so on.

© Springer International Publishing Switzerland 2015
J. Yang et al. (Eds.): CCBR 2015, LNCS 9428, pp. 186–192, 2015.
DOI: 10.1007/978-3-319-25417-3_23

On the contrary, the local approaches generally divide the facial image into several components from which can extract features separately. The Local Binary Pattern (LBP) [4] as well as its extension versions, such as Local Gradient Pattern (LGP) [5] and Center-Symmetric Local Binary Patterns [6] have been considered to extract the local features in face images. Weber Local Descriptor (WLD) [7] is a simple but powerful local operator. Nevertheless, those methods mentioned above are dense descriptors computed for every pixel and depend on the local intensity variation and the center pixel's intensity, in this paper, we present a novel descriptor, called Weber Local Gradient Pattern (WLGP), for face recognition. The proposed WLGD operator, through taking gradients into account from horizontal, vertical and diagonal respectively, acquires the encoding features.

The remainder of this article is organized as follows. Section 2 gives the brief review of the WLD technology, and then introduces our proposed WLGD method in detail. In section 3, we demonstrate the experimental results on both ORL and infrared face database, and analysis to account for the superiority of our proposed algorithm. Finally, conclusion is given in Section 4.

2   Proposed Method

In this section, we firstly introduce the basic method of Weber Local Descriptor (WLD) briefly. And then, the proposed method, called Weber Local Gradient Descriptor (WLGD) operator, is described for face representation.

2.1   Weber Local Descriptor

Weber's Law suggests that the ratio between the perceptual increment threshold and the background intensity is a constant, and it can be defined as Eq. (1):

$$\frac{\Delta I}{I} = k, \tag{1}$$

where I is the background intensity, ΔI is the perceptual increment threshold. And k is a constant, which is usually regarded as Weber fraction.

Inspired from Weber's Law, Chen et al. presented Weber Local Descriptor (WLD), and this local pattern operator empirically justified to be more effective than LBP and other local algorithms. The WLD can be expressed as Eq. (2):

$$WLD\,(x_c) = \arctan\left[\sum_{i=0}^{P-1}(\frac{x_i - x_c}{x_c})\right], \tag{2}$$

where P is the neighborhood size, x_i represents the surrounding pixels which equally sampled from x_0 to x_{P-1}, and x_c denotes the center pixel value surrounded by x_i . arctan is the arctangent function that contributes to increase the robustness of WLD against noise. A slight modification of the approach describes as:

$$WLD\,(x_c) = \arctan\left[\alpha\sum_{i=0}^{P-1}(\frac{x_i - x_c}{x_c + \lambda})\right]. \tag{3}$$

here, α is a factor which is able to magnify or shrink the difference between neighbors. To avoid division by zero, λ is assigned a small constant value.

2.2   Proposed WLGD

The WLD method is certainly a simple and robust local descriptor. However, with the limitation that it only considered the gray relationship between the center pixel and neighboring pixels, the more effective and discriminative information among the surrounding pixels is ignored.

Therefore, for the above shortcomings, in this article, a novel and more stable local operator, which is called Weber Local Gradient Descriptor, is proposed.

The algorithm formula is expressed in Eq. (3)-(4) below, using the 3×3 neighborhood template as shown in Fig.1, comparing the level of eight peripheral pixels, horizontal and diagonal gradients, and then we get the WLGD value.

x_0	x_1	x_2
x_7	x_c	x_3
x_6	x_5	x_4

Fig. 1. A 3×3 template of WLGD operator

$$WLGD = \arctan\left[\alpha \frac{1}{x_m + \lambda}\left((x_0 - x_2) + (x_7 - x_3) + (x_6 - x_4) + (x_0 - x_4) + (x_2 - x_6)\right)\right] \quad (4)$$

$$x_m = \frac{1}{8}\sum_{i=0}^{7} x_i \quad (5)$$

where x_m is the mean of the neighboring pixels, the default values for α and λ are empirically 3 and 1×10^{-7} [8], respectively, in our experiments.

The presented WLGD method has the following properties:

- The WLGD manner can bring into correspondence with the trends of the other feature points in facial images, such as mouth, facial muscles, eyes and so on, meanwhile, it also takes fully account of the effects that face texture changes in different directions on the expression.
- Unlike WLD exploits the contrast information, the presented encoding method uses the gradient-based remainder which shows more effective information and is more stable and reliable against the illumination variations.
- Comparing with the conventional LBP operator which generates a binary string at first and then converts this sequence to a decimal value, the proposed encoding algorithm directly takes the intensity values to calculate the transformation instead of producing intermediate binary sequence values. So it can effectively avoid the loss of information during the conversion.

As can be observed from Fig. 2 which illustrates the WLD and WLGD, the WLD operator extracts prominent features while neglecting details. Whereas, the WLGD considers more detailed structures, such as eyes, forehead and mouth, and fully utilizes the gradient texture information in the facial images.

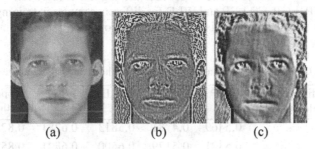

(a)   (b)   (c)

Fig. 2. (a) Original image from ORL database; (b) WLD (c) WLGD

3   Experimental Results

We carried out our experiments on the public ORL face database and the infrared face database to evaluate the effectiveness of the WLGD method.

The ORL face database is composed of 400 visible light facial images. It contains 40 individuals with various illuminations and poses. The examples of ORL face database are demonstrated in Fig. 3. The infrared face database is captured by Thermo Vision A40 infrared camera [9]. This database consists of 50 subjects with 20 images per person. Every original image size is 320×240, after face detection and normalization, the image size is 60×80. And the samples of the database are revealed in Fig. 4.

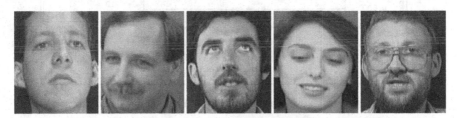

Fig. 3. Some samples in ORL database

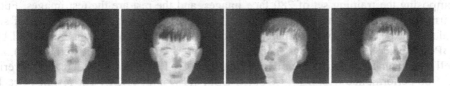

Fig. 4. Part of infrared face samples

3.1   Experiments on ORL Database

In this paper, we firstly make a series of simulation experiment with different training samples number from 2 to 9, and the remaining images will be taken as the testing samples correspondently. From Table 1. and Fig. 5, we can easily observe the fact that our proposed method is the best one which has the highest recognition rate among others, such as LBP, LGP, CS-LBP and WLD for different samples in training set. And when the training samples number is 8 and 9, the recognition rate utilizing WLGD operator can arrive at 100% .

Table 1. Comparison experiments of different methods on ORL database

Methods of different training samples	LBP	LGP	CSLBP	WLD	Proposed method
2	0.5469	0.4781	0.5813	0.6281	0.8281
3	0.5321	0.5179	0.6500	0.6821	0.8536
4	0.6417	0.5750	0.7208	0.7375	0.9167
5	0.6800	0.6400	0.7550	0.8150	0.9400
6	0.7063	0.6875	0.8000	0.8250	0.9500
7	0.7333	0.7333	0.8083	0.8667	0.9917
8	0.7375	0.7125	0.8000	0.9000	1.0000
9	0.8250	0.7750	0.8000	0.9250	1.0000

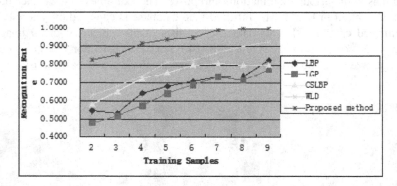

Fig. 5. Comparison experiments of different methods on ORL database

Then, we take the former 7 face images of each person as the trained samples, composing the training set of 280 face images, and the rest are the test images. Furthermore, to measure the superiority of the proposed operator, through a mass of simulation experiments, we compare the recognition rates of our method with WLD, LBP and other variant versions of LBP, which are Local Gradient Pattern (LGP), as well as Center-Symmetric Local Binary Pattern (CS-LBP). Table 2. depicts the verification performance with LBP, LGP, CS-LBP, WLD and WLGD. The results of each method demonstrate that our proposed method archives much better recognition rate, 99.17%. Thus we conclude that WLGD is more effective and robust than other ones.

Table 2. Performance comparison using different methods on ORL database

Method	LBP	LGP	CS-LBP	WLD	Proposed method
Accuracy	0.7333	0.7333	0.8083	0.8667	0.9917

3.2   Experiments on Infrared Face Database

To explain the stability of the WLGD operator, we also make simulation experiments on infrared face database. In these experiments, for each person, 10 images for training, and the rest 10 images for testing. Table 3. illustrates that compared with LBP, LGP, CS-LBP and WLD, the recognition rate of our proposed method can reach 97.40%, which is more discriminative and efficient than other algorithms.

Table 3. Performance comparison using different methods on infrared face database

Method	LBP	LGP	CS-LBP	WLD	Proposed method
Accuracy	92.40	93.00	93.28	95.40	97.40

4   Conclusion

This paper proposes the Weber Local Gradient Descriptor (WLGD) method, and applies it to face recognition. And this operator can exploit gradient information from horizontal and diagonal direction separately. By this way, the most discriminative and effective texture features extracted with some special directions can contribute to the further investigation. At the same time, WLGD directly takes the intensity values to calculate the transformation instead of converting a binary string to a decimal value of LBP, which can effectively avoid the loss of information during the conversion. And the experimental results prove that, in comparison with original WLD, LBP and other existing LBP-based methods conducted on ORL face database and infrared face database, the WLGD is significantly superior to other methods even in the extreme condition of illumination variation and facial expression.

Acknowledgement. This paper was supported by the National Natural Science Foundation of China under Grant 61402332 and the 2015 key projects of Tianjin science and technology support program No.15ZCZDGX00200.

References

1. Zhao, W., Chellappa, R., Phillips, P.J., Rosenfeld, A.: Face recognition: a literature survey. ACM Comput. Surv. (CSUR) **35**, 399–458 (2003)
2. Turk, M., Pentland, A.: Eigenfaces for recognition. J. Cognitive Neuroscience **3**, 71–86 (1991)
3. Belhumeur, P.N., Hespanha, J.P., Kriegman, D.J.: Eigenfaces vs. fisherfaces: Recognition using class specific linear projection. IEEE Trans. Pattern Analysis and Machine Intelligence **20**, 71–86 (1997)
4. Ahonen, T., Hadid, A., Pietikainen, M.: Face description with local binary patterns: Application to face recognition. IEEE Transactions on Pattern Analysis and Machine Intelligence **28**(12), 2037–2041 (2006)
5. Jun, B., Kim, D.: Robust face detection using local gradient patterns and evidence accumulation. Pattern Recognit. **45**(9), 3304–3316 (2012)
6. Heikkilä, M., Pietikäinen, M., Schmid, C.: Description of interest regions with center-symmetric local binary patterns. In: Kalra, P.K., Peleg, S. (eds.) ICVGIP 2006. LNCS, vol. 4338, pp. 58–69. Springer, Heidelberg (2006)
7. Chen, J., Shan, S., He, C., Zhao, G., Pietikainen, M., Chen, X., Gao, W.: WLD: a robust local image descriptor. IEEE Trans, On PAMI **32**(9), 1705–1720 (2010)
8. Wang, B., Li, W., Yang, W., Liao, Q.: Illumination normalization based on weber's law with application to face recognition. IEEE Signal Process. Lett. **18**(8), 462–465 (2011)
9. Wu, S.Q., Jiang, L.J., Xie, S.L., et al.: Infrared face recognition by using blood perfusion data. In: Audio and Video-based Biometric Person Authentication, New York, pp. 320–328 (2005)
10. Wu, Y., Jiang, Y.Y., Zhao, Y.C., Li, W.F., Lu, Z.Q., Liao, Q.M.: Generalized Weber-face for illumination-robust face recognition. Neurocomputing **136**, 262–267 (2014)
11. Chen, C.J., Ross, A.: Local Gradient Gabor Pattern (LGGP) with Applications in Face Recognition, Cross-spectral Matching and Soft Biometrics. In: Proc. of SPIE Biometric and Surveillance Technology for Human and Activity Identification X, (Baltimore, USA), May 2013
12. Jiang, Y.Y., Wang, B., Zhou, Y.C., Li, W.F., Liao, Q.M.: Patterns of Weber magnitude and orientation for uncontrolled face representation and recognition. Neurocomputing **165**, 190–201 (2015)
13. Zhu, C., Bichot, C.E., Chen, L.M.: Image region description using orthogonal combination of local binary patterns enhanced with color information. Pattern Recognition **46**, 1949–1963 (2013)

Multi-task Attribute Joint Feature Learning

Lu Chang, Yuchun Fang[⊠], and Xiaoda Jiang

School of Computer Engineering and Science, Shanghai University, Shanghai 200444, China
ycfang@shu.edu.cn

Abstract. Recognizing face attributes can improve face recognition as well as provides useful information in face image retrieval. Usually the attributes are studied separately. Considering that the attributes are inter-related, they can be regarded as sharing common data structure. In this paper, we propose to take advantage of Multi-task learning (MTL) framework to learn attribute feature simultaneously. Specifically, the attributes are divided into several tasks. The attribute feature information can be better shared across the tasks with MTL. According to the value of weight vectors of all features learnt by MTL, we can select much lower number of feature dimension for attribute recognition without losing the prediction precision. The experiments are conducted on LFW database with nine face attributes from three tasks to verify our method. The experiment results compared with Single Task Learning (STL) show the effectiveness of the proposed method.

Keywords: Face attribute · Joint feature learning · Multi-task learning · Attribute recognition

1 Introduction

Facial attributes (e.g., gender, race, expression) are high level semantic descriptions of human face. Face attribute classification has become one of the most active research topics in recent years with various applications such as face verification [1], image retrieval [2] and similar attribute search [8]. However, attributes are usually learnt independently. The interrelation among the attributes is often ignored in practice.

In many machine learning problems, we usually have multiple correlated learning tasks. Traditionally we train a model using samples of each task individually, that is, Single Task Learning (STL), as shown in Fig. 1(a). When there are n kinds of attributes, STL takes every attribute as a task. We train a model for each task independently, thus we obtain n models for attribute recognition, and no relationship exists among tasks. However, the learning problems among tasks are often related in practice. Instead of learning the tasks independently, Multi-Task Learning (MTL) considers each learning problem as a separate task. It can learn them together by capturing the intrinsic correlation among tasks, as illustrated in Fig. 1(b). When there are n kinds of attributes, MTL divides them into m tasks according to their characteristics. We train models using the samples of all tasks simultaneously and obtain m models for attribute recognition. They are learnt by sharing the data information of all

© Springer International Publishing Switzerland 2015
J. Yang et al. (Eds.): CCBR 2015, LNCS 9428, pp. 193–200, 2015.
DOI: 10.1007/978-3-319-25417-3_24

samples. MTL has been widely applied in various fields, such as visual tracking [3], action recognition [4], neural semantic basis discovery [5].

In [7], multi-task learning is applied in race and gender classification of human. But it considers only binary-class problem. In reality, many facial attributes are multi-class problem. In multi-class problem, we need to explore more complex factors to learn the relationships among them. The richness of face attribute information makes the research on multi-class attribute becomes realizable. So in this paper, inspired by the work of [7], we propose multi-task attribute joint feature learning. By analyzing the relationship among attributes, we classify the attributes into several tasks. Then through sharing data structure information among related tasks with MTL, we can select more effective feature for feature components of different attributes

The rest part of this paper is organized as follows. Section 2 presents a brief review of related work in attribute learning and multi-task learning. In Section 3, we introduce the algorithm in detail. In Section 4, we evaluate our method on the challenging dataset LFW, which shows the effectiveness of our method. At last, Section 5 concludes our paper.

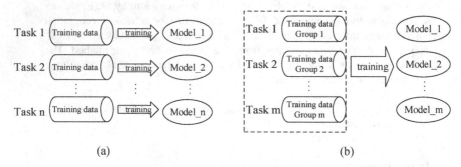

(a)   (b)

Fig. 1. STL (a) vs. MTL (b)

2   Related Work

Facial attributes possess rich information about people and automatically detected human attributes has attracted significant interest in different applications recently. Kumar et al. [1] proposed a learning framework to automatically detect visual attributes and achieve excellent performance on keyword-based face image retrieval. Siddiquie et al. [9] extended the framework to deal with multi-attribute queries. To further improve the quality of attributes, Luo et al. [10] estimated facial attributes by organizing discriminative decision trees into a sum-product network. In [11], a novel deep learning framework was proposed. It cascaded two convolutional neural networks for face localization and attribute prediction respectively. Fang and Chang [14] utilized multi-instance feature learning with sparse representation for facial expression attribute recognition. However, the relationship among attributes is rarely considered. In our work, we try to exploit the correlations among the attributes so as to learn more sophisticated feature representation for face attribute prediction.

Multi-task learning has drawn a lot of interest in the machine learning community. It is used in situations where one has to solve a few related learning problems. It enables a task to be learnt using the data from multiple related tasks, thus information can be better shared across tasks. This can result in a better predictive performance than the individual task. Many approaches have been proposed to design various MTL algorithms effectively by capturing the similarity among them. Chen et al. [12] proposed a linear MTL formulation in which the model parameter can be decomposed into a sparse component and a low-rank component. Zhang et al. [16] proposed a robust Multi-task Feature Learning algorithm (rMTFL) which can recognize abnormal task in the related tasks. As facial attributes can also be seen as sharing common data structure, in this paper, we apply the MTL framework of [15] in multi-class attribute feature learning to obtain the weight vectors of all features, thus we can select a much lower dimensional feature representation according to the value of weights for recognition without losing the prediction precision.

3   Proposed Method

Different from [7], we consider more than a simple binary classification problem. Given P tasks $S=\{s_1, s_2,...,s_P\}$ with each task s_i containing k_i kinds of attributes. In binary classification problem, the value of k_i is equal to 2. But in our proposed method, the value of k_i can be greater than 2. So there are a total of $n = \sum_{i=1}^{P} k_i$ kinds of attributes. Denote the M dimension training samples of the i-th kind attribute as $A^{(i)} = [z_1^{(i)},...,z_{N_i}^{(i)}]^T \in R^{N_i \times M}$. Each row of A represents a sample; N_i represents the number of training samples. The task s_i can be denoted as $s_i = [A^{(1)},...,A^{(k_i)}]^T$. The combination of all P tasks is written as $S=[s_1, s_2,...,s_P]^T \in R^{N \times M}$, where $N = \sum_{i=1}^{n} N$ is the total number of samples. The response label vector is denoted as

$$y = [\overbrace{l_1,...,l_1}^{N_1}, \overbrace{l_2,...,l_2}^{N_i}, ..., \overbrace{l_n,...,l_n}^{N_n}]^T \in R^n,$$

where l_i represents the label of the i-th kind attribute. The object loss function of the multi-task feature learning model can be defined as the following problem:

$$\min_{W} \left\{ \sum_{i=1}^{P} \| s_i w_i - y_i \|^2 + \lambda r(W) \right\} \qquad (1)$$

where $W=[w_1,...,w_P] \in R^{M \times P}$ is the weight matrix with the i-th column w_i belonging to the weight vector of the i-th task s_i; $\lambda > 0$ is a regularized parameter; $r(W)$ is a model-specific regularizer (for example, a non-convex regularizer). Here we adopt l_2-norm restriction to get the equation of the objective function, as shown in Eq. (2):

$$\min_{W} \left\{ \sum_{i=1}^{P} \| s_i w_i - y_i \|^2 + \lambda \sum_{k=1}^{M} \| w^k \|_2 \right\} \qquad (2)$$

Through Eq. (2), we get the optimal solution W. For the i-th task s_i, the higher value of w_i means that it is more effective for feature components. Then we can select the feature according to the descending order of w_i. When the number of tasks is 1, the multi-task learning problem will convert into single task problem. In our experiments, the framework of process is shown in Fig. 2. The number of tasks P is 3. The number of attributes n is 9. We set $l_i=i$ to differentiate the labels. Then, we can get the weight vectors of features through optimizing the objection function of multi-task learning. We can select features by the weights. In the prediction step, we train models by using the learned feature to perform attribute recognition.

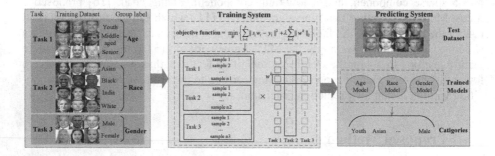

Fig. 2. Framework of our proposed method.

4   Experimental Protocol and Results Analysis

4.1   Experiment Results and Discussion

In this paper, we use the challenging LFW database [17] to evaluate the performance of our proposed method. LFW consists of 13233 images from 5749 subjects, which varies in pose, illumination and environment. We aligned the faces based on the eye positions through the locations of 10 facial feature points [6], and normalized them to 140 * 160. We select 9 kinds of attributes which are considered as important biometric traits for human recognition and divide these attributes into 3 tasks. The specific information is shown in Table 1. The sample set forms our facial attribute database in experiment.

Recently, both Uniform Local Binary Pattern (ULBP) features [18] and Local Difference (LD) features [19] have shown good performance in face recognition. In our study, we want to use advanced features for facial attribute representation, thus we extract ULBP and LD features of the whole face respectively for our method. The ULBP is obtained by dividing the face image into several regions from which the LBP histograms are extracted and concatenating them into an enhanced feature vector. In this experiment, the face images are divided into 56 blocks. In every block, we collect 59 pixels. Thus, we get 3304 dimensional ULBP features. LD considers the local variations of facial images. Unlike other local coding approaches, it extracts direction information of both first-order and second-order difference. Here the direction of the parameter is set to 17, blocking number is 7 * 8 and finally we get the 952 dimensional LD feature. In our experiments, the libsvm [13] is used to train the classifiers.

Table 1. The distribution of the subset for classification

Task	Attribute	# of sample
	Middle Aged	1000
Age	Senior	1000
	Youth	1000
	Asian	800
Race	Black	1000
	Indian	1000
	White	1000
Gender	Male	1000
	Female	1000

4.2   Experiment Results and Discussion

To evaluate the robustness of the proposed method, we compare the experiment results from two aspects as descripted in section 4.2.1 and section 4.2.2. To verify our
method, we repeat the experiments 5 times. Every time for each attribute we choose
500 samples randomly from the attribute database to constitute the training set and the
rest of this attribute as test data. The average recognition rate is used to measure the
performance of the algorithm. The baseline is obtained by raw feature without learning information. For both methods, the SVM with an RBF kernel was employed.

4.2.1   Comparison under ULBP, LD

In this experiment, we aim to justify that MTL is helpful for the attribute featuring
problem. As illustrated in Fig. 3, with the increase of dimensions, all the recognition
rates gain gradually and maintain steadiness at a high value. It is worth noting that in
race task, the recognition rates of the attributes "Black", "Indian" and "White" are not
very good when compared with other attributes. It is maybe due to the fact that the
number of categories of race is 4. While the number of categories is small, for example, the gender task, the recognition rate can reach much higher value than race task.
Besides, from Fig.3, we can also see that ULBP features show better recognition rate
than the LD in all 9 attributes in general, therefore, comparison between MTL and
STL uses ULBP features as an instance.

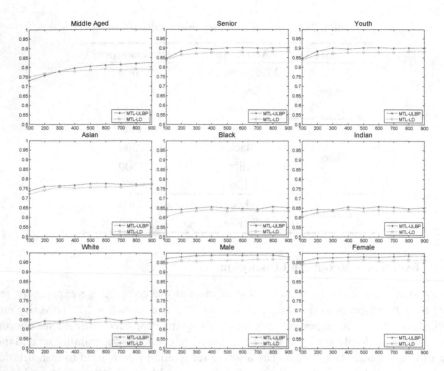

Fig. 3. Performance comparison of ULBP and LD with respect to the feature dimensionality after MTL on the LFW database. For each subfigure, the horizontal axis represents the dimensions selected, and vertical axis is the recognition rate.

4.2.2   Comparison with Single-Task Learning

In this part, the test is to further verify the importance and effectiveness of MTL in attribute learning. MTL trains the models of 3 tasks simultaneously. In STL, models of 3 tasks are trained separately. The baseline is raw ULBP feature without dimensionality reduction. We compare the proposed method with both the STL and baseline. The experimental results are illustrated in Table 2. In age and gender task, the average recognition rate of MTL is slightly improved compared with STL and baseline. But in "Black", "Indian" and "White", it is obviously higher than STL. This indirectly indicates that the tasks in MTL can interact with each other. The effect of this interaction is that for some attribute, the rate is slightly improved; but for some attribute it can achieve a great degree of increase. In general, the recognition rate of multi-task learning is superior to that of single task learning and baseline. The advantage of MTL shows that knowledge sharing among related tasks can have a significant impact for better generalization ability.

Table 2. Performance comparison of MTL, STL and Baseline

Task	Attribute	AVG Rate		Baseline
		MTL	STL	
	Middle Aged	79.91%	79.45%	79.68%
Age	Senior	89.76%	89.68%	89.72%
	Youth	89.65%	89.54%	89.59%
	Asian	76.80%	76.35%	76.57%
Race	Black	64.20%	60.71%	62.45%
	Indian	64.11%	60.71%	62.41%
	White	64.03%	60.71%	62.37%
Gender	Male	98.36%	97.93%	98.15%
	Female	97.71%	97.59%	97.65%

5   Conclusion

In this work, we present the method of joint multi-class attribute feature learning based on MTL. We apply nine facial attributes including two of gender (Male, Female), three of age (Middle Aged, Senior, Youth) and four of race (Asian, Black, Indian, White) in multi-task learning framework to learn features together. The attributes are classified into three tasks. Thus, the training samples of these tasks can share a common data structure in MTL. Through the weight vector learnt by MTL we can find the importance of all features. So we can select much lower dimensions for attribute feature representation without losing precision in attribute recognition. The experiment results on LFW show that the proposed method can increase recognition rate with much lower number of feature dimension. The results comparison with STL verify the effectiveness of the proposed method.

Acknowledgments. The work is funded by the National Natural Science Foundation of China (No.61170155)

References

1. Kumar, N., Berg, A.C., Belhumeur, P.N., Nayar, S.K.: Describable visual attributes for face verification and image search. IEEE Trans. Pattern Anal. Mach. Intell. **33**(10), 1962–1977 (2011)
2. Chen, B.C., Chen, Y.Y., Kuo, Y.H., Hsu, W.H.: Scalable face image retrieval using attribute-enhanced sparse codewords. IEEE Trans. Multi. **15**(5), 1163–1173 (2013)
3. Hong, Z., Mei, X., Prokhorov, D., Tao, D.: Tracking via robust multi-task multi-view joint sparse representation. In: 2013 IEEE International Conference on Computer Vision, pp. 649–656. IEEE Press (2013)
4. Zhu, F., Shao, L.: Weakly-supervised cross-domain dictionary learning for visual recognition. Int J Comput Vision **109**(12), 42–59 (2014)

5. Liu, H., Palatucci, M., Zhang, J.: Blockwise coordinate descent procedures for the multi-task lasso, with applications to neural semantic basis discovery. In: Proceedings of the 26th Annual International Conference on Machine Learning, pp. 649–656. ACM (2009)
6. Dantone, M., Gall, J., Fanelli, G., Van Gool, L.: Real-time facial feature detection using conditional regression forests. In: 2012 IEEE Conference on Computer Vision and Pattern Recognition, pp. 2578–2585. IEEE Press (2012)
7. Yu, C., Fang, Y., Li, Y.: Multi-task learning for face ethnicity and gender recognition. In: Sun, Z., Shan, S., Sang, H., Zhou, J., Wang, Y., Yuan, W. (eds.) CCBR 2014. LNCS, vol. 8833, pp. 136–144. Springer, Heidelberg (2014)
8. Scheirer, W.J., Kumar, N., Belhumeur, P.N., Boult, T.E.: Multi-attribute spaces: Calibration for attribute fusion and similarity search. In: 2012 IEEE Conference on Computer Vision and Pattern Recognition, pp. 2933–2940. IEEE Press (2012)
9. Siddiquie, B., Feris, R.S., Davis, L.S.: Image ranking and retrieval based on multi-attribute queries. In: 2011 IEEE Conference on Computer Vision and Pattern Recognition, pp. 801–808. IEEE Press (2011)
10. Luo, P., Wang, X., Tang, X.: A deep sum-product architecture for robust facial attributes analysis. In: 2013 IEEE International Conference on Computer Vision, pp. 2864–2871. IEEE Press (2013)
11. Liu, Z., Luo, P., Wang, X., Tang, X.: Deep Learning Face Attributes in the Wild. arXiv preprint (2014). arXiv:1411.7766
12. Chen, J., Liu, J., Ye, J.: Learning incoherent sparse and low-rank patterns from multiple tasks. ACM Trans. Knowl. Discov. Data 5(4), 1–31 (2012)
13. Chang, C.C., Lin, C.J.: LIBSVM: A library for support vector machines. ACM Trans. Intell. Syst. Technolog. 2(3), 1–27 (2011)
14. Fang, Y., Chang, L.: Multi-instance feature learning based on sparse representation for facial expression recognition. In: He, X., Luo, S., Tao, D., Xu, C., Yang, J., Hasan, M.A. (eds.) MMM 2015, Part I. LNCS, vol. 8935, pp. 224–233. Springer, Heidelberg (2015)
15. Liu, J., Ji, S., Ye, J.: SLEP: Sparse Learning with Efficient Projections (2009). http://www.public.asu.edu/~jye02/Software/SLEP
16. Gong, P., Ye, J., Zhang, C.: Robust multi-task feature learning. In: Proceedings of the 18th ACM SIGKDD international conference on Knowledge discovery and data mining, pp. 895–903. ACM (2012)
17. Huang, G.B., Mattar, M., Berg, T., Learned-Miller, E.: Labeled faces in the wild: A database for studying face recognition in unconstrained environments. In: Workshop on Faces in 'Real-Life' Images: Detection, Alignment, and Recognition (2008)
18. Ahonen, T., Hadid, A., Pietikainen, M.: Face description with local binary patterns: Application to face recognition. IEEE Trans. Pattern Anal. Mach. Intell. 28(12), 2037–2041 (2006)
19. Cheng, G., Fang, Y., Tan, Y., Dai, W., Cai, Q.: A Local Difference coding algorithm for face recognition. In: 2011 4th International Congress on Image and Signal Processing, vol. 2, pp. 828–832. IEEE Press (2011)

Person-specific Face Spoofing Detection for Replay Attack Based on Gaze Estimation

Lijun Cai[✉], Lei Huang, and Changping Liu

Institute of Automation Chinese Academy of Sciences, Beijing, China
cailijun2013@ia.acs.cn

Abstract. Based on gaze estimation, we propose an effective person-specific spoofing detection method to counter replay attack using a non-invasive challenge and response technique. The points on the computer screen create the challenge, and the gaze positions of the user as they look at the computer screen form the response. Firstly, face identification is conducted to recognize identity. Secondly, gaze estimation model is trained for each subject by adaptive linear regression with incremental learning and used to predict gaze positions when user is looking at the computer screen. Finally, difference between predicted gaze positions and system point locations is used as fake score to evaluate the liveness of user. Our basic assumption is that a genuine access can be attacked by salient objects and follow them. Therefore, the lower the fake score is, the more probable the user is genuine. Experimental results show that proposed method obtains competitive performance in distinguishing replay attacks from genuine accesses.

Keywords: Face spoofing detection · Replay attack · Incremental learning · Gaze estimation

1 Introduction

Due to the requirement of information security, face spoofing detection is attracting more and more attention and research nowadays. Generally speaking, there are three common manners to spoof face recognition system: print photograph, replayed video and 3D model of a valid user. Compared with real faces, print photograph faces are planar, as well as having quality degradation and blurring problems. Replayed video faces are reflective and 3D face models are rigid. Based on these clues, face anti-spoofing techniques can be roughly classified into three categories: motion-based [1–5], texture-based [6–9] and fusion methods combing motion and texture [10,11]. Almost all these methods are effective for simple spoofing attacks for example, print photograph. However, very little attention has been paid to replay attacks. Existing methods dealing with replay attacks either by combing other biometric mode such as voice, gesture with face information [12–14] or by multiple spectrum device [15,16] or operating in controlled environment such as a darkened room [17].

© Springer International Publishing Switzerland 2015
J. Yang et al. (Eds.): CCBR 2015, LNCS 9428, pp. 201–211, 2015.
DOI: 10.1007/978-3-319-25417-3_25

Considering that gaze is a kind of behavioral biometrics which is difficult to be detected by the surveillance due to the ambiguity of visual attention process, it can be used as a clue for anti-spoofing with the following characteristics [18]. Firstly, it does not require physical contact between user and device. Secondly, gaze is difficult to be obtained by surveillance camera and other equipment. Ali et al. [19–21] present the first time to use gaze clue for anti-spoofing, in which user is required to follow a moving point showed on the computer screen. Features based on the collinearity of gaze are used to discriminate between genuine access and print photographs attack. However, they are invalid for still photographs and uncooperative users. We previously provided the first investigation in research literature on the use of gaze estimation model for face spoofing detection in [22], in which nonlinear regression model is trained including multiple subjects and used for gaze estimation, then information entropy on predicted gaze positions under the stimulus of random points suggests the uncertainty level of user's gaze movement. The higher the information entropy is, the more probable the user is genuine. Experimental results show the effectiveness of this method on photographs and replay attacks with still gaze (user in the video almost only watch one direction). However, it does not work to replay attacks with moving gaze. That is to say, this method misjudges relay attack in which video user changes his gaze directions frequently as genuine access.

In this paper, based on gaze estimation, we propose an improved version of [22] to counter replay attack using a noninvasive challenge and response technique. The points on the computer screen create the challenge, and the gaze positions of the user as they look at the computer screen form the response. Face spoofing detection is performed by evaluation the difference of the gaze positions and system point locations. Compared with [22], the different points and improvements in this proposed method are as follows. 1) Proposed method is person-specific. In this paper, gaze estimation model is trained for each subject, which dismisses the interferences among different subjects. 2) Compared with nonlinear regression, adaptive linear regression is adopted to estimate gaze positions for reducing computation complexity. To meanwhile obtain lower gaze error, incremental learning is integrated into adaptive linear regression for dynamically increasing the calibration-free training PoG (point of gaze). 3) Considering that moving point locations too random makes it impossible for the eyes to follow it, system points in this paper are generated following some distribution with random parameters, for example, Gaussian distribution with random mean and variance.

2   Proposed Face Spoofing Detection Method

The general framework of proposed method is illustrated in Fig. 1, which consists of three main steps: face identification, gaze estimation and liveness judgement.

For a test sample, his identity should be obtained firstly. Note that face identification is not the focus of this paper, any effective face identification methods, for example [23,24], can be used here to identify the test sample.

After obtaining the identity of the input face images, person-specific gaze estimation model is trained and used to predict the gaze positions of input images. Finally, Euclidean distance between predicted gaze positions and system points locations is computed as the fake score of the test sample. According to the visual attention mechanism, people are always attracted by some certain regions or objects. Therefore, the lower the fake score is, the more possible the user is judged as a genuine access. Next we will detail the gaze estimation and liveness judgement.

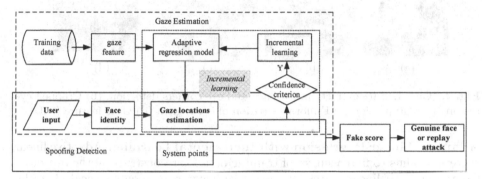

Fig. 1. System architecture.

2.1 Gaze Estimation

Existing gaze estimation methods can be roughly classified into two categories: feature-based methods and appearance-based methods. Feature-based methods [25,26] map the gaze feature (for example iris outline, pupil, cornea) to gaze position. However, this kind of methods generally require high quality camera, even multiple light sources. Appearance-based [27,28] methods directly map the whole eye region to gaze position, which takes full advantage of gaze information. Considering proposed method is conducted under the condition of nature light and a generic camera, we choose an effective appearance-based method, adaptive linear regression [28], to establish gaze estimation model. Generally speaking, the gaze error will become lower with the increasing of training PoG (Point of Gaze) number which, however, brings more users' calibration burden. To get lower gaze error meanwhile not bring additional burden on user, incremental learning is added to adaptive linear learning in this work for online dynamically increasing the number of calibration-free training PoG.

Gaze Feature Extraction. Gaze feature extraction consists of two steps: eye region crop and feature generation. In the first step, face region and inner and outer eye corners are detected by adaptive boosting algorithm [29] (Fig. 2(a), left eye is used in this paper). To deal with small head motion, an additional alignment procedure is performed. Firstly we define an eye image template with 60×40 pixels, and the location of inner eye corner is set at (55, 25) and outer corner (5, 25). The aligned eye region is obtained by rotating and scaling the face region based on the locations of eye corners in template (Fig. 2(b)).

In the feature generation step, similar to [28], the cropped eye region is further divided into $r \times c$ subregions (here 8×12, Fig. 2(c)). Let S_j denote the sum of pixel intensities in j-th subregion, then gaze feature is generated by $e = \frac{[S_1, S_2, \cdots, S_{r \times c}]^T}{\sum_j S_j}$ (Fig. 2(d)).

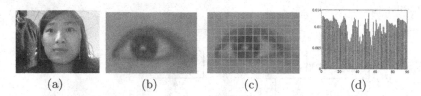

(a)   (b)   (c)   (d)

Fig. 2. Gaze feature extraction. (a) Face and eye corners detection. (b) Cropped eye region (60×40 pixels). (c) Uniform partition of eye region. (d) Gaze feature (96D)

Adaptive Linear Regression with Incremental Learning. Adaptive linear regression aims to find a subset of training data for reconstructing the test data. Compared with linear regression, adaptive linear regression can neglect irrelevant training data, thus is helpful to predict. Based on adaptive linear regression, incremental learning is combined for lower gaze error. The mathematical definition of adaptive linear regression with incremental learning is described as follows.

Let matrices $F = [f_1^d, \cdots, f_n^d] \in \mathrm{R}^{m \times n}$ and $P = [p_1^d, \cdots, p_n^d] \in \mathrm{R}^{2 \times n}$ include all the gaze features and gaze positions of training samples belonging to the person with identity d (d is obtained by face identification), where m is the feature dimension and n is the samples number. For a test frame I_t with identity d and gaze feature $\hat{f}$, the corresponding gaze position can be estimated as $\hat{p} = P\hat{w}$ by adaptive linear regression

$$\hat{w} = \arg\min_w \|w\|_1 \quad s.t. \quad \|Fw - \hat{f}\|_2 < \epsilon, \sum_i w_i = 1 \tag{1}$$

Assuming $\{Q_0, \cdots, Q_N\}$ are the system points and Q_{j_0} is appearing on the computer screen when I_t is captured by system camera. If confidence criterion $\|\hat{(p)} - Q_{j_0}\|_2 < \varepsilon$ (ε is a small positive number) is met, F and P can be extended to $\tilde{F} = [F \hat{f}]$ and $\tilde{P} = [P \hat{p}]$. Therefore, for the next captured image I_{t+1} with gaze feature f^*, its gaze position can be estimated as $p^* = \tilde{P}\hat{w}$ by solving

$$\hat{w} = \arg\min_w \|w\|_1 \quad s.t. \quad \|\tilde{F}w - f^*\|_2 < \epsilon, \sum_i w_i = 1 \tag{2}$$

Based on above description, system points satisfying confidence criterion in the test phase can be added into the training PoG set one by one without calibration, which is the main idea of adding incremental learning to adaptive linear regression.

2.2 Liveness Judgement

In this paper, system points $\{Q_1, \cdots, Q_N\}$ are generated by Gaussian distribution with random mean μ and standard deviation σ. Given another random positive number a, Q_i can be represented as $Q_i = (Q_x^{(i)}, Q_y^{(i)})^T$, where $Q_x^{(i)} = \mu - a + \frac{2a}{N}i$ and $Q_y^{(i)} = \frac{1}{\sqrt{2\pi}\sigma}e^{-\frac{(Q_x^{(i)} - \mu)^2}{2*\sigma^2}}$. That is to say, system points are different for each of the test runs and their locations are determined by three random parameters: μ, σ and a. From above analysis, $Q_x^{(i)} \in [\mu - a, \mu + a], Q_y^{(i)} \in [\frac{1}{\sqrt{2\pi}\sigma}e^{-\frac{a^2}{2\sigma^2}}, \frac{1}{\sqrt{2\pi}\sigma}]$. In order to be showed on the computer screen in a suitable way, the coordinate range of system random points have to be transformed according to the original training PoGs.

Assuming original training PoGs are $\{P_1, \cdots, P_M\}$ (in this paper, $M = 9$) and $P_j = (P_x^{(j)}, P_y^{(j)})^T \in R^{2 \times 1}$. The locations of training PoGs are shown in Fig. 3a, which are uniformly distributed on the computer screen. In this paper, linear transformation is used as follows.

$$\hat{Q}_x^{(i)} = \frac{PH_x - PL_x}{QH_x - QL_x}(Q_x^{(i)} - QL_x) + PL_x$$
$$\hat{Q}_y^{(i)} = \frac{PH_y - PL_y}{QH_y - QL_y}(Q_y^{(i)} - QL_x) + PL_y$$

(3)

where $\hat{Q} = (\hat{Q}_x^{(i)}, \hat{Q}_y^{(i)})^T$ is the transformed system random point. $AH_c = \max A_c^{(i)}$, $AL_c = \max A_c^{(i)}$, $A = \{P, Q\}$, $c = \{x, y\}$. An example of system random point is shown in Fig. 3b. Green big circles are training PoG and red small circles are system random points. The arrows represent the movement direction of system random points.

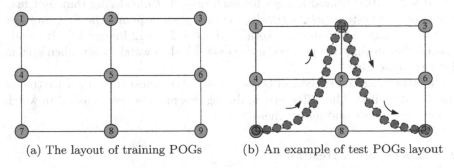

(a) The layout of training POGs   (b) An example of test POGs layout

Fig. 3. Data collection system for gaze estimation.

Based on gaze estimation model, gaze positions of user can be predicted under the guide of system random points. Euclidean distance is used here as fake score to evaluate the matching degree between system point locations and predicted gaze positions. The lower the score is, the more probable the user is genuine.

3   Experiments

3.1   Database

Publicly available databases such as CASIA [10] and Replay-attack [22] don't contain gaze information, thus they are unsuitable for evaluating our proposed method. In this paper, we collect a database composed of 18 subjects. For each subject, there are four kinds of data: training data for gaze estimation model, test data for gaze estimation model, data of genuine face and data of replay attack. In the following section, we use Data-Train-Gaze, Data-Test-Gaze, Data-Test-Genuine and Data-Test-Replay to represent these four kinds of data. Data-Train-Gaze and Data-Test-Gaze are used to train and test gaze estimation model. Data-Test-Genuine and Data-Test-Replay are Genuine access and replay attack data and used for evaluating proposed spoofing detection method.

In order to collect data, we develop a system on a desktop composed of a 19-inch computer screen with 1440×900 pixels resolution and a generic webcam with 640×480 pixels resolution. To collect Data-Train-Gaze, $M = 9$ fixed markers are showed on the computer screen (Fig. 3a). The system captures user's frontal appearance while his gaze is focusing on every marker shown on the screen. In this paper there are 20 images are captured at each marker for each user, totally $20 \times 9 \times 18 = 3240$ frontal images. By artificially removing eye-closed images, there are 2917 frontal images left. Considering the negative effect of optical reflection, users are required to remove glasses during the data collection.

To collect Data-Test-Genuine and Data-Test-Replay, $N = 51$ system points following Gaussian distribution with random mean and variance appear one by one (Fig. 3b) on the computer screen. The system camera captures user's frontal appearance while these points are shown on the screen. In this paper there are 10 images are captured at each system point and each kind of data, totally $51 \times 10 \times 2 = 1020$ frontal images for each subject. Considering that user may not respond to system points timely, for each system point, the first and last two frontal images are removed, Totally $51 \times 6 \times 2 = 612$ images left. It should be noted that during this process, user is not asked to watch point when system points are appearing.

The data collection process of Data-Test-Gaze is almost the same with that of Data-Test-Genuine. The difference is, during this process user is asked to watch these system points and follow them.

3.2   Experimental Results

In this section, we will verify the effectiveness of proposed method from the following three aspects: 1) Effectiveness of adaptive linear regression with incremental learning; 2) Effectiveness of proposed method for distinguishing replay attacks from genuine accesses; 3) Effectiveness of Euclidean distance based liveness score.

Effectiveness of Incremental Learning. Gaze error [28] is commonly used to evaluate the gaze estimation model.

$$error = arctan\left(\frac{\|y - \hat{y}\|_2}{d_{user}}\right) \tag{4}$$

where $\|y - \hat{y}\|_2$ represents the Euclidean distance between ground truth and predicted value, and d_{user} refers to the distance between user's eye with computer screen.

In order to verify the effectiveness of incremental learning, we compare proposed adaptive linear regression with incremental learning with that without incremental learning. In addition, to show the effectiveness of person-specific gaze estimation model, we also compare proposed method with subject-dependent adaptive linear regression. Subject-dependent experiment is conducted by training samples of all subjects instead of one subject. Compared results are illustrated in Fig. 4, which shows that 1) compared with original adaptive linear learning, proposed method with incremental learning achieves lower average gaze error; 2) compared with subject-dependent method, subject-specific methods obtain lower gaze error. Therefore, proposed method for gaze estimation is effective. Considering the gaze errors for 18 subjects are tolerated, adaptive linear regression with incremental learning can be embedded into proposed spoofing detection system.

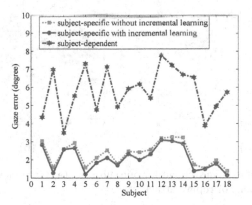

Fig. 4. Compared results on gaze error.

Effectiveness of Proposed Face Spoofing Detection Method. EER (Equal Error Rate) and recognition accuracy are adapted as evaluation metrics. EER is the value when FRR (False Rejection Rate) equals to FAR (False Acceptance Rate). Recognition accuracy is reported based on cross-validation sets. 18 subjects are divided into 6 cross-validation sets and for each set there are 30 training samples (15 sequences of genuine faces and 15 sequences of replay attacks) for 15 subjects and 6 test samples (3 sequences of genuine faces and 3 sequences of replay attacks) for another 3 subjects. At each round, thresh is selected on training samples and used on test samples. The final recognition accuracy is achieved by averaging all the results on 6 sets of test samples. what's more, FRR values are also reported when FAR = 0.1, 0.01 and 0.001. Experimental results are listed in Table 1, which shows that proposed method perform excellent in distinguishing replay attacks from genuine accesses.

Table 1. EER FRR and recognition accuracy.

EER	FRR(FAR=0.1)	FRR(FAR=0.01)	FRR(FAR=0.001)	accuracy
0%	0%	0%	0%	100%

To further verify the effectiveness of proposed method, predicted gaze trajectories of genuine access and replay attack for one subject under the system point challenge are given in Fig. 5. Fig. 5a shows that genuine face is completely attracted by system points and follows them well. However, the replay video collected can not respond the challenge and predicted gaze trajectory is disorder (Fig. 5b). Therefore, proposed method is reasonable and effective.

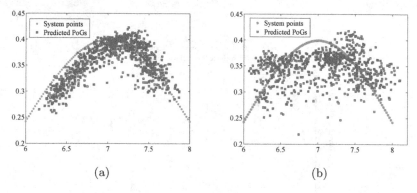

(a)   (b)

Fig. 5. An example of gaze movement for one subjects. (a) Gaze movement of Genuine face. (b) Gaze movement of replay attack.

Effectiveness of Euclidean Distance Based Fake Score. Fig. 6 illustrates the fake scores of samples for 18 subjects and shows that scores of real faces are averagely lower than that of replay attacks. Considering the fact that different from replay attacks, genuine accesses can be attracted by some objects or regions even in a long while. Experimental results show that the hypothesis of proposed method matches the real case, therefore, Euclidean distance based fake score is a good indicator.

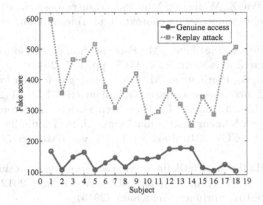

Fig. 6. Fake scores of real faces and replay attacks for 18 subjects.

4 Conclusion and Future Work

In this paper we propose an effective spoofing detection method for replay attack based on gaze estimation. Proposed spoofing detection method contains three key stages: face identification, gaze estimation and liveness judgement. In order to obtain lower gaze error, gaze estimation model is trained for each subject which dismisses the interferences among different subjects. In addition, adaptive learning regression is used for gaze estimation and improved with incremental learning. Then Euclidean distance based fake score is used to evaluate the difference between predicted gaze positions and system random point locations. Experimental results on collected database show that proposed method can effectively distinguish replay attacks from genuine accesses. We believe that with gaze estimation becoming more and more accurate, proposed spoofing detection method based on gaze estimation will have a good applicant prospect. However, how to deal with head pose in this work is still an challenge problem that we will research on.

References

1. Kollreider, K., Fronthaler, H., Bigun, J.: Non-intrusive liveness detection by face images. Image and Vision Computing **27**, 223–244 (2009)
2. Bao, W., Li, H., Li, N., Jiang, W.: A liveness detection method for face recognition based on optical flow field. In: Proc. Int. Conf. Image Analysis and Signal Processing, pp. 233–236 (2009)
3. Anjos, A., Marcel, S.: Counter-measures to photo attacks in face recognition: a public database and a baseline. In: Proc. IJCB, pp. 1–7 (2011)
4. Anjos, A., Mohan, M., Marcel, S.: Motion-based counter-measures to photo attacks in face recognition. Institution of Engineering and Technology Journal on Biometrics (2014) (to be published)

5. Pan, G., Sun, L., Wu, Z., Wang, Y.: Monocular camera-based face liveness detection by combining eyeblink and scene context. J. of Telecommunication Systems **47**, 215–225 (2011)
6. Jukka, M.P., Hadid, A., Pietikinen, M.: Face spoofing detection from single images using micro-texture analysis. In: Proc. IJCB, pp. 1–7 (2011)
7. Maatta, J., Hadid, A., Pietikainen, M.: Face spoofing detection from single images using texture and local shape analysis. IET Biometrics **1**, 3–10 (2012)
8. Tan, X., Li, Y., Liu, J., Jiang, L.: Face liveness detection from a single image with sparse low rank bilinear discriminative model. In: Daniilidis, K., Maragos, P., Paragios, N. (eds.) ECCV 2010, Part VI. LNCS, vol. 6316, pp. 504–517. Springer, Heidelberg (2010)
9. Komulainen, J., Hadid, A., Pietikäinen, M.: Face spoofing detection using dynamic texture. In: Park, J.-I., Kim, J. (eds.) ACCV Workshops 2012, Part I. LNCS, vol. 7728, pp. 146–157. Springer, Heidelberg (2013)
10. Yan, J.J., Zhang, Z.W., Lei, Z., Yi, D., Li, S.Z.: Face liveness detection by exploring multiple scenic clues. In: Proc. Int. Conf. Control Automation Robotics and Vision, pp. 188–193 (2012)
11. Komulainen, J., Hadid, A., Pietikainen, M., Anjos, A., Marcel, S.: Complementary countermeasures for detecting scenic face spoofing attacks. In: Proc. ICB, pp. 1–7 (2013)
12. Frischholz, R.W., Dieckmann, U.: Bioid: A multimodal biometric identification system. Computer **33**, 64–68 (2000)
13. Eveno, N., Besacier, L.: Co-inertia analysis for "liveness" test in audio-visual biometrics. In: Proc. Int. Symp. Image and Signal Processing and Analysis, pp. 257–261 (2005)
14. Chetty, G., Wagner, M.: Liveness verification in audio–video speaker authentication. In: Proc. Australian Int. Conf. Speech Science and Technology, pp. 363–385 (2004)
15. Zhang, Z.W., Yi, D., Lei, Z., Li, S.Z.: Face liveness detection by learning multi-spectral reflectance distributions. In: Proc. IEEE Int. Conf. Automatic Face and Gesture Recognition and Workshops, pp. 436–441 (2011)
16. Kim, Y., Na, J., Yoon, S., Yi, J.: Masked fake face detection using radiance measurements. J. of the Optical Society of America A **24**, 760–766 (2009)
17. Smith, D.F., Wiliem, A., Lovell, B.C.: Face Recognition on Consumer Devices: Reflections on Replay Attacks. IEEE Trans. Inf. Foren. Sec. **10**, 736–745 (2015)
18. Sireesha, M.V., Vijaya, P.A., Chellamma, K.: A survey on gaze estimation techniques. In: Chakravarthi, V.S., Shirur, Y.J.M., Prasad, R. (eds.) Proceedings of International Conference on VLSI, Communication, Advanced Devices, Signals and Systems and Networking (VCASAN-2013). LNEE, vol. 258, pp. 353–361. Springer, Heildelberg (2013)
19. Ali, A., Deravi, F., Hoque, S.: Liveness detection using gaze collinearity. In: Proc. Int. Conf. Emerging Security Technologies, pp. 62–65 (2012)
20. Ali, A., Deravi, F., Hoque, S.: Directional sensitivity of gaze-collinearity features in liveness detections. In: Proc. Int. Conf. Emerging Security Technologies, pp. 8–11 (2013)
21. Ali, A., Deravi, F., Hoque, S.: Spoofing attempt detection using gaze colocation. In: Proc. Int. Conf. Biometrics Special Interest Group, pp. 1–12 (2013)
22. Cai, L., Xiong, C., Huang, L., Liu, C.: A novel face spoofing detection method based on gaze estimation. In: Cremers, D., Reid, I., Saito, H., Yang, M.-H. (eds.) ACCV 2014. LNCS, vol. 9005, pp. 547–561. Springer, Heidelberg (2015)

23. Taigman, Y., Yang, M., Ranzato, M., Wolf, L.: Deepface: closing the gap to human-level performance in face verification. In: Proc. CVPR, pp. 1707–1708 (2014)
24. Lu, C., Tang, X.: Learning the face prior for bayesian face recognition. In: Fleet, D., Pajdla, T., Schiele, B., Tuytelaars, T. (eds.) ECCV 2014, Part IV. LNCS, vol. 8692, pp. 119–134. Springer, Heidelberg (2014)
25. Sigut, J.F., Sidha, S.A.: Iris center corneal reflection method for gaze tracking using visible light. IEEE Trans. on Biomedical Engineering **58**, 411–419 (2011)
26. Xiong, C.S., Huang, L., Liu, C.P.: Gaze estimation based on 3D face structure and pupil centers. In: Proc. ICPR, pp. 24–28 (2014)
27. Williams, O., Blake, A., Cipolla, R.: Sparse and semi-supervised visual mapping with the S3GP. In: Proc. IEEE Computer Society Conf. Computer Vision and Pattern Recognition, pp. 230–237 (2006)
28. Feng, L., Sugano, Y., Takahiro, O., Sato, Y.: Inferring human gaze from appearance via adaptive linear regression. In: Proc. ICCV, pp. 153–160 (2011)
29. Viola, P., Jones, M.: Robust Real-time Face Detection. Int. J. of Computer Vision **57**, 137–154 (2004)

Fingerprint and Palmprint

Palmprint Feature Extraction Method
Based on Rotation-invariance

Jinghui Feng[1], He Wang[1], Yang Li[2], and Fu Liu[1(✉)]

[1] College of Communication Engineering, Jilin University, Changchun 130022, China
liufu@jlu.edu.cn
[2] College of Electrical Engineering,
Changchun Automobile Industry Institute, Changchun 130011, China

Abstract. Feature extraction is one of most basic problems in the research of palmprint recognition. Extracting effective palmprint feature is the crucial problem in the field of palmprint recognition. There was a research focus on how to select the feature. The lacking of main orientation for palmprint recognition system will lead to an incorrect feature extraction and matching. In order to extract more precise palmprint feature, a new method for feature extraction of palmprint was proposed in the research of palmprint recognition, which could improve the efficiency of identification. Firstly, calculating the main orientation of the whole image, and then adjusting the gradient of each pixel according to the main orientation to ensure this method has rotation invariance. Secondly, combining with the method of histogram of oriented gradient and dominant orientation. Finally, the feature value of palmprint was obtained. A reasonable threshold is set to estimate the similarity between the experimental images and the sample images. The experimental results showed that the method proposed in this paper can improve the efficiency of identification.

Keywords: Feature extraction · Histogram of oriented gradient · Dominant orientation · Main direction · Image matching

1 Introduction

The security of personal information has been concerned along with the rapid economic development and the continuing elevation of people's living standards. Biometric identification technology could protect personal privacy, which was more convenient. The existing biometric identification technologies mainly include fingerprint identification, hand shape identification and iris identification. But palmprint recognition as a biometric identification technology has been the focus of the research. Comparing with other biometric identification technologies, palmprint identification technology has the characteristics of uniqueness、 stability and high accuracy [1-4], which was a research hotspot for a long time.

Extracting the feature of palmprint is the key link in the process of palmprint recognition, which determines the recognition rate. There are several typical algorithms

© Springer International Publishing Switzerland 2015
J. Yang et al. (Eds.): CCBR 2015, LNCS 9428, pp. 215–223, 2015.
DOI: 10.1007/978-3-319-25417-3_26

of palmprint at present: recognition method based on line feature、 method based on subspace and method based on spatial-frequency domain [5-7]. Li [8] proposed a method based on feature coding. This method computed the orientation code and imaginary part's characteristic code, which had a better ability to distinguish. Though this method was an effective method, as a result of the angle deviation in the process of acquisition, it would decrease the recognition rate. To the issue, this paper proposed a method of palmprint recognition based on rotation invariant, and then combined with the histogram of oriented gradient (HOG) and predominant direction. The algorithm could improve the accuracy of palmprint recognition. Above all, we should extract the region of interest (ROI).The key points between the fingers are positioned via a boundary-tracking algorithm and two key points are lined to obtain the Y-axis of the palmprint coordinates system. A line drawn through their midpoint is regarded as the X-axis, which is perpendicular to the Y-axis. In the middle of the image, a sub-image is extracted. Then, a new feature extraction method is proposed. Firstly, the main direction of the image is determined. Secondly, this paper get the feature code of the palmprint image. Finally, using Hamming Distance to match the feature. The flow chart of the algorithm is as shown in Fig. 1.

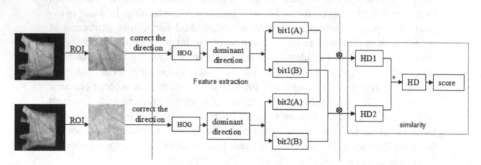

Fig. 1. The flow chart of the algorithm

2   Feature Extraction

We adopt the HOG to calculate the gradient magnitude and gradient orientation after the extraction of the ROI, which can be defined as follows:

$$G_x(i, j)=I(i, j) * W \tag{1}$$

$$G_y(i, j) = I(i, j) * W^T \tag{2}$$

$$Mag(i, j) = \sqrt{G_x^2 + G_y^2} \tag{3}$$

$$Ang(i, j) = \tan^{-1}(G_y / G_x) \tag{4}$$

where I stands for the region of interest image, whose size is 128×128, G_x is the horizontal gradient, G_y is the vertical gradient, $*$ is the convolution operation, $W=[-1,0,1]$ is the convolution template. The experiment results showed that the template have the best effect. $Mag(i,j)$ and $Ang(i,j)$ is the gradient magnitude and gradient orientation for each pixel on the image [9].

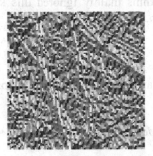

Fig. 2. The orientation of gradient°

Fig. 2 shows the orientation of gradient for an image. According to the Fig. 2, we divided the image into 16×16 blocks firstly. Namely, each block has 8×8 pixels. Secondly, we obtain the histogram of oriented gradient for each block. The weighted of gradient magnitude as ordinate and the abscissa represents gradient orientation with different region.

2.1 Rotation-Invariant

In the process of acquisition, there is no consideration of rational invariance. So there will be some interference factors in the matching process. After analyzing this situation, this paper proposed a method of correcting direction. We need to calculate the main orientation of the whole image, then correct each pixel. The steps are as follows:

Regional Division

$360°$ is divided in average into 36 regions, which each region is $10°$. And then we calculated the weighted gradient amplitude value in each region. The formula is as follows:

$$F = \sum Mag(i,j), \ k\pi/18 < Ang(i,j) < (k+1)\pi/18 \tag{5}$$

where $k=0,1,2\ldots35$, the weighted value of gradient magnitude is calculated in each directional unit.

The Main Orientation of the Whole Image

$$D_m = \arg\max_{0,1,\ldots35} (F) \tag{6}$$

where D_m represent the directional unit corresponding to the maximum amplitude of the gradient. Obviously, which value is $0, 1\ldots35$.

Adjusting the Gradient Orientation

$$Ang_m(i,j) = Ang(i,j) - D_m * 10 \tag{7}$$

Rotation invariant is particularly important for a palmprint image. Existing palmprint recognition algorithms mainly ignored this kind of situation, which will lead to the error identification.

2.2   HOG

We ensure the rotation invariance through the above steps. After that we use the HOG method to extract feature.

$$F_k = \sum Mag(i,j), k\pi/4 < Ang(i,j) < (k+1)/4 \tag{8}$$

where $k=0, 1, 2...7$. Then normalized the F_K by $F_k = F_K / \Sigma F_k$. Each block can be expressed as $F(i) = (F_0, F_1, F_2, ... F_7)$. Fig. 3 shows the HOG method in a block.

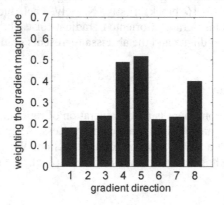

Fig. 3. The histogram of oriented gradient for F (1)

The whole image of palmprint is composed of 16×16 blocks, which each block has its own histogram of gradient orientation, namely $F=(F(1), F(2),...F(16\times16))$. An image can be represented by these arrays. Orientation histogram of gradient of each block hang together as characteristics of the whole image. Due to the large amount of calculation, we introduce dominant orientation to calculate characteristics of the HOG.

2.3   Dominant Direction

The generation process of HOG may be long-winded, so in order to improve the robustness, we want to estimate the dominant orientation of the image. This idea has been applied to the fingerprint identification [10]. The dominant orientation can be more accurate and faster to describe the change of trend, so we calculate the dominant orientation after extracting HOG.

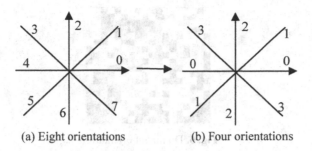

(a) Eight orientations   (b) Four orientations

Fig. 4. Divide the gradient direction

Firstly, we adjust the gradient orientation from 2π to π, the calculation formula is as follows:

$$FN=(F_{no},F_{n1},F_{n2},F_{n3})=\begin{cases} F_{no}=F_0+F_4, & 0<Ang\leq\pi/4 \\ F_{n1}=F_1+F_5, & \pi/4<Ang\leq\pi/2 \\ F_{n2}=F_2+F_6, & \pi/2<Ang\leq3\pi/4 \\ F_{n3}=F_3+F_7, & 3\pi/4<Ang\leq\pi \end{cases} \quad (9)$$

According to the formula, we recalculate HOG by four orientations of image and then get the following histogram:

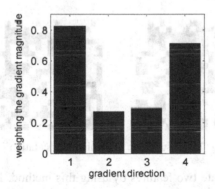

Fig. 5. The histogram of oriented gradient with four direction

The maximum value of the corresponding orientation is the dominant orientation, which can be computed as follows:

$$D = \arg\max_{0,1,2,3}(FN) \quad (10)$$

where the values of D is 0,1,2,3, which represent the dominant orientation of each block. As shown in Fig. 6, it is a figure, which size is 128×128. There are four values in the figure, the range of elements in the figure is from 0 to 3.

Fig. 6. Dominant orientation

Fig. 6 can be encoded by the following two palmprint feature codes. The coding principles are as follows:

Table 1. The principle of the dominant orientation coding

Dominant direction	bit1	bit2
0	0	0
1	0	1
2	1	0
3	1	1

On the basis of the coding principle, the dominant orientation split into two binary images. As is shown in Fig. 7.

Fig. 7. The subgraph of dominant orientation

Any image can calculate two features by using this method. In fact, the method is very efficient in our experiments.

3   Palmprint Recognition

The extracted feature have the same size, which can be represented by vector. So we can use Hamming Distance to match the similarity of two images. Let, $P=(P_1^b, P_2^b)$, $Q=(Q_1^b, Q_2^b)$ be the characteristics of two images [11]. We define $HD(P,Q)$ as follows:

$$HD(P,Q) = (P_1^b \otimes Q_1^b) + (P_2^b \otimes Q_2^b) \tag{11}$$

where $\otimes$ represent XOR operation, '+' represent the addition operation. We compare the characteristic value of the two image to judge whether they are come from the same person. The value of HD can be 0, 1, 2. '2'represent the wrong matching, '0' represent the correct matching. In the case of $HD=1$, we should further calculate its matching degree. Here we need to normalize correlation coefficient to recalculate the similarity between the two images, which is defined as follows:

$$NCC = \frac{\sum (F^1 - \mu_1)(F^2 - \mu_2)}{\sigma_1 \sigma_2 l} \tag{12}$$

where F^1 and F^2 represent the feature of HOG in the case of $HD=1$, μ_1 and μ_2 represent the mean of F^1 and F^2, σ_1 and σ_2 represent standard deviation, and l represent the length of F^1 and F^2. According to the Eq. (12), we define the matching scores are as follows:

$$S(i,j) = \begin{cases} 1 & if \quad HD = 0 \\ NCC & if \quad HD = 1 \\ 0 & if \quad HD = 2 \end{cases} \tag{13}$$

where $S(i,j)$ stands for the matching score between two test images.

4   Experimental Results

In the experiment, we use the PolyU palmprint database, which size is 384×284. The gray level is 256. The database of test image is consist of 250 images (The database come from 50 volunteers, and 5 images each person). After pretreatment, each sample can obtain the region of interest which size is 128×128.

Then we obtain the characteristic of each image. In the end, the matching score is calculated by using Hamming Distance. Fig. 8 and Fig. 9 represent the statistical graph of the intra-class correlation coefficient and inter-class correlation coefficient. Most of the intra-class correlation coefficient are more than 0.6. However, the inter-class correlation coefficient are less than 0.3 at the same time. We can easily find that this method is easy to distinguish two palm images, and the effect of recognition is obvious.

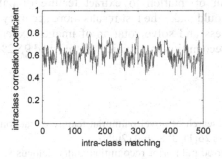

Fig. 8. Intra-class correlation coefficient

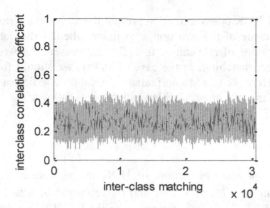

Fig. 9. Inter-class correlation coefficient

Recognition results as shown in Table 2. There are many reasons for the cause of the error identification. For example, error in image acquisition process; Different position of the palm will cause failure when extracting the ROI; Complex recognition process will also lead to calculation error. While the method based on rotation-invariant has long training time, its recognition rate has improved significantly. The recognition rate is increased by 7.8%.

Table 2. The effect of recognition

Comparative item	HOG	HOG+ dominant orientation	Rotation-invariant
Threshold	55	60	65
Training time/s	0.26	0.73	0.92
The number of matching	500	500	500
The correct matching	398	437	476
The recognition rate/%	79.6	87.4	95.2

5   Conclusion

This paper analyze the shortcomings of existing methods, in order to improve the recognition rate, a new method based on rotation-invariant is proposed, we combine the HOG and dominant orientation to extract feature of palmprint. The method proposed in this paper could make the test results more accuracy, it is an effective tool to improve the robustness and solve rotation of image. Experiments show that the algorithm has a higher recognition rate, which can reached 95.2%.

References

1. Wu, X., Wang, T.: Research of novel palmprint feature extraction method. J. Application Research of Computers **26**(1), 398–400 (2009)
2. Lin, S., Fan, W.: Blurred palmprint recognition under defocus status. J. Optics Precision Engineering **21**(3), 734–740 (2003)

3. Qiu, X.G., Liu, J., Zhang, D.P.: Representation and recognition of palmprints based on line minutia features. J. **25**(6), 44–47 (2006)
4. Peng, Q.S., Chen, H.H.: Based on template matching and morphology method of Palmprint feature extraction. J. Journal of Hangzhou Dianzi University **33**(3), 22–24 (2013)
5. Zhang, Y., Shang, L.: Survey of feature extraction algorithms in palmprint recognition. J. Journal of Suzhou Vocational University **21**(3), 7–12 (2010)
6. Yuan, W.Q., Huang, J., Sang, H.F.: Palmprint recognition based on wavelet decomposition and PCA. J. Application Research of Computers **25**(12), 3671–3673 (2008)
7. Li, P., Jing, R.Z.: Palmprint recognition based on invariant moments. J. Electronic Design Engineering **21**(17), 11–13 (2013)
8. Guo, Z.H., Zhang, L., Zhang, D.: Hierarchical multiscale LBP for face and palmprint recognition. In: Proceedings of the IEEE Conference on Image Processing, pp. 4521–4524 (2010)
9. Feng, J., Liang, X.X., Miu, Z.C.: Ear recognition with histogram of oriented gradient features. J. Journal of Nanjing University (Natural Sciences) **48**(4), 452–458 (2012)
10. Yin, Y.L., Tian, J., Yang, X.K.: Ridge distance estimation in fingerprint images: algorithm and performance evaluation. EURASIP J. Appl. Signal Process. **24**, 495–502 (2004)
11. Kong, A., Zhang, D., Kamel, M.: Palmprint identification using feature-level fusion. Pattern Recognit. **39**(3), 478–487 (2006)

CPGF: Core Point Detection from Global Feature for Fingerprint

Dejian Li, Xishun Yue, Qiuxia Wu, and Wenxiong Kang[✉]

School of Automation Science and Engineering,
South China University of Technology, Guangzhou, China
lidjwork@163.com, auwxkang@scut.edu.cn

Abstract. To detect the core point more accurately and quickly has always been the focus for the fingerprint recognition. In this paper, we propose a novel core point detecting algorithm with global information, core point detection from global feature (CPGF). Firstly, we extract a set of points with high curvature according to the statistics of the fingerprint orientation distribution. Secondly, a reference line is fitted on the point set with certain orientation distribution. Finally, the core point is detected by the Poincare Index around the reference line. The experimental results demonstrated that our algorithm is low time-consuming and it is able to produce convincing core point coordinates from the ROI provided by the reference line which is valuable to be investigated for further optimizing other core point algorithms.

Keywords: Core point detection · Global feature · Orientation distribution

1 Introduction

In recent years, the fingerprint recognition has become an important application in the security domain. Due to the ability of locating the features and improving fingerprint matching[1], the core point detection has played an important role in fingerprint recognition. Nevertheless, it also can be used for measuring the quality of fingerprint images[2]. Hence, the core point has become an outstanding feature in the biometric of fingerprint. Most of the core point detecting algorithms are local feature-based but ignore the global information from the fingerprint. These algorithms may not be easily adapted to complex noise, especially in the case of a fracture or fuzzy fingerprint. In order to overcome the disturbance of noise and other pseudo-feature points, a statistical analysis of fingerprint orientation is performed in this paper. Inspired by the statistical analysis, we propose a novel method for core point detection from global feature, CPGF. Compared with raw Poincare index, CPGF narrows down the detection region in order to resistent the disturbance form the noise, which will result in improved detecting performance. The contribution of this paper can be divided into three aspects: (1) the orientation distribution of the fingerprint is noticed by our statistical analysis; (2) a reference line is obtained by fitting the point set with a certain orientation distribution; (3) an accurately and quickly core point detection algorithm from gobal information, CPGF, is proposed in this paper.

© Springer International Publishing Switzerland 2015
J. Yang et al. (Eds.): CCBR 2015, LNCS 9428, pp. 224–232, 2015.
DOI: 10.1007/978-3-319-25417-3_27

Our paper is organized as follows. A short introduction on the related work is conducted in Sec. 2. In Sec. 3, we make a statistical analysis on the orientation distribution of the fingerprint. The fitting of the reference line and the detection of the core point are described in Sec. 4. The evaluation experiments are followed in Sec. 5. Finally, the paper is concluded in Sec. 6.

2   Related Work

Core point is the key feature of fingerprint recognition, which can be detected by means of the fingerprint's special orientation distribution. Generally speaking, core point detecting algorithms can be divided into two categories, one is based on multi-resolution detection, and the other is by slided-window.

Multi-resolution based core point detection firstly divides the fingerprint image into several blocks with the same size, and then detects the core point through narrowing and screening the blocks. Kawagoe [3] detected the core point with convergence test, but the algorithm was sensitive to the noise even with complex preprocessing. However, Kawagoe's method draws more attention from many researchers. Waimunkoo [4] calculated the curvature on the blocks for core point detection, but the accuracy can be easily affected by the stain on the fingerprint and more pesudo-core points may be detected in the result. Van [5] proposed a method based on orientation consistency of core point, but it cannot handle the fracture and the adhesion of the ridge.

The core point detection algorithm by slided-window has also been widely used. Core points can be detected when the result calculated in the sliding window reaches to a threshold. Poincare index is the most commonly used mathematical model[6-7] for detecting core point. Hong [8] implemented a core point detection algorithm with Poincare index and achieved desirable performance, but it was sensitive to noise. J Zhou [9] improved Poincare index by analyzing the ridge feature, but raised the computational cost. In addition, based on the sine distribution around the core point, AK Jain [10] proposed to detect the core point with multi-orientation Gabor filter. Jin Qi [11] proposed a complex polynomial model for the sliding window to detect the core point which achieved superior performance, but it was difficult to satisfy the real time requirement for the complexity of its model. Although these methods can restrain noise to some extent, they increase the time consumption.

Whether the method is based on multi-resolution or sliding window, the noise and other pseudo-feature points are the main issues need to be eliminated. In [12], it assumed that there is a line joined the core point and delta point and this line can be obtained from global information. Inspired by [12], we propose the CPGF by means of adding global information. After analyzing the orientation distribution of the fingerprint, the reference line is obtained and the final core point is detected by Poincare index on designated region of interest. The CPGF is based on global information, which is insensitive to noise and achieves desirable performance.

3   Statistical Analysis on Fingerprint Orientation

Although the local feature around the core point can be detected easily, the detection results prone to be affected by the noise, such as fracture, adhesion, stain, which are similar to the core point. We conduct the fingerprint orientation distribution analysis in this section and manage to find a way to weaken the interference of noise. The statistical analysis on orientation is showed in Fig. 1(b). *X axis* is the angle of fingerprint orientation and the *y axis* is the summation of the pixel associated with the angle. As the graphic shows, the curve has two peaks which are generated by the flat ridge distributed on two sides of the core point. These ridges distributed in the intervals from 10 to 30 degrees and from 150 to 180 degrees which contribute to the summation of the peaks. The ridges from the core point to the fingertip are composed of the pixels with large curvature. These ridges distributed in the interval from 50 to 140 degrees lead to the valley of the curve. And each angle in interval from 50 to 140 degrees can be used for finding a point set which has straight-line distribution. Fig. 1 (c) shows the distribution of a point set with the orientation of 90 degrees. It is noticed that the points on the left are distributed as straight line and the points on the right are scattered. In order to get a point set distributed as straight-line, the detection region is restricted to the half of the fingerprint image so that we can get rid of the scattered points (Fig. 1(d)). With the orientation field from core point to the fingertip, we can fit a straight line which goes across the core point. This reference line plays the critical role in CPGF. The improved experimental result is given in section 5.

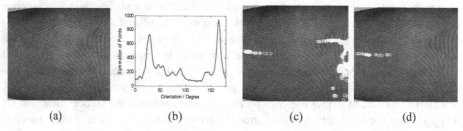

| (a) | (b) | (c) | (d) |

Fig. 1. (a) is the raw fingerprint image and (b) is the orientation distribution curve. (c) is the distribution of all 90 degrees points and (d) eliminates the scattered points in (c).

4   Core Point Detection

In this section, we will introduce our proposed algorithm, CPGF, in details. The block diagram of the proposed detection approach is shown in Fig. 2. It should be noted that the aim of our algorithm is to detect the sole core point. Two core points may appear in some fingerprints. And the core point, which is closest to the fingertip, is defined as the key core point. Without any special instruction, the core point detected by our algorithm is the key core point in our paper.

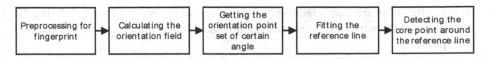

Fig. 2. Overview of the proposed detection approach.

4.1   Angle Interval Selection

According to the statistical analysis of the fingerprint orientation, each integer angle in the interval from 50 to 140 corresponds to a point set (a total of 91 point sets). One of these point sets can be used for fitting a reference line that goes across the core point. However, the points in this interval are distributed in half of the fingerprint image from the core point to the fingertip. Detecting a core point in such a large region needs a long time and we should narrow the search interval. Considering the orientation distribution above the core point, the point sets with largest curvature correspond to the angle from 85 to 95 degree. These point sets distribute as a straight line which is close to the core point. The point sets from 50 to 85 degrees and from 95 to 140 degrees are also distributed as a straight line. However, the ridges above the core point are not strictly a semi-circle and their shape becomes flat when it extends on both side of the core point. In Fig. 3, (a) is the raw fingerprint. (b), (c) and (d) circle the distribution of points with 134, 90 and 46 degree, respectively. The 90 degree point set, obviously, has the best distribution as a straight line. So the optimal angle in our method is selected in the interval from 85 to 95 degrees.

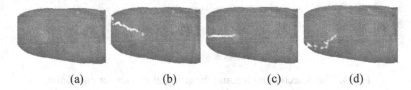

(a)   (b)   (c)   (d)

Fig. 3. Sample images from our database for different degree.

4.2   Reference Line Fitting

In this section, we describe the optimal angle selection and reference line fitting. The optimal angle selection consists of two steps, the first step is to remove the noise points, and the second step is to select the optimal point set in the interval from 85 to 95 degrees. Two types of noise point will affect the line fitting, the first type is the irregular orientation field from the core point to the knuckle (Fig. 1(c)), and the second type is the noise points (fracture, adhesion or stain) from the core point to the fingertip. In order to eliminate the first type of noise, our algorithm selects the point set in an effective region from the middle of the fingerprint image to the fingertip. On the other hand, the orientation of the ridge cannot change suddenly so that the point sets can be purified to remove the second type of noise. During the purification, each point in the interval from 85 to 95 degree is subtracted by its eight neighborhoods.

All the differences are translated to absolute values which are used for generating the summation. If the summation exceeds the threshold level, the point is evaluated as a noise point.

After the above processing on the noise, the following step is to select an optimal angle in the optimal interval to confirm a point set for fitting the reference line. The interval from 85 to 95 degrees has 11 point sets. Due to the ridge above the core point is not strictly a semi-circle, not all point sets distribute as straight line. Screening is needed to achieve the optimal point set. In order to solve this problem, for each point set, every two adjacent points in the point set are used for calculating tangent. All the results of tangents are used for calculating the variances, and the point set with the minimum variance will be the optimal point set to fit the reference line. To improve the computational efficiency, the least square method is applied to fit the reference line.

4.3   Core Point Detection

This section describes the core point detection with reference line. Because the ridge above the core point is not strictly a semi-circle, the reference line may not go across the core point accurately. To be more robust, the detection region is extended to the neighborhoods of the reference line. In Fig. 4, the black point is the real core point marked artificially. The white line is the reference line. The core point may not be detected on the reference line. Our algorithm becomes more robust with this extended region (the red rectangular). And the core point can be detected in this region by Poincare index [6].

Fig. 4. The detection region and the artificial marker for core point.

5   Experiments

In this section, we are going to evaluate the accuracy and speed of our proposed core point detection algorithm. This part firstly introduces the database and evaluation standard used in our experiments, and then shows the experimental results of CPGF compared with other algorithms. Nevertheless, it is also demonstrated that the experiments on the AMI [11] optimized by the reference line are able to achieve superior performance. And the time consumption is discussed in the last part. All the algorithms mentioned in the experiments are implemented with C++.

5.1   Database and Evaluation Standard

In order to prove the CPGF has the ability to resist noise, contactless fingerprint database is adopted for the evaluation. It contains complex noise and difficult to be removed in practice. We build a contactless fingerprint database with our contactless fingerprint acquisition equipment. The database contains 393 fingerprint images and the rotation is less than 30 degrees. To prove the efficiency of reference line on eliminating noise, the fingerprint images do not have any preprocesses except segmentation and removing the background. Samples are shown in Fig. 5.

The exist core point detecting algorithms are almost singular point detecting or delta point detection, but we focus on core point detection in this paper. So the evaluation standard for singular point detection is not suitable for our experiments. In order to be more intuitive on reflecting the performance of CPGF, the distance distribution curve is utilized as a criteria. In the experiments, the distance between the output coordinate and ground truth core point is recorded in each test, as well as the test time. On the curve, the x *axis* is the distance between the output coordinate to the ground truth core point. The y *axis* is the summation of the test time for the distance. For example, if there are n detected core points have the distance of m pixel to the real core point(ground truth core point), the coordinate ($x = m$, $y = n$) on the distribution curve is achieved. Obviously, if the curve distributes more to the left and narrower interval, the algorithm will achieve higher accuracy. In the experiments, the first detected core point is designated as the key core point. If another core point is close to the first core point (within 4 pixels), the key core point is the average of them. Otherwise, the test of the sample image terminates, i.e., only one core point is detected in every test. The ability of resisting noise is demanded in this standard.

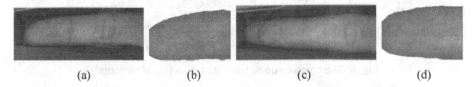

| (a) | (b) | (c) | (d) |

Fig. 5. (b) and (d) are the preprocess image of (a) and (c) respectively

5.2   The Evaluation of CPGF

To demonstrate the performance of CPGF, comparison experiments between Poincare index, AMI and our algorithm are conducted in this part. And three point sets selected from intervals 55 to 70 degrees, 85 to 95 degrees and 115 to 140 degrees, can be used for fitting three reference lines. Calculating the average of their intersections is able to obtain the coordinate of core point, noted as three reference lines intersection core point (TLI), which also achieves desirable performance.

As the graph shown in Fig. 6(a), the highest peak is on the curve of CPGF from the distance between 0 to 20 pixels, which proves that CPGF achieves the highest accuracy, because the reference line narrows down the detection region and eliminates the noise of other region. The curve of Poincare index has two peaks in the intervals from 0 to 20 pixels and from 100 to 150 pixels, but the first peak is smaller than the CPGF. Most detected points in the interval from 100 to 150 pixels shows that the accuracy of Poincare index is low. And the AMI has more false detection in the interval from 50 to 100 pixels because of the noise. The output images on comparison between CPGF and Poincare index are shown in Fig. 7.(a) and (b) are the result of CPGF. (c) and (d) are the result of Poincare Index. It can be found that for the same fingerprint image, CPGF can detect the core point accurately while Poincare Index detects the false core point caused by the noise. From the Fig. 6(a), we can see that the TLI's accuracy is lower than CPGF, but higher than the other two algorithms, which also proves the effectively of the reference line.

The AMI[11] is a novel core point detection algorithm based on complex polynomial model. It achieves good performance in high quality fingerprint image, but it cannot handle the image with complex noise. This experiment also shows that AMI can be optimized by reference line proposed in our paper. During the experiments, the optimized algorithm calculates the reference line, and then AMI is used for detecting the core point in the neighborhood of the reference line. The detecting regulation is also the same as ection 5.1. As the graph shown in Fig. 6(b), the peak of optimized AMI in the interval between 0 to 20 pixels is higher than the raw AMI, which proves that the reference line plays an important role in improving the accuracy of AMI.

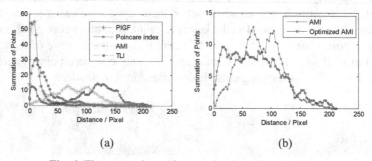

(a)   (b)

Fig. 6. The comparison of core point detection algorithms.

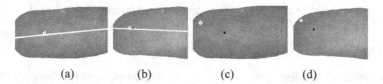

(a)   (b)   (c)   (d)

Fig. 7. (a) and (b) are the result of CPGF, (c) and (d) are the result of Poincare index.

All above core point detection algorithms are also evaluated in this paper according to the instructions from the first fingerprint singular points detection competitions (SPD2010) [13]. Due to our algorithm focuses on core point detection, detection rate and miss rate are calculated for quantitatively measuring the performance. The definitions of such metrics can be found in [13]. If the distance between a detected core point and a ground truth core point is less than 10 pixels, the detected core point is said to be truly detected and, otherwise, it is called a miss.

The experimental results are listed in table 1. Our algorithm yields the best performance over other algorithms. Compared with other algorithms, our algorithm achieves 85.75% in detection rate. It is important to note that the reference line in our algorithm narrows down the detection region and eliminates the noise interference in other region. This makes our algorithm achieve satisfactory performance. The comparison on time consumption amount of CPGF, TLI, optimized AMI, Poincare index and AMI is also shown in Table 1. It demonstrates that CPGF achieves the least time consumption, that is because the reference line narrows down the detection region. Besides, the time consumption is much lower while AMI is optimized by the reference line, which demonstrates that the reference line is valuable for application.

Table 1. Performance ranking of five algorithms.

Algorithm	CPGF	Optimized AMI	Poincare index	AMI	TLI
Detection rate(%)	85.75	20.36	34.35	6.16	21.63
Average time consumption [ms]	11.41	88.8	16.5	1921.4	19.29

6   Conclusion

This paper proposes a novel core point detection method adding the global information from the fingerprint orientation field. The reference line is adopted according to the statistical analysis of the orientation field, which can be used for narrowing down the detection region and eliminating the noise in other region. Compared with other algorithms based on local feature, CPGF achieves higher accuracy and least time consumption.

Acknowledgments. This work was supported by the National Natural Science Foundation of China (No. 61105019, No. 61573151), the Science and Technology Program of Guangzhou (No. 0201510010088), the Fundamental Research Funds for the Central Universities, SCUT (No. 2014ZG0041, No. 2015ZM080).

References

1. Babatunde, I.G.: Fingerprint Matching Using Minutiae-Singular Points Network. International Journal of Signal Processing, Image Processing and Pattern Recognition **8**(2), 375–388 (2015)
2. Wang, J., Olsen, M.A., Busch, C.: Finger image quality based on singular point localization. In: SPIE Defense+ Security. International Society for Optics and Photonics, pp. 907503–907503 (2014)
3. Kawagoe, M., Tojo, A.: Fingerprint pattern classification. Pattern Recognition **17**(3), 295–303 (1984)
4. Koo, W.M., Kot, A.C.: Curvature-based singular points detection. In: Bigun, J., Smeraldi, F. (eds.) AVBPA 2001. LNCS, vol. 2091, pp. 229–234. Springer, Heidelberg (2001)
5. Van, T.H., Le, H.T.: An efficient algorithm for fingerprint reference-point detection. In: Computing and Communication Technologies, pp. 1–7. IEEE Press, Kottayam (2009)
6. Sherlock, B., Monro, D.: A model for interpreting fingerprint topology. Pattern Recognition **26**(93), 1047–1055 (1993)

7. Vizcaya, P.R., Gerhardt, L.A.: A nonlinear orientation model for global description of fingerprints. Pattern Recognition **29**(7), 1221–1231 (1996)
8. Hong, L.: Automatic personal identification using fingerprints. Michigan State University (1998)
9. Zhou, J., Chen, F., Gu, J.: A novel algorithm for detecting singular points from fingerprint images. Pattern Analysis & Machine Intelligence **31**(7), 1239–1250 (2009)
10. Jain, A.K., Prabhakar, S., Hong, L.: Filterbank-based fingerprint matching. Image Processing **9**(5), 846–859 (2000)
11. Qi, J., Liu, S.: A robust approach for singular point extraction based on complex polynomial model. In: Computer Vision and Pattern Recognition Workshops (CVPRW), pp. 78–83. IEEE Press, Columbus (2014)
12. Gupta, P., Gupta, P.: A robust singular point detection algorithm. Applied Soft Computing **29**, 411–423 (2015)
13. Spd 2010 - fingerprint singular points detection competition database. http://paginas.fe. up.pt/~spd2010/

Fingerprint Liveness Detection Based on Pore Analysis

Mengya Lu, Zhiqiang Chen, and Weiguo Sheng$^{(\boxtimes)}$

School of Computer Science and Technology, Zhejiang University of Technology,
Hangzhou 310023, People's Republic of China
wsheng@zjut.edu.cn

Abstract. Fingerprint scanners can be spoofed by using artificial fingerprints made from Play-Doh, gelatin and silicone molds. It is, thus, necessary to offer protection for fingerprint systems against such threats. Since it is difficult to replicate pores during the fake fingerprints fabrication, in this paper, we propose a pore based liveness detection method. In our method, we firstly extract the sweat pores from a grayscale fingerprint image using the Mexh wavelet transform and adaptive Gaussian filters. Based on the obtained pore information, we compute five statistical features of the image to quantify the pore distribution. Finally, the support vector machine (SVM) technique is used for classification. Our experimental results show the proposed method can achieve an average classification error rate (ACE) of 7.11%, 11.4% on ATVS-FFp and LiveDet2011 data sets, respectively, generally outperforming conventional liveness detection schemes to be compared.

Keywords: Fingerprint · Liveness detection · Pore extraction · Image processing

1   Introduction

Personal identification is a very important issue in today's security systems. Benefiting from the largely accepted uniqueness of fingerprints and the availability of low cost acquisition devices, fingerprints are perhaps the most widely used biometric [1] for secure applications. However, like other biometrics, fingerprint based security systems are usually subjected to various attacks at the sensor level [6-8]. Previous studies have shown that many fingerprint capture devices can be deceived by well-made fake fingerprints [7], created from latent fingerprints or with the collaboration of fingerprint owner. Also it is not difficult to make molds of fake fingerprints with Play-Doh, gelatin and silicone materials. Thus, it is essential for fingerprint systems have the ability to defeat the spoof attack from fake fingerprints.

Liveness detection, ensuring that only live fingerprints are captured for further identification, has become a mean to circumvent attacks from fake fingerprints. Practically, a variety of liveness detection solutions have been proposed. Based on the different types of the liveness features, the software-based solution can be generally divided into several categories: skin distortion based methods, texture based methods, pore based methods, perspiration-based methods and combined method.

© Springer International Publishing Switzerland 2015
J. Yang et al. (Eds.): CCBR 2015, LNCS 9428, pp. 233–240, 2015.
DOI: 10.1007/978-3-319-25417-3_28

These methods used a variety of technologies including power spectrum energy, ridgelet transformation, statistical features of fingerprint texture, middle valley signal, gray intensity and local descriptor (LD) based detectors, etc.

Among the software based methods, the sweat pore based method is viable. Pores, which are the most obvious level-3 fingerprint feature, are very small (80-$200\mu m$) circular-like structures on the ridges of the fingertip. As the pore size is much less than 1 mm, making it very difficult to replicate during the fabricating of fake fingerprints [7]. A large number of pores can be easily detected in live fingerprint images whilst, on average, a much lower number of pores is present in fake fingerprint images [4]. A few proposed methods make detection of sweat pores on fingertip images as a sign of liveness.

Manivanan et al. [2] proposed a method for extraction and location of active sweat pores in high-resolution fingerprint images. They applied highpass filter to extract active sweat pore, then used a correlation filter to locate the position of pores. Memon et al. [3] extended the previous study [2]. They developed a newly image processing algorithm based on High-Pass and Correlation filtering technique for sweat pore detection. Espinoza et al. [4] observed that the difference in pore quantities between a reference image and a query image (genuine or fake) can be used as a discriminating factor for fingerprint liveness detection. In their study they have only focused on the presence or absence of visualized pores with a linear discriminant analysis. Marcialis et al. [5] developed a method based on pore distribution between two images captured at time 0s and 5s. Johnson et al. [9] presented a fingerprint pore analysis approach, which combines the analysis of the detected pores distribution with the analysis of gray level distribution around each pore center. There are obvious drawbacks in these previously developed pore-based methods. For Espinoza's method [4], it required comparing the pore quantity between query image (real or fake) and the recorded one to do the liveness detection, which is intricate and time-consuming. The method proposed in [5] needs two images captured at 0s and 5s, which is not efficient for real-time system and user-friendly.

In this paper, we also present a liveness detection method based on fingerprint pore analysis. In contrast to previous pore-based methods, our method combines the usage of Mexh wavelet transform with an adaptive Gaussian filter, which can extract pores accurately and robustly with the adaptive parameters setting. We demonstrate the performance of our method on ATVS-FFp Database and the 2011 International Fingerprint Liveness Detection competition Dataset with a promising performance. Additionally, we need only one fingerprint image on 500dpi, which is used for identification, to extract the feature to for liveness detection. This makes it easier than previous method to be integrated into the existing fingerprint system.

2   Proposed Method

The live and fake fingerprints are different considering on pore quantity. Reasons include the perspiration pattern of live fingers and differences in the properties of the spoof materials compared to human skin. Therefore we utilize image processing techniques to quantify sweat pores patterns along ridges to discriminate between live and fake fingerprints. The procedure of the proposed method can be divided into three stages: pore detection, statistical features extraction and classification. Pore detection is achieved by combining the Mexh wavelet transform and an adaptive Gaussian filter. Specifically, we first enhance the pore feature with the Mexh wavelet transform. Secondly, the enhanced fingerprint image is segmented into blocks, from which the orientation fields and ridge periods are computed of each block. Then an adaptive Gaussian filter, which can adjust its parameter value adaptively according to the local ridge period, is introduced to extract the sweat pores from each block. Based on the obtained pore information, we subsequently compute five statistical features of the image: pore number, pore density, mean pore space, its variance and variation coefficient feature, which combine into a pore feature vector. Finally, SVM is used to distinguish the fake fingerprints from the live ones.

2.1   Pore Detection

Wavelet analysis is a time-frequency analysis method based on Fourier transform. It can realize the localization of the time domain and the frequency domain at the same time and can adjust the frequency window adaptability. Mexh wavelets have good localization ability both in time domain and frequency domain, and it is suitable for detecting entrained instantaneous abnormal phenomenon in normal signal. The intensity of the pore positions always change abruptly from black to white, which sudden change can be enhanced by Mexh wavelet transform. Therefore we firstly apply the Mexh wavelet transform to the fingerprint image, which is defined as follow:

$$\varphi(x,y) = -2\pi(x^2 + y^2)^{p/2} \exp\left(-\frac{|(\sigma_x x)^2 + \sigma_y y^2|}{2}\right) \tag{1}$$

where $\sigma_x \in R$, $\sigma_y \in R$, $p > 0$. Here we set the $p=2$, $\sigma_x = \sigma_y = 1.5$.

The second step is the image segmentation. In the fingerprint image, compared with background region, the difference of gray level between the ridge and valley of the interested region is large. Thus, the statistical variance of the gray level in interested region is significant, while it is much smaller in background area. Based on this characteristic, we utilize local variance method to segment the fingerprint image. This segmentation allows ignoring potential contaminations as well as decreasing the effect of the fingerprint deformation. The segmentation process is shown as follows:

1) Divide the input fingerprint image into non-overlapping $w*w$ sub-block (we set the $w=16$ here);

2) Calculate the average grey value of every block using the following formula:

$$M(k,l) = \frac{1}{w*w}\sum_{j=1}^{w}\sum_{i=1}^{w} G(i,j) \quad k = 1, \ldots, M, l = 1, \ldots, M \tag{2}$$

where $G(i,j)$ refers to the grey value of the image elements in the ith row j^{th} column in the image sub-block(k, l). $M(k, l)$ indicates the average grayscale of the sub-block. We divide the fingerprint image into $w*w$ block. Let the width of the image be "Width" pixels, the high of the image be "Height" pixels, then the $M= Height/w$, $N=Width/w$.

3) Calculate the gray variance of each fingerprint image block using the formula 3:

$$V(k,l) = \frac{1}{w*w} \sum_{j=1}^{w} \sum_{i=1}^{w} [G(i,j) - M(k,l)]^2 \tag{3}$$

4) For each fingerprint image sub-block, when the value of $V(k, l)$ is less than a predefined threshold T, then set it as the background region. Otherwise, set it as interested area.

Based on the each image block, we further compute the local orientation field and the local ridge period. It is performed according to the following steps:

1) Calculate the gradient component of each pixel, and use the Sobe$_1$ template (formula 4) of the size 3×3 to calculate gradient amplitude value ($Gx(s, t)$, $Gy(s, t)$) of the pixel (i, j).

$$Sobel_x = \{(-1,0,1), (-2,0,2), (-1,0,1)\} \tag{4}$$

2) Calculate the local direction θ (i, j) of each block whose center at (i, j) using formula 5.

$$\begin{cases} \theta(i,j) = \frac{1}{2} tan^{-1}\left(\frac{V_x(i,j)}{V_y(i,j)}\right) \\ V_x(i,j) = \sum_{s=i-\frac{w}{2}}^{i+\frac{w}{2}} \sum_{t=j-\frac{w}{2}}^{j+\frac{w}{2}} 2G_x(s,t)G_y(s,t) \\ V_y(i,j) = \sum_{s=i-\frac{w}{2}}^{i+\frac{w}{2}} \sum_{t=j-\frac{w}{2}}^{j+\frac{w}{2}} \left(G_x^2(s,t) - G_y^2(s,t)\right) \end{cases} \tag{5}$$

3) Set k for the distance from the spectrum center to the spectrum peak (in pixels), N for the image size, the ridge period $p=N/k$.

After obtaining the mean orientation θ and the median ridge period p of each block, we proceed to extract the pores. As the spatial distributions of the pores are similar to two-dimensional Gaussian functions, we use a Gaussian filter with adaptive parameter to extract the pores within each block. We set the standard deviation parameter σ of the Gaussian filter to cp_i, where the p_i is the ridge period of the ith block and c is a regulation constant. So each image block enhanced by the Mexh wavelet pass through the Gaussian filter to extract the pores, which produce an images S_1. We apply the Gabor filter[11] to the image enhanced by the Mexh wavelet to separate fingerprint ridges from valleys, which produce an images S_2. After converting image S_1 and S_2 into binary images, we add the two images and output the extracted pore information.

The last step is to remove the possible spurious pores. In many instances, spurious pores can be found on the valleys in fingerprint images. To avoid this, we employ the following constraints to post-process the extracted pores. Firstly, pores should reside on ridges only. To implement this constraint, we use the binary ridge image as a mask to filter the extracted pores. Secondly, the mean intensity of a true pore should be large enough. In our experiments, we discarded the last smallest 5% pores. An example of the resulting image is shown in Fig. 1.

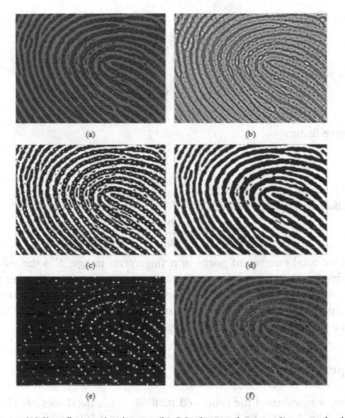

Fig. 1. (a) A partial live fingerprint image. (b) Mexh wavelet transform on the image (a) to enhance the pores. (c)Image (b) pass through the Gaussian filter to extract the pores. (d) Enhancement of ridges of image (b) using Gabor filters. (e) Get the pore information by adding the image(c) to image (d). (f) Extracted pores of image (e) (pink circles) add to the original image (a).

2.2   Features Extraction

Fig. 1 shows the example of the typical processing steps with the proposed method. For normal live fingerprints, it is easy to get a clear pore distribution structure when fingertip touches on the senor plane with a normal pressure, as shows in Fig. 1(f). However, it is very difficult to replicate the pore distribution during the fabrication of fake fingerprints. Based on the extracted pore information, we subsequently compute five statistical features of the image: pore number, pore density, pore space and its mean, variance and variation coefficient feature, which quantify the pore distribution of the fingerprint. These statistical features defined as follow:

F_1: pore number feature:

$$C_1 = N \tag{6}$$

F_2: pore density feature:

$$C_2 = \frac{N}{S} \tag{7}$$

F_3: mean pore space feature:

$$C_3 = \frac{\sum_{i=1}^{N} D_i}{N} \tag{8}$$

F_4: variance feature:

$$C_4 = \sum_{i=1}^{N} (D_i - \mu)^2 \tag{9}$$

F_5: variation coefficient feature:

$$C_5 = \frac{\sigma}{\mu} \tag{10}$$

where N is the total number of pores in a fingerprint image, S is the valid area of a fingerprint image, D_i is the minimum distance of a pore(x_i, y_i) with other pores in the image, μ is the mean and σ is the standard deviation of D_i. After statistical feature values are computed, which combine into a pore features vector, SVM is used to separate fake fingerprints from the live fingerprints.

3   Experiments

In this paper, we evaluated the proposed method on the databases of ATVS-FFp and LivDet2011. The ATVS-FFp Databases contain over 4,500 real and fake fingerprint images specifically thought to evaluate the performance of liveness detection methods. Fake samples were captured from gummy fingers generated both with and without the cooperation of the user. Three different sensors were used to acquire the database: flat-optical (512 dpi), flat-capacitive (500 dpi), and sweeping-thermal (500 dpi).The LivDet2011 dataset is used for the 2011 International Fingerprint Liveness Detection competition. LivDet2011 consists of images from four different devices including Biometrika, Digital Persona, Italdata and Sagem [10]. There are 4000 images for each of these datasets, 2000 live images and 2000 spoof images.

The following rates are used to evaluate the system performance of liveness detection. False accept ratio (FAR) is defined as the percentage of fake fingerprints that are detected as live. False reject ratio (FRR) is defined as the percentage of live fingerprints that are detected as fake. Average Classification Error rate (ACE) is the average of FAR and FRR weighted by the number of spoof and live samples, respectively. SVM is used to classification on the two databases. For each database, half of the data is used for training and the other for testing. Table 1 shows the performance of the proposed method on ATVS-FFp Databases. It shows the proposed method works well on the three scanners, especially on the optical and capacitive scanners, and the average classification error rate is 7.11%. The results for the LivDet2011 datasets are presented in Table 2.The performance of the proposed approach is compared to the top performer on each of the four datasets from the LivDet2011 competition and the state of the art approaches. Dermalog, Federico and CASIA are the top performers on each dataset from LivDet2011[10]. The experimental data shows that the proposed method gets better results than the these method for ItalData and Swipe database in LivDet2011.The average classification error of the proposed approach is 11.44% for all datasets in LivDet2011, and the winner in LiveDet2011 is 23.3%. The performances of the LBP method and the newly pore detection method [9] are also compared with our method. Our method gets better results on some datasets.

Table 1. Performance of the proposed method on ATVS-FFp databases.

Type of scanners	FAR	FRR	ACE
Optical scanner	1.64%	7.13%	4.39%
Capacitive scanner	8.08%	3.28%	5.68%
Thermal scanner	10.11%	12.39%	11.25%

Table 2. Comparing ACE performance of the proposed method with LBP, pore detetion method [9], Dermalog, Federico and CASIA on LivDet 2011 databases.

Databases(columns) Algorithm(rows)	Biometrika	ItalData	Crossmatch	Swipe	Ave. ACE
Proposed method	14.4%	10.6%	13.0%	7.6%	11.4%
LBP	11.0%	19.0%	10.6%	8.4%	12.3
Pore Detecion	27.4%	28.8%	35.9%	41.6%	33.4%
Dermalog	20.0%	21.8%0	36.1%	15.3%	23.3%
Federico	40.0%	40.0%	8.9%	13.5%	25.6%
CASIA	33.9%	26.7%	25.4%	22.9%	27.2%

In general, our experiments show significant performance improvement in fingerprint system security using the proposed method. The advantages of our proposed method as the following: First, we combines the adaptive Gaussian filters with Mexh wavelet transform, which would can extract pores accurately and robustly. Second, our method does not need to compare between the query image (real or fake) and the stored one in the database. This makes it much easier than previous methods to be integrated into the existing fingerprint system. Finally, our method requires only one fingerprint image with 500dpi. This makes the real-time authentication possible and user friendly. For future works, our method can be improved by fusing with an existing liveness detection method.

4   Conclusions

A pore-based fingerprint liveness detection method has been proposed in this paper. As the pore distribution in fake and live fingerprints is significantly different, we extract the pore information from the grayscale fingerprint image as the features for liveness detection. Our method combines the Mexh wavelet transform with an adaptive Gaussian filter, which can extract pores accurately and robustly. Additionally, we need only one fingerprint image with 500dpi, which is used for identification, to extract the feature for liveness detection. The proposed method is evaluated on the ATVS-FFp and LivDet2011 databases with very promising performance and generally outperformance related methods.

Acknowledgments. This work was supported in part by the National Natural Science Foundation of China (Grant No. 61203288, 61573316) and the Zhejiang Provincial Natural Science Foundation of China (Grant No. LY12F02031).

References

1. Derakhshani, R., Schuckers, S., Hornak, L., O'Gorman, L.: Determination of Vitality from A Noninvasive Biomedical Measurement for Use in Fingerprint Scanners. Pattern Recognition **36**, 383–396 (2003)
2. Manivanan, N., Memon, S., Balachandran, W.: Automatic Detection of Active Sweat Pores of Fingerprint Using Highpass And Correlation Filtering. Electronics letters **46**(18), 1268–1269 (2010)
3. Memon, S., Manivannan, N., Balachandran, W.: Active pore detection for liveness in fingerprint identification system. In: 19th Telecommunications forum, pp. 619–622 (2011)
4. Espinoza, M., Champod, C.: Using the number of pores on fingerprint images to detect spoofing attacks. In: 2011 International Conference on Hand-Based Biometrics, pp. 1–5 (2011)
5. Marcialis, G., Roli, F., Tidu, A.: Analysis of fingerprint pores for vitality detection. In: 20th International Conference on Pattern Recognition, pp. 1289–1292 (2010)
6. Sandstrom, M.: Liveness Detection in Fingerprint Recognition Systems (2004)
7. Matsumoto, T., Matsumoto, H., Yamada, K., Hoshino, S.: Impact of Artificial 'Gummy' Fingers on Fingerprint Systems. In: Proceedings of SPIE, vol. 4677 (2002)
8. Vander Putte, T., Keuning, J.: Biometrical fingerprint recognition: don't get your fingers burned. In: Proceedings of IFIP TC8/WG8.8 Fourth Working Conference on Smart Card Research and Advanced Applications, pp. 289–303. Kluwer Academic Publishers, Dordrecht (2000)
9. Johnson, P., Schuckers, S.: Fingerprint pore characteristics for liveness detection. In: Proceedings IEEE BIOSIG (2014)
10. Yambay, D., Ghiani, L., Denti, P., Marcialis, G., Roli, F., Schuckers, S.: LivDet 2011 fingerprint liveness detection competition 2011. In: IAPR/IEEE Int. Conf. on Biometrics, pp. 208–215 (2012)
11. Hong, L., Wan, Y., Jain, A.: Fingerprint Image Enhancement: Algorithms and Performance Evaluation. IEEE Trans. PAMI **20**(8), 777–789 (1998)

A DCNN Based Fingerprint Liveness Detection Algorithm with Voting Strategy

Chenggang Wang, Ke Li, Zhihong Wu, and Qijun Zhao[(⊠)]

School of Computer Science, Sichuan University, Chengdu 610000, China
{chenggang.wang,ke.li007}@stu.scu.edu.cn,
{wuzhihong,qjzhao}@scu.edu.cn

Abstract. The concern of the safety of fingerprint authentication system is rising with its widely using for it is easy to be attacked by spoof (fake) fingerprints. Fake fingerprints are usually made of Ploy-Doh, silicon or other
artifacts. So most current approaches rely on fingerprint liveness detection as
main anti-spoofing mechanisms. Recently, researchers propose to use local feature descriptor for fingerprint liveness detection, but the results are still not satisfying the real world application requirement. Inspired by the newly trend of
application of Deep Convolution Neural Network (DCNN) in computer vision
field and its outstanding performance in face detection and image classification,
we propose a novel fingerprint liveness detection method based on DCNN and
voting strategy, which performs better than handcraft feature and optimize the
process of feature extraction and classifier training simultaneously. The experimental results on the datasets of LivDet2011 and LivDet2013 show that the
proposed algorithm has great improvement compare to the former state-of-the-
art algorithm, and keep highly real-time performance at the same time.

Keywords: Fingerprint liveness detection · Fingerprint anti-spoofing · Deep
learning · Deep convolution neural network · Voting strategy

1 Introduction

Fingerprint technology [1] has widely used for it offers authentication service and
avoids typical problems of systems based on the use of passwords, meanwhile the
safety demands of fingerprint technology is also growing. Many studies have been
reported [1-3] that fingerprint system is vulnerable to be spoofed by fake fingerprints.
These fake fingerprints are usually made by reproducing the fingerprint pattern on
artificial materials such as silicone, Play-Doh, gelatin and so on. Thus, people try to
solve fingerprint anti-spoofing problem by study fingerprint liveness detection algorithm [4]. Liveness detection is the ability of a system that can distinguish live fingerprints from fake ones. However, as was reported in Liveness Detection Competition
[5-7], the fingerprint liveness detection error rate is still not low enough to meet safety
requirement of fingerprint authentication system.

© Springer International Publishing Switzerland 2015
J. Yang et al. (Eds.): CCBR 2015, LNCS 9428, pp. 241–249, 2015.
DOI: 10.1007/978-3-319-25417-3_29

Two main stream methods of fingerprint anti-spoofing are hardware based method and software based method. Software based method become popular for it is much cheaper, more flexible and less invasive. A lot of software based methods have been done on analyzing static or dynamic features of fingerprint images which can distinguish live samples from fake ones. The extraction of static features is more popular for its efficiency. Only one or a few images rather than an image sequences [12] will be needed to extracting the static features.

Recently, the application of image local feature analysis has gained a lot of popularity for its outstanding performance. Some fingerprint liveness detection methods are based on gradients, such as LBP [15], while others are study local phase, which is able to preserve the correlation between neighborhood samples better and can give a more precise pattern description. In paper [16], Ghi et al first propose to use a kind of local phase named LPQ for fingerprint liveness detection. LPQ has similar structure to LBP, but it encodes the phase information by performing STFT on the local patch rather than gradients. Latter, a further improvement of this method named LCPD is proposed in [17], which combines gradient and local phase information together to form a better liveness detector. Compare to LBP and LPQ approaches, Ghiani et al have studied the application of BSIF[18] in fingerprint liveness detection task, which was first proposed by Kannala[14] inspired by LBP and LPQ method and learns a filter set by using statistics of natural images.

We notice that most of existing fingerprint liveness detection algorithms are based on handcraft features. In fact, the success of an anti-spoofing method is usually rely on expert knowledge to engineer features that are able to distinguish the live samples from the fake ones. However, the need of custom-tailored solutions is really expensive and not suit to handle countless possible attacks. Furthermore, small changes in the spoofing attack could require the redesign of the entire system.

Recently, Deep Convolution Neural Network (DCNN) has been successfully implemented in image classification[9], object detection[10], and many other tasks[11], and proved to have great power of extracting local feature of images[20]. The differences between traditional machine learning algorithms and DCNN are illustrated in Fig. 1. In paper [19], DCNN was firstly attempted to solve fingerprint liveness detection problem. However, feature extraction and classification are designed into two separate part in that work [19], which makes the whole system can not be optimized simultaneously. And it was also designed to take the whole image as the input, so obviously the introducing of the useless background information into the training stage is inevitable, which will compromise the performance of the DCNN.

Inspired by previous work [19], here we propose a novel DCNN based fingerprint liveness detection algorithm with voting strategy. We designed a DCNN structure named Finger-Net and employ Softmax as the last layer and classifier of the DCNN model to optimize the process of feature extraction and classifier training simultaneously through back propagation pass. We also adopt segmentation technique as the preprocessing procedure to avoid useless background information input. Experimental results on the LivDet2011 [6] and LivDet2013 [7] databases have shown that the performance of proposed approach outperforms state-of-the-art algorithms in terms of Half Total Error Rate.

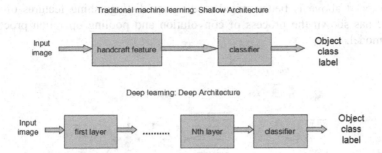

Fig. 1. Comparison of processing procedure between traditional machine learning algorithms and DCNN algorithm

2   The Proposed Method

2.1   Training Data Preparation

We train and test our DCNN model on the benchmarks of LivDet2011 [6] and LivDet2013 [7] databases. As we can see from table 1, the training sample on both databases is relatively small, and the fingerprint image includes useless background information as well. So we cannot just put the raw images into the DCNN directly without any preprocessing procedures. The procedures are as follows. Firstly, we cut the images into non-overlapped small patches as big as 32×32 pixels, then calculate the variance of all the pixel value of each patch. Next we adopt threshold based image segmentation method to segment fingerprint images. We try to make the segmented image include no background part by carefully selecting the threshold value. After a series experiments, in this paper, we set the threshold value equal to half of the mean value of all the variance. Then we use those patches whose variance value is above selected threshold to train DCNN model.

2.2   DCNN Architecture

Deep Convolution Neural Network is a type of artificial neural network inspired from biology. The three prominent feature of DCNN are localized receptive fields, weight sharing and spatial pooling. By combing the three ideas above, DCNN achieve some extend of drift, scaling and deformation invariability [20]. In DCNN, receptive field means that each output neuron are only respond to a local region of input neurons, which is pretty much like human visual cortex. We can consider the idea of receptive field as convolution operation. Each neuron of the hidden layer can be seen as one type of convolution operation, this is called feature mapping. Obviously, learning a classifier with a huge input features is really difficult and easy to get over-fitted. So, spatial pooling operation is adopted to avoid this situation in DCNN. The mechanism we mentioned above is better suited to discover distinguishing features of images. Figure 2 has shown the process of convolution and pooling operation process of a DCNN model.

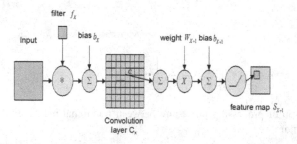

Fig. 2. The convolution and pooling operation process of a DCNN model.

The architectures of DCNN model which are used in this paper, named Cifar10-Net and Finger-Net are shown in Figure 3. They are consisted of data layer, convolution layer, pooling layer, local response normalization layer, innerproduct layer and Softmax. In this paper we use ReLU as the activation function.

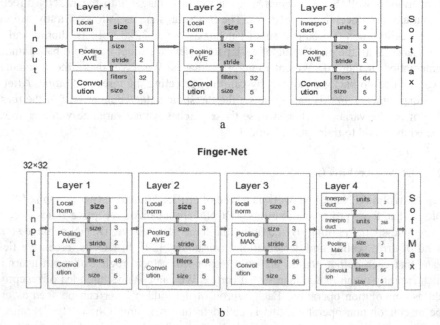

Fig. 3. The architecture of DCNN model used in this paper: (a) Cifar-10; (b) proposed Finger-Net. Finger-Net architecture suits the fingerprint liveness detection better.

DCNN training process can be divided into two stages: feed forward pass and back propagation pass, which enables to optimize the process of feature extraction and classifier training simultaneously. We put the fingerprint patch and its corresponding label into the DCNN, and then use DCNN to extract the image features. SoftMax was adopted in this paper as the final layer as well as classifier, which predicts the probability distribution of every label and defined as:

$$y_i = \exp(x_i) / \sum\nolimits_{j=1}^{N} \exp(x_j)$$

(1)

Where x_i and y_i are the input and output, respectively, of the ith neuron at the output layer. The training process is illustrated in Fig. 4.

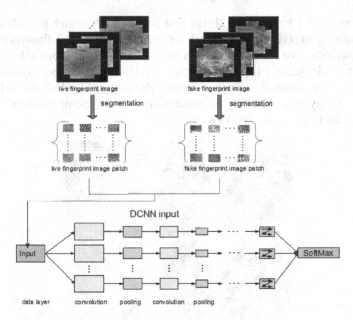

Fig. 4. The training process of proposed algorithm.

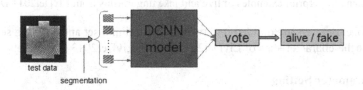

Fig. 5. The testing process of proposed algorithm.

2.3   Voting Strategy

After we finish the DCNN model training, we test the model as shown in Fig. 5. Firstly, we divided the testing fingerprint images into 32*32 pixel non-overlapped patches as well. Then we use the pre-trained DCNN model to predict the label of them. After we obtained the label of all the patches within a fingerprint image, we use voting strategy to decide the label of the fingerprint image. That is the label with biggest vote is chosen as the label of the image. If the number of alive labels is equal to fake ones within a fingerprint image, we consider the label of this fingerprint image is fake. That is because it is more risky to classify a fake fingerprint sample to a alive one in real life application.

3   Experiments

3.1   Liveness Detection Challenge

Liveness Detection Challenge [5-7] was first held in 2009, which provide open dataset and common experimental protocol for evaluating different fingerprint liveness detection methods. We decided to assess the performance of proposed algorithm on the datasets of LivDet2011 [6] and LivDet2013 [7], for they are used frequently in the current study. But we avoid using the Crossmatch dataset of LivDet2013 [7] for it was known that it may be affected by an acquisition problem. Some examples from Liv-Det2011 [6] database is present in Fig. 6.

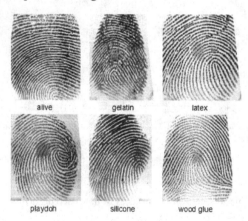

Fig. 6. Some fingerprint examples of live and fake fingerprints from LivDet2011 Database.

All LivDet datasets are divided into two parts: a training set and a testing set. Table 1 summarize the characteristics of LivDet2011 [6] and LivDet2013 [7] datasets.

3.2   Parameter Setting

As mentioned above. After the preprocessing, the size of input images is 32×32 pixel. We employ Caffe [23] implementation as our experiment platform, which is a very popular DCNN framework. Caffe [23] has a uniform data structure, which makes it possible to exchange data between GPU and CPU freely. Enhanced by GPU parallel computing power, Caffe can finish DCNN training very fast. The training of DCNN model is conducted on a Linux server with NVIDIA Geforce GTX 780.

Two types of DCNN models are trained in this paper to analysis the impact of neural network complexity to the final classification performance. They are Cifar-10[22] and our own proposed Finger-Net. As we can see in Fig. 3, Finger-Net has more complex structure than Cifar-10 for it has increased the complexity of convolution layer and pooling layer, and adds one more innerproduct layer. We can see from the experimental results that the Finger-Net performance much better.

In this paper, we set the iteration to 200,000 times. The initial learning rate was set to 0.01. And the learning rate will decrease by 0.1 times every 50,000 iterations.

Table 1. The database used in this paper (Bio, Dig, Ita, Sag, Swi represents for Biometrika, Dig. Pers., Italdata, Sagem and Swipe respectively)

Datasets	LivDet2011				LivDet2013		
Scanner	Bio	Ita	Sag	Dig	Bio	Ita	Swi
Res. (dpi)	500	500	500	500	569	500	96
Image size	312×3 72	640×4 80	352×3 84	355× 391	312×3 72	480×6 40	1500× 208
Live samples	2000	2000	2000	2000	2000	2000	2500
Fake samples	2000	2000	2000	2000	2000	2000	2000
Materials	5	5	5	5	5	5	4

Table 2. Performance comparisons of different algorithm on LivDet2011 and LivDet2013 databases (Bio, Dig, Ita, Sag, Swi represents for Biometrika, Dig. Pers., Italdata, Sagem and Swipe respectively)

%	ref.	LivDet2011				LivDet2013			
		Bio	Dig	Ita	Sag	Bio	Ita	Swi	AVE
Compet. winner		14.7	20.0	36.1	21.8	1.7	0.8	3.5	(-)
CNN	[19]	9.9	1.9	5.1	7.9	4.6	47.7	6.0	11.9
LCPD	[17]	4.9	4.7	12.3	3.2	1.2	1.3	4.7	4.6
BSIF	[18]	6.8	4.1	13.9	5.6	1.1	3.0	5.2	5.7
Cifar-10	[22]	11.5	0	0	0	0	0	21.5	4.7
Finger-Net		3.5	0	0	0	2.5	0	0.2	0.9

3.3   Result Comparisons

The fingerprint liveness detection results are illustrated in Table 2. We evaluate our algorithm on both LivDet2011 [6] database and LivDet2013 [7] database and compare our result with competition winner. Also, we have compared with three other public published algorithms: CNN [19], BSIF [18] and LCPD [17] at the same time. In this paper, all results are in terms of Half Total Error Rate (HTER):

$$HTER = (FGR+FER)/2 \qquad (2)$$

where *FGR* is the False Genuine Rate, which is the percentage of fake samples mis-classified as genuine; *FER* is the False Fake Rate, which is the percentage of genuine samples mis-classified as fake.

The experimental results show that the proposed approach outperforms the state-of-the-art algorithm [17] and former CNN [19] as well. The results also show that, after we utilize a more complex DCNN model, the overall performance gets better. The performance of Finger-Net on Biometric2011 dataset drops a little, which is caused by its relatively small data set. We can not tuning the neural network very well if we do not feed it with enough data.

We also evaluate the time performance of proposed algorithm. We test it on a PC with Inter(R) Core(TM) i7-4770K CPU 3.50GHz, 32GB RAM, Ubuntu 14.04 LTS. It takes 1 minute to process 40 fingerprint images on average. So, the proposed algorithm can meet the real-time processing requirement.

4   Conclusion and Future Work

In this paper, we proposed a novel fingerprint liveness detection based on DCNN and voting strategy. We designed a Deep Convolution Neural Network to fulfill fingerprint image feature extraction and classification. To enlarge the number of training data and avoid disturbance of image background information, we cut the image in to small patches and use threshold to ensure that the training data is background free. We adopt voting strategy to fusion the results of all the patches within one fingerprint image. Experiments on LivDet2011 [6] and LivDet2013 [7] database have shown that the performance of proposed algorithm outperforms the state-of-the-art algorithm [17].

Experiment results also show that the DCNN model complexity has big impact on the final classification performance. However, like other machine learning algorithms, we can not get better result by simply increase the complexity of the model. In future, we will discuss the parameters of DCNN model, such as the number of hidden layer, units of each layer, and its impact on the final result.

At last, although we have achieved really good results, fingerprint liveness detection is still an open question, and a lot of work need to be done. For example, fingerprint sensor and spoofing finger material is newly everyday, thus makes the study of how to make a well trained DCNN model to suit a new dataset very import.

References

1. Marcel, S., Mark, S.: Nixon: Handbook of Biometric Anti-Spoofing. Springer, New York (2014)
2. Gragnaniello, D., Poggi, G.: An Investigation of Local Descriptors for Biometric Spoofing Detection. J. IEEE Trans. Inf. Foren. Secur. **10**(4), 849–863 (2015)
3. Maltoni, D., Maio, D., Jain, A.K., et al.: Handbook of Fingerprint Recognition, Springer (2009)
4. Schuckers, S.: Spoofing and anti-spoofing measures. Information Security Technical Report **7**(4), 56–62 (2002)

5. Marcialis, G.L., Lewicke, A., Tan, B.: First international fingerprint liveness detection competition - LivDet 2009. In: 15th International Conference on Image Analysis and Processing, pp. 12-23, Vietri sul Mare, Italy (2009)
6. Yambay, D., Ghiani, L., Denti, P.: LivDet 2011 - fingerprint liveness detection competition 2011. In: 5th International Conference on Biometrics, pp. 208-215, New Delhi, India (2012)
7. Ghiani, L.,Yambay, D., Tocco, S.: LivDet 2013 fingerprint liveness detection competition 2013. In: 6th International Conference on Biometrics, pp. 1-6, Madrid, Spain (2013)
8. LeCun, Y., Boser, B., Denker, J.S., Henderson, D.: Back propagation applied to handwritten zip code recognition. Neural Computation (1989)
9. Krizhevsky, A., Sutskever, I., Hinton, G.E.: Imagenet classification with deep convolution neural networks. In: 22th Annual Conference on Neural Information Processing Systems, pp. 1097-1105. IEEE Press, Columbus (2012)
10. Girshick, R., Donahue, J., Darrel, T., Malik, J.: Rich feature hierarchies for accurate object detection and semantic segmentation. In: 27th IEEE Conference on Computer Vision and Pattern Recognition, pp. 580-587. IEEE Press, Columbus (2014)
11. Zhang, N., Paluri, M., Ranzato, M., Darrell, T.: Panda: pose aligned networks for deep attribute modeling. In: 27th IEEE Conference on Computer Vision and Pattern Recognition, pp. 1637-1644. IEEE Press, Columbus (2014)
12. Galbally, J., Alonso-Fernandez, F., Fierrez, J.: A high performance fingerprint liveness detection method based on quality related features. J. Future Generation Computer Systems 28, 311-321 (2012)
13. Galbally, J. Alonso-Fernandez, F.: Fingerprint liveness detection based on quality measures. In: 2009 Int. Conference on Biometrics, Identity and Security, pp. 1-8. IEEE Press, Tampa (2009)
14. Kannala, J., Rahtu, E.: Bsif: Binarized statistical image features. In: 21st Int. Conference on Pattern Recognition, pp. 1363-1366. IEEE Press, Tuskuba (2012)
15. Ojala, T., Peitikainen, M., Maenpaa, T.: Multiresolution gray-scale and rotation invariant texture classification with local binary patterns. J IEEE Trans. Pattern Anal. Mach. Intell. 24(7), 971-987 (2002)
16. Ghiani, L., Marcialis, G.L., Roli, F.: Fingerprint liveness detection by local phase quantization. In: 21st Int. Conf. Pattern Recognit, pp. 537-540. IEEE Press, Tsukuba (2012)
17. Gragnaniello, D., Poggi, G., Sansone, G., Verdoliva, L.: Local contrast phase descriptor for fingerprint liveness detection. J. Pattern Recognit. 48(4), 1050-1058 (2015)
18. Ghiani, L., Hadid, A., Marcialis, G.: Fingerprint liveness detection using binarized statistical image feature. In: 6th IEEE Int. Conference on Biometrics: Theory Application and Systems, pp. 1-6. IEEE Press, Arlington (2013)
19. Nogueira, R.F., Alencar Lotufo, R.: Evaluting software-based fingerprint liveness detection using convolutional networks and local binary patterns. In: IEEE Workshop Biometric Meas. Syst. Secur. Med. Appl., pp. 22-29. IEEE Press, Rome (2014)
20. Sun, Y., Wang, X., Tang, X.: Hybrid deep learning for face verification. In: 2013 IEEE International Conference on Computer Vision, pp. 1489-1496. IEEE Press, Sydney (2013)
21. Bengio, Y.: Learning deep architectures for AI. Foundations and Trends(r) in Machine Learning 2(1), 1-127 (2009)
22. Wan, L., Zeiler, M., Zhang, S., Cun, Y.L., Fergus, R.: Regularization of neural networks using dropconnect. In: 30th International Conference on Machine Learning, pp. 1058-1066. Atlanta (2013)
23. Github, https://github.com/BVLC/caffe/

Slap Fingerprint Recognition for HD Mobile Phones

Yongliang Zhang[1(⊠)], Hongtao Wu[2], Congmin Huang[3], Jinlei Yang[4], and Xiaoli Jiang[3]

[1] College of Computer Science and Technology,
Zhejiang University of Technology, Hangzhou 310023, China
titanzhang@zjut.edu.cn
[2] School of Computer Science and Engineering,
Hebei University of Technology, Tianjin 300130, China
[3] Hangzhou Jinglianwen Technology Co., Ltd, Hangzhou 310014, China
[4] Xinchang Branch of China Telecom Co., Ltd, Shaoxing 312500, China

Abstract. This paper proposes an efficient recognition algorithm for the four finger slaps captured by HD mobile phones. Firstly, statistical histogram is used to segment the minutiae set extracted from a slap image; secondly, RST-invariant feature descriptor (RST-IFD) is proposed to match two minutiae sets. Experimental results show that the proposed algorithm has the characteristics of higher compatibility and higher speed, not only for the slaps captured by live-scan sensors but also for those captured by HD mobile phones.

Keywords: Statistical histogram · RST-Invariant Feature Descriptor · Four finger slap · HD mobile phones

1   Introduction

Based on the motivation that the dramatic improvement of the false accept rate and false reject rate can be obtained if more than one finger is used to reference an individual[1], slap fingerprint is helpful to design a more secure and robust Automatic Fingerprint Identification System (AFIS). Besides increasing the recognition accuracy, use of slap fingerprint can also reduce the problem of spoofing as it is difficult to forge all fingerprints[2].Therefore, slap fingerprint based personal recognition has become a new research direction[3-6].

A four slap fingerprint contains four fingers as shown in Fig. 1 and needs to be segmented into individual fingerprints for personal recognition. Accurately extracting and labeling individual fingerprints from a slap image termed as slap fingerprint segmentation are crucial. Several algorithms for slap fingerprint segmentation have been proposed in the existing literature. Hodl et al. used a combination of mean-shift and ellipse-fitting algorithm to extract fingerprint components[1]. Zhang et al. extracted knuckle line information to improve the segmentation accuracy[7]. The existing slap fingerprint recognition algorithms usually include the steps of segmenting the slap image into individual fingerprints, extracting the minutiae from each individual fingerprint, and matching two slaps based on the extracted minutiae. The high complexity of the existing algorithms leads to poor real-time performance.

© Springer International Publishing Switzerland 2015
J. Yang et al. (Eds.): CCBR 2015, LNCS 9428, pp. 250–257, 2015.
DOI: 10.1007/978-3-319-25417-3_30

Fig. 1. Slap fingerprint

This paper proposes an efficient recognition algorithm for the slap fingerprint captured by HD mobile phones (mobile phones with high-definition camera). In the proposed algorithm, the minutiae set segmentation is used to increase its real-time performance. In addition, RST-invariant feature descriptor (RST-IFD) is used to overcome the influences of the rotation, translation and scaling between two slaps captured by HD mobile phones. Experimental results show that the proposed algorithm has the characteristics of higher compatibility and higher speed, not only for the slaps captured by live-scan sensors but also for those captured by HD mobile phones.

2   Statistical Histogram Based Slap Fingerprint Segmentation

The process of our proposed slap fingerprint segmentation algorithm is shown in Fig. 2. The minutiae extracted from a slap image are divided into four minutiae sets based on statistical histogram. Let $M_i^I = (x_i^I, y_i^I)$ be the ith minutia of a slap image I, where (x_i^I, y_i^I) is the coordinates of M_i^I.

2.1   Minutiae Set Segmentation

A slap image is much larger than the plain image captured by a single-finger sensor. The maximum of x_i^I may be more than 2000, especially when a slap image is captured by a high resolution sensor or a high-definition camera. To improve the processing speed, the x coordinate of the original slap image is re-sampled to its 1/10.

In statistical histogram, y indicates the number of minutiae when x_i^I is equal to the x coordinate value. It is clear that there are fewer minutiae between two adjacent fingers. So, threshold segmentation is used to evaluate the cut line between two adjacent fingers. For a four slap image, there are ideally three cut lines. But, there are some abnormal cases in some accidental circumstances. For example, the slap is divided into 5 fingers. Therefore, post-processing is needed. Let x_{min} and x_{max} be the minimum and maximum in the sequence $\{x_i^I\}_{i=1}^N$, where N is the minutia number of a slap image. The average width w_{ave} of each finger is calculated:

$$w_{ave} = (x_{max} - x_{min})\Big/4 \qquad (1)$$

And the corresponding intervals of four fingers are obtained:

$$[x_{min}, x_{min} + w_{ave}) \; [x_{min} + w_{ave}, x_{min} + 2w_{ave}) ,$$
$$[x_{min} + 2w_{ave}, x_{min} + 3w_{ave}) \; [x_{min} + 3w_{ave}, x_{max}) \qquad (2)$$

2.2   Minutiae Selection

The minutiae number N of a slap image is usually more than 255. The time complexity of the matching algorithm will increase when all minutiae are used. So minutiae selection is necessary. Our experiments demonstrate that the minutiae above the first knuckle line are enough for matching two fingers. The main steps of the minutiae selection are as follows: 1) minutiae of each finger are sorted from top to bottom and from left to right; 2) if the number of the minutiae of each finger is larger than a given threshold N_{max}, the top N_{max} minutiae are selected.

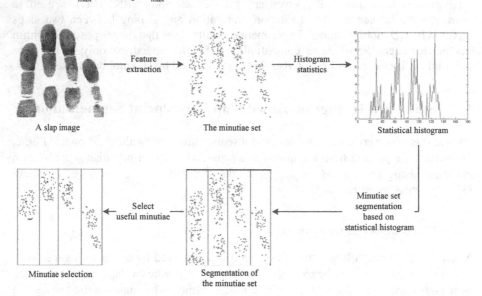

Fig. 2. Flow chart of slap fingerprint segmentation

3   Slap Fingerprint Matching Based on RST-IFD

In order to recognize the slaps collected from different types of slap fingerprint scanners, or captured by mobile phones as shown in Fig. 3, a matching algorithm is proposed in this paper, which is based on RST (Rotation, Scale, Translate)-invariant feature descriptor (RST-IFD).

3.1 Sextant Nearest Minutiae Structure (SNMS)

In order to speed up the matching speed, Sextant Nearest Minutiae Structure (SNMS) is used as the RST-IFD in this paper inspired by Octantal Nearest-Neighborhood Structure (ONNS) proposed in [8]. As shown in Fig. 4, each minutia is taken as the center, and its direction as the X-axis. The image is divided into six equal sectors by counterclockwise, and then the nearest minutia in each sector is selected. To be invariable to scaling, the difference between this paper and the reference [8] in calculating the similarity of two SNMS is to omit the distance between the center and the nearest minutia. For further details, please refer to the reference [8].

Fig. 3. One slap fingerphoto captured by a mobile phone

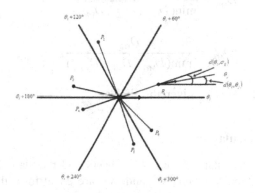

Fig. 4. SNMS

3.2 Corresponding Minutiae Pairs (CMP)

Ideally, one minutia M_i^I in the image I is corresponding to at most one minutia M_j^T in the image T. However, as described in [8], the SNMS of M_i^I may have more than one possible corresponding SNMS of T. Let M_{ik}^I and M_{jk}^T are the CMP, and the similarity $S(M_{ik}^I, M_{ik}^T)$ between the SNMS of M_{ik}^I and that of M_{ik}^T is bigger than a given threshold. Let $\Theta = \left\{ \left(ik, jk, S(M_{ik}^{I}, M_{jk}^{T}) \right) \big| k = 1, 2, ..., N \right\}$ be all the CMP between I and T. The selection rules of CMP are as follows:

1) Let Υ^{I}, Υ^{T} and Θ' be the null set;
2) Θ is sorted in descending order according to the value of $S(M_{ik}^{I}, M_{ik}^{T})$;
3) If $ik \notin \Upsilon^{I}$ and $jk \notin \Upsilon^{T}$, ik is added into Υ^{I} and jk is added into Υ^{T}, and $\left(ik, jk, S(M_{ik}^{I}, M_{ik}^{T}) \right)$ is added into Θ'.

1. Here, Θ' is the set of selected candidates.

3.3   Validation of CMP

Inspired by the reference [9], similar triangle theorem is used to eliminate the incorrect CMP. Let $\left(MI_{k}, MT_{k} \right), k \in N'$ be the selected CMP. Let $\left(MI_{k1}, MT_{k1} \right)$, $\left(MI_{k2}, MT_{k2} \right)$ and $\left(MI_{k3}, MT_{k3} \right)$ be three arbitrary CMP. Let TR_{k}^{I} and TR_{k}^{T} be the triangles formed by $(MI_{k1}, MI_{k2}, MI_{k3})$ and $(MT_{k1}, MT_{k2}, MT_{k3})$ respectively. Angles of TR_{k}^{I} are denoted as $A_{MI_{k1}}$, $A_{MI_{k2}}$, $A_{MI_{k2}}$, and the three edges are denoted as $D_{MI_{k1}}$, $D_{MI_{k2}}$, $D_{MI_{k3}}$. In the same way, $A_{MT_{k1}}$, $A_{MT_{k2}}$, $A_{MT_{k2}}$ are the angles of TR_{k}^{T} and $D_{MT_{k1}}$, $D_{MT_{k2}}$, $D_{MT_{k3}}$ are the three edges. The validation rules are as follows:

$$A_{k} = \left| A_{MI_{k}} - A_{MT_{k}} \right| < TA_{A}, k = 1, 2, 3 \tag{3}$$

$$D_{k} = \left| D_{MI_{k}}' - D_{MT_{k}}' \right| < TA_{D}, k = 1, 2, 3 \tag{4}$$

$$D_{MI_{k}}' = \frac{D_{MI_{k}}}{\min(D_{MI_{k1}}, D_{MI_{k2}}, D_{MI_{k3}})} \tag{5}$$

$$D_{MT_{k}}' = \frac{D_{MT_{k}}}{\min(D_{MT_{k1}}, D_{MT_{k2}}, D_{MT_{k3}})} \tag{6}$$

where TA_{A} and TA_{D} are two given thresholds.

3.4   Similarity Calculation

Let us suppose that the slap A has N^{A} fingers and the slap B has N^{B} fingers after segmentation. Ideally when N^{A} and N^{B} are equal to 4, the matching is just done in turn. Sometimes $N^{A} \neq N^{B}$ because of segmentation errors. Let sim be the similarity and its initial value is 0. The algorithm of similarity calculation between two slaps is described as follows:

```
sim=0
If  N^A == N^B  and  N^A ==4
For i=1 to N^A
Calculate the similarity a_i between the i^th finger of A and
the i^th finger of B. If a_i > T_1, then  sim = sim + a_i
```

```
Else
```
$F_i^A = 0, i = 1,2,\ldots,N^A$, $F_j^B = 0, j = 1,2,\ldots,N^B$
```
For i=1 to  N^A
    For j=1 to  N^B
```
        If $F_i^A == 0$ `&&` $F_j^B == 0$, calculate the similarity a_{ij} of the ith finger of A and the jth finger of B. If $a_{ij} > T_1$, then $sim = sim + a_{ij}$ and set $F_i^A = 1$, $F_j^B = 1$.

where T_1 is a given threshold.

4   Experimental Results

4.1   Evaluation Data

The S700 4-fingerprint live scanner manufactured by Changchun Hongda is used to establish three slap fingerprint databases, i.e. a four-slap database, a double-slap database and a single-finger database. The four-slap database consists of 198 slaps from 28 different hands. The other two databases are obtained by manually cutting samples of the four-slap database, wherein the double-slap database is established by segmenting the crack between second and third fingers, and the single-finger database is established by cutting the four slap samples into four separate fingerprints which only retain the part above the first knuckle line. Samples of three databases are shown in Fig. 5. To prove that our proposed algorithm can be applied to HD mobile phones, we have established another dataset named as slap_ZJUT_ HD, in which 113 four-slap images is contained. The samples of slap_ZJUT_ HD are captured by HD mobile phones when the distance between the phone and the slap is in range of 10 to 20cm.

4.2   Evaluation

Our proposed matching algorithm is tested on the four-slap database, double-slap database and single-finger database. The experimental results are listed in Tab. 1, where EER (Equal Error Rate) is an important indicator to denote the error value where false match rate (FMR) and false non-match rate (FNMR) are identical. In order to obtain more accurate results, N_{max} is set to 100 in this test. As shown in Tab. 1, our proposed algorithm has a better accuracy on the four-slap database, and can meet the requirements of real-time applications.

    As shown in Tab. 2, we can easily find that with the increase of minutiae number N_{max}, EER is gradually decreased and the time of single matching is gradually increased. The performance of our algorithm can reach high level when the value of N_{max} is between 60 and 100. To ensure the reliability of the algorithm and the higher recognition rate and efficiency, the optimal value of N_{max} is 75.

We also test our proposed algorithm on slap_ZJUT_ HD database, and the value of EER is 4.39%. Testing results show that the proposed method has high accuracy for four-slap fingerprints captured by HD mobile phones.

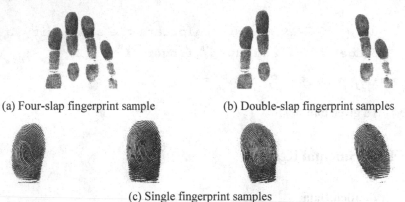

(a) Four-slap fingerprint sample   (b) Double-slap fingerprint samples

(c) Single fingerprint samples

Fig. 5. Slap fingerprint samples

Table 1. The test results on three databases

Databases	Samples	EER	Time cost(s)
Single fingerprint	792	0.0149	0.001185
Double-slap fingerprint	396	0.0131	0.00617
Four-slap fingerprint	198	0.0066	0.006286

Table 2. The performance of our proposed algorithm tested on different N_{max}

N_{max}	EER	Time cost(s)
45	0.0316	0.004547
55	0.0150	0.005365
60	0.0133	0.005830
65	0.0133	0.005938
70	0.0100	0.006037
75	0.0066	0.006049
80	0.0066	0.006127
90	0.0066	0.006231

5   Conclusion

A novel slap fingerprint segmentation and matching algorithm is proposed in this paper, which is based on statistical histogram and RST-IFD. Experimental results show that the algorithm has high accuracy and good real-time performance for four-slap fingerprints, and can be applied to the slap fingerprints obtained by live slap sensors and those captured by HD mobile phones. A limitation of our algorithm is that the rotation angle of slap fingerprints is needed to be less than 20 degrees. In future, we will do our best to tackle this problem.

References

1. Kyriacou, E., Kounoudes, A., Paraskeva, L., Konstantinides, A., Pattichis, C., Jossif, A., Pattichis, M., Vogiatzis, D.: Continuous monitoring of children with suspected cardiac arrhythmias. In: Weerasinghe, D. (ed.) eHealth 2008. LNICST, vol. 1, pp. 1–8. Springer, Heidelberg (2009)
2. Gupta, P.: Slap fingerprint segmentation using symmetric filters based quality. In: 2015 Eighth International Conference on Advances in Pattern Recognition (ICAPR), pp.1-6 (2015)
3. Ye, X.Y., Zhuang, Z.Q., Zhang, Y.C., et al.: Fingerprint Identification Based on Multi-Templet Characters Fusion. Journal of Image and Graphics. **10**, 170–174 (2005)
4. Li, Y., Yin, J.P., Zhu, E., et al.: A Comparative Study of Multiple Fingerprint Recognition. Computer Engineering & Science **30**, 32–35 (2008)
5. Yang, F., Pu, Z.B., Wang, Z.L.: Information Fusion Technology of Multi-Fingerprints Based on D-S Evidence Theory. Computer Engineering **31**, 175–177 (2005)
6. Sun, X.H., Ji, L.P.: An Fingerprint Identification Based on The Five-Fingerprint Data Fusion. Fujian Computer **25**, 87–88 (2009)
7. Zhang, Y.L., Xiao, G., Li, Y.M., et al.: Slap fingerprint segmentation for live-scan devices and ten-print cards. In: 2010 International Conference on Pattern Recognition, pp. 1180–1183 (2010)
8. Zhang, Y.L.: Algorithm Study on Swipe Fingerprint Mosaicking and Fingerprint Matching. Shanghai Jiao Tong University (2006)
9. Chai, H.Y., Tian, D.P., Fan, J.L., et al.: Fingerprint Minutia Matching Algorithm Based on Similar Triangle Theory. Communications Technology 42, 57-59, 62 (2009)

A Palmprint Recognition Algorithm Based on GIDBC

Mengqi Jia, Weibo Wei$^{(\boxtimes)}$, Danfeng Hong, and Gang Wang

College of Information Engineering, Qingdao University, Qingdao, China
{dorisj1991,njustwwb,hellowangxiaogang}@163.com,
hongdanfeng1989@gmail.com

Abstract. As fractal dimension could not describe the information of palmprint accurately as a characterization, differential box dimension (DBC) is improved by using a custom fractal operator, and a novel palmprint recognition algorithm based on Gabor transform and improved differential box dimension (GIDBC) is proposed in this paper. Firstly, Gabor transform is used for palmprint images in frequency domain to get the information of multi-scale and multi-direction, and the ideas of block is used to divide palmprint images into blocks. Then every block's feature vector is extracted by using improved differential box dimension (IDBC) algorithm, and features of all blocks are fused in the parallel. Finally, chi-square distance is used for classification. Compared with those traditional algorithms by experiments in PolyU palmprint database, recognition rate can reach 99.78%, feature extraction and matching time is 338ms, which demonstrates the validity and efficiency of the proposed algorithm.

Keywords: Palmprint recognition · Fractal dimension · Improved differential box dimension · Gabor transform · Fractal operator

1 Introduction

As an emerging biometrics technology, palmprint recognition has become an important complement of personal identification due to its merits, e.g. high accuracy, low-cost, and easy availability. [1-4] As principal lines and wrinkles can be captured with low resolution devices which are cheap and also have a fast matching speed, low resolution palmprint recognition is more suitable for civilian and commercial applications, as well as a focus of research interest in the field of palmprint recognition.

The algorithm based on geometrical feature is the original low resolution palmprint recognition method. Liu et al. [5] proposed a wide line detector. Considering the location and width, this method can obtain the rough location of the palm-lines. However, there're also many shortcomings such as large calculating quantity, poor anti-noise performance and easy to lose ridge information. Dai et al. [6] used palm texture energy as the image representation of feature vectors with the application of M-band wavelet. Kong and Zhang[7] proposed a method of real value Gabor filter in six directions, which can preferably describe the directional information as well as get better recognition rate. Zhou[8] et al. proposed a face recognition algorithm based on energy adaptive local Gabor feature extraction. This method can reduce the dimension of

© Springer International Publishing Switzerland 2015
J. Yang et al. (Eds.): CCBR 2015, LNCS 9428, pp. 258–265, 2015.
DOI: 10.1007/978-3-319-25417-3_31

feature vector and ensure the accuracy of recognition, however, Gabor transform is only for analysis of the image scale feature and direction feature, failed to well reflect the changes in texture characteristics of the surface of images. On this basis, Feng [9] extracted texture features by using fractal dimension as feature vectors, made a comparison between local fractal algorithm and global fractal algorithm, and then demonstrated that local fractal algorithm can pick the regions which complicatedly transformed up conveniently from the images. However, high complexity rate of local fractal algorithm states that it must be not applied better in the large and medium data. Zhao et al. [10] extracted fractal feature with scale and direction information which is a multilevel description of textural images. It provides a new idea to the research on recognition of fractal palmprint.

On the basis of above studies, this paper puts forward a new method based on Gabor transform and improved differential box dimension(GIDBC). Firstly, Gabor transform is applied to image features to obtain characteristics of different scales and directions. In order to extract the Gabor feature accurately, the differential box counting method is improved. We use fractal operator as Gabor feature vector and parallel fusion to form a new feature vector. Finally, general chi-square distance is used to match the features.

2   Box Dimension Method

2.1   Differential Box Counting

The concept of fractal geometry is first proposed by A French American mathematician called Mandelbrot in 1975. Graphic fractal model is adapted to the method of calculating fractal dimension of the image. Here, we list three common graphic fractal models, the ε-blanket model, the fractional geometric Brownian motion model and the box counting model.

What differs from other estimation algorithm based on covering is that the Box Counting model regards the minimum box number N_r which can cover the surface of the image as the measurement. Since the algorithm is proposed, it has been widely used because of its simplicity, and many scholars have improved it. Among them, the most important is the differential box dimension method proposed by Sarkar and Chaud-huri[11].

The differential box counting method can be described as follows.

A given image which size is $M \times M$ pixels is divided into non-overlapping grids, the size of each grids is $s \times s$ pixels, where s is the current image scale. In the three-dimensional space (x,y,z), (x,y) represents a point in the plane of the coordinate system, z corresponds to the gray value at position (x,y). The grid is filled with boxes of size $s \times s \times s$, if the maximum and the minimum gay value of each grid is located in the l-th box and k-th box, the number of boxes in the grid is

$$n_r(i,j) = l - k + 1 \tag{1}$$

The number of boxes in the whole image I can be calculate by

$$N_r = \sum_{m,n} n_r(i,j); r = s/M \tag{2}$$

Hence, we can get the fractal dimension D by

$$D = \log(N_r)/\log(1/r) \tag{3}$$

2.2   Improved Differential Box Counting, IDBC

The basic idea of traditional DBC algorithm is as follows. Firstly, using different size of boxes to cover the image. Secondly, getting fractal dimension by fitting the results. Finally, using the fractal dimension as the feature vector to recognize. Fractal dimension is used to describe surface roughness of two-dimensional images by numbers between 2 and 3, although fractal dimension can distinguish different image texture in some degree, it cannot accurately reflect local feature information of different images and global feature information of similar images.

The DBC algorithm is improved in this paper. We use a customized fractal operator as the feature vector instead of fractal dimension. The improved algorithm is as follows. An image is divided into several sub-images of size $m \times m$, each sub-image is divided into several grids of size $s \times s$, and each grid is recorded as $n(i,j)$, boxes of different sizes are used to fill the same grid respectively. The number of box categories in this paper is $t = \log_2^m$, m is the side length of sub-image. The number of boxes with different sizes which are occupied the same grid are record as $h_1, h_2, \ldots, h_t$. Parallel fusion respectively to get the box distribution $H_1, H_2, \ldots, H_t$. Then histogram statistics are used to get feature vector $T_1, T_2, \ldots, T_t$. Finally parallel fused preliminary feature vectors are used as the final feature vector.

It can be seen from the definition above that fractal operator can well describe surface texture distribution of an image and accurately distinguish different palmprint images, which eliminate the defects of inaccurate recognition when use fractal dimension as feature vectors. Without curve fitting, the algorithm complexity is also reduced.

In order to describe fractal operator vividly and get the optimal size of the sub-image, we compared the following results. We take two different palmprint images (palmprint A and B), divide them into sub-images of different size to obtain different fractal operator, which is shown in Fig. 1, Fig. 2. The horizontal axis represents the image feature information category, the vertical axis represents the image characteristic information of the weight percentage. In Fig. 1(a) and Fig. 2(a), the types of feature information is little and feature weight is concentrated, therefore, fractal features operator are similar for different palmprint, the inter-class and intra-class have poor distinguish ability. In Fig. 1(b), (c) and Fig. 2(b), (c), the kinds of feature is increased, and feature weight changed obviously, which can describe the texture fluctuation of rough surface better and see the classification of different palmprint operator clearly. Therefore, it can distinguished the image of inter-class and intra-class accurately. In Fig. 1(d) and Fig. 2(d), although contain more feature kinds, the information of feature weights is redundancy, and concentrated together, as a result, different palmprints have similar fractal operator, which can not well described the distinguish ability between inter-class and intra-class. Therefore, the sub-image of size 8×8、16×16 are used in this paper, processing the Gabor.mat, and verify the algorithm to get higher recognition rate.

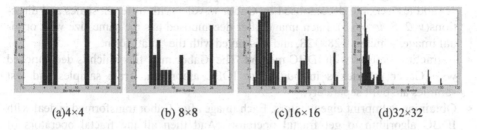

(a)4×4　　　　　(b) 8×8　　　　　(c)16×16　　　　　(d)32×32

Fig. 1. Fractal operator with different block size of palmprint A

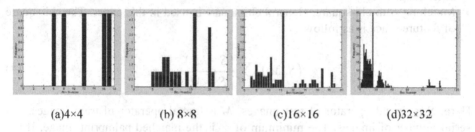

(a)4×4　　　　　(b) 8×8　　　　　(c)16×16　　　　　(d)32×32

Fig. 2. Fractal operator with different block size of palmprint B

3   Palmprint Recognition Algorithm Based on GIDBC

Framework of palmprint recognition algorithm based on GIDBC is illustrated in Fig. 3, and the process is as follows.

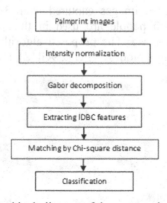

Fig. 3. The block diagram of the proposed algorithm.

- Preprocessing palmprint images. This paper uses the palmprint ROI images (128×128) directly which have been well handled in PolyU palmprint database[17], so we just need to do intensity normalization with ROI images.
- Decomposing with Gabor wavelet. The preprocessed images are divided into train set and test set, and decomposed by Gabor wavelet with different scales and directions(v=2~5, u=4,6,8). Each image after decomposed has the same size with original image, which is 128×128, and it is saved with the '.mat' form.
- Extracting features with IDBC method. The 'Gabor.mat' file which is decomposed with Gabor wavelet is introduced to IDBC algorithm. Train samples and test samples are built separately.
- Obtaining palmprint eigenvectors. Each image after Gabor transformed is deal with IDBC algorithm to get fractal operators. And then all the fractal operators of images with different scales and directions are parallel fused. The feature weight of each image is 1.
- Matching with chi-square. General chi-square is used in this paper. The chi-square of feature space is as follows.

$$\chi^2(S,M) - \sum_i \frac{(S_i - M_i)^2}{S_i + M_i} \tag{4}$$

Here, S is fractal operator of test images, M is fractal operator of train images, i is serial number of images. The minimum of χ^2 is the matched palmprint image. If the label belongs to the same person, it means that the recognition is right.

4   Experimental Results and Analysis

4.1   Database

In this section, all the experiments are performed involve PolyU palmprint database, which includes 7752 palmprint images captured from 386 people. 1000 palmprint images which belong to 100 people are used in this paper. Fig. 4 shows some palmprint images in test database. The proposed algorithm was implemented using MATLAB2010a on a PC with a modest CPU (2.9GHZ), and 4GB RAM.

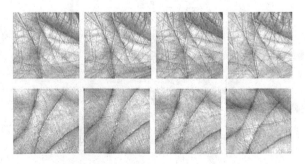

Fig. 4. ROI images in PolyU Database

4.2   Comparison and Analysis

This paper selected 100 palmprint images from PolyU palmprint database as a sample, take 10 images of each person, thus, there are 1000 palmprint images totally, we randomly select one image of each person as the training set and the rest nine as the test set. Table 1 shows the recognition rate of GIDBC in three different scales and directions of Gabor transform. Obviously, the best recognition rate can achieve when the block size is 16×16, and in 4 scales and 4 directions.

As shown in table 1, when Gabor transform use 4 scales and 4 directions, the recognition rate is better than other scales and directions. The reason is that the distribution of image texture is regarded as feature vector in IDBC and to distinguish different images by describing surface roughness which request image surface contains rich information. Too much decomposition scales and directions make image information less, so IDBC cannot describe texture distribution of image. What's more, too little decomposition scales and directions is also infeasible. When Gabor algorithm in 4×4 blocks, the decomposed images are best suited for IDBC algorithm. The recognition rate of IDBC algorithm in 8×8 is better than 16×16 blocks. Finally the fusion results of Gabor 4×4 and IDBC 16×16 blocks can achieve very good effect.

Table 1. The recognition rate of GIDBC with different scales, directions and grids

Gabor(direction)		Gabor(scale)	IDBC(grid)	Recognition rate
4	directions	3scales	8×8	95.56%
			16 × 16	97.78%
		4scales	8×8	99.33%
			16 × 16	99.78%
		5scales	8×8	98.11%
			16 × 16	98.44%
6	directions	3scales	8×8	95.67%
			16 × 16	95.56%
		4scales	8×8	94.33%
			16 × 16	92.89%
		5scales	8×8	94.56%
			16 × 16	93.67%
8	directions	3scales	8×8	92.00%
			16 × 16	89.11%
		4scales	8×8	94.22%
			16 × 16	97.56%
		5scales	8×8	96.67%
			16 × 16	96.89%

The algorithm in this paper is superior to the traditional fractal dimension algorithm such as FD, LFD, Contourlet and CLFD, under PolyU palmprint database. As shown in Fig. 5, the recognition rate of GIDBC is the highest.

In table 2, it is seen that although FD algorithm cost less time in features extraction and matching, FD represents the dimension of the whole image. Since fractal dimension of two-dimensional images is just between 2 and 3, the fractal dimension of different palmprint are relatively close for the palm, we cannot correctly recognize the palmprint if we directly put the fractal dimension as the characteristic, which means that those algorithms based on the traditional fractal dimension cause the larger error identification. In this paper, the improved IDBC we proposed extends and improves the fractal dimension into the form of histogram, which can effectively improve the feature representation ability and meanwhile reduce the error rate. In addition, computation time to extract features of the proposed method is the shortest, but the recognition rate is low. The combination of Gabor transform and IDBC can guarantee the recognition rate as well as short recognition time. In summary, GIDBC not only has a high recognition rate, but also the recognition time is shorter.

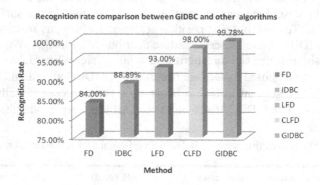

Fig. 5. Recognition rate comparison between GIDBC and other algorithms

Table 2. Speed comparison

Algorithms	Extraction(ms)	Matching(ms)
FD	150	0.391
LFD	8085	0.596
CLFD	25180	4.035
IDBC	52	0.316
GIDBC	336	2.453

5   Conclusion

Although the IDBC algorithm can better describe the surface roughness of the images and maximize the accuracy of features information from palmprint images that have been acquired, but the recognition rate is low if we use this algorithm directly due to the comparatively simple features so that it cannot give a better description to palmprint images with multi-resolution In this paper, Gabor transform is well introduced to the scale and direction, and the GIDBC algorithm is proposed. Experiments show that compared with the traditional algorithms, the GIDBC algorithm can reduce the complexity of the algorithm while ensuring high recognition accuracy. The main work next step is to improve the algorithm, so that it can be applied to large palmprint database.

Acknowledgements. This work was financially supported by Shandong Province Higher Educational Science and Technology Program (J14LN39).

References

1. Liu, Y.Q., Yuan, W.Q., Guo, J.Y.: On-Line Palmprint Recognition Based on Wavelet Decomposition and High and Low Hat Rransform. Application Reasearch of Computers. **28**(6), 2355–2357 (2011)
2. Guo, J.Y., Liu, Y.Q., Yuan, W.Q.: Palmprint Recognition Using Local Information From a Single Image Per Person. Journal of Computational Information Systems. **8**(8), 3199–3206 (2012)
3. Hong, D.F., Pan, Z.K., Wu, X.: Improved Differential Box Counting with Multi-scale and Multi-direction: A New Palmprint Recognition Method. Optik-International Journal of Light Electron Optics. **125**(15), 4154–4160 (2014)
4. Pan, X., Ruan, Q.Q., Wang, Y.X., et al.: Palmprint Recognition Using Gabor Local Relative Features. Computer Engineering and Applications **48**(15), 34–38 (2012)
5. Liu, L., Zhang, D.: Palm-line detection. In: Proceedings of International Conference on Image Processing, pp. 269-272. IEEE, Washington D. C (2005)
6. Dai, Q., Bi, N., Huang, D., Zhang, D., Li, F.: M-Band wavelets application to palmprint recognition based on texture features. In: Proceedings of IEEE International Conference on Image Processing, vol. 11(2), pp. 893-896 (2004)
7. Kong, W., Zhang, D.: Competitive coding scheme for palmprint verification. In: Proceedings of International Conference Pattern Recognition, vol. 11(1), pp. 520–523 (2005)
8. Zhou, L.J., Ma, Y.Y., Sun, J.: Face recognition with adaptive local-gabor features based on energy. Journal of Computer Applications **33**(3), 700–703 (2013)
9. Feng, X.H.: Image Processing Method Based on Local Fractal Dimension. Digital technology and Application **33**(3), 700–703 (2013)
10. Zhao, Y., Gao, J., Chen, G., et al.: Multi-scale and Multi-orientation Texture Feature Extraction Method Based on Fractal Theory. Chinese Journal of Scientific Instrument. **29**(4), 787–791 (2008)
11. Sarkar, N., Chaudhuri, B.B.: An Efficient Differential Box-Counting Approach to Compute Fractal Dimension of Image. IEEE Transactions on System Man and Cybernetics **SMC-24**(1), 115–120 (1994)
12. PolyU Palmprint Palmprint Database. Biometric Research Centre, HongKong Polytechnic University. http://www.comp.polyu.edu.hk/biometrics/S

Structural Feature Measurement Using Fast VO Model for Blurred Palmprint Recognition

Gang Wang, Weibo Wei$^{(\boxtimes)}$, Zhenkuan Pan, Danfeng Hong, and Mengqi Jia

College of Information Engineering, Qingdao University, Qingdao, China
{hellowangxiaogang,qduwwb,dorisj1991}@163.com,
zkpan@qdu.edu.cn, hongdanfeng1989@gmail.com

Abstract. It is inevitable for non-contact palmprint recognition to obtain the low resolution image when capturing the image, which leads to poor recognition accuracy. In order to solve this problem effectively, a blurred palmprint recognition method based on Structure Feature (SF) is proposed in the paper. Firstly, fast Vese-Osher (VO) decomposition model is utilized to decompose blurred images in order to obtain stable feature of blurred images which is regarded as SF. Next, a non-overlapping sampling method based on Structure Ratio (SR) for SF is used to further improve recognition accuracy. Finally, Structural Similarity Index Measurement (SSIM) is used to measure the similarity of palmprints and judge the palmprint category for classification. The recognition results of proposed method are stable in the PolyU palmprint database and the Blurred-PolyU palmprint database, moreover, the Equal Error Rate (EER: 0.9069%) of proposed method is lower than other classical algorithms in Blurred-PolyU palmprint database.

Keywords: Blurred palmprint recognition · Structure feature · Fast VO decomposition model · Structure ratio · Structural similarity index measurement

1 Introduction

Palmprint is a kind of effective method to verify the identity of a person, its study has attracted more attention and some fruitful research achievements have been obtained in the past decades [1]. Research on non-contact palmprint image acquisition and recognition has gradually become the mainstream due to its various merits, e.g. low-cost, easy availability and high accuracy [2-3]. However, there are some inherent defects in non-contact system, e.g. the palmprint image easily produces blurriness when it is captured by non-contact device, which possibly reduces the performance of system recognition. Researchers proposed some methods to solve these problems, Yuan [4] designed a non-contact online palmprint simulation system, however, this method cannot be used in large-scale palmprint database. Sang [5] directly extracted the feature from blurred palmprint images, but the accuracy of identification is not very high. Lin [6] considered that stable features exist during the process from clear images to blurred images, as a result, they extracted stable features by using Laplacian Smoothing Transform (LST), and achieved good recognition results. Wang [7]

© Springer International Publishing Switzerland 2015
J. Yang et al. (Eds.): CCBR 2015, LNCS 9428, pp. 266–274, 2015.
DOI: 10.1007/978-3-319-25417-3_32

proposed an image restoration method based on normalized super Laplace, which achieves good experimental results. Lin [8] put forward Discrete Cosine Transform (DCT), recognition accuracy has been further improved compared with reference [6], but they did not propose a specific guideline for the part of feature fusion and explain how to select stable features.

In order to effectively extract stable features in palmprint blurred process, fast VO decomposition model and non-overlapping sampling method are used to the image. Finally, the effectiveness of proposed method is verified in the experimental results.

2   Stable Features in Image Blur Process

2.1   Fast VO Model Based on the Split Bergman Algorithm

Meyer pointed out that an image f can be divided into structure layer u and texture layer v using image decomposition [9]. This can be expressed as

$$f = u + v \tag{1}$$

Vese and Osher established VO decomposition model, however, the process of solving VO model is complicated, therefore, split bergman algorithm [10] is introduced to simplify the model, we called fast VO model in this paper.

$$\inf_{u, g_1, g_2, w} \left\{ \begin{aligned} & E(u, g_1, g_2, w) = \int_\Omega |w| \, dxdy + \lambda \int_\Omega (f - u - \nabla \cdot \vec{g})^2 \, dxdy \\ & + \theta \int_\Omega (w - \nabla u - b^{n+1}) \, dxdy + \mu \int_\Omega (\sqrt{g_1^2 + g_2^2}) \, dxdy \end{aligned} \right\} \tag{2}$$

$$b^{n+1} = b^n + \nabla u^n - w^n \tag{3}$$

where $\vec{g} = (g_1, g_2)$, $v(x,y) = \partial_x g_1(x,y) + \partial_y g_2(x,y)$, λ and μ are positive penalty parameters. $b = (b_1, b_2)^T$ is a bergman iteration parameter, θ is a penalty parameter, $w = (w_1, w_2)^T$ is auxiliary variable to replace ∇u. The corresponding Euler-Lagrange equation is as follows:

$$\begin{cases} u = f - \partial_x g_1 - \partial_y g_2 + \dfrac{\theta}{2\lambda}(\nabla \cdot (\nabla u) + \nabla \cdot b^{n+1} - \nabla \cdot w) \\[2mm] w^{n+1} = (\nabla u + b^{n+1}) - \dfrac{1}{\theta} \dfrac{w^{n+1}}{|w^{n+1}|} \\[2mm] \mu \dfrac{g_1}{\sqrt{g_1^2 + g_2^2}} = 2\lambda \left[\dfrac{\partial(u - f)}{\partial x} + \partial_{xx}^2 g_1 + \partial_{xy}^2 g_2 \right] \\[2mm] \mu \dfrac{g_2}{\sqrt{g_1^2 + g_2^2}} = 2\lambda \left[\dfrac{\partial(u - f)}{\partial y} + \partial_{xy}^2 g_1 + \partial_{yy}^2 g_2 \right] \end{cases} \tag{4}$$

Here, w^{n+1} can be solved by using soft threshold formula as follows:

$$w^{n+1} = Max\left(|\nabla u + b^{n+1}| - \frac{1}{\theta}, 0\right)\frac{\nabla u + b^{n+1}}{|\nabla u + b^{n+1}|}, 0\frac{0}{0} = 0 \tag{5}$$

Finite difference method is used to solve (4) and (5) via alternative optimization procedure. Thus, u and v can be obtained. It is obvious that convergence rate of fast VO model is much faster than that of normal VO model in Fig. 1.

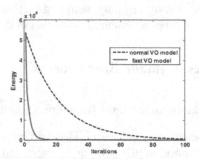

Fig. 1. Comparison of convergence rate between normal VO model and fast VO model.

2.2   Results of Image Decomposition

Fig. 2 is the region of interest (ROI) with different scale of blurring, (a) is the ROI of original palmprint, (b)~(f) are the ROI of σ =1,2,3,4,5 respectively.

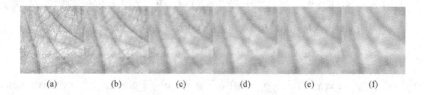

    (a)   (b)   (c)   (d)   (e)   (f)

Fig. 2. ROI with different scale of blurring in the PolyU palmprint database.

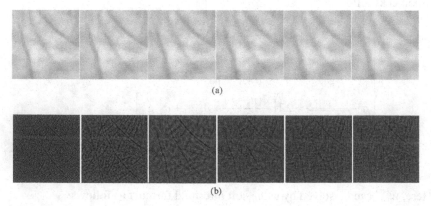

Fig. 3. Structure layer (a) and texture layer (b) of original image and different degrees of blurring (σ =1,2,3,4,5) obtained using fast VO decomposition model

Fig. 3 shows that structure layer remains unchanged when the degree of blur (σ) changed, however, texture layer changes dramatically. Namely, the information in texture layer is extremely unstable, it cannot be regarded as stable image features.

According to the example of fast VO decomposition, we know that structure layer of palmprint image remains stable even if an image suffers from different degree of blurring. As a result, structure layer can be treated as stable feature to recognize.

3   Blurred Palmprint Recognition Based on SR-SF Algorithm

3.1   Image Down-Sampling Based on Structure Ratio

Although structure layer can be kept relatively stable, the recognition results are not good because structure layer, whose dimension is too large, has low effectiveness of feature matching and low recognition accuracy. Therefore, a non-overlapping sampling method based on Structure Ratio (SR) for SF is used to further improve the discrimination of feature, and obtain the SR-SF. This can be expressed as

$$M = \frac{\sum_{i=1}^{m} \sum_{j=1}^{n} I(i, j)}{m \times n} \tag{6}$$

$$S = \frac{\sum_{i=1}^{m} \sum_{j=1}^{n} (I(i, j) - M)^2}{m \times n} \tag{7}$$

$$SR = \frac{M}{S} \tag{8}$$

where I is a size of $m \times n$ non-overlapping sampling area, i and j is corresponding pixel location of sampling area, M stands for average gray value of sampling area, S is variance of sampling area, SR is structure ratio of sampling area. From Eqs. (6), (7) and (8), we can see that the size of sample area has a great impact to SR value. Therefore, the size of sampling area should be determined by experiments.

In this section, structure layer of blurring palmprint image ($\sigma = 3$) is chosen to test by using SR method, results can be seen from Figs. 4 (d)~(f) is the RISF obtained by fast VO model, which could better distinguish the similar blurring image, (g)~(i) is the SR-SF whose dimension is small enough to further improve the discrimination of features   for the palmprint image.

3.2   Feature Matching for Blurring Palmprint Image

Structural Similarity Index Measurement (SSIM)[11] is introduced in this paper to measure the similarity between palmprint features. SSIM describe structure features from brightness (L), contrast (C) and structure (S). Specifically shown as follows

$$L(x,y) = \frac{2\mu_x\mu_y + c1}{\mu_x^2 + \mu_y^2 + c1} \tag{9}$$

$$C(x,y) = \frac{2\sigma_x\sigma_y + c2}{\sigma_x^2 + \sigma_y^2 + c2} \tag{10}$$

$$S(x,y) = \frac{\sigma_{xy} + c3}{\sigma_x\sigma_y + c3} \tag{11}$$

Here, x and y represent two structural features to be matched, small constants c_1, c_2, c_3 are used to increase the stability of calculation results. SSIM value is determined by L, C, S, therefore, SSIM is defined as

$$SSIM(x,y) = L(x,y) \times C(x,y) \times S(x,y) \tag{12}$$

As can be seen from Fig. 5, the smaller intersects area between inner-class and intra-class curves it is, the smaller correlation they are. Therefore, an appropriate threshold of *thres* (we can obtained the size of threshold by equal error rate curve [12], *thres*=0.4251) can separate the palmprint more accurately and effectively.

(a)palmprint ① for volunteer A (b)palmprint② for volunteer A (c)palmprint③ for volunteer B

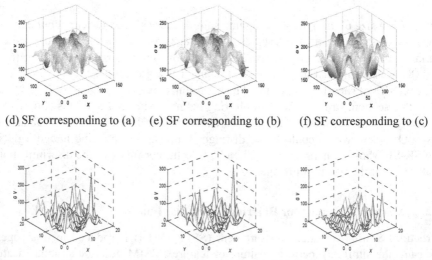

(d) SF corresponding to (a)   (e) SF corresponding to (b)   (f) SF corresponding to (c)

(g) SR-SF corresponding to (a) (h) SR-SF corresponding to (b) (i) SR-SF corresponding to (c)

Fig. 4. Blurred palmprint feature examples among the same people and different people

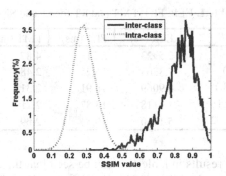

Fig. 5. Curves of inter-class and intra-class

4   Experiment Results and Analysis

The proposed method is implemented using MATLAB2010a on a desktop PC with a modest CPU (2.9GHZ), and 4GB of random access memory. We carried out 2 experiments on PolyU and Blurred-PolyU database to verify the effectiveness of the method.

4.1   Experiment 1

It is difficult to describe the characteristics if structure layer is directly used as the features to recognize. Because the size of sampling area has a great influence on the recognition results, therefore, blocks of different size (4×4 , 8×8 , 16×16 , 32×32) are tested in the Blurred-PolyU palmprint database to choose the optimal regional block. Fig. 6 shows the ROC curve of different size sampling area for SR-SF method and ROC curve of SF method.

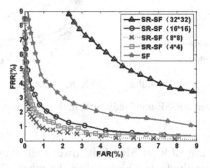

Fig. 6. ROC curves obtained using different block size

As can be seen from Fig. 6, the EER obtained using 8×8 is the lowest, and the EER of 32×32 is higher than obtained using SF method. Table 1 gives the corresponding equal error rate (EER), feature extraction time (FET), feature matching time (FMT) and recognition time (RT), RT is the time for an identity[7].

Table 1. EER, FET, FMT and RT for SF and SR-SF

Algorithm	EER (%)	FET (ms)	FMT (ms)	RT (ms)
SF	2.5923	5.71	4.87	1885.53
SR-SF (4×4)	1.3363	25.25	2.48	982.53
SR-SF (8×8)	0.9069	16.91	2.31	908.57
SR-SF (16×16)	1.6118	13.87	2.21	866.93
SR-SF (32×32)	5.1760	10.54	2.09	817.28

By considering the results in table 1, it can be seen that the recognition time of SF algorithm is the longest, the bigger of block is, the smaller of recognition time it is, and the EER of SR-SF (8×8) is the lowest, the RT is only 908.57ms (less than 1 s) which can satisfy the real-time requirements. Therefore, the optimal size of sampling size in this paper is 8×8.

4.2   Experiment 2

In order to verify the proposed SR-SF method could extract stable feature of the palmprint image, we performed experiments using PolyU and blurred-PolyU palm-print databases, and making comparison with some high-performance methods on PolyU palmprint database (Palm Code, Fusion Code, Competitive Code, RLOC, FCM+ Competitive Code).

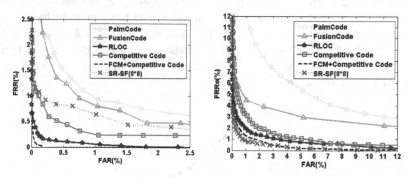

(a) ROC curves on the PolyU databa   (b) ROC curves on the Blurred-PolyU database

Fig. 7. ROC curves between SR-SF and traditional high-performance algorithms on different palmprint databases

Fig. 7(a) shows that the EER of SR-SF is lower than those obtained using Palm Code and Fusion Code methods, but higher than the others. Fig. 7(b) shows that the EER of SR-SF is lower than those obtained using other classical algorithm on blurred-PolyU database. Therefore, a conclusion can be obtained when compared Fig. 7(a) with Fig. 7(b) that the EER of SR-SF method is stable both in PolyU and blurred-PolyU databases, meanwhile, EER values of other algorithm has larger increased on the Blurred-PolyU   database. Table 2 lists the EER values corresponding to Fig. 7.

Table 2. EER values corresponding to Fig. 7

algorithm	EER (%)	
	PolyU database	Blurred-PolyU database
PalmCode	0.9706	5.2653
FusionCode	0.8876	3.5215
Competitive Code	0.4792	2.0812
RLOC	0.1657	1.5250
FCM+ Competitive Code	0.0716	1.1979
SR-SF (8×8)	0.8283	0.9069

Palmprint recognition methods based on coding (Palm Code, Fusion Code, Competitive Code, RLOC, FCM+ Competitive Code) can better describe texture information of palmprint, and gain a higher recognition accuracy. However it is difficult to represent texture information for blurred images due to the loss of texture information. Therefore, identification results of coding method are generally poor on the Blurred-PolyU palmprint database; the proposed method (SR-SF) can extract relatively stable features of blurred images. As a result, the identification accuracy and robustness of the SR-SF is higher than those of traditional high-performance algorithms.

5   Conclusions

A blurred palmprint recognition method based on Structure Feature (SF) is proposed in the paper. The method could obtain higher identification accuracy when compared with traditional recognition methods; meanwhile, the robustness is higher for noise, blurriness and illumination. Moreover, fast VO model is utilized in this method, and experiments demonstrate the performance of the proposed method.

Acknowledgements. The work was supported by Shandong Province Higher Educational Science and Technology Program (J14LN39).

References

1. Yue, F., Zuo, W.M., Zhang, D.P.: Survey of Palmprint Recognition Algorithms. Acta Automatica Sinica **36**(3), 353–365 (2010)
2. Hong, D.F., Pan, Z.K., Wu, X.: Improved differential box counting with multi-scale and multi-direction: A new palmprint recognition method. Optik-International Journal of Light Electron Optics **125**(15), 4154–4160 (2014)
3. Hong, D.F., Pan, Z.K., Su, J., Wei, W.B., Wang, G.D.: VO Decomposition Model Method for Blurred Palmprint Recognition. Journal of Computer-Aided Design & Computer Graphics **26**(10), 1737–1746 (2014)
4. Yuan, W.Q., Feng, S.Y.: Simulation system of improved non-contact on-line palmprint recognition. Acta Optica Sinica **31**(7), 0712003 (2011)

5. Sang, H.F., Liu, F.: Defocused palmprint recognition using 2DPCA. In: Proceedings of International Conference on Artificial Intelligence and Computational Intelligence, Shanghai, China, pp. 611–615 (2009)

6. Lin, S., Yuan, W.Q.: Blurred palmprint recognition under defocus status. Optics and Precision Engineering **21**(3), 734–741 (2013)

7. Wang, G.D., Xu, J., Pan, Z.K., Liu, C.L., Yang, J.B.: Blind image restoration based on normalized hyper laplacian prior term. Optics and Precision Engineering **21**(5), 1341–1347 (2013)

8. Lin, S., Yuan, W.Q., Wu, W., Fang, T.: Blurred palmprint recognition based on DCT and block energy of principal line. Journal of Optoelectronics Laser **23**(11), 2200–2206 (2012)

9. Meyer, Y.: Oscillating patterns in image processing and nonlinear evolution equations. American Mathematical Society Academic Publishers (2010)

10. Wei, W.B., Pan, Z.K., Zhao, Z.F.: VO model and its spilt bregman method for color texture image decomposition. Chinese Journal of Scientific Instrument **33**(10), 2279–2284 (2012)

11. Ye, S.N., Su, K.N., Xiao, C.B., Duan, J.: Image Quality Assessment Based on Structural Information Extraction. Acta Electronica Sinica **36**(5), 856–861 (2008)

12. Hong, D.F., Liu, W.Q., Su, J., Pan, Z.K., Wang, G.D.: A Novel Hierarchical Approach for Multispectral Palmprint Recognition. Neurocomputing **151**, 511–521 (2015)

Palmprint Liveness Detection by Combining Binarized Statistical Image Features and Image Quality Assessment

Xiaoming Li[1], Wei Bu[2], and Xiangqian Wu[1(✉)]

[1] School of Computer Science and Technology,
Harbin Institute of Technology, Harbin 150001, China
{csxmli,xqwu}@hit.edu.cn
[2] Department of New Media Technologies and Arts,
Harbin Institute of Technology, Harbin 150001, China
buwei@hit.edu.cn

Abstract. This paper proposes a method based on Binarized Statistical Image Features (BSIF) and Image Quality Assessment for palmprint anti-spoofing approach. Firstly, BSIF computes a binary code for each pixel by filters, whose basis vectors are learnt from natural images via independent component analysis. For palmprint, it provides more texture information than the features in the original image. Image Quality Assessments are suitable measures since the re-captured images have features of blur and less details. Secondly, a new feature vector is formed by the former feature vectors. Finally, a SVM classifier is trained to discriminate the live and fake palmprint image. We collect a new database using iphone5 and iphone5s, which is the first one for palmprint liveness detection. Experiments on this database show great efficiency and high accuracy.

Keywords: Biometrics technology · Live palmprint detection · BSIF · Image quality assessment

1 Introduction

Nowadays, with the rapid development of biometrics technology, a large amount of applications have been used for personal authentication in our daily life. Biometrics, such as face, palmprint, fingerprint and iris, have gotten its popularity in various of security aspects. For instance, the fingerprint recognition in the function of unblocking in iphone5s, the palmprint authentication used in the Time Card Machines, and the face identification in the online shopping which is still in testing phase. With characters of unique for individuals, it is widely used in large amount of areas instead of traditional identification authentication which has the disadvantages of easily being forged and loss. However, most of these applications only use the 2-D images to analysis whether it is authenticated successfully. Unfortunately, once such personal biometric data is duplicated or stolen, imposters without access privileges can try to authenticate themselves as valid users. Therefore, it is necessary for us to detect whether the user is an imposter or an authorized person. Studies about liveness detection have been developed to determine where a biometric image is from the real person, a photograph, a video or

© Springer International Publishing Switzerland 2015
J. Yang et al. (Eds.): CCBR 2015, LNCS 9428, pp. 275–283, 2015.
DOI: 10.1007/978-3-319-25417-3_33

other material. In this paper, we have concentrated on the palmprint liveness detection which is the first attempt to distinguish the liveness in palmprint.

Recently, more and more researches have been proposed to detect liveness. These researches can be categorized into 3 types as follows. Firstly, specific devices are used in the most security approach, such as near infrared images or thermal images [1]. The 3D information could also be used to provide additional information which can easily identify whether the object is a 2-D planar or a 3-D cube. Experiments show that these methods are extraordinarily efficient no matter what the way of attack is, image, video, or mask model. However, such devices as 3-D cameras or multiple 2-D cameras need extra high expense. Secondly, the most commonly used cues include the motion of biometric images such as eye-blinking and small movements of parts of face or head. In [2], the author detects the eye regions and calculates the variation of eyes from the input images to determine whether it is a live face or not. User's cooperation are also used to satisfy the command of the system. Although no additional devices are required in these methods, they may face such difficulties, for instance, the imposters can use a short video of the valid people before the system to make such movement that is re-quired [3]. Imposters also can cut off the part of mouth and eyes from the images of valid people, then show this image on his face to make such movement, eye-blinking or mouth-moving. In [4], the author gives an interesting example that eye-blinking and some mouth movement can be easily simulated using only two photographs. In the end, lots of methods concentrating on the surface texture of biometric have been proposed. Features such as Local Binary Pattern (LBP) [5], Local Phase Quantization (LPQ) [6], and Binarized Statistical Image Features (BSIF) [7], focus on using only a single image to detect liveness. In [5], the author used LBP to extract texture features. Combined with frequency analyses, the features used SVM classifiers to detect the live face. In [6, 7], the author uses LPQ and BSIF to extract texture features to distinguish the fingerprint liveness.

In this paper, the first database for palmprint liveness detection has been proposed. Compared with face and fingerprint, the palmprint has less texture, that gives us great high challenge for distinguishing the liveness. Because of the rapid development of biometrics in the mobile phone and the high resolution of iphone, iphone5 is used to capture valid palmprint and recapture the fake palmprint from the iphone5's screen in order to get the higher resolution in not only the live palmprint but also the fake palmprint. In the experiment, we used BSIF to extract the texture feature, and then got the histogram of this image. Combined with 8 image quality measures, these features were merged into a new vector. Lastly, SVM classifier were trained to distinguish live palmprint and fake palmprint. The experimental results on our database demonstrate that our method gets better performance than many previous methods.

2   Methodology

This is the first attempt to use the features combined by BSIF and image quality measures to detect liveness. For an input image, BSIF is used to extract the histogram of palmprint, and then the image quality is used to extract the difference between the gradient image and the gradient image after Gaussian filter. At last we get the feature vector combined with the BSIF histogram and the quality feature, SVM is used to train the classification model. The total work is shown in Figure 1.

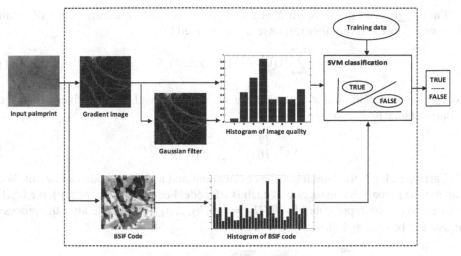

Fig. 1. The process of our method.

2.1   Binarized Statistical Image Features (BSIF) Extraction

Local image descriptors have been widely used in local feature extraction during the recent years. Local binary pattern (LBP) [8], and local phase quantization (LPQ) [9, 10] are extensively applied in texture description and classification. Furthermore, combined with other features, such as Fourier Analysis and Gaussian Distribution, these local image descriptors also show extraordinary results in liveness detection including face and fingerprint [5-7, 11].

Fig. 2. Examples of learnt filters with the size of 15 × 15 and the bit of 5 that used in our experiment.

Inspired by LBP and LPQ, which is regarded as statistics of labels computed in local pixel neighborhoods through filtering and quantization, and then gets a binary code by convolving the image with linear filters, BSIF learn a set of filters from natural images through independent component analysis (ICA) [12], instead of using hand-crafted filters. The filters trained from natural images are illustrated in Figure 2. In [13], the author uses the BSIF and Gaussian distribution to detect the fingerprint liveness, and the experimental result indicates that the BSIF is a better descriptor for liveness detection. Since the palmprint has many thin lines, differences between the live and fake palmprint can be better extracted by the BSIF code. The set of filters that used in our experiment are provided by [12]. The process of BSIF descriptors is briefly demonstrated as below.

Firstly, given an image patch X of size $l \times l$ pixels and a pre-learnt filter W_i with the same size $l \times l$, the filter response s_i is obtained by:

$$s_i = \sum_{u,v} W_i(u,v)X(u,v) = w_i^T x \qquad (1)$$

where the vector w_i and x represent the pixels of W_i and X respectively. Then the binary feature b_j is expressed as follows:

$$b_j = \begin{cases} 1, & s_i > 0 \\ 0, & s_i \leq 0 \end{cases} \qquad (2)$$

Lastly, each pixel of the image has been computed and BSIF code can be got. We can get the probability histogram of each BSIF code. For each image $f(x,y)$, the BSIF histogram can be represented by $BSIF_f = \{h_1, h_2, \dots h_{32}\}$. The code after the process above can be seen as follows:

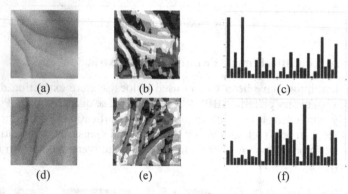

(a)   (b)   (c)

(d)   (e)   (f)

Fig. 3. The palmprint images, the corresponding BSIF codes with the filter size of 15×15 and the bit of 5 and the corresponding histogram. The first row is the live palmprint information: (a) live palmprint image; (b) the BSIF code of live palmprint image (a); (c) the histogram of BSIF code (b). And the second row is the fake palmprint information that is similar to the first row.

2.2 Image Quality Assessment

After observing the live and fake palmprint images carefully, we found that the fake palmprint images recaptured from the screen of Iphone5 and Iphone5s have the features of blur and less detail which can be seen from the Lambertian model [14, 15]. According to this model, the image can be described as follows:

$$I(x,y) = \rho(x,y)n(x,y)^T s \qquad (3)$$

where ρ is the albedo of surface texture, $n(x,y)^T$ is the surface normal of 3-D object, and s is the information of point. Because of the 2-D object which means the recaptured images from screen or image is a planer structure, the $n(x,y)^T$ is a constant. We can draw a conclusion from equation (3) that the recaptured image from screen or image has less intensity contrast compared with the captured image from live object under the same illumination. In the collecting process of our database, even though we tried our best to capture the palmprint from screen clearly, the fake image also had a low image quality. That is why image quality assessment is chose to distinguish the liveness.

8 image quality assessments are selected which are shown in Table 1. I denotes the gradient image, while $\bar{I}$ represents the reference image of I. Experiments from [16] show that these measures of image quality did great contribution for liveness detection.

Table 1. List of 8 image quality measures.

Name	Description	Ref.
Mean Squared Error	$MSE(I,\bar{I}) = \dfrac{1}{MN}\sum_{i=1}^{N}\sum_{j=1}^{M}(I_{i,j} - \bar{I}_{i,j})^2$	[17]
Peak Signal to Noise Ratio	$PSNR(I,\bar{I}) = 10log(\dfrac{max(I^2)}{MSE(I,\bar{I})})$	[18]
Signal to Noise Ratio	$SNR(I,\bar{I}) = 10log(\dfrac{\sum_{i=1}^{N}\sum_{j=1}^{M}(I_{i,j})^2}{N \cdot M \cdot MSE(I,\bar{I})})$	[19]
Structural Content	$SC(I,\bar{I}) = \dfrac{\sum_{i=1}^{N}\sum_{j=1}^{M}(I_{i,j})^2}{\sum_{i=1}^{N}\sum_{j=1}^{M}(\bar{I}_{i,j})^2}$	[20]
Maximum Difference	$MD(I,\bar{I}) = max\lvert I_{i,j} - \bar{I}_{i,j}\rvert$	[20]
Average Difference	$AD(I,\bar{I}) = \dfrac{1}{MN}\sum_{i=1}^{N}\sum_{j=1}^{M}(I_{i,j} - \bar{I}_{i,j})$	[20]
Normalized Absolute Error	$NAE(I,\bar{I}) = \dfrac{\sum_{i=1}^{N}\sum_{j=1}^{M}\lvert I_{i,j} - \bar{I}_{i,j}\rvert}{\sum_{i=1}^{N}\sum_{j=1}^{M}\lvert I_{i,j}\rvert}$	[20]
Normalized Cross-correlation	$NXC(I,\bar{I}) = \dfrac{\sum_{i=1}^{N}\sum_{j=1}^{M}(I_{i,j} \cdot \bar{I}_{i,j})}{\sum_{i=1}^{N}\sum_{j=1}^{M}(I_{i,j})^2}$	[20]

In consideration of the characters of palmprint having lots of thin lines, we can extract them by the gradient image for what the gradient of live palmprint has much more details than the fake palmprint. In addition, the gradient of image could better reflect the tiny difference compared with other edge detectors whose result shows that there is little difference between the image and its reference image. In our experiment, we found that the loss of quality produced by the Gaussian filtering differs from the live palmprint to the fake palmprint. These difference can be reflected from two levels. For the pixel level, we computed the distortion between two images on the basis of the pixel difference. These measures include MSE, PSNR, SNR, SC, MD, AD and NAE which are inspired by the difference between the live and fake palmprint after Gaussian filtering. For the correlation level, the similarity of two images can also been quantified by the correlation. A common correlation measure is the NXC that is listed in Table 1. The gradient image I is filtered with a low-pass Gaussian kernal ($\sigma = 0.6$) in order to get the reference image $\bar{I}$ for using the full-reference image quality assessment.

We can get a vector with 8 dimensions for each image, and then normalize these vectors. $IQA_f = \{q_1, q_2, \dots q_8\}$. After normalizing, the last feature vector can be obtained by combining the $BSIF_f$ and IQA_f, which can be described by $F = \{h_1, \dots h_{32}, q_1, \dots q_8\}$.

3   Experiments

3.1   The Palmprint Database

In consideration of the higher pixels and much more stable in capturing, the iphone5 is used to collect our live palmprint. In the same time, with the higher resolution of the iphone's screen, iphone5 is used to recapture the fake palmprint from the screen of iphone5s. Our database of palmprint images is divided into 3 sessions and contains 2654 images of live palmprint and 2887 images of fake palmprint. Images of the first session are taken from 48 students that include their left hand and right hand. Then using the iphone5 to recapture these palmprint images from the screen of iphone5s. The second session of images comes from 16 students which are randomly selected from the first session to detect whether time will affect the result or not. The images from third session are taken from the hands of 103 students for whom is the first time to be captured, and then recapture them. In the process of collecting, in order to take all of factors into account, different backgrounds and lights are selected for ensuring the high quality of captured and recaptured images. Some example images are shown in Figure 4.

Fig. 4. Examples of palmprint from our database. The first row: the live palmprint images. The second row: the fake palmprint images.

3.2   Experimental Result

In our experiments, the BSFI histogram and 8 image qualities are combined to form the last feature vector. we select the filters of BSIF with different size and bit in order to detect the best result. The accuracy is shown in Table 2.

Table 2. The accuracy of BSIF with different size and bit used in our database.

	3×3	5×5	7×7	9×9	11×11	13×13	15×15	Dimension
5	87.5%	88.2%	88.8%	90.4%	90.8%	90.8%	**92.0%**	32
6	84.6%	83.5%	89.8%	89.0%	90.6%	87.6%	90.5%	64
7	83.9%	83.0%	85.9%	89.9%	88.3%	88.7%	90.2%	128
8	81.9%	83.9%	81.9%	84.8%	87.6%	86.0%	89.2%	256

The first row represents the filter size and the first column means the filter bit which directly decide the feature dimension in the last column. The accuracy is gotten by this BSIF and the image quality measures with 8 feature dimensions. From Table 2, the best accuracy can be acquired in our database with the size of 15 and bit of 5.

Table 3. The result on our palmprint database.

Approach	Accuracy	Rate for live face	Rate for fake face	Feature dimensions
LBP-F[11]	83.2%	84.9%	81.7%	91
Ours	**92.0%**	**85.3%**	**93.3%**	**40**

In order to compare with other method in liveness detection, LBP-F [11] is selected whose result has the highest accuracy in NUAA database [21] in last year. In the experiment, we implement the LBP-F by ourselves that may have some deviation. Table 3 shows our result in palmprint database in detail with the size of 15 and bit of 5 and the result of LBP-F used in our database.

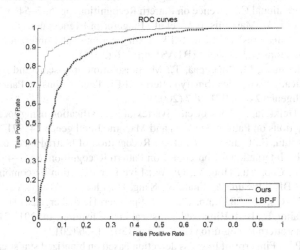

Fig. 5. ROC Curves for our method and LBP-F.

From Figure 5, it can be found that our method outperforms the LBP-F, for what we consider that the images not only for live palmprint but also for fake palmprint have much higher resolution so that the Fourier analysis can't distinguish the difference between the live and fake palmprint images.

4   Conclusions

The primary contribution of this paper is that we propose a first database for palmprint liveness detection in which the fake image is from the electronic screen. Databases in liveness detection have ranged from face, iris, to fingerprint which have at least two different database respectively. Our experiments combined with the BSIF and Image Quality Assessment have shown great efficiency and high accuracy.

In the later work, we plan to collect fake palmprint images from different mobile phones and different size of photograph.

References

1. Socolinsky, D.A., Selinger, A., Neuheisel, J.D.: Face recognition with visible and thermal infrared imagery. Computer Vision and Image Understanding **91**(1), 72–114 (2003)
2. Jee, H.K., Jung, S.U., Yoo, J.H.: Liveness detection for embedded face recognition system. International Journal of Biological and Medical Sciences **1**(4), 235–238 (2006)
3. Pan, G., Sun, L., Wu, Z.: Liveness detection for face recognition. INTECH Open Access Publisher (2008)
4. Joshi, T., Dey, S., Samanta, D.: Multimodal biometrics: state of the art in fusion techniques. International Journal of Biometrics **1**(4), 393–417 (2009)
5. Kim, G., Eum, S., Suhr, J.K., et al.: Face liveness detection based on texture and frequency analyses. In: International Conference on Biometrics, pp. 67–72 (2012)
6. Ghiani, L., Marcialis, G.L., Roli, F.: Fingerprint liveness detection by local phase quantization. In: International Conference on Pattern Recognition, pp. 537–540 (2012)
7. Ghiani, L., Hadid, A., Marcialis, G.L., et al.: Fingerprint liveness detection using binarized statistical image features. In: 2013 IEEE Sixth International Conference on Biometrics: Theory, Applications and Systems (BTAS), pp. 1–6 (2013)
8. Ojala, T., Pietikäinen, M., Mäenpää, T.: Multiresolution gray-scale and rotation invariant texture classification with local binary patterns. IEEE Transactions on Pattern Analysis and Machine Intelligence **24**(7), 971–987 (2002)
9. Ojansivu, V., Heikkilä, J.: Blur insensitive texture classification using local phase quantization. Transactions on Pattern Analysis and Machine Intelligence **24**, 971–987 (2002)
10. Ahonen, T., Rahtu, E., Ojansivu, V., et al.: Recognition of blurred faces using local phase quantization. In: International Conference on Pattern Recognition, pp. 1–4 (2008)
11. Wu, L., Xu, X., Cao, Yu., Hou, Y., Qi, W.: Live face detection by combining the fourier statistics and LBP. In: Sun, Z., Shan, S., Sang, H., Zhou, J., Wang, Y., Yuan, W. (eds.) CCBR 2014. LNCS, vol. 8833, pp. 173–181. Springer, Heidelberg (2014)
12. Kannala, J., Rahtu, E.: Bsif: Binarized statistical image features. In: 2012 21st International Conference on Pattern Recognition (ICPR), pp. 1363–1366 (2012)
13. Li, Q., Chan, P.P.: Fingerprint liveness detection based on binarized statistical image feature with sampling from Gaussian distribution. In: 2014 International Conference on Wavelet Analysis and Pattern Recognition (ICWAPR), pp. 13–17 (2014)
14. Basri, R., Jacobs, D.W.: Lambertian reflectance and linear subspaces. IEEE Transactions on Pattern Analysis and Machine Intelligence **25**(2), 218–233 (2003)
15. Li, J., Wang, Y., Tan, T., et al.: Live face detection based on the analysis of fourier spectra. In: Defense and Security, pp. 296–303. International Society for Optics and Photonics (2004)
16. Galbally, J., Marcel, S.: Face anti-spoofing based on general image quality assessment. In: 2014 22nd International Conference on Pattern Recognition (ICPR), pp. 1173–1178 (2014)
17. Sayood, K.: Statistical evaluation of image quality measures. Journal of Electronic Imaging **11**(2), 206–223 (2002)
18. Huynh-Thu, Q., Ghanbari, M.: Scope of validity of PSNR in image/video quality assessment. Electronics Letters **44**(13), 800–801 (2008)

19. Yao, S., Lin, W., Ong, E., et al.: Contrast signal-to-noise ratio for image quality assessment. In: IEEE International Conference on Image Processing. ICIP 2005, pp. I-397–400 (2005)
20. Eskicioglu, A.M., Fisher, P.S.: Image quality measures and their performance. IEEE Transactions on Communications **43**(12), 2959–2965 (1995)
21. Tan, X.Y., Li, Y., Liu, J., et al.: Face liveness detection from a single image with sparse low rank bilinear discriminative model. In: European Conference on Computer Vision, pp. 504–517 (2010)

Vein Biometrics

Study of Heterogeneous Dorsal Hand Vein Recognition Based on Multi-device

Yiding Wang and Linlin Xu[✉]

College of Electronic Information Engineering,
North China University of Technology, Beijing, China
wangyd@ncut.edu.cn, xul11014@126.com

Abstract. The effectiveness of dorsal hand vein recognition technology depends on image quality. The problem of dorsal hand vein image heterogeneity is becoming increasingly prominent in the era of big data. In the multi-device acquisition process, image ROI size, contrast, sharpness, position shift and image rotation are the main parameters of image heterogeneity. In order to explore the effects of different parameters on the image multi-device recognition, we adjusted 5 quality parameters of dorsal hand vein image individually first of all. Then, we used different recognition algorithms for experiment, and quantitatively analyzed the effect of different parameters on the heterogeneous dorsal hand vein image recognition by the improvement of recognition rate. Finally, the method of multi-parameter adjustment was proposed to improve recognition rate.

Keywords: Biometric recognition · Dorsal hand vein image · Image heterogeneity · Quality parameters · Multi-device

1 Introduction

Dorsal hand vein recognition is a recently developed technology based on biometric dorsal hand vein texture information. And dorsal hand vein recognition technology has attracted wide attention and become a research hotspot. However, in the image acquisition process, the dorsal hand vein images acquired by various devices get significant differences, such as too bright, too dark, position shift and undersize target area, resulting in the heterogeneous dorsal hand vein image recognition problem.

In actual application, we hope the images captured by different devices can be identified by different devices, which is what we call distributed dorsal hand vein recognition system. Now, either fingerprint or face recognition are moving in this direction, and have achieved some achievements. Obviously, it is urgent to address the problem of distributed recognition system in the domain of the dorsal hand vein recognition. In this work, we individually adjusted 5 quality parameters of dorsal hand vein image and used different recognition algorithms for experiment, and quantitatively analyzed the effect of different parameters on the heterogeneous dorsal hand vein image recognition by the improvement of recognition rate. Finally, the method of multi-parameter adjustment was proposed to improve recognition rate.

© Springer International Publishing Switzerland 2015
J. Yang et al. (Eds.): CCBR 2015, LNCS 9428, pp. 287–296, 2015.
DOI: 10.1007/978-3-319-25417-3_34

2   Heterogeneous Dorsal Hand Vein Image

2.1   Multi-device Heterogeneous Dorsal Hand Vein Image Database

The different acquisition devices have differences between the collection environments (lighting) and between the devices themselves (contrast, brightness, focal length, and optical properties of the lens). Moreover, in the acquisition process, due to different acquisition mode such as left or right hand, acquired image quality will be varied. In this work, the left and right dorsal hand vein images of 50 individuals were collected by three devices. The same person was collected left and right dorsal hand vein images 10 times by each device, so each person have 60 dorsal hand vein images. The original image size is 640×480. Fig. 1 is the acquired dorsal hand vein images of the same individual at different acquisition devices.

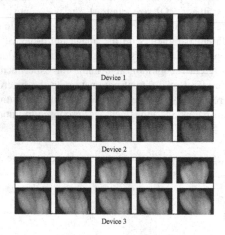

Fig. 1. Dorsal hand vein images of the same individual at different acquisition devices.

2.2   The Evaluation of Multi-device Heterogeneous Dorsal Hand Vein Image

As can be seen from the chart, the brightness, contrast of dorsal hand vein images captured by three devices are markedly different, the original image contains an amount of redundant information; there are also significant differences in image clarity, texture, and angle among dorsal hand vein images captured by different devices. Structural similarity of the image (SSIM) [1] [2] [3] can be a good proxy of similarity relation between two images. SSIM model includes brightness, contrast, and structure of the three evaluation factors. It can be expressed respectively as follows:

$$l(x,y) = \frac{2\mu_x\mu_y + C_1}{\mu_x^2 + \mu_y^2 + C_1},$$

$$c(x,y) = \frac{2\sigma_x\sigma_y + C_2}{\sigma_x^2 + \sigma_y^2 + C_2}, \tag{1}$$

$$s(x,y) = \frac{\sigma_{xy} + C_3}{\sigma_x\sigma_y + C_3}$$

where l, c, s respectively represent the brightness, contrast and structure. x, y represent two images. μ_x, μ_y, σ_x, σ_y respectively represent the means and variances of two images; σ_{xy} is the covariance of x and y; C_1, C_2, C_3 respectively represent the constants. Thus, SSIM evaluation model can be expressed as:

$$Q = [l(x,y)]^\alpha [c(x,y)]^\beta [s(x,y)]^\gamma \tag{2}$$

where α, β, $\gamma > 0$, they are used to adjust the proportion of three components, and the value is 1.

The dorsal hand vein image similarity between different devices calculated by the SSIM model is shown in Table 1.

Table 1. Structural similarity of the image.

Q_{12}	Q_{13}	Q_{23}
0.3736	0.5053	0.4102

The Q_{12} represents the average structure similarity between the 1st and the 2nd image databases. As can be seen from Table 1, there are differences among three dorsal hand vein image databases and image structure similarity among them is low. Where, there is a great difference of image structure between the 1st and the 2nd image databases, and the image structure is more similar between the 1st and the 3rd image databases. In summary, in this work, the three multi-device heterogeneous dorsal hand vein image databases we established are obviously different. The images are heterogeneous, and there are in line with the condition of multi-device heterogeneous dorsal hand vein image research.

3   The Image Quality Parameters Optimization and Adjustment

When acquiring the dorsal hand vein image using different devices, there are quality problems such as ROI undersize, poor contrast, image blurring, position shift, image rotation and so on. The fundamental way to solve the image heterogeneous recognition problems is to reduce the differences among images captured by different devices. Perspective from the causes of dorsal hand vein image heterogeneity, we optimized five quality parameters of dorsal hand vein image respectively: ROI size, contrast, image sharpness, positional shift and image rotation, so that different dorsal hand vein images acquired by different devices are similar in structural character.

3.1   Image Rotation

Image rotation means clockwise or counterclockwise rotating the image a certain angle around the center point. Dorsal hand vein images of the same individual acquired by different devices will be shifted because of different dorsal hand posture. Referring to one dorsal hand vein image database among them, this work correct the image angle of other two databases respectively. The original and rotated heterogeneous dorsal hand vein images are shown in Fig. 2.

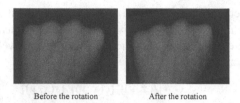

Before the rotation   After the rotation

Fig. 2. The original and rotated heterogeneous dorsal hand vein image.

3.2   Extraction of Effective ROI

Dorsal hand vein image characters center on specific region, so there is amount of redundancy information for the acquired dorsal hand vein image. Extract the correct, stable ROI size is capable of removing most of the redundant information, while reducing image processing time. In this work, we used image centroid [4] [5] to extract the ROI of dorsal hand vein image. The centroid (x_0, y_0) of vein image $f(x, y)$ can be calculated as shown in equation (3) .

$$x_0 = \frac{\sum_{i,j} i \times f(i,j)}{\sum_{i,j} f(i,j)}; y_0 = \frac{\sum_{i,j} j \times f(i,j)}{\sum_{i,j} f(i,j)} \tag{3}$$

We get the region of size $R \times R$ with the centroid as the center according to our dorsal hand vein images. Fig. 3 is the ROI of one dorsal hand vein image extracted by centroid.

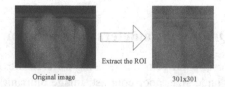

Original image   301x301

Fig. 3. ROI of dorsal hand vein image extracted by centroid.

3.3   Position Shift

In the process of dorsal hand vein image acquisition, because of the dorsal hand placement, the acquired image may be upper, downward, center-left or center-right. Thus, in the ROI extraction section, extracted ROI will be position shift, referring to the image acquired by one device, this work respectively adjusted the ROI position of image captured by other two devices. The original and adjusted ROI position images are shown in Fig. 4.

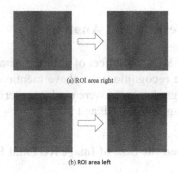

(a) ROI area right

(b) ROI area left

Fig. 4. The original and adjusted ROI position images.

3.4   Contrast

Contrast refers to the brightness levels difference between the lightest part and the darkest part of an image. In this work, the linear gray transform method is used to adjust the contrast of the image, the image captured by one device as a reference; images captured by the other two devices were adjusted. Since the maximum gray value of the dorsal hand vein image of this work selected is 179, so when the gray-scale transformation coefficient k is 1.6, the maximum gray value of converted image has been more than 255, which would lose part of the information. The contrast effects were shown in Fig. 5 when gray transform coefficients k was selected 0.4, 0.8, 1, and 1.4.

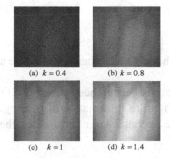

(a) $k = 0.4$ (b) $k = 0.8$

(c) $k = 1$ (d) $k = 1.4$

Fig. 5. The contrast.

3.5   Sharpness

In the process of dorsal hand vein image acquisition, due to the influence of dark current noise of acquisition device, dust on the lens, hand hairs and other factors, the image can be very blurred. Among them, the dark current noise belongs to white noise; noise caused by lens dust and hand hairs belongs to salt and pepper noise. In this work, the median filter algorithm and mean filter algorithm, which are simple and efficient, were used to complete the image de-noising and reduce the blur of the image.

4   Experimental Results and Analysis

In order to quantitatively analyze the effect of different parameters on the heterogeneous dorsal hand vein image recognition, the above mentioned multi-device heterogeneous dorsal hand vein image databases were used to experiment. And the experimental methods are deep learning, PCA, LBP and SIFT.

4.1   Relationship between the Size of Image ROI and Rate

The ROI extraction principle is to retain the useful image feature information and remove unwanted interference information. For the dorsal hand vein images acquired by different devices, selection of the ROI should contain the collective feature information of heterogeneous images. In this work, PCA, LBP and deep learning methods were used to recognition experiment for the ROI images of different sizes. The relationships between ROI size and recognition rate were shown in Fig. 6.

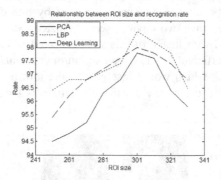

Fig. 6. The relationship between ROI size and rate.

As shown in Fig. 6, the rate is getting best when the ROI size is 301×301. Because the ROI contains collective feature information of heterogeneous images in this case. However, when the ROI size becomes larger or smaller, the rate actually has dropped.

4.2   Relationship between Single Parameter Optimization and Rate

Image ROI size, contrast, image sharpness, position shift and image rotation are the main parameters of image heterogeneity. In this work, we adjusted 5 quality parameters of dorsal hand vein image individually and experiment in different recognition algorithms. Table 2 is the experiment result.

Table 2. Single parameter optimization.

Mode	Parameter	PCA	LBP	SIFT	DL
Device 1 training/device 2 recognition	Original image	6%	2.6%	43%	42.4%
	Image rotation	16%	4%	44.5%	45.1%
	ROI extract	12.5%	5.2%	32.5%	51.5%
	Position shift	16%	6.5%	35%	59.6%
	Contrast	21%	4.8%	48%	46.8%
	Sharpness	7.2%	2.83%	43.9%	43.7%
Device 1 training/device 3 recognition	Original image	10%	5.2%	47.8%	48.9%
	Image rotation	19.5%	5.8%	49.6%	51.2%
	ROI extract	15%	8.6%	38.2%	57.8%
	Position shift	18.5%	10.2%	40.3%	64.6%
	Contrast	24%	6.5%	53.5%	54.9%
	Sharpness	11.4%	5.48%	48.2%	50.4%
Device 2 training/device 3 recognition	Original image	8%	4%	45.5%	45.4%
	Image rotation	16.5%	4.5%	46.8%	48.2%
	ROI extract	14.5%	6.4%	36.2%	53.8%
	Position shift	18%	8.5%	38.4%	62.8%
	Contrast	22.5%	5.2%	51.2%	50.6%
	Sharpness	9.6%	4.21%	46.3%	46.5%

As shown in Table 2, the recognition rates of different algorithms have been improved with the optimization of the quality parameters of the dorsal hand vein image, which demonstrated that the image quality is an important factor affecting the rate of recognition algorithm. However, the recognition rate actually fell for SIFT with the extraction of ROI. The recognition rate declined, because of the destruction of the image information in some ways and the reduction of the SIFT characteristic points with the extraction of ROI. In order to see the sensitivity of different algorithms for each quality parameter more clearly, we obtained the average improvement of recognition rates above the three modes. The result is shown in Table 3.

Table 3. The average improvement of recognition rate.

Parameter	PCA	LBP	SIFT	DL
Image rotation	9.3%	0.8%	1.5%	2.6%
ROI extract	6%	2.8%	-9.8%	8.8%
Position shift	9.5%	4.5%	-7.5%	16.8%
Contrast	14.5%	1.6%	5.5%	5.2%
Sharpness	1.4%	0.24%	0.7%	1.3%

From Table 3, we can see different recognition algorithms have different sensitive degrees on the five quality parameters. And to the specific recognition algorithm, the recognition performance depends on a key parameter, which plays a decisive role in the improvement of recognition performance. Therefore we can adjust the corresponding key parameters accordingly to improve the recognition performance effectively. What is more, the key parameters should be adjusted to reduce the difference between images in the process of dorsal hand vein images acquisition. In this way we can reduce the heterogeneous problem from the source.

From Table 3, we also can see the impact of contrast is the largest on the PCA algorithm, that is to say it is a key parameter which decides the improvement of PCA recognition algorithm. The reason is that PCA is sensitive to the influence of light, so the contrast improvement can make greatest degree to improve the recognition rate of PCA algorithm. For LBP and deep learning, the ROI extraction and the position shift have a bigger influence on recognition effect. Extracting ROI can remove redundant information and reserve effective characteristics. And the improvement of position shift is on the basis of the ROI extraction. Therefore both of them play a decisive role to the improvement of the recognition effect. Lastly, for SIFT algorithm, the contrast improvement has a certain effect on recognition effect. However, the SIFT features have certain robustness to illumination, rotation, scale. Therefore, the image quality parameters optimization has a little influence on SIFT performance.

4.3   Relationship between Multi-parameter Optimization and Rate

In order to verify the effectiveness of image parameters optimization for heterogeneous dorsal hand vein recognition, in this work, the method of multi- parameter optimization was used to recognition experiment. First of all, we will complete the adjustment of the first parameter. Then we will adjust the second parameter based on the first step. Similarly, we will complete the adjustment of the third parameter. The result is shown in Table 4.

Table 4. Multi-parameter optimization.

Mode	Status	PCA	LBP	DL
Device 1 training/device 2 recognition	Original image	6%	2.6%	42.4%
	Multi-parameter	24.5%	8.2%	62.8%
Device 1 training/device 3 recognition	Original image	10%	5.2%	48.9%
	Multi-parameter	28%	12.6%	68.2%
Device 2 training/device 3 recognition	Original image	8%	4%	45.4%
	Multi-parameter	26.2%	9.6%	66.3%

As shown in Table 4, the recognition rate of multi-device heterogeneous dorsal hand vein image has been significantly improved after multi-parameter optimization. Moreover, the deep learning algorithm has been the better recognition effect for the heterogeneous dorsal hand vein image, which indicates a clear direction to the recognition question of the heterogeneous image. For this problem, the most fundamental thing is to reduce the difference of the dorsal hand vein image. Therefore, the parameters optimization plays an important role to the recognition of heterogeneous dorsal hand vein image.

5   Conclusion

For multi-device heterogeneous dorsal hand vein image, firstly, perspective from the causes of dorsal hand vein image heterogeneity, we optimized 5 quality parameters of dorsal hand vein image respectively, this work put forward an algorithm of optimizing a single quality parameter, and quantitatively analyzed the effect of different parameters on the heterogeneous dorsal hand vein image recognition; Then, we used different recognition algorithms for experimental analysis, including PCA, LBP, SIFT and deep learning; Finally, the method of multi-parameter adjustment was proposed to improve recognition rate. The results of the experiment are very good to analyze the causes of image heterogeneity. The data is real and reliable, and provides a reference for the quality optimization of the dorsal hand vein image.

The study of heterogeneous dorsal hand vein image is a relatively novel area. And the recognition of heterogeneous dorsal hand vein is an urgent problem. The next step of this work is to study the standardization of acquisition device to effectively solve the heterogeneous problem caused by multi-device.

Acknowledgments. This work is supported by the National Natural Science Foundation of China (No.61271368) and the Beijing Natural Science Foundation of China (No.KZ201410009012). The authors would also like to thanks for Zhao Zepeng, Duan Qiangyu for their constructive advices and grateful for comments from the anonymous associate editor and reviewers.

References

1. Wang, Z., Bovik, A.C., Sheikh, H.R.: Image Quality Assessment: from Error Visibility to Structural Similarity. J. IEEE Transactions on Image Processing **13**(4), 600–612 (2004)
2. Xie, X.F., Zhou, J., Qin-Zhang, W.U.: No-reference Quality Index for Image Blur. J. Journal of Computer Applications **30**(4), 921–924 (2010)
3. Miao, J.F., Wu, Q., Zhu, H., Hu, G.Y.: An Improved Image Quality Assessment Method Based on Structural Similarity. J. Computer Technology and Development **24**(3) (2014)
4. Kumar, A., Prathyusha, K.V.: Personal Authentication Using Hand Vein Triangulation and Knuckle Shape. J. IEEE Transactions on Image Processing **18**(9), 2127–2136 (2009)
5. Wang, Y., Li, K., Cui, J.: Study of Hand-dorsal Vein Recognition Based on Partition Local Binary Pattern. In: 10th International Conference on Signal Processing (2010)

Finger Vein Recognition Based on Local Opposite Directional Pattern

Ying Xie, Jucheng Yang[✉], Xi Zhao, and Xiaoli Zhang

College of Computer Science and Information Engineering,
Tianjin University of Science and Technology, Tianjin, China
jcyang@tust.edu.cn

Abstract. Local operator has already been used in the finger vein recognition. But the traditional algorithms, such as Local Binary Pattern (LBP), Local Directional Pattern (LDP) and so on, are lack of effective extraction of the gradient information of the image. In order to overcome the shortcomings of the traditional methods, this paper proposed a Local Opposite Directional Pattern (LODP) operator for finger vein recognition motivated from the Local Gradient Pattern (LGP), LDP, local Ternary Pattern (LTP) operators. The LODP operator mainly extracts the gradient information of the finger vein images. This operator uses local 3×3 masks to make the convolution with the images. After comparing the opposite pixels, three-valued encoding mode has been used. Then the center pixel will be set with a new binary value. The experimental results showed that the LODP operator behaves better than LGP, LDP, LTP operators in extracting the features of finger vein images.

Keywords: Finger vein · Gradient · Opposite direction pattern

1   Introduction

Nowadays, Biometric technologies [1] have played a very important role in the information security technology. It has been widely used in our daily life. There are a lot of biometric can be used, such as finger print, face, iris, finger vein and so on. Among which, finger vein recognition technology is one of the most representative techniques.

Finger vein recognition has been developed rapidly in recent years. Not only it has a great increase in the recognition rate and accuracy, but also the method of obtaining the finger vein images has made a great development. Among the large number of finger vein recognition algorithms, the approaches which based on local pattern recognition have attracted a lot of attention. Because this type of operator has a high robustness while dealing with the change of the images, and it also can make full use of the characteristics of the finger vein images. More important, it shows better results than the holistic approaches in the accuracy of the finger vein recognition. Recently, LBP operator [2] has been widely concerned because of its superiority. LBP Operator uses the information of the center pixel and its neighborhood pixels through encoding to get a new binary code of the center pixel in the 3x3 mask. The LBP operator takes

© Springer International Publishing Switzerland 2015
J. Yang et al. (Eds.): CCBR 2015, LNCS 9428, pp. 297–304, 2015.
DOI: 10.1007/978-3-319-25417-3_35

the texture features of the image into account, and it also possess a very high flexibili-ty. So it can be modified to be adapting to different needs. LGP operator [3] is the improvement of the LBP operator. It takes the gradient information of images into account, which enables the operator to extract richer feature information of gradient. LDP operator [4] uses directional operator to get more information of the gradient, and it is not sensitive to the noise. LTP operator [5] takes three value coding mode to encode the images and it has the ability to resist the noise.

However, all these methods will lose a part of the gradient information, which will affect the final recognition rate. In order to solve these problems, this paper puts for-ward the Local Opposite Directional Pattern (LODP) operator. It takes the informa-tion of the diagonal line into consideration to get more gradient information. The experimental results have been proved that it will show better performances than LGP, LDP, LTP operators.

The rest of the paper is organized as follows: Section 2 introduces the methods of LGP, LDP, LTP briefly; The proposed method for finger vein recognition based on LODP is shown in Section 3; Section 4 shows the experimental results; The conclu-sion is given in Section 5.

2   Related Theory

2.1   LGP

LGP operator extracts the gradient information of the images which based on the improvement of the LBP operator. It takes the 3×3 neighborhood from the images at first. Then the center pixel will be used to minus its neighbor pixels and we'll get 8 values. After averaging the 8 values, the mean value will be given to the center pixel, the comparison between the center pixel and the neighbor pixels will be carried on. If the neighbor pixel is greater than or equal to the average value, it will set to be 1, and if it is less than the average value, it will set to be 0. The specific calculation process of LGP operator is shown as Fig. 1:

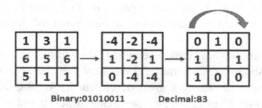

Binary:01010011   Decimal:83

Fig. 1. LGP Operator

2.2   LDP

By using the Kirsch Gradient Operator [6] to process the images in 8 directions, LDP operator will get the edge response values through the calculation. The 8 masks are shown as Fig. 2:

-3	-3	5
-3	0	5
-3	-3	5

-3	5	5
-3	0	5
-3	-3	-3

5	5	5
-3	0	-3
-3	-3	-3

5	5	-3
5	0	-3
-3	-3	-3

5	-3	-3
5	0	-3
5	-3	-3

-3	-3	-3
5	0	-3
5	5	-3

-3	-3	-3
-3	0	-3
5	5	5

-3	-3	-3
-3	0	5
-3	5	5

Fig. 2. Kirsch Gradient Operator

A new neighborhood will be gotten after the calculation of the image. The value of the K has been determined after getting the 8 values. Then the maximum of the first k value is set to 1, the other value is set to 0. The specific calculation process of LDP operator is shown as Fig. 3:

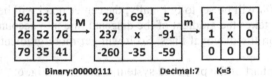

Binary:00000111   Decimal:7   K=3

Fig. 3. LDP Operator

2.3   LTP

LTP operator is the improvement of the LBP operator which has been changed into three value coding mode. The basic idea of LTP is still the same as the LBP operator. The center pixel value and the adjacent pixel values are compared at first. Then the limit value of t will be settled down. The neighbor pixels which are in the limits of the $[ic-t, ic+t]$ will be set to 0. If the pixels are larger than the limits, it will be set to 1. And if the pixels are smaller than the limits, it will be set to -1. The specific calculation process of LTP operator is shown as Fig. 4 ($t=5$):

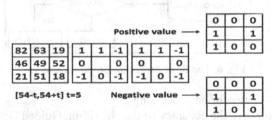

Fig. 4. LTP Operator

3   Proposed Method

This paper proposed a LODP operator for finger vein recognition. In order to take full use of the gradient information, this operator is motivated from the main idea of LDP, LGP and LTP.

LODP operator:

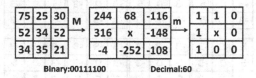

Fig. 5. LODP Operator

In order to take full use of the information of the gradient, the LODP operator uses the Kirsch Gradient Operator which has been used in LDP operator, to deal with the 3×3 neighborhood of the image. The 8 values will be gotten after the convolution. Then the values should be compared with each other if two of them are on the diagonal line. Learning from the LTP operator, a new encoding method has been used in the proposed method. Just as the Fig. 5 shows, 244 is greater than -108, so 244 will be set to 1, and -108 will be set to 0. Finally, the center pixel will be set to a new value. The new value takes the gradient of the diagonal line into account. It compares the pixels which are on the diagonal lines. So it will get more gradient information than the LGP operator.

The main flow chart of the proposed system is shown as Fig. 6:

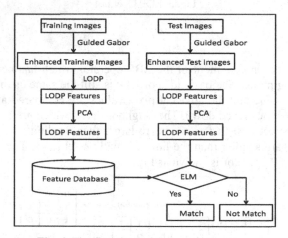

Fig. 6. The flowchart of the proposed system

1). Guided Gabor filter for preprocessing
   In order to improve the accuracy of the algorithm, Guided Gabor filter has been chosen to preprocess the finger vein images. The Guided Gabor filter can reduce the effect of the recognition results by removing the redundant information and keeping the gradient information.

2). LODP feature extraction process
   Step1: The finger vein image is processed by the 3 × 3 neighborhood template. The gradient values of the 8 directions are obtained by using Gradient Operator Kirsch.

Step2: The values should minus each other if the two of them are on the diagonal line. If two elements are the same, they are both set to be 0. If one   of the elements is larger than the other, the larger one will be set to be 1 and the smaller one will be set to be 0. The new binary code will be assigned to the central pixel.

Step3: After the convolution of the template and the image, a feature vector will be obtained.

3). PCA to reduce the dimension of feature matrix

Because the feature vector dimension is too large which is not easy to deal with, the PCA[8] has been used to reduce the dimension. Usually PCA algorithm can choose the specific dimension or choose the contribution rate to set the method of reducing dimension. In order to get a better result, the contribution rate of PCA has been chosen and it is set to be 0.95.

4). ELM classification

Based on the Extreme Learning Machine (ELM) [9,10,11] classifier's excellent classification performance, ELM was chosen as a classifier for finger vein classification. Through experiments, the hidden layer node is chosen to be 2000[10,11].

4   Experiments

4.1   Experimental Database

In order to prove the effectiveness of the algorithm, the database used here is named Homologous Multi-modal Traits Database (SDUMLA-HMT Database) [12] provided by the Shandong University. SDUMLA-HMT Database contains face, fingerprint, iris, and gait vein and other biometrics. In this paper, only the finger vein database is used in the experiments.

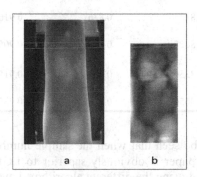

Fig. 7. Examples of preprocessing (a) Original image (b)ROI image

The finger vein image database has 600 images from 100 fingers, and each finger has 6 pictures, and the size of each picture is 320×240. Specific images are shown in Fig. 7.

4.2   Determine the Best Block Manner

In order to improve the recognition rate and to achieve the best experimental results, block manner has been used in this experiment. The different block manner of the images will be determined the number of the sub-images. So it also has an effect on the dimension of the feature matrix, and influences the recognition rate.

For each finger, we use 4 training samples and 2 testing samples. So the total training and test images are 400 and 200, respectively. The results of the experiments have been shown as Table 1. From the Table 1, we can draw a conclusion that the best block manner is 32×4 and the highest recognition rate is 93.5%.

Table 1. Recognition Rate of Different Block manner

Block Manner	1×1	4×4	8×8	16×16	32×4	64×4
Recognition Rate	0.8900	0.8950	0.9000	0.9200	0.9350	0.9150

4.3   Compares with Different Algorithms

In order to prove the effectiveness of the proposed method, three traditional algorithms are compared. Table 2 shows that the performance of the proposed algorithms with the other traditional LGP, LDP, LTP algorithms on the same finger vein database. The block manner of 32×4 is chosen.

Table 2. Recognition Rate of Different Algorithms

	N=2	N=3	N=4	N=5
LGP	0.8175	0.8367	0.9100	0.9800
LTP	0.8625	0.8833	0.9050	0.9800
LDP	0.8350	0.8533	0.9150	0.9700
LODP	0.8650	0.8867	0.9350	0.9900

From Table 2, it can be seen that when the sample number is 2, 3, 4, 5; the proposed algorithm in this paper is obviously superior to LGP, LDP, LTP operators. The ROC curves achieved using the different algorithms have also been shown in the Fig. 8. From Fig. 8, the curves of the LGP, LDP, LTP algorithms are above on the curve of the LODP algorithm. Table 3 showed that the LODP algorithm achieved the lowest EER of 2.68%.

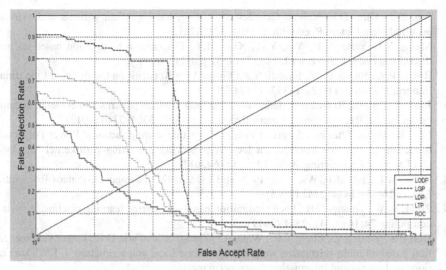

Fig. 8. ROC curves achieved using different algorithms

Table 3. ERRs of Different Algorithms

Methods	LGP	LDP	LTP	LODP
ERRs	5.52%	4.02%	3.61%	2.68%

5   Conclusion

In this paper, we proposed an LODP operator for finger vein recognition. This operator takes the information of the gradient into account, and it makes full use of the
gradient information of each part. This operator uses local 3 x 3 masks to make the
convolution with the images. After comparing the opposite pixels, three-valued encoding mode has been used. Then the center pixel will be set with a new binary value.
The results of the experiments show that the LODP algorithm has better performances
than other traditional methods for finger vein recognition. The next step is to extract
the gradient information of the adjacent pixels which will make the algorithm become
more robustness for the noise.

Acknowledgement. This paper was supported by the National Natural Science Foundation of China under Grant No.61202415, No.61402332, No.61502338 and the 2015 key projects of Tianjin science and technology support program No.15ZCZDGX00200, the TJSFC: 15JCQNJC00700.

References

1. Yang, J.F.: Finger-vein image restoration based on skin optical property. In: Proceedings of 2012 IEEE 11th International Conference on Signal Processing (ICSP) (2012)
2. Bo, Y.G., Chen, S.C.: A comparative study on local binary pattern (LBP) based face recognition: LBP histogram versus LBP image. J. Neurocomputing, 65–379 (2013)

3. Jun, B.J., Kim, D.J.: Robust face detection using local gradient patterns and evidence accumulation. Pattern Recognition, 3304–3316 (2012)
4. Meng, X.J., Yang, G.P., Yin, Y.L., Xiao, R.Y.: Finger vein recognition based on local directional code. J. Sensors **12**, 14937–14952 (2012)
5. Rosdi, B.A., Shing, C.W., Suandi, S.A.: Finger Vein Recognition Using Local Line Binary Pattern. J. Sensors **11**(12), 11357–11371 (2011)
6. Jun, B., Kim, D.: Robust face detection using local gradient patterns and evidence accumulation Pattern Recognition. J. Pattern Recognition **45**(9), 3304–3316 (2012)
7. Li, J.B.: Gabor filter based optical image recognition using Fractional Power Polynomial model based common discriminant locality preserving projection with kernels. J. Optics and Lasers in Engineering **50**(9), 1281–1286 (2012)
8. Chen, W.L., Er, M.J., Wu, S.Q.: PCA and LDA in DCT domain. J. Pattern Recognition Letters **26**(15), 2474–2482 (2005)
9. Zong, W.W., Huang, G.B.: Face recognition based on extreme learning machine. J. Neuro-computing **74**(16), 2541–2551 (2011)
10. Dong, S., Yang, J.C., Chen, Y.R., Wang, C., Zhang, X.Y., Park, D.S.: Finger vein recognition based on multi-orientation weighted symmetric local graph structure. J. KSII Transactions on Internet and Information Systems (in press)
11. Chen, Y.R., Yang, J.C., Wang, C., Park, D.S.: Variational Bayesian Extreme Learning Machine. J. Neural Computing and Applications, 1–12 (2014)
12. http://mla.sdu.edu.cn/sdumla-hmt.html

Finger Vein Recognition Based on Cycle Gradient Operator

Song Dong, Jucheng Yang(✉), Xi Zhao, and Xiaoli Zhang

College of Computer Science and Information Engineering,
Tianjin University of Science and Technology, Tianjin, China
jcyang@tust.edu.cn

Abstract. The finger vein recognition technology, using the finger vein feature for identification, due to its liveness, easy collection features, becomes more popular. In order to overcome the shortcomings of the traditional local feature extraction methods, a Cycle Gradient Operator (CGO) for finger vein recognition is proposed in this paper. Compared with LBP (Local Binary Pattern), LGP (Local Gradient Pattern) and other traditional operators, CGO calculates an overall gradient direction and the cycle gradient direction, and not only considers the relationship between the target pixel and the surrounding pixels, but also considers the relationship between the surrounding pixels, therefore, the operator can improve the efficiency of feature extraction. Experiment results show that the proposed algorithm has advantages in terms of recognition rate.

Keywords: Biometrics · Finger vein · Gradient · Cycle

1 Introduction

With the rapid rise of e-commerce around the world, people can do on-line electronic trading and other business activities through the Internet and other open networks. Also, as there is a lot of sensitive personal, military, government information in network, the information can only be accessed by authorized people, network security has become a key issue for network development. As the body's biological characteristics are not likely to be stolen, forgotten or cracked, it has unique advantages in identity authentication. Biometrics [1] use the inherent personal characteristics for identity authentication. Biometrics is more secure, private and convenient than the traditional method of identification.

Among the existing biological recognition technology, finger vein recognition [2-3] makes use of human finger vein feature for identity authentication, with liveness, characteristics of internal, non-contact and other unique advantages, and has widely application prospects. As the finger vein image is easily influenced by the light, humidity and other factors, it has difficulties to a certain extent. The finger vein image contains rich directional information, therefore, in recent years, finger vein feature extraction algorithm based on direction information is widely used in the field of finger vein recognition, such as LBP [4], LLBP [5], LGP [6], LDC [7]. In 2012, Lin et. al. [8]

© Springer International Publishing Switzerland 2015
J. Yang et al. (Eds.): CCBR 2015, LNCS 9428, pp. 305–311, 2015.
DOI: 10.1007/978-3-319-25417-3_36

proposed a finger vein recognition algorithm based on gradient-correlation, which used the maximum curvature model to extract the gradient image of finger vein. In 2014, Dong et. al. [9] proposed the Multi-Orientation Weighted Symmetric Local Graph Structure (MOW-SLGS), which assigned weight according to the positional relationship between the edge and the target pixel for each edge, and extended to 4 directions, and applied the MOW-SLGS to finger vein recognition. Dong et. al. [10] proposed the Difference Symmetric Local Graph Structure (DSLGS), which took the contribution of difference value into consideration. However, these traditional local feature extraction methods do not make full use of the relationship between the surrounding pixels, and take not full account of the overall gradient trend as well as the gradient information between the surrounding pixels.

Therefore, this paper proposes a Cycle Gradient Operator (CGO) for finger vein recognition. Compared with LBP, LGP and other traditional operators, CGO calculates an overall gradient direction and the cycle gradient direction, and not only considers the relationship between the target pixel and the surrounding pixels, but also considers the relationship between the surrounding pixels, therefore, the operator can improve the efficiency of feature extraction. Experimental results show that the method has better robustness to the light and temperature, and improves the recognition efficiency of the finger vein recognition system.

The remaining paper is structured as follows: section 2 introduces the theoretical basis of LGP, section 3 describes the proposed method; section 4 shows the experimental results; section 5 gives the summary.

2   Related Theory

2.1   Local Gradient Pattern

LGP (Local Gradient Pattern) [6], compared with the traditional operator, uses the gradient information instead of the traditional pixel value information, moreover, the gradient information is more stable, and therefore, LGP has certain advantages in terms of feature extraction. This calculation procedure is shown below.

First, we calculate the difference value between surrounding pixels and the target pixel, i.e. the gradient value, and then, calculate the average value of the gradient. The gradient value is compared with the average value, if greater than the average value, it set to 1. Otherwise, it set to 0. Through the above process, we can get 8-bit binary number, which can be converted to a decimal number, and then we can get the feature value of the target pixel.

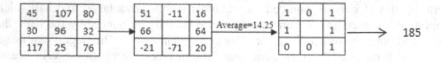

Fig. 1. Calculation process of LGP

3   Proposed Method

3.1   The Finger Vein Recognition System

The finger vein recognition system constructed in this paper consists of the following major steps, and the flowchart is shown in Figure 2.

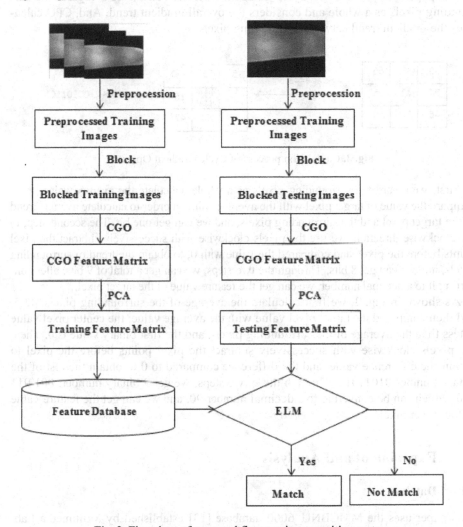

Fig. 2. Flowchart of proposed finger vein recognition system

The specific process is described as follows. The first step is feature extraction. We use the proposed Cycle Gradient Operator above for feature extraction. The second step is dimension reduction. The dimension of feature matrix after feature extraction is too large, therefore, we use PCA[11] to reduce the dimension of feature matrix. The third step is the training and classification. We use Extreme Learning Machine (ELM) [12] for training and classification, and the number of hidden layer node is 2000.

3.2   Cycle Gradient Operator

In this paper, we propose the Cycle Gradient Operator (CPO). CPO regards the surrounding pixels as a whole and considers the overall gradient trend. And, CPO calculates the gradient trend between surrounding pixels.

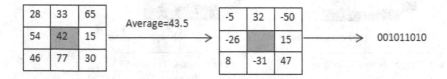

Fig. 3. Calculation process of Cycle Gradient Operator

First, we regard the surrounding pixels as a whole, calculate the average value, then, compare the value of target pixel with the average value in order to calculate average trend of the target pixel and the surrounding pixels, and we can get one bit. The second step, in the clockwise direction, we use the pixels clockwise with successively subtract the pixel points before the pixel, and compared the value with 0, to obtain the trend of surrounding pixels, and we can get 8 bits. Through the two steps, we can get a total of 9 bits, after converting it to a decimal number, we can get the feature value of the target pixel.

As shown in Fig. 3, we first calculate the average of the surrounding pixels, 43.5, and then compared the target pixel value with the average value; the center pixel value is less than the average of the surrounding pixels, and the first binary value is 0. Then, the pixels clockwise with successively subtract the pixel points before the pixel to obtain the difference value, and the difference compared to 0 to obtain the rest of the binary number 01011010. Through these two steps, we get 9 binary number, 001 011 010, which can be converted to a decimal number 90, and we can get the feature value of the target pixel.

4   Experiment and Analysis

4.1   Database

This paper uses the MMCBNU_6000 database [13] established by Multimedia Lab, Chonbuk National University, Republic of Korea. The database consists of 100 volunteers with middle finger, index finger, ring finger of left hand, right hand. Each finger has 10 images, 6000 images in total, and the image is shown in Figure 4(a).

ROI region extraction method mention [14] is used here, and the finger vein ROI image is shown in Figure 4(b).

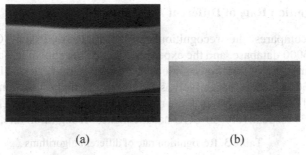

(a)   (b)

Fig. 4. Finger vein image. (a) Finger vein image in MMCBNU_6000 database (b) Finger vein ROI image

4.2 Determine the Best Block Manner

In order to enhance feature extraction's efficiency and improve the pertinence of feature extraction algorithm, this paper carried out experiments to determine the best way of blocking the image. The block manner of image determines the number of sub-images, influence the size of feature matrix, and finally impact feature extraction. And the number of sub-images should be less than 10.

In this paper, we select seven training samples, three test samples, and the results are shown in Table 1. The recognition rate is different in different block manner, and when the block manner is 2×4, the recognition rate is 94.39%, and it is the highest.

Table 1. Recognition rate of different block manner

Block Manner	1×1	1×2	2×1	2×2	2×4	4×2
Recognition Rate	0.6433	0.7894	0.8144	08678	0.9439	0.9422

4.3 Processing Time of Different Algorithms

Finger vein recognition system, as a real-time system, has high demands for time-consuming. Therefore, this paper compares processing time of different algorithms for a same image, and the concrete result is shown in the following table. The experiments are implemented with MATLAB 7.0, and performed on a PC with a 2.8 GHz CPU and 2.0 G memory in windows 7 OS.

From Table 2 we can see that, compared with other operators, CGP operator takes 0.5453 second and it is slightly higher than the LBP operator, but far lower than other operators. The proposed operator has certain advantages in terms of time-consuming.

Table 2. Processing time of different algorithms

Algorithm	LBP	LGP	DSLGS	CGO
Processing time(second)	0.5054	0.7387	0.7152	0.5453

4.4   Recognition Rate of Different Algorithms

This paper compares the recognition rate of LBP, LGP and CGO under the MMCBNU_6000 database, and the experiment results are shown in Table 3 and Figure 5. When the number of training sample is 5, the recognition rates of LBP, LGP, CGO are 70.07%, 66.8%, 86% respectively, so CGO has the highest recognition rate. When the number of training sample is 8, the recognition rate of LBP, LGP, CGO is 89.83%, 88.58%, 96.5% respectively, so CGO has the highest recognition rate, too.

Table 3. Recognition rate of different algorithms

Algorithm\ Number of Training Sample	LBP	LGP	CGO
4	0.4778	0.3956	0.6589
5	0.7007	0.6680	0.8600
6	0.8117	0.7854	0.9138
7	0.8717	0.8417	0.9439
8	0.8983	0.8858	0.9650
9	0.9350	0.9150	0.9767

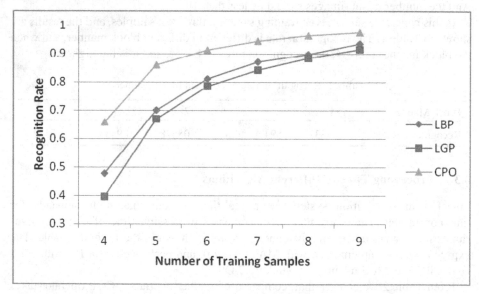

Fig. 5. Recognition rate of different algorithms

5   Conclusion

In this paper, we propose a Cycle Gradient Operator, and apply it to the finger vein recognition. Compared with LBP, LGP and other traditional operators, CGO calculates an overall gradient direction and the cycle gradient direction, and not only considers the relationship between the target pixel and the surrounding pixels, but also considers the relationship between the surrounding pixels, therefore, the operator can improve the efficiency of feature extraction. Experimental results show that the operator has advantages in recognition rate comparing with other traditional methods.

Acknowledgement. This paper was supported by the National Natural Science Foundation of China under Grant No.61202415, No.61402332, No.61502338 and the 2015 key projects of Tianjin science and technology support program No.15ZCZDGX00200.

References

1. Sim, H.M., Asmuni, H., Hassan, R., Othman, R.M.: Multimodal biometrics: Weighted score level fusion based on non-ideal iris and face images. J. Expert Systems with Applications **41**(11), 5390–5404 (2014)
2. Gupta, P., Gupta, P.: An accurate finger vein based verification system. J. Digital Signal Processing **38**, 43–52 (2015)
3. Liu, F., Yang, G.P., Yin, Y.L., Wang, S.Q.: Singular value decomposition based minutiae matching method for finger vein recognition. J. Neurocomputing **145**(5), 75–89 (2014)
4. Lee, E.C., Kang, B.J., Lee, E.C.: Finger vein recognition using weighted local binary pattern code based on a support vector machine. J. Journal of Zhejiang University: Science C. **07**, 514–524 (2010)
5. Rosdi, B.A., Shing, C.W., Suandi, S.A.: Finger Vein Recognition Using Local Line Binary Pattern. J. Sensors **11**(12), 11357–11371 (2011)
6. Jun, B., Kim, D.: Robust face detection using local gradient patterns and evidence accumulation Pattern Recognition. J. Pattern Recognition **45**(9), 3304–3316 (2012)
7. Meng, X.J., Yang, G.P., Yin, Y.L., Xiao, R.Y.: Finger vein recognition based on local directional code. J. Sensors **12**, 14937–14952 (2012)
8. Lin, C.Y., Li, M.Z., Sun, X.: A finger vein recognition algorithm based on gradient correlation. In: AASRI Conference on Computational Intelligence and Bioinformatics, pp. 40–45. AASRI Procedia, China (2012)
9. Dong, S., Yang, J.C., Wang, C., Chen, Y.R., Sun, D.: A New Finger Vein Recognition Method Based on the Difference Symmetric Local Graph Structure (DSLGS). J. International Journal of Signal Processing, Image Processing and Pattern Recognition (in press)
10. Dong, S., Yang, J.C., Chen, Y.R., Wang, C., Zhang, X.Y., Park, D.S.: Finger Vein Recognition Based on Multi-Orientation Weighted Symmetric Local Graph Structure. J. KSII Transactions on Internet and Information Systems (in press)
11. Chen, W.L., Er, M.J., Wu, S.Q.: PCA and LDA in DCT domain. J. Pattern Recognition Letters **26**(15), 2474–2482 (2005)
12. Chen, Y.R., Yang, J.C., Wang, C., Park, D.S.: Variational Bayesian Extreme Learning Machine. J. Neural Computing and Applications, 1–12 (2014)
13. Wang, Z., Park, D.S.: An available database for the research of finger vein recognition. In: 6rd International Congress on Image and Signal Processing (CISP 2013), China, pp. 386–392 (2013)
14. Lu, Y., Xie, S.J., Yoon, S., Yang, J.C., Park, D.S.: Robust Finger Vein ROI Localization Based on Flexible Segmentation. J. Sensors **13**, 14339–14366 (2013)

Hand-dorsa Vein Recognition Based on Improved Partition Local Binary Patterns

Kefeng Li[1(✉)], Guangyuan Zhang[1], Yiding Wang[2], Peng Wang[1], and Cui Ni[1]

[1] School of Information Science and Electric Engineering,
Shandong Jiaotong University, Jinan, China
seafrog1984@hotmail.com, xdzhanggy@163.com,
{121602121,81001630}@qq.com
[2] College of Information Engineering, North China University of Technology, Beijing, China
wangyd@ncut.edu.cn

Abstract. In this paper, a new feature descriptor is presented and proposed for personal verification based on near infrared images of hand-dorsa veins. This new feature descriptor is a modification of the previously proposed partition local binary patterns (PLBP) by adding feature weighting, combining multi-scale PLBP and fusion with structure information. While addition of feature weighting aims to reduce the influence of insignificant local binary patterns, combination of multi-scale features aims to get more texture information and fusion with structure feature aims to increase binary information. Testing on a large database with more than two thousand hand-dorsa vein images, Multi-scale PLBP (MPLBP) is shown to be more effective than the original PLBP and Weighted PLBP (WPLBP), and offers a better performance in recognition of hand-dorsa vein images with a correct recognition rate reaching approximately 99% using a simple nearest neighbor (NN) classifier.

Keywords: Biometrics · Hand-dorsa vein images · Local binary patterns

1 Introduction

Personal verification is fundamental in any identity based access control system, and there is an increasing use of biometric features to authenticate individuals by measuring some inherent physiological or behaviour characteristics. Compared to the traditional authentication modes such as password or identification code, biometric features offer the advantages of not only high security and reliability as they are hard to forge, but also user convenience without the need to remember passwords or carry identity cards.

Hand vein patterns have attracted significant attention in the research community recently, as a new means of biometric based recognition. Compared to more established biometric patterns, such as fingerprints, facial characteristics and iris patterns, hand vein patterns have higher user convenience as the manner of image acquisition is perceived to be less intrusive and more user friendly; and higher security as it does not rely on surface or appearance based features [1-3] .

© Springer International Publishing Switzerland 2015
J. Yang et al. (Eds.): CCBR 2015, LNCS 9428, pp. 312–320, 2015.
DOI: 10.1007/978-3-319-25417-3_37

2   Vein Image Acquisition

The acquisition of hand vein images using near IR (NIR) imaging has been studied in [4-6] and [7]. In this work, a low-cost reflection-mode NIR imaging device developed by the authors was employed for hand-dorsa vein image acquisition. Fig. 1 shows the photo and schematic of the vein image acquisition device, where the back of the hand is seen to be illuminated from two sides by two LED arrays acting as the infrared sources and the light reflected from the hand is captured by the camera placed directly above the hand. Attached to front of the camera is an infrared filter to prevent unwanted visible light from entering the camera.

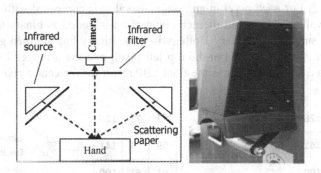

Fig. 1. Schematic and picture of vein image acquisition device

A database of hand-dorsa vein images has been built using the vein image acquisition device developed. It contains 2,040 images from 102 individuals in which 52 are female and 50 are male. Ten images of each hand were captured for every individual with each individual placing alternately the left hand and right hand under the image acquisition device. Some image samples in the database are illustrated in Fig. 2.

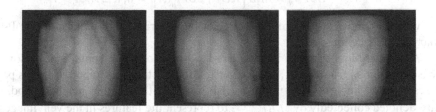

Fig. 2. Sample images acquired

3   Partition Local Binary Patterns (PLBP)

General approaches to hand vein pattern recognition are based on the use of various shape descriptors to represent the vein structure extracted through image segmentation[8-9]. With all of these methods based on features extracted from the segmented images, segmentation errors cannot be avoided. Some thin vessels could be missed, and some dark regions could be considered as vein patterns by mistake. As a result, a texture descriptor based on Partition Local Binary Patterns (PLBP) was previously proposed by the authors for improved vein pattern recognition.

Proposed by Ojala et al [10], Local Binary Patterns (LBP) provides an efficient rotation-invariant texture descriptor, and an illustration of the basic LBP operator is shown in Fig.3. For each pixel in an image, its value is compared with all the neighboring pixel values. The result of each comparison is coded as binary 0 if the center pixel value is smaller and binary 1 otherwise. The binary bits are then grouped in the clockwise direction starting from the top left pixel, and the arranged binary string is converted to a decimal number as the final LBP result for the center pixel.

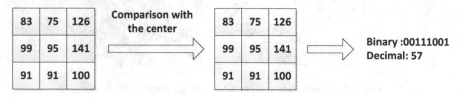

Fig. 3. Example of basic LBP operator

To remove the effect of image rotation resulting in different binary patterns to be generated, each LBP is rotated to a position that acts as the common reference for all rotated versions of the binary patterns, and this involves the use of the rotation invariant LBP operator, $LBP_{P,R}^{ri}$, defined as

$$LBP_{P,R}^{ri} = \min\left\{ ROR(LBP_{P,R}, i) \mid i = 0, 1, 2, \ldots, P - 1 \right\} \qquad (1)$$

where $ROR(x, i)$ performs the circular bitwise right shift i times on the P-bit binary number denoted by x.

A circular binary pattern is considered to be uniform if it contains at most two bitwise transitions from 0 to 1, or vice versa [10]. For the work reported in this paper, it uses rotation invariant and uniform LBP based on the circular neighborhood, which are denoted collectedly by $LBP_{P,R}^{riu2}$, to represent the features in the vein images.

To allow not only micro-patterns but also macro-patterns in a vein image to be represented, Partition LBP (PLBP) is used in the implementation, whereby each vein image is scaled to M and divided into N non-overlapping rectangular regions as shown in Fig. 4.

Fig. 4. Rectangular partition

After partition, $LBP_{8,2}^{riu2}$ (rotation invariant uniform patterns calculated from 8 sampling points on a circle of radius 2) features are extracted from each sub images. Here, we use H_i denotes the LBP histogram of the ith sub-image.

$$H_i = [h_{i,1} \quad h_{i,2} \quad \cdots \quad h_{i,10}] \quad (i = 1, 2, \ldots, N) \quad (2)$$

Then N LBP features are connected to form a 10×N dimensions vector V to describe the vein pattern.

$$V = [H_1 \quad H_2 \quad \cdots \quad H_N] \quad (3)$$

The feature histograms of them are shown in Fig. 5, which shows that PLBP features describe vein patterns more minutely than the original LBP.

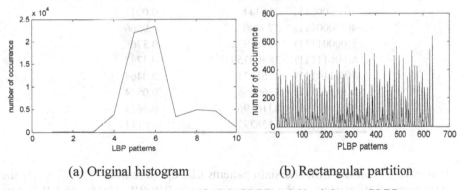

(a) Original histogram   (b) Rectangular partition

Fig. 5. Feature histograms of original LBP and 64 sub-images PLBP

4 Improved Partition Local Binary Patterns

4.1 Weighted Partition Local Binary Patterns (WPLBP)

To improve the Rectangular Partition LBP (RPLBP) with M=256 and N=64, feature histograms of sub-images are studied separately. From the histogram of one sub-image shown in Fig. 6 Feature histogram of sub-image 1, it is seen that the fifth and sixth binary patterns (corresponding to 00001111 and 00011111) have much higher occurrences than other binary patterns.

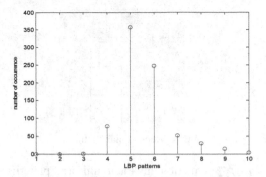

Fig. 6. Feature histogram of sub-image 1

Further analysis of all the sub-image histograms reveals this as a common phenomenon with the occurrence of fifth and sixth binary patterns found to be more than others. The proportions of different patterns are given in Table 1 by add up them from all sub-images of all the 2040 images.

Table 1. Proportions of patterns

Patterns	Number of occurrence	Proportion
1(00000000)	7538	0.0001
2(00000001)	53171	0.0005
3(00000011)	116344	0.0011
4(00000111)	5796903	0.0566
5(00001111)	38485992	0.376
6(00011111)	38305358	0.3742
7(00111111)	4751973	0.0464
8(01111111)	5366668	0.0524
9(11111111)	8316796	0.0813
10(others)	1158297	0.0113

It is obvious that the fifth and sixth patterns take up more than 75%. To study the contributions of 10 patterns to the recognition result, RPLBP (M=256, N=64) feature is divided into 10 vectors, which consist of each pattern respectively. They can be obtained by:

$$V_k = [h_{1,k} \quad h_{2,k} \quad \cdots \quad h_{N,k}] \quad (k = 1, 2, \cdots, 10) \tag{4}$$

where, $h_{i,k}$ denotes the kth pattern of the ith sub-image histogram. Recognition experiments with these feature vectors were carried out on the database. The results are shown in Table 2.

Table 2. Results of sub-features

Patterns	1(00000000)	2(00000001)	3(00000011)	4(00000111)	5(00001111)
RR(%)	2.06	10.98	26.67	93.24	96.47
Pattern	6(00011111)	7(00111111)	8(01111111)	9(11111111)	10(others)
RR(%)	96.08	93.82	90.59	85.98	42.84

Use w_k (k=1,2,…,10) describes the weights of 10 patterns, r_k denotes the corresponding recognition rate, then:

$$w_k = r_k / \sum_{i=1}^{10} r_i \qquad (5)$$

So that WPLBP feature could be calculated from (6) as follows:

$$V_w = \begin{bmatrix} H_1' & H_2' & \cdots & H_N' \end{bmatrix} \qquad (6)$$

$$H_i' = [h_{i,1} \times w_1 \quad h_{i,2} \times w_2 \quad \cdots \quad h_{i,10} \times w_{10}] \qquad (i = 1, 2, \ldots, N) \qquad (7)$$

4.2   Multi-scale Partition Local Binary Patterns (MPLBP)

To get more information, RPLBP features from different scales are combined. According the results shown in section 0, the numbers of sub-images N for each scale size (M=64, 128, 256) are set to 32, 64 and 64 respectively. V_{64}, V_{128}, and $V256$, denote the feature vectors of selected RPLBPs (M=64, N=32; M=128, N=64; M=256, N=64) and w_1, w_2, w_3 are the corresponding weights. Then the MPBLP could be obtained by:

$$V_M = [V_{64} \times w_1 \quad V_{128} \times w_2 \quad V_{256} \times w_3] \qquad (8)$$

The simplest combination method is to set w_1=w_2=w_3=1, which means the three selected RPLBPs are seen to has equal contribution to recognition. However, this assume is not correct according to Table . As the recognition results of these RPLBPs are r_1=96.96, r_2=97.84, r_3=98.33, the weights are set by:

$$w_i = \frac{r_i}{r_1 + r_2 + r_3} (i = 1, 2, 3) \qquad (9)$$

Thus the weights are set to 0.3308, 0.3338 and 0.3354 for RPBLPs (M=64, N=32; M=128, N=64; M=256, N=64) respectively.

5   Experiments and Results

To test the proposed feature descriptor based on coded and weighted PLBP, the database containing 2,040 hand-dorsa vein images from 102 individuals was divided into two sets with set A containing five images of every hand and set B the other five.

Using set A as the reference set and the nearest neighborhood classifier, the PLBP feature vector of each image in set B is compared with all of those in set A and the minimum Euclidean distance produced by a particular pair is considered as a match to yield the recognition result. As this is done without thresholding, all recognition errors belong to the category of false acceptance.

5.1   PLBP

To make the image easy to be divided, the images size M are scaled to 2^m and the number of sub-images N is set to 2^n. PLBP with $M=2^6, 2^7, 2^8$ and $N=2^2, 23, \ldots, 28$ are tested, the recognition rates (RR) are shown in Table 3.

Table 3. Results of PLBP with different M and N

N	RR(%)		
	M=64	M=128	M=256
4	84.41	82.16	85.69
8	94.41	93.04	94.61
16	96.18	96.86	96.71
32	96.96	97.65	97.83
64	96.76	97.84	98.33
128	-	97.25	97.75
256	-	97.16	97.25

It can be seen from the results, if an image is divided into more sub-images, it can be described in more details. But it is dare not to say more details means better recognition rate because too much details means the feature vector is sensitive to noise and distortion. From the experimental results the suitable number of sub-images can be found that N=64 and M=256 is the best.

5.2   Improved PLBP

Some improved PLBP, such as WPLBP, MPLBP and FPLBP are carried out on the database. The weights of WPBLP ($M=256$, $N=64$) are set by equation (5) and Table 2, so that we can get:

$$w_1=0.0032, w_2=0.0172, w_3=0.0418, w_4=0.1460, w_5=0.1510;$$
$$w_6=0.1504, w_7=0.1469, w_8=0.1418, w_9=0.1346, w_{10}=0.0671 \qquad (10)$$

MPLBP feature combined with PLBP ($M=64$, $N=32$), PLBP ($M=128$, $N=64$) and PLBP ($M=256$, $N=64$) features, and the weights are set to 0.3308, 0.3338 and 0.3354 correspondingly. The results of these features are listed in Table 4 and compared with integral histogram, Hu's moments [11] and Key points [8] methods.

Table 4. Results of improved PLBP

Method	RR (%)
Integral histogram	95.39
Hu's moments	95.20
Key points	98.14
WPBLP	98.43
MPBLP	98.83

As these improved PLBP contain more useful information for recognition, they perform better than RPLBP. And MPLBP combined with RPLBP (M=64, N=32), RPLBP (M=128, N=64) and RPLBP (M=256, N=64) reaches the best recognition result of 98.83%.

6   Conclusions

Some new feature descriptors based on improved PLBP are presented in this paper for hand-dorsa vein recognition. This could be seen as a natural extension of the original PLBP with weighting introduced to suppress insignificant micro-patterns in vein images and combination of multi-scale features to get more texture information. From the classification experiments performed on a large database of more than two thousand hand-dorsa vein images, the proposed improved PLBP descriptors have been shown to be more effective than original LBP. In particular, MPLBP reaches the highest recognition rate of 98.83%, with an improvement of 0.5% in recognition rate is achieved by using MPLBP.

Acknowledgements. This work is supported by National Natural Science Foundation of China (61271368).

References

1. Ding, Y., Zhuang, D., Wang, K.: A study of hand vein recognition method. In: 2005 IEEE International Conference on Mechatronics and Automations, pp. 2106–2110 (2005)
2. Delac, K., Grgic, M.: A survey of biometric recognition methods. In: 46th International Symposium Electronics in Marine, pp. 184–193 (2004)
3. Wang, R., Wang, G., Chen, Z., Zeng, Z.: A palm vein identification system based on Gabor wavelet features. Neural Computing & Applications **24**(1), 161–168 (2014)
4. Wang, Y., Li, K., Cui, J.: Hand-dorsa vein recognition based on partition local binary pattern. In: 10th International Conference on Signal Processing, Beijing, pp. 1671–1674 (2010)
5. Zhao, S., Wang, Y.: Extracting hand vein patterns from low-quality images: a new biometric technique using low-cost devices. In: 4th International Conference on Image and Graphics, Sichuan, pp. 667–671 (2007)

6. Cross, J.M., Smith, C.L.: Thermo graphic imaging of the subcutaneous vascular network of the back of the hand for biometric identification. In: International Carnahan Conference on Security Technology (1995)

7. Wang, L., Leedham, G.: Near- and far-infrared imaging for vein pattern biometrics. In: IEEE International Conference on Video Signal Based Surveillance, Sydney, pp. 52–57 (2006)

8. Wang, Y., Fan, Y., Liao, W., Li, K., Lik-Kwan, S., Martin, V.: Hand vein recognition based on multiple keypoints sets. In: International Conference on Biometrics (2012)

9. Hu, Y., Wang, Z., Yang, X., Xue, Y.: Hand vein recognition based on the connection lines of reference point and feature point. Infrared Physics & Technology **62**, 110–114 (2014)

10. Ojala, T., Pietikäinen, M., Mäenpää, T.: Multiresolution Gray-Scale and Rotation Invariant Texture Classification with Local Binary Patterns. IEEE Transactions on Pattern Analysis and Machine Intelligence **24**(7), 971–987 (2002)

11. Flusser, J.: On the Independence of Rotation Moment Invariants. Pattern Recognition Letters **33**, 1405–1410 (2000)

Research on Finger Vein Recognition Based on NSST

Kejun Wang, Xianglei Xing[✉], and Xiaofei Yang

College of Automation, Harbin Engineering University, Harbin 150001, China
xingxl@hrbeu.edu.cn

Abstract. In the finger vein image collection procedure, there are always two kinds of negative factors: the first is unstable illumination, the second is information loss caused by bad collection operation. There are not yet special methods for the above-mentioned question for now. We adopt the Non-Subsampled Shearlet Transform (NSST) coefficients for feature extraction, since the NSST transform domain coefficients are affected less by unstable illumination. For the question of information loss, we first introduce an improved ROI extraction method for database extension. We further propose an improved robust regression classification method for vein recognition. The experimental results show that: compared with traditional methods, our proposed method based on NSST does better in recognizing finger vein images which lack some information and are influenced by the unstable illumination.

Keywords: Finger vein · NSST · Feature extraction · ROI extraction · Robust regression classification

1 Introduction

In finger vein image acquisition process, the finger vein image is frequently prone to be influenced by the unstable illumination due to the finger's random movement. In this case, the finger vein image's pixel value will be different at the same location. Furthermore, general finger vein image is obtained in a certain collection operation specification, i.e. all the finger vein image translates or rotates in a small range, every finger vein image has enough structural information for pattern recognition. But in exceptional circumstances, some finger vein image lack too much information since the greater degree of finger movement, in this case, the traditional recognition method will be powerless to some extent.

There are two kinds of feature extraction methods for now, the first is based on picture pixel value, such as feature point MHD distance [1], feature point MHD relative distance [1], template feature [2], etc. This type of method can extract finger vein feature effectively, but its utilization of structural information insufficiency, moreover, it's prone to unstable illumination.

The second is based on transforming domain coefficients, such as wavelet [3] [4], ridgelet [5], and curvelet [6], etc. this type of existing method can seize picture's frequency, directions, and location information, but are sensitive for translation and have frequency aliasing. In this article, we employ NSST to overcome the general methods' shortcoming.

© Springer International Publishing Switzerland 2015
J. Yang et al. (Eds.): CCBR 2015, LNCS 9428, pp. 321–330, 2015.
DOI: 10.1007/978-3-319-25417-3_38

2   NSST Feature Extraction

Shearlet transform is based on composite Wavelet theory [7]. For 2-dimentional signal, the affine systems with composite dilations are the collections as follows:

$$M_{AB}(\psi) = \left\{ \psi_{i,j,k}(x) = \left| \det A \right|^{i/2} \psi \left(B^j A^i x - k \right) : i, j \in Z, k \in Z^2 \right\} \quad (1)$$

where A, B are the 2×2 invertible matrix, A is anisotropic expansion matrix, B is shearlet transform matrix. ψ is generation function, and $\psi \in L^2(R^2)$, for any $\xi = (\xi_1, \xi_2) \in R^2$, $\xi_1 \neq 0$, the fourier transform of ψ is as follows:

$$\hat{\psi}(\xi) = \hat{\psi}_1(\xi_1) \hat{\psi}_2 \left(\frac{\xi_1}{\xi_2} \right) \quad (2)$$

where ψ_1 is continuous wavelet which meet the standard wavelet admission condition, and $\hat{\psi}_1 \in C^\infty(R)$. ψ_2 is continuous wavelet and meet the condition : $\| \psi_2 \|_2 = 1$, $\hat{\psi}_2 \in C^\infty(R)$, $\mathrm{supp} \hat{\psi}_2 \subset [-1, 1]$. If $M_{AB}(\psi)$ is a tight frame, elements in $M_{AB}(\psi)$ can be called synthesized wavelet.

The discrete process of NSST was divided into two parts, which are scale and direction decomposition, and Non-subsampled pyramid (NSP) decomposition is used to perform the scale decomposition. Each source image can be decomposed by a NSP to generate a low-frequency sub-band image and a high-frequency sub-band image, after each level of NSP decomposition, the low-frequency component will perform iterations to obtain singular points of the image. Therefore, after the k levels NSP decomposition for a two-dimensional image, we can obtain $k+1$ sub-band images which have the same size with the source image, they included a low-frequency image and k high-frequency sub-bands images which have the same size but different frequency scale with source image. It applies the specific discrete re-sampling transform converting from the pseudo polar to Cartesian coordinate system. The whole process can be done directly through the two-dimensional convolution, thus effectively abandoned the link of decimated, this process achieved shift invariance for NSST. For $n \times n$ image, NSST's decomposition coefficient size is shown as Table 1.

Table 1. The NSST coefficients size of n × n image

Decomposition scale	Coefficient size
1 scale	n × n × 1
2 scale (horizontal tiling/vertical tiling)	n × n × 5/ n × n × 5
3 scale (horizontal tiling/vertical tiling)	n × n × 5/ n × n × 5
4 scale (horizontal tiling/vertical tiling)	n × n × 9/ n × n × 9
5 scale (horizontal tiling/vertical tiling)	n × n × 9/ n × n × 9

As Table 1 shows, if the size of a finger vein image is 64 × 64, the sum total of NSST coefficients is 950272. This number is too big for feature extraction, so the NSST coefficients can not be used for feature directly. In the next subsection, this article will analyze the most important characteristic of NSST and propose a new feature extraction method based on NSST.

2.1   The NSST Coefficients Energy Distribution Characteristic of Finger Vein Image

Compared with other images, finger vein image has a lower contrast gradient, which implies that the number of decomposition scales of finger vein need not to be too big. To illustrate this point, the distribution of NSST coefficients energy of finger vein image is plotted in Fig. 1.

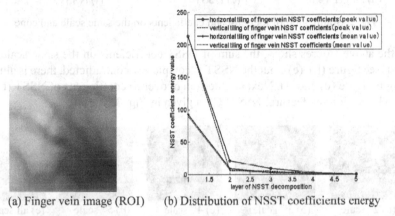

(a) Finger vein image (ROI)   (b) Distribution of NSST coefficients energy

Fig. 1. Distribution of NSST coefficients energy of finger vein image

We can see from the picture above, the lower the NSST decomposition layer is, the higher the coefficients energy is, which is in connection with the quantity of image information. When the decomposition layer is greater than or equal to 5, the NSST coefficients energy is too small, therefore in this article the total layer of NSST decomposition is set to 4.

2.2   The Anti-aliasing in Frequency Domain of NSST Coefficients

In this article, we solve the problem of information loss by extending the finger vein database. The translation of ROI is essential, therefore, the translation invariance property of NSST is very important, which is the most primary cause of the raise of NSST.

In addition, as shown in Table 1, the number of the NSST coefficients is too big to extract features, in this article, we intend to incorporate all the sub-band coefficients into one coefficient matrix, and then the most important problem is to verify the reasonableness of this operation. In contrast, we also use DSST as a comparison. The zone plate is a standard test image with full types of frequency information and suitable for the contrast test. In addition, due to the different size of DSST coefficients on a different scale, this article just give one of the same layer's coefficients adding experiment. The result is shown in Fig. 2.

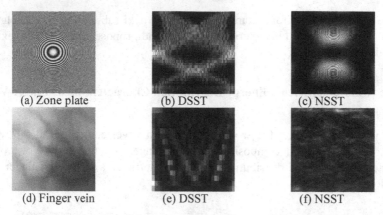

| (a) Zone plate | (b) DSST | (c) NSST |
| (d) Finger vein | (e) DSST | (f) NSST |

Fig. 2. Summation of the sub-band coefficients on the same scale and cone

As the above figures show, the sum of DSST coefficients on the same scale is disordered (see figure (b), (e)), but the NSST is completely contradicted, there is almost no aliasing in figure (c) and (f). Next up, the sum of overall coefficients of NSST (be short for NSST coefficients feature, NSSTFC) is given in Fig. 3.

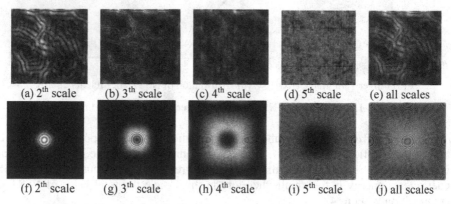

| (a) 2th scale | (b) 3th scale | (c) 4th scale | (d) 5th scale | (e) all scales |
| (f) 2th scale | (g) 3th scale | (h) 4th scale | (i) 5th scale | (j) all scales |

Fig. 3. Summation of the NSST sub-band coefficients on different scale

Several results can be summarized through Fig. 3: (1) There is little aliasing in different sub-band coefficients of NSST.n (2) There are too many noise interference in the fifth scale of finger vein, which is shown in figure (d). (3) Although the noise interference of high scale coefficients is too much, but its' negative influence isn't enough to disturb the last structural feature, because its energy is small.

Compared with the original finger vein image, the NSST coefficients feature is constructed by frequency information, so the interference of unstable illumination is tiny. Since the first scale of NSST coefficients is the image by removing high frequency information, which is also prone to be sensitive to unstable illumination, therefore not be considered. Fig. 4 chooses a severely contaminated finger vein image by unstable illumination as a comparison, from which the robustness of NSSTFC is reflected.

(a) Original finger vein ROI image   (b) NSSTFC image

Fig. 4. The robustness of NSSTFC matrix for the interference of unstable illumination

As Fig. 4 shows, NSSTFC has an excellent quality of anti-unstable illumination: the original vein (please see Fig. 4 (a)) is clearly reflected in the NSSTFC image (please Fig. 4 (b)), while both the bright spot on the left of Fig. 4 (a) and the black fuzzy part on the right of Fig. 4 (a) have consistent performance in the NSSTFC image, whose values are all small.

3   Improved Robust Regression Classifying Method Based on MM Estimation

Imran proposes a linear regression classifier to solve the face recognition problem in reference [8], this method translate the pattern recognition problem into linear regression problem. The brief summary is as follows:

For test sample y, the parameter vector is $\hat{\beta} = \left(W_i^T W_i\right)^{-1} W_i^T y$, W_i is the training sample collection of ith class and $W_i (= [w_{i,1}, w_{i,2}, \cdots, w_{i,p_i}]) \in R^{n \times p_i}$. Then the estimation of test sample y on the ith training sample is:

$$\hat{y}_i = W_i \hat{\beta}_i = H_i y, \quad i = 1, 2, \cdots, N \tag{3}$$

where H_i is test sample's symmetrical projection matrix, and $H_i = W_i \left(W_i^T W_i\right)^{-1} W_i^T$. Thus, the category of test sample y is i^*:

$$i^* = \arg\min_i \|\hat{y} - y\|, \quad i = 1, 2, \cdots, N \tag{4}$$

Imran [9] further proposes a robust linear regression classifying method based on Huber estimation which is used to replace least square method, in which, the parameter vector is:

$$\hat{\beta}_i = \arg\min_{\hat{\beta}} \sum_{j=1}^{n} \rho_H \left(r_j(\hat{\beta}_i)\right) \tag{5}$$

where ρ_H is Huber weight function, $r_j(\hat{\beta}_i)$ is j-th element of residual error vector: $r_j(\hat{\beta}_i) = y - X_i \hat{\beta}_i, \quad i = 1, 2, ..., N$.

The Robust estimation is used to solve two kinds of outliers: univariate outlier and regression outlier. The univariate outlier is the observed value which is far from the other in training database; the regression outlier (also known as vertical outlier) is dependent variables which have big difference with values in the training database. In reference [9], the problem of different illumination and noise pollution belong to regression outlier, in this article, the ROI translation in the test sample belongs to regression outlier too. In fact, there are always univariate outliers in training database, but the regression estimation method based on Huber function doesn't have a good performance for univariate outliers.

MM estimation is a most widely applying robust regression method proposed by Yohai [10] at present. It has highest breakpoint and excellent efficiency, Wilcox proved that MM estimation is most worthy in all robust estimation methods in reference [11]. In this article, we choose MM estimation to improve general robust regression classifying method by estimating parameter vector $\hat{\beta}$:

$$\hat{\beta} = \arg \min_{\hat{\beta}} \sum_{j=1}^{n} \rho_M \left(\frac{r_j(\hat{\beta})}{\hat{\sigma}_e} \right) \tag{6}$$

where ρ_M is loss weight function, in this paper ρ_M is Huber weight function; $\hat{\sigma}_e$ is residual error dissemination.

The only difference between Imran's method and our proposed method is the computation of $\hat{\beta}$, the other procedure is same as paper [9].

4   The Sample Database Expansion Based on ROI Extraction

In this article, another primary purpose is to ensure the recognition performance when some finger vein images lack a part of information. To simulate this scenario, we take interception action at different levels to the original finger vein image and do ROI extraction again. The ROI method in this article is proposed by improving the traditional method in paper [12]. Four cutting lines l_1, l_2, l_3, l_4 are shown in Fig. 5.

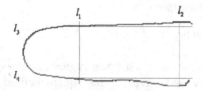

Fig. 5. The ROI cutting line of finger vein

The concrete calculation of cutting lines l_1, l_2, l_3, l_4 is omitted here, which can refer to paper [12]. In order to extend the database, we obtain 4 group ROI samples by translate l_1 10%, 20%, 30%, as shown in Fig. 6.

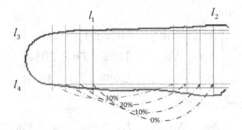

Fig. 6. The expansion of training sample

The biggest difference from the general ROI method is that the lines l_3, l_4 (the horizontal red dashed line) which are determined by the 30% left cutting line based on l_1. In accordance with the method shown in Fig.6, the original training sample is expanded into 4 groups, therefore, when the test sample's ROI has a certain degree of translation between 0%-30%, two groups training samples will be chosen for classification.

There are two different situations for test sample: the first is actual condition and the second is simulation condition. In actual condition, the degree of ROI translation can be tested by:

$$Tp = \begin{cases} 0, & d_l \geq 124 \\ (124 - d_l)/124, & d_l < 124 \end{cases} \tag{7}$$

In the above formula, d_l is the distance between l_1 and right boundary. In the simulation condition, this article divides test sample into three groups: the first, 2.5%, 5%, 7.5%; the second, 12.5%, 15%, 17.5%; the third, 22.5%, 25%, 27.5%. There are two main reasons for database expansion:

(1) Although the four groups training sample database have a common area, but the common area is not big enough and the information loss is severe if we only use the common area to perform the recognizing. So the database expansion is necessary.

(2) The image for NSST decomposition must be the size of $2^j \times 2^j$, in this paper all the size of ROI image should be converted into $2^j \times 2^j$, then there is a problem when NSST is used to extract feature: the size of ROI must be the same, otherwise the converted image will be distorted   for the same finger vein.

5   The Matching Scheme Based on Sample Database Expansion

In this section, the specific matching procedure is as follows:

1) Four groups finger vein ROI samples are gained by method in Fig. 6, denoted by Nu_0, Nu_1, Nu_2, Nu_3.
2) Perform NSST to Nu_0, Nu_1, Nu_2, Nu_3 and get 4 groups NSSTFC matrix, perform PCA and get 4 groups PCA feature: FNu_0, FNu_1, FNu_2, FNu_3.
3) Choose training samples. When the degree of ROI translation is given, only two training sample is needed, the selection rules are as follows:

In actual condition:

$$\begin{cases} Nu_0 \, , \ Nu_1 \, , & 0\% \le Tp \le 10\% \\ Nu_1 \, , \ Nu_2 \, , & 10\% \le Tp \le 20\% \\ Nu_2 \, , \ Nu_3 \, , & 20\% \le Tp \le 30\% \end{cases} \tag{8}$$

In simulation condition:

$$\begin{cases} Nu_0 \, , \ Nu_1 \, , & Tp{=}2.5\%, 5\%, 7.5\% \\ Nu_1 \, , \ Nu_2 \, , & Tp{=}12.5\%, 15\%, 17.5\% \\ Nu_2 \, , \ Nu_3 \, , & Tp{=}22.5\%, 25\%, 27.5\% \end{cases} \tag{9}$$

4) After the confirmation of training samples Nu_i, Nu_{i+1}, i=0, 1, 2, two PCA feature (denoted by FY_i, FY_{i+1}, i=0, 1, 2) can be obtained based on FNu_i, FNu_{i+1}, i=0, 1, 2.

5) By using FNu_i and FY_i, we can obtain N_c (the number of categories) residual value $r = \| \hat{y} - y \|$; likewise, by using FNu_{i+1} and FY_{i+1}, we can obtain another N_c residual values. The corresponding category with minimal value in these $2 \times N_c$ is the category of the test sample.

6   Experiments

The finger vein database in this article is obtained by a self-made collecting device in pattern recognition research institute of Harbin Engineering University. There are 299 categories, every category have 5 images, 1495 images in all.

The experimental setup is as follows: for every category, 4 random images are used for training, the rest 1 image is used for testing, the experiment is repeated for 10 times, the experiment result is the mean value of the 10 experiments' recognition rate. The nearest neighbor classifier is used for classification.

The comparative methods in this article are: method based on feature point MHD distance (abbr. MHDD) [1]; method based on feature point MHD relative distance (abbr. MHDRD) [1]; method based on the template (abbr. Template) [2]; method based on wavelet moment and PCA (abbr. wavelet& PCA) [3]; method based on wavelet energy and feature point (abbr. wavelet&FP) [4]; NSSTFC using Huber estimation (NSSTFC&Hu); and NSSTFC using MM estimation (NSSTFC&MM). The experimental results are shown in Table 2. From Table 2, we can see that

- The recognition performance of MHDD and MHDRD depend on the number of useful feature points, when the degree of interception is severe, the number of useful feature points may be too little to extract feature. The recognition rate is rarely 82.07% and 82.27% in the third group experiment.
- Template feature has a higher utilization ratio of the finger vein image, when the degree of interception is higher. The recognition rate falls slowly and performs stability.

- Wavelet & PCA. This method takes right shift operation for image blocking, then performs feature extraction to image block. This method has a high utilization of finger vein feature information and has a fine recognition performance. The recognition rate is 90.54% in the third group experiment.
- Wavelet & FP. The interception has a higher influence to feature point. In addition, as a feature, the wavelet energy feature is relatively single. Therefore, in this experiment, the recognition performance is not good; the recognition in the third group is only 85.42%.
- NSSTFC & Hu and NSSTFC & MM, both these two methods have a good recognition performance. The NSSTFC & MM is better, its main reason is that Huber estimation only has a robust effect for the regression outlier (test sample), but MM estimation also has a robust effect for the univariate outliers (training sample).

Table 2. The average recognition rate (%) of different feature extraction methods

Feature extraction method	Recognition rate(%)		
	The first group	The second group	The third group
MHDD	88.16	85.42	82.07
MHDRD	89.03	85.92	82.27
Template	91.27	90.50	89.53
wavelet& PCA	92.17	91.14	90.54
wavelet&FP	90.03	88.60	85.42
NSSTFC&Hu	92.74	92.31	91.57
NSSTFC&MM	**93.58**	**93.11**	**92.47**

7 Conclusion

In this article, a new finger vein feature extraction method based on NSST is proposed. Our proposed method utilizes the NSST's shift invariance and frequency anti-aliasing sufficiently, and gives a solution for the problem that the number of coefficients from the NSST is too large. In addition, the features extracted by our method are insensitive to unstable illumination. Then, we expand the sample database using the ROI extraction method and propose an improved robust classification strategy, which provides a good solution for the information loss of finger vein image.

Acknowledgement. This work was supported by the Postdoctoral Sustentation Fund and Natural Science Fund of Heilongjiang Province of China under Grant LBH-Z14051 and 42400621-1-15114.

References

1. Li, X.F.: Research of Dual-Mode Recognition Algorithm Based on Fingerprint and Finger Vein. Master's thesis, Harbin Engineering University, pp. 42–46 (2010)
2. Yuan, Z.: The Study of Finger Vein Recognition Methods. Master's thesis, Harbin Engineering University, pp. 36–39 (2007)
3. Wang, K., Yuan, Z.: Finger Vein Recognition Based on Wavelet Moment Fused with PCA Transform. Pattern Recognition and Artificial Intelligence **20**(5), 692–697 (2007)
4. Lv, C., Cheng, C.: Dorsal Hand Vein Recognition Based on Wavelet Energy Feature Fused with Feature Points. Computer Measurement & Control **19**(3), 630–632 (2011)
5. Wang, K., Yang, X., Tian, Z., Yan, T.: The research of finger vein feature extraction based on the ridgelet transform. In: IEEE International Conference on Mechatronics and Automation (IEEE ICMA), pp. 1378–1383 (2013)
6. Wang, K., Yang, X., Tian, Z., Du, T.: The finger vein recognition based on curvelet. In: Chinese Control Conference (CCC 2014), pp. 4706–4711 (2014)
7. Guo, K., Labate, D.: Optimally Sparse Multidimensional Representation using Shearlets. Siam Jmath. Anal. **39**(1), 298–318 (2007)
8. Imran, N.: Linear Regression for Face Recognition. IEEE Transactions on Pattern Analysis and Machine Intelligence **32**(11), 2106–2112 (2010)
9. Imran, N., Roberto, T., Mohammed, B.: Robust regression for face recognition. Pattern Recognition **45**(1), 104–118 (2012)
10. Yohai, V.J.: High Breakdown Point and High Efficiency Robust Estimations for Regression. Annals of Statistics **15**, 642–656 (1987)
11. Wilcox, R.R.: Introduction to Robust Estimation and Hypothesis Testing, 3rd edn, p. 608. Elsevier Academic Press, New York (2012)
12. Ma, H., Wang, K.: A Region of Interest Extraction Method using Rotation Rectified Finger Vein Images. Transactions on Intelligent Systems **7**(3), 230–234 (2012)

A New Finger-Vein Recognition Method Based on Hyperspherical Granular Computing

Zhiyuan Liu, Guimin Jia, Yihua Shi, and Jinfeng Yang[✉]

Tianjin Key Lab for Advanced Signal Processing,
Civil Aviation University of China, Tianjin, China
jfyang@cauc.edu.cn

Abstract. Finger-vein (FV) recognition is an emerging biometric identification technique and has been receiving increasing attention. In this paper, a new finger-vein recognition method is proposed which combines the hyperspherical granular computing with principle component analysis (HSGrC-PCA). We firstly use PCA to obtain the principle components of the FV images. The FV components are then represented as hyperspherical granules. For the training samples, the hyper-spheres corresponding to the classes of training samples can be built using the granular computing classification, thus all of the hyper-spheres form a granule set. For a testing sample, we can classify it into one of the trained hyper-sphere by distance measures. The experimental results show that the proposed method has a good performance in finger-vein recognition efficiency and accuracy.

Keywords: Finger-vein · Hyperspherical granule · Granular computing · PCA

1 Introduction

Finger-vein recognition as an accurate and fraud-proof biometric technique has drawn increasing attention from biometrics community in recent years [1-3]. Compared with other traditional biometrics (e.g. face, fingerprint, and iris), the finger-vein pattern itself is forgery-proof, high live, high acceptable for users [4]. Thus, the recognition methods based on finger-vein are promising in personal identification.

For identification performance, the key problem is how to categorize a sample into its corresponding classes. Viewing a sample as a granule, thus the classification can be regarded as granular matching in high-dimensional space. For granule clusters, a hyperspherical granularity scheme, a special case of granular computing (GrC), can be adopted in practice.

As for GrC, the basic idea is to use information granulation for complex problem solving. Since Zadeh published papers in 1979, information granularity had attracted the interests of many researchers [5]. Now, GrC has been rapidly developed and widely used [6-8]. However, how to represent a granule has been always a key problem for GrC, especially in high-dimensional space [9]. Actually, for biometric features, they are always very high in dimension. So it is hard to granulate the samples by

J. Yang et al. (Eds.): CCBR 2015, LNCS 9428, pp. 331–337, 2015.
DOI: 10.1007/978-3-319-25417-3_39

hyperspherical granularity scheme in practice. To solve this problem, reducing dimensions of high dimensional space is necessary. It is well-known that PCA is a very succinct and efficient dimension-reduction method to reduce the complexity and obtain the informative aspects of high-dimensional datasets [10]. Here   we adopt PCA to reduce dimensions for two reasons. On one hand, PCA is the most convenient and fastest dimension-reduction method. On the other hand, it should be more favorable to verify the performance of hyperspherical granular computing using a simple dimension-reduction method. After this processing, a hyper-sphere is used to represent an information granule. For a hyper-sphere, its center is offered by the PCA component of a FV image and its initial granularity is set to zero.

In this paper, we first improve the image quality using Gabor filter, and then obtain the principle component of each image by PCA. Second, the finger-vein images that represented by the principle component are granulated using hyper-sphere. Third, the classification algorithms based on distance measures is adopted. The experimental results show that the proposed method HSGrC-PCA is feasible and valid.

2   Finger-Vein Image Acquisition

The finger-vein images we employed are captured automatically by our homemade imaging system, as shown in Fig.1(a). An open window ($70 \times 25mm^2$) centered in the width of imaging plane is set for finger-vein imaging [11]. And the luminaire we adopt is infrared light. Due to the different size of ROI images, FV images are normalized to 46*102 (4692) pixels, as shown in Fig.1(b).

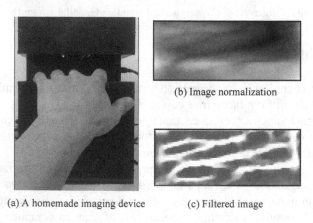

(b) Image normalization

(a) A homemade imaging device   (c) Filtered image

Fig. 1. A homemade imaging device and enhanced FV results

3   The Proposed Method

3.1   Image Enhancement and PCA

According to Fig.1(b), it is obvious that the FV image features are not clear. So we adopt Gabor filter to enhance the image, the result is shown in Fig.1(c). Here considering the variations of vessels in orientation and diameter alone a finger, we use oriented Gabor filters in multiscale [12]. Thus, the FV images are enhanced and the features are clearer.

However, if the image that shown in Fig.1(c) is treated as a hyper-sphere directly, the dimension of the feature space is too high. As a result, it will be very hard to compute hyperspherical granularity. Hence, for simplifying calculation and increasing efficiency, it is necessary to reduce the dimensionality. By now, the most common and simplest dimension-reduction method is PCA. So it is adopted here to reduce the dimensionality and to extract the principle component of FV images. Due to the dimension after PCA will have a great influence on the accuracy and efficiency of hyperspherical granular computing, thus it is also important to choose a suitable dimensionality. As for dimensionality, it is only related to the value of the cumulative energy on a percentage basis. In this paper, seven thresholds of the cumulative energy are tested, as shown in Table. 1.

Table 1. The dimensionality after PCA

Cumulative energy	99%	95%	90%	85%	80%	75%	70%
Dimensionality k	714	195	113	81	62	49	39

3.2   Granulation

It is well known that any point regarded as atomic granules are indivisible, the union process is the key to obtain the larger granules compared with atomic granules. The present work treats each FV image as an atomic granule which expressed as a hyper-sphere with a radius of 0 and a vector as center.

For two hyper-sphere granules $G_1=(C_1, r_1)$ and $G_2=(C_2, r_2)$, where $C_1=(x_1, x_2, ..., x_n)$ and $C_2=(y_1, y_2, ..., y_n)$ are the centers of hyper-sphere granules G_1 and G_2 and r_1 and r_2 are granularities of hyper-sphere granules G_1 and G_2, the union hyper-sphere granule is described in Eq(1)[13-15]:

$$G = G_1 \vee G_2 = [C,R] = \left[\frac{1}{2}(P+Q), \frac{1}{2}\|P-Q\| \right]$$ (1)

where R is the granularity of the union hyper-sphere granule, $P=C_1-r_1(C_{12}/\|C_{12}\|)$, $Q=C_2+r_2(C_{12}/\|C_{12}\|)$, $C_{12}=C_2-C_1$,the vector from C_1 to C_2. The union between two granules is explained in Fig. 2 for 2-dimensional space. Two granules $G_1=(2,6,2)$ and $G_2=(5,7,3)$ represent two hyperspherical granules in 2-dimensional space, the union hyperspherical granule is $(3.97,6.66,4.08)$ and represented as the red line in Fig. 2.

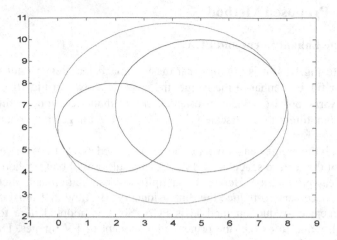

Fig. 2. Union between two granules [13]

Here, the hyperspherical granulation is shown as the following procedure.

Step 1. The principle component of a FV sample is considered as an atomic granule with a class label.

Step 2. Calculate the distance d_j between the atomic granule G_j and the other granules using Euclidean distance which is defined as Eq. (2):

$$d(G_1, G_2) = \|C_1 - C_2\|_2 - r_1 - r_2 \tag{2}$$

All the distance values d_j should be recorded and kept in an ascending order in the jth column.

Step 3. Set a larger threshold ρ. In the jth column, we choose the granules which are satisfied with $d \leq \rho$, compare the label of these granules with the tag of the granule G_j, and keep the atomic granules in the jth class cell if they have the same label. Thus we can obtain all the classes. It is obvious many classes may have the same elements, but one will be retained and other classes that same with it will be rejected, so it can be ensured that every class is different.

Step 4. Unite the granules that belong to the same class by Eq. (1). Then the granule set is composed of all the union granules, and the number of the union granules equals to the classes of the samples.

3.3   Recognition

After granulation, we obtain the union granule set and the corresponding class labels, the label of testing samples can be predicted by measuring the distance between testing samples and the granule set. However, due to different application fields, there are so many metric function of distance measure, such as Minkowski Distance Measure, Cosine Distance Measure and so on.

Minkowski Distance Measure is:

$$d(G_1, G_2) = \left(\sum_{i=1}^{n} |x_i - y_i|^p \right)^{1/p} \tag{3}$$

when $p=1$, the measure is called Manhattan Distance Measure; when $p=2$, it turns into Euclidean Distance Measure; when $p=\infty$, we call it Chebyshev Distance Measure. Cosine Distance Measure is

$$sim(G_1, G_2) = \cos\theta = \frac{\vec{x} \cdot \vec{y}}{\|x\| \cdot \|y\|} \tag{4}$$

Comparing these distance measures, we prefer to choose the simplest one, Euclidean Distance Measure, for it can be more favorable to verify the performance of hyperspherical granular computing. As for the result of recognition, if the prediction label of the testing simple is the same as the real class label, the testing simple is correctly recognized.

In this paper, we first compute the distance between test granule g and each granule in the granule set by Eq. (1), then find the granule g_m that has the minimal distance with g. So the corresponding class label of the g_m as the prediction label of g is obtained.

4   Experiments and Analysis

Here, a self-built database including training data and testing data that contains 1850 finger-vein images from 185 fingers is used. We view three FV images of each finger as training data and others as testing. Hence, a training set of 555 images and a testing set of 1295 images are formed.

In the experiments, the first judging rule is the fusion method, it means if the distance value between the testing granule g and g_m is negative and minimal, then g and g_m can be fused, so they share the same label. But the result, as shown in Table 2 is not fine. Thus another way is chosen here, the minimal distance without limiting positive or negative, we can see the testing accuracy (Ts) is better, thus this method will be taken in the next experiment. To verify these two methods efficiently, only 600 images from 60 individuals are adopted in this experiment.

Table 2. Performance from different discriminant rule

Method	Tr (%)	Ts (%)
Fusion method	100	99.44
Minimal distance method	100	100

We mainly analyze and discuss the recognition method based on hyper-sphere GrC combining with PCA from Tr, Ts, training time (tr), testing time (ts). The performances of this method with seven different percentages of energy are listed in Table 3. From the table, we can see that HSGrC-PCA with 75% of energy can achieve the optimal performance because of the suitable dimensionality of the feature space after PCA. As for 99%, the poor Ts may caused by the high dimensionality which leads to over-matching. These prove that dimension has a big influence on the accuracy of hyperspherical granular computing. And the performance *tr* shows similar from 95% to70%, it means PCA can do well in a wider range. The training time and testing time are related to the dimensionality, so the HSGrC-PCA algorithm with the lowest dimensionality is our pursuit in the same conditions for the maximal test accuracy.

Table 3. Recognition performance

Performance	Cumulative energy						
	99%	95%	90%	85%	80%	75%	70%
$Tr(\%)$	94.13	94.13	94.13	94.13	94.13	94.13	94.13
$Ts(\%)$	92.61	96.22	96.22	96.22	96.76	96.76	96.4
$tr(s)$	36911	36114	35780	35518	35371	35107	35016
$ts(s)$	16.45	9.32	8.79	8.76	8.65	8.38	7.73

5   Conclusion and Future Work

In this paper, a new finger-vein recognition method based on hyper-sphere granule computing was proposed. We combined hyper-sphere granular computing with PCA, and conducted a series of experiments based on the same database. The results showed that finger-vein recognition based on HSGrC-PCA can obtain a good identification performance. However, the algorithm still has much room to improve, such as, reducing the training time for high-efficiency, considering other dimension-reduction methods to get a better test accuracy.

Acknowledgements. This work is jointly supported by National Natural Science Foundation of China (Nos.61379102, U1433120) and the Fundamental Research Funds for the Central Universities (No. 3122014C003).

Reference

1. Kono, M., Ueki, H., Umemura, S.: Near-infrared finger vein patterns for personal identification. Appl. Opt. **41**, 7429–7436 (2002)
2. Liu, Z., Yin, Y.L., Wang, H.J., Song, S.L., Li, Y.L.: Finger vein recognition with manifold learning. J. Network Comput. Appl. **33**, 275–282 (2010)
3. Lee, E.C., Jung, H., Kim, D.: New finger biometric method using near infrared imaging. Sensors **11**, 2319–2333 (2011)
4. Yang, J.F., Shi, Y.H., Yang, J.L.: Personal identification based on finger-vein features. Computers in Human Behavior **27**(5), 1565–1570 (2010)
5. Wang, G.Y., Zhang, Q.H., Hu, J.: An overview of granular computing. CAAI Transactions on Intelligent Systems **2**(6), 8–26 (2007)
6. Xie, G., Liu, J.: A Review of the Present Studying State and Prospect of Granular Computing. Software **32**(3), 5–10 (2011)

7. Liu, Q., Liu, Q.: Approximate reasoning based on granular computing in granular logic. In: Int'l Conf. on Machine Learning and Cybernetics, Hoboken, USA (2002)
8. Liu, Q.: Granular language and its deductive reasoning. Communications of Institute of Information and Computing Machinery **5**(2), 63–66 (2002)
9. Zhang, L., Zhang, B.: The theory and application of problem solving. Tsinghua University Press (1990)
10. Maadooliat, M., Huang, J.Z., Hu, J.H.: Integrating data transformation in principal components analysis. Journal of Computational and Graphical Statistics **24**(1), 84–103 (2015)
11. Yang, J.F., Shi, Y.H.: Towards finger-vein image restoration and enhancement for finger-vein recognition. Information Sciences **268**, 33–52 (2014)
12. Yang, J.F., Shi, Y.H., Wu, R.B.: Finger-vein recognition based on Gabor features. In: Riaz, Z. (ed.) Biometric Systems, Design and Applications, 17–32 (2011)
13. Liu, H.B., Liu, C.H., Wu, C.A.: Granular computing classification algorithms based on distance measures between granules from the view of set. Computational Intelligence and Neuroscience (2014)
14. Liu, H.B., Li, L., Wu, C.A.: Color image segmentation algorithms based on granular computing clustering. International Journal of Signal Processing, Image Processing and Pattern Recognition **7**(1), 155–168 (2014)
15. Liu, H.B., Zhang, F., Wu, C.A., Huang, J.: Image superresolution reconstruction via granular computing clustering. Computational Intelligence and Neuroscience (2014)

Iris and Ocular Biometrics

An Iris Recognition Method
Based on Annule-energy Feature

Guang Huo[1,2], Yuanning Liu[1], Xiaodong Zhu[1(✉)], Chun Huang[1,3], Fei He[1],
Si Gao[1], Hongxing Dong[1], Lijiao Yu[1], and Xia Yang[1]

[1] College of Computer Science and Technology, Jilin University, Changchun 130012, China
zhuxd@jlu.edu.cn
[2] Informatization Office, Northeast Dianli University, Jilin 132012, China
[3] China Mobile Group Heilongjiang Co., Ltd., Harbin 150000, China

Abstract. Different annulus regions of iris texture have various distribution characteristics. All the previous feature extraction methods are unable to make a difference between relevance of intra-annulus feature and difference of inter-annulus feature. With an analysis of relevance of intra-annulus, this paper proposes a kind of feature extraction method based on texture regions. The method firstly uses 2D-Gabor filter to independently extract and encode texture features from different regions respectively, and then the set of feature vectors are applied to classification and recognition by SVM classifier. The experimental results show that the proposed method has quite high recognition accuracy.

Keywords: Iris recognition · Annulus partition · 2D-Gabor filter

1 Introduction

The iris images contain rich texture information. Since these texture information have such advantages as stability, uniqueness and non-invasiveness, iris is considered as a more promising and valuable biometric traits to identify individuals than other modalities. The first iris recognition system was introduced by Daugman. He used multi-scale Gabor filter to extract binary phase features of iris and adopted hamming distance for matching [1,2]. The method Daugman proposed regarded an iris image as an overall but ignored the distribution differences in various regions. Therefore, for the sake of improve the integral performance of algorithms many scholars tried to use different partition strategies to divide an iris image into many local regions with more distinguishable [3]. However, so far there has not yet been a unified and universal standard.

As for the above problems, from physiological structure perspective, this paper puts forward an iris recognition method based on multi-annulus energy feature on the basis of analysis of iris texture feature. Firstly, this paper divides the iris region into several annules, and then uses 2D-Gabor filter to extract the local energy information of each annule. Finally the process of recognition is done by SVM classifier. The recognition system framework of the proposed algorithm is shown in Fig. 1.

© Springer International Publishing Switzerland 2015
J. Yang et al. (Eds.): CCBR 2015, LNCS 9428, pp. 341–348, 2015.
DOI: 10.1007/978-3-319-25417-3_40

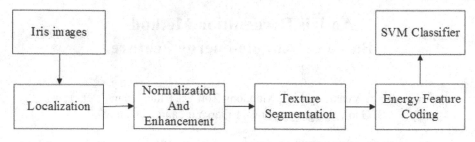

Fig. 1. The recognition system framework

2 Iris Texture Segmentation

Iris is located between pupil and sclera, which contains a large number of texture features. These texture structures generally present radiated distribution centered on pupil [4].If we segment the iris region with equidistant annulus, it is not difficult to find that the texture details with the same annulus have higher similarity and the texture details among different annules have greater diversity. The result is shown in Fig. 2.

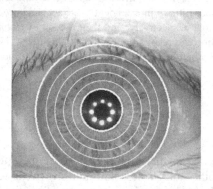

Fig. 2. Iris texture segmentation

In addition, the direction and the complexity of the texture with the same annules are more similar in the frequency. Therefore we divide the located iris image into multiple annular regions and encode the segmented annules from inside out. In order to facilitate the subsequent feature extraction, the segment is performed on the normalized and enhanced iris images.

Fig. 3. Segmentation results with normalization and enhancement

As shown in Fig. 3, each segmented annules after normalized will become a rectangular region where the internal texture is similar. The paper regards the feature of each rectangle region as a matching unit. The multiple rectangular regions can make up of the overall feature vector.

3   Annulus-Energy Feature Extraction

3.1   2D-Gabor Filter

The majority of the iris texture and horizontal direction shows larger angle distribution, using multiple directions, multiple scales filters can accurately express the texture information. Therefore this paper 2D-Gabor filter bank analyses multi-scale texture and direction, achieving iris encoding. The form of 2D-Gabor filter is shown in equation (1).

$$G(x,y) = \exp(-\pi[(x-x_0)^2]\alpha^2 + (y-y_0)^2\beta^2) * \exp(-2\pi j[u_0(x-x_0) + v_0(y-y_0)]) \quad (1)$$

where (x_0, y_0) is the filter center, (u_0, v_0) is the frequency domain center, α and β are standard deviations of the elliptical Gaussian along the x and y axes, respectively. The real and imaginary parts of 2D-Gabor filter are shown in Fig. 4.

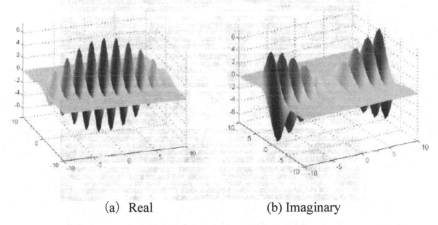

(a) Real   (b) Imaginary

Fig. 4. The real and imaginary parts of 2D-Gabor filters

3.2   Feature Extraction and Encoding

Iris textures are rich in content and various in forms. Due to superior performance for image details extraction, the energy value of multi-direction is chosen for matching. By filtering the result of the real part R and imaginary part I, we calculate the amplitude information, as shown in equation (2).

$$Mag(x,y) = \sqrt{R^2(x,y) + I^2(x,y)} \quad (2)$$

Thus, we can construct a filter bank, and the number of direction and scale are m and n, respectively. The amplitude information of multi-directional and multi-scale are shown in Fig. 5.

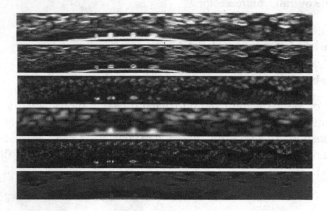

Fig. 5. Amplitude image

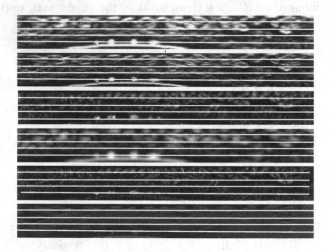

Fig. 6. Regional energy distribution

In order to facilitate for observing energy distribution of different annules, we divide the normalization images into many tracks, as shown in Fig. 6. The similarity of energy distribution in each track is obvious. We take mean as the average level of the tracks. The result of filtering characteristics is described as equation (3):

$$e_i = \{m_1, m_2, \cdots, m_j\} \qquad (3)$$

where e_i stands for i^{th} filter, obtaining sequence of Regional energy value: m_1, m_2, …, m_j respectively represent the mean of intensity of the iris region from inside to outside edges, the calculation equation is as follows:

$$m_j = \frac{1}{l \times h} \sum_{k=1}^{l \times h} Mag(x,y) \tag{4}$$

where l and h represent the length and height of the sub-block regions respectively.

Since the 2D-Gabor filter bank is composed by the $m \times n$ filters. Therefore, energy feature E of the endless belt of an image also should have the $m \times n$ elements, as the equation (5). We will combine Euclidean distance (ED) of two iris images each endless belt together as the input feature vectors V of SVM model.

$$E = \{e_1, e_2, \cdots, e_{m \times n}\} \tag{5}$$

$$\left\{ \begin{array}{l} V = \{ED_1, \cdots, ED_j, \cdots, ED_{m \times n}\} \\ ED_j = \sqrt{\sum_{k=1}^{j} \left[e_j(input) - e_j(enrolled) \right]^2} \end{array} \right. \tag{6}$$

4   The Classification Based on SVM Model

Because SVM is capable of handling problems brought about by small samples and is a nonlinear and high dimensional model, it is employed in this study [5].

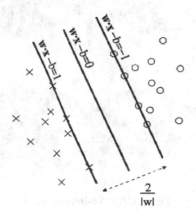

Fig. 7. The principle of SVM

As shown in Fig.7, assumed the hyperplane expression is $w \cdot x - b = 0$, which was a vector that plumbed to the hyperplane, x as a sample, b as a shift amount. The n samples of training set and the corresponding class label were expressed as $(x_1, y_1), \ldots, (x_l, y_l)$, which y as the corresponding category. In two categories of this figure, the two lines which closest to the classified plane and parallel to each other were expressed as $w \cdot x - b = 1$ and $w \cdot x - b = -1$, and the known maximum distance between the two lines was $2/\|w\|$. Then you can ensure that the sample data points which all are in the hyperplane spacer met $w \cdot x - b \leq -1$ or $w \cdot x - b \geq 1$. The SVM is defined as follows:

$$\begin{cases} \dfrac{1}{2}\|w\|^2, \ \min(w,b) \\ y_i((w \cdot x_i)+b) \geq 1 \end{cases} \tag{7}$$

In this paper, the training set $\{V_{train}\}$ feature vectors were trained for SVM model, the trained SVM model was applied to the test set $\{V_{test}\}$ for classification. This identification process belongs to a typical two-class problem that is the inter-class or intra-class. Thus, for any pair of vectors x and x_i from the training and test set, if the result is $f(x) = 1$, it is considered to be intra-class; if the result is $f(x) = -1$, it is considered to be inter-class.

5   The Experimental Results and Analysis

We randomly selected 100 class (7 per class) from the CASIA V4-Interval database to test the algorithm performance [6], shown as Fig. 8. Then, we take the former five in each class (the total iris image is 500) as the training sample, and the other two as the test samples.

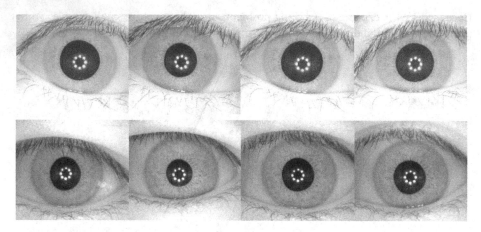

Fig. 8. CASIA4-Interval iris images.

The experiment steps as follow: First, find the optimal annules. In this paper, we choose the parameters ($f_{max} = 64$, $d_f = 2$, $M = 6$, $N = 4$) to structure Gabor filters, and select the radial basis function (RBF) as the SVM kernel function. For the specific selection method, please refer to our earlier paper [7]. Since this paper choose the filter window size 4 as the minimum of the ring, and 512×64 as the size of normalization. In order to easily divisible, select the power factor of 2 to increase to the half of the annule width, and the experimental results are shown in Table 1. It can be seen that the normalization images which divided into four regions can achieve better recognition result.

Table 1. The multi-annulus division results.

No. of annules	FRR (%)	FAR (%)
2	0.5775	0.5312
4	**0.4905**	**0.4895**
8	0.5466	0.5265
16	0.5418	0.5379

Second, the iris texture will be encode by blocks based on the optimal number of annules. Then we use the training set to build SVM model. The number of training samples is 124750, among   which the number of intra-class is 1000, and the number of samples of inter-class is 123750. Then, the trained SVM model will be used to classify the test set. The number of test samples is 19900, among which the number of intra-class is 100, and the number of inter-class is 19800. The CRR of the proposed method is 99.17%, the EER is 0.08%, as shown in Table 2. Compared with the classical iris recognition algorithms, the proposed method achieves higher performance.

It has to be pointed out that neither Mask nor ROI are employed to eliminate the negative effects brought about by blocking of eyelids and eyeslashes. Nor there is requirement on quality of images. The algorithms of Daugman and Yao perform sligtly lower than the algorithms of other literatures. These factors effect our algorithm, so it has no influence on their comparisons.

Table 2. Comparison of methods.

Method	CRR (%)	EER (%)
Daugman[3]	98.98	0.68
Boles[8]	92.64	8.13
Wildes et al.[9]	N/A	1.76
Yao P [10]	99.06	0.65
Proposed	99.17	0.49

6   Conclusion

According to the characteristics of the regional distribution of iris texture, we proposed an iris recognition method based on annulus features. The method of feature extraction transforms the whole object to several similar local regions, so that the 2D-Gabor filters can extract more targeted texture features. The experimental results imply that the proposed method outperforms some classical iris recognition methods.

References

1. Daugman, J.G.: How iris recognition works. IEEE Trans. Circuits Syst. Video Technol. **14**(1), 21–30 (2004)
2. Daugman, J.G.: New methods in iris recognition. IEEE Trans. Syst. Man Cybern. B **37**(5), 1167–1175 (2007)
3. Vatsa, M., Singh, R., Noore, A.: Improving iris recognition performance using segmentation, quality enhancement, match score fusion, and indexing. IEEE Trans. Syst. Man Cybern. B **38**(4), 1021–1035 (2008)
4. Ma, L., Tan, T., Wang, Y., Zhang, D.: Personal identification based on iris texture analysis. IEEE Trans. Pattern Anal. Mach. Intell. **25**(12), 1519–1533 (2003)
5. Ding, S.F., Qi, B.J., Tan, H.Y.: An overview on theory and algorithm of support vector machines. J. Univ. Electron. Sci. Technol. China **40**(1), 2–10 (2011)
6. CASIA V4-Interval Iris Image Database. http://www.cbsr.ia.ac.cn/irisdatabase.htm
7. He, F., Liu, Y., Zhu, X.: Score level fusion scheme based on adaptive local Gabor features for face-iris-fingerprint multimodal biometric. J. Electron. Imag. **23**(3), 572–579 (2014)
8. Boles, W.W., Boashash, B.: A Human Identification Technique Using Images of the Iris and Wavelet Transform. IEEE Trans. Signal Processing **46**(4), 1185–1188 (1998)
9. Wildes, R.P., et al.: A machine-vision system for iris recognition. In: Machine Vision and Applications. Springer, Heidelberg (1996)
10. Yao, P., Ye, X.Y., Zhuang, Z.: An iris recognition algorithm combining local frequency features with local orientation features. Acta Electron. Sinica **35**(4), 663–667 (2007)

An Efficient Iris Recognition Method
Based on Restricted Boltzmann Machine

Guang Huo[1,2(✉)], Yuanning Liu[2], Xiaodong Zhu[2], and Jianfeng Wu[2]

[1] Informatization Office, Northeast Dianli University, Jilin 132012, China
huoguang@mail.nedu.edu.cn
[2] College of Computer Science and Technology, Jilin University, Changchun 130012, China

Abstract. As one of major methods for iris feature extraction, 2D-Gabor filter is capable of texture features in different directions and scales. Restricted Boltzmann Machine (RBM) is quite favored because of its simple structure and fastness in classification. However, due to conflicts between the feature vector dimension and the complexity of the network structure, rarely few combine them for iris recognition. This paper proposes a multi-class iris recognition method which combines 2D-Gabor feature extraction and classification model of RBM together. Firstly, 2D-Gabor filter is employed to extract energy-orientation feature of iris texture, whose dimension will not increase with the increasing number of filters. In this case, as the number of nodes in hidden layers of RBM network is determined to a definite value, complexity of the whole RBM design is simplified. Experiments show that this method displays high recognition accuracy on sample sets.

Keywords: Iris recognition · 2D-Gabor filter · RBM

1 Introduction

Iris recognition is a technique using iris texture of human eyes for identification. It has advantages of good stability, high recognition accuracy, capability of biopsy, etc. Therefore, iris recognition becomes the focus of academic research in this field and classical recognition algorithms are designed [1-5].

One of the most representatives is the 2D-Gabor transform by Daugman, using 2D-Gabor filter to extract iris texture on multi-scales and from multi-orientations before binary phase encoding and matching with Hamming distance [1]. Filtering an iris image with a family of filters resulted in 1024 complex-valued phasors which denote the phase structure of the iris at different scales. Each phasor was then quantized to one of the four quadrants in the complex plane. The resulting 2048-component iris coding was used to describe an iris [6]. But there are two drawbacks with this recognition mode: firstly, the phase encoding only expresses independent features extracted by filters on different scales, ignoring the correlation among these features. Subsequent experiments show distinguishable features of such correlation. Secondly, the accuracy of judgment method based on a threshold value is highly dependent on the

© Springer International Publishing Switzerland 2015
J. Yang et al. (Eds.): CCBR 2015, LNCS 9428, pp. 349–356, 2015.
DOI: 10.1007/978-3-319-25417-3_41

training set of data which only works in one-to-one recognition pattern. Based on those considerations above, this paper presents a multi-class iris recognition method by combining the 2D-Gabor feature extraction method and the classification model of RBM. This method has better robustness and high recognition accuracy on a small sample set.

2   Iris Feature Extraction

Prior to the extraction, IRIS image preprocessing is needed to eliminate negative impact on subsequent recognition brought about by factors such as light intensity, palpebral occlusion, iris deformation. Iris image preprocessing includes iris localization, normalization, enhancement, ROI selection and resizing, as it is shown in Fig. 1. Iris image preprocessing should be carried out before feature extraction to eliminate negative impact on subsequent recognition caused by factors such as illumination intensity, eyelid occlusion, and iris deformation, etc.

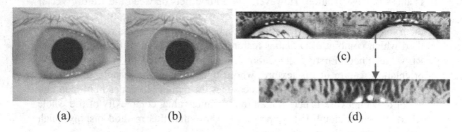

(a)   (b)   (d)

Fig. 1. Iris image pre-processing; (a) original iris image; (b) iris localization; (c) iris normalization and enhancement; (d) ROI selection and resizing.

2.1   2D-Gabor Filter

The texture features of an iris image are sufficient to represent the uniqueness of each individual, so we extract the texture features by 2D-Gabor filters with different scales and orientations. 2D-Gabor function is a product of an elliptical Gaussian and a complex plane wave. It can be represented by the following equation in the spatial domain:

$$G(x, y) = e^{-\frac{\pi}{\sigma^2}\left[(x-x_0)^2 + (y-y_0)^2\right]} \cdot e^{-2\pi i\left[\omega(x-x_0)\cos\theta + \omega(y-y_0)\sin\theta\right]} \tag{1}$$

where (x_0, y_0) is the center of the receptive field in the spatial domain, σ is the standard deviations of the Gaussian function, ω is the central frequency and θ indicates the orientation of the Gabor filter.

2.2   Energy-Orientation Encoding

The iris feature extracted through 2D-Gabor filter has both imaginary and real components, as shown in equations (2) and (3) below. Through different operations on the imaginary part and the real part, we can derive a number of new features, such as phase, amplitude and cosine. In this paper, a combination of amplitude and filter direction generates a new form of feature expression, that is, ability direction feature. Such feature reflects the relationship among magnitude features on the same scale but in different directions. Experiments show that Energy-Orientation Feature (EOF) is capable of high distinguishability on small sample set. Specific operations are shown in equation (4) and (5):

$$\mathrm{Im} = \frac{\omega^2}{\sigma^2} \exp(-\frac{\omega^2(x^2+y^2)}{2\sigma^2}) \times [\sin(\omega x \cos\theta + \omega y \sin\theta)] \tag{2}$$

$$\mathrm{Re} = \frac{\omega^2}{\sigma^2} \exp(-\frac{\omega^2(x^2+y^2)}{2\sigma^2}) \times [\cos(\omega x \cos\theta + \omega y \sin\theta) - \exp(-\sigma^2/2))] \tag{3}$$

$$Mag_k = \sqrt{\mathrm{Re}_k^2 + \mathrm{Im}_k^2} \tag{4}$$

$$EOF_k = x_k = \arg \max_{x \in [0,5]} Mag_k(\frac{\pi}{6}x) \tag{5}$$

where ω is the central frequency, θ is the angle of the filter, σ is the Gaussian standard deviation, $\exp(-\sigma^2/2)$ is the DC component. Im and Re are the imaginary and real of the filter, Mag_k is the magnitude filtered by the kth sampling point in ROI, EOF is the matrix composed of 0,1,2,3,4,5. 0,1,2,....,5 denote the orientation symbols at 0, $\pi/6$, $\pi/3$, $\pi/2$, $2\pi/3$, $5\pi/6$ orientations when the magnitude of the six is largest.

3   Training of Restricted Boltzmann Machine

3.1   Restricted Boltzmann Machines

RBM is a restricted type of BM (Boltzmann Machines) which has been introduced as bidirectionally connected networks of stochastic processing units [7]. Different from BM, in practical applications RBM solve complex time-consuming process of learning better. Meanwhile, RBM is a special Markov Random Field (MRF). As shown in Fig. 2, RBM is a neural network consists of two layers, m visible units

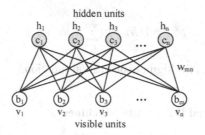

Fig. 2. The undirected graph of RBM

$v=\{v_1,v_2,...,v_m\}$ and n hidden units $h =\{h_1,h_2...h_n\}$. Its energy function $E(v,h)$ is defined as follows:

$$E(v,h) = -\sum_{i=1}^{m}\sum_{j=1}^{n} v_i h_j w_{ij} - \sum_{i=1}^{m} b_i v_i - \sum_{j=1}^{n} c_j h_j \qquad (6)$$

where w_{ij} is a real valued weight associated with the edge between units v_i and h_j, and b_i and c_j are real valued bias terms associated with the ith visible and the jth hidden variable, respectively. We focus on binary RBMs where the random variables (v, h) take values from $\{0, 1\}$. The probability distribution of (v, h) is defined as follows:

$$p(v,h) = \frac{1}{z} e^{-E(v,h)} \qquad (7)$$

$$z = \sum_{v,h} e^{-E(v,h)} \qquad (8)$$

where z is a normalization factor. Assuming there are m visible cells and n hidden units, in order to 2^{m+n} calculations are needed for the normalization factor z. Even if we can get parameter w through the training model, but we still cannot figure out the distribution determined by the parameter w efficiently.

Because there are only connections between the layer of visible and hidden variables but no connections between two variables from the same layer. The hidden variables are independent given the state of the visible variables and vice versa [8], as in function (9) and (10).

$$p(h|v) = \prod_{j=1}^{n} p(h_j,v), \quad p(v|h) = \prod_{i=1}^{m} p(v_i,h) \qquad (9)$$

When a visible given node is determined, the activation probability of jth node in hidden layer is:

$$p(h_j = 1|v) = g(\sum_{i=1}^{m} w_{ij} v_i + c_i) \qquad (10)$$

After obtaining all nodes in the hidden layer and based on the limitations of symmetrical structure of Boltzmann machine, the activation probability of visible node is calculated as:

$$p(v_i = 1|h) = g(\sum_{j=1}^{n} w_{ij} h_j + b_j) \qquad (11)$$

where $g(x) = 1/(1+e^{-x})$ is the sigmoid activation function.

3.2   Learning Restricted Boltzmann Machines

The task of learning restricted Boltzmann machine is to find the parameter θ (including b_i, c_j, w_{ij}) to fit a given learning sample. The parameter θ is obtained by restricting the maximization of log likelihood of Boltzmann machine on learning set (assuming the number of learning data is T), the specific equation is as follows:

$$\theta = \arg \max \sum_{t=1}^{T} \log p(v^{(t)} \mid \theta) \tag{12}$$

This paper calculates the optimal parameters by random rising gradient whose critical step is to calculate the partial derivatives with respect to each of the model parameters.

$$L(\theta) = \sum_{t=1}^{T} \log p(v^{(t)} \mid \theta) = \sum_{t=1}^{T} \log \sum_{h} p(v^{(t)}, h \mid \theta) \tag{13}$$

Let θ denote a member of the parameter set, the log-likelihood function with respect to the gradient of θ is:

$$\frac{\partial L}{\partial \theta} = \sum_{t=1}^{T} \frac{\partial}{\partial \theta} \left(\log \sum_{h} e^{-E(v^{(t)}, h \mid \theta)} - \log \sum_{v} \sum_{h} e^{-E(v, h \mid \theta)} \right) \tag{14}$$

where $<\cdot> p$ stands for the average about distribution p. $p(h \mid v^{(t)}, \theta)$ denotes the probability distribution of the hidden layer when the visible cells define the learning samples $v(t)$. Therefore, the former part in equation (14) is relatively easy for calculation. $p(h \mid v, \theta)$ prepresents the joint distribution of the visible and the unit cell in hidden layer. Because of the normalization factor z, the latter part in the equation (14) couldn't be calculated. Therefore, we use to Gibbs sampling method to get an approximate value.

This paper employs contrastive divergence of learning algorithms to quickly train the corresponding parameters in RBM. Suppose there is only one training sample, data and model are used to mark the probability distributions of $p(h \mid v^{(t)}, \theta)$ and $p(h \mid v, \theta)$ respectively. The partial derivatives of log-likelihood function with respect to the connection matrix w_{ij}, the bias b_i of visible layer node and the bias c_j of hidden layer node are:

$$\Delta w_{ij} = \frac{\partial \log p(v \mid \theta)}{\partial w_{ij}} = \langle v_i h_j \rangle_{data} - \langle v_i h_j \rangle_{model} \tag{15}$$

$$\Delta b_i = \frac{\partial \log p(v \mid \theta)}{\partial b_i} = \langle v_i \rangle_{data} - \langle v_i \rangle_{model} = v_i - \sum_{v} p(v) v_i \tag{16}$$

$$\Delta c_j = \frac{\partial \log p(v \mid \theta)}{\partial c_j} = p(h_j = 1 \mid v) - \sum_{v} p(v) p(h_j = 1 \mid v) \tag{17}$$

The parameter w_{ij} is often updated in an optimized rule, as in function (18).

$$w_{ij}^{(t+1)} = w_{ij}^{(t)} + \varepsilon \times \Delta w_{ij}^{(t)} - \eta \times w_{ij}^{(t)} + \lambda \times \Delta w_{ij}^{(t-1)} \tag{18}$$

The constant ε is the learning rate and the term $-\eta \times w^{(t)}$, called weight decay, penalizes the weights with large magnitude. The update rule can be further extended by a momentum term $\Delta w_{ij}^{(t-1)}$, weighted by the parameter λ. Using a momentum term helps against oscillations in the iterative update procedure and can speed-up the learning process as known from feed-forward neural network training [9]. The update rule can also be applied to b_i and c_j similarly.

4   Experimental Results

In this paper, the performance of algorithms is verified in iris databases CASIA V1.0 and JLU 3.0. The CASIA V1.0 database consists of 108 iris images of 80 individuals with different grayness, and there are seven images for each eye with a total of 756 [10]. Four images are selected from each set to construct training sets and the rest are testing sets. JLU 3.0 includes 1,800 left and right eye images from 30 individuals wherein each eye contains 30 images, with a resolution of 640×480 [11]. 5 images are selected from each category as training set and the rest are for test with specific parameters shown in Table 1.

Table 1. Construction of the experimental iris databases

Iris Databases	Resolution	Normalization Size	ROI Selection	ROI Resizing	Training Set	Testing Set
CASIA V1.0	320×280	512×64	(256, 0, 256, 20)	256×32	4×108	3×108
JLU 3.0	640×480	512×64	(256, 0, 256, 30)	256×32	5×30	5×30

Firstly, based on the experimental data, parameter optimization is carried out for multi-directional filter banks on a single scale. Then, the optimized filter banks are used for feature extraction of all ROI to obtain the characteristic matrix in size of 32×216, shown in Fig. 3. Next, this matrix is transformed into a feature vector of 1×6912, and function as input in visible layer of RBM network. Because the code length of EOF is only related to the size of ROI, the encoding length for CASIA V1.0 and JLU 3.0 is 6912. The three most important parameters in constructing RBM network are the numbers of nodes on visible layer and hidden layer nodes, and maxim number of training times. Due to the number of nodes on visible layer is determined, 6192, the number of nodes on hidden layer can be approximated to one-third on visible one. Maximum number of training times can be obtained according to the refactoring error distribution curve, as shown in Figure 4. Therefore, as for iris bank in the same size of ROI, the basic parameters for building RBM in this design can remain unchanged. Thus the problems such as network reconfiguration and parameter adjustment resulting from the changing number of nodes in visible layer in constructing RBM are avoided.

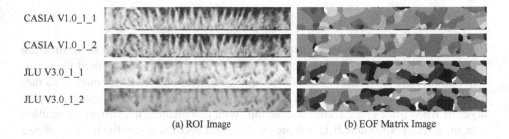

CASIA V1.0_1_1		
CASIA V1.0_1_2		
JLU V3.0_1_1		
JLU V3.0_1_2		
	(a) ROI Image	(b) EOF Matrix Image

Fig. 3. EOF encoding

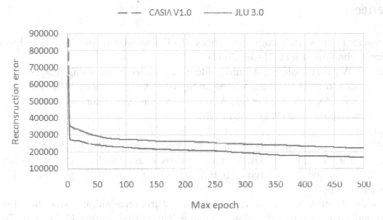

Fig. 4. The curve of reconstruction error

Finally, based on the trained network of RBM, test sets are then identified, and the specific training parameters are shown in Table 2. Note that this paper does not perform the classical binary recognition with SVM, instead, multi-class recognition characterized as fewer matching and faster recognition. Due to the number of samples identified by multi-class method is far less than those by binary methods, the recognition accuracy of the former is slightly lower than that of the latter. Therefore, recognition rates our proposed algorithm on iris banks CASIA V1.0 and JLU 3.0 are 98.15% and 98.67% respectively. It is enough to show this algorithm on a small sample set is of better versatility and higher recognition accuracy.

Table 2. Parameters of the RBM

Iris Databases	Visible layer nodes	Hidden layer nodes	Max epoch	No. of Error/ total	CRR (%)
CASIA V1.0	6192	2064	440	6/324	98.15
JLU 3.0	6192	1935	460	2/150	98.67

5   Conclusion

Based on a detailed analysis of expression characteristics of 2D-Gabor construction method of RBM, this paper presents a multi-class iris recognition method that combines the feature extraction of 2D-Gabor and classification of RBM model. This method greatly reduces complexity of designing RBM by determining nodes on display layer of RBM prior to the feature extraction. With this method, the correct recognition rate on CASIA V1.0 and JLU 3.0 are 98.15% and 98.67% respectively. This shows that the proposed method is feasible and effective on small sample set.

References

1. Daugman, J.: How iris recognition works. IEEE Transactions on Circuits and Systems for Video Technology 14(1), 21–30 (2004)
2. Boles, W.W., Boashash, B.: A human identification technique using images of the iris and wavelet transform. IEEE Transactions on Signal Processing 46(4), 1185–1188 (1998)
3. Wildes, R.P., Asmuth, J.C., et al.: A machine-vision system for iris recognition. Machine Vision and Applications 9(1), 1–8 (1996)
4. Ma, L., Tan, T.N., Wang, Y.N., et al.: Efficient iris recognition by characterizing key local variations. IEEE Transactions on Image Processing 13(6), 739–750 (2004)
5. Sun, Z., Tan, T., Qiu, X.: Graph matching iris image blocks with local binary pattern. In: Zhang, D., Jain, A.K. (eds.) ICB 2005. LNCS, vol. 3832, pp. 366–372. Springer, Heidelberg (2005)
6. Nabti, M., Bouridane, A.: An effective and fast iris recognition system based on a combined multiscale feature extraction technique. Pattern Recognition 41(3), 868–879 (2008)
7. Tieleman, T., Hinton, G.: Using fast weights to improve persistent contrastive divergence. In: Proceedings of the 26th Annual International Conference on Machine Learning, pp. 1033–1040. ACM, New York (2009)
8. Fischer, A., Igel, C.: Training restricted Boltzmann machines: An introduction. Pattern Recognition 47(1), 25–39 (2014)
9. Rumelhart, D.E., Hinton, G.E., Williams, R.J.: Learning internal representations by error propagation. In: Parallel Distributed Processing: Explorations in the Microstructure of Cognition, vol.1, pp.318–362. MIT Press (1986)
10. CASIA V1.0 Iris Image Database. http://www.cbsr.ia.ac.cn/irisdatabase.htm
11. JLU 3.0 Iris Image Database. http://biis.jlu.edu.cn/irisdatabase/

Iris Cracks Detection Method Based on Minimum Local Gray Value and Dilating Window of Regional Mean Gray Value

Bo Zhang[1,2](✉) and Weiqi Yuan[1]

[1] Visual Inspection Institute, Shenyang University of Technology, Shenyang, China
zber@163.com
[2] College of Computer Science and Technology, Shenyang University of Chemical Technology, Shenyang, China

Abstract. Iris crack has the characteristics of minimum local gray value and regional meoan gray value. Its gray value is lower than those of the surrounding area and from the edge to the inside the gray value is shown a trend of decline gradually. A method is proposed based on Minimum local Gray value and Dilating Window of Regional Mean Gray value. The initial starting point of the dilating window is determined by the minimum local gray value, and the dilating windows is configured with the regional mean gray value, and the areas of iris cracks will be found. Thirdly, the iris crack is segmented at the area according to minimum local gray value again. Finally, the result is found with the connection and de-noising. Compared method with single minimum local gray value method and Gaussian filter method, this method has low misdetection rate and simple threshold selection, and can meet the expected requirement.

Keywords: Minimum local gray value · Dilating window · Regional mean gray value · Iris crack

1 Introduction

The iris is one of the most common biometric identification and authentication, the rich texture of the iris has uniqueness and stability in a period, therefore, it is a valid individual feature for identification.

Since iris recognition idea was developed, texture feature extraction has been one of the key issues. Three classic iris texture feature extraction methods included using multi-scale two-dimensional Gabor filter, using one dimensional wavelet zero method, and the Gaussian - Laplace filter method[1-3]. In recent years, two classes of improvements have been developed[4].The first one employs the filter or signal transformation to express iris texture. These techniques obtain the iris texture feature coding by analyzing the resolution or using signal transformation method. However, they can't get the size or location information of the textures such as cracks and pigment spots. Therefore, this class of methods can't be utilized in evidence examination such as identity authentication. In order to overcome the drawbacks of the first class methods, the second class methods detect texture information in spatial domain.

© Springer International Publishing Switzerland 2015
J. Yang et al. (Eds.): CCBR 2015, LNCS 9428, pp. 357–364, 2015.
DOI: 10.1007/978-3-319-25417-3_42

These methods can obtain iris texture features, the characteristics features with low gray values, and the gray value map. On the other hand, this class of methods lacks the pertinence of various textures. If a method can detect various iris textures and extract the characteristic features such as sizes, shapes and locations, to be used as fundamental parameters of the iris recognition, it will be very valuable complement to the existing iris texture feature extraction methods.

In this study, according to the shapes, the iris textures are classified to four modes, i.e., crack, ring line, hole, and patch. The crack is used as the detecting object in the visible iris image. An innovative approach is proposed based on minimum local gray value and the average regional gray value. According to the shape and grayscale distribution of the crack, the crack area is initially positioned with the minimum local gray value, then a search window is constructed and image segmentation in the window is manipulated to examine the iris crack.

2   Iris Crack Detection Method

2.1   The Iris Crack Texture Feature Analysis

Divided by the frill, the internal part of iris is pupil area, and the external part is collarette area. The texture in collarette area can be classified as crack, ring line, hole, and patch.

The iris crack is in wheel or radial shape, and it may cover the entire iris. The cracks appear in different colors, various lengths. The longest crack can cross over the pupil to the edge of the iris. In Fig. 1(a), where the arrow points is the crack. The Crack is zoomed in as shown in Fig. 1(b). Remarkable changes of the gray value are demonstrated in Fig. 1(c), which shows the crack's gray level significantly lower than the surrounding area and its internal grayscale distribution is declined from the edge of the crack to the middle. Therefore, the crack has the minimum gray value, and the grayscale distribution of the iris is in a valley shape Fig. 1(d).

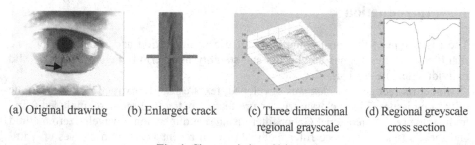

(a) Original drawing   (b) Enlarged crack   (c) Three dimensional   (d) Regional greyscale
                                                  regional grayscale   cross section

Fig. 1. Characteristics of iris crack

2.2   The Iris Image Preprocess

Because the original cracks are radially distributed in the iris region, normalizing and unfolding processes can make them, distributed in vertical direction which will simplify the computation. The method in [5] is employed in this study to local iris, and

Daugman method is adopted to normalize the image to 200×720. The preprocess of the iris image is shown in Fig. 2.

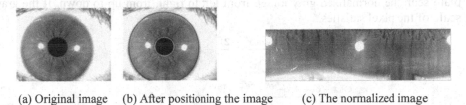

(a) Original image   (b) After positioning the image   (c) The normalized image

Fig. 2. The preprocessed iris image

2.3   The Method Based on Minimum Local Gray Value

A few cracks are shown in Fig. 3(a)①②③④⑤⑥is cross points of six cracks and the corresponding grayscales are s shown in Fig. 3(b), ①②③④⑤⑥has minimum local gray value.

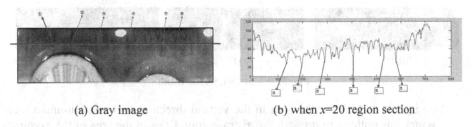

(a) Gray image   (b) when $x=20$ region section

Fig. 3. The section of the gray image

Since the cracks in the preprocessed iris image are distributed in vertical direction, the template should be built in perpendicular direction to the vertical direction, i.e., 0°. The template consists of an odd number of pixels, and the center pixel is the one to be detected by scanning the image along the template direction. To find the location of the target pixel, the center pixel is subtracted with neighbor adjacent pixels, if the center pixel is the minimum point, the difference is bigger; otherwise, the value is smaller. The difference is judged by the set threshold. The computation accuracy is determined by the template size and the selection of the threshold.

It is found that the width of the crack in the iris image is commonly in 3 to 7 pixels in the normalized image. According to the characteristics of the crack width, the template is designed in the way that the pixels are not involved in the operation, as shown in Fig. 4.

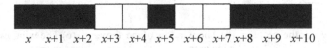

x $x+1$ $x+2$ $x+3$ $x+4$ $x+5$ $x+6$ $x+7$ $x+8$ $x+9$ $x+10$

Fig. 4. The template of the minimum local gray value difference

The pixels are marked as $(x, x+1, x+2,..., x+10)$ from left to right. The white parts are vacant pixels, located in $(x+3),(x+4)$, and $(x+7)$, $(x+8)$ do not participate in the operation.

The grayscale of the point $(x+5)$ is set as A, and the threshold is set as T. The template scan the normalized gray image from left to right, from up to down. If the gray scale of the pixel satisfies.

$$\frac{A(x) + A(x + 1) + A(x + 2)}{3} - A(x + 5) \geq T \cdot \quad (1)$$

$$\frac{A(x + 8) + A(x + 9) + A(x + 10)}{3} - A(x + 5) \geq T \cdot \quad (2)$$

This pixel is selected as the alternative point .

In this paper, the threshold is set in the range from 1 to 10. It is found that the connectivity of white area of the normalized image (the alternative area) varies from T. The smaller T is, the better the connectivity is. But it doesn't mean to make threshold as small as possible. The threshold T is also related to the number of the noise. Smaller T results in higher noise. After comparing different thresholds, threshold T = 5 is selected as it maintains the good connectivity with low noise, as shown in Fig. 5.

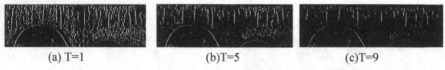

(a) T=1   (b)T=5   (c)T=9

Fig. 5. When T=1,5,9 the result

The target is to find out the area in the vertical direction with the minimum local gray, which has nothing to do with the average gray. Even in the area of the asymmetrical illumination and low contrast, the edge pixel will be detected if its gray scale is lower than the surrounding area. Therefore, besides all the cracks, some parts which are not cracks will be detected as well. Further selection is necessary.

2.4   The Dilating Window Based on Regional Mean Gray Level

The edge of the crack can be determined according to the minimum local gray values. A group of the dilating windows based on mean regional grayscale are proposed to detect the crack. Dilating windows for crack detection are configured because the position and the dimension of the cracks vary in the iris images, as shown in Fig. 6.

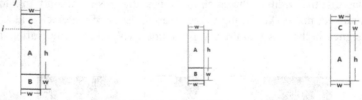

(a) The window for the   (b) The window of the above   (c) The window of the down
common area   edge area   edge area

Fig. 6. A group of the dilating windows

Fig. 6(a) shows the window for the common area, which is used in searching for the common area in the iris image except upper and lower edge. The dilating window is rectangular and divided into three segments: A, B and C. A is the center area and is the initial window, of which width and height are w and h respectively. B and C are squared extension window, of which edge size of.

The starting point of the initial window (A) is located at the upper left corner with the pixel coordinate of (i, j). The unit of the dimensions is pixel, namely the range in the row direction is from row i to row $i+h$ and in the column direction is from column j to column $j+w$. Window B is the bottom extension of the initial window, whose row range is from $i+h$ to $i+h+w$, while column range is the same to A. Window C is the top extension window of A, whose row range is from row $i-h$ to row i, and column range is the same to A and B.

Because the cracks may appear in the top or bottom edge of the preprocessed iris image, the dilating window as Fig. 5(a) is modified to those in Fig. 5(b) and Fig. 5(c), aiming at the top edge and the bottom edges respectively.

The mean grayscale of the center of the crack is smaller than both ends of the cracks according to the characteristics of the iris image gray spatial distribution. If the initial window A belongs to a part of the crack, the mean gray value of the window A is larger than it in B or C, that is the distribution of the grayscales of the initial window A, extension window B and extension window C should satisfy equation(3) or equation(4).

$$\mu_A > \mu_B. \tag{3}$$

$$\mu_A > \mu_C. \tag{4}$$

In equation(3) and (4), μ_A, μ_B, μ_C respectively refer to the mean gray value of the window A,B and C. The definition of μ_A, μ_B, μ_C can calculated by equation (5),(6) and(7). In the equations, $I(x, y)$means the gray matrix of the preprocessed iris image.

$$\mu_A = \frac{1}{w \cdot h} \sum_{x=i}^{x=i+h} \sum_{y=j}^{y=j+w} I(x, y) \tag{5}$$

$$\mu_B = \frac{1}{w \cdot w} \sum_{x=i+h}^{x=i+h+w} \sum_{y=j}^{y=j+w} I(x, y) \tag{6}$$

$$\mu_C = \frac{1}{w \cdot w} \sum_{x=i-w}^{x=i} \sum_{y=j}^{y=j+w} I(x, y) \tag{7}$$

(1) If the window A and B satisfy Eq.(3), merge A and B, to form a new initial window A, then create a new window B, and repeat this step.

(2) If the window A and C satisfy Eq.(4), merge A and C to form a new initial window A, then create a new window C, and repeat this step.

(3) When window A, window B and C don't satisfy the Equations, this area don't belong to no crack present in the area.

Because the minimum width of the crack is 3 pixels, the dimensions of window A is defined as $3×10$, extension window B is $3×3$, and C is $3×3$.

In all, this study designed the dilating window based on the minimum local grayscale, the dimension, shape and gray level distribution of the crack in the iris image.

3   Experimental Process and Results

3.1   Algorithmic Flow

The algorithm of detecting iris crack is as follows:

*Step a: preprocess the captured iris image: locate the iris using the method in [5], then normalize and expend the located image.

*Step b: translate the color image to gray image.

*Step c: minimum local gray value search: search the iris gray image in row direction traversal by the window in $0°$ direction, then mark the pixel of the minimum local gray value and find the initial point of crack.

*Step d: the dilating window (initial window, top extension window, bottom extension window) carry on search after step c, then mark the crack region that satisfies the condition of the dilating window.

*Step e: target selection: use the method of step c to carry on binarization of the crack area that marked by step d, then place the result to the black background which redesigned.

*Step f: connect the breakage of the crack area: design a connected window to connect the breakage of the crack area.

*Step g: remove the noise: count the area of the connected region, and remove the small area noise. Then filter the crack by the width/height ratio.

*Step h: output the result: output the result in binarization image form, in which white area is the crack.

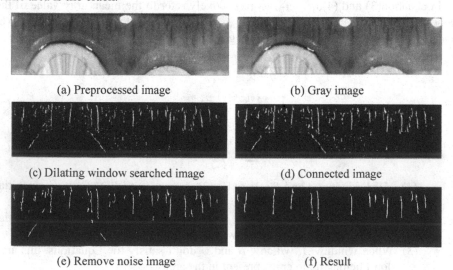

(a) Preprocessed image   (b) Gray image

(c) Dilating window searched image   (d) Connected image

(e) Remove noise image   (f) Result

Fig. 7. Iris crack image detected result step by step

The result is as shown in Fig. 7.

4   Experimental Comparison and Discussion

4.1   Experimental Comparison

Fig. 8 displays the results achieved by various methods.

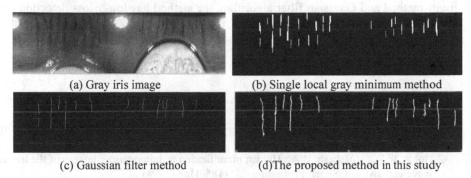

(a) Gray iris image	(b) Single local gray minimum method
(c) Gaussian filter method	(d)The proposed method in this study

Fig. 8. Comparison with several methods

The single minimum local gray value method missed several cracks and the shapes of the crack are not similar. While the threshold in the Gaussian filter method is difficult and need manually selecting threshold.

Up to date, there are several types of technologies in the iris recognition, such as the CASIA, ICE, MMU and UBIRIS. However, these libs can't meet the demand of subject due to the inherent drawbacks. Firstly, the resolution isn't enough. Iris texture detail information is very limited. Near infrared acquisition device is used in most of the libs. When the texture feature of the melanin formation under near infrared cannot be achieved, iris pigment can lead to better imaging result in visible light. SUT iris image lib is used to evaluate the proposed and published methods. Total 112 images, including 485 cracks, are examined, The new method correctly detected the in 447 cracks, 28 cracks in errors, and missed 45 cracks. Table 1 lists the testing results.

Table 1. Testing results.

Method	Detected rate	Loss detection rate	False detection rate
The proposed method	92.2%	5.8%	9.3%
Single MLG method	85.7%	11.3%	10.1%
Gaussian filter method	91.3%	9.7%	9.8%

In the table, the detection rate means that the percentage of the correctly detected cracks to the actual total cracks. Loss detection rate means that the percentage of un-detected cracks to the actual total cracks. False detection rate means the percentage of wrongly detected cracks to the total. Table 1 evidences that the proposed method is superior in loss detection rate and the threshold selection to the Gaussian filter.

5   Conclusion

This study proposed an innovative method that employs minimum local grayscale and average regional grayscale of dilating window to detect cracks. Experiment confirmed that this method can obtain high accuracy. Compared with the single local gray minimum method and Gaussian filter algorithm, the method has lower loss detection rate, and easier threshold selection.

References

1. Daugman, J.: Recognizing people by their iris patterns. Information Security Technical Report **3**, 33–39 (1998)
2. Widles, R.P.: Iris recognition: An emerging biometric technology. Proceedings of the IEEE **85**, 1348–1363 (1997)
3. Boles, W.W., Boashash, B.A.: Human identification technique using images of the iris and wavelet transform. Signal Processing **46**, 1185–1188 (1998)
4. Yuan, W.Q., Liu, X.N.: A kind of iris image block texture detection algorithm. Chinese Journal of Scientific Instrument **35**, 1093–1099 (2014)
5. Yuan, W.Q., Lin, Z.H.: A novel iris localization algorithm based on human eye structure characteristics. Electro-Optical Engineering **34**, 116–125 (2007)
6. Yuan, W.Q., Wang, N.: Based on local gray minimum palm vein image segmentation method. Journal of Optoelectronics Laser **7**, 1091–1096 (2011)
7. Shen, B., Xu, Y., Lu, G.M., Zhang, D.: Detecting iris lacunae based on gaussian filter. In: Third International Conference on International Information Hiding and Multimedia Signal Processing (2007)
8. Bo, S.: Iris pathological feature extraction research. In: HIT (2007)
9. Yuan, W.Q., Liu, X.N.: Iris image block texture detection based on the combined windows. Chinese Journal of Scientific Instrument **35**, 1900–1906 (2014)
10. Bowyer, K., Hollingsworth, K.P., Flynn, P.J.: A survey of iris biometrics research: 2008–2010. In: Handbook of Iris Recognition, pp. 15–54. Springer, London (2013)
11. Yuan, W.Q., Liu, B.: Defocused iris recognition based on stable feature fusion in spatial and frequency domains. Chinese Journal of Scientific Instrument **34**, 2300–2308 (2013)

Extraction of Texture Primitive
of the Iris Intestinal Loop

Jing Huang[✉] and Weiqi Yuan

School of Information Science and Engineering, Shenyang University of Technology,
Shenyang, China
hj4393@gmail.com

Abstract. Iris images have rich texture features and there are significant differences between inner and outer texture in the area of intestinal loop. The texture
of intestinal loop dominated the whole iris images, and they are applied to iris
recognition and evaluation of health. This paper presents a novel approach to
extraction intestinal loop based on textures primitive. First, using texture primitive to count rhythmicity of texture variation, then counting the frequency modes in the windows by defining the boundary and non-boundary mode, and finally to identify the specified window which containing the intestinal loop round
to extract intestinal loop by frequency variation. Experimental results indicate
that extraction with fuzzy textures which can effectively turn the IRIS intestinal
loop, provide a favorable basis for application based intestinal loop.

Keywords: Iris intestinal loop · Fuzzy texture · Primitive

1 Introduction

Iris images have rich texture features with different shapes such as block, strip, fleck,
etc[1]. These textures are spread unevenly and people can see that there is a transition
boundary from the vision. The boundary in Iris images is blurry for most people. The
entire iris boundary is divided into inner and outer portions, the area from pupil to the
transition boundary is called intestinal loop [2], as shown in Figure 1. There are significant differences between inner and outer texture in the area of intestinal loop.
While, the distribution and texture of Iris images' intestinal loop region vary from
different types of human. These differences dominated the whole iris images and they
are applied to iris recognition and IRIS-based computer-aided diagnosis.

In addition, the intestinal loop region of iris images is not sheltered from eyelid and
eyelash when collecting information so that it is conducive to recognize information
features in applications and extract them stably.

In recent years, only few domestic scholars do some research about extracting outer boundary of intestinal loop. Xin guodong [3], who use gradient method of gray-
scale on the normalized iris image to search for the largest gradient gray-scale to
extract the boundary. Yu Li, who use the improved method of snake to extract it [4,5].
The algorithms are all trying to detect boundary, but it is unsatisfactory for the large

J. Yang et al. (Eds.): CCBR 2015, LNCS 9428, pp. 365–372, 2015.
DOI: 10.1007/978-3-319-25417-3_43

number of image detection results of boundary blur. The outer boundary of intestinal loop locate on the iris have kinds of shapes. The gray-scale of image varies slowly within a certain range of pixels. There are more gray-scale of pixels that vary fast within a certain range than a non-edge regions. So the center of the range is regarded as the edge. This paper establishes a certain size of window and traverses the image firstly. Secondly, it counts the variation of pixels in the window. Finally, it obtains the maximum value of the variation of the line. The center where the value of the window locates is the intestinal loop boundary points of the line. Based on the above idea, the method of texture primitives is adopted in this paper.

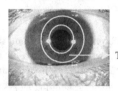

The Intestinal Loop of Iris

Fig. 1. The Intestinal Loop of Iris

2   Image Preprocessing

Determines the IRIS in the human eye image position and size are extracted outer boundary of intestinal loop the first step is the most crucial step. Iris location finds out between the pupil and iris, Iris and sclera the two inside edges and the outside community. These two boundaries are usually similar as two circles. Iris location is therefore determined the two circles of center and radius. This paper is based on gray distribution features of eye images for iris location method.

The iris's eyes' image are different and at the same time the influence of light and other factors may also cause changes in the size of the iris region. We must normalize iris in order to extract intestinal loop and map the two boundaries of the iris ring to a fixed shape texture map [9]. This mapping is normalization of iris image. Therefore, this paper transforms the original cartesian coordinates into polar coordinates by the method of coordinates' conversion. Divide the iris area from the inner radius to the outer radius into 150 parts so using the above methods to normalize iris image. The normalized image's size is 360 ×150, as shown in Figure 2.

Fig. 2. Normalized iris image

3   The Outer Boundary of Intestinal Loop's Extraction

3.1   Extraction Principal

3.1.1   Structure and Mode of Primitive

Primitives are a basic unit for describing the gray level change between pixels of an image [11]. The structure of the primitives is defined by the horizontal direction of the center pixel and the adjacent 4 pixels. As shown in Figure 3. Where X represents the center pixel and 1,2,3,4 are defined the order of pixels in the primitives. In order to describe the extent of pixels' gray change, the gray difference between each pixel and the center pixel of the pixel is calculated. According to the serial number of each pixel, the gray difference is recorded as $q_i(i=1,2,3,4)$. The absolute values of the difference between different thresholds and $q_i(i=1,2,3,4)$ are defined as the primitive model. The primitive model is regarded as $P=\{p_1, p_2, p_3, p_4\}$. $p_i(i=1,2,3,4)$ is set to 0, 1, 2. Where 0 means the absolute value of q_i is not less than the threshold a. 2 means the absolute value of q_i is less than the threshold b. 1 means the absolute value of q_i is between a and b.

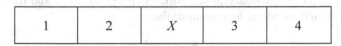

1	2	X	3	4

Fig. 3. The structure of the primitives

3.1.2   Eigenvector of Image

In order to count the frequency of each mode in the window, the number of each primitive mode is established. The number is defined as $n=\sum_i p_i\times 3^{i-1}(i=1,2,3,4)$. The total of possible modes in the image is 3^4, because p_i is three possible values for 0, 1, 2 in the primitive model. The frequency of all modes in the window forms a vector. It is a eigenvector $V=\{F(P(n))\}$, $n=0,1,2,....3^4-1$, where $P(n)$ is a mode of n, $F(P(n))$is the frequency of $P(n)$. To ensure feature vector the same length, the frequency mode did not appear in the image is represented by 0.

3.2   Extraction Process

The value of $P=\{0,0,0,0\}$ represents the gray level difference of the center pixel of the primitive and the other pixels is the maximum. This mode appears in the image edge. It named as boundary mode. The value of $P=\{2,2,2,2\}$ represents the gray level difference of the center pixel of the primitive and the other pixels is the minimum. This mode appears in the image edge. It named as non-boundary mode. Given an image, the frequency of the boundary mode is high, and the frequency of the non-boundary mode is low. It is represented by quotient of two modes. So we obtains the maximum value of quotient of the line. The center where the value of the window locates is the intestinal loop boundary points of the line.

In consideration, using the quotient of two mode ({0000},{2222})frequency to determine boundary is unitary. It cannot fully represent the boundaries. Several modes of the boundary and the non-boundary are also added. That is {2221} {2212} {2122} {1222} are represent the boundary and {0001} {0010} {0100} {1000} are represent the non-boundary. We calculate the sum of the frequency of all the modes S_{BF}, S_{NBF} in the boundary range and the non-boundary rang. At last, we use the size of the quotient D to determine the boundary of a certain direction.

3.3   Extraction Step

As shown in Figure 4 of the normalized calculation window within a window of a certain size on the image characteristic values to determine the intestinal loop boundary position. The steps are as follows:

Step 1. Based on primitive is defined, calculate eigenvector of different scales within the window, and the quotient D.

Step 2. Slide window in the row direction as shown. Calculated value of D of each window to obtain the maximum value of D of the line. The center where the value of the window locates is the intestinal loop boundary points of the line.

Step 3. The window is moved downward one pixel, repeating steps (2), until you find the boundary points of all the lines.

Step 4. Connect all boundary points which step (3) obtain in and this is the outer boundary of the iris intestinal loop contour line.

Fig. 4. Illustration of Searching Process

4   Experiments Results and Discussion

Ours iris image capture device uses a handheld iris instrument. This equipment can collect 24-bit color image. Image size is 800×600. In our paper, we randomly select 300 samples (150 people, everyone has 2 samples). The iris images were taken from student volunteers at the Shenyang University of Technology. We named database 1. There are 220 samples taken from the Central Hospital Affiliated to Shenyang Medical College. We named database 2.

4.1   Extraction Based on Primitive's Pattern Statistics

4.1.1   Threshold Selection

We make a threshold selection experiment in our database. When we select the threshold a is too large, the boundary mode is less. When we select the threshold b is too small, the non-boundary mode is less. The above theoretical analysis can be known. In the window, the boundary mode and the non-boundary mode should appear. That is, S_{BF}, S_{NBF} are not to 0. So, in this paper, the results show that the threshold value of a is no more than 10, and the threshold value b is no less than 3.

At last, the threshold a is 9 and the threshold value b is 4. The correct detection rate is the highest under this threshold.

4.1.2   Window Block Division

This paper represents the texture characteristics of a certain window size. According to this paper, obtain the window where the outer boundary of intestinal loop locate and center the window as the outer boundary points of the intestinal loop. So the selection of window's size will not only affect the accuracy of the trend but also affect the running speed. Without affecting the accuracy of the extraction, window's selection should meet the needs which the time of computation is short.

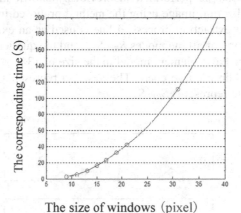

The size of windows (pixel)

Fig. 5. Relationship between the size of windows and intestinal loop extraction time

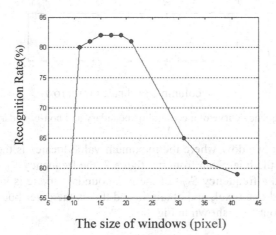

The size of windows (pixel)

Fig. 6. Relationship between the size of windows and intestinal loop extraction accuracy

The experiment is realized by Matlab2011b and its toolbox on the PC of Window7. Figure 5 shows the relations between the window's size and extraction's time of the outer boundary of intestinal loop. The above data indicates that the extraction time increases as the window size .When the window size is 31×31, extraction time was 111.301s. Figure 6 shows the relation between the window size and the outer boundary extraction rate of correct of intestinal loop. Because this paper see the center point of the window as the detected outer boundary of the intestinal loop, then when the window is too large, the center position of window has great difference with the actual position, resulting in a lower accuracy rate; When the window is small, less involved in the statistics window and then affect its efficiency. Combining these results, the paper size is selected window 13×13.

4.1.3   Extraction Results

Intestinal loop extraction is performed in previously shown in iris pre-processing method of iris normalization image using the method proposed in this paper. In order to illustrate the whole extraction process, a line is used as an example. We calculate the sum of the frequency of all the modes S_{BF}, S_{NBF} and the quotient D according to the above definition of the basic element model in the size of 13×13. Slide window in the row direction and obtain a curve chart. The abscissa represents column coordinates for a row. The ordinate represents S_{BF}, S_{NBF}, D.

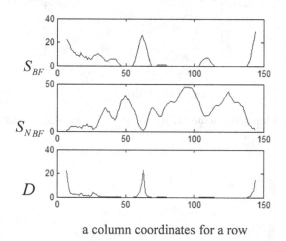

a column coordinates for a row

Fig. 7. Frequency curve of a certain line boundary and non-boundary mode

The center of the window where the maximum value locates is the intestinal loop boundary points of the line. Seen from the figure 7, the frequency S_{BF} of the boundary mode is high, and the frequency S_{NBF} of the non-boundary mode is low. The window is moved downward one pixel, and obtain in and this is the outer boundary of the iris intestinal loop contour line, shown in Fig. 8.

Fig. 8. Results of extraction

4.2   The Comparison of Results of Extraction

In order to further verify the effectiveness of the proposed algorithm, the comparison with the maximum gray gradient method is carried out. Our experiment begins with our database. The experimental results of the extraction of the outer boundary of the iris image are shown in figure 9. Fig. 9(a) is extraction results in this paper; Fig. 9(b) is extraction results the maximum gray level gradient method. The results can be seen that the gray gradient method for blur boundary extraction is not ideal, is unable to obtain the real intestinal loop position.

(a) The proposed algorithm   (b) The maximum gray level gradient method

Fig. 9. Results of intestinal loop extraction

It can be seen from Table 1 that recognition Rate is 86% by our method. The maximum gray level gradient method is lower than our method.

Table 1. Experimental data of comparison of different method

	Iris images	Correctly extraction the number of images		Recognition Rate（%）	
		Gray gradient method	The proposed method	Gray gradient method	The proposed method
Database 1	80	55	74	68.75	92.5
Database 2	220	112	184	50.9	83.6
total	300	167	258	55.67	86

5   Conclusion

This paper proposes that a feature extraction method based on texture primitive method for iris intestinal loop. In this method, the frequency of the boundary patterns and non-boundary patterns are statistically based on the texture primitives. The law of frequency variation reflects the fuzzy boundary, so the outer boundary of iris intestinal loop is extracted. Our method is compared with the maximum gray level gradient method, can more accurately extract iris intestinal loop outer boundary.

References

1. Yang, Z.H., Zhang, D., Li, N.M.: Kernel false-colour transformation and line extraction for fissured tongue image. Journal of Computer-Aided Design & Computer Graphics **22**(5), 771–776 (2010)
2. Wang, L.: Known health by iris observation: illustration of holographic iridology. Liaoning Science and Technology Publishing House, Shenyang (2010)
3. Jiang, F., Jiang, N.: Interpretation of the iris visible sub-health. China Citic Press, Beijing (2010)
4. Li, F.M.: System of ophthalmology. People's Medical Publishing House, Beijing (1996)
5. James, C., Sheelagh, C.: Iridology: Health Analysis and Treatments from the Iris of the Eye. Element Books, Incorporated (1996)
6. Xin, G., Wang, W.: Study on collarette extraction. Computer Engineering and Design **29**(9), 2290–2292 (2008)
7. Ma, L., Wang, K.Q., Han, Y.X., et al.: Study on computational system of diagnosis. In: Proceedings of the Seventh Conference on Four Diagnostic Methods Based on Integrative of Chinese and Modern Medicine. Chinese Association of Integrative Medicine, Beijing, pp.121–124 (2004)
8. Yu, L., Wang, K.Q., Li, N.M., et al.: Texture feature extraction for iris diagnosis. In: Proceedings of Computer Application and Study in Diagnosis. Chinese Association of Integrative Medicine, Beijing, pp.110–114 (2005)
9. Yu, L., Wang, K.Q., David, Z.: Extracting the autonomic nerve wreath of iris based on an improved snake approach. Neurocomputing **70**(4–6), 743–748 (2007)
10. Yuan, W.Q., Zhang, K.Y., Yang, R.R., et al.: Iris recognition algorithm based on extracting stable feature points of sequence images. Chinese Journal of Scientific Instrument **32**(5), 1069–1076 (2011)

Texture Enhancement of Iris Images Acquired under Natural Light

Boyan Hou, Yuqing He$^{(\boxtimes)}$, Mengmeng Liang, and Xue Wang

Key Laboratory of Photoelectronic Imaging Technology and System, Ministry of Education of China, School of Optoelectronics, Beijing Institute of Technology, Beijing 100081, China
yuqinghe@bit.edu.cn

Abstract. The iris image acquired under natural light may be degraded by non-uniform illumination, which results in the iris texture's low resolution and low contrast. The recognition accuracy may be affected. This paper describes a method for enhancing the iris textures on the V channel of HSV space. The enhancement has two steps. First, the image is divided into small blocks and luminance enhancement is carried out in each block by using nonlinear transfer function and bilinear interpolation. Secondly, contrast enhancement by multi-scale Gaussian convolution is applied to improve the quality of the image. We test the proposed method on UBIRIS.v2 database. Experimental results show that the proposed method has better texture enhancement performance and can achieve higher recognition accuracy.

Keywords: Iris recognition · Natural light · Luminance enhancement · Contrast enhancement · Nonlinear transfer function · Gaussian convolution

1 Introduction

Among the biometrics traits, iris recognition achieves particularly high recognition accuracy. Most near-infrared illumination iris recognition systems may have heavy imaging constraints to get good quality images. These may bring inconvenience to users or limit the working distance. Recently, with the high resolution and high performance of mobile imaging device or ordinary cameras, the iris image captured under natural light or visible wavelength may be used for recognition. Natural light iris verification has drawn substantial attention due to the feasibility, convenience and acceptable performance. The iris image acquired under natural light may be degraded by some factors such as the light reflection from the eye's surface, non-uniform illumination, which results in the iris texture's low resolution and low contrast. Texture enhancement can increase the availability of distinctive features needed for proper recognition and promote the recognition accuracy.

Some enhancement techniques such as histogram equalization and contrast stretching have been used in grey level iris images acquired under near-infrared illumination [1]. For color iris images acquired under natural light, methods should be different with above. R. Szewczyk et al.[2] used histogram equalization procedure to

© Springer International Publishing Switzerland 2015
J. Yang et al. (Eds.): CCBR 2015, LNCS 9428, pp. 373–380, 2015.
DOI: 10.1007/978-3-319-25417-3_44

reduce the influence of illumination in R and G channel. Gil Santos et al.[3] and Ning Wang et al.[4] converted the RGB iris image to gray level and enhanced it by histogram equalization. Aditya Nigam et al.[5] used the contrast-limited adaptive histogram equalization to enhance the micro texture in the grey level of the image. Kwang Yong Shin et al.[6] and Chun-Wei Tan et al.[7] presented the Retinex algorithm to eliminate the illumination variation and perform the luminance enhancement and contrast enhancement. T. Tan et al.[8,9] adopted super-resolution of iris image sequences or multiple cues to get higher recognition result.

Most of the image enhancement methods discussed above treat the input image globally by considering the global illumination. These methods may not achieve the best results since they didn't consider the local information. In this paper, we propose a method for enhancing the iris textures on the value (V) channel of HSV space. We divide the image into blocks and utilize nonlinear transfer function and bilinear interpolation for luminance enhancement. Then multi-scale Gaussian convolution is used for the contrast enhancement.

The rest of paper is organized as follows. In Section 2, we introduce the proposed method for iris enhancement. In Section 3, different enhancement methods are compared and the experimental results are described. Finally, some conclusions are drawn in Section 4.

2   Iris Texture Enhancement Method

The illumination over the whole image is not uniform, some regions may be dark and some may be bright. So the image's local information should be considered. Here we mainly do the process in the V channel of HSV space image. The image is divided into small blocks. Nonlinear transfer function is applied for each block to enhance the luminance. Then we also consider the local image and use multi-scale Gaussian convolution to realize the contrast enhancement. Fig.1 shows the block diagram of the proposed method.

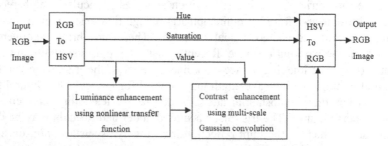

Fig. 1. Block diagram of the iris texture enhancement method

2.1   Luminance Enhancement

The luminance enhancement, also known as dynamic range compression, is applied to the V channel of the input image using specially designed nonlinear transfer function

[10]. Suppose that $V_1(x,y)$ denote the normalized V channel in HSV space and $V_2(x,y)$ be the transferred value by applying nonlinear transfer function defined below.

$$V_2 = \frac{V_1^{(0.75z+0.25)} + 0.4(1-z)(1-V_1) + V_1^{(2-z)}}{2} \qquad (1)$$

where z is the image dependent parameter and is define as follows.

$$z = \begin{cases} 0, & L \le 50 \\ \dfrac{L-50}{100}, & 50 < L \le 150 \\ 1, & L > 150 \end{cases} \qquad (2)$$

where L is the value level of V corresponding to probability distribution on cumulative distribution function of 0.1 [11].

In Equation (1) the parameter z defines the shape of the transfer function or the amount of luminance enhancement for each pixel value. In most images the illumination in all regions are not uniform. So estimating the parameter z globally for transfer function can't preserve the image details.

To solve this problem we divide the V component image into equal sized small blocks and find the parameter z for each block. Again, to solve the problem of blocking artifacts and region transition we further subdivide the blocks into sub blocks and find the parameter z for each sub block by interpolating the previously calculated z for each block. Bilinear interpolation is used for interpolating the parameter z from blocks to sub blocks. We assume the parameter z as the center coordinate parameter value of the corresponding block. The four values of parameter z from neighboring blocks are taken and then interpolated for all the sub blocks inside the centre coordinate position of the neighboring blocks. Now the shape of transfer function for each sub block is different depending upon the value of parameter z of that sub block.

2.2   Contrast Enhancement

In order to improve the quality of the whole image, contrast enhancement is also applied after the luminance enhancement. In this process, the multi-scale Gaussian convolution using Gaussian function $G(x, y)$ is carried out. The convolution can be expressed as:

$$V_3(x,y) = \sum_{m=0}^{M-1} \sum_{n=0}^{N-1} V_1(m,n) G(m+x, n+y) \qquad (3)$$

The convolution result V_3 contains the luminance information from the surrounding pixels. The amount of contrast enhancement of the centre pixel is now determined by comparing centre pixel value with the Gaussian convolution result. This process is described in the following equation:

$$V_4(x,y) = 255 V_2(x,y)^{E(x,y)} \qquad (4)$$

where

$$E(x,y) = \left[\frac{V_3(x,y)}{V_1(x,y)}\right]^g \tag{5}$$

where g is the parameter determined from the original V component image for tuning the contrast enhancement process. This parameter g is determined using following equation:

$$g = \begin{cases} 1.75, & \sigma \le 2 \\ \dfrac{27-2\sigma}{13}, & 2 < \sigma < 10 \\ 0.5, & \sigma \ge 10 \end{cases} \tag{6}$$

where σ denotes the standard deviation of the individual block of the original value component image.

In the original implementation of this contrast enhancement [10], the standard deviation is determined globally. The relationship between σ and g defined by Equation (6) is linear. Here again due to different illumination in different region of the input image, the same value of g for contrast enhancing each pixel of the input image is not appropriate. The image details may be distorted in some cases. To solve this problem, we apply the same procedure as described above by dividing the image into smaller block. Then we find the parameter g for each block of the image independently and perform the contrast enhancement procedure.

For the better performance multi-scale convolution is carried out. If we take the small scale Gaussian function for convolution with input image, nearest neighbor pixel luminance information is considered. On the other hand, if we take the Gaussian function with large scale, whole luminance information is considered. The convolved images into multiple scales are collected and we calculate the average image as the final multi-scale result.

3   Experiments and Performance Evaluation

To evaluate the performance of the proposed iris image enhancement procedure, we test the iris images in UBIRIS.v2 database [12]. We select 200 degraded iris images to the test database which consists of 40 person and 5 samples for each. We enhance the images in V channel and restore them back to RGB.

3.1   Block Size and Gaussian Parameter Selection

The output image will lose some texture information and obvious edge may occur if the block is big. Fig.2 shows the enhancement results with different size of block. We can see that with the size of block getting bigger, the edge of the block is more clear. In order to preserve the details we divide the image into blocks with size 4×4. Then we find the value of parameter z used in luminance enhancement procedure, and the value of parameter g used in contrast enhancement procedure. Each block is further divided into 2×2 pixel size sub block and parameter z and g are interpolated for those sub blocks. The interpolation procedure removes the problem of blocking artifacts and region transition as well as saves the computation time for finding parameter for each sub blocks individually.

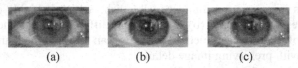

(a)   (b)   (c)

Fig. 2. Enhancement images with different size of block. (a) block size 20×20 and sub block size 10×10 (b) block size 10×10 and sub block size 5×5 (c) block size 4×4 and sub block size 2×2

For the better performance multi-scale convolution is carried out. The parameters of the Gaussian function include Gaussian random matrix M and standard deviation σ_1. Here, we use 200×200 as the matrix size and 6 scale of the $\sigma1$ from 10 to 60 with interval of 10. The multiple scales convolved images are collected and final average image is calculated. In the following process, we enhance the images in V channel and restore them back to RGB. Fig.2 shows the results of gray level image of the output RGB images using different Gaussian parameters and multi-scale convolution.

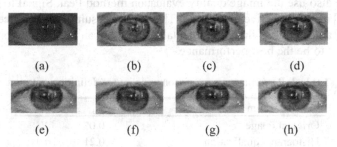

(a)   (b)   (c)   (d)

(e)   (f)   (g)   (h)

Fig. 3. Enhanced images with different parameters. (a) original image (b)~(g) σ_1=10~60 with interval of 10 (h) result of multi-scale convolution

To determine the quality of enhanced images with different σ_1, and image convolved by multi-scale Gaussian function, we use modified Banner operator as the quality evaluation. The operator is often used for image definition criterion. Lager value indicates better image quality. For an image $f(x, y)$, which is $M \times N$ piexls, the modified Banner operator can be described as[13]:

$$F_{\text{Banner}} = \sum_M \sum_N |f(x+1, y) - f(x, y)| - \sum_M \sum_N |f(x+2, y) - f(x, y)| \quad (7)$$

Table 1 shows the image quality results enhanced by different parameter of Gaussian function. From Fig. 2 and Table 1 we can see the multi-scale Gaussian convolution has the highest performance.

Table 1. Performance comparison of different Gaussian parameters

σ_1	10	20	30	40	50	60	multi-scale
F_{Banner}	0.07	0.10	0.16	0.19	0.23	0.27	0.31

3.2   Image Quality Evaluation

We compare the performance of the proposed method with Histogram equalization [3], Histogram equalization with RG components [2] and Retinex [6]. Fig.3 (a) shows an original iris image captured under visible light, which is highly degraded and the textural features are not clear. (b)-(e) shows the different enhancement results. In the output image of the proposed method in (e), we can see both local and global contrast increase well with preserving image details.

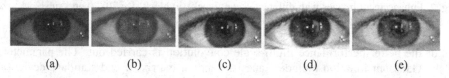

(a)   (b)   (c)   (d)   (e)

Fig. 4. Result of image enhancement with different methods. (a) original iris image, (b) Retinex enhancement, (c) histogram equalization, (d) histogram equalization with RG components, (e) proposed method

Modified Banner operator can also be used to evaluate the output image quantificationally. We also use the image quality evaluation method Peak Signal to Noise Ratio (PSNR) [14] as the objective evaluation. The average result of all enhanced images is calculated. Table 2 shows the experimental result. We can see that the proposed method turns out to be the best performance.

Table 2. Performance comparison using image definition criterion

algorithm	F_{Banner}	PSNR
Original image	0.07	/
Histogram equalization	0.21	10.3
Histogram equalization (RG)	0.24	12.5
Retinex	0.15	9.6
Proposed method	0.35	14.1

3.3   Recognition Result Evaluation

We also do the recognition to evaluate the enhancement result. First, we enhance the images using the proposed method. Then the iris images are located and normalized. Finally, we use 2D-Gabor [15] filters to extract features in gray level of output RGB images, and use Hamming distance for recognition. We draw the ROC curve which illustrates the verification performance of all the mentioned schemes and the proposed scheme for enhancement of degraded iris images respectively. Fig.5 presents the recognition results of different enhancement algorithms, The EER for original image is 6.2%, for the proposed method is 2.9%. The proposed method turns out to be the best performance.

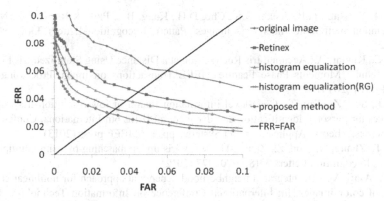

Fig. 5. Verification performance for enhanced iris images

4   Conclusion

In this paper, a strategy for image enhancement using degraded iris images acquired under visible lighting is presented. The method provides a process which combines nonlinear transfer function and bilinear interpolation for luminance enhancement and multi-scale Gaussian convolution for contrast enhancement.

We compared our method with other algorithms both in image definition evaluation and recognition. Experimental results show that our method has better texture enhancement performance and can achieve higher recognition accuracy. Future work should use more images acquired from different sensors under the natural light.

Acknowledgments. This work is supported by National Science Foundation of China (No.60905012, 60572058) and International Fund of Beijing Institute of Technology.

References

1. Lttadi, A., Jain, M.: Iris Recognition Algorithm Using Effective Localized Fuzzy Features. International Journal of Advanced Research in Computer Science **4**(5), 1681–1697 (2013)
2. Szewczyk, R., Grabowski, K., Napieralska, M., Sankowski, W., Zubert, M., Napieralski, A.: A reliable iris recognition algorithm based on reverse biorthogonal wavelet transform. Pattern Recognition Letters **33**(8), 1019–1026 (2012)
3. Santos, G., Hoyle, E.: A fusion approach to unconstrained iris recognition. Pattern Recognition Letters **33**(8), 984–990 (2012)
4. Wang, N., Li, Q., El-Latif, A., Yan, X., Niu, X.: A novel hybrid multibiometrics based on the fusion of dual iris, visible and thermal face images. In: International Symposium on Biometrics and Security Technologies, pp. 217–223. IEEE press (2013)
5. Nigam, A., Krishna, V., Bendale, A., Gupta, P.: Iris recognition using block local binary patterns and relational measures. In: International Joint Conference on Biometrics, pp. 1–6. IEEE press (2014)

6. Shin, K.Y., Nam, G.P., Jeong, D.S., Cho, D.H., Kang, B.J., Park, K.R., Kim, J.: New iris recognition method for noisy iris images. Pattern Recognition Letters **33**(8), 991–999 (2012)
7. Tan, C., Kumar, A.: Accurate Iris Recognition at a Distance Using Stabilized Iris Encoding and Zernike Moments Phase Features. IEEE Transactions on Image Processing **23**(9), 3962–3974 (2014)
8. Liu, J., Sun, Z., Tan, T.: Code-level information fusion of low-resolution iris image sequences for personal identification at a distance. In: IEEE 6th International Conference on Biometrics: Theory, Applications and Systems, pp. 1–6. IEEE press (2013)
9. Tan, T., Zhang, X., Sun, Z., Zhang, H.: Noisy iris image matching by using multiple cues. Pattern Recognition Letters **33**(8), 970–977 (2012)
10. Li, T., Asari, V.: An integrated neighborhood dependent approach for nonlinear enhancement of color images. In: International Conference on Information Technology: Coding and Computing, vol. 2, pp. 138–139. IEEE press (2004)
11. Ghimire, D., Lee, J.: Color image enhancement in HSV space using nonlinear transfer function and neighborhood dependent approach with preserving details. In: 4th Pacific-Rim Symposium on Image and Video Technology, pp. 422–426. IEEE press (2010)
12. Proenca, H., Filipe, S., Santos, R., Oliveira, J., Alexandre, L.A.: The UBIRIS.v2: A Database of Visible Wavelength Iris Images Captured On-the-Move and At-a-Distance. Pattern Analysis and Machine Intelligence, IEEE Transactions on Biometrics Compendium **32**(8), 1529–1535 (2010)
13. Wang, J., Chen, H.: An Improved Brenner Algorithm for Image Definition Criterion. Acta Photonica Sinica **41**(7), 855–858 (2012)
14. Ren, H., He, Y., Wang, S., Gan, C., Wang, J.: Defocused iris image restoration based on spectral curve fitting. In: Sun, Z., Shan, S., Yang, G., Zhou, J., Wang, Y., Yin, Y. (eds.) CCBR 2013. LNCS, vol. 8232, pp. 338–344. Springer, Heidelberg (2013)
15. Wang, Q., Zhang, X., Li, M., Dong, X., Zhou, Q., Yin, Y.: Adaboost and multi-orientation 2D Gabor-based noisy iris recognition. Pattern Recognition Letters **33**(8), 978–983 (2012)

Behavioral Biometrics

Facial Expression Recognition Based on Multiple Base Shapes

Lijun Cai[✉], Lei Huang, and Changping Liu

Institute of Automation Chinese Academy of Sciences, Beijing, China
cailijun2013@ia.ac.cn

Abstract. Geometric variation is one of the important components deteriorating the facial expression recognition performance. Aligning the face image to a base shape is a commonly used preprocess step to alleviate the variation. However, the assumption of single base shape can not necessarily guarantee the best performance. In this paper, we propose for the first time a facial expression recognition framework based on multiple base shapes, which aims to minimize the geometric variation between face images with the same facial expression and retain the geometric shape difference between face images with different facial expressions. For a new sample, a weighed vote based criterion is used to give the final predicted facial expression given multiple base shapes. Experimental results on CK+ (Extended Cohn-Kanade) and JAFFE (Japanese Female Facial Expression databases) show the effectiveness of proposed method.

Keywords: Facial expression recognition · Multiple base shapes · Hybrid feature · Weighted vote

1 Introduction

Facial expression is an effective way to express human emotion states, such as anger, sadness and happiness, therefore perceiving facial expression can be helpful to human interaction. With the development of artificial intelligence, researchers pay more and more attention on automatic facial expression recognition which plays an important role in human-machine interaction.

For two face images having the same facial expression, the differences include varying identities, gestures, illuminations, geometric variation and noise which is randomly distributed in face images. Geometric variation indicates that for a specific expression, face component displacements are not the same for different people, even for the same person at different time. Identity, geometric variation, gesture and illumination are four components deteriorating the facial expression recognition performance. Normally, noise is of small energy. In this paper, we focus on the geometric variation.

Face alignment is widely used to alleviate the geometric variation. Face alignment has been one of the most hot issues for many years and there are a lot of effective methods achieved so far [17]. When it comes to facial expression recognition, a common way for face alignment is to normalize images to a canonical

© Springer International Publishing Switzerland 2015
J. Yang et al. (Eds.): CCBR 2015, LNCS 9428, pp. 383–392, 2015.
DOI: 10.1007/978-3-319-25417-3_45

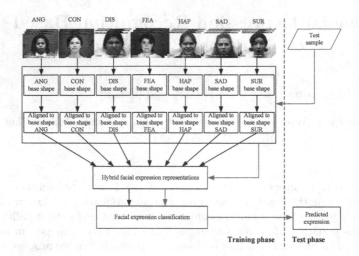

Fig. 1. The flowchart of our proposed method. ANG, CON, DIS, FEA, HAP, SAD and SUR are the acronym of Anger, Contempt, Disgust, Fear, Happiness, Sad and Surprise expressions.

template by an affine transformation. Particularly, face images are normalized by keeping the distances between two eye centers the same for all images [3–5,13,16]; face images are aligned to the mean shape of all facial expressions [7,8,14] or a fixed expression geometric shape with larger size in mouth/eyes regions [9].

To the best of my knowledge, all the current facial expression recognition methods simply adopt one base shape to be the canonical template, such as the mean shape of all facial expressions or a fixed expression geometric shape. However, from another perspective, decreasing the geometric variation between face images with different facial expressions can reduce the separability. In this paper, we propose a novel facial expression recognition method based on multiple base shapes aiming to decrease the geometric variation between face images having the same facial expression and retain the geometric variation between face images having different facial expressions. The generalized framework of proposed method is illustrated in Fig. 1 (take CK+ (Extended Cohn-Kanade) database [8] for example). It can be observed from the flowchart that each of multiple base shapes is generated based on samples with the same expression. In training phase, after aligned to its corresponding base shape, face image is described by the hybrid feature combining geometric and appearance feature. Then classifier is obtained based on SVM (Support Vector Machine) [18]. For a new sample, how to classify it into one category of expression given multiple base shapes? We will give a feasible solution to this question in the next section. Our contribution in this paper is to propose for the first time an assumption of one expression one base shape for facial expression recognition.

2 Generalized Framework of Facial Expression Recognition Based on Multiple Base Shapes

2.1 AAM Derived Representations

Representations derived from AAM (Active appearance model) [10] used in [7] will be adopted in this paper. Here, we briefly explain these representations as follows.

- Shape s: the shape s of AAM is described by a 2D triangulated mesh. In particular, the coordinates of the mesh vertices define the shape s (see Fig. 2(a)), which correspond to a source appearance image (see Fig. 2(d)).
- Base shape s_0: shape s can be described as a base shape s_0 plus a linear combination of finite shapes. Procrustes alignment [10] is used to estimate the base shape s_0 (see Fig. 2(c)).
- Rigid normalized shape s_n: s_n gives the vertex locations after all rigid geometric variation (translation, scale, rotation), relative to the base shape s_0, has been removed (see Fig. 2(b)).
- Rigid normalized appearance a_n: it represents the appearance after all rigid geometric variation removed (see Fig. 2(e)) and is obtained by affine warping pixels of the source appearance image into s_n.
- Non-rigid normalized appearance a_0: we can obtained a_0 by affine warping pixels of the source appearance image into s_0 (see Fig. 2(f)).

Different from [7] using a single base shape s_0, we propose a method based on multiple base shapes, each of which is generated by the Procrustes alignment from the shapes belong to the same expression (see Fig. 1). To emphasize the different expressions, in this paper, we use s_i^c, $s_{i,n}^c$, $a_{i,n}^c$, $a_{i,0}^c$, $c = 1, \cdots, C$, to indicate above mentioned AAM derived representations of sample i belonging to expression c, and s_0^c to indicate the base shape of expression c, where C is the total number of expressions.

2.2 Hybrid Feature

In this paper, hybrid feature concatenating normalized geometric and appearance feature is adopted to represent the facial expressions.

For the geometric feature, based on the assumption that a data can be locally approximated by linear Euclidean subspace, Roweis et al. [11] present to describe each data point by coefficients that linearly reconstruct the data point from its neighbors, and they gave an algorithm to solve these linear coefficients. For an face image i with rigid normalized shape $s_{i,n}$ and the set of its neighbors N^K (K-nearest neighbors), the reconstruction error on the cth expression space is calculated by

$$e_i^c = \min_{w_{i,j}^c} ||s_{i,n} - \sum_{s_{j,n}^c \in N^K} w_{i,j}^c s_{j,n}^c||^2 \tag{1}$$

It is commonly used that image i is classified as class $\hat{c}$ if $\hat{c} = \min_c e_i^c$ [3,4]. Therefore, we believe that $w_i^c = [w_{i,1}^{\hat{c}}, \cdots, w_{i,K}^{\hat{c}}]^T$ satisfying equation (1) can

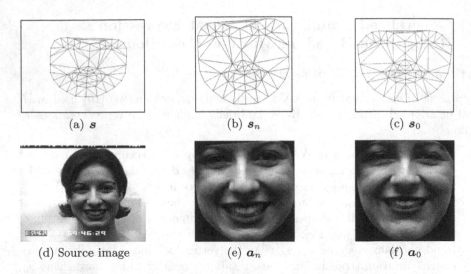

(a) s (b) s_n (c) s_0

(d) Source image   (e) a_n (f) a_0

Fig. 2. AAM derived representations. (a)Face shape s; (b)Rigid normalized shape s_n; (c)Base shape s_0; (d)Source image; (e) Rigid normalized appearance a_n; (f) Non-rigid normalized appearance a_0.

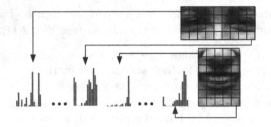

Fig. 3. Appearance feature.

be taken as the geometric feature to describe the shape information of samples belonging to expression $\hat{c}$.

For the appearance feature, according to the experimental results in [7], poor performance was gained by using rigid normalized appearance, thus only non-rigid normalized appearance is used in this paper. Considering that the micro-texture information of eye, nose and mouth regions plays an important role in facial expression recognition [9], patch-based local binary pattern histograms are extracted and concatenated to a long feature to form the appearance feature (see Fig. 3). As we know that LBP (Local Binary Pattern) [5] is an effective texture descriptor, to improve the generalization of training model, we use an improved version of LBP, DH-LBP (Dual Histogram Local Binary Pattern) [19], which has lower feature dimensions and remains the discriminative ability of LBP. In this paper, there are $36 + 35 = 71$ subresions and each subregion has 16-dimensional DH-LBP feature, totally $71 \times 16 = 1136$ dimensions.

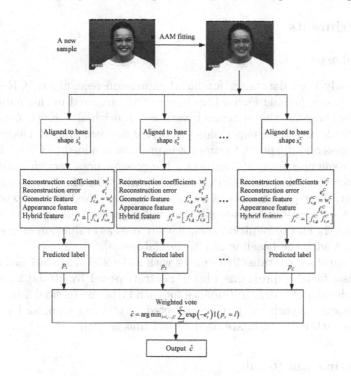

Fig. 4. Test phase of proposed method.

2.3 Classification Based on Multiple Base Shapes

Given multiple base shapes, we propose a weighted vote based criterion to fulfill the classification of a new sample. The flowchart is illustrated in Fig. 4.

For a new sample, its shape s_t is firstly obtained by AAM fitting. Given the multiple base shape $\{s_0^c\}_{c=1}^C$ obtained in the training phase, s_t is aligned to each of them. Then multiple groups of reconstruction coefficients $\{w_t^c\}_{c=1}^C$, reconstruction error $\{e_t^c\}_{c=1}^C$, geometric feature $\{f_{t,g}^c\}_{c=1}^C$, appearance feature $\{f_{t,a}^c\}_{c=1}^C$ and hybrid feature $\{f_t^c\}_{c=1}^C$ are obtained. For each group of hybrid features, a predicted label p_c is obtained by support vector machine with Radius basic function kernel. Then the following weighted vote based criterion determines the finally predicted class.

$$\hat{c} = \text{argmax}_{l=1,\cdots,C} \sum_{c=1}^C \exp(-e_t^c) * I\{p_c = l\} \tag{2}$$

where $\exp(-e_t^c)$ is the weight, the smaller the reconstruction error is, the bigger the weight. $I(p_c = l)$ is 1 if $p_c = l$, else is 0. Equation (2) allows each base shape contributes a weighted vote to a specific class $l, l = 1, \cdots, C$, and the new sample is assigned to the class with the most weighted vote.

3   Experiments

3.1   Databases

Two commonly used databases for facial expression recognition, CK+ [8] and JAFFE (Japanese Female Facial Expression) [20], are used in this paper.

CK+ database is the extended version of original CK (Cohn-Kanade) database. Aside from six expressions in CK database: Anger, Disgust, Fear, Happy, Sadness and Surprise, Contempt expression is added to CK+. There are totally 593 sequences from 123 subjects. Image sequences vary in duration and each sequence starts from the neutral face to peak frame of a specific expression. In this paper, three peak frames of every sequence are used for our experiments, and leave-one-subject-out cross-validation configuration is adopted. what's more, confusion matrix and recognition accuracy are uses as evaluation metrics, which are consistent with the baseline of CK+ database [8].

JAFFE database contains 213 images with 256×256 pixels of 7 facial expressions (6 basic facial expressions plus 1 neutral) posed by 10 Japanese female models. Each subject has 3 or 4 images for each facial expression. 2 images from each expression for each subject are selected in training step, and the rest of images from each expression are used as test images [21].

3.2   Experimental Results

Experimental section consists of three parts: 1) the sensibility of proposed method to the choose of nearest neighbors size K in equation (1). 2) Comparison with facial expression recognition based on single base shape. 3) Comparison with the state-of-the-arts.

Firstly, we will demonstrate the sensibility of proposed method to the nearest neighbors size K. The range of K is determined by the least number of samples for each expression. For CK+, $K \in [1, 54]$ and for JAFFE, $K \in [1, 29]$. Experimental

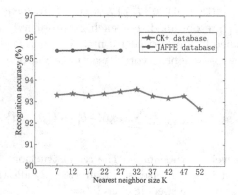

Fig. 5. Sensibility of proposed method to the choice of nearest neighbors size K.

results on two databases with step 5 are shown in Fig. 5. It can be seen that proposed method is not sensible to the size K over a range of values. The result is not surprising because the idea of reconstruction coefficients and errors comes from [11], in which the authors have obtained the similar conclusion. In this paper, considering both the recognition accuracy and computation complexity, $K = 12$ is adopted in the following experiments.

Table 1 and Table 2 illustrate the confusion matrix on two databases. It can be observed that proposed method achieves good performance on both two public facial expression databases. However, recognition of Sadness expression in CK+ database is still difficult because of the database characteristics.

Table 1. Confusion matrix of proposed method on CK+ database(%).

	ANG	DIS	FEA	HAP	SAD	SUR	CON
ANG	**94.07**	2.96	0	0	0	0.74	0.22
DIS	2.96	**96.05**	0	0	0	1.09	0
FEA	5.33	0	**81.34**	5.33	4	2.67	1.33
HAP	0	0.96	0	**99.03**	0	0	0
SAD	10.71	5.95	0	0	**78.57**	1.19	3.57
SUR	0	0	0	0	0	**98.90**	1.20
CON	5.56	0	0	0	0	0	**94.44**

Average **93.37**

Table 2. Confusion matrix of proposed method on JAFFE database(%).

	ANG	DIS	FEA	HAP	SAD	SUR
ANG	**100**	0	0	0	0	0
DIS	0	**100**	0	0	0	0
FEA	0	0	**91.67**	0	0	8.33
HAP	0	0	0	**90.91**	0	9.09
SAD	0	0	0	9.09	**90.91**	0
SUR	0	0	0	0	0	**100**

Average **95.38**

Secondly, comparison between proposed method based on multiple base shapes and method based on single base shape is performed. Single base shape based method has only one base shape (mean shape) which is acquired according to the Procrustes alignment based on all training samples. Given the same facial expression representation and classifier training, recognition accuracies on two databases are shown in Table 3. It can be observed that proposed method based on multiple base shapes achieves better performance than the method based on single base shape. Therefore, retaining the geometric shape difference between face images with different facial expressions is helpful to facial expression recognition.

Table 3. Compared recognition accuracies of method based on single base shape and proposed method based on multiple base shapes(%).

Method	CK+	JAFFE
Single base shape	90.32	93.33
Proposed method	**93.37**	**95.38**

Table 4. Compared accuracy with State-of-the-Arts.

Methods	Class number	Accuracy(%)	Cross validation
Proposed method	7	**93.37**	leave-one-subject-out
Proposed method	6	**94.31**	leave-one-subject-out
Proposed method	7	**96.22**	10-fold
Proposed method	6	**96.33**	10-fold
Proposed method	7	**95.82**	5-fold
Proposed method	6	**96.01**	5-fold
Lucey[8]	7	88.33	leave-one-subject-out
Islam[12]	7	90.10	10-fold
Ptucha[13]	7	91.40	leave-one-subject-out
Shan[5]	7	88.9	10-fold
Shan[5]	6	92.6	10-fold
Sadeghi[9]	6	94.48	10-fold
Sadeghi[9]	6	94.16	5-fold
Jain[14]	6	95.79	4-fold
Khan[15]	6	95.3	10-fold

Table 5. Compared accuracy with State-of-the-Arts on JAFFE database.

Methods	Class number	Accuracy(%)
Proposed method	6	**95.38**
Sadeghi[21]	6	91.23

Lastly, compared results with the state-of-the-arts on two databases are given in Table 4 and Table 5. For CK+ databse, to compare with existing methods, proposed method is performed using different class numbers and cross validations. Class number is 6 means that all expressions except Contempt are involved into the experiment. It is demonstrated in Table 4 and 5 that compared with existing popular methods, proposed method obtains a comparable performance given the same class number and cross validation. All the experimental results illustrated above shows that our proposed method based on multiple base shapes are effective.

4   Conclusion

In this paper, we propose a novel facial expression recognition method based on multiple base shapes. Compared with most existing methods utilizing single base shape, this method performs face shape alignment on the assumption of one facial expression one base shape. In the training phase, each of multiple base shapes is generated based on the shapes with the same facial expression, which can minimize the geometric variation between intra-expression face images and retain the geometric shape difference between extra-expression face images. In the test phase, a new sample are firstly aligned to all the base shapes respectively and then weighted vote based criterion is used to determine the final predicted facial expression. Experimental results on CK+ and JAFFE databases show the effectiveness of proposed multiple base shape based method. However, this method is not limited to facial expression recognition and will be applied to other face attributes recognition in our next work, for example the age estimation.

References

1. Kotsia, I., Pitas, I.: Facial expression recognition in image sequences using geometric deformation features and support vector machines. IEEE Trans. Image Proc. **16**, 172–187 (2007)
2. Pai, N.S., Chang, S.P.: An embedded system for real-time facial expression recognition based on the extension theory. Comput. Math. Appl. **61**, 2101–2106 (2011)
3. Xiao, R., Zhao, Q.J., Zhang, D., Shi, P.F.: Facial expression recognition on multiple manifolds. Pattern Recog. **44**, 107–116 (2011)
4. Zafeiriou, S., Petrou, M.: Sparse representations for facial expressions recognition via l1 optimization. In: IEEE Computer Society Conference on Computer Vision and Pattern Recognition Workshops, pp. 32–39. IEEE Press, San Francisco (2010)
5. Shan, C.F., Gong, S.G., McOwan, P.W.: Facial expression recognition based on local binary patterns: A comprehensive study. Image Vision Computing **27**, 803–816 (2009)
6. Buciu, I., Kotropoulos, C., Pitas, I.: ICA and Gabor representation for facial expression recognition. In: International Conference on Image Processing, pp. 855–858. IEEE Press (2003)
7. Ashraf, A.B., Lucey, S.C., Jeffrey, F., Chen, T., Ambadar, Z.P., Kenneth, M., Solomon, P.E.: The painful face-pain expression recognition using active appearance models. Image Vision Computing **27**, 1788–1796 (2009)
8. Lucey, P., Cohn, J., Kanade, T., Saragih, J., Ambadar, Z., Matthews, I.: The extended Cohn-Kanade Dataset (CK+): a complete dataset for action unit and emotion-specified expression. In: IEEE Computer Society on Computer Vision and Pattern Recognition Workshops, pp. 94–101. IEEE Press, San Fransico (2010)
9. Sadeghi, H., Raie, A.A., Mohammadi, M.R.: Facial expression recognition using geometric normalization and appearance representation. In: 8th Iranian Conference on Machine Vision and Image Processing, pp. 159–163. IEEE Press, Zanjan (2013)
10. Cootes, T., Edwards, G., Taylor, C.: Active appearance models. IEEE Trans. Pattern Anal. Machine Intell. **23**, 681–685 (2001)
11. Roweis, S.T., Saul, L.K.: Nonlinear dimensionality reduction by locally linear embedding. Science **290**, 2323–2326 (2000)

12. Islam, M.S., Auwatanamongkol, S.: A novel feature extraction technique for facial expression recognition. Int. J. Comput. Science **10**, 9–14 (2013)
13. Ptucha, R., Savakis, A.: Manifold based sparse representation for facial understanding in natural images. Image Vision Computing **31**, 365–378 (2013)
14. Jain, S., Hu, C., Aggarwal, J.: Facial expression recognition with temporal modeling of shapes. In: IEEE International Conference on Computer Vision Workshops, pp. 1642–1649. IEEE Press, Bacilona (2011)
15. Khan, R.A., Meyer, A., Konik, H., Bouakaz, S.: Human vision inspired framework for facial expressions recognition. In: International Conference on Image Processing, pp. 2593–2596. IEEE Press, Orlando (2012)
16. Jeni, L., Girard, J., Cohn, J., Fernando D.L.T.: Continuous AU intensity estimation using localized, sparse facial feature space. In: 10th IEEE International Conference on Automatic Face and Gesture Recognition, pp. 1–7. IEEE Press, Shanghai (2013)
17. Cao, X.D., Wei, Y.C., Wen, F., Sun, J.: Face alignment by explicit shape regression. Int. J. Comput. Vision **107**, 177–190 (2014)
18. Chang, C.C., Lin, C.J.: LIBSVM: a library for support vector machines. ACM Trans. Intell. Syst. Techno. **2**, 27 (2011)
19. Ma, W.H., Huang, L., Liu, C.P.: Advanced local binary pattern descriptors for crowd estimation. In: Pacific-Asia Workshop on Computational Intelligence and Induatrial Application, pp. 958–962. IEEE Press, Wuhan (2008)
20. Lyons, M., Akamatsu, S., Kamachi, M., Gyoba, J.: Coding facial expressions with Gabor wavelets. In: Third IEEE International Conference on Automatic Face and Gesture Recognition, pp. 200–205. IEEE Press, Nara (1998)
21. Sadeghi, H., Raie, A.A., Mohammadi, M.R.: Facial Expression Recognition Using Texture Description of Displacement Image. J. Inf. Syst. Telecom. **2**, 205–212 (2014)

A Novel Speech Emotion Recognition Method via Transfer PCA and Sparse Coding

Peng Song[1]($\boxtimes$), Wenming Zheng[2], Jingjing Liu[3], Jing Li[3],
and Xinran Zhang[3]

[1] School of Computer and Control Engineering, Yantai University,
Yantai 264005, China
pengsongseu@gmail.com
[2] Key Laboratory of Child Development and Learning Science of Ministry
of Education, Southeast University, Nanjing 210096, China
[3] School of Information Science and Engineering, Southeast University,
Nanjing 210096, China

Abstract. In practice, the training data and testing data are often from different datasets, which have an adverse impact on speech emotion recognition rates. To tackle this problem, in this paper, a novel transfer principal component analysis (TPCA) and sparse coding based speech emotion recognition method is proposed. The TPCA approach is first presented for feature dimension reduction, then the sparse coding algorithm is introduced to learn the robust feature representations for both labeled source and unlabeled target corpora. To evaluate the performance of our proposed method, the experiments are conducted on two public datasets. Experimental results demonstrate that our proposed approach significantly outperforms the automatic recognition method, and obtains better performance than the state-of-the-art method.

Keywords: Dimension reduction · Sparse coding · Transfer learning · Speech emotion recognition

1 Introduction

Speech emotion recognition is a hot research topic in affective computing and speech signal processing fields, and its main task is to automatically recognize emotions from speech. It can be applied in many fields [1], e.g., monitoring the driver's mood swings to avoid accidents in intelligent transportation systems, helping diagnose the patient's diseases in healthcare field, and managing the customer's moods in call centres.

Many studies have been done for speech emotion recognition during the last decades. All kinds of classification methods, popular in pattern recognition and machine learning fields, are employed for emotional label classification or prediction [1], e.g., support vector machine (SVM), hidden Markov model (HMM), Gaussian mixture model (GMM), neural network (NN) and some regression methods. Recently, the deep learning techniques, successfully applied in speech

J. Yang et al. (Eds.): CCBR 2015, LNCS 9428, pp. 393–400, 2015.
DOI: 10.1007/978-3-319-25417-3_46

recognition and image classification fields, are also introduced for speech emotion recognition [2]. All these approaches can obtain satisfactory recognition performance to some degree. However, they are carried out on single dataset. In practical situations, it is too hard to collect a large emotional speech dataset, and the training data and testing data are often from different corpora, this discrepancy will obviously influence the recognition performance.

To realize the cross-corpus speech emotion recognition, some efforts have been taken in recent years. Schuller et al. [3] conduct experiments on six different datasets, and preliminary results show that the case using more datasets for model training can improve the recognition rates. Zhang et al. [4] propose an unsupervised approach for cross-corpus speech emotion recognition. Deng et al. [5] present a domain adaptation method to reduce the discrepancy between the training and testing datasets. These methods can achieve better performance than traditional automatic recognition methods. However, they have some obvious shortcomings, e.g., most of the current methods do not take into account the different distributions of different corpora, and the difference of the different emotional datasets is always very large, which will significantly affect the recognition performance [6].

Different from the above mentioned methods, in this paper, an efficient transfer PCA and sparse coding approach is presented for cross-corpus speech emotion recognition. First, a transfer PCA approach is proposed for dimension reduction. Then, the sparse coding algorithm is introduced to obtain the robust feature representations for source and target datasets, respectively. Finally, the learned sparse features are adopted for emotion classification.

The subsequent paper is structured as follows. In Section 2 and Section 3, the transfer PCA and sparse coding methods are given, respectively. In Section 4, the experimental results and discussions are presented. Finally, the conclusions and future work are discussed in Section 5.

2   Transfer Dimension Reduction

Feature dimension reduction is an important step for many pattern classification problems. Many dimension reduction methods [7], e.g., PCA, linear discriminant analysis (LDA), locally linear embedding (LLE), locality preserving projections (LPP), have been employed for emotional feature dimension reduction. All these algorithms can obtain satisfactory results to some degree. However, in practice, the training data and testing data are often from different datasets, in which, the features follow different distributions, and will lead to a significant drop of the recognition rates. In this paper, a novel transfer PCA algorithm is presented for dimension reduction, in which the similarity of the feature distributions of different corpora is considered when the PCA algorithm is conducted.

Let $X_S = [x_1, x_2, \ldots, x_{n_l}]$ and $X_T = [x_{n_l+1}, x_{n_l+2}, \ldots, x_{n_l+n_u}]$ be the labeled source and unlabeled target features, respectively, the PCA approach is chosen for dimension reduction. Let $X = [X_S, X_T] \in R^{m \times n}$, $Y = 1 - \frac{1}{n}\mathbf{1}$ ($\mathbf{1}$ is an $n \times n$ matrix of ones, and $n = n_l + n_u$) be the centering matrix, and the covariance matrix be XYX^T, the goal of PCA is to maximize the variance of the embedded data via an orthogonal transformation matrix P as

$$\max_{P^T P=1} tr(P^T XYX^T P) \tag{1}$$

where $tr(\cdot)$ is the trace of the matrix. Furthermore, to better perform dimension reduction, the kernel PCA algorithm is further adopted. By introducing the non-linear mapping function $\phi(X)$, the eq. (1) will become as

$$\max_{V^T V=1} tr(V^T KYK^T V) \tag{2}$$

where $K = \phi(X)^T \phi(X)$ is a kernel matrix, and $V \in R^{n \times k}$ is a transformation matrix for the kernel PCA. After dimension reduction, the optimal feature representation is obtained as $V^T K$.

It should be noted that, to cross-corpus speech emotion recognition, X_S and X_T often have different distributions, which will influence the reconstruction performance of the input features. In this paper, the similarity between the distributions of X_S and X_T is considered, and the empirical maximum mean discrepancy (MMD) [8] is used for the distance measurement. In the reproducing kernel Hilbert space (RKHS) $\mathcal{H}$, the distance between source and target feature distributions is given as

$$D = \left\| \frac{1}{n_l} \sum_{i=1}^{n_l} V^T k_i - \frac{1}{n_u} \sum_{j=n_l+1}^{n} V^T k_j \right\|_{\mathcal{H}}^2$$
$$= tr(V^T KMK^T V) \tag{3}$$

where $M = [m_{i,j}]_{i,j=1}^n$ is the MMD matrix satisfying

$$m_{ij} = \begin{cases} \frac{1}{n_l^2} & \text{if } x_i, x_j \in X_S \\ \frac{1}{n_u^2} & \text{if } x_i, x_j \in X_T \\ \frac{-1}{n_l n_u} & \text{otherwise} \end{cases} \tag{4}$$

In this paper, our goal is to make dimension reduction while minimizing the distance D. By incorporating eq. (2) and eq. (3), the following optimization problem will be obtained as

$$\min_{V^T KYK^T V=I} tr(V^T KMK^T V) + \lambda \|V\|_F^2 \tag{5}$$

where $\|\cdot\|_F$ is a Frobenius norm, and λ is a regularization parameter. The above equation can be solved by the Lagrange function as

$$L = tr(V^T KMK^T V) + \lambda \|V\|_F^2 + tr(\mathbf{I} - V^T KYK^T V\alpha) \tag{6}$$

where $\alpha = [\alpha_1, \alpha_2, \ldots, \alpha_k] \in R^{k \times k}$ is a Lagrange multiplier matrix. By employing the zero gradient condition, we will obtain the following equation as

$$\frac{\partial L}{\partial V} = 2KMK^T V + 2\lambda V - 2KYK^T V\alpha = 0 \tag{7}$$

Then, the above equation can be expressed as a generalized eigen-decomposition problem

$$(KMK^T + \lambda\mathbf{I})V = KYK^TV\alpha \tag{8}$$

By computing the k smallest eigenvectors, the optimal matrix V can be easily obtained.

3   Sparse Coding for Speech Emotion Recognition

Sparse coding has been successfully applied to many pattern classification and signal processing fields [9]. Inspired by its recent progress, in this paper, we introduce the sparse coding algorithm to learn the robust feature representations of labeled source and unlabeled target datasets. Given the features after dimension reduction as $Z = [z_1, z_2, \ldots, z_n] \in R^{p \times n}$, each feature vector can be represented by a linear combination of basis vectors in the dictionary, and the objective function of the sparse coding is written as follows

$$\min_{D,S} \left\| Z - DS \right\|_F^2 + \beta \sum_{i=1}^{n} f(s_i) \tag{9}$$

$$\text{s.t. } \| d_j \|^2 \leq c, \forall j = 1, 2, \ldots, q$$

where $D = [d_1, d_2, \ldots d_q] \in R^{p \times q}$ is the dictionary, $S = [s_1, s_2, \ldots, s_n] \in R^{q \times n}$ is the coefficient matrix, c is a constant, and $f(\cdot)$ is a function for the sparsity measurement. To function $f(s_i)$, a straightforward choice is adopting L_0 norm, in which the non-zero entries of S are counted. However, it has been proved to be an NP-hard problem to compute the unknown parameters [10]. To solve this problem, a common practice is to replace the L_0 norm with L_1 norm, so the eq. (9) can be rewritten as

$$\min_{D,S} \left\| Z - DS \right\|_F^2 + \beta \sum_{i=1}^{n} \| s_i \|_1 \tag{10}$$

$$\text{s.t. } \| d_j \|^2 \leq c, \forall j = 1, 2, \ldots, q$$

To better learn the sparse representations of the data, the graph regularized sparse coding algorithm is adopted [10], in which the geometrical structure of the data is considered. Given the data points $z_1, z_2, \ldots, z_n$, the graph G can be constructed with each vertex referring to a data point. Let $W = [w_{i,j}]_{i,j=1}^{n}$ be the weight matrix, if z_i is among the N nearest neighbors of z_j, then $w_{ij} = 1$, otherwise, $w_{ij} = 0$. The degree of vertex z_i is given as $d_i = \sum_{j=1}^{n} w_{ij}$, and $D = \text{diag}(d_1, d_2, \ldots, d_n)$. A reasonable criterion to describe the geometric structure of G is to minimize

$$\frac{1}{2} \sum_{i=1}^{n} \sum_{j=1}^{n} (s_i - s_j)^2 w_{ij} = tr(SLS^T) \tag{11}$$

where $L = D - W$ is a Laplacian matrix. Integrating the eq. (11) with eq. (10), the objective function becomes

$$\min_{D,S} \left\| Z - DS \right\|_F^2 + \beta \sum_{i=1}^{n} \left\| s_i \right\|_1 + \gamma tr(SLS^T)$$

(12)

$$\text{s.t. } \left\| d_i \right\|^2 \leq c, \forall i = 1, 2, \ldots, p$$

where β and γ are the regularization parameters. By employing the feature-sign search algorithm [11], the above equation can be efficiently solved.

4   Experiments

4.1   Experimental Setup

To evaluate the performance of our proposed method, two popular corpora, i.e., Berlin dataset [12] and eNTERFACE dataset [13], are chosen. The Berlin dataset is a pubic speech emotion corpus, it consists of 377 utterances with 6 basic emotions, i.e., anger, disgust, fear, happiness, neutral and sadness. The eNTERFACE dataset is another public audio-visual emotion corpus, it has totally 1287 video samples with 6 basic emotions, i.e., anger, disgust, fear, happiness, sadness and surprise. Two types of experiments are considered, in the first case, the lableled Berlin dataset is chosen as the training corpus, and the unlabeled eNTERFACE dataset is used as the testing corpus. While in the second case, the labeled eNTERFACE dataset is chosen for training, and the unlabeled Berlin dataset is used for testing. The common emotion categories, including anger, disgust, fear, happiness and sadness, are chosen for evaluation.

The openSMILE toolkit [14] is chosen for feature extraction, and totally 1582 dimensional emotional feature set, which is the standard feature set of Interspeech 2010 Paralinguistic challenge [15], is adopted for the experiments. The popular SVM is employed for emotion classification, and the PCA algorithm is used for dimension reduction. Four kinds of recognition methods are compared, they are the automatic recognition method (PCA), in which the classifier trained in one corpus is directly applied to emotion recognition in another corpus, the TPCA based recognition method (TPCA), the transfer component analysis method (TCA) [16], our proposed TPCA and sparse coding based recognition method (TPCA-SC), and the baseline method (Baseline), in which the training and testing procedures are conducted on single corpus.

In our experiments, a 10-fold cross validation strategy is adopted to obtain the optimal values of the parameters, e.g., λ, β, γ. Meanwhile, in the experiments, each dataset is divided into 5 parts, among which random 4/5 are used for training, while the others are for testing, and the experiments are repeated 20 times to cover all the possible cases in the training corpus.

4.2   Experimental Results

The average recognition results of our proposed TPCA-SC method and the other four methods are illustrated in Table 1 and Table 2. As can be seen from the tables, the TPCA method can significantly outperform the PCA method. This can be attributed to that, compared to the PCA method, the TPCA approach makes the dimension reduction considering the distance between different feature distributions of different corpora. It can be also noticed that, combining with sparse coding algorithm can further improve the recognition rates. Meanwhile, compared to the classic TCA approach, our proposed method always obtains higher recognition rates. It can be concluded that our proposed TPCA-SC approach is effective for cross-corpus speech emotion recognition.

Meanwhile, it can be also observed that the average recognition rates of our proposed method in these two cases are 51.36% and 43.97%, while the recognition rates of the corresponding baseline approach are 75.06% and 61.94%, respectively. Although the proposed approach can achieve better performance than the other methods, it is still far from satisfactory compared with the baseline method.

Table 1. The recognition rates of different methods in the 1st case (eNTERFACE dataset for training, Berlin dataset for testing).

Methods	Recognition rates (%)					
	Anger	Disgust	Fear	Happiness	Sadness	Average
Baseline	73.05	81.67	68.73	52.65	79.23	75.06
PCA	31.24	52.72	17.13	19.86	47.52	34.13
TPCA	34.02	71.02	18.45	24.35	68.35	41.95
TCA	35.16	73.28	19.01	26.32	70.28	50.72
TPCA-SC	35.89	74.36	19.35	26.53	71.10	51.36

Table 2. The recognition rates of different methods in the 2nd case (eNTERFACE dataset for training, Berlin dataset for testing).

Methods	Recognition rates (%)					
	Anger	Disgust	Fear	Happiness	Sadness	Average
Baseline	74.48	55.29	53.89	60.02	61.09	61.94
PCA	37.72	19.14	18.02	27.26	28.35	22.95
TPCA	47.62	25.24	29.54	43.68	41.46	36.52
TCA	50.56	28.85	34.89	45.72	43.92	41.83
TPCA-SC	52.31	29.43	37.26	46.42	44.25	43.97

5   Conclusions and Discussions

In this paper, a new speech emotion recognition method using transfer PCA and sparse coding is presented. First, the transfer PCA approach, which considers the similarity between the distributions of source and target datasets, is proposed for dimension reduction. Then, the graph sparse coding algorithm is employed to obtain the efficient sparse representations of source and target features. Finally, the proposed method is evaluated on the public datasets, and preliminary experimental results demonstrate the efficacy of our proposed approach.

It should be noted that there still exist many problems in current method, e.g., the classifier is trained only using the labeled features of source dataset, without considering the unlabeled information from the target dataset, and the TPCA or sparse coding method may lessen the class discrimination of each dataset. In the future, we will focus on addressing these problems.

Acknowledgments. The authors acknowledge that this study is partly supported by NSFC (61231002, 61201444), and partly supported by the Natural Science Foundation of Shandong Province (ZR2014FQ016), the Natural Science Foundation of Jiangsu Province (BK20130020), the Ph.D. Program Foundation of Ministry Education of China (20120092110054), the National Basic Research Program of China (2015CB351704), and the Fundamental Research Funds for the Southeast University (CDLS-2015-04).

References

1. El Ayadi, M., Kamel, M.S., Karray, F.: Survey on Speech Emotion Recognition: Features, Classification Schemes, and Databases. Pattern Recognition **44**, 572–587 (2011)
2. Kim, Y., Lee, H., Provost, E.M.: Deep learning for robust feature generation in audiovisual emotion recognition. In: IEEE International Conference on Acoustics. Speech and Signal Processing (ICASSP), pp. 3687–3691. IEEE Press, Vancovour (2013)
3. Schuller, B., Vlasenko, B., Eyben, F., Wollmer, M., Stuhlsatz, A., Wendemuth, A., Rigoll, G.: Cross-corpus Acoustic Emotion Recognition: Variances and Strategies. IEEE Transactions on Affective Computing **1**, 119–131 (2010)
4. Zhang, Z., Weninger, F., Wollmer, M.: Unsupervised learning in cross-corpus acoustic emotion recognition. In: IEEE Workshop on Automatic Speech Recognition and Understanding (ASRU), pp. 523–528, IEEE Press, Hawaii (2011)
5. Deng, J., Zhang, Z., Eyben, F., Schuller, B.: Autoencoder-based Unsupervised Domain Adaptation for Speech Emotion Recognition. IEEE Signal Processing Letters **21**, 1068–1072 (2014)
6. Song, P., Jin, Y., Zhao, L., Xin, M.: Speech Emotion Recognition Using Transfer Learning. IEICE TRANSACTIONS on Information and Systems **97**, 2530–2532 (2014)
7. Bishop, C.M.: Pattern Recognition and Machine Learning. springer, New York (2006)
8. Gretton, A., Borgwardt, K.M., Rasch, M., Schlkopf, B., Smola, A.J.: A kernel method for the two-sample-problem. In: Advances in Neural Information Processing Systems, pp. 513–520. NIPS Foundation, Vancovour (2006)
9. Wright, J., Yang, A.Y., Ganesh, A., Sastry, S.S., Ma, Y.: Robust Face Recognition Via Sparse Representation. IEEE Transactions on Pattern Analysis and Machine Intelligence **31**, 210–227 (2009)
10. Zheng, M., Bu, J., Chen, C., Wang, C., Zhang, L., Qiu, G., Cai, D.: Graph Regularized Sparse Coding for Image Representation. IEEE Transactions on Image Processing **20**, 1327–1336 (2011)

11. Lee, H., Battle, A., Raina, R., Ng, A.Y.: Efficient sparse coding algorithms. In: Advances in Neural Information Processing Systems, pp. 801–808. NIPS Foundation, Vancovour (2006)
12. Burkhardt, F., Paeschke, A., Rolfes, M., Sendlmeier, W., Weiss, B.: A Database of german emotional speech. In: Interspeech, pp. 1517–1520. ISCA, Lisbon (2005)
13. Martin, O., Kotsia, I., Macq, B., Pitas, I.: The eNTERFACE 2005 audio-visual emotion database. In: International Conference on Data Engineering Workshops, pp. 8–8. IEEE Press, Atlanta (2006)
14. Eyben, F., Wöllmer, M., Schuller B.: Opensmile: the munich versatile and fast open-source audio feature extractor. In: ACM Multimedia, pp. 1459–1462. ACM Press, Firenze (2010)
15. Schuller, B., Steidl, S., Batliner, A., Burkhardt, F., Devillers, L., Muller, C.A., Narayanan S.S.: The interspeech 2010 paralinguistic challenge. In: Interspeech, pp. 2794–2797. ISCA, Makuhari (2010)
16. Pan, S.J., Tsang, I.W., Kwok, J.T., Yang, Q.: Domain Adaptation via Transfer Component Analysis. IEEE Transactions on Neural Networks 22, 199–210 (2011)

Sparse Facial Expression Recognition Algorithm Based on Integrated Gabor Feature

Yang Liu[✉], Lei Ren, and Hong Shao

School of Information Science and Engineering, Shenyang University of Technology,
Shenyang, China
liuyangxx@sut.edu.cn

Abstract. Facial expression recognition has been widely applied in the field of medicine and civil, and is a very active research area. Gabor wavelet transform is a classical and effective method of expression feature extraction, but the original facial expression images after the Gabor transform generate high dimension feature, which must be processed through effective feature fusion and selection, otherwise it will cause data redundancy. In this paper, in order to overcome the shortcoming of data redundancy of the traditional Gabor feature, sparse facial expression recognition algorithm based on integrated Gabor feature is proposed. Firstly, by means of two integration methods, mean fusion and differential binary encoding, the original Gabor feature images are integrated in a multi-scale and multi-angle way and 26 integrated Gabor feature images are obtained; then use feature selection method based on the facial expression recognition contribution coefficient, selecting 4 images from 26 integrated Gabor feature images as the final feature vector. Finally, the feature vector is fed to sparse representation classifier for facial expression recognition. Experimental results indicate that sparse facial expression recognition algorithm based on integrated Gabor feature can separate and express the facial expression features facial features effectively, and reduce dimension and present expression data compactly, meanwhile the expressions are classified correctly.

Keywords: Integrated gabor feature · Mean fusion · Differential binary encoding · Expression recognition · Contribution coefficient

1 Introduction

Facial expression contains rich personal emotional information, and plays an important role in daily communication. The research findings of facial expression recognition can explain and demonstration of new methods, new theories and new phenomena [1]. With the same characteristics of 2-dimensional reflex zone of simple cells in the human brain cortex, Gabor wavelet transform is a classic and efficient facial feature extraction method and are widely used in the field of computer vision and image analysis. However, the feature dimension of the original facial expression image after Gabor transform is very high, and the data redundancy of Gabor feature is caused without the reasonable feature selection.

For the above problem, many researchers propose the improvement scheme. In addition to using traditional dimension reduction methods, Zavaschi Thiago H.H. and

© Springer International Publishing Switzerland 2015
J. Yang et al. (Eds.): CCBR 2015, LNCS 9428, pp. 401–408, 2015.
DOI: 10.1007/978-3-319-25417-3_47

Britto Alceu S. Jr. et al. use two kinds of feature sets, local binary pattern and Gabor feature, and search the combination mode with error minimization through multi-objective genetic[2]; Shuaishi Liu and Yantao Tian et al. use Gabor multi-direction feature fusion method combined with block histogram to extract facial expression features, effectively give expression to the global image features, achieve good recognition effect[3]; Ebenezer Owusu and Yonzhao Zhan et al. use Adaboost algorithm for feature selection from the Gabor feature, adding the processing link of discrete cosine transform [4].The above algorithms, on the basis of the original Gabor features, add the other facial features and new process links. During the process, facial features newly added increases the number of features again; the contributions to expression recognition of different types of features are not clear, therefore it is still essential to design the improved scheme.

In this paper, sparse facial expression recognition algorithm based on integrated Gabor feature is proposed. The main advantages of the algorithm: (1) Based on the grey value, the original Gabor features are integrated, and in the integration methods the whole operation process involves all pixels, including pixel location information, save the expression features and reduces the feature dimension effectively. (2) With a lot of experimental data as the basis, contrast the feature extraction results of the different integration methods; select the expression characteristics, which are the most beneficial for classification.

The overall process of the proposed algorithm in this paper is as follows. (1) Image preprocessing. (2) Facial expression feature extraction. (3) Facial expression recognition.

2   Image Preprocessing

Japanese female facial expression database (JAFFE) is taken advantage of as the experimental object. First of all, make use of Adaboost face detection algorithm [5] for facial expression area segmentation, as shown in Fig. 1. Then the facial expression region image is converted into 100×100 gray level image. Finally, the histogram equalization is used to ray normalization.

Fig. 1. Facial expression region segmentation

3   Facial Expression Feature Extraction

Firstly, extract multi-scale and multi-angle Gabor features of a pure facial expression image. Then integrate the original Gabor features using two kinds of integration methods, including mean fusion and differential binary encoding, to obtain 26 integrated Gabor feature images. Finally take advantage of feature selection method based on the facial expression recognition contribution coefficient, select 4 integrated Gabor feature images for mosaic, and convert the mosaic image to a column vector, which is as the final feature vector.

3.1 Gabor Feature Extraction

As the different types of facial expressions need to use different-scale and different-angle Gabor features for analysis, on the basis of the traditional Gabor feature extraction method [6], select 5 scales and 8 angles of 2D Gabor filter banks, and the convolution operation of the pure facial expression image in Fig. 1 and Gabor kernel function is carried out, whose result is complex number and the real part of complex number is taken as the Gabor feature of expression image. As shown in Fig. 2, 40 five-scale and eight-angle Gabor feature images.

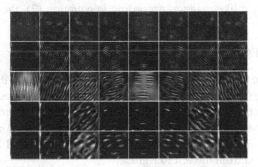

Fig. 2. 40 Gabor feature images corresponding to facial expression image

3.2 Gabor Feature Integration

Grouped by scale, 40 original Gabor feature images are divided into 5 groups, and each group includes 8 angle feature images, corresponding to a row of images in Fig. 2; grouped by angle, divided into 8 groups, each group includes 5 scale feature images, corresponding to a column of images in Fig. 2.

3.2.1 Mean Fusion
(1) Scale Mean Fusion

Scale mean fusion is to fuse 8 angle Gabor feature images of the same scale into the corresponding scale mean fusion images following mean fusion rule. According to equation (1), the corresponding scale mean fusion image is constructed pixel by pixel.

$$\text{MFS}_u\left(x,y\right) = \frac{\sum_{v=0}^{7} G_{u,v}\left(x,y\right)}{8}, u \in \left(0,\dots,4\right) \tag{1}$$

where $G_{u,v}$ is the u-scale and v-angle Gabor feature image, MFS_u represents u-scale mean fusion image($u \in (0,\dots,4)$), and $\text{MFS}_u(x,y)$ is pixel value corresponding to(x,y).

Through respectively fuse 8 angle Gabor feature images of the same scale, 5 scale mean fusion images MFS_u, ($u \in (0,\dots,4)$) are constructed. As shown in Fig. 3, 0-scale, 1-scale, 2-scale, 3-scale and 4-scale mean fusion images are arranged from the left to right.

Fig. 3. Scale mean fusion images

(2) Angle Mean Fusion
Similar to the scale mean fusion, angle mean fusion is to fuse 5 scale Gabor feature images of the same angle into the corresponding angle mean fusion images following mean fusion rule. In like manner, according to equation (2), the corresponding angle mean fusion image is constructed.

$$MFA_v(x, y) = \frac{\sum_{u=0}^{4} G_{u,v}(x,y)}{5}, v \in (0, \dots, 7). \tag{2}$$

where $G_{u,v}$ is the the u-scale and v-angle Gabor feature image, MFA_v represents v-angle mean fusion image ($v \in (0, \dots 4)$), and $MFA_v(x,y)$ is pixel value corresponding to (x,y).

Through respectively fuse 5 scale Gabor feature images of the same angle, 8 angle mean fusion images $MFA_v(x,y)(v \in (0, \dots, 4))$ are constructed. As shown in Fig. 4, 0-angle, 1-angle, 2-angle, 3-angle, 4-angle, 5-angle, 6-angle and 7-angle mean fusion images are arranged from the left to right.

Fig. 4. Angle mean fusion images

3.2.2   Differential Binary Encoding

(1) Scale Differential Binary Encoding
Regard the 8 angle Gabor feature images of the u scale, $G_{uv}(x, y)(u \in (0, \dots, 4)$, $v \in (0, \dots, 7))$, as the information source, and successively calculate the difference $d_{u,j}(x, y)$ of pixel values corresponding to (x, y) in two adjacent Gabor feature images, where $j \in (0, \dots, 7)$, $u \in (0, \dots, 4)$ following the equation (3) and totally obtain 8 differences.

$$d_{u,j}(x, y) = \begin{cases} G_{u,j}(x,y) - G_{u,j+1}(x,y), & 0 \leq j < 7 \\ G_{u,j}(x,y) - G_{u,0}(x,y), & j = 7 \end{cases} \tag{3}$$

According to the equation (4), obtain binary encoding $t_{u,j}(x,y)$ corresponding to $d_{u,j}(x,y)$, where $u \in (0, \dots, 4)$.

$$t_{u,j}(x, y) = \begin{cases} 1, & |d_{u,j}(x,y)| > 0 \\ 0, & |d_{u,j}(x,y)| = 0 \end{cases} \quad j \in (0, \dots, 7) \tag{4}$$

8 binary encoding $t_{u,j}(x, y)(j \in (0, \dots, 7))$ obtained by calculation are arranged in accordance with the ascending order of j, occupying the binary digit from low to high, which generates the 8-bit binary number corresponding to pixel (x, y). Finally convert

the 8-bit binary number into a decimal number, as scale differential binary encoding value $DCS_u(x,y)$, according to the equation (5).

$$DCS_u(x,y) = \sum_{j=0}^{7} t_{u,j}(x,y) \times 2^j, \ u \in (0,\dots,4) \tag{5}$$

According to the above algorithm, 5 scale differential binary encoding images $DCS_u(u \in (0,\dots,4))$ are constructed. As shown in Fig. 5, 0-scale, 1-scale, 2-scale, 3-scale and 4-scale differential binary encoding images are arranged from the left to right.

Fig. 5. Scale differential binary encoding images

(2) Angle Differential Binary Encoding

Regard the 5 scale Gabor feature images of the v angle, $G_{uv}(x, y)$ ($u \in (0,\dots,4)$, $v \in (0, \dots, 7)$), as the information source, and successively calculate the difference $d_{i,v}(x, y)$ of pixel values corresponding to pixel in two adjacent Gabor feature images, where $i \in (0,\dots,4)$, $v \in (0,\dots,7)$, following the equation (6) and totally obtain 5 differences.

$$d_{i,v}(x,y) = \begin{cases} G_{i,v}(x,y) - G_{i+1,v}(x,y), & 0 \le i < 4 \\ G_{i,v}(x,y) - G_{0,v}(x,y), & i = 4 \end{cases} \tag{6}$$

According to the equation (7), obtain binary encoding $t_{i,v}(x,y)$ corresponding to $d_{i,v}(x,y)$, where $v \in (0,\dots,7)$.

$$t_{i,v}(x,y) = \begin{cases} 1, & |d_{i,v}(x,y)| > 0 \\ 0, & |d_{i,v}(x,y)| = 0 \end{cases} \ i \in (0,\dots,4) \tag{7}$$

5 binary encoding $t_{i,v}(x,y) i \in (0,\dots,4)$ obtained by calculation are arranged in accordance with the ascending order of i, occupying the binary digit from low to high, and the remaining binary digit positions are set to 0, which generates the 8-bit binary number corresponding to pixel (x, y). Finally convert the 8-bit binary number into a decimal number, as angle differential binary encoding value $DCA_v(x, y)$, according to the equation (8).

$$DCA_v(x,y) = \sum_{i=0}^{4} t_{i,v}(x,y) \times 2^i, \ v \in (0,\dots,7) \tag{8}$$

According to the above algorithm, 8 angle differential binary encoding images $DCA_v(x, y) v \in (0,\dots,7)$ are constructed. As shown in Fig. 6, 0-angle, 1-angle, 2-angle, 3-angle, 4-angle, 5-angle, 6-angle and 7-angle differential binary encoding images are arranged from the left to right.

Fig. 6. Angle differential binary encoding images

Through feature integration of 40 Gabor feature images, obtained 26 feature images, including 5 scale mean fusion images, 8 angle mean fusion images, 5 scale differential binary encoding images and 8 angle differential binary encoding images, are collectively called integrated Gabor feature images. As shown in Table 1, grouping mechanism and serial number of 26 integrated Gabor feature images.

Table 1. Grouping mechanism and serial number of 26 integrated Gabor feature images

Group	number	1					2				
	name	Scale mean fusion					Scale differential binary encoding				
Serial number		1	2	3	4	5	6	7	8	9	10
Image		MFS_0	MFS_1	MFS_2	MFS_3	MFS_4	DCS_0	DCS_1	DCS_2	DCS_3	DCS_4

Group	number	3				4			
	name	Angle mean fusion group				Angle differential binary encoding			
Serial number		11	12	13	14	19	20	21	22
Image		MFA_0	MFA_1	MFA_2	MFA_3	DCA_0	DCA_1	DCA_2	DCA_3
Serial number		15	16	17	18	23	24	25	26
Image		MFA_4	MFA_5	MFA_6	MFA_7	DCA_4	DCA_5	DCA_6	DCA_7

3.3   Feature Selection

Since the feature number of the 26 integrated Gabor feature images is still large, it is necessary to conduct further feature selection. The proposed feature selection method based on facial expression recognition contribution coefficient is used for feature selection.

Firstly, according to each integrated Gabor feature image's recognition rate of each kind of expression and the average recognition rate, calculate $R_{n,c}$ of each integrated Gabor feature image, and $R_{n,c}$ represents recognition rate rank of c expression, where n is the serial number of integrated Gabor feature image and different value of c corresponds to different expression, c represents anger, disgust, fear, happiness, neutral, sadness, and surprise expression respectively when value of c is 1, 2, 3, 4, 5, 6 and 7.

Table 2. The recognition effect of three kinds of selection schemes

feature selection scheme	Scheme number	Selected reasons
inner group selection scheme	1-4	the top 4 in descending order of ERCC in the same group
inter group selection scheme	5-10	select arbitrarily 2 groups from 4 groups ,and select the top 2 in descending order of ERCC in each selected group
overall selection scheme	11	the top 4 in descending order of ERCC
	12	the top 2 of each facial expression recognition rate

Then use the equation (9) to calculate the facial expression recognition contribution coefficient (ERCC_n) of each integrated Gabor feature image, where n (($n \in$ (1,...,26))is serial number of 26 integrated Gabor feature images.

$$\text{ERCC}_n = 210 - \sum_{c=1}^{7} R_{n,c} \ , \ n \in (1, \dots, 26) \tag{9}$$

As shown in Table 2, according to ERCC_n of 26 integrated Gabor feature images, combined with their grouping mechanism and serial number in Table 1, choose 4 images from 26 integrated Gabor feature images.

Finally, on the basis of 12 different feature selection schemes, select 4 integrated Gabor feature images for mosaic, and convert the mosaic image to a column vector as the final feature vector.

4   Facial Expression Recognition

Sparse representation classifier (SRC) [7] is used for facial expression recognition, and JAFFE is as experimental data, including 213 facial expression images of 10 different women and each kind of expression contains 3 or 4 images. Over complete dictionary [7] of sparse representation classifier is composed of corresponding feature vectors of 140 training samples, including 7 expressions of 10 different women, where each expression contains 2 images. Except for 3 images sampled repeatedly, training samples include 137 expression images, the remaining 76 images are test samples (10 anger, 11 disgust, 12 fear, 12 happiness, 10 neutral, 11 sad and 10 surprised expression images).

Table 3. The recognition effect of three kinds of selection schemes

Scheme number	Series number				Average recognition rate
1	4	5	3	2	84.48%
2	8	9	7	6	85.97%
3	17	14	12	13	79.46%
4	25	22	20	21	**88.25%**
5	4	5	8	9	87.06%
6	4	5	17	14	86.00%
7	4	5	25	22	85.74%
8	8	9	17	14	82.89%
9	8	9	25	22	80.84%
10	17	14	25	22	81.00%
11	25	4	17	22	80.89%
12	25	4	17	5	86.00%

5   Experimental Results

The experimental platform is Microsoft Visual Studio 2012. The selection scheme information and the recognition effect of these three kinds of selection schemes are shown in Table 3, where integrated Gabor feature images are arranged in accordance with descending order of ERCC from left to right and the highest average recognition rate is 88.25%.

Table 4. The comparison of recognition effect of the proposed algorithm and other algorithm

Algorithm	The proposed algorithm	Gabor + SRC	LBP + SVM
Average recognition rate	88.25%	83.25%	71.04%

6   Conclusions

In order to solve the problem of data redundancy of Gabor feature, two kinds of Gabor feature integration methods and feature selection method based on facial expression recognition contribution coefficient are proposed. Experimental results indicate that the proposed sparse facial expression recognition algorithm based on integrated Gabor feature, can separate and express the facial expression features facial features effectively, and reduce dimension and present expression data compactly; meanwhile the expressions are classified correctly. The focus of the subsequent work is to improve the expression recognition rate, and attempt to use more efficient classifier.

Acknowledgments. This work was sponsored by Natural Science Foundation of Liaoning Province (No.201202162)and Program for Liaoning Excellent Talents in University (No.LJQ2013013).

References

1. Li, D., Tian, Y., Wan, C., Liu, S.: Facial expression feature selection based on rough set. In: Liu, B., Ma, M., Chang, J. (eds.) ICICA 2012. LNCS, vol. 7473, pp. 159–166. Springer, Heidelberg (2012)
2. Zavaschi, T., Oliveira, L.S., Souza Jr., A.B., Koerich, A.: Fusion of Feature Sets and Classifiers for Facial Expression Recognition. Expert Systems with Applications **40**, 646–655 (2013)
3. Shuaishi, L., Yantao, T., Chuan, W.: Facial Expression Recognition Method Based on Gabor Multi-orientation Features Fusion and Block Histogram. Acta Automatica Sinica **12**, 1457–1458 (2011)
4. Ebenezer, O., Yonzhao, Z., Qirong, M.: An SVM-AdaBoost Facial Expression Recognition System. Applied Intelligence **40**, 536–545 (2014)
5. Viola, P., Jones, M.: Robust real time object detection. In: 8th IEEE International Conference on Computer Vision, pp. 151–184. IEEE Press, Vancouver (2001)
6. Li, W., Ruifeng, L., Ke, W., Chuqing, C.: OLPP-based gabor feature dimensionality reduction for facial expression recognition. In: IEEE International Conference on Information and Automation, pp. 455–460. IEEE Press, Hailar (2014)
7. Shiqing, Z., Xiaoming, Z., Bicheng, L.: Robust Facial Expression Recognition via Compressive Sensing. Sensors **12**, 3747–3761 (2012)

Robust Gait Recognition Based on Collaborative Representation with External Variant Dictionary

Wanjiang Xu[1,2], Can Luo[1], Aiming Ji[1], and Canyan Zhu[1(✉)]

[1] Institute of Intelligent Structure and System, Soochow University, Suzhou 215006, China
xuwanjiang0821@163.com, 20134246004@stu.suda.edu.cn,
{jiaiming,qiwuzhu}@suda.edu.cn
[2] Teachers University, Yancheng 224002, China

Abstract. Existing methods for gait recognition mainly depend on the appearance of human. Their performances are greatly affected by variation outside of human body. To solve the problem, we proposed a collaborative representation classification (CRC) based approach by which gait under different condition is decomposed into normal gait ingredient and variant ingredient. An external variant dictionary is constructed to linear represent variant. The normal gait ingredient is directly classified by CRC. Experiments on CASIA gait database show that the proposed method achieves a satisfactory recognition result.

Keywords: Biometric · Gait recognition · Collaborative representation · External variant dictionary

1 Introduction

Gait is an important biometric feature for human identification in video-surveillance based applications since it is difficult to conceal, imitate and perceived unobtrusively from a distance. Results from the field of psychology demonstrated that humans can be indeed recognized by their gait [1]. However, there are various factors significantly affecting recognition of gait, such as carrying bag, wearing a coat. A practical gait recognition system should be robust to these variations.

The existing methods for human gait recognition fall roughly in two categories: model-based and appearance-based approaches. In model-based approaches [2,3], features of human is represented as model parameters, e.g. swing angle of leg, position of gravity, stride length. However, they are sometimes difficult to obtain for self-occlusion of body. In appearance-based approaches [4,5], features are extracted from gaits by different descriptors. Gait energy image (GEI) [6] is one of most widely used gait features, which also is adopted in this paper. GEI is defined as $G(x,y)=\sum_i^N I(x,y)/N$, where N is number of frames in complete cycle(s), and x and y are values in image coordinate. PCA and LDA are taken to reduce the dimension, by which probe GEI is represented as linear combination of eigen-vectors.

© Springer International Publishing Switzerland 2015
J. Yang et al. (Eds.): CCBR 2015, LNCS 9428, pp. 409–415, 2015.
DOI: 10.1007/978-3-319-25417-3_48

Sparse representation (SR) based classification approaches seek to find a sparse linear representation for gallery sample. SRC [7, 12] was firstly employed successfully for robust face recognition. There were also some approaches based on SRC in gait recognition [5, 8, 9]. The work [8] divided GEI into three parts (upper, medium, lower). Each part was represented by corresponding dictionary. They recognized gait by minimizing sum reconstruction error. Zheng et al. [5] decomposed GEI as low-rank part and noise, then construct view transformation model to recognize gait. Xu et al. [9] proposed locality-constrained group sparse representation method to classify gait which incorporating locality-constraint and group information to get a high recognition rate.

Pattern recognition based on SRC has achieved excellent results. However, Zhang et al.[10] pointed out that CR is more important than sparseness in classifying. And they proposed CRC to obtain a competitive recognition result.

Gallery samples usually act as dictionary in SRC or CRC. However, because of external variant, probe sample may be too different from gallery samples to recover. Therefore, the recognition rates cannot achieve much improvement by SRC or CRC. In this paper, we add an external variant dictionary for representation of variant ingredient. Probe sample is recovered by combination of gallery samples and external variant dictionary. Our method is robust to external variation (e.g. carrying and wearing).

2   External Variant Dictionary

2.1   Problem

Denote the gallery samples as the matrix $X=[X_1, X_2,...,X_c]$, where the vector X_i represent a training sample. Then a probe sample y can be rewritten as follow:

$$y = X\alpha + \varepsilon \tag{1}$$

where α is a linear combination coefficient of dictionary X, and ε is a noise term. However, some outer factors such as bag and coat are impossible to be composed as noise ε, since they lead to a great gap between gallery and probe samples.

2.2   Proposed External Variant Dictionary

Since the variation is not inherent in human being, we could work to get rid of them. In this paper, all of the variant factors are included in a dictionary. Then gaits under different conditions were decomposed into two ingredients: normal gaits and variant factors. For example, as shown in Fig. 1, gait under the condition of carrying bag consist two ingredients: normal gait and bag (similar to wearing condition).

Let V be external variant dictionary, X be normal gallery set, a gait can be represented as follows:

$$y = X\alpha + V\beta + \varepsilon \tag{2}$$

where ε is a noise term, and V usually represents bag carried, coat, hat and so on. Hence, α and β can be recovered simultaneously by L1-minimization.

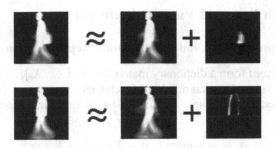

Fig. 1. Gaits under carrying and wearing conditions are decomposed into two ingredients.

2.3 Construction of External Variant Dictionary

In this paper, the external variant dictionary is constructed by difference values of gait samples of same person under various kinds of conditions. Let us take, for example, the external variant of carrying bag and wearing coat. For subject i, d is dimension of vectorized GEI, a total of n_i normal gaits form matrix $G_i^{nm} \in \Re^{d \times n_i}$; a total of m_i gaits carrying bag form a matrix $G_i^{bg} \in \Re^{d \times m_i}$; a total of l_i gaits wearing coat form a matrix $G_i^{cl} \in \Re^{d \times l_i}$. The external variant vectors can be obtained by subtracting the normal gait from other gait of the same class as following.

$$V_{bg} = [G_1^{bg} - \overline{G}_1^{nm}, G_2^{bg} - \overline{G}_2^{nm}, ... G_c^{bg} - \overline{G}_c^{nm}] \in \Re^{d \times n_i} \tag{3}$$

$$V_{cl} = [G_1^{cl} - \overline{G}_1^{nm}, G_2^{cl} - \overline{G}_2^{nm}, ... G_c^{cl} - \overline{G}_c^{nm}] \in \Re^{d \times l_i} \tag{4}$$

Let columns of matrix $V_i^{bg} \in \Re^{d \times (m_i \times n_i)}$ be pairwise difference vectors between the carrying bag samples and the normal samples of class i. The carrying variation set (the same to wearing variation set) could be constructed as follows:

$$V_{bg} = [V_1^{bg}, V_2^{bg}, ..., V_c^{bg}] \in \Re^{d \times \sum_i m_i n_i} \tag{5}$$

$$V_{cl} = [V_1^{cl}, V_2^{cl}, ..., V_c^{cl}] \in \Re^{d \times \sum_i l_i n_i} \tag{6}$$

In gait recognition problem, recognition performance is greatly affected by shadow, carrying, clothing, wearing and other variants. The final dictionary V as follows.

$$V = [V_{bg}, V_{cl}, ..., V_{shadow}] \tag{7}$$

3   CRC with External Variant Dictionary

3.1   Sparse Representation and Collaboration Representation

Let all gallery samples form a dictionary matrix $X=[X_1,X_2,\ldots,X_c]$, , where each column of X_i is a sample of class i, a total number of c classes.

Once a probe sample y comes, we code it based on sparse representation as follows:

$$\hat{\alpha} = \arg \min_{\alpha} \parallel y - X\alpha \parallel_2^2 + \lambda \parallel \alpha \parallel_1 \tag{8}$$

where λ is a scaling factor. E.q (8) was improved [10] using L2-norm as follows.

$$\hat{\alpha} = \arg \min_{\alpha} \parallel y - X\alpha \parallel_2^2 + \lambda \parallel \alpha \parallel_2 \tag{9}$$

E.q. (9) is solved by regularized least square as:

$$\hat{\alpha} = (X^T X + \lambda \cdot I)^{-1} X^T y \tag{10}$$

Clearly, $(X^T X + \lambda \cdot I)^{-1} X^T$ can be pre-calculated as a projection. We can simply project y to get $\hat{\alpha}$. Let $\hat{\alpha}_i$ be a coefficient vector to class i. Then, y is classified by minimum recover residual using sparse coefficients as following.

$$identify(y) = \arg \min_i \parallel y - X_i\hat{\alpha}_i \parallel_2 \tag{11}$$

Table 1. Algorithm of CRC with external variant dictionary

---

1) Input : a matrix X formed by all gallery samples, an external variant dictionary matrix V , and a probe sample y.

2) Dimension reduction and normalization by principal component analysis

3) Solve the problem: $\begin{bmatrix} \hat{\alpha} \\ \hat{\beta} \end{bmatrix} = ([X \ \ V]^T [X \ \ V] + \lambda \cdot I)^{-1} [X \ \ V]^T y$

4) Compute the residuals for each class i: $r_i(y) = \left\| y - [X,V] \begin{bmatrix} \delta_i(\hat{\alpha}) \\ \hat{\beta} \end{bmatrix} \right\|_2$

5) Output: $identify(y) = \arg \min_i r_i(y)$

3.2   Algorithmic Process

We extend CRC incorporating external variant dictionary to recognize gaits. After external variant dictionary is constructed as section 2, any probe gait is represented as a collaboration of gallery gaits adding a collaboration of variation. In the end, probe gait is classified by residual minimization.

The proposed algorithm is summarized as shown in table 1. In first step, the external variants of carrying bag, wearing coat, etc. are obtained by subtracting the normal gaits from these abnormal gaits of the same class. These variants are gathered in a set then entire external variant dictionary is constructed. In Second step, PCA is used in this paper to reduce the dimension of gait feature. In the next few steps, CRC with the external dictionary V is employed to recognize the probe gait y.

4   Experimental Results

The CASIA gait database B [11] is used in our experiments. This database contains 124 subjects from 11 views. There are six normal, two carrying and two wearing gait sequences for each subject from each view. The first 62 subjects' normal, carrying, wearing sequences of each view are used to construct variant dictionary. The rest 62 subjects' sequences are used to evaluate.

In our experiments, for a fair comparison, we have carried out experiments based on these methods and our proposed method on the same gallery and probe data sets. A comprehensive experiment is conducted to compare the performance of the proposed method (CRC-V) with that of NN, SRC [7], CRC [10], and SRC-V (SRC with external variant dictionary). After tune, we set parameter λ as 0.001.

4.1   Probe Gaits Under Carrying Bag Condition

Table 2 enumerates the recognition rates for this experiment. Under each view angle, CR based approach (CRC and CRC-V) do better than corresponding SR (SRC and SRC-V), which explains collaboration work better than sparseness in carrying gait recognition.

Table 2. Recognition rates of probe gaits under carrying bag condition

Probe view	0°	18°	36°	54°	72°	90°	108°	126°	144°	162°	180°	Avg
NN	0.71	0.69	0.61	0.53	0.38	0.30	0.36	0.51	0.52	0.63	0.73	0.54
SRC	0.56	0.44	0.35	0.41	0.35	0.34	0.36	0.34	0.42	0.49	0.55	0.42
CRC	0.81	0.77	0.73	0.62	0.44	0.44	0.53	0.56	0.57	0.66	0.73	0.62
SRC-V	0.85	0.78	0.78	0.70	0.70	0.60	0.65	0.62	0.74	0.81	0.83	0.73
CRC-V	0.86	0.88	0.85	0.87	0.83	0.84	0.79	0.83	0.88	0.87	0.89	0.85

SRC do worst from the table, which shows that sparsity is ill-advised in recognizing gaits carrying bag. SRC-V performs better than SRC, and our proposed method CRC-V performs better than CRC. This illustrates the external variant dictionary is useful in gait recognition.

4.2   Probe Gaits Under Wearing Coat Condition

The result from Table 3 illustrates that the recognition rates of the four methods is too low to be unworthy to apply. Big coat shuts off some body parts which usually are useful in classification.

Table 3. Recognition rates of probe gaits under wearing coat condition

Probe view	0°	18°	36°	54°	72°	90°	108°	126°	144°	162°	180°	Avg
NN	0.11	0.15	0.21	0.16	0.10	0.12	0.10	0.12	0.14	0.10	0.10	0.13
SRC	0.23	0.24	0.27	0.19	0.29	0.34	0.30	0.27	0.29	0.23	0.18	0.27
CRC	0.26	0.20	0.26	0.31	0.25	0.28	0.29	0.23	0.22	0.19	0.23	0.25
SRC-V	0.26	0.26	0.31	0.42	0.40	0.50	0.39	0.30	0.32	0.27	0.32	0.33
CRC-V	0.58	0.73	0.67	0.76	0.85	0.83	0.63	0.58	0.60	0.57	0.60	0.67

Though SRC-V get a higher average rate than NN, SRC and CRC, it is also too low to put into use. This indicates that sparsity is not that important in this problem. However, the proposed method (CRC-V) performs at relatively high level (recognition rates of each view are more than 57%), which indicate that both external variant dictionary and CR play the vital role in this recognition. Under some view (e.g. 72° and 90°), satisfactory results (0.85 and 0.83) is achieved by CRC-V.

4.3   Computational Burden Analysis

In the application of gait recognition, probe subject should be recognized in real time. In this section, we compare the time cost of proposed method. Probe view 90° is adopted in this experiment. All experiments are conducted with Matlab code on a HP 4421s personal computer (2.4GHz CPU with 2G RAM).

Table 4. Running time(in second) of NN, SRC,CRC,SRC-V and CRC-V on gallery carrying and wearing gaits.

	Probe Gait Wearing Coat					Probe Gait Wearing Coat				
	NN	SRC	CRC	SRC-V	CRC-V	NN	SRC	CRC	SRC-V	CRC-V
Construct Dictionary V	-		1.20			-		1.24		
Recognition	0.04	20.22	0.10	26.02	0.24	0.03	20.79	0.10	24.53	0.25

From Table 4, we observe that SR based methods (SRC and SRC-V) take more time than others. This is because l_1-norm based sparsity need iteration for a long time. Time of constructing external variant dictionary takes about 1.2 second. Once this dictionary is constructed, we will never speed time on testing. Our proposed method spends about 0.25 second in recognition, which can be implemented in real time.

5   Conclusion

This paper proposes a robust method for human gait recognition, which uses collaborative representation classifier incorporating external variant dictionary. External variant dictionary is constructed by difference between normal gait and abnormal gait under conditions of carrying bag and wearing coat. The experiment results show that our method is robust to external variant factors (e.g. carrying, wearing) of human being.

Acknowledgement. This project is supported by the Funding of Jiangsu Innovation Program for Graduate Education (Grant No. KYZZ_0340).

References

1. Sarkar, S., Phillips, P.J., Liu, Z., Vega, I.R., Grother, P., Bowyer, K.W.: The humanid gait challenge problem: data sets, performance, and analysis. IEEE Transactions on Pattern Analysis and Machine Intelligence 27(2), 162–177 (2005)
2. Bobick, A.F., Johnson, A.Y.: Gait recognition using static activity-specific parameters. IEEE Conference on Computer Vision and Pattern Recognition 1, 423–430 (2001)
3. Zeng, W., Wang, C.: Human gait recognition via deterministic learning. Neural Networks 35, 92–102 (2012)
4. Nie, D., Ma, Q.: Identification of people at a distance using effective block list. In: Sun, Z., Shan, S., Yang, G., Zhou, J., Wang, Y., Yin, Y. (eds.) CCBR 2013. LNCS, vol. 8232, pp. 402–408. Springer, Heidelberg (2013)
5. Zheng, S., Zhang, J., Huang, K., He, R., Tan, T.: Robust view transformation model for gait recognition. In: IEEE International Conference on Image Processing, pp. 2073–2076 (2011)
6. Han, J., Bhanu, B.: Individual recognition using gait energy image. IEEE Transactions on Pattern Analysis and Machine Intelligence 28(2), 316–322 (2006)
7. Wright, J., Yang, A., Ganesh, A., Sastry, S., Ma, Y.: Robust face recognition via sparse representation. IEEE Transactions on Pattern Analysis and Machine Intelligence 31(2), 210–227 (2009)
8. Gong, M., Xu, Y., Yang, X., Zhang, W.: Gait identification by sparse representation. In: IEEE 8th Eighth International Conference on Fuzzy Systems and Knowledge Discovery, pp. 1719–1723 (2011)
9. Xu, D., Huang, Y., Zeng, Z., Xu, X.: Human gait recognition using patch distribution feature and locality-constrained group sparse representation. IEEE Transactions on Image Processing 21, 316–326 (2012)
10. Zhang, L., Yang, M., Feng, X.: Sparse representation or collaborative representation: which helps face recognition. In: IEEE International Conference on Computer Vision, pp. 471–478 (2011)
11. Yu, S., Tan, D., Tan, T.: A framework for evaluating the effect of view angle, clothing and carrying condition on gait recognition. In: IEEE 18th International Conference on Pattern Recognition, vol. 4, pp. 441–444 (2006)
12. Deng, W., Hu, J., Guo, J.J.: Extended SRC: undersampled face recognition viaintraclass variant dictionary. IEEE Transactions on Pattern Analysis and Machine Intelligence 34(9), 1864–1870 (2012)

Facial Expression Recognition
Based on Gabor Feature and SRC

Xiaojun Lu, Lingmei Kong, Mengzhu Liu, and Xiangde Zhang[⊠]

School of Sciences, Northeastern University, Shenyang 110819, China
luxiaojun@mail.neu.edu.cn, {18742435988,zhangxdneu}@163.com,
741511507@qq.com

Abstract. We present a facial expression recognition algorithm in this paper, which is based on a combination of the Gabor Feature and the Sprase Representation based Classification(SRC). First, improved Gabor filter is used to extract features. Then we use Principle Component Analysis (PCA) to reduce the dimension of Gabor feature to avoid redundancy. Finally, SRC is used to recognize and classify facial expression. Experiments on facial expression database JAFFE and Cohn-Kanade show that our approach is effective for both dimension reduction and recognition performance. The proposed method achieve 97.68% recognition accuracy on JAFFE.

Keywords: Facial expression recognition · Gabor feature · Principle Component Analysis(PCA) · Sparse Representation based Classification(SRC)

1   Introduction

Facial Expression Recognition (FER) is an important application of computer vision, which has been applied to many areas. The basic process of facial expression recognition is shown in Fig.1. The advantage of Gabor wavelet in expression feature extracting has been proved by S.Bashyal in 2008[1], it is capable to detect multi-orientation and multi-scale's texture changes, and little affected by light, while the Gabor feature impact the performance of face recognition algorithm as it needs large amount of calculation with high-dimension and information redundancy. Robust face recognition in [10] acquires better result by using sparse representation which represents the test sample in an over-complete dictionary whose base elements are the training samples themselves, and the represent is naturally sparse, but it is still difficult to determine which feature is suitable for SRC.

In order to make full use of the benefits of Gabor feature with sparse representation, we present a facial expression recognition based on combination of the Gabor Feature and SRC. First, we code the facial expression images by a multi-orientation, multi-resolution set of Gabor filters at some fixed geometric positions of the facial landmarks, then we use PCA to reduce redundant information of Gabor feature, the features after PCA are effective to classify 7 expressions based on SRC.

© Springer International Publishing Switzerland 2015
J. Yang et al. (Eds.): CCBR 2015, LNCS 9428, pp. 416–422, 2015.
DOI: 10.1007/978-3-319-25417-3_49

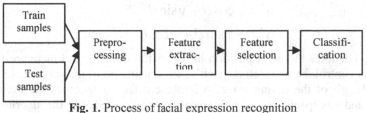

Fig. 1. Process of facial expression recognition

2   Preprocessing

An essential step of facial expression recognition is preprocessing, including face detection, face alignment, illumination processing, ect.

First, we use Adaboost algorithm [3] and Active Shape Model (ASM) [4] to detect face and locate facial feature point respectively, and we implement geometry normalization and grey level normalization on the basis of eye coordinate which transform face to the same location and size. Each image has a fixed size of 105×105 in this paper.

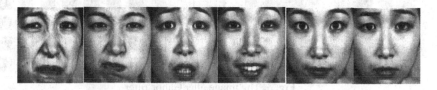

Fig. 2. Expression faces after preprocessing

3   Gabor Feature

A Gabor Wavelet filter is an essential tool for extracting local features both in spatial and frequency domain which can be applied on images to extract features aligned at particular orientations. Gabor filter is a linear filter used for edge detection. Frequency and orientations of Gabor filters are similar to those of the human visual system, they have been found particularly appropriate for texture representation and discrimination. In the spatial domain, a 2D Gabor filter is a Gaussian kernel function modulated by a sinusoidal plane wave. Simple cells in the visual cortex of mammalian brains can be modeled by Gabor functions [5]. Therefore, image analysis with Gabor filters is thought to be similar to perception in the human visual system.

The Gabor Wavelets kernel can be defined by equation (1):

$$W\left(x,y,\theta,\lambda,\phi,\sigma,\gamma\right) = e^{-\frac{x'^2+\gamma y'^2}{2\sigma^2}} \cos\left(2\pi\frac{x'}{\lambda}+\phi\right) \tag{1}$$

The parameters x' and y' can be defined by the following equations:

$$x' = x\cos\theta + y\sin\theta$$
$$y' = -x\sin\theta + y\cos\theta \qquad (2)$$

where (x,y) denotes the pixel position in the spatial domain, and there are five para-meters that control the wavelet: θ specifies the orientation of the wavelet, λ represents the wavelength of the cosine wave. φ is phase offset. σ specifies the radius of the Gaussian and γ is spacial aspect ratio, most wavelets tested with the algorithm use an aspect ratio of 1.0.

Gabor filter bank of various frequencies and orientations has been frequently used to extract features of face image[6,7]. In our work, a forty Gabor filter bank at five scales and eight orientation is used, where $\lambda \in \{4,4\sqrt{2},8,8\sqrt{2},16\}$,and $\theta \in \{0,\pi/8, 2\pi/8, 3\pi/8, 4\pi/8, 5\pi/8, 6\pi/8, 7\pi/8\}$ with $\varphi=0,\gamma=1,\sigma=\lambda$.

We improve the efficiency of Gabor filter by reducing the size of the Gabor kernel. We choose the center area of Gabor kernel rather than the complete one, which con-tains 95% energy of the Gabor kernel, since the major energy of Gabor kernel is con-centrated in the center area.

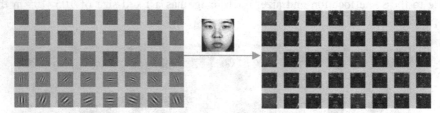

Fig. 3. The image after Gabor filter

4   Feature Selection

4.1   Feature Selection Based on Sampling Point

As is shown in section 4, we use Gabor filter bank at five scales and eight orientations, the dimension of Gabor feature is $M \times N \times 40$, where M, N is the size of an image. We choose both M and N as 105, the dimension of Gabor feature is as high as $105 \times 105 \times 40$. Considering the high correlation of adjacent pixels, and that the Gabor filter is not sensi-tive to the position of the gray value, we extract the Gabor features of some fixed geo-metric positions of the facial landmarks[8] as shown in Fig.4, the Gabor features of each sampling point form feature vector with dimension $8 \times 8 \times 40 = 2560$.

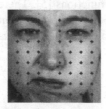

Fig. 4. The distribution of the sampling points on face

4.2   PCA Feature Extracting

After sampling, the dimension of Gabor feature vector has been significantly reduced, but is still quite high for recognition, the principal component analysis (PCA) finds orthogonal basis for data, sorts dimensions in the order of importance and discard low significance dimensions and has been used in many pattern recognition applications such as FER and face recognition[9,10]. So we use PCA to reduce the dimension of feature.

Supposing there are N samples: x_i (i =1,2,..., N)and each sample is T-dimensional, for the training data X, we firstly center the data:

$$X = (X - \bar{X}) / \sqrt{D} \tag{3}$$

where, X is the mean of each feature, D is the covariance matrix of the data. The principal components of training set can be calculated as following:

$$U^T (XX^T)U = \Lambda \tag{4}$$

Where Λ is the diagonal matrix of eigenvalues , U is corresponding eigenvectors of X X^T, we sort feature values: $\lambda_1 \geq \lambda_2 \geq ... \geq \lambda_N$, the corresponding eigenvectors are U_i (i =1,2,..., N).

The full principle components deposition of X can be given as:

$$X_{pca} = W_{pca} X^T \tag{5}$$

where W_{pca} is a p-by-p matrix whose columns are the eigenvector of $X X^T$, and p is the number of principle component. Feature set X_{pca} is the new training set, PCA reduces dimension from T to p , p can be decided by the cumulative energy content for each eigenvector:

$$R = \left. \sum_{k=1}^{p} \lambda_k \middle/ \sum_{k=1}^{N} \lambda_k \right. \quad (i=1,2,...,N) \tag{6}$$

where $R \in [85\%, 95\%]$, we choose $R=95\%$ in this paper.

5   The SRC Algorithm

The classification method based on (SRC) has been widely applied in many areas such as face recognition [11,12], and its basic idea is simple: in complex multidimensional spaces, some data and feature may only be closely related to very tiny part of large number of potentially relevant data and features. This may make the sparse representation theory greatly simplify the process of facial expression recognition. When recognizing the expression of test image using the SRC framework, examples of seven expression classes are available and used to construct a training set. Each example is Gabor feature extracted from the facial expression images. Assuming that the given training sample $X=[X_1,X_2,...,X_k] \in R \text{ d} \times \text{n}$, where d is feature of each sample , n is the number of training samples, $X_i \in R \text{ d} \times \text{n}^i$ represents n_i training samples of ith class, and $n=\sum_{i=1}^{k} n_i$. The test sample $y \in R \text{ d}$ can be presented by sparse linear combination of training samples X:

$$y = X\alpha + z \qquad (7)$$

where, $\alpha=[0,...,0,\alpha_{i1},...,\alpha_{in},0,...,0]^T \in R^n$ is coefficient vector whose entries are zero except those associated with the ith class, and $\|Z\|_2 \leqslant \varepsilon$. Since the linear representation is sparse, which means that the α can be calculated by solving an l^0-minimization problem as shown in formation:

$$(l^0): \min \|\alpha\|_0, s.t. \quad \|y-X\alpha\|_2 \leq \varepsilon \qquad (8)$$

If the solution α sought is sparse enough, the solution of the l^0-minimization problem (8) is equal to the solution to the following l^1-minimization problem:

$$(l^1): \min \|\alpha\|_1 , s.t. \quad \|y-X\alpha\|_2 \leq \varepsilon \qquad (9)$$

The class of testing sample can be predicted from coefficient. The specific steps of SRC is given below:

Algorithm. Sparse Representation-based Classification(SRC)

Input:a matrix of training samples $X=[X_1,X_2,...,X_k] \in R \text{ d} \times \text{n}$ for k class, a test sample $y \in R \text{ d}$.

Output: class label of y.

1: Normalize the columns of X to have unit l^2-norm.

2: Solve l^1-minimization problem(9) to get coefficient vector α of y.

3: Calculate the value of residual between y and $X\delta_i(\alpha)$:
$$r_i(y)= \|y - X\delta_i(\alpha)\|_2, i=1,...,k$$
$\delta_i(\alpha)$ is a new vector whose only nonzero entries are the entries in α that are associated with class i.

4:The classification decision can be obtained
$$i^* = \arg \min r_i(y).$$

---

6   Experiment

All the experiments are carried out in MATLAB R2014a environment running on a desktop with CPU Intel Core i5 3.10GHz and 4 GB RAM and conducted on the JAFFE and Cohn-Kanade database. JAFFE database contains 213 images of seven expressions for 10 Japanese female models, each female has two to four examples for each facial expression, and the size of each image is 256×256. Cohn-Kanade database includes 2105 digitized facial expression image sequences from 182 adult subjects. We choose the whole JAFFE database and part of Cohn-Kanade database to get the final results by using cross validation.

Certain local binary patterns(LBP) are fundamental properties of local image texture and their occurrence histogram is proven to be a very powerful textual feature, but it is too local to be robust. The result based on LBP and Gabor feature is shown in Table 1.

Table 1. Recognition rates of different features

Feature	Recognition rate(%)	
	JAFFE databse	Cohn-Kanade database
LBP+PCA+SRC	81.19	88.45
Block LBP+PCA+SRC	91.96	95.48
Improved Gabor+PCA+SRC	97.68	99.12

When the size of Gabor kernel is reducing, part of energy is lost, so the recognition rate of Improved Gabor feature is a little lower than original Gabor feature, but the speed is faster. The result is shown in Table 2.

Table 2. Recognition rates of Gabor feature on JAFFE database

Feature extracting	Recognition rate/%	Time /s
Gabor feature	98.09	0.32
Improved Gabor feature	97.68	0.13

In order to demonstrate the efficiency of the combination of PCA with SRC, Table 3 shows the results of different feature dimension reduction and classification methods. From Table 3, it can be seen that our method outperforms other methods.

Table 3. Recognition rate of different methods on JAFFE database

Method	Recognition rate (%)
Gabor+Adboost+SVM[9]	97.18
Gabor+PCA-LDA[3]	92
Ours	97.68

Table 4. Recognition rate of each class of facial expression on JAFFE database

Expression	Anger	Disgust	Fear	Happy	Neutral	Sadness	Surprise
Recognition rate(%)	100	96.67	93.33	97.5	100	96.67	100

The results of every class of facial expression are shown in Table 4, among which, the recognition rate of angry, neutral and surprise are highest, since these expressions are more different, but fear and sadness are similar sometimes and changed a little, so they are not easily identified.

7   Conclusion

We proposed a method combining improved Gabor feature with SRC for facial expression recognition, which performs well on JAFFE and Cohn-Kanade database. Although Gabor feature is capable to detect multi-orientation and multi-scale's texture changes, and little affected by light, but it needs large amount of calculation with high-dimension. The selection of sampling points and PCA reduce the dimension of feature greatly, and make the feature more suitable for SRC, then improve speed and accuracy of recognition.

References

1. Zhang, Z., Lyons, M., Schuster, M., Akamatsu, S.: Comparison between geometry-based and gabor-wavelets-based facial expression recognition using multi-layer perceptron. In: 3rd IEEE International Conference on Automatic Face and Gesture Recognition, pp. 454–459. IEEE Press, Nara (1998)
2. Lyons, M.J., Budynek, J., Akamatsu, S.: Automatic Classification of Single Facial Images. IEEE Trans. Pattern Anal. Mach. Intell. 21, 1357–1362 (1999)
3. Viola, P., Jones, M.J.: Robust real-time face detection. In: 8th IEEE International Conference on Computer Vision, pp. 747. IEEE Press (2001)
4. Milborrow, S., Nicolls, F.: Locating facial features with an extended active shape model. In: Forsyth, D., Torr, P., Zisserman, A. (eds.) ECCV 2008, Part IV. LNCS, vol. 5305, pp. 504–513. Springer, Heidelberg (2008)
5. Marcelja, S.: Mathematical Description of the Responses of Simple Cortical Cells. J. Opt. Soc. Am. 70, 1297–1300 (1980)
6. Lyons, M., Akamatsu, S., Kamachi, M., Gyoba, J.: Coding facial expressions with gabor wavelets. In: 3rd IEEE International Conference on Automatic Face and Gesture Recognition, pp. 200–205. IEEE Press, Nara (1998)
7. Wiskott, L., Fellous, J.M., Kuiger, N., Von Der Malsburg, C.: Face recognition by elastic bunch graph matching. In: 7th International Conference on Computer Analysis of Images and Patterns, pp: 129–132. IEEE Press, Santa Barbara (2002)
8. Zhu, J.X., Su, G.D., Li, Y.E.: Facial Expression Recognition Based on Gabor Feature and Adaboost. J. Optoelectronics Laser 17, 993–998 (2006)
9. Turk, M., Pentland, A.: Eigenfaces For Recognition. J. Cognitive Neurosci. 3, 71–86 (1991)
10. Abdulrahman, M., Gwadabe, T.R., Abdu, F.J., Eleyan, A.: Gabor wavelet transform based facial expression recognition using PCA and LBP. In: 22nd Signal Processing and Communications Applications Conference, pp. 2265–2268. IEEE Press, Trabzon (2014)
11. Wright, J., Yang, A.Y., Ganesh, A., Sastry, S.S., Ma, Y.: Robust Face Recognition via Sparse Representation. IIEEE Trans. Pattern Anal. Mach. Intell. 31, 210–227 (2008)
12. Yang, M., Zhang, D., Yang, J.: Robust sparse coding for face recognition. In: 2011 IEEE Conference on Computer Vision and Pattern Recognition, pp. 625–632. IEEE Press, Providence (2011)

Feature Fusion of Gradient Direction and LBP
for Facial Expression Recognition

Yu Li$^{(\boxtimes)}$ and Liang Zhang

Tianjin Key Lab for Advanced Signal and Image Processing,
Civil Aviation University of China, Tianjin, China
liyuld2009@163.com

Abstract. Feature extraction is an important step in facial expression recognition. A novel method is proposed based on feature fusion which combines gradient direction and LBP features. Firstly, eyes are located through the integration projection method. And the operation of image rotating, cropping and normalizing is conducted based on eyes' position. Secondly, the image is partitioned into nine non-overlapping regions with different weight, then the gradient direction and LBP features are extracted and fused. The fused features generated from each of the regions are concatenated to form the feature vector which represents the facial expression. Finally, K-nearest neighbor algorithm is performed for classification. Experiments on JAFFE and Cohn-Kanade facial expression databases show that the proposed method achieves better performance for facial expression recognition.

Keywords: Facial expression recognition · LBP(Local Binary Pattern) · Gradient direction · K-nearest neighbor algorithm

1   Introduction

As a kind of nonverbal communication, facial expression recognition is of great importance in human communication and loaded with rich psychological and emotional information [1]. According to American psychologist Mehrabian [2], the contribution of verbal information in a face to face communication is usually limited to only 7% of the total information, whereas conventional signals such as voice contributes 38% and facial expression contributes 55%. With the development of human-computer interaction system, the facial expression recognition has become a hot research topic as well as a difficult issue in the field of pattern recognition and artificial intelligence. Generally, a facial expression recognition system includes three parts: face detection, expression feature extraction and expression classification. Among them, expression feature extraction is the key to face recognition. An effective feature extraction method not only helps to simplify the classification of follow-up design, but also can enhance the recognition accuracy.

At present, the main method of expression feature extracting are: Principal Component Analysis (PCA) [3], Active Appearance Model (AAM) [4], Gabor wavelet [5], Local Binary Pattern (LBP) [6-7], etc. Among them, PCA utilizes only the holistic information of an image. Features extracted by AAM are relatively reliable and have a high recognition rate, but the disadvantages are that the calculation is complex and

© Springer International Publishing Switzerland 2015
J. Yang et al. (Eds.): CCBR 2015, LNCS 9428, pp. 423–430, 2015.
DOI: 10.1007/978-3-319-25417-3_50

the initial parameters are difficult to obtain. The method based on Gabor wavelet extracts multi-scale and multi-direction information, while the time-consuming and large amount of memory-requiring make it difficult to establish an efficient human-computer interaction system. Compared to Gabor wavelet features, the LBP-based method is well-accepted due to its low computational complexity yet powerful feature for analyzing local texture structures. It is invariant to any monotonic gray scale transformation and is robust to illumination changes. However, it also has some deficiencies, such as rather long histograms, lower discrimination, and sensitivity to noise.

Considering the deficiency of LBP operator, the researchers put forward a lot of improved LBP operators. In order to make LBP features more distinguishing, Zhang et al. utilize the Boosting algorithm [8] to select features. Tan et al. extended the original LBP to a version with 3-value codes, which is called local ternary patterns (LTP) [9]. The LTP codes are more resistant to noise, but no longer strictly invariant to gray-level transformations. More recently, Guo et al. proposed a complete LBP (CLBP)[10], which enhanced the capability of LBP operator to describe features. Another method is to combine Gabor wavelet with LBP [11], so as to solve the problem that the dimension of the Gabor wavelet features is too high.

In this paper, a novel feature extraction method that fuses gradient direction and LBP features is proposed. Due to the influence of head deflection and illumination changes, face image is preprocessed firstly and partitioned into nine non-overlapping regions according to facial feature. Then, the gradient direction [12] and LBP features are extracted and fused. Histograms generated from each region are concatenated to form the feature vector. Finally, k-nearest neighbor (KNN) algorithm is performed for classification. Experiments on JAFFE and Cohn-Kanade (CK) facial expression databases show that it is an effective method for facial expression recognition.

The rest of the paper is organized as follows: Section 2 introduces the preprocessing work; Section 3 describes the proposed method; Section 4 presents detailed experiments and results; and finally conclusions are given.

2   Preprocessing Procedure

In order to improve the efficiency of extracting facial features, face image must be preprocessed. The ideal output is to obtain pure facial expression images with normalized intensity, uniform size and shape.

As the image in the database is not completely aligned, the operation of angle normalized is needed. So the method of horizontal and vertical integral projection are conducted on input images respectively to locate the eyes' position, the angle between two eyes' center and horizontal line is the degree the image should be rotated. Besides, the areas, such as hair, ears, neck and shoulder, that are not useful for expression classification should be removed. If not, it will increase the amount of calculation and influence the recognition accuracy. According to the eyes' position, the cutting rule is: set the distance between the two eyes' center for d , and the image's upper-left corner is the origin; the center point of the two eyes here we define as (x_c, y_c); the top-left comer can be defined as $(x_c-0.9d, y_c-0.5d)$ and the top-right comer can be defined as $(x_c+0.9d, y_c-0.5d)$; the bottom-left and bottom-right corner here are $(x_c-0.9d, y_c+1.5d)$ and $(x_c+0.9d, y_c+1.5d)$ respectively. The last step is normalized the image to size of128×128pixe1s. Some sample images are shown in Fig. 1:

Angry   Disgust   Fear   Sad   Surprise   Happy

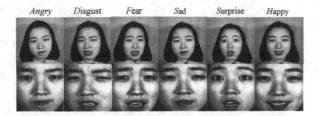

Fig. 1. The first level is original images, the second level is preprocessed images

3 Feature Extraction

Facial expression information mainly lies in the change of eyes, nose and mouth, so expression features should contain the texture's direction information. A novel feature extraction method that combines gradient direction and LBP operator is proposed. LBP operator is used to describe the texture information and gradient orientation operator is used to describe the change of texture's direction. Fusion of the two features can effectively describe the expression information.

3.1 Local Binary Pattern (LBP)

LBP operator is a simple yet effective way to describe the local texture. It can describe as: each pixel is compared with its eight neighbors by subtracting the center pixel value; the resulting strictly negative values are encoded with 0, and the others encoded with 1. For each given pixel, a binary number is obtained by concatenating all these binary values in a clockwise direction, which starts from the one of its top-left neighbor. The corresponding decimal value of the generated binary number is then used for labeling the given pixel. The binary number and decimal number can be obtained as shown in Fig. 2.

A limitation of the original LBP operator is that it only covers a small neighborhood area and can only get very limited local information. In order to obtain more local information by covering larger neighborhood area, and therefore to increase discriminative power of the original LBP, multi-scale LBP operator is applied by combining different LBP operators which use a circular neighborhood with different radius and different number of neighboring pixels. As illustrated in Fig. 3.

Formally, the resulting LBP can be expressed in decimal form as follows:

$$LBP_{P,R} = \sum_{p=0}^{P-1} s\left(g_p - g_c\right) 2^p \tag{1}$$

where g_c and g_p are, respectively, gray-level values of the central pixel and P surrounding pixels in the circle neighborhood with a radius R, and function $s(x)$ is defined as:

$$s(x) = \begin{cases} 1, & x \geq 0 \\ 0, & x < 0 \end{cases} \tag{2}$$

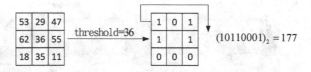

Fig. 2. The basic LBP operator

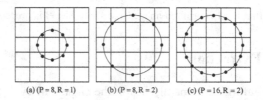

(a) (P = 8, R = 1)   (b) (P = 8, R = 2)   (c) (P = 16, R = 2)

Fig. 3. The LBP operator with different radius and the number of neighbors.

The operator $LBP_{P,R}$ produces 2^P different output values, corresponding to 2^P different binary patterns. For example: if $P=8$, the total patterns is $2^8=256$; if $P=16$, the total patterns is $2^{16}=65536$. However, too much kinds of pattern will make the data volumes too large and the histogram too sparse. Therefore, in order to reduce the dimension of original LBP patterns, one extension to the original LBP operator is the uniform LBP which contains at most two bitwise transitions from 0 to 1 or vice versa in a circular sequence of bits. Formally, the uniform LBP operator can be described as:

$$U\left(LBP_{P,R}\right) = \left|s(g_{p-1}-g_c)-s(g_0-g_c)\right| + \sum_{p=1}^{P-1}\left|s(g_p-g_c)-s(g_{p-1}-g_c)\right| \le 2 \quad (3)$$

Through such improvement, uniform LBP owns only $P(P-1)+3$ possible patterns, the binary patterns are reduced greatly. Meanwhile, uniform LBP can well reduce the effect of noise and makes the extracted features more accurately.

3.2   Gradient Direction (GD) Operator

The gradient direction is about the ratio of the change in horizontal directions to that in vertical direction of an image. Which is computed as:

$$\theta(g_c) = \arctan\left(\frac{v_1}{v_2}\right), \text{ and } v_1 = g_7 - g_3 , v_2 = g_5 - g_1$$

$$(4)$$

For simplicity, θ is further quantized into T dominant orientations. Before the quantization, we perform the mapping: $f: \theta \to \theta'$

$$\theta' = \arctan 2\left(v_1, v_2\right) + \pi \quad (5)$$

$$\arctan 2\left(v_1, v_2\right) = \begin{cases} \theta , & v_1 > 0, v_2 > 0 \\ \theta + \pi, & v_1 > 0, v_2 < 0 \\ \theta - \pi, & v_1 < 0, v_2 < 0 \\ \theta , & v_1 < 0, v_2 > 0 \end{cases} \quad (6)$$

where $\theta\in[-\pi/2, \pi/2]$ and $\theta'\in[0,2\pi]$.The quantization function is then as follows:

$$\varphi_t = f_q(\theta') = \frac{2t}{T}\pi , \; and \; t = \mathrm{mod}\left(\left\lfloor \frac{\theta'}{2\pi/T}+\frac{1}{2}\right\rfloor,T\right) \tag{7}$$

For example, if $T=8$, these T dominant orientations are $\varphi_t=(t\pi/4)$ $(t=0,1,\ldots,7)$.In other words, those orientations located within the interval $[\varphi_t-\pi/T,\varphi_t+\pi/T]$ are quantized to φ_t.

3.3   Features Fusion

Firstly, the preprocessed image is partitioned into nine non-overlapping regions; Then, the LBP and gradient direction features are extracted respectively and fused; Finally, the fused feature generated from each of the regions are concatenated to form the expression feature vector. The detail process is shown in Fig. 4:

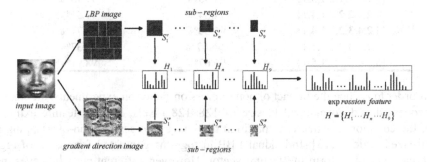

Fig. 4. The process of feature fusion

4   Experimental Results

Experiments are performed on JAFFE and CK databases to testify the effectiveness of the proposed method for facial expression recognition. JAFFE database is a set of 213 images of 7 different expressions (Anger, Disgust, Fear, Happy, Sad, Surprise and Neutral) posed by 10 Japanese females with 2-4 images for each expression. CK database consists of 100 university students in age from 18 to 30 years, of which 65% were female, 15% were African-American, and 3% were Asian or Latino. Subjects were instructed to perform a series of 32 facial expressions with seven prototypic emotions; namely, Anger, Disgust, Fear, Happy, Neutral, Sad, and Surprise. In our study, six basic expressions (except for the neutral) of ten people from JAFFE database are picked up. Then we select one image from each person's each expression as test samples, the others as training samples. In order to ensure that each image is used as a test, we run this experiment three times and take the mean value as the final recognition accuracy. For another, we choose 40 subjects of CK and select four images from image sequences per expression (except for the neutral), totaling 960 images. The same experiments are also done in CK database, and the only difference is taking the mean value of four experiments as the recognition accuracy.

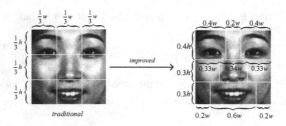

Fig. 5. segmentation of face image

Table 1. The relationship between the weights and recognition accuracy.

The weights	Recognition accuracy on JAFFE	Recognition accuracy on CK
{1,1,1,1,1,1,1,1,1}	90.89%	92.32%
{3,1,3,2,1,2,1,3,1}	94.33%	97.15%
{4,2,4,2,2,2,1,4,1}	94.54%	97.51%
{4,2,4,3,2,3,1,4,1}	95.00%	97.74%
{5,2,5,3,2,3,1,5,1}	96.67%	98.37%
{5,2,5,3,2,3,1,5,1}	96.67%	98.91%

In order to reduce the impact of non-expression factor on experiments, the image is preprocessed and normalized to size of 128×128 pixels. In LBP feature extraction step, the common practice is to partition the image into several non-overlapping and equal-sized regions [13]. Individual LBP histograms generated from each of region are concatenated to form the feature vector. However, different parts like eyes, nose and mouth which does not contribute equally to facial expression recognition. So a novel partitioned method (see Fig. 5) is proposed and different weights are set for different regions according to their contribution to expression recognition. In our experiments, we adapt $LBP_{8,1}^{u_2}$ and the dominant orientation T is set for 8. Table 1 shows that the highest recognition accuracy is achieved when weights are {5, 3, 5, 3, 2, 3, 1, 5, 1} .The final expression features are $H=\{5*H_1, 3*H_2, 5*H_3, 3*H_4, 2*H_5, 3*H_6, H_7, 5*H_8, H_9\}$,and $H_i(i=1,\dots,9)$is the ith regions' histogram. In this paper, the total dimension of the facial expression feature vector is 603. In expression classification step, a simple KNN method is adopted. The performance of KNN is close related to the value of k. It can be seen from Fig. 6 that the highest recognition rate is achieved at $k=3$ on JAFFE database and $k=5$ on CK database.

From Table 2 we can visually see that the recognition accuracy improves a lot when the image is partitioned into nine regions. In the same 3×3 regions condition, LBP+GD features have higher recognition accuracy. Furthermore, regular partition way is easily distract the expression information of eyes、 mouth and other important parts, so our method which adapts an irregular partitioned way and extracts LBP+GD features shows better recognition performance.

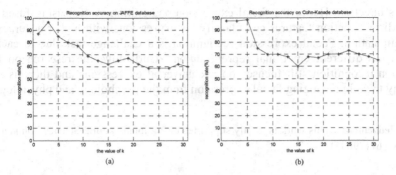

Fig. 6. The relationship between k and recognition rate

Table 2. Experiments on different conditions

method	Recognition accuracy on JAFFE	Recognition accuracy on CK
LBP(1×1region)	76.11%	81.13%
LBP(3×3regions)	85%	89.38%
LBP+GD(3×3regions)	90.16%	94.55%
Our method	96.67%	98.91%

Table 3. Compare with other methods

method	Recognition accuracy
LBP+DCT[14]	92.83%
Gabor+LBP[15]	96.1%
AAM	93.43%
Our method	98.91%

Table 3 shows that our method can classify six expressions with higher accuracy, compared with other methods. The main reasons are: 1) partition the image into nine regions and higher weights are allocated to the regions which contribute more than others in classification; 2) the features extracted by the proposed method both contain the texture information and texture's direction information which can well describe the expression characteristics; 3) the dimensions of the expression feature vector are lower; 4) Due to convolving face images with multi-banks of Gabor filters in order to extract multi-scale and multi-direction coefficients, the computation of Gabor wavelet is both time and memory expensive; 5) AAM-based approaches can obtain more reliable facial feature parameters but have the drawbacks of complex computation and difficulties in obtaining initial parameters.

5   Conclusion

This paper proposed a novel feature extraction method to improve facial expression recognition. LBP operator can well describe the image texture information and gradient direction operator shows a good performance on describing the change of texture's direction. Hence the facial expression recognition system using fused LBP and gradient direction features can classify six expressions with higher accuracy and less computation. Facial expression recognition is a challenge task due to each expression has different emotional representations. Until now, the research on facial expression recognition still focuses on six universal expressions and there is still a long way to go in cognizing facial expression from the psychology and physiology.

Acknowledgements. This work is jointly supported by National Natural Science Foundation of China (No.61179045).

References

1. Jabid, T., Kabir, M.H., Chae, O.: Robust facial expression recognition based on local directional pattern. ETRI Journal **32**(5), 784–794 (2010)
2. Wang, L., Li, R.F., Wang, K.: Multi-scale local binary pattern fourier histogram features for facial expression recognition. Journal of Computer Application **34**(7), 2036–2039 (2014)
3. El-Hori, I.H., El-Momen, Z.K., Ganoun, A.: PCA facial expression recognition. In: Proceedings of Sixth International Conference on Machine Vision (ICMV 2013), International Society for Optics and Photonics, pp. 906712–906712–5 (2013)
4. Tang, F., Deng, B.: Facial expression recognition using AAM and local facial features. In: Proceedings of the Third IEEE International Conference on Natural Computation, Haikou, China, pp. 632–635 (2007)
5. Ahsan, T., Jabid, T., Chong, U.P.: Facial expression recognition using local transitional pattern on Gabor filtered facial images. IETE Technical Review **30**(1), 47–52 (2013)
6. Ojala, T., Pietikäinen, M., Harwood, D.: A comparative study of texture measures with classification based on featured distributions. Pattern Recognition **29**(1), 51–59 (1996)
7. Liu, W., Wang, Y., Li, S.: LBP feature extraction for facial expression recognition. Journal of Information & Computational Science **8**(3), 412–421 (2011)
8. Zhang, G., Huang, X., Li, S.Z., Wang, Y., Wu, X.: Boosting local binary pattern (LBP)-based face recognition. In: Li, S.Z., Lai, J.-H., Tan, T., Feng, G.-C., Wang, Y. (eds.) SINOBIOMETRICS 2004. LNCS, vol. 3338, pp. 179–186. Springer, Heidelberg (2004)
9. Tan, X., Triggs, B.: Enhanced local texture feature sets for face recognition under difficult lighting conditions. IEEE Transactions on Image Processing **19**(6), 1635–1650 (2010)
10. Guo, Z., Zhang, D.: A completed modeling of local binary pattern operator for texture classification. IEEE Transactions on Image Processing **19**(6), 1657–1663 (2010)
11. Zhang, W., Shan, S., Gao, W.: Local gabor binary pattern histogram sequence (lgbphs): a novel non-statistical model for face representation and recognition. In: Proceedings of Tenth IEEE International Conference on Computer Vision-ICCV, vol. 1, pp.786–791 (2005)
12. Chen, J., Shan, S., He, C.: WLD: A robust local image descriptor. IEEE Transactions on Pattern Analysis and Machine Intelligence **32**(9), 1705–1720 (2010)
13. Shan, C., Gong, S., McOwan, P.W.: Facial expression recognition based on local binary patterns: A comprehensive study. Image and Vision Computing **27**(6), 803–816 (2009)
14. Li, R., Zhao, X.: Fusing DCT and LBP features for expression recognition. Computer Engineering and Applications **49**(15), 171–174 (2013)
15. Zhang, Z., Fang, C., Ding, X.Q.: A hierarchical algorithm with multi-feature fusion for facial expression recognition. In: Proceedings of 21st International Conference on Pattern Recognition (ICPR 2012), pp. 2363–2366 (2012)

A Mahalanobis Distance Scoring with KISS Metric Learning Algorithm for Speaker Recognition

Zhenchun Lei[✉], Jian Luo, Yanhong Wan, and Yingen Yang

School of Computer and Information Engineering, Jiangxi Normal University,
Nanchang, China
{zhenchun.lei,luo.jian}@hotmail.com, wyanhhappy@126.com,
ygyang@jxnu.edu.cn

Abstract. The cosine similarity scoring is often used in the i-vector model for its computational efficiency and performance in text-independent speaker recognition field. We propose a new Mahalanobis distance scoring with distance metric learning algorithm in this paper. The Mahalanobis metric matrix is learned using the KISS (keep it simple and straightforward!) method, which is motivated by a statistical inference perspective based on a likelihood-ratio test. After whitening and length-normalization, the i-vectors extracted from the development utterances were used to train the metric matrix. Then, the score between the target i-vector and the test i-vector is based on the Mahalanobis distance. The results on NIST 2008 telephone data show that the performance of new scoring is obviously better than the cosine similarity scoring's.

Keywords: Speaker recognition · I-vector model · Mahalanobis distance · Distance metric learning

1 Introduction

I-vector model [1] has become the state of the art technique for text-independent speaker recognition in recent years. The i-vector is a compact, low-dimensional representation of any speech segment, which turn a complex high-dimensional speaker recognition problem into a low-dimensional classical pattern recognition one. First of all, different scoring approaches have been proposed in order to make decision from i-vectors extracted from both training and testing utterances. Among these scoring approaches, we can differentiate the simple Cosine Similarity Scoring (CSS) [1] and derived distances to deal with score normalization [2] from more advanced Gaussian-based scoring approaches like two covariance scoring [3], Mahalanobis scoring [4], and Gaussian Probabilistic Linear Discriminant Analysis (PLDA) [5], or from Heavy Tailed PLDA [6].

The basic speaker recognition task seeks to determine whether the test utterance and the target utterance are from the same speaker. In other words, the goal is to determine the proximity between the test utterance and the target utterance are close enough or not. Thus we can view the speaker verification system as a distance metric

© Springer International Publishing Switzerland 2015
J. Yang et al. (Eds.): CCBR 2015, LNCS 9428, pp. 431–438, 2015.
DOI: 10.1007/978-3-319-25417-3_51

learning problem [7]: given speaker labels of training utterances, we aim to find a good distance metric that brings "similar" data points (belonging to the same speaker) close together while separating "dissimilar" data points (belonging to different speakers) [8]. A particular class of distance functions that exhibits good generalization performance for many machine learning problems is Mahalanobis metric learning. The goal is to find a global, linear transformation of the feature space such that relevant dimensions are emphasized while irrelevant ones are discarded. The metric adapts to the desired geometry by arbitrary linear rotations and scalings.

Learning a Mahalanobis metric on a large scale dataset raises further issues on scalability and the required degree of supervision. Kostinger propose a KISS (keep it simple and straightforward!) [9] learning algorithm, which is motivated by a statistical inference perspective based on a likelihood-ratio test. The resulting metric is not prone to over-fitting and very efficient to obtain. Compared to other approaches, it is not rely on a tedious iterative optimization procedure, and it is scalable to large datasets, as it just involves computation of two small sized covariance matrices.

In the i-vector framework, we propose a new Mahalanobis distance scoring model with the metric matrix trained by the KISS learning algorithm. The classical CSS operates by comparing the angles between two i-vectors, and our method is based on the Mahalanobis distance.

This paper is structured as follows: We review the i-vector model in section 2. We present our new Hahalanobis scoring model in section 3. Section 4 provides the results of our experiments on NIST 2008 telephone data. Finally, section 5 is devoted to the main conclusions and our future work.

2   The I-Vector Model

I-vectors, whether through the simpler CSS approach, or the more complex length-normalized Gaussian PLDA (GPLDA) [1] approach are considered the state-of-the-art for speaker verification research. Such systems typically involve three phases: i-vector feature extraction, session variability compensation and scoring.

2.1   I-Vector Feature Extraction

In contrast to the separate speaker and session dependent subspaces of the previous state-of-the-art JFA [10] technique, i-vectors represent the GMM supervector using a single total-variability subspace. This single-subspace approach was motivated by the discovery that the session variability space of JFA contains information which can be used to distinguish between speakers. In an i-vector based speaker recognition system, the speaker and session dependent GMM supervector can be represented by

$$\mu = m + Tw \tag{1}$$

where m is the speaker and session independent UBM supervector, T is a low rank matrix representing the primary directions of variation across a large collection of development data, and w is normally distributed with parameters $N(0,I)$, and is the i-vector representation used for speaker verification. The supervector is assumed to be normally distributed with mean vector m and covariance matrix $T*T^T$. This model can be viewed like a principal component analysis of the larger supervector space which project the speech utterances onto the total variability space. The factor analysis plays the role of features extraction where we now operate on the total factor vectors. The details of the total-variability subspace training and subsequent i-vector extraction is given by Dehak et al. [1].

2.2   Inter-Session Compensation

2.2.1   Linear Discriminant Analysis

LDA [11] is used as session variability compensation technique, which attempts to find a reduced set of axes A that minimizes the within-class variability while maximizing the between-class variability through the eigenvalue decomposition of

$$S_b \mathrm{v} = \lambda S_w \mathrm{v} \tag{2}$$

where the between-class scatter, S_b, and within-class scatter, S_w, can be calculated as follows,

$$S_b = \sum_{s-1}^{S} n_s (\overline{w}_s - \overline{w})(\overline{w}_s - \overline{w})^T \tag{3}$$

$$S_w = \sum_{s=1}^{S} \sum_{i=1}^{n_s} (w_i^s - \overline{w}_s)(w_i^s - \overline{w}_s)^T \tag{4}$$

where S is the total number of speakers, n_s is number of utterances of speaker s. The mean i-vectors, $\overline{w}_s$ for each speaker, and $\overline{w}$, the mean across all speakers.

2.2.2   Within Class Covariance Normalization

WCCN [2] is then used as an additional session variability compensation technique to scale the subspace in order to attenuate dimensions of high within-class variance. The WCCN transformation matrix (B) is trained using the LDA-projected i-vectors from the first stage. The WCCN matrix is calculated using Cholesky decomposition of $B \cdot B^T = W^{-1}$, where the within-class covariance matrix W is calculated using

$$\mathrm{W} = \frac{1}{\mathrm{S}} \sum_{s=1}^{S} \sum_{i=1}^{n_s} (w_i^s - \overline{w}_s)(w_i^s - \overline{w}_s)^T \tag{5}$$

The final subspace compensation is carried out through LDA followed by WCCN,

$$\widetilde{w} = B^T A^T w \tag{6}$$

2.3   Cosine Similarity Scoring without Score Normalization

The simple cosine similarity scoring [1] has been applied successfully to compare two i-vectors for making a speaker detection decision. Dehak [2] propose a scoring technique that combines the effects of z- and t-norm score normalization, and it does not require test-time score normalization compared to the classical cosine similarity scoring. Given two i-vectors via the projection of two supervectors in the total variability space and the LDA-WCCN compensation for inter-session variabilities, a target w_{target} from a known speaker and a test w_{test} from an unknown speaker, the cosine similarity score is given as:

$$score(w_{t\arg et}, w_{test}) = \frac{(w_{t\arg et} - \overline{w}_{imp})^T g(w_{test} - \overline{w}_{imp})}{\left\| C_{imp} g w_{t\arg et} \right\| \left\| C_{imp} w_{test} \right\|} \tag{7}$$

where $\overline{w}_{imp}$ the mean of the impostor i-vectors. C_{imp} is a diagonal matrix that contains the square root of the diagonal covariance matrix of the impostor i-vectors.

3   The Mahalanobis Distance Scoring Model

In the classical i-vector model, the cosine similarity scoring is used, and the scoring is based on the Mahalanobis distance in our model. After the i-vectors were extracted from the training utterances, a metric matrix M is trained using the KISS[9] learning algorithm on the whitened i-vectors. Finally, the score between two vectors is based on the Mahalanobis distance.

3.1   Whitening and Length-Normalization

The i-vectors from the extractor are to be normalized by a linear whitening and length-normalization [12]. A linear-whitened i-vector can be estimated as follows,

$$w_{wht} = d^{-\frac{1}{2}} U^T w \tag{8}$$

where Σ is a covariance matrix, estimated using development i-vectors. U is an orthonormal matrix containing the eigenvectors of Σ and d is a diagonal matrix containing the corresponding eigenvalues. The length-normalized i-vector feature w_{norm}, can be calculated as follows,

$$w_{norm} = \frac{w_{wht}}{\left\| w_{wht} \right\|} \tag{9}$$

3.2   KISS Metric Learning [9]

Learning a distance or similarity metric based on the class of Mahalanobis distance functions has gained considerable interest. In general, a Mahalanobis distance metric measures the squared distance between two data points x_i and x_j:

$$d^2(x_i, x_j) = (x_i - x_j)^T M(x_i - x_j) \tag{10}$$

where $M \geq 0$ is a positive semidefinite matrix and $x_i, x_j \in R^d$ is a pair of samples (i, j). Further, for the following discussion we introduce a similarity label y_{ij}, $y_{ij}=1$ for similar pairs, i.e., if the samples share the same class label $(y_i=y_j)$ and $y_{ij}=0$ otherwise.

From a statistical inference point of view the optimal statistical decision whether a pair (i, j) is dissimilar or not can be obtained by a likelihood ratio test. Thus, we test the hypothesis H_0 that a pair is dissimilar versus the alternative H_1:

$$\delta(x_i, x_j) = \log(\frac{p(x_i, x_j \mid H_0)}{p(x_i, x_j \mid H_1)}) \tag{11}$$

A high value of (x_i, x_j) means that H_0 is validated. In contrast, a low value means that H_0 is rejected and the pair is considered as similar. In the KISS metric learning algorithm [9], the problem is casted in the space of pairwise differences $(x_{ij} = x_i - x_j)$ with zero mean for the independent of the actual locality in the feature space.

$$\delta(x_{ij}) = \log(\frac{p(x_{ij} \mid H_0)}{p(x_{ij} \mid H_1)}) = \log(\frac{f(x_{ij} \mid \theta_0)}{f(x_{ij} \mid \theta_1)}) \tag{12}$$

where $f(x_{ij}|\theta_0)$ is a pdf with parameters for hypothesis H_1 that a pair(i, j) is similar $(y_{ij}=1)$ and vice-versa H_0 for a pair being dissimilar. Assuming a Gaussian structure of the difference space, the maximum likelihood estimate of the Gaussian is equivalent to minimizing the Mahalanobis distances from the mean in a least squares manner.

$$\delta(x_{ij}) = \log(\frac{\frac{1}{\sqrt{2\pi|\Sigma_{y_{ij}=0}|}}\exp(-1/2x_{ij}^T \Sigma_{y_{ij}=0}^{-1} x_{ij})}{\frac{1}{\sqrt{2\pi|\Sigma_{y_{ij}=1}|}}\exp(-1/2x_{ij}^T \Sigma_{y_{ij}=1}^{-1} x_{ij})}) \tag{13}$$

where

$$\Sigma_{y_{ij}=1} = \sum_{y_{ij}=1}(x_i - x_j)(x_i - x_j)^T \tag{14}$$

$$\Sigma_{y_{ij}=0} = \sum_{y_{ij}=0} (x_i - x_j)(x_i - x_j)^T \qquad (15)$$

This allows us to find respective relevant directions for the two independent sets. Finally, the Mahalanobis distance metric can be obtained, which reflects the properties of the log-likelihood ratio test, M is a positive semidefinite matrix.

$$d_M^2(x_i, x_j) = (x_i - x_j)^T M (x_i - x_j) \qquad (16)$$

where

$$M = (\Sigma_{y_{ij}=1}^{-1} - \Sigma_{y_{ij}=0}^{-1}) \qquad (17)$$

3.3   Mahalanobis Distance Scoring

Motivated by the distance metric learning algorithm, we use the Mahalanobis metric for the speaker scoring. If the distance between two i-vectors is smaller, the probability that they belong to a unique class is higher. The scoring function between a target and test is the negative distance:

$$score(w_{target}, w_{test}) = -d_M^2(w_{target}, w_{test}) = -(w_{target} - w_{test})^T M (w_{target} - w_{test}) \qquad (18)$$

This equation is Euclidean distance when $M=I$, and we will also compare their performances.

4   Experiment

4.1   Set-Up

The features were derived from the waveforms using 13 mel-frequency cepstral coefficients on a 20 millisecond frame every 10 milliseconds. Delta and delta-delta coefficients were computed making up a thirty nine dimensional feature vector. And the band limiting was performed by retaining only the filter bank outputs form the frequency range 300-3400 Hz. Mean removal, preemphasis and a hamming window were applied, and energy-based end pointing eliminated nonspeech frames.

Our experiments were performed on the 2008 NIST SRE dataset. NIST SRE2004 1side training corpus was used to train two gender-dependent UBMs with 512 Gaussian components. The rank of the total variability matrix T was chosen to be 400. NIST SRE2004, SRE 2005, and SRE 2006 telephone datasets were used for estimating the total variability space, LDA transformation matrix, the WCCN transformation matrix and Mahalanobis metric matrix. For measuring the performance, we used equal error rate (EER) and the minimum decision cost function (DCF).

In the KISS learning algorithm, the input are similar pairs and dissimilar pairs of samples, but the NIST SRE provide the speech labels from the development dataset. So we need to construct the pairs of samples according the speech segment labels. A simple way is using utterance labels belonging to the same speaker construct the similar pairs with each other. For example, if one speaker has 10 utterance segments, we can get 10×9/2=45 similar pairs. For dissimilar pairs, we use the segment labels belonging to the different speaker, and the size of dissimilar pair dataset is very big. In our experiment, there are 61,625 similar pairs and 41,667,055 dissimilar pairs for female speakers, 47,182 similar pairs and 21,788,954 dissimilar pairs for male speakers.

4.2 Results

The experiment was run on the 1conv-1conv 2008 SRE core phonecall condition. The classical cosine similarity scoring, Euclidean distance scoring and Mahalanobis distance scoring were compared. Table 1 shows the results. We can see that the performance of our new method is obviously better than the cosine similarly scoring's. The performance of Euclidean distance model is worst, which can be predictable.

In our experiments, learning the Mahalanobis metric matrix take about three hours for the large scale pairs on a dell server with one 4-core cpu using matlab. Compared to some minutes the LDA and WCCN used, that is time consuming. But in test phase, its computational efficiency is comparable with the classical cosine similarity scoring's because the matrix computations are also very efficient in the model.

Table 1. Comparison results between the classical cosine similarity scoring and our Mahalanobis distance scoring. The results are on the female portion of NIST 2008 telephone dataset.

Model	EER(%)	minDCF
Cosine similarity	6.78	0.0342
Euclidean distance	9.31	0.0436
Mahalanobis distance	5.77	0.0287

Table 2 show the performance of models on the male portion of NIST 2008 telephone dataset. We can see that the performance of the new scoring is the best also.

Table 2. Comparison results between the classical cosine similarity scoring and our Mahalanobis distance scoring. The results are on the male portion of NIST 2008 telephone dataset.

Model	EER(%)	minDCF
Cosine similarity	5.29	0.0262
Euclidean distance	7.86	0.0356
Mahalanobis distance	5.05	0.0246

5   Conclusions

We propose a new Mahalanobis distance scoring with KISS metric learning algorithm. The results on NIST 2008 telephone dataset show that our new method is better than the classical cosine similarity scoring. Many machine leaning algorithms heavily rely on the distance metric for the input data patterns. We will apply the others distance metric learning algorithms to speaker recognition in future.

Acknowledgements. This work is supported by National Natural Science Foundation of P.R.China (61365004), Educational Commission of Jiangxi Province of P.R.China (GJJ12198).

References

1. Dehak, N., Kenny, P., Dehak, R., Dumouchel, P., Ouellet, P.: Front-end factor analysis for speaker verification. IEEE Trans. Audio Speech Lang. Process **19**(4), 788–798 (2011)
2. Dehak, N., Dehak, R., Glass, J., Reynolds, D., Kenny, P.: Cosine similarity scoring without score normalization techniques. In: Proc. of Odyssey - The Speaker and Language Recognition Workshop, Brno, Czech Republic, 71–75 (2010)
3. Brummer, N., Villalba, J., Lleida, E.: Fully bayesian likelihood ratio vs i-vector length normalization in speaker recognition systems. In: NIST SRE Analysis Workshop (2011)
4. Bousquet, P.-M., Matrouf, D., Bonastre, J.-F.: Intersession compensation and scoring methods in the i-vector space for speaker recognition. In: Proc. of International conference on Speech Communication and Technology (2011)
5. Prince, S.J.D.: Probabilistic linear discriminant analysis for inferences about identity. In: Proc. of International Conference on Computer Vision (ICCV), Rio de Janeiro, Brazil (2007)
6. Kenny, P.: Bayesian speaker verification with heavy-tailed priors. In: Proc. of Odyssey - The Speaker and Language Recognition Workshop, Czech Republic (2010)
7. Fang, X., Dekhak, N., Glass, J.: Bayesian distance metric learning on i-vector for speaker verification. In: INTERSPEECH 2013 – Proceedings of the 14th Annual Conference of the International Speech Communication Association, August 25–29, 2013, Lyon, France, pp. 2514–2518 (2013)
8. Xing, E., Ng, A., Jordan, M., Russell, S.: Distance metric learning with application to clustering with side-information. In: Neural Information Processing Systems, pp. 505–512 (2002)
9. Kostinger, M., Hirzer, M., Wohlhart, P., Roth, P.M., Bischof, H.: Large scale metric learning from equivalence constraints. In: Proceedings of the 2012 Computer Vision and Pattern Recognition., pp. 2288–2295 (2012)
10. Kenny, P.: Joint factor analysis of speaker and session variability: theory and algorithms, Tech. rep., CRIM (2005)
11. McLaren, M., van Leeuwen, D.: Source-normalised and weighted LDA for robust speaker recognition using i-vectors. In: 2011 IEEE International Conference on Acoustics, Speech and Signal Processing (ICASSP), pp. 5456–5459 (2011)
12. Garcia-Romero, D., Espy-Wilson, C.Y.: Analysis of i-vector length normalization in speaker recognition systems. In: Annual Conference of the International Speech Communication Association (Interspeech), pp. 249–252 (2011)

Automatic Facial Expression Analysis of Students in Teaching Environments

Chuangao Tang, Pengfei Xu[✉], Zuying Luo[✉], Guoxing Zhao, and Tian Zou

Beijing Key Laboratory of Digital Preservation and Virtual Reality for Cultural Heritage, College of Information Science and Technology, Beijing Normal University, Beijing 100875, China
{xupf,luozy}@bnu.edu.cn

Abstract. Based on students' facial expressions, the teacher in class can know the students' comprehension of the lecture, which has been a standard of teaching effect evaluation. In order to solve the problem of high cost and low efficiency caused by employing human analysts to observe classroom teaching effect, in this paper we present a novel and high-efficiency prototype system, that automatically analyzes students' expressions. The fusion feature called Uniform Local Gabor Binary Pattern Histogram Sequence (ULGBPHS) is employed in the system. Using K-nearest neighbor (KNN) classifier, we obtain an average recognition rate of 79% on students' expressions database with five types of expressions. The experiment shows that the proposed system is feasible, and is able to improve the efficiency of teaching evaluation.

Keywords: Teaching effect evaluation · Facial expression recognition · ULGBPHS · Feature fusion

1   Introduction

Classroom teaching evaluation has been a hot spot in recent years. It has been widely used to promote the classroom teaching quality and teachers' skills [1]. Students' grasp of the lecture and students' emotional involvement, both of which are indexes of the teaching effect evaluation, are correlated with their facial expressions. For instance, students usually smile after comprehending the lecture and finding it interesting, and they form negative expressions when they find that the content is too abstruse to understand. The research [2] indicated that facial expression ranks top of the mode of nonverbal communication, followed by body language, gestures and hands. Experienced instructors often adjust their teaching according to students' expressions during the lectures. Currently, the classical methods of instructional measurement like tests, exams, questionnaires, interviews, observations are applied in classroom teaching evaluation. It is a common phenomenon that dozens of professors are invited every semester to form a supervision team to observe the classroom sessions of required and elective courses. After the observation, the feedback reports with the ratings and comments are written by the office and provided to the corresponding faculties within a few weeks. However, these manual evaluation methods often come with high cost and low efficiency [1, 2].

© Springer International Publishing Switzerland 2015
J. Yang et al. (Eds.): CCBR 2015, LNCS 9428, pp. 439–447, 2015.
DOI: 10.1007/978-3-319-25417-3_52

As our research motivation is to realize evaluating classroom teaching effect automatically, we conduct an exploratory research based on the recognition results of students' facial expressions in class. Since the late 1990s, an increasing number of efforts toward automatic affect recognition were reported in literature [3]. AFER technology has been successfully applied in the areas such as human-computer interaction (HCI), driver fatigue detection, e-learning, etc. [3]. Most of the existing facial expression recognition approaches are based on posed expression databases, like Japanese Female Facial Expression (JAFFE) database, Cohn-Kanade (CK) database. Due to lack of facial expression database in pedagogical environments, the researchers in our college firstly built the students' spontaneous expressions database in classroom teaching environments. Then, we propose a prototype system to automatically analyze students' expressions in class. In this system, a fusion feature ULGBPHS is employed. K-nearest neighbor (KNN) method based on Euclidean distance is employed for classification. The proposed method obtains a high recognition rate of 96.7% on JAFFE database, which outperforms some existing methods, and a recognition rate of 79% on self-build database. Furthermore, to the best of our knowledge, using the recognition results of students' facial expressions in class for traditional classroom teaching effect evaluation is first proposed in this paper.

The rest of this paper is organized as follows. Section 2 reviews the related work. Section 3 describes the self-build students' expressions database and an overview of the proposed system is given in section 4. Details of the proposed system are presented in section 5, followed by the experimental results in section 6. In the last section we conclude this paper with discussion.

2   Related Work

In this section, we offer an overview of some recent literature about facial expression recognition (FER) and some FER systems used in learning environments. Because of the importance of face in emotion expression and perception [3], extracting an efficient representation of the face is a key step for successful FER [4]. There are two main streams in the current research of extracting features for facial expression recognition: geometric based methods and appearance based methods [4]. Geometric features contain information about the location and shape of facial features. In general, a shape model defined by 58 facial landmarks is used during the process of geometric feature extraction, in which noise and tracking errors often decline the recognition performance. Appearance based features examine the appearance change of the face (including wrinkles, bulges and furrows) and are extracted by image filters applied to the face or sub regions of the face [3, 4]. Appearance based features are less reliant on initialization and can encode micro patterns in skin texture that are important for facial expression recognition. Gabor feature [6] and extended LBP feature [5] are widely used as appearance based features in facial expression recognition approaches. Hua Lu et al. [5] presented a method of divided local binary pattern (DLBP) and obtained a recognition rate of 95.7% on JAFFE database. Seung Ho Lee et al. [6] proposed a new sparse representation based FER method and got the highest overall recognition rate of 94.7% on JAFFE database under their experimental scenarios, compared with SRC+LBP and SRC+ Gabor, where the recognition rate of the former is 90.30% with the latter 91.21%. Recently, deep learning technology has attracted many researchers' interest. Ping Liu et al. [7] presented a novel Boosted Deep Belief Network (BDBN) framework for facial expression recognition, and obtained impressive recognition results. In their study, it took about 8 days to complete the overall training for 6 expressions in an 8-fold experimental setup on a 6-core 2.4GHz PC using Matlab implementation.

Some researchers have been focusing on facial expression and facial affect in the lab or wild [8]. In the lab environment, Whitehill et al. [9] used Gabor features with a SVM classifier to detect engagement as students interacted with cognitive skills training software. Labels used in their study were obtained from retrospective annotation of videos by human judges. While in the wild environment, Nigel Bosch et al. [8] collected the data of students' facial expressions, including videos containing students' faces and affect labels in the real-world environment of a school computer lab, where the students were interacting with a game-based physics education environment called Physics Playground.

3   Students' Spontaneous Expressions Database

Having enough labeled data of facial expressions is a prerequisite in designing automatic facial expression recognition system [3]. The self-build facial expression database in this paper contains the students' spontaneous expressions [18], as opposed to posed expressions in current mainstream databases. Since we focus on the spontaneous facial behavior correlated to learning, we predefine the labels of expression as follows: joviality, surprise, concentration, confusion, fatigue. The corresponding face images are demonstrated in Fig.1.

joviality   surprise   concentration   confusion   fatigue

Fig. 1. Five types of facial expressions

As [3] pointed out, current techniques for detection and tracking of facial expressions are sensitive to head pose, clutter, and variations in lighting conditions. Thus the experiment of self-build expression database was conducted under controlled condition to get rid of some above mentioned variations, with 23 youthful college students from different majors invited to participate in the experiment. There were 17 participants wearing glasses. They received a short-term training that the behaviors like extreme pose or position, occlusions from hand-to-face gestures, and rapid movements should be avoided during the process of experiment. All the participants sat on the seats in a common classroom, where the light condition was normal. The task for them was to watch 6 short videos, which lasted about 15 minutes. A 1080p HD camera was used for capturing their facial expressions. Another task for participants was to label their own expressions, respectively.

4   System Overview

In this paper, we propose a prototype system of AFER to analyze students' expressions for classroom teaching effect evaluation. The system consists of 5 modules: data acquisition module, face detection module, face recognition module, facial expression recognition module and post-processing module. The schematic diagram of the system is demonstrated in Fig. 2.

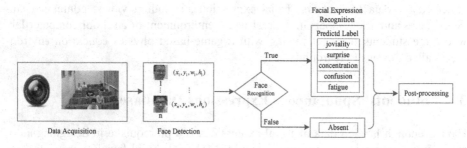

Fig. 2. Schematic diagram of proposed facial expression analysis system

Data Acquisition: A full 1080p HD camera is configured at the front of the classroom. Using HD camera can ensure every student's face enough resolution.

Face Detection: We use AdaBoost method to detect faces. The face images are segmented based on the location and size. We use canthi positions returned by the Structured Output Support Vector Machines (SO-SVM) [10] method to calculate the angle of tilt, which is used to normalize face rotation. Finally, the region of interest is cropped with geometry rules of face to remove background. We resize the cropped image region to 66×66 pixels.

Face Recognition: The location and size of the face are used to speed up computation if the face is recognized in the current frame, instead of repeating face recognition for the same student in the next frame. Here, we use location and size feature, known in advance, of the faces to sort the detected faces for facial expression recognition. If and only if the face is verified, facial expression recognition will be conducted. Otherwise, our system outputs an 'Absent' label.

FER: In this paper, the fusion feature ULGBPHS outperforms onefold feature. The details of the facial expression recognition will be illustrated in section 5.

Post-processing: In this stage, the results of facial expression recognition are used to evaluate classroom teaching effect, which will be analyzed in section 6.

5 Facial Expression Recognition

In this section, two main parts of our expression recognition system, feature extraction and expression classifier, are described. Feature extraction aims to build derived values, which is informative, non-redundant, and facilitates the subsequent learning steps. Expression classifier identifies which of a set of classes a new observation belongs to, on the basis of a training set containing observations whose class is known. In this system, we employ fused feature based on Gabor [11, 13] and LBP [12, 14].

Gabor feature: Gabor features have been widely used in many pattern analysis applications. C.J.Liu et al. [11] pointed that Gabor feature performs the best in classification of expression units. *2D* Gabor filter is a Gaussian kernel function modulated by a complex sinusoidal plane wave [13], defined as:

$$\varphi_{\Pi}(f,\theta,\gamma,\eta) = \frac{f^2}{\pi\gamma\eta}\exp(-(\alpha^2 x'^2 + \beta^2 y'^2))\exp(j2\pi fx')$$

$$\begin{cases} x' = x\cos\theta + y\sin\theta \\ y' = -x\sin\theta + y\cos\theta \end{cases} \tag{1}$$

Gabor features with different orientations and scales are obtained by convolving the images with *2D* Gabor filters. Due to limitations on space, we only list the kernel function in this paper. More details for Gabor feature extraction are presented in paper [13].The filters are more prominent at expression-rich positions like eyebrows, eyes, mouth and nose.

LBP feature: LBP is firstly proposed by Ojala [14]. LBP is computational efficient and robust to rotation and light variations, and has been successfully used in many object classification and detection applications. The operator labels the pixels of an image by thresholding a 3×3 neighborhood of each pixel with the center value and considering the result as a binary number [5]. Given a pixel at (x_c, y_c), the resulting LBP can be expressed in decimal form as follows:

$$LBP_{P,R}(x,y) = \sum_{p=0}^{P-1} S(i_p - i_c)2^p, \quad S(i_p - i_c) = \begin{cases} 1 & \text{if } i_p - i_c \geq 0 \\ 0 & \text{if } i_p - i_c < 0 \end{cases} \tag{2}$$

where i_c is the gray value of the pixel at (x_c, y_c), similarly, i_p (p=0, ..., p-1) are the gray values of P equally spaced pixels on a circle of radius R. This operator was extended to use neighborhoods of different sizes and capture dominant features at different scales. A Local Binary Pattern is called uniform, which is defined in Eq. (3), if it contains at most two bitwise transitions from 0 to 1 or 1 to 0 when the binary string is considered circular [12, 14].

$$LBP_{P,R}^{u2}(x,y) = \begin{cases} F(LBP_{P,R}(x,y)) & \text{if } U(LBP_{P,R}) \leq 2, \\ F(z) \in [0,(P-1)P+1], z \in [0,255] & \tag{3} \\ (P-1)P+2 & \text{otherwise} \end{cases}$$

where $U(LBP_{P,R}) = |S(i_{P-1} - i_c) - S(i_0 - i_c)| + \sum_{p=1}^{P-1}|S(i_p - i_c) - S(i_{p-1} - i_c)|$, $F(z)$ is an index function. A spatially enhanced feature histogram of the image $f_l(x, y)$ is defined as follows:

$$H_{i,j} = \sum_{x,y} I\{f_i(x,y) = i\} I\{(x,y) \in R_j\}, \quad i = 0, \cdots, L-1; j = 0, \cdots, m-1;$$

$$I(A) = \begin{cases} 1, & A \text{ is true} \\ 0, & A \text{ is false} \end{cases}$$

(4)

where L is the number of different bins produced by the LBP operator. Using uniform local binary pattern (ULBP) for a neighborhood where P=8, reduces the histogram from 256 to 59 bins (58 bins for uniform patterns and 1 bin for non-uniform patterns). Usually, images are divided into non-overlapping sub-regions $\{R_0, R_1, \ldots, R_{m-1}\}$ with the size of m. Then histogram for each sub-region is calculated and concatenated into a histogram sequence, which is Uniform Local Binary Pattern Histogram Sequence.

ULGBPHS feature: The proposed system employs a fused feature called Uniform Local Gabor Binary Pattern Histogram Sequence (ULGBPHS), which has been shown to be very robust to illumination changes and misalignment. The winner of the FERA 2011 AU detection sub-challenge adopted this architecture [15-16]. Firstly, Gabor filtering is performed on target expression image. Secondly, LBP is employed to filter the magnitudes in face regions, and the output is called Uniform Local Gabor Binary Pattern (ULGBP) image. Thirdly, the ULGBP image is partitioned into non-overlapping sub-regions. Then, histogram for each sub-region is calculated and concatenated into a histogram sequence, which is the fused feature ULGBPHS used in our system. The framework of ULGBPHS approach is demonstrated in Fig.3.

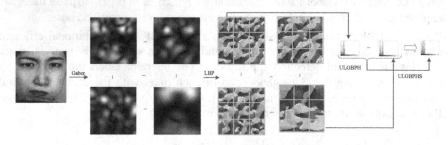

Fig. 3. The framework of ULGBPHS feature

Classification: Due to the high dimension $O(10^5)$ of the fusion feature vector, the system applies two steps of dimension reduction, which are principal component analysis (PCA) and linear discriminant analysis (LDA) respectively. PCA is often considered as revealing the internal structure of the data in a way that best explains the variance in the data. LDA aims to find a linear combination of features that characterizes or separates two or more classes of data. It is proved that PCA + LDA based dimension reduction performs better than using PCA only [17]. The reduction step is defined as:

$$z_i = W_{LDA}^T \cdot W_{PCA}^T x_i \quad (i = 1, 2, \cdots, M),$$

(5)

where x is fusion feature vector corresponding to feature extraction, z is final feature vector corresponding to feature selection, M is the number of samples. In our system, we classify the data of expression into 5 categories, thus the dimension of vector z is at most 4. Last but not the least, K-nearest neighbors algorithm (K-NN) is used as our classifier. Given a test sample, K-NN firstly finds k closest training samples in the feature space, and then uses the class membership of these k training samples to vote for the class membership of the given sample. The distance measure is often calculated based on Euclidean distance.

6   Experimental Results

Firstly, we tested our algorithm on JAFFE database. The dataset contains ten females with six types of prototypical expressions (happiness, anger, sadness, fear, surprise, disgust) and a neutral expression. There are 213 pictures with each person having 2-4 pictures of onefold expression. We selected 211 pictures which were labeled correctly. These pictures were cropped and resized to the size of 66×66 pixels for 3-fold cross-validation experiments. 2-3 pictures of each facial expression for each person were used for training and the remaining pictures were used as the test set. The intensity of each picture in the experiment was normalized. The recognition rate was obtained under person-dependent condition, as person-independent FER had not obtained satisfied results compared with person-dependent FER. The recognition results of KNN (K=3) are demonstrated in Table 1. We performed the experiment on a 4-core 3.2GHz PC with 16GB memory using Matlab implementation. As can been seen from the Table 1, the fusion feature outperforms onefold feature.

Table 1. Comparisons of different methods with corresponding recognition rate on JAFFE database. Time represents time consumption while performing feature extraction on our experimental platform, Pro. Mat$_{PCA(95\%)}$ and Pro. Mat$_{LDA}$ are the projection matrixes for PCA and LDA, respectively. LBP operator means using only Eq.(2) method without histogram for extracting features,ULBPHS$_{8x8}$ means that the partition grid for the image is 8x8 while extracting corresponding features, as well as ULGBPHS$_{8x8}$, Gabor$_{5x8}$ means calculating Gabor filter responses at five different scales and eight different orientations.

Methods	Recognition (%)	Dimensions	Time(ms)	Pro. Mat. PCA(95%)	Pro.Mat. LDA
LBP operator	75.2	4096	63.7	4096 × 121	121 × 6
ULBPHS$_{8x8}$	81.0	3776	23.8	3776 × 108	108 × 6
Gabor$_{5x8}$	95.2	174240	412.4	174240 × 65	65 × 6
ULGBPHS$_{8x8}$	96.7	151040	633.7	151040 × 115	115 × 6

Table 2. The average recognition rate of 4-fold cross-validation (K=3) on self-build expression database (%)

Methods	Expressional		Labels			
	fatigue	confusion	concentration	surprise	joviality	Mean
LBP operator	60.0	57.5	47.5	50.0	82.5	59.5
ULBPHS$_{8x8}$	47.5	67.5	65.0	65.0	87.5	66.5
Gabor$_{5x8}$	72.5	72.5	60.0	72.5	95.0	74.5
ULGBPHS$_{8x8}$	67.5	80.0	72.5	82.5	92.5	79.0

Secondly, we performed the same methods on our self-build facial expression database. Different participants have different feelings while watching the same video clip. Due to lack of expressional labels of some participants, we selected 10 qualified participants as our research objects. The participants' expressions with peak frames were selected for expression recognition. Thus, the whole dataset size is 4×5×10=200. Similarly, we used 3 pictures of each facial expression for each person to form training set, and the remaining samples for testing. The intensity of each picture in the experiment was normalized. The recognition rate is demonstrated in Table 2.

In the comparison of 5 types of expressions, joviality expression has been classified with a higher accuracy, as there is a similar laugh among different persons, which has been proven by the well- known Facial Action Coding System (FACS). While fatigue expression has been classified with the lowest accuracy, for its intensity is relatively low. Besides, compared with the other expressions, it is related to head pose as far as the participants in our experiment are concerned and it changes from person to person.

In the last stage, based on participants' expressions changing slightly within 2-3 seconds, the video frames are analyzed by the proposed system with a sampling ratio of 1:100, which also decreases the computational quantity. In this way, the system can analyze students' expressions in class in a fair short time.

7   Conclusion and Discussion

Although AFER is widely used in e-learning currently, there are few systems for analyzing students' expressions in classroom teaching environments. In this paper, we firstly explore applying the results of AFER to traditional classroom teaching effect evaluation. Compared with manual methods of analyzing teaching effect, the computer-aided facial expression analysis system improves the efficiency of evaluation substantially.

In this paper, we focus on improving the recognition rate of expression in classroom environments, and the fusion feature ULGBPHS is employed. The proposed system gets higher accuracy compared with onefold feature at the cost of increased computational consumption. In the future, we would further improve the efficiency and accuracy of this expression recognition system, and collect more data of spontaneous facial expression in the real-world environment. Since deep learning has robust performance in many machine learning applications, we will also employing this hot technology in our system, thus increase practical value of our system in instructional evaluation.

Acknowledgments. We wish to thank 23 participants and Professor Bo Sun in our university for their support. This paper is supported by the Fundamental Research Funds for the Central Universities (No. 2013YB71).

References

1. Wen, S.H., Xu, J.S., Carline, J.D., Zhong, F., Zhong, Y.J., Shen, S.J.: Effects of a teaching evaluation system: a case study. J. International Journal of Medical Education **2**, 18–23 (2011)
2. Sathik, M., Jonathan, S.G.: Effect of facial expressions on student's comprehension recognition in virtual educational environments. SpringerPlus **2**(1), 1–9 (2013)

3. Zeng, Z., Pantic, M., Roisman, G., Huang, T.S.: A survey of affect recognition methods: Audio, visual, and spontaneous expressions. IEEE Transactions on Pattern Analysis and Machine Intelligence 31(1), 39–58 (2009)
4. Moore, S., Bowden, R.: Local binary patterns for multi-view facial expression recognition. Computer Vision and Image Understanding 115(4), 541–558 (2011)
5. Lu, H., Yang, M., Ben, X., Zhang, P.: Divided Local Binary Pattern (DLBP) Features Description Method For Facial Expression Recognition. J Journal of Information & Computational Science 11(07), 2425–2433 (2014)
6. Lee, S.H., Plataniotis, K., Konstantinos, N., Ro, Y.M.: Intra-class variation reduction using training expression images for sparse representation based facial expression recognition. IEEE Transactions on Affective Computing 5(3), 340–351 (2014)
7. Liu, P., Han, S., Meng, Z., Tong, Y.: Facial expression recognition via a boosted deep belief network. In: 2014 IEEE Conference on Computer Vision and Pattern Recognition (CVPR), pp. 1805–1812. IEEE (2014)
8. Bosch, N., D'Mello, S., Baker, R., Ocumpaugh, J., Shute, V., Ventura, M., Wang, L., Zhao, W.: Automatic detection of learning-centered affective states in the wild. In: Proceedings of the 20th International Conference on Intelligent User Interfaces, pp. 379–388. ACM (2015)
9. Whitehill, J., Serpell, Z., Lin, Y.C., Foster, A., Movellan, J.R.: The Faces of Engagement: Automatic Recognition of Student Engagement from Facial Expressions. IEEE Transactions on Affective Computing 5(1), 86–98 (2014)
10. Uřičář, M., Franc, V., Hlaváč, V.: Detector of facial landmarks learned by the structured output SVM. VISAPP 12, 547–556 (2012)
11. Liu, C., Wechsler, H.: A gabor feature classifier for face recognition. In: Eighth IEEE International Conference on Computer Vision 2, pp. 270–275. IEEE (2001)
12. Chan, C.-H., Kittler, J., Messer, K.: Multi-scale Local Binary Pattern Histograms for Face Recognition. In: Lee, S.-W., Li, S.Z. (eds.) ICB 2007. LNCS, vol. 4642, pp. 809–818. Springer, Heidelberg (2007)
13. Shen, L.L., Bai, L., Fairhurst, M.: Gabor wavelets and general discriminant analysis for face identification and verification. Image and Vision Computing 25(5), 553–563 (2007)
14. Ojala, T., Pietikäinen, M., Mäenpää, T.: Multiresolution gray-scale and rotation invariant texture classification with local binary patterns. IEEE Transactions on Pattern Analysis and Machine Intelligence 24(7), 971–987 (2002)
15. Zhang, W., Shan, S., Gao, W., Chen, X., Zhang, H.: Local gabor binary pattern histogram sequence (lgbphs): a novel non-statistical model for face representation and recognition. In: Tenth IEEE International Conference on Computer Vision 1, pp. 786–791. IEEE (2005)
16. Almaev, T.R., Valstar, M.F.: Local gabor binary patterns from three orthogonal planes for automatic facial expression recognition. In: 2013 Humaine Association Conference on Affective Computing and Intelligent Interaction (ACII), pp. 356–361. IEEE (2013)
17. Deng, H.B., Jin, L.W., Deng, H.B., Jin, L.W.: Facial Expression Recognition Based on Local Gabor Filter Bank and PCA+ LDA. J. Journal of Image and Graphics 12(02), 322–329 (2007)
18. BNU-LSVED Database. http://www.bnusei.net:8080/BNULSVED/cn_index.html

Modified Marginal Fisher Analysis for Gait Image Dimensionality Reduction and Classification

Shanwen Zhang[1], Zhen Wang[1], Jucheng Yang[2], and Chuanlei Zhang[2(✉)]

[1] XiJing University, Xi'an 710123, Shanxi, China
[2] Tianjin University of Science & Technology, Tianjin 300222, China
97313114@tust.edu.cn

Abstract. Gait is a kind of biometric feature to identify a walking person at a distance. As an important biometric feature, human gait has great potential in video-surveillance-based applications, which aims to recognize people by a sequence of walking images. Compared with other biometric feature identifications such as face, fingerprint or iris, in medium to long distance security and surveillance applications in public space, the most important advantage of gait identification is that it can be done at a distance. As gait images are complex, time-varying, high-dimensionality and nonlinear data, many classical pattern recognition methods cannot be applied to gait recognition directly. The main problem in gait recognition asks is dimensionality reduction. Marginal Fisher analysis (MFA) is an efficient and robust dimensionality reduction algorithm. However, MFA does not take the data distribution into consideration. Based on original MFA, a modified MFA is proposed for gait recognition. Firstly, the discriminant classification information is computed to guide the procedure of extracting intrinsic low-dimensional features and provides a linear projection matrix, and then both the between-class and the within-class scatter matrices are redefined by the classification probability. Secondly, through maximizing the between-class scatter and minimizing the within-class scatter simultaneously, a projection matrix can be computed and the high-dimensional data are projected to the low-dimensional feature space. The experimental results on gait database demonstrate the effectiveness of the proposed method.

Keywords: MFA · Modified MFA · Gait recognition · Dimensionality reduction

1 Introduction

Gait recognition is a kind of foreground biometric feature recognition technology and has recently attracted much attention in many applications, such as video-surveillance-related, medical diagnostics, biometric identification and forensics, pedestrian information collection systems [1-3]. Compared with other biomechanics, such as fingerprint, palm print and iris requiring physical touch or proximal sensing etc., gait-based human identification is a challenging problem and has gained significant attention. Using gait feature i.e., walking posture, to recognize person does not need the user's interaction

© Springer International Publishing Switzerland 2015
J. Yang et al. (Eds.): CCBR 2015, LNCS 9428, pp. 448–455, 2015.
DOI: 10.1007/978-3-319-25417-3_53

other than walking. Human gait is an important physiological biometric feature. The advantage of gait is that it does not require subject's cooperation and can operate without interrupting or interfering with the subject's activity, which makes gait ideal for situations where direct contact or cooperation with the subject is not possible. Gait can be captured secretly at a distance, which naturally advances users' acceptance. From the surveillance perspective, gait is the most attractive feature for human recognition at a distance. Furthermore, in the applications of biometric recognition, many biometrics can be obscured, altered or hidden, while human gait is usually visible, i.e., and people generally do not disguise or hide their gaits purposely. For example, the terrorists can change their appearance, but it is very difficult to change their gait. Whenever the police catch criminals, they could record the way they walk and put it into a database. The gait can be highly individual and recognizable. We can recognize a person by the way they walk a long time before they are near enough to recognize their face. Although gait recognition is noninvasive and effective from a distance, the performance of gait analysis suffers from the high-dimensionality, nonlinear and low-resolution problems. Moreover, if the gait data are projected into a non-optimal low-dimensional subspace, the performance of gait recognition will decline. By now, numerous gait recognition methods and technologies have been proposed for various applications, especially in video surveillance, human-computer interaction and medical diagnosis [4-6]. The subspace methods are widely used to reduce the high dimensionality of the gait data based on principal component analysis (PCA) and linear discriminant analysis (LDA), etc. [7-10]. A modified MFA algorithm is presented for gait data reduction [13]. In this paper, a new modified MFA algorithm is proposed and we will compare its performance with that of the PCA+LDA (linear discriminant analysis) [7], gait energy images (GEI) [11, 12], and MFA [13], to verify the effectiveness of the method.

The remainder of this paper is organized as follows: Section 2 introduces the MFA algorithm. We give a short introduction to modified MFA in section 3. In section 4, the proposed method is examined on the well-known databases to show its effectiveness. The conclusions are presented in section 5.

2   Marginal Fisher Analysis (MFA)

The common supervised generic dimensionality reduction problem can be described as follows. A dataset of n data points $x^i \in R^D$ could be represented as a $D \times n$ matrix $X = \{X_1, X_2, \ldots, X_n\} \subset R^{D \times n}$, c_i is the class label of X_i, where D denotes the original dimensionality of any sample of the dataset. The goal of dimensionality reduction is to project the high-dimensional data into a low-dimensional feature space R^d, where $d << D$. Then the corresponding set of n samples in the reduced subspace could be represented as $Y = \{Y_1, Y_2, \ldots, Y_n\} \subset R^{d \times n}$, where Y_i is the low-dimensional representation of x_i in R^d space $Y_i = A^T X_i$, A is a transformation matrix. Then, the marginal Fisher analysis (MFA) method is introduced as follows [13]:

In MFA, two weighted adjacency graphs G_1 and G_2 are designed by using k nearest neighbor criterion to characterize the within-class G_2 and the between-class G_2, respectively. In G_1, the vertex pair is connected if two points are the k_1-nearest neighbors and they belong to the same class. In G_2, the vertex pair is connected if two points are the k_2-nearest neighbors but they are in different classes. The within-class scatter matrix and between-class scatter matrix in MFA are defined as follows,

$$S_w = \sum_i^n \sum_j^n H_{ij}^w \left(Y_i - Y_j \right)^2$$

$$S_b = \sum_i^n \sum_j^n H_{ij}^b \left(Y_i - Y_j \right)^2$$

(1)

where H_{ij}^w and H_{ij}^b denote respectively two neighborhood matrices with the following:

$$H_{ij}^w = \begin{cases} 1, \text{if } X_i \in N_{k_1}(X_j) \text{ or } X_j \in N_{k_1}(X_i) \\ 0, \text{otherwise} \end{cases}$$

$$H_{ij}^b = \begin{cases} 1, \text{if } X_i \in N_{k_2}(X_j) \text{ or } X_j \in N_{k_2}(X_i) \\ 0, \text{otherwise} \end{cases}$$

(2)

where $N_{k1}(X_i)$ is the set of the k_1 within-class nearest neighbors of X_i, $N_{k2}(X_j)$ is the set of the k_2 between-class nearest neighbors of X_i.

By some simple algebraic steps, we can get

$$S_w = \sum_i^n \sum_j^n H_{ij}^w \left(A^T X_i - A^T X_j \right)^2 = 2A^T X (D^w - H^w) X^T A$$

$$S_b = \sum_i^n \sum_j^n H_{ij}^b \left(A^T X_i - A^T X_j \right)^2 = 2A^T X (D^b - H^b) X^T A$$

(3)

where D^w and D^b are two diagonal matrices with $D_{ii}^w = \sum_j H_{ji}^w$, $D_{ii}^b = \sum_j H_{ji}^b$, and $H^w = \{ H_{ij}^w \}$, $H^b = \{ H_{ij}^b \}$.

MFA aims to find an optimal projection that optimizes the marginal Fisher criterion, and the objection function is

$$A^* = \arg\max_A \frac{A^T X (D^b - H^b) X^T A}{A^T X (D^w - H^w) X^T A}$$

(4)

3   Modified Marginal Fisher Analysis

To improve the classifying performance of the classical MFA algorithm, we propose a modified MFA in this section. In this paper, we shall address the method of learning with local and global consistency. A classifying function is designed with respect to discover the intrinsic structure collectively revealed by the known labeled points. A simple algorithm is presented to obtain such a smooth solution. In this section, a modified learning with local and global consistency is presented to make use of the label information and class prior knowledge for supervised learning.

The graph-based supervised manifold learning methods model the whole dataset as a graph. Although constructing the graph is a main task of the graph-based methods, their construction has not been studied extensively. These methods are a promising family of the techniques based on Gaussian fields, which assume that nearest neighbors(according to some similarity measure) in the high-dimensional input space will have similar 'outputs' or be close to each other in the low-dimensional manifold. Most of these methods adopted a Gaussian distance metric to calculate the edge weights of the graph. *i.e.* the edge links data X_i and X_j is computed as,

$$w_{ij} = \exp(-\left\| X_i - X_j \right\|^2 / \beta) \tag{5}$$

Where β is an adjustment parameter.

The range of the parameter β of the Gaussian function is from zero to infinity, so finding the best β is very time-consuming. The label and class prior information, which can be more beneficial to classification, is ignored. Though the labeled samples could be few, the label and the class prior information, as the prior knowledge, are very important to improve the classification efficiency. To address the above issues, a novel adaptive weight is proposed to add the label information and class prior knowledge. Zhu et al. [14] firstly advised to incorporate the class prior knowledge. Let c denote the label of any sample. To go from c to labels, the obvious decision rule is to assign label 1 to node i if $c(i) > 1/2$, and label 0 otherwise. In terms of the random walk interpretation, if $c(i) > 1/2$, starting at i, the random step is more likely to reach a positive labeled point before a negative labeled point. This decision rule works well when the classes are well separated. However in the real datasets, the classes are often not ideally separated, and using c tends to produce severely unbalanced classification. Assume the desirable proportions for classes 1 and 0 are q and $1-q$, respectively, where these values are estimated from labeled data. Zhu et al. [14] adopt a simple procedure called class mass normalization to adjust the class distributions to match the priors. This method can extend naturally to the general multi-label case. In the following section, we make use of the prior label probability to improve the classification performance of the dimensionality reduction.

In traditional dimensionality reduction methods, data relation is often represented by their Euclidean distance. A shorter distance means a closer relationship between two data points. In some real datasets, most data points of the same class generally lie together. Therefore, we construct an adjacent neighboring matrix to demonstrate local property [15]. First we put edges between each data points and its k nearest neighbors. The weights of edges represent the similarity and correlation of the data pairs, which are defined as Eq. (5). Hence, the sum of k weights $D_{ii} = \sum_{j=1}^{k} w_{ij}$ provides a natural measure on the data points. The large D_{ii} implies a high local density, which means the outliers on the edge of each class often have small D_{ii} s and are prone to cause misclassification. For each data class, we repeat the procedure above N_c times to obtain all D_{ij} as $\{D_{11}, D_{22}, ..., D_{N_cN_c}\}$.

In our proposed modified MFA, we firstly try to minimize the maximum risk of error classification by setting high penalties to the noise points and outliers, and transform $\{D_{11}, D_{22}, ..., D_{N_cN_c}\}$ to $\{1/D_{11}, 1/D_{22}, ..., 1/D_{N_cN_c}\}$, and normalize it to $\{p_1^c, p_2^c, ..., p_{N_c}^c\}$, named as probability. Secondly, we use the probability to design two weighted adjacency graphs G_1 and G_2 by the k-nearest neighbor criterion. According to the probability, two weighted are defined as follows, respectively

$$W_{ij}^w = \begin{cases} p_i^c \exp(-\|X_i - X_j\|^2 / \beta), \text{if } X_i \in N_{k_1}(X_j) \text{or } X_j \in N_{k_1}(X_i), \\ \qquad\qquad \text{and } c_i \text{ is the class label of } X_i \\ 0, \text{otherwise} \end{cases} \qquad (6)$$

$$W_{ij}^b = \begin{cases} \exp(-\|X_i - X_j\|^2 / \beta), \text{if } X_i \in N_{k_2}(X_j) \text{ or } X_j \in N_{k_2}(X_i) \\ 0, \text{otherwise} \end{cases}$$

In Eq. (6), the corresponding penalty is denoted as p_i^c. It is obvious that the smaller D_{ii} associate with heavier penalty when conducting the objective function which would be subjected to the heaviest penalty. Then the weighted between-class scatter and weighted within-class scatter matrix are redefined as that like the above Eq. (3), where the weighted values are replaced by W_{ij}^w, W_{ij}^b and the objection function like Eq. (4).

Computing the eigenvector and eigenvalue for the generalized eigenvalue problem:

$$X(E^b - W^b)X^T a = \lambda X(E^w - W^w)X^T a \qquad (7)$$

where E^w is a diagonal matrix with $E_{ii}^w = \sum_j W_{ji}^w$, $W^w = \{W_{ij}^w\}$, E^b is a diagonal matrix with $E_{ii}^b = \sum_j W_{ji}^b$, $W^b = \{W_{ij}^b\}$.

It has been proved that if $E^b - E^w$ is a nonsingular matrix, the ratio can be maximized when projection matrix A is constructed by the d column eigenvectors of $(E^b - W^b)^{-1}(E^w - W^w)$, where the d generalized eigenvectors $\{\alpha_1, \alpha_2, ..., \alpha_d\}$ of $E^b - W^b$ and $E^w - W^w$ are selected according to the d largest generalized eigenvalues $\{\lambda_1, \lambda_2, ..., \lambda_d\}$, $A = [\alpha_1, \alpha_2, ..., \alpha_d]$.

The low-dimensional representation of X in the subspace is defined as follows:

$$X \to Y = A^T X \qquad (8)$$

4   Experimental Results and Discussions

A typical gait analysis laboratory has several cameras (video or infrared) placed around a walkway or a treadmill, which are linked to a computer [16]. The subject has markers located at various points of reference of the body (e.g., iliac spines of the pelvis, ankle malleolus, and the condyles of the knee), or groups of markers applied to half of the body segments. The subject walks down the catwalk or the treadmill and the computer calculates the trajectory of each marker in three dimensions. A model is applied to calculate the movement of the underlying bones. In this section, the gait database CASIA-A is used to show the performance of the proposed algorithm. The dataset consists of the data from 124 subjects under 11 viewing angles. For each subject there are 10 walking sequences consisting of six normal walking sequences where the subject does not carry a bag or wear a bulky coat. The dataset also contains two sequences from each normal walking subject wearing overcoat or carrying a bag under one of the 11 viewing angle. We select some human subjects in the video sequences who do not carry handbag, nor wear large jacket. Since the complexity of recognition system becomes enormously increased as the number of subject increases, we divide the 80 subjects into eight different groups (each group with 10 subjects).

Gait is sensitive to various covariate conditions, which are circumstantial and physical conditions that can affect either gait itself or the extracted gait features. Example of these conditions include clothing, surface, carrying condition (backpack, briefcase, handbag, etc.), view angle, speed, and shoe-wear type to name a few. We use the gait energy images (GEI) to overcome the noise and to conduct our experiments. GEI [12] is a gray level image which stores important spatiotemporal information in a gait cycle, which can be computed by Eq. (9).

$$GEI = B(x,y) = \frac{1}{T} \sum_{k=1}^{T} f(x,y,k) \tag{9}$$

where T is the number of frames in a complete gait cycle, x and y are the horizontal and vertical coordinates of the binary silhouette image respectively. Some examples of gait images and GEI are given shown in Fig. 1.

A. Gait image sequences   B. GEI

Fig. 1. Gait image sequences of a period and responding GEI

Based on above observation, the classifying feature selection method is developed to select the most informative gait features from the GEI. The GEI data are reduced by the proposed method.

The correlation coefficient criterion can be used to classify issues. To classify an unknown sample Y, compute the correlation coefficient between Y and each known labeled samples from the training set, and makes decision that the class label of Y is the same as the class label of the known sample corresponding to the maximum coefficient.

From above analysis, the gait recognition steps are listed as follows:

(1) Gait image acquisition.
(2) Image preprocessing, and image segmentation.

(3) GEIs are computed.
(4) Dimensionality reduction by the modified MFA.
(5) Statistical analysis.
(6) Classification based the correlation coefficient.

In gait recognition experiments, all GEI data are computed from the original gait sequences. GEI data are reduced by the proposed Modified MFA. The Leave One Out (LOO) classification method is adopted. By this method, one of the low-dimensional GEIs is left out and a model is fitted based on all but the left-out sample. The fitted model is then used to predict the left-out sample. This procedure is repeated for all the low-dimensional GEIs. A comparison of the classification performance of GEI [12], PCA+LDA [7] and Marginal Fisher Analysis(MFA)[13] are provided in Table 1. From Table 1, the proposed approach outperforms PCA+LDA and MFA. When the number of images is much smaller than image vector dimension, we can apply PCA preprocessing to avoiding the singularity of the objection function.

Table 1. The gait recognition results and variances in CASIA-A gait database

Method	0°	45°	90°
GEI	97.51±2.05	96.23±4.03	96.40±4.19
PCA+LDA	96.62±3.52	97.13±3.83	96.12±3.46
MFA	96.15±4.11	97.72±4.34	96.28±4.30
Modified MFA	96.78±3.73	98.33±3.92	96.37±3.66

5   Conclusions

There is a challenge to reduce the data dimensionality to study the gait recognition method. Marginal Fisher analysis (MFA) is an efficient and robust dimensionality reduction algorithm. But it does not consider the data distribution. In this paper, a modified MFA algorithm is proposed for gait data reduction. The method takes advantage of the label prior probability of each sample. Experimental results demonstrate the feasibility of the proposed approach. In future, we will analyze these problems and pay more attention to the feature space for describing and recognizing the human gait on the larger database of subjects.

Acknowledgments. This work is supported by the grants of the higher education development special fund of Shaanxi Private (XJ13ZD01), the basic research project of Natural Science of Shaanxi Province (2014JM2-6096), Tianjin City High School Science & Technology Fund Planning Project 20140802, the young academic team construction projects of the 'twelve five' integrated investment planning in Tianjin University of Science and Technology and the 2015 key projects of Tianjin science and technology support program No.15ZCZDGX00200.

References

1. Choudhary, A., Chaudhury, S.: Gait recognition based online person identification in a camera network. In: Jawahar, C.V., Shan, S. (eds.) ACCV 2014 Workshops. LNCS, vol. 9008, pp. 145–156. Springer, Heidelberg (2015)
2. Hu, M., Wang, Y., Zhang, Z., Little, J.J., Huang, D.: View-invariant Discriminative Projection for Multi-view Gait-based Human Identification. IEEE Transactions on Information Forensics and Security (T-IFS) 8(12), 2034–2045 (2013)
3. Yu, S., Tan, T., Huang, K., et al.: A Study on Gait-Based Gender Classification. IEEE Transactions on image processing 18(2), 1905–1910 (2009)
4. Bashir, K., Xiang, T., Gong, S.: Gait recognition without subject cooperation. Pattern Recognition Letters 31, 2052–2060 (2010)
5. Ben Abdelkader, C., Culter, R., Davis L.: Stride and cadence as a biometric in automatic person identification and verification. In: Proc. Int. Conf. Automatic Face and Gesture Recognition, Washington, pp. 372–376 (2002)
6. Matovski, D., Nixon, M., Mahmoodi, S., et al.: The Effect of Time on Gait Recognition Performance. IEEE Transactions on Information Forensics and Security 7(2), 543–552 (2012)
7. Cheng, Q., Fu, B., Chen, H.: Gait recognition based on PCA and LDA. In: Proceedings of the Second Symposium International Computer Science and Computational Technology, Huanshan, China, pp. 124–127 (2006)
8. Okumura, M., Iwama, H., Makihara, Y., et al: Performance evaluation of vision-based gait recognition using a very large-scale gait database. In: Fourth IEEE International ConferenceBiometrics: Theory Applications and Systems (BTAS), pp. 1–6 (2010)
9. Xu, D., Yan, S., Tao, D., et al.: Marginal Fisher Analysis and Its Variants for Human Gait Recognition and Content- Based Image Retrieval. IEEE Transactions on image processing 16(11), 2811–2821 (2007)
10. Sugiyama, M.: Dimensionality Reduction of Multimodal Labeled Data by Local Fisher Discriminant Analysis. Journal of Machine Learning Research 8, 1027–1061 (2007)
11. Han, J., Bhanu, B.: Individual recognition using gait energy image. IEEE Transactions on Pattern Analysis and Machine Intelligence 28(2), 316–322 (2006)
12. Ali, H., Dargham, J., Ali, C., et al.: Gait Recognition using Gait Energy Image. International Journal of Signal Processing, Image Processing and Pattern Recognition 4(3), 141–152 (2011)
13. Yi, S., Chen, C., Cui, J., Ding, Yu.: Robust marginal fisher analysis. In: Sun, Z., Shan, S., Yang, G., Zhou, J., Wang, Y., Yin, Y. (eds.) CCBR 2013. LNCS, vol. 8232, pp. 51–61. Springer, Heidelberg (2013)
14. Zhu, X., Ghahramani, Z., Lafferty, J.: Semi-supervised learning using gaussian fields and harmonic functions. In: Proceedings of the Twentieth International Conference on Machine Learning, Washington DC (2003)
15. Wang, L., Tan, T., Hu, W., Ning, H.: Silhouette Analysis-Based Gait Recognition for Human Identification. IEEE Trans on Pattern Analysis and Machine Intelligence 25(12), 1505–1518 (2003)
16. Lee, H., Hong, S., Kim, E.: An Efficient Gait Recognition with Backpack Removal. Hindawi Publishing Corporation. EURASIP Journal on Advances in Signal Processing 1, 1–7 (2009)

Gait Recognition Based on Energy Accumulation Images

Chuanlei Zhang[1], Shanwen Zhang[2], Jucheng Yang[1(✉)], and Weijun Cheng[3]

[1] Tianjin University of Science & Technology, Tianjin 300222, China
jcyang@tust.edu.cn
[2] XiJing University, Xi'an Shanxi 710123, China
[3] Minzu University of China, Beijing 100081, China

Abstract. Human identification in a distance by the analysis of gait patterns extracted from video has recently become a research topic. In this paper, a feature fusion method is proposed for gait recognition. Firstly, four energy accumulation images of gait energy image (GEI), change energy images (CIE), are generated from a sequence of silhouettes of a gait cycle. Secondly, Orthogonal locally discriminant projection (OLDP) is applied to four sequence of energy accumulation images and four low-dimensionality vectors are obtained, respectively. Thirdly, the classifying feature vector is established by fusing the four vectors. Then nearest neighbor criterion is employed to recognize gait. The experimental results on Chinese CASIA database A show the effectiveness and feasibility of the method proposed in this paper.

Keywords: Gait recognition · Energy accumulation images · OLDP · Feature fusion

1   Introduction

Global security concerns have raised an important application of video surveillance devices. Intelligent surveillance systems aim to detect possible threats automatically and raise alerts [1-4]. Gait is an individual biometric feature determined by his or her weight, limb length, footwear, and posture combined with characteristic motion [5-8]. Hence, gait can be used as a biometric measure to recognize known persons and classify unknown subjects. Gait recognition is a method of identifying an individual based on his style of walking, which is considered to be unique among individuals. Gait recognition is attractive since it requires no subject contact, in common with automatic face and fingerprint recognition and other biometrics. Unlike other biometrics identification methods, gait recognition is noninvasive and effective and can be obtained unobtrusively at a distance video, and may be performed at a distance or at low resolution, while other biometric recognition needs higher resolution [9-12].

There are two main methods to model human motion. The first one is model-based: after the human body model is selected, the 3-D structure of the model is recovered from image sequences with [13] or without moving light displays [14]. The second one emphasizes determining features of motion fields without structural reconstruction [15]. Ideas from human motion studies [16] can be used for modeling the movement of human walking. However, the methods of gait recognition will suffer in the low-resolution

© Springer International Publishing Switzerland 2015
J. Yang et al. (Eds.): CCBR 2015, LNCS 9428, pp. 456–463, 2015.
DOI: 10.1007/978-3-319-25417-3_54

(LR) case. Furthermore, when gait sequences are projected onto a non-optimal low-dimensional subspace to reduce the data complexity, the performance of gait recognition will also decrease. In this paper, we introduce a gait feature fusion methods for gait recognition.

2   Gait Image Preprocess

To extract walking images from the background image, gait detection is the first step for gait recognition [4-6]. Change detection based on background subtraction is employed. The processing steps are given as (1) the background subtraction method is used to extract the moving object; (2) morphological operators are used to remove noise and small holes; (3) the images are normalized. The normalized size is 128×40. Fig. 1 shows an example of silhouette extraction processes. Fig. 1(c) is the results of silhouette extraction directly subtracting the foreground image from original image, and (d) is the amended silhouettes.

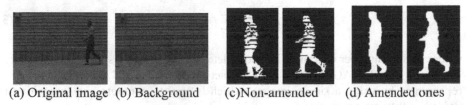

(a) Original image (b) Background   (c)Non-amended   (d) Amended ones

Fig. 1. The example of silhouette extraction

3   Gait Energy Accumulation Images

To classify the different person by their gait easily, some kinds of gait energy accumulation images (GAI) have been defined. In comparison to the gait representation by binary silhouette sequence, GAI not only saves storage space and computation time, but also is less sensitive to silhouette noise in individual frames.

3.1   Gait Energy Image (GEI)

The human gait is a broad form of periodic motion. Gait cycle is the time between the successive peak values of the width (height), which is one of features for the latter recognition. Based on gait sequences extracted from background and gait cycle estimation T, GEI is computed as gait representation to characterize human walking properties for individual recognition by gait with the information in spatial and temporal domain by averaging the silhouettes extracted over a complete gait cycle [17]. GEI is a gray level image which stores important spatiotemporal information in a gait cycle and GEI can be computed as follows

$$GEI = \frac{1}{T} \sum_{k=1}^{T} G(x, y, k) \tag{1}$$

where $G(x, y, k)$ is the total gait image serial numbers representative, x and y are the horizontal and vertical coordinates of the binary silhouette image respectively.

3.2 Average Gait Differential Image (AGDI)

The difference between two adjacent gait silhouettes was accumulated to get the average gait differential image (AGDI) [18] which is used as the feature image of one walking. Suppose that $G(x, y, i)$ and $G(x, y, i+1)$ are two adjacent images aligned by the centroid; the gait differential image can then be defined as follows:

$$D_i(x, y) = \begin{cases} 0, \text{ if } G(x, y, i) = G(x, y, i+1) \\ 1, \text{ if } G(x, y, i) \neq G(x, y, i+1) \end{cases} \tag{2}$$

where $G(x, y, i)$ is the frame number in the image sequence and x and y are values in the 2D gait image coordinate.

By overlapping all the differential images in a gait cycle, AGDI is expressed as

$$GEI = \frac{1}{N-1} \sum_{i=1}^{N-1} D(x, y, i) \tag{3}$$

where N is the number of frames in a complete gait cycle(s) of a silhouette sequence.

Similar as GEI, AGDI is also a compact representation of gait (a gait cycle is represented by using a single image), which is easy to compute and insensitive to noise in silhouette extraction.

Based on the above observation, the classifying feature selection method is developed to select the most informative gait features from the GEI and AGDI.

3.3 Change Energy Images (CIE)

To capture energy variations in the static and dynamic part in a gait sequence of a gait cycle, change energy images **(CIE)** is computed to extract discriminative feature values for gait recognition. Change energy images from pre-processed silhouettes for each gait cycle are generated as follows. Let $G(x, y, k)$ $(k=1,2,...,N)$ be the N silhouette images in a given gait cycle. For a gait cycles consisting of N silhouettes, a set of N-1 change energy images are obtained. Let $CEI=\{CEI_1, CEI_2,..., CEI_{N-1},\}$ be the set of change energy images, where,

$$\begin{cases} CEI_1 = \frac{1}{2}(G(x, y, 1) + G(x, y, 2)) \\ CEI_i = \frac{1}{2}(G(x, y, i-1) + G(x, y, i+1))(i = 2, 3, ..., N-2) \\ CEI_{n-1} = \frac{1}{2}(G(x, y, n-2) + G(x, y, n)) \end{cases} \tag{4}$$

3.4   Active Energy Image (AEI)

When one is walking, the moving parts are external protrusions (such as the limbs) and the primary body (such as the trunk) is almost stationary relative to the centroid corresponding to the previous and the next frames. Active energy image (AEI)[19] not only concentrates on dynamic regions, but also eliminates or suppresses the impact of carrying bag and clothing variety. To solve the above problems, we introduce AEI in the following. Given a preprocessed binary gait silhouette sequence, $f_t(x, y)$ represents the tth silhouette and N is the number of frames in this sequence. We firstly compute the difference image between two adjacent silhouettes as follows:

$$D_t = \begin{cases} f_t(x, y), & t = 0 \\ \| f_t(x, y) - f_{t-1}(x, y) \|, & t > 0 \end{cases} \tag{5}$$

From Eq. (1), it is found that $D_t(x, y)$ is the difference between $f_t(x,y)$ and $f_{t-1}(x,y)$, i.e., $D_t(x,y)$ is the active region in time t, and it is desirable to use difference image to extract the dynamic parts of the moving body. Then AEI is defined as follows:

$$A(x, y) = \frac{1}{N} \sum_{t=0}^{N-1} D_t(x, y) \tag{6}$$

AEI not only concentrates on the dynamic parts of the body, but also remains the walking information when the person is walking. The intensity of a pixel in AEI reflects the frequency (i.e., the energy) of active parts occurring in the position of this pixel in a walking procedure.

4   Orthogonal Locally Discriminant Projection (OLDP)

Ideal features should maximize inter-class variance and minimize within-class variance. Orthogonal locally discriminant projection (OLDP) [20] is an effective manifold learning method by combining neighbor information and class information, and a locality discriminant criterion is employed to find the projections that well preserve the within-class local structures while decrease the between-class overlap. OLDP is introduced as follows.

Suppose $X = \{X_1, X_2, \dots, X_n\} \subset R^{D \times n}$ is n high-dimensional data points, C is the number of data sample classes, C_i is the class label of X_i, $N(X_i)$ is the k nearest neighbors of X_i, A is a transformation matrix, and $Y_i = A^T X_i$ is the mapping of X_j, define the intra-class and inter-class weights respectively as follows,

$$W_{ij}^I = \begin{cases} 1, \text{ if } X_i \in N(X_j) \text{ or } X_j \in N(X_i), \text{and } c_i = c_j \\ 0, \qquad\qquad \text{otherwise} \end{cases} \tag{7}$$

$$W_{ij}^B = \begin{cases} 1, \text{ if } X_i \in N(X_j) \text{ or } X_j \in N(X_i), \text{and } c_i \neq c_j \\ 0, \qquad\qquad \text{otherwise} \end{cases} \tag{8}$$

For the purpose of classification, we try to find a projection A which will draw the within-class samples mapped closer together while simultaneously making the between-class samples mapped even more far from each other. From this point of view, a reasonable criterion for choosing a "good" projection is to optimize the two following objective functions

$$\begin{cases} \min \sum_i \sum_j W_{ij}^I \left\| Y_i - Y_j \right\|^2 \\ \max \sum_i \sum_j W_{ij}^B \left\| Y_i - Y_j \right\|^2 \end{cases} \tag{9}$$

Following some simple algebraic steps, Eq. (9) is transformed as

$$\max_{A^T A = I} \frac{A^T X L^B X^T A}{A^T X L^I X^T A} \tag{10}$$

where $L^I = D^I - W^I$, D^I is a diagonal matrix with $D_{ii}^I = \sum W_{ji}^I$, W^I is the intra-class weight matrix with W_{ij}^I; D_{ii}^I measures the local density around X_i; $L^B = D^B - W^B$, D^B is a matrix with $D_{ii}^B = \sum W_{ji}^B$, and W^B is the inter-class weight matrix with W_{ji}^B.

After the generalized eigenvalue equation is solved, we obtain a set of eigenvalues and eigenvectors that span the canonical space where the classes are much better separated and the clusters are much smaller. Let $\{A_1, A_2, ..., A_d\}$ be the orthogonal basis vectors, define $A^{(i-1)} = [A_1, A_2, ..., A_{i-1}]$. The orthogonal basis vectors $\{A_1, A_2, ..., A_d\}$ can be computed by step-by-step procedure [12]. After calculating the projections $\{A_1, A_2, ..., A_{i-1}\}$, the ith projection A_i is computed by solving the following optimization problem

$$A_i = \arg \max_{A_{i-1}^T A_{i-1} = 0} \frac{A_{i-1}^T X L^B X^T A_{i-1}}{A_{i-1}^T X L^I X^T A_{i-1}} \tag{11}$$

Once A has been learnt, the projection of any new test point X_{new} is projected by

$$Y_{new} = A^T X_{new} \tag{12}$$

where $A \in R^{n \times d}$, $X_{new} \in R^D$, $Y_{new} \in R^d$, $d \ll D$.

5   Experimental Results and Discussions

The motivation of this paper is to capture gait energy data in static and dynamic part in a gait sequence of a gait cycle by generating GEI, AGDI, CIE and AEI and to extract discriminative features for gait recognition. Input data is a sequence of silhouettes of a gait cycle. The process of the gait recognition is shown in Fig. 2.

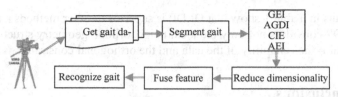

Fig. 2. Gait recognition processes

The Institute of Automation, Chinese Academy of Sciences (CASIA) provided a CASIA Gait Dataset A, which was created on Dec. 10, 2001, including 20 persons. Each person has 12 image sequences, 4 sequences for each of the three directions, i.e. parallel, 45 degrees and 90 degrees to the image plane.

In this section, we conduct a set of experiments on the CASIA Dataset A to verify the effectiveness of the proposed method, and compare it with two representative dimensionality reduction methods PCA+LDA[12] and GEI [17] and two other dimensionality reduction methods, average neighborhood margin (ANM) [20] and modified orthogonal discriminant projection (MODP) [21]. ANM, MODP and OLDP are three recently proposed supervised manifold learning methods. The input data of PCA+LDA are GEI. The input data of ANM, MODP and OLDP are GACA.

The original gait images need to be preprocessed to segment, crop, align and resize the gait silhouettes before constructing templates and dimensionality reduction, because the closer the walking person gets to the camera, the bigger the gait silhouette image will be. We resize gait silhouettes so that all silhouettes have the same height, and then centralize each silhouette image according to the horizontal center C_i. Supposed the number of the training samples per class is known, denoted as l, the number of nearest neighbor k can be set to $k=l-1$. The justification for this choice is that each sample should connect with the remaining l-1 samples of the same class. The justification for this choice is that each data point should connect with the remaining l-1 data points of the same class. The features GEI and GACA are matched by nearest neighborhood using the simple city block distance. The city block distance between the two gait feature vectors is defined as:

$$D(F_1, F_2) = \sum_{i=1}^{P} |F_{1i} - F_{2i}| \qquad (13)$$

where F_1, F_2 are any two feature vector sequences, F_{1i}, F_{2i} is ith element of F_1, F_2, respectively, P is the dimension of F_1, F_2.

Table 1. The recognition results on CASIA-A database

Algorithm	Recognition rate		
	0°	45°	90°
PCA+LDA	92.20±5.13	93.27±3.37	93.76±4.19
GEI	91.32±2.64	92.01±3.62	92.84±3.26
ANM	95.08±2.54	95.53±4.35	95.14±4.12
MODP	96.53±2.38	96.84±2.63	96.48±4. 06
OLDP	98.02±5.52	98.12±4.05	97.53±4.08

The results in Table 1 show that OLDP is superior to other methods and the reason is that OLDP considers not only the local neighborhood geometry structure and class labels, but also the reliability of the data and the orthogonal constraint.

6   Conclusions

The feature fusion of gait is promising in real world application because the gait images are quite different between gait sequences. So far, gait recognition research is still in the exploratory phase, rather than at an established one. Gait image analysis and recognition offers a rich avenue of research opportunity. In terms of technique, analysis of gait image sequences is at a very rudimentary stage, especially for the purposes of moving-feature extraction. As yet there are few techniques aimed primarily to integrate the whole image sequence for the recognition. In this paper, a feature fusion based gait recognition method is proposed. Four energy accumulation image sequences are applied to gait recognition. OLDP is employed to reduce the dimensionality of the fusion feature vectors. The experimental results on CASIA dataset A show that the method is effective and feasible. In future, we will pay more attention to the feature space for describing and recognizing the gait on the larger database of subjects.

Acknowledgments. The study uses the CASLA gait database collected by Institute of Automation. This work is supported by the grants of the higher education development special fund of Shaanxi Private (XJ13ZD01), basic research project of Natural Science of Shaanxi Province (2014JM2-6096),Tianjin Research Program of Application Foundation and Advanced Technology 14JCYBJC42500,Tianjin City High School Science & Technology Fund Planning Project 20140802, the young academic team construction projects of the 'twelve five' integrated investment planning in Tianjin University of Science and Technology and the 2015 key projects of Tianjin science and technology support program No.15ZCZDGX00200.

References

1. Yu, S., Tan, T., Huang, K., et al.: A Study on Gait-Based Gender Classification. IEEE Transactions on image processing **18**(2), 1905–1910 (2009)
2. Tanawongsuwan, R., Bobick, A.: Modeling the effects of walking speed on appearance based gait recognition. In: Proceedings of the 2004 IEEE Computer Society Conference on Computer Vision and Pattern Recognition (CVPR 2004), vol. 2, pp. 783–790 (2004)
3. Ben Abdelkader, C., Culter, R., Davis, L.: Stride and cadence as a biometric in automatic person identification and verification. In: Proc. Int. Conf. Automatic Face and Gesture Recognition, Washington, pp. 372–376 (2002)
4. Tao, D., Li, X., Wu, X., Maybank, S.J.: General tensor discriminant analysis and gabor features for gait recognition. IEEE Trans. Pattern Anal. Mach. Intell. **29**(10), 1700–1715 (2007)
5. Matovski, D., Nixon, M., Mahmoodi, S., et al.: The Effect of Time on Gait Recognition Performance. IEEE Trans. on Info. Forensics and Security **7**(2), 543–552 (2012)

6. Han, J., Bhanu, B.: Individual recognition using gait energy image. IEEE Transactions on Pattern Analysis and Machine Intelligence **28**(2), 316–322 (2006)

7. Ali, H., Dargham, J., Ali, C., et al.: Gait Recognition using Gait Energy Image. International Journal of Signal Processing, Image Processing and Pattern Recognition **4**(3), 141–152 (2011)

8. Lee, H., Hong, S., Kim, E.: An Efficient Gait Recognition with Backpack Removal. Hindawi Publishing Corp. EURASIP Journal on Advances in Signal Processing **1**, 1–7 (2009)

9. Wang, L., Tan, T., Hu, W., Ning, H.: Silhouette Analysis-Based Gait Recognition for Human Identification. IEEE Trans. on Pattern Analysis and Machine Intelligence **25**(12), 1505–1518 (2003)

10. Amin, T., Hatzinakos, W.: Determinants in Human Gait Recognition. Journal of Information Security **3**, 77–85 (2012)

11. Hong, S., Lee, H., Nizami, I.F., Kim, E.: A new gait representation for human identification: mass vector. In: Proc. IEEE Conference on Industrial Electronics and Applications, pp. 669–673 (2007)

12. Cheng, Q., Fu, B., Chen, H.: Gait recognition based on PCA and LDA. In: Proceedings of the Second Symposium International Computer Science and Computational Technology, Huanshan, China, pp. 124–127 (2006)

13. Okumura, M., Iwama, H., Makihara, Y., et al: Performance evaluation of vision-based gait recognition using a very large-scale gait database. In: Fourth IEEE International Conference Biometrics: Theory Applications and Systems (BTAS), pp. 1–6 (2010)

14. Xu, D., Yan, S., Tao, D., et al.: Marginal Fisher Analysis and Its Variants for Human Gait Recognition and Content- Based Image Retrieval. IEEE Transactions on Image Processing **16**(11), 2811–2821 (2007)

15. Wu, J.: Automated recognition of human gait pattern using manifold learning algorithm. In: 2012 8th International Conference on Natural Computation (ICNC 2012), pp. 199–202 (2012)

16. Wang, L., Tan, T.N., Hu, W.M., Ning, H.Z.: Automatic Gait Recognition Based on Statistical Shape Analysis. IEEE Transactions on Image Processing **12**(9), 1120–1129 (2003)

17. Ali, H., Jamal, D., Ali, C., Moung, E.G.: Gait Recognition using Gait Energy Image. International Journal of Signal Processing, Image Processing and Pattern Recognition **4**(3), 141–152 (2011)

18. Chen, J., Liu, J.: Average Gait Differential Image Based Human Recognition. Hindawi Publishing Corporation e Scientific World Journal, 8 (2014)

19. Zhang, J., Pu, J., Chen, C., Fleischer, R.: Low-resolution gait recognition. IEEE Trans. Syst. Man Cybern B Cybern. **40**(4), 986–996 (2010)

20. Wang, F., Zhang, C.: Feature extraction by maximizing the average neighborhood margin. In: IEEE Conference on Computer Vision and Pattern Recognition, CVPR 2007, pp. 1–8 (2007)

21. Zhang, S.W., Lei, Y.K., Wu, Y.H., et al.: Modified orthogonal discriminant projection for classification. Neurocomputing **74**(17), 3690–3694 (2011)

Speaker Verification Based on TES-PCA Classifier and SVM plus FCM Clustering

Xing Yujuan(✉), Tan Ping, and Zhang Chengwen

School of Digital Media, Lanzhou University of Arts and Science, Lanzhou 730000, China
xyj19811010@126.com

Abstract. Speaker verification is an important branch of speaker recognition. In this paper, a novel hierarchical speaker verification method based on TES-PCA Classifier and support vector machine plus Fuzzy c-means clustering was proposed for the sake of improving performance of speaker verification. In this algorithm, we utilized PCA and Fuzzy c-means clustering to select more discriminant and lower dimensional feature vectors firstly. And then, the truncation error space(TES) was obtained from PCA transformation matrix. The R target speakers were selected fleetly from TES-PCA classifier. Finally, support vector machine was used to make final decision. The experimental results showed that our proposed method could improve recognition accuracy remarkably and the system has better robustness compared with traditional methods.

Keywords: Speaker recognition · Support vector machine · Principal component analysis · Truncation error space classifier

1 Introduction

Automatic speaker verification is a process which a machine authenticates the claimed identity of a person from his or her voice characteristic [1]. It has been a research hotspot in the past decades. The key problems of speaker verification are the extraction of more discriminant feature vectors and the design of efficient recognition algorithm.

In the feature extraction, principal component analysis (PCA) is a classical statistics technique. It analyses the structure of covariance, which is generated by observing the multi-class statistics data, in order to present statistics data compactly with some principal components which could show the interdependence of the data. PCA transform is not only a data reduction method, but also a classifier. In [2], M A. El-Gamal et al utilized PCA to reduce the dimensions of feature vectors, and experiments showed that PCA could reduce the computational complexity effectively. In reference [3], a speaker recognition system based on PCA classifier was proposed. Although the recognition accuracy was lower than traditional methods, PCA classifier carries out easily and fast. Also, Fuzzy c-means clustering technique is based on the concept of fuzzy C-partition. It is the best known and most widely used method to select training data. Hong-Jie Xing et al [4] applied FCM into several synthetic and real-world data sets, and good experiment results were achieved.

© Springer International Publishing Switzerland 2015
J. Yang et al. (Eds.): CCBR 2015, LNCS 9428, pp. 464–471, 2015.
DOI: 10.1007/978-3-319-25417-3_55

In the research of recognition algorithms, statistical methods are dominant approach in speaker verification because of their superior performance. Support vector machine (SVM)[5] has many desirable properties inherently, including the ability to classify patterns with least expected risk principle, to classify sparse data without over-training problem and to make non-linear decisions via kernel function. As a typical statistical analysis technique, it has been applied to solve many pattern recognition problems and its good performances are available. Abderrahmane Amrouche[6] proposed a novel speaker recognition based on GMM-PCA-SVM. PCA was used as dimensionality reduction in the front-end process. SVM was adopted as final classifier accordingly. The experimental results on TIMIT database showed that SVM had excellent classification performance. KAWTHAR YASMINE ZERGAT [7] investigates on the influence of the dialect and the size of database on the text independent speaker verification task using the SVM and the hybrid GMM/SVM speaker modeling. John H.L. Hansen [8] focuses on determining a procedure to select effective negative examples for development of improved Support Vector Machine (SVM) based speaker recognition. However, with the increasement of samples, the training of SVM will become slow. Thereby, this problem will influence the performance of SVM. How to accelerate the training speed of SVM could make a better applied to speaker verification.

Inspired by above related researches, we propose a hierarchical speaker verification method based on TES-PCA classifier and SVM via FCM. The advantages of PCA and FCM clustering could reduce the dimension of input vectors and selected more discriminant features. The combination of them will help a lot in applying SVM to speaker verification. In addition, we design hierarchical classifier based on PCA and FCM clustering. We established the truncation error space classifier (TES-PCA) for each registered speaker according to their PCA transformation matrix firstly. And then, the R target speakers were selected fleetly from TESC. Finally, the coarse classification results are adopted as input of SVM to decide target speaker. By doing so, we expected that the training time of SVM would be shortened and system recognition performance also would be improved simultaneously.

The reminder of this paper is organized as follows. In section 2, feature extraction based on PCA and FCM clustering was presented, followed by a hierarchical speaker verification based on TES-PCA classifier and SVM was proposed in section 3. Experimental evaluation and results are presented in section 4. Finally, conclusions are drawn in section 5.

2 Feature Extraction

To solve the problem that the training of SVM descends while the number of training samples increases, we utilized PCA and FCM clustering to obtain denoised, lower dimensional and more useful feature vectors.

2.1   Dimension Reduction

Given a set of centered input vectors $x_t=(t=1,\ldots, n)$, each of which is of m dimensions $x_t=(x_{t1}, x_{t2},\ldots, x_{tm})^T$ (usually $m<n$), PCA linearly transforms each vector x_t of m dimensions into a new one y_t of s dimensions ($s<<m$) by

$$y_t = U^T x_t \tag{1}$$

where U is the $m\times m$ orthogonal matrix whose i^{th} column u_i is the ith eigenvector of the sample covariance matrix $C = 1/l\sum_{t=1}^{l} x_t x_t^T$, $y_t = (y_{t_1}, y_{t_2},\cdots, y_{t_s})^T$.

Thus, we could conclude that PCA firstly solves the eigenvalue problem, and describe as following:

$$\lambda_i u_i = C u_i, i = 1,\cdots, m \tag{2}$$

where λ_i is one of eigenvalues of C, u_i is eigenvector corresponding to λ_i. We sorted the eigenvalues of C in descending order $\lambda_1 \geq \lambda_2 \geq \ldots \lambda_m \geq 0$, so the corresponding eigenvector also sorted in this order $U=[u_1, u_2,\ldots,u_m]$. Based on the estimation of u_i, the components of y_t could be calculated as the orthogonal transformations of x_t by the following formula:

$$y_{t_i} = u_i^T x_t, i = 1,\cdots, m \tag{3}$$

We only used the first several eigenvectors (for example, first s eigenvectors) sorted in descending order of the eigenvalues; the number of principal components in y_t can be reduced. This is the dimensional reduction characteristic of PCA.

2.2   Data Selection

Fuzzy c-means (FCM) clustering technique can get rid of the less important data and partition the whole training set into several clusters which has its own cluster center to constitute the input feature vector set.

We suppose that the data set $X = \{x_i\}_{i=1}^n$ with $x_i \in R^d$ represent the training samples of n register speakers, the FCM clustering algorithm minimizes the objective function below [9].

$$J_f(D,U,C) = \sum_{j=1}^{c} \sum_{i=1}^{n} [u_j(x_i)]^b d_{ij}^2 \tag{4}$$

where c is the scheduled number of clusters, and $M = \{m_1,m_2,\ldots,m_c\}$ is the cluster centers of corresponding clusters. The fuzzy matrix $U = (u_j(x_i))_{c\times n}$ makes up of the fuzzy memberships of the each training sample x_i to each cluster m_j. Moreover, $b>1$ is the weighting exponent which is used to control the amount of fuzziness of the resulting classification. $d_{ij}^2 =\| x_i - m_j \|^2$ is the square Euclidean distance between data object x_i to center m_j. By definition, each sample x_i satisfies the constraint:

$$\sum_{j=1}^{c} \mu_j(x_i) = 1, \ 0 \le \mu_j(x_i) \le 1 \tag{5}$$

The objective function (4) is minimized subjected to the constraint (5). This is a constrained optimization problem, which can be converted to an unconstrained optimization problem using the Lagrange multiplier technique.

$$m_j = \frac{\sum_{i=1}^{n} [u_j(x_i)]^b x_i}{\sum_{i=1}^{n} [u_j(x_i)]^b}, j = 1, 2, \ldots, c \tag{6}$$

$$u_j(x_i) = \frac{(1/\|x_i - m_j\|^2)^{\frac{1}{b-1}}}{\sum_{k=1}^{c} (1/\|x_i - m_j\|^2)^{\frac{1}{b-1}}},$$
$$i = 1, 2, \ldots, n, j = 1, 2, \ldots, c \tag{7}$$

The data selection algorithm is described as follows:

Step1: Determine the number of cluster c, choose the value of b (b=2), give converging error ε which is a small positive constant, and set t=0 to record the cluster centers.

Step2: Initialize the centers m_j^t, $j = 1, 2, \ldots, c$ by random and initialize $u_j(x_i)^t$;

Step3: Update m_j^t and $u_j(x_i)^t$;

   Step31: Compute new m_j^{t+1} using equation (6);

   Step32: Compute new $u_j(x_i)^{t+1}$ using equation (7);

Step4: If $\|U^t - U^{t-1}\| < \varepsilon$ then stop FCM, otherwise return to step3.

3   Speaker Verification Based on TES-PCA Classifier and SVM Plus FCM

Truncation error space (TES) was obtained by PCA transformation matrix. In stage of recognition, a novel TES-PCA classifier was proposed to make a coarse decision for the sake of selecting the R possible target speakers firstly, and then the target speaker is finally found out from these R speakers by SVM classifier. The framework of our proposed hierarchical speaker verification is shown in figure 1.

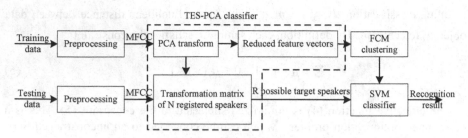

Fig. 1. The system block diagram of our proposed speaker verification algorithm

3.1   TES-PCA Classifier for Coarse Decision

For each registered speaker, we selected first q eigenvectors to form principal component space (PCS) after PCA transformation. The PCS was denoted as follows.

$$P^{(s)} = \{\boldsymbol{\mu}_1^{(s)}, \boldsymbol{\mu}_2^{(s)}, \ldots, \boldsymbol{\mu}_q^{(s)}\}, s = 1, \ldots, N \tag{8}$$

Accordingly, the rest of the eigenvectors that was not chosen as PCS would form truncation error space (TES):

$$Q^{(s)} = \{\boldsymbol{\mu}_{q+1}^{(s)}, \boldsymbol{\mu}_{q+2}^{(s)}, \ldots, \boldsymbol{\mu}_m^{(s)}\}, s = 1, \ldots, N \tag{9}$$

After the input vectors were mapped to TES, truncation error of vectors was obtained as follows.

$$\boldsymbol{TE}^{(s)}(X) = \left\| Q^{(s)\mathrm{T}}(X - \boldsymbol{m}_s) \right\|^2, s = 1, \ldots, N \tag{10}$$

where $\boldsymbol{m}_s = 1/l \sum_{t=1}^{l} \boldsymbol{x}_t^{(s)}$ is mean vector of the sth speaker. According to the definition of PCA transformation, speaker's samples is closer to target speaker, truncation error $\boldsymbol{TE}^{(s)}(X)$ on TES is smaller. So, we computed truncation error on TES for each speaker, and sorted $\boldsymbol{TE}^{(s)}(X)$ in ascending order $\boldsymbol{TE}^1(X) < \boldsymbol{TE}^2(X) < \ldots < \boldsymbol{TE}^N(X)$, we select speakers that are corresponding to first $R\,\boldsymbol{TE}^{(s)}(X)$ as the coarse decision of TES-PCA classifier.

3.2   Support Vector Machine for Final Decision

Support Vector Machine (SVM), invented by Vapnik [10], is powerful tool for data classification. The new feature vectors of target speaker and imposters are used to train SVM, so the class decision function for each speaker can be obtained as follows.

$$f(x) = \sum_{i=1}^{l} y_i \alpha_i K(x_i, x) + b \tag{11}$$

where $x_i \in R^n$, i=1, 2, ..., l is a new training Fisher feature vector. Each x_i belongs to one of two classes identified by the label $y_i \in \{-1,1\}$. The coefficients α_i and b are the solution of a quadratic programming problem. α_i is non-zero for support vectors (SV) and is zero otherwise. $K(\cdot)$ is the kernel function. In this paper, we selected the Radial Basis Function (RBF) kernel which is more like GMM [11]. Radial Basis Function (RBF) kernel is described as follows.

$$K(x_i, x_j) = \exp(- \|x_i - x_j\|^2 / 2\sigma^2) \tag{12}$$

4   Experiments

4.1   Experimental Database

We performed our testing experiments on the TIMIT speech database [12] to verify the effectiveness and feasibility of our proposed method. This corpus contains broad-band recordings of 630 speakers including 438 male and 192 female. And all speakers had 8 major dialects of American English. Each speaker was asked for reading 10 phonetically rich sentences. The signal was sampled at 16 kHz, on 16 bits, on a linear amplitude scale. We combine 12 dimensional Mel-Frequency Cepstral Coefficients (MFCCs) and their first derivatives into 24 dimensional vectors as input vectors. In our experiment, the training set contains 5 utterances of each speaker that is randomly chosen from ten sessions, and the testing set contains the rest 5 utterances. The first-order digital filter was $H(z)$=1-0.95z^{-1}. We adopted equal error rate (EER) and minimum decision cost value (minDCF) as metrics for evaluation.

4.2   Experiment Results and Discussion

Experiment 1: In this experiment, we compared different common kernel functions applied in our proposed hierarchical classifier, including radial basis function (RBF) kernels ($\sigma = 0.6$), polynomial kernels and linear kernels. By doing this, we expected to seek for kernel which performed very well.

Table 1. Comparison of EER and minDCF for different kernels

kernels	%EER	minDCF
Linear kernels	10.14	0.0703
polynomial kernels	8.22	0.0497
RBF kernels ($\sigma = 0.6$)	5.02	0.0382

As shown in table 1, the EER of RBF kernels is 5.02%, and minDCF is 0.0382. Obviously, comparing with the linear kernels and polynomial kernels, substantial reduction of RBF kernels is achieved in EER and minDCF. Compared with linear kernels, EER of RBF had gone down 5.12%, and minDCF had reduced 0.0321.

Meanwhile, compared with polynomial kernels, EER had gone down 3.2%, and minDCF had gone down 0.0115. So, we could easily conclude that the RBF kernels significantly outperform the other kernels.

Experiment 2: In this experiment, we test the performance of our proposed hierarchical speaker verification method compared with GMM, TES-PCA classifier and SVM. In order to test the robustness of our proposed method, we also had corrupted the speech signal with "babble" noise extracted from the NOISEX database [13]. The experimental results were shown as table 2.

Table 2. Comparison of EER and minDCF for Different classifiers

classifier	clean speech			noise speech		
	EER (%)	minDCF	RR(s)	EER (%)	minDCF	RR(s)
GMM	9.72	0.0836	3.04	9.93	0.0925	4.52
SVM	5.04	0.0542	2.77	6.12	0.0668	3.18
TES-PCA classifier	6.13	0.0601	1.53	7.33	0.0727	2.04
hierarchical classifier	4.11	0.0443	1.86	4.83	0.0504	2.39

From Table 2, we could get conclusions as follows. In the case of clean speech, SVM outperformed GMM with 4.68% lower in EER, 0.0294 lower in minDCF and 0.27s improved in RR as illustrated in Table 1. Though the EER and minDCF of TES-PCA classifier were higher than SVM, its RR had shortened 1.24s than SVM. This suggested that TES-PCA classifier had simpler computation than other classifiers, so it had shorter training time. The performance of our proposed hierarchical classifier was best. The EER, minDCF and RR of the hierarchical classifier were 4.11%, 0.0443, 1.86s respectively. Compared with SVM, the EER, minDCF and RR of our method had reduced 0.93%, 0.0099, and 0.91s. Similarly, in the case of noise speech, our proposed method also performed very well both in EER, minDCF and RT. EER and minDCF of our method had approximately 2.5% and 0.0223 reduction respectively compared with system based on TES-PCA classifier. In the same way, EER and minDCF of our method had approximately 1.29% and 0.0164 reduction respectively compared with system based on SVM. The EER of our method under clean speech was 0.72% lower than EER under noise speech. And the reduction of minDCF is 0.0061. RR had shortened 0.53s. All in all, our proposed method was effective and high-powered, and had better robustness.

5   Conclusions

In this paper, a novel speaker verification method based on TES-PCA and SVM plus FCM clustering is proposed. With the aids of PCA and FCM clustering, the scope of speech recognition was narrowed and the number and dimension of input vectors were reduced. TES-PCA was designed based on truncation error space of PCA transformation matrix to select possible R target speakers fleetly. By doing so, it speeded up the training of support vector machine (SVM) and reduced the computational complexity. Simulation experiment results show that our method has good recognition performance.

Acknowledgments. This paper is supported by Education Foundation of Gansu (2014A-125), China.

References

1. Chao, Y.H.: Using LR-based discriminant kernel methods with applications to speaker verification. International Journal of Speech Communication 57(2), 76–86 (2014)
2. El-Gamal, M.A., Abu El-Yazeed, M.F., El Ayadi, M.M.H.: Dimensionality reduction for text-independent speaker identification using gaussian mixture model. In: IEEE International Symposium on Micro-Nano Mechatronics and Human Science, pp. 625–628. IEEE, Cairo (2003)
3. Zhang, W.F., Yang, Y.C., Wu, Z.H.: Exploiting PCA classifiers to speaker recognition. In: International Joint Conference on Neural Networks, pp. 820–823. IEEE, Portland (2003)
4. Xing, H.J., Hu, B.G.: An adaptive fuzzy c-means clustering-based mixtures of experts model for unlabeled data classification. Neurocomputing 71, 1008–1021 (2008)
5. Vapnik, V.: Universal Learning Technology: Support Vector Machines. NEC Journal of Advanced Technology 2(2), 137–144 (2005)
6. Zergat, K.Y., Amrouche, A.: New scheme based on GMM-PCA-SVM modelling for automatic speaker recognition. International Journal of Speech Technology 17(4), 373–381 (2014)
7. Zergat, K.Y., Amrouche, A.: SVM against GMM/SVM for dialect influence on automatic speaker recognition task. International Journal of Computational Intelligence and Applications 13(2), 1450012-1–1450012-10 (2014)
8. Suh, J.W., Lei, Y., Kim, W., Hansen, J.H.L.: Effective background data selection for SVM-based speaker recognition with unseen test environments: more is not always better. International Journal of Speech Technology 17(3), 211–221 (2014)
9. Vapnik, V.: The Nature of Statistical Leaning Theory, 2nd edn. Springer, New York (2000)
10. Renjifo, C., Barsic, D., Carmen, C., Norman, K., Peacock, G.S.: Improving radial basis function kernel classification through incremental learning and automatic parameter selection. Neurocomputing 72(13), 3–14 (2008)
11. Byrd, D.: Preliminary results on speaker-dependent variation in the TIMIT database. Journal of the Acoustical Society of America. 92(1), 593–596 (1992)
12. Gales, M.J.F., Young, S.J.: Robust continuous speech recognition using parallel model combination. IEEE Transactions on Speech & Audio Processing 4(5), 352–359 (1996)

Preliminary Study on Self-contained UBM Construction for Speaker Recognition

Yingchun Yang$^{(\boxtimes)}$ and Yongkun Sun

College of Computer Science and Technology, Zhejiang University, Hangzhou 310027, China
{yyc,alwaysyk}@zju.edu.cn

Abstract. Although speaker recognition technology has evolved into some new stages recently, GMM-UBM (Gaussian Mixture Model-Universal Background Model) has always been the base module for the newly developed methods such as SVM, JFA and i-vector. Because of its simplicity, flexibility and robustness, GMM-UBM has been used as a benchmark system for research reference. For traditional UBM construction, speech data from a lot of speakers other than the target speakers should be obtained, which means much cost of data collection. In this paper, we make preliminary exploration on a new approach to train the UBM, named as self-contained UBM, in which only the target speakers' training data were used. We study several strategies of speaker selection for the self-contained UBM construction, gradually reduced from 50 to 3 speakers. Experiments on MASC@CCNT show that our self-contained UBM obtain considerable recognition rate compared with traditional UBM, while needing far less training data thus less training time. Furthermore, we find out that the obtained good ternary UBM speakers have an interesting characteristic of spanning a triangle (UBM speaker triangle) after dimension reduction of MFCC features with PCA.

Keywords: Speaker recognition · GMM (Gaussian Mixture Model) · Self-contained UBM (Universal Background Model) · UBM speaker triangle

1 Introduction

In recent years, there have developed several novel speaker recognition methods, including SVM (Support Vector Machine), JFA (Joint Factor Analysis) and i-vector [1], however, GMM-UBM framework is still the basis for the above newly evolved models, which using Gaussian mixture model (GMM) for likelihood function, and a UBM (universal background model) for alternative speaker representation [3]. The UBM is a speaker-independent Gaussian mixture model trained with speech acoustic features from a large set of speakers to represent the general, speaker independent distribution of features and is assumed to be a very large GMM[3, 4]. As an important element, UBM construction is computationally expensive. Therefore, some work has been taken to reduce the UBM construction cost, including two approaches: one is order reduction to reach lower order UBM and then lower computing complexity [5], the other is data selection according to data variation, sub-sampling and speaker

© Springer International Publishing Switzerland 2015
J. Yang et al. (Eds.): CCBR 2015, LNCS 9428, pp. 472–479, 2015.
DOI: 10.1007/978-3-319-25417-3_56

variation[4]. It's shown experimentally that increasing the inter-speaker variability in the UBM data while maintaining the overall total data size constant gradually improves system performance [4].

In this paper, we propose a novel approach for UBM construction, i.e. self-contained UBM, which utilizing only the training speech of the target speakers rather than other background speakers. This paper is organized as follows. Sec. 2 proposes our research motivation. The experiment setup is given in Sec. 3. The ternary UBM speaker sets are detailed in Sec.4. In sec.5, we further explore the interesting characteristics of the ternary UBM speaker, i.e. UBM speaker triangle. Finally, conclusions are presented in Sec.6.

2 Motivation

GMM (Gaussian mixture model) is a stochastic speaker model to describe the target speaker's feature distribution, treating the speaker as a random source producing the observed speech feature vectors [6].

In terms of the parameters of an M-state statistical speaker model, the GMM pdf (probability density function) is

$$p(x|\lambda) = \sum_{i=1}^{M} p_i b_i(x) \qquad (1)$$

The pdf for state i as a function of the D-dimensional feature vector x is

$$b_i(x) = \frac{1}{(2\pi)^{D/2}|\Sigma_i|^{1/2}} \times \exp\left\{-\frac{1}{2}(x-\mu_i)^T \Sigma_i^{-1}(x-\mu_i)\right\} \qquad (2)$$

where μ_i is the state mean vector and Σ_i is the sate covariance matrix. $\lambda=(p_i, \mu_i, \Sigma_i)$, for $i = 1, L, M$ represents the parameters of the speaker model and are obtained in an unsupervised manner by using the expectation-maximization (EM) algorithm[6].

In theory, to create a complete GMM for each speaker, the speaker's training speech should cover all sorts of variabilities from phones, channel, environments, health and emotions etc. However, that's impossible to reality. Adaptation of the acoustic model to a new operating condition is an effective and common means to deal with speech variability. In GMM-based speaker recognition, a speaker-independent UBM is first trained with the EM algorithm from a large amount of background speakers' speech to represent the general, speaker independent distribution of speech features [1, 3]. Each target speaker model is adapted from the UBM by the maximum a posteriori (MAP) method [3]. Therefore, the MAP-adapted model and the UBM are coupled and the model is commonly named as GMM-UBM. The match score depends on both the target model (λ_{tar}) and the background model (λ_{UBM}) via the average log likelihood ratio:

$$LLR_{avg} p(X|\lambda_{tar}) - p(X|\lambda_{UBM}) = \frac{1}{T}\sum_{t=1}^{T}\left\{\log p(x_t|\lambda_{tar}) - \log p(x_t|\lambda_{UBM})\right\} \qquad (3)$$

where $X=\{x_1, x_2, L, x_T\}$ is the test speech feature vectors.

A UBM is first trained with the EM algorithm from tens or hundreds of hours of speech data gathered from a large number of speakers. The general guideline for choosing UBM training speech is to select speech that is representative of the expected alternative speech to be encountered during recognition in the views of the type, quality and the composition of speakers. There are no objective measures to determine the right number of speakers or amount of speech to use in training a UBM. Empirically, no performance loss was observed using a UBM trained with one hour of speech compared to one trained with six hours of speech [6]. Since UBM is a large GMM trained typically with large amount of speech data thus requires extensive resource, there have been some works devoted to reduce the UBM construction cost. Except the direct UBM order reduction [5], the recent research is data selection according to data variation, sub-sampling and speaker variation [4]. It's shown experimentally that the sub-sampling methods can retain the baseline EER (Equal Error Rate) using only 1% of the original UBM data and less than 30% of the original UBM speakers (60 and 100 speakers vs. original 320 speakers) [4].

Since the previous work [5,6] tell us that the UBM data is not so consuming as it seemed to be, we further consider the problems of UBM construction: What are the necessary and sufficient conditions for UBM construction? Is there least complete data set for UBM construction? Here, we research on a new UBM construction approach named as self-contained UBM, which means UBM training data is from the target speakers themselves without extra data requirement for other speakers. In our experiments, we gradually reduce the number of UBM speakers from 50 to 3 and find out that the recognition performance deteriorate most often but still remain the same level with such reduction for some special speaker groups.

3 Experiments

All our experiments are taken on the MASC@CCNT corpus [2], which contains 68 speakers' data, each speaker has five emotions including anger, elation, neutral, panic and sadness. For each speaker, we have collected 2 neutral paragraphs (18~25s) and 20 utterances (1~5s) three times in the other 4 emotions. These materials cover all the phonemes in Chinese. The contents of utterances are: simple statements, a declarative sentence with an enumeration, general questions (yes/no question), alternative questions, imperative sentences, exclamatory sentences, special questions (wh-questions).

In all the following experiments, the last 50 speakers' utterances (the 19-68th speaker) of 5 emotions are used as the test data. The speech is pre-emphasized and framed with a 16 ms Hamming window. A 34-order MFCC feature is extracted and 64-component GMM is trained.

In the baseline experiment, the first 18 speakers' two neutral paragraphs (the 1-18th speaker) are selected to train the UBM, and the remaining 50 speakers' two neutral paragraphs are utilized to adapt their own target models from the UBM. We name the resulting system as S_{basic}.

Firstly, we try to train a UBM by using the 19-68th speaker's neutral paragraph data, and do the adaption and testing steps as the baseline experiment. In this way, we need no extra data to train a UBM and get a 19-68th speaker's self-contained UBM. The system is called S_{50}. Then we try two smaller UBM training datasets respectively, one containing only the 19-43th speaker's neutral paragraphs data (first 25 speakers, f25 for short) and another containing 44-68th speaker's neutral paragraphs data (last 25 speakers, l25 for short). It can be seen as a simple binary partition of the whole 50 speakers (19-68th). We named the two systems as S_{f25} and S_{l25} respectively. Table 1 show the UBM training time, identification rate and equal error rate of the basic system, S_{50}, S_{f25} and S_{l25}.

Table 1. Training Time, Identification Rate (IR) and Equal Error Rate (EER) of S_{basic} S_{50} S_{f25} S_{l25}

System	UBM Training Time(s)	IR(%)	EER(%)
S_{basic}	29	51.89	18.45
S_{50}	83	50.61	19.39
S_{f25}	39	49.44	20.15
S_{l25}	41	51.55	19.30

From Table 1, we can see that the recognition rates of new systems are a little bit lower than the basic system, and their EERs are higher than basic system. However, we can also see that identification rate of the S_{l25} is very close to that of the basic system S_{basic}, which is better than that of S_{50} and S_{f25}. In addition, we try a simple linear fusion of S_{50}, S_{f25} and S_{l25}'s and achieve 51.73% identification rate and 19.07% EER. We can make our first conclusion that our proposed self-contained UBM really work for speaker recognition, especially for speaker identification. From table 1, we can also get the conclusion that the selection of target speaker set may result in a big change on the recognition rate. Take S_{f25} and S_{l25} for example, both of them have 25 training speakers which are exclusive to each other, but their performances have about 2 points difference. And at the same time, the performance of difference system is not closely related to the capacity of the UBM training set because S_{50} has a lower recognition rate compare to S_{l25} and higher recognition rate to S_{f25}. Based on such fact, we further consider the problem of least complete data set for UBM construction i.e. are there such minimum training UBM speaker sets, using which we could get comparable performance with the baseline system S_{basic}. Therefore, we'll lay out the new UBM data selection by reducing speaker number gradually.

4   The Ternary UBM Speaker Set

In order to find the least complete UBM speaker sets, we next try to use a partition of ten and five of the whole 50 speakers to train the UBM. In each of the divided 5 system, there are 10 different UBM training speakers, and similarly each divided 10 system has 5 extinct UBM training speakers. And both of the four systems' UBM training speaker sets are selected at random. Table 2 and Table 3 show the results of those systems.

From Table 2 and able 3, we can get the conclusion that 5 is a relative minimum volume of UBM training set. To move forward, we can change it lower from 5 to 1 to get a more minimum value. Then we take account of experiments in which we select randomly 1-5 speakers from the 19-68 speakers. Finally, we get the ideal number 3, which will have a better recognition rate than the basic experiment when chosen properly. The Table 4 lists some ternary UBM speaker set and their results, from which we can find out that some systems with ternary set trained UBM even obtain a higher identification rate than the basic system. Also, the UBM training time reduce from 29 seconds to 5 seconds, very close to six-fold reduction.

Table 2. Training Time, Identification Rate (IR) and Equal Error Rate (EER) of partition 5 systems

System	UBMTraining Time(s)	IR(%)	EER(%)
S_{basic}	29	51.89	18.45
S_{div5-1}	16	47.71	19.50
S_{div5-2}	15	48.87	19.47
S_{div5-3}	16	47.65	21.30
S_{div5-4}	16	50.58	18.89
S_{div5-5}	17	51.45	20.50

Table 3. Training Time, Identification Rate (IR) and Equal Error Rate (EER) of partition 10 systems

System	UBM Training Time(s)	IR(%)	EER(%)
S_{basic}	29	51.89	18.45
$S_{div10-1}$	8	47.35	19.83
$S_{div10-2}$	9	47.33	20.67
$S_{div10-3}$	7	48.60	19.41
$S_{div10-4}$	8	49.03	19.81
$S_{div10-5}$	8	47.14	21.66
$S_{div10-6}$	9	45.90	21.31
$S_{div10-7}$	8	50.88	21.93
$S_{div10-8}$	7	44.71	21.81
$S_{div10-9}$	7	49.22	19.95
$S_{div10-10}$	9	52.11	21.22

From Table 1 to Table 4, we can observe that there remain some good UBM speaker sets (highlighted in red), e.g. S_{125} (in Table 1), S_{div5-5} (in Table 2), $S_{div10-10}$ (in Table 3), 66-58-65 (in Table 4), 59-50-28 (in Table 4). We can further conclude that there do exist the least complete UBM speaker sets, which are named as the ternary UBM speaker sets and the set volume is three. Since different speakers play different roles in UBM construction, can we find some hints for finding those ternary UBM speaker sets? Thus, we then make shallow investigation on the characteristics on those speaker sets by feature visualization.

Table 4. Training Time, Identification Rate (IR) and Equal Error Rate (EER) of ternary UBM speaker systems

System	UBMTraining Time(s)	IR(%)	EER(%)
S_{basic}	29	51.89	18.45
66-58-65	5	52.45	20.58
59-50-28	5	51.66	24.85
66-23-62	5	50.98	20.62
63-66-37	4	50.46	25.09
52-45-61	5	49.14	23.72
49-36-31	6	48.24	21.73
59-49-58	4	46.63	22.01
67-63-46	6	44.66	21.31
60-24-51	5	42.70	25.51
43-58-29	5	42.24	25.87

5   UBM Speaker Triangle

The ternary UBM speaker sets in the last section are selected at random. Now we could say that it does exist, but how can we find it before the model training? We do find some interesting phenomena on the different ternary speaker sets.

We visualize the feature distribution of the three speakers in ternary set by PCA on their training paragraph speech features. And we found that speakers in the good ternary sets are distribute as a triangle (ref. Fig. 1 (a) and (b)), while the bad ternary speaker sets always have overlapped speakers (ref. Fig. 1 (c) and (d)). Fig. 1 shows this interesting phenomenon: the obtained good ternary UBM speakers have an interesting characteristic of spanning a triangle (UBM speaker triangle) after dimension reduction of MFCC features with PCA.

We also reduce their features to three dimensions by PCA in order to get more information. But it shows the same results as in two dimensions. Furthermore, we try to get three speaker by their distribution which formed a triangle in two dimension PCA picture, but it is not always a good ternary set (refer to Fig. 1 (e) and (f)). That means UBM speaker triangle is an important characteristic for the good UBM speaker sets but not unique for them.

Further work might be done by analyzing the KL divergence of the ternary set speakers or using the GMM token information to explore their dynamic relation.

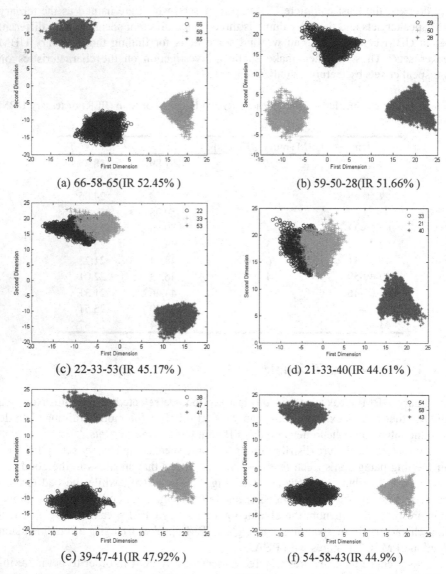

(a) 66-58-65(IR 52.45%)

(b) 59-50-28(IR 51.66%)

(c) 22-33-53(IR 45.17%)

(d) 21-33-40(IR 44.61%)

(e) 39-47-41(IR 47.92%)

(f) 54-58-43(IR 44.9%)

Fig. 1. Feature distribution of different ternary UBM speakers after transformation by PCA

6   Conclusions

In this paper, we make preliminary exploration on a new UBM construction approach, i.e. self-contained UBM, in which UBM training data comes only from the target speakers compared with extra background speakers in the traditional approach. The experiments on the MASC@CCNT corpus show that the systems with our new UBM can retain their IR (Identification Rate) in spite of the reduction of the speaker account from 50 to 3 with training time reduction by up to almost six-fold. We further make feature visualization and find out that the good ternary UBM speakers' features constitute a triangle (UBM Speaker Triangle) after dimension reduction with PCA. Our preliminary study shows that our self-contained UBM is effective for speaker identification tasks and the good ternary UBM speakers present a distinctive characteristic of triangle. More corpuses would be tested in the future. Applying the self-contained UBM to speaker verification task and the problem of selection of the good ternary UBM speakers remain to be considered in our future. Also, extend this work to speaker gender recognition [7] is to be considered. In fact, our preliminary study is just the beginning for the problems of UBM construction: What are the necessary and sufficient conditions for UBM construction? The goal is to find the objective measures to determine the right number of speakers or amount of speech to use in training a UBM, which is still an open problem in the field of speaker recognition.

Acknowledgement. This work is supported by the National Basic Research Program (973) of China (No. 2013CB329504), the National Natural Science Foundation of China (No. 60970080), and the National HighTech R&D Program (863) of China (No. 2006AA01Z136).

References

1. Kinnunen, T., Li, H.Z.: An overview of text-independent speaker recognition: From features to supervectors. Speech Commun. **52**, 12–40 (2010)
2. Wu, T., Yang, Y.C., Wu, Z.H.: A speech corpus in mandarin for emotion analysis and affective speaker recognition. In: IEEE Odyssey Speaker and Language Recognition Workshop, pp. 1–5. IEEE Press, New York (2006)
3. Reynolds, D.A., Quatieri, T.F., Dunn, R.B.: Speaker Verification Using Adapted Gaussian Mixture Models. Digit. Signal Proces. **10**, 19–41 (2000)
4. Hasan, T., Hansen, J.H.L.: A study on universal background model training in speaker verification. IEEE T. Audio Speech Lang. Proces. **19**, 1890–1899 (2011)
5. Shan, Z.Y., Yang, Y.C.: Universal back ground model reduction based efficient speaker recognition. J. Zhejiang Univ.(Eng. Sci.) **43**, 978–983 (2009). (in Chinese)
6. Reynolds, D.A.: Automatic speaker recognition using Gaussian Mixture speaker model. Lincoln Lab. J. **8**, 173–192 (1996)
7. Huang, T., Yang, Y.C., Wu, Z.H.: Combining MFCC and pitch to enhance the performance of the gender recognition. In: 8th International Conference on Signal Processing, pp. 1–4. IEEE Press, New York (2006)

The Comparison of Denoising Methods Based on Air-ground Speech of Civil Aviation

Zhihui Zhang, Yihua Shi, Guimin Jia, and Jinfeng Yang[✉]

Tianjin Key Lab for Advanced Signal Processing,
Civil Aviation University of China, Tianjin, China
jfyang@cauc.edu.cn

Abstract. With the rapid development of the civil aviation industry, the air traffic flow is increasing greatly. At the same time, the expansion of telecommunication business has made the problem of electromagnetic interference more and more serious. Consequently, the communication between pilots and air traffic controllers may interfere by other signals, which poses a potential threat to flight safety. So we compare several denoise methods based on the original algorithm in order to find which is optimal in noise reduction for air-ground communication. Comparison tests are performed on actual air-ground communication data, and the experiment results show the improved subtraction algorithm is optimal to reduce the noise interference effectively, while wiener filtering is worst.

Keywords: Speech enhancement · Civil aviation air-ground communication · Improved spectral subtraction algorithm · Masking model algorithm

1   Introduction

VHF (Very High Frequency Communication), one of the most significant communication system used in the field of civil aviation, implements the communication between pilots and traffic controllers on the ground. It is an important way to know the position of planes and other basic information for ground crew. However, as the electromagnetic environment becomes more and more complex, the interference to civil aviation air-ground communication is increasing greatly. Though the device of restraining interference is equipped on the plane, the communication quality can not be protected effectively, especially during the thirteen minutes when an airplane just takes off or begins to descend [1]. Once the communication was interrupted and even lost, serious accidents may happen unexpectedly.

As we all know, there are many interfacing source for civil aviation air-ground communication, but the main source comes from electromagnetic environment [2]. Unfortunately, we can not find the right kind of noise to simulate this electromagnetic interference, so it is impossible to use the traditional method of clean speech adding noise. In order to evaluate the effect of the usually used denoise algorithm, we use the actual air-ground communication records collected from airlines directly in this paper. Quantitative experiments are carried out to find out a suitable method for air-ground denoising.

J. Yang et al. (Eds.): CCBR 2015, LNCS 9428, pp. 480–487, 2015.
DOI: 10.1007/978-3-319-25417-3_57

In this paper, we first introduce the principle of four noise reduction methods briefly and point out the using range of it. Second, denoising the speech records by using four different methods, we make some comparisons. Third, we draw a conclusion and give the future work for air-ground communication speech denoising and recognition.

2   Principle of Algorithm

2.1   Improved Spectrum Subtraction

In the field of speech enhancement, spectral subtraction algorithm is widely used due to its simple principle. However, with the default of the narrow range of SNR, it greatly reduces the speech intelligibility [3] when the value of SNR is low. Besides, it creates "music noise" obviously at the time of reconstructing speech. So it limits the use of spectral subtraction to some extent.

B.F.Boll put forward an improved spectrum subtraction algorithm [4] in 1979. In order to reduce the residual noise as much as possible, this algorithm retains the maximum of noise in the process of spectrum subtraction and reconstruction. Its principle is shown as:

$$\left|\hat{X}_i(k)\right|^\gamma = \begin{cases} \left|X_i(k)\right|^\gamma - a \times D(k) & \left|X_i(k)\right|^\gamma \geq a \times D(k) \\ \beta \times D(k) & \left|X_i(k)\right|^\gamma < a \times D(k) \end{cases} \tag{1}$$

where $\left|X_i(k)\right|^\gamma$ is the value of noising speech spectral, $D(k)$ is the value of noise spectral, α is spectral subtraction factor, β is gain compensation factor. γ can be valued 1 or 2 ($\gamma = 1$ equals to use of amplitude spectrum in spectrum subtraction, $\gamma = 2$ equals to use power spectrum).

The improved spectrum subtraction algorithm have two obvious advantages. First, the principle is very simple, we just need to estimate the value of noise. Second, it reduces "musical noise" obviously. So it is widely used due to its advantages above.

2.2   Wiener Filter

As the speech signal is not stationary, so the filter should be different for each frame signal. Therefore, wiener filter should be designed as:

$$H(i,k) = \frac{\left|S(i,k)\right|^2}{\left|S(i,k)\right|^2 + \left|D(i,k)\right|^2} \tag{2}$$

where $\left|S(i,k)\right|^2$ is estimated power spectrum of i-th frame speech signal, $\left|D(i,k)\right|^2$ is estimated power spectrum of i-th frame noise signal.

In order to ensure the speech signal between two adjacent frames can transit smooth, the estimated power spectrum of the i-th frame speech signal is defined as [5,6]:

$$\left|\tilde{S}(i,k)\right|^2 = \tau \left|\tilde{S}(i-1,k)\right|^2 + (1-\tau)\left|S(i,k)\right|^2 \tag{3}$$

where τ is an introduced smooth factor and the classic value is 0.85. $H(i, k)$ is wiener filter designed as the principle above. For a noising speech $Y(i, k)$, we can obtain a estimated value after the noising speech pass through this filter:

$$\hat{S}(i,k) = H(i,k)Y(i,k) \tag{4}$$

The advantage of wiener filter is that it hardly produce "musical noise". However, it does not consider the importance of the speech spectral component to human hearing, so this algorithm has some distortion to speech signal.

2.3   MMSE Algorithm

Expressions of noisy speech is generally shown as: $y(n)=x(n)+d(n)$, where $y(n)$ is noisy speech, $x(n)$ is clear speech and $d(n)$ is noise signal. Frequency spectral components of $y(n)$ and $x(n)$ is shown as:

$$Y_k = R_k \exp(j\alpha_k) \qquad X_k = A_k \exp(j\theta_k) \tag{5}$$

Assume that each spectral component is statistical independent, we can obtain estimated value $\hat{A}_k$ of A_k by Bayes formula readily

$$\hat{A}_k = E\{A_k \mid Y_k\} = \frac{\int_0^{2\pi} \int_0^{\infty} a_k p\left(Y_k \mid a_k, \alpha_k\right) p\left(a_k, \alpha_k\right) da_k d\alpha_k}{\int_0^{2\pi} \int_0^{\infty} p\left(Y_k \mid a_k, \alpha_k\right) p\left(a_k, \alpha_k\right) da_k d\alpha_k} \tag{6}$$

As the speech and noise are random signals and difficult to get their statistical distribution, *Yariv* and *David* proposed a STSA-MMSE approach [7]. Assume that the noise signal is statistical independence of zero mean Gaussian process [8].

$$p(Y_k \mid a_k, \alpha_k) = \frac{1}{\pi\lambda_d(k)} \exp\left\{-\frac{1}{\lambda_d(k)}\left|Y_k - a_k e^{j\alpha_k}\right|^2\right\} \tag{7}$$

$$p\left(a_k, \alpha_k\right) = \frac{a_k}{\pi\lambda_s(k)} \exp\left\{-\frac{a_k^2}{\lambda_s(k)}\right\} \tag{8}$$

where $\lambda_s(k) = E[|S(k)|^2]$ and $\lambda_d(k) = E[|D(k)|^2]$ are the k-spectrum component of speech and noise respectively, taking Eq. (7) and Eq. (8) into Eq. (6), we can obtain:

$$\hat{A}_k = \Gamma(1.5)\frac{\sqrt{v_k}}{\gamma_k} M(-0.5; 1; -v_k) R_k \tag{9}$$

where $\hat{A}_k$ is the estimated value of noisy speech after reduction, we can obtain the enhanced signal after adding the phase of noising speech to it. $\Gamma(\cdot)$ is gamma function and $\Gamma(1.5) = \sqrt{\pi}/2$, $M(a, b, c)$ is superfluid function [9,10]. v_k is shown as:

$$v_k = \frac{\xi_k}{\xi_k + 1}\gamma_k \tag{10}$$

where $\xi_k = \lambda_s(k)/\lambda_d(k)$ is priori SNR, $\gamma_k = R_k^2/\lambda_d(k)$ is posteriori SNR.

2.4   Masking Model Combined with Spectral Subtraction

Unlike traditional methods, auditory masking model considers both improving SNR and the effect of masking to noise when design gain function. Since the late 90s, more and more scholars begin to import auditory masking model into speech enhancement [11-13]. *Virag* combined masking model and traditional spectral subtraction together, then he proposed a new speech enhancement method [14]:

$$X'(k) = \begin{cases} \left(1 - \alpha\left[\dfrac{N(k)}{Y(k)}\right]^{\gamma_1}\right)^{\gamma_2} \times Y(k), & \left[\dfrac{N(k)}{Y(k)}\right]^{\gamma_1} < \dfrac{1}{\alpha + \beta} \\[4mm] \left(\beta\left[\dfrac{N(k)}{Y(k)}\right]^{\gamma_1}\right)^{\gamma_2} \times Y(k), & else \end{cases} \tag{11}$$

where $X'(k)$ is the valued spectrum of clear speech, $Y(k)$ and $N(k)$ are spectrum of noisy speech and noise respectively, α is spectral subtraction threshold and increase this coefficient will improve SNR, while it will also damage the speech signal at the same time. β is noise spectral subtraction coefficient, whose role is to mask the residual musical noise by adding a little background noise. Increasing β will reduce musical noise, but it will make the energy of background noise increase and decline the value of SNR.

It is not ideal when fix spectrum subtraction coefficient in noise reduction process. Therefore we need adjust spectrum subtraction coefficient α and β dynamically in order to match different speech frame:

$$\frac{T_{max} - T}{\alpha(T) - \alpha_{min}} = \frac{T - T_{min}}{\alpha_{max} - \alpha(T)} \qquad \frac{T_{max} - T}{\beta(T) - \beta_{min}} = \frac{T - T_{min}}{\beta_{max} - \beta(T)} \tag{12}$$

where T is the masking threshold of each critical band, T_{max} is the maximum masking threshold and T_{min} is the minimum masking threshold. α_{max}, α_{max}, β_{max}, and β_{max} are ceil and floor of two coefficient, and they are known.

3   Experiments and Analysis

The following result of simulations are based on MATLAB platform. Speech samples are real recordings from an airline, we choose 50 samples with clear noise from nearly

600 recordings for comparison tests. Qualitative experiments and quantitative experiments are both carried out in order to compare the four algorithms.

For qualitative analysis, the waveforms of the 50 samples are produced by the four different denoising algorithms. Take one recording for example, Fig. 1 shows some processed waveforms of recording civil aviation speech. The first one is the original waveform of the recording, the others are the waveforms which are produced by the four noise reduction algorithms respectively.

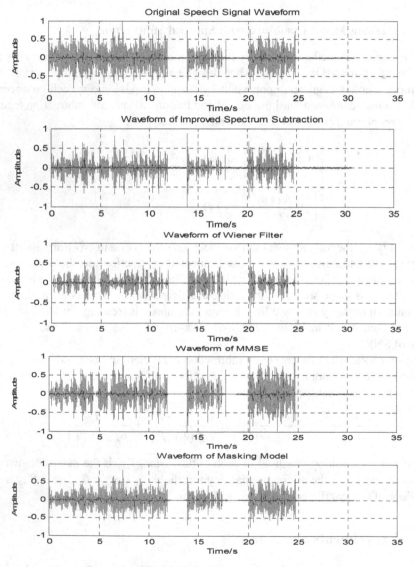

Fig. 1. Waveforms produced by four speech denoising algorithms

From Fig. 1, we can see that wiener filter reduces more noise than any other methods. However, speech distortion is obvious. We can hardly obtain any useful information from processed speech signal. It means that the distortion from denoisng beyond the original noise impact to speech. As to auditory masking model, we can observe that it save more residual noise than other three algorithm. Therefore, the background noise makes speech intelligibility decrease obviously, so its noise reduction effect is not good. From Fig. 1, we also get that the improved spectrum subtraction is similar to the result of MMSE algorithm.

In order to evaluate the four algorithms quantitatively, SNR value of the denosied samples are calculated. Because the real air-ground communication recordings are used in the experiments, the ideal noise power can not be computed. So the theory of spectrum subtraction principle is employed and the noise power is estimate through the recording dops without speech communication. The experiment results are demonstrated in Fig. 2 and Table 1.

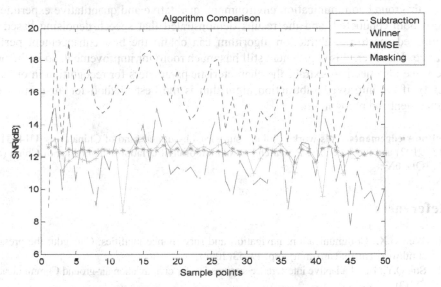

Fig. 2. SNR of the 50 Denoised Recording smaples by four algorithms

Fig. 2 shows the SNR of each sample after denoising. From Fig. 2, we can easily see that SNR of the improved subtraction algorithm is super to other algorithm, almost all of the SNR value is higher to other three algorithm. SNR of MMSE algorithm and masking auditory is stable, while the worst result is wiener algorithm due to is low SNR and unsteadiness.

Table 1. Average SNR value of 50 Recording samples Denoised by four algorithms

Processing Method	Average Value of SNR(dB)
Spectrum Subtraction	15.7690
Wiener Filter	11.7715
MMSE Algorithm	12.3628
Auditory Masking	12.1799

Table 1 shows the average SNR of the 50 samples after denoising. From Table 1, we can observe a quantitative evaluate of these four algorithm. Through the comparison of the SNR displayed in the Table 1, we can clearly see that SNR of the improved subtraction algorithm is super to other methods, and the speech intelligibility is good. The effect of MMSE algorithm is near to masking auditory, while wiener filter is worst among these four algorithms. From the experimental results, we can draw the conclusion that the improved subtraction algorithm can be applied to civil aviation air-ground communication enhancement.

4   Conclusion and Future Work

In this paper, we introduced four different methods that usually used in the field of air-ground speech enhancement. In order to find the optimal denoised algorithm for real air-ground communication environment, qualitative and quantitative experiments were both conducted, and the results demonstrated that speech denoising based on improved spectrum subtraction algorithm can obtain the best enhancement performance. However, this experiment still has much room for improvement, so in the next step, we also need to extract the characteristic parameters for recognition in order to verify if the improved subtraction algorithm is the best method for air-ground enhancement and recognition.

Acknowledgements. This work is jointly supported by united fund of China (Nos. U1433120, 61379102) and the Scientific Research Foundation of civil aviation Universities of China (No. 2013QD26X).

References

1. Wei, G.X.: Communication, navigation and surveillance facilities. Chengdu: the press of southwest Traffic University, pp. 49–53(2004)
2. Shi, Q.Y.: Blind adaptive interference suppression for civil aviation air-ground Communication (2012)
3. Wang, J., Fu, F.L., Zhang, Y.W.: Summarize of speech enhancement algorithm **77**(1), 22–26 (2005)
4. Zhang, P.: Research of speech enhancement algorithms (2007)
5. Lu, G.H., Peng, X.Y., Zhang, R.L., et al.: Random signal processing. The press of electronic science and technology university of Xi'an (2002)
6. Yang, X.J., Chi, H.S.: Digital processing of speech signal. Press of electronic industry university (1995)
7. Cappe, O.: Elimination of the musical noise phenomenon with the Ephraim and Malah noise suppressor. IEEE Transactions Speech and Audio Processing **2**(2), 345–349 (1994)
8. Lin, B.: Speech recognition technology research under low SNR (2006)
9. Yang, C.F., Chen, J.: Real-time improvement of MMSE speech enhancement algorithm **82**(2), 24–27(2006)

10. Liu, J.: Airborne noise suppression technology for speech research and implementation (2008)
11. Cai, B., Guo, Y., Li, H.W., et al.: A modified MMSE speech enhancement method **20**(1), 68–72(2004)
12. Ephraim, Y.: Statistical-Model-Based Speech Enhancement Systems. Proceedings of IEEE **80**(10), 1526–1555 (1992)
13. Cai, H.T., Yuan, B.T.: A speech enhancement algorithm based on auditory masking model. Journal of Communications **23**(8), 93–98 (2002)
14. Chen, X.: Research and implementation of speech enhancement algorithm (2007)

Application and System of Biometrics

The K-F Ring Detection Method
Based on Image Analysis

Le Chang[1,2(✉)] and Weiqi Yuan[1]

[1] Computer Vision Group, Shenyang University of Technology, No.111, ShenLiao West Road,
Economic & Technological Development Zone, Shenyang 110087, People's Republic of China
changle1105@163.com
[2] Guidaojiaotong Polytechnic Institute, No.13 Street, Economic and Technological
Development Zone, Shenyang 110023, People's Republic of China

Abstract. Medical trials show that individuals with Wilson disease develop recurrently a distinctive golden brown pigmentation around their corneas. This characteristic sign is known as Kayser-Fleischer ring (K-F ring). The purpose of this article is carrying on the detection method of K-F ring by image analysis. Our research has an important significance in screening and diagnosis of WD. Firstly, extracting the ROI region of iris image by pretreatment. Secondly, locate the boundary of K-F ring by the integral optimal of gradient algorithm and boundary tracking algorithm. Finally, detect the K-F ring of the image by color features which we defined in this paper. Experimental results show the validity of this approach.

Keywords: K-F ring · Wilson's disease · Image processing

1 Introduction

Wilson's disease (WD) is an inherited disorder of copper metabolic disturbance. It an abnormality of human copper metabolism, copper in blood will deposit in the cornea, liver and brain [1-2]. The cornea is a layer of transparent film in front of the lens. The function of Corneal is to provide the majority of refractive power for the eyes and protect interior tissue. Moreover, many individuals with Wilson disease develop Kayser-Fleischer (K-F) ring in their eyes. It is a distinctive golden brown pigmentation with outer circle shape which affects the patient cornea. K-F ring can be used as important adjunct in the diagnosis of WD. The WD is mainly occurs in 6~20 year olds. When patients with WD often show signs of abnormal behavior, slow, depression and anxiety, if the patients not have treatment timely will lead to life-threatening [3-5]. The symptoms of people is quite obvious before they went to the hospital. Unfortunately, most of patients have missed the best treatment time. In order to confirm the suspicion, magnetic resonance imaging of brain is suggested to understand the real origin of disease. Moreover, blood or urine tests allow physician to estimate the amount of copper in body. Finally, genetic test is performed to detect the defected gene [6-7]. Because the image of K-F ring can be acquitted by noninvasive way, Image-based K-F ring detection method is of great significance to discover and diagnose

J. Yang et al. (Eds.): CCBR 2015, LNCS 9428, pp. 491–498, 2015.
DOI: 10.1007/978-3-319-25417-3_58

WD. In 2013, the scholar Rosario Morello in Italy give a K-F ring detection method based on JSEG segmentation algorithm and design a K-F ring detection system applied in mobile application [8-10]. The performance of this method is affected if the boundary of K-F ring is not clear enough or the K-F ring is covered by the eyelids. In our country, Yuan Weiqi [11] and Chang le proposes a K-F ring detection method based on HSI color space in 2013, this method used the fixed area to detect target and have higher percentage of false accepts rate. The main purpose of this study gives a robustness detection method of K-F ring.

2   Image Acquisition and Preprocessing

2.1   Image Acquisition

Because the eyes are sensitive to the outside environment especially the changes of light, it has brought difficulties to the image acquisition. There are many kinds of image acquisition equipment shown on the market, these devices capable of acquiring iris image clearly. In order to collect enough images for testing our algorithm, our research groups cooperate with Shenyang Medical College Fengtian Hospital assistance. All images are collected by noninvasive way and participant 'eyes are opened naturally. We collected more than 2234 iris images, and the size of each image is 600×800 pixels. The database contains 40 images with K-F ring.

2.2   Iris Preprocessing

K-F ring is mainly on the outer boundary of the iris, because the iris usually covered by the eyelids when people's eyes are opened naturally. In order to detect the K-F ring accurately we need to preprocess the image and extract the detection area of the image, which mainly consists of two steps: location and segmentation

(1) Location
This paper used the method describe in reference [12] to locate the iris. The specific steps are as follows: first of all, we need to find a point P in the pupil by gray projection operator. Secondly, locate other three edge points of the pupil named A, B, C by horizontal gradient template and vertical gradient template. Finally, get the center of the pupil O through A, B and C.

(2) Segmentation
From the beginning of the point O, by using horizontal gradient template we get another two iris outer boundary points E, F. As shown in Fig. 1, assuming that R_1 is the distance of EO, R_2 is the distance of FO and R is the radius of the pupil. The area we used to detect the K-F ring includes two regions S_L and S_R. The height of each region is $2*R$, the width of the region $d=max(R_1,R_2)-R$.

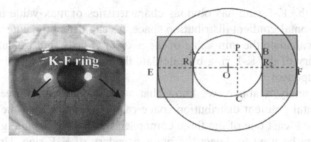

Fig. 1. Iris color image with K-F ring and the detection area of K-F ring

3   The K-F Ring Detection Method

3.1   Image Representation and Boundary Analysis

Many methods have been used in edge detection of color image. In HSI color space, the image F can be described as follows:

$$F(x,y) = H(x,y)i + S(x,y)j + I(x,y)k \tag{1}$$

The equation of $H(x, y)$ represents the H component of the color image F, the $S(x, y)$ represents the S component of the color image F and $I(x, y)$ represents the I component of color image F.

In order to detect the inner and outer boundary of K-F ring accurately, we analyzed the horizontal gradient distribution of the boundary in HSI space and RGB space. Fig. 2 (a) shows that the segmentation results of the iris image and the analyzed area we selected in left ROI area.

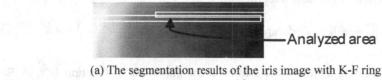

(a) The segmentation results of the iris image with K-F ring

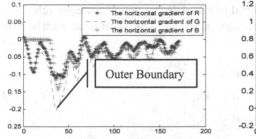

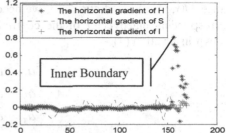

(b) The horizontal gradient distribution of analyzed area in RGB space

(c)The horizontal gradient distribution of analyzed area in HSI space

Fig. 2. The distribution of K-F ring RGB and HSI space

Fig. 2 (b) shows that the outer boundary of the K-F ring has obvious characteristics of min-value in the G component or B component. Fig. 2(c) shows that the inner boundary of the K-F ring has obvious characteristics of max-value in the H component. In horizontal gradient distribution space, we can detect the outer boundary of the K-F ring by calculate the min-value of the pixel in G or B, and we can also detect the inner boundary of the K-F ring by calculate the max-value of the pixel in H component or I component.

From the analysis above, we know that at least one of the three components in RGB horizontal gradient distribution space can be used to detect the outer boundary of K-F ring. At least one of the three components in HSI horizontal gradient distribution space can be used to detect the outer boundary of K-F ring. Unfortunately, the components we choose are not the same about different images. To solve this problem, based on reference [13] we proposed a common model named the integral optimal of gradient algorithm.

3.2   The Integral Optimal of Gradient Algorithm

The integral optimal of gradient algorithm includes the following steps:

(1) Vector projection
Assume the vector $\mu=n_1i+n_2j+n_3k$ is a unit vector, its means $|\mu|=1$. The operation of the vector projection can be achieved by equation (2). $W(x,y)$ represent the projection of the $F(x,y)$ in the unit vector μ.

$$W(x,y)=\mu \bullet F(x,y)=n_1H(x,y)+n_2S(x,y)+n_3I(x,y) \tag{2}$$

According to the equation (2), the different selection of vector μ will get different results. The boundary of the K-F ring is mainly in the vertical direction. We defined an optimal function of gradient integral named $M(x, y)$.

$$M(x,y)=\iint_S | grad(W(x,y))|^2\, dxdy =\iint_s [\frac{\partial(n_1H(x,y)+n_2S(x,y)+n_3I(x,y))}{\partial x}]^2\, dxdy \tag{3}$$

Our purpose is finding a unit vector μ to make the maximum of function $M(x, y)$. Because $M(x, y)$ is a quadratic form, we need to calculate the maximum eigenvalue and corresponding eigenvector of the coefficient matrix A. The coefficient matrix V is shown in equation (4).

$$A=\begin{bmatrix} a_{11} & a_{12} & a_{13} \\ a_{21} & a_{22} & a_{23} \\ a_{31} & a_{32} & a_{33} \end{bmatrix} \tag{4}$$

The elements of matrix A calculate by the following equation:

$$a_{11}=\iint(\frac{\partial H}{\partial x})^2\, ds \quad a_{12}=a_{21}=2\iint(\frac{\partial H}{\partial x}\frac{\partial S}{\partial x})ds \quad a_{22}=\iint(\frac{\partial S}{\partial x})^2\, ds \tag{5}$$

$$a_{13}=a_{31}=2\iint(\frac{\partial H}{\partial x}\frac{\partial I}{\partial x})ds \quad a_{33}=\iint(\frac{\partial I}{\partial x})^2\, ds \quad a_{32}=a_{23}=2\iint(\frac{\partial I}{\partial x}\frac{\partial S}{\partial x})ds \tag{6}$$

By using the integral optimal of gradient algorithm, the inner boundary of the K-F ring in our database is shown an obvious maximum distribution. By using our method in RGB space, the outer boundary of the K-F ring is shown an obvious maximum distribution.

(2) The gradient filter design

Due to the influence of iris texture, there are still some noises exist in $W(x,y)$. The gradient filter and filtered results of $W(x,y)$ as shown in Fig. 3.

1	1	0	-1	-1
1	1	0	-1	-1
1	1	0	-1	-1
1	1	0	-1	-1
1	1	0	-1	-1

(a) The gradient filter we used in our method

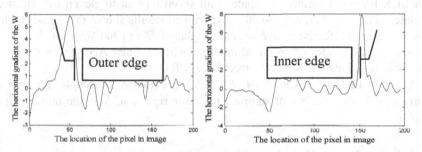

(a) Filtered results of $W(x,y)$ in RGB space   (b) Filtered results of $W(x,y)$ in HSI space

Fig. 3. Filter and Filtered results of $W(x,y)$

(3) The edge tracking

The tracking steps are as follows: firstly, find the starting position. Because the bottom of the edge point is not interfering by eyelid, we defined this point as starting position of tracking. Subsequently, by calculating the maximum of three candidates point shown in Fig. 4 then determine the next edge point. Thirdly, repeat the step 2 until to the first line of the image.

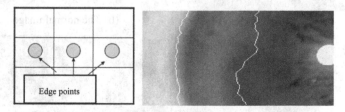

Fig. 4. Tracing template and tracking results of K-F ring

3.3   Quantization and Algorithm Evaluation

By analyzed, the influence of light to H channel and S channel is smaller than I, the proportion of I reached 72.21%. By using H channel and S channel to extract the K-F ring can reduce the effect of illumination effectiveness. The quantization result R can be calculated by equation (7):

$$R = \frac{\sum_{x,y \in \Omega}(a \times H(x,y) \times f(x,y) + b \times S(x,y))}{K} \tag{7}$$

$$f(x,y) = \begin{cases} 1 & h_{min} < H(x,y) < h_{max} \\ 0 & \text{other} \end{cases} \tag{8}$$

The function $H(x,y)$ is the H values of selected iris area, $S(x,y)$ is the S values of selected iris area, function $f(x,y)$ is used to detect the color information. h_{min} and h_{max} is the minimum and maximum values of the K-F ring color information. Because the color of K-F ring is mainly distribute from seven o'clock to eleven o'clock in color template, so $h_{min} =0.547$, $h_{max} =0.708$. Experiment results shown this value can locate the K-F ring area effectively. a, b are the weights of $H(x,y)$ and $S(x,y)$, $a+b=1$.

The evaluation index of proposed method includes: False Acceptance Rate (FAR), False Rejection Rate (FRR) and Correct Rate (CR).

$FAR=A/N$, $FRR=R/N$, $CR=1-(A+R)/N$, A is the number of samples for error identification, R is the number of samples for error rejection, N is the number of total samples.

4   Experiment Results and Analysis

To test the proposed tracking method, 2234 visual light iris image in our database are used, 40 images with K-F ring. Finally, 2151 images are tracking correctly and 83 images are tracking wrong by our method and the correct rate is 96.3%. There are

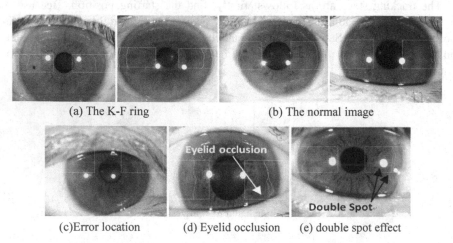

(a) The K-F ring   (b) The normal image

(c)Error location   (d) Eyelid occlusion   (e) double spot effect

Fig. 5. The tracing results of part image in database

three main reason of error for our method: error location, eyelid occlusion and double spot effect. 61 images failed in locating, 14 images are failed for eyelid occlusion. The tracing results are shown in Fig. 5.

In order to verify the effectiveness of the proposed K-F ring detection method, The quantization result R are used to decide weather the tracing results has the K-F ring or not. Two different methods are used in same database to compare with our method. The experimental results are shown in Table 1.

Table 1. The comparison of different algorithms

Method	False accept	FAR	False reject	FRR	CR
Our method	96	4.3%	0	0.0%	95.7%
Reference [11]	188	8.4%	2	0.1%	91.5%
Reference [8]	164	7.3%	0	0.0%	92.7%

5   Conclusions

In this paper, we propose a K-F ring detection method aimed at screening and diagnosis of WD timely. The experimental results reasonably demonstrate the effectiveness of proposed method. From all 2234 iris images only 40 iris images have K-F ring, the scale of the database still needs to be increased. Because all images are collected while the participant's eyes are opened naturally, proposed method still not performance well if the image has the characteristic of Corneal Arcus, error location, eyelid occlusion or double spot effect. These issues will be the main content of our future research.

Acknowledgments. This work is supported by the National Natural Science Foundation of China (No.61271365).

References

1. Gustavo, G., Frauens, B.J.: Corneal Copper Deposition Secondary to Oral Contraceptives. J. Optometry and vision Science **9**, 802–807 (2008)
2. Mimi, L., Elisabeth, J.C., George, J.B., Peter, R.L.: Kayser-Fleischer ring as the presenting sign of Wilson disease. J. American Journal of Ophthalmology **9**, 832–836 (2002)
3. Srinivas, K., Sinha, A.T.: Dominant psychiatric manifestations in Wilson's disease: A diagnostic and therapeutic challenge. J. Neurol. Sci. **26**, 104–108200 (2008)
4. Benhamla, Y.D., Tirouche, A., Abaoub-Germain, F.T.: The onset of psychiatric disorders and Wilson's disease. J. Encephale **33**, 924–932 (2007)
5. Chakor, R.T., Santhosh, N.S.: Severe neuropsychiatric presentation of Wilson's disease. Indian J. Psychiatry **53**(2), 170–171 (2011)
6. Ang, M., Wong, W., Lavanya, R.: Corneal Arcus is a Sign of Cardiovascular Disease, Even in Low-Risk Persons. J. American Journal of Ophthalmology **152**, 5 (2011)

7. Eller, A., Gorovoy, I.R., Mayercik, V.A.: Yellow Corneal Ring Associated with Vitamin Supplementation for Age-Related Macular Degeneration. J. Ophthalmology **119**(5), 1011–1016 (2012)
8. Rosario, M., Claudio, D.: Image-Based Detection of Kayser-Fleischer Ring in Patient with Wilson Disease. IEEE press (2013)
9. Rosario, M., Claudio, D.: Ocular Biometric Measurements to Diagnose Neurological Disorders Due to Wilson Disease. J. IEEE Sensors Journal **13**(9), 3203–3205 (2013)
10. Claudio, D., Laura, F.: A web service-based mobile application for detecting Kayser-Fleischer ring in eye corneal. J. Instrumentation Science and Technology **42**, 95–108 (2014)
11. Yuan, W.Q., Chang, L., Sun, X., Teng, H.: Venous congestion detection method based on HSI color space. In: Sun, Z., Shan, S., Yang, G., Zhou, J., Wang, Y., Yin, Y. (eds.) CCBR 2013. LNCS, vol. 8232, pp. 378–385. Springer, Heidelberg (2013)
12. Yuan, W., Lin, Z., Xu, L.: Novel iris location algorithm based on the structure of human eyes. J. Opto-Electronic Engineering **34**, 112–116 (2007)
13. Lang, W., Zhou, J.: Quaternion and Color Image Edge Detection. J. Computer science **34**, 212–216 (2007)

A Panoramic Video System Based on Exposure Adjustment and Non-linear Fusion

Linlin Yang[1], Dandan Du[1], Baochang Zhang[1](✉), and Wankou Yang[2]

[1] School of Automation Science and Electrical Engineering, Beihang University,
Beijing 100191, China
{yanglin,bczhang}@buaa.edu.cn, ddnszbd@163.com
[2] School of Automation, Southeast University, Nanjing 210096, China
wkyang@seu.edu.cn

Abstract. This paper proposes a new video stitch method based on the exposure adjustment and nonlinear fusion. To solve the challenging problem of exposure difference between cameras, we propose the exposure adjustment method to deal with luminance difference among images in the YCrCb color space; As for the ghosting problem in the video stitch, we propose a nonlinear fusion algorithm based on, which achieves a much better performance than traditional linear fusion method, especially when there is a big disparity between cameras. The proposed method is real-time and efficient for a video surveillance system.

Keywords: Panoramic video · Image stitching · Image registration · Image fusion · SIFT

1 Introduction

Panorama, as an new technology, can expand view and display a wider range of scenarios at the same time [1]. The traditional video surveillance systems are generally using the fixed cameras with limited range of view, which can only monitor a fixed angle of space in front of the camera, thus fail to deal with all the events occurring within the range of around 360°. Currently, static panoramic image systems, except for a few applications using ultra-wide-angle lens or fisheye directly, mainly use software methods such as image stitching and fusion algorithms. In contrast, Dynamic video systems are largely rely on specific hardware: one solution is to use fast ball system, using a high-speed moving ball to capture a wide range of scenarios. But due to the limitation of rotational speed, it inevitably exists blind areas. Another approach is to use professional camera system equipped with panoramic cameras, but such systems are expensive, complicated to use and cannot be extended. In recent years, panoramic video surveillance system has aroused great attention [2][3]. Panoramic video surveillance system can simultaneously monitor all targets within the range of 360° at any time, and virtually eliminates monitoring blind spots and areas.

This paper focuses on the static monitoring system, and we briefly review the existing image stitching and fusion technologies [4][5], which can be used to show

J. Yang et al. (Eds.): CCBR 2015, LNCS 9428, pp. 499–507, 2015.
DOI: 10.1007/978-3-319-25417-3_59

the dynamic scene of a large-scale view in real time. The technology of stitching and fusion firstly conduct registration of a sequence of images which have overlapping regions between each other capturing by several cameras. And then those images are fused into a wide view mosaic image containing all the information of the image sequences, the so-called panoramic video. We do this from two images in the image registration process by extracting feature points in the overlapping region. Through matching the corresponding points, we can estimate image transformation relationship between them, and then do coordinates alignment according to the transformation. And after the boundary smooth transition of the jointing image, we form a confluent image containing the information of two images. The technology is different from the panoramic video technology using special instruments and PTZ video surveillance technology, which combines the advantages of both, thus it is of significant practical significance.

The rest of the paper is organized as follows, in section 2, we give a brief overview of our system, including the hardware components, the framework of our system and the specific algorithms we use for each step; in section 3, we briefly introduce the image stitching method used in our system, in section 4, we give some results to show the effectiveness of our system.

2   The Proposed Panoramic System

This paper designs a system which consists of several cameras with fixed installation in the relative positions, and the adjacent lens have certain overlapping scenes, so we can get multi-channel video streams at the same time. We discuss the process of the flow of camera video mosaic. The input is the four separate video cameras used to capture videos; the captured videos can enter the PC through the USB port for further processing, and then the wide-angle video will be displayed on the PC screen in real-time. Cameras used in the experiment are fixed on a tripod, the angle and direction of each camera can be adjusted within a certain range.

Fig. 1. The framework of camera video mosaic

The framework of our method is shown in Fig. 1, and each part will be descried in details as shown in the following subsections.

2.1   Image Preprocessing Based on Exposure Adjustment

In the process of the video acquisition and transmission, the image quality of the video is often affected by many unexpected factors. For example, the minor differences between two machines or the discrepancy in light, results in the difference among the several collected videos in terms of brightness and chromaticity; most of these noises are a random distribution. The existence of the above problems will not only affect the image matching precision in the process of image stitching, but also make the result of video stitching unsatisfactory. They can result in the discontinuity of the joint video images on both sides, and make the picture not clear enough to be seen. The image preprocessing is very necessary before jointing two images together to guarantee the quality of the video image stitching. The commonly used methods for preprocessing are histogram equalization, or other filter-based methods. In this paper, we propose to preprocess the image based on Exposure Adjustment method in the YCrCb color space.

Supposed there are two images, one is the standard image $img0$, another is to-be-adjusted image $img1$. Different from direct calculation of the mean of luminance Y for each image, we firstly divide the image into three blocks of different size, and then get the overall brightness mean $Iavg\_Y0$, $Iavg\_Y1$ in different weightings of each block and the standard deviation std_Y0, std_Y1. And then we calculate the average exposure $Savg\_Y0$, $Savg\_Y1$ of the two images according to formula(1). Y_curr is the current brightness value of $img1$, Y_new refers to the new brightness value. The methods are shown in following equations.

$$Savg\_Y = \frac{-(log^{\frac{255}{Iavg\_Y}} - 1.0)}{std\_Y}, \tag{1}$$

$$Y\_new = \frac{255}{1 + exp(-std\_Y1 \times S\_curr)}, \tag{2}$$

$$S\_curr = \frac{-log^{\frac{255}{Y\_curr}} - 1}{std\_Y1} + (avg\_Y0 - avg\_Y1) \times (1 + \frac{sign \times (Iavg\_Y1 - Y\_curr)}{255})$$

where

$$sign = \begin{cases} 1 & if(Savg\_Y0 - Savg\_Y1 \geq 0) \\ -1 & otherwise \end{cases} \tag{3}$$

To illustrate the effectiveness of the proposed method, we show samples as in Fig. 2.

(a)   (b)

Fig. 2. (a) The pictures before preprocessing (b) The pictures after preprocessing

It can be seen from the pictures, the exposure difference between two images decreased significantly after preprocessing. And thus we lay a good foundation for the following steps.

2.2 Image Registration

Image registration [6] is one of key steps of image mosaic. The current generic image registration methods can be divided into three categories: the image registration algorithm based on pixel values; based on transform domain, or feature-based image registration algorithm [7]. Considering that the geometric relationships between multiple cameras only need calibration once in the beginning step, we can adopt the methods with higher alignment accuracy. Among existing video mosaic methods, the SIFT algorithm based on multi-scale space theory is widely used. The SIFT method has a good robustness of translation, rotation, scale change, illumination change and so on [8], and enables our method handle images with varying orientation and zoom. Note that this is impossible to use traditional feature matching techniques such as correlation of image patches around Harris corners [9], Ordinary (translational) correlation. The reasons lie in that they are not invariant under rotation, or not invariant to changes in scale. Once features have been extracted from all images (number is n, with linear complexity), they must be matched. Since multiple images may overlap a single ray, each feature is matched to its k nearest neighbours (we use k = 2). This can be done in O(nlog n) time by using a k-d tree to nd approximate nearest neighbours [10]. If the ratio of the closest distance(d1) verse the second-closest distance(d2) is less than 0.4, we call that these matching is an inlier(correct matches) and preserve these matching. On the contrary, it will be called outlier (false matches) and discard these matches. The next step is to use the matched points to calculate the transformation matrix H which can warp from image I to image I'.

2.3 Robust Homography Estimation Using RANSAC

RANSAC(random sample consensus) [11]is essentially a sampling approach to estimating H. It is a robust estimation procedure that uses a minimal set of randomly sampled correspondences to estimate image transformation parameters, and nds a solution that has the best consensus with the data. In the case of panoramas we select sets of r = 4 feature correspondences and compute the homography H between them using the direct linear transformation(DLT) [12] method. We repeat this with n = 500 trials and select the solution that has the maximum number of inliers (whose projections are consistent with H within tolerance pixels). Given the probability that a feature match is correct between a pair of matching images (the inlier probability) is p_i, the probability of finding the correct transformation after n trials is

$$p(\text{H is correct}) = 1 - (1 - (p_i)^r)^n \,, \tag{4}$$

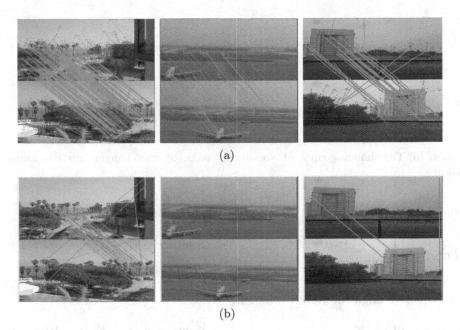

(a)

(b)

Fig. 3. (a) The results of SIFT feature detection (b) The results of Harris corner detection

then

$$n = \frac{\log(1 - p)}{\log(1 - (1 - p_i^r))} . \tag{5}$$

The image matching results in Fig. 3 show that the SIFT algorithm can well adapt to various circumstances, despite a few false matching points, it has a good robustness of translation, rotation, scale change, illumination change and so on. Finally, after calculating a best-fit image transform from image feature correspondences using RANSAC, we finally get the perspective transformation matrix H. With the matrix H, we get the warp image.

2.4   A Non-linear Algorithm for Image Fusion

Images sampling in different time, under different light intensity could result in obvious seam in overlap on the stitched images. Fusion strategies should meet the requirements of two aspects: boundary transition should be smooth and can eliminate split seams to achieve seamless splicing; as far as possible to ensure no loss of original image information due to the split processing. Commonly used fusion algorithms include average fusion, linear fusion, multi-resolution fusion [13], etc. Our system adopts a kind of nonlinear fusion method, and the results show it can effectively eliminate the image ghosting caused by luminance difference and movement objects in the images.

$$I_{overlap}(x, y) = \alpha(x, y) \times I_1(x, y) + (1 - \alpha(x, y)) \times I_2(x, y) . \tag{6}$$

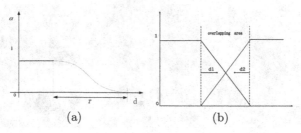

(a)   (b)

Fig. 4. (a) The changing curve of Non-linear fusion (b) The changing curve of Linear fusion

There are two cases for $\alpha(x,y)$,when we align the left image to the right,

$$\alpha(x,y) = \begin{cases} 1 & \text{if } \min(x,y,|x-W|,|y-H|) > T) \\ \frac{\cos(\pi \cdot (\frac{\min(x,y,|x-W|,|y-H|)}{T}-0.5))+1}{2} & \text{otherwise} \end{cases},$$

(7)

else, when we align the right to the left,

$$\alpha(x,y) = \begin{cases} 1 & \text{if } \min(x,y,|x-W|,|y-H|) > T) \\ \frac{\sin(\pi \cdot (\frac{\min(x,y,|x-W|,|y-H|)}{T}-0.5))+1}{2} & \text{otherwise} \end{cases},$$

(8)

where W and H represent the width and height of the original frame, T is the width of the nonlinear transition region, here it refers to the width of the overlapping area, as shown above. Since the non-overlapping area does not need to be weighted, we will resize the registrated weight templates according to the shape of the overlapping region, so that the weighting function only applies to the overlapping region. The value of a remains the same in the center of the frame, when getting closer to the boundary, namely into transition region of T, it will decline rapidly in a nonlinear form, and the decreasing rate can be controlled by the parameter T. We call this fusion method as nonlinear fusion. The comparison results of traditional linear method and our nonlinear method are as Fig. 5.

From the results under various situations as shown above, we can see that linear fusion algorithm contains ghost and fuzzy phenomenon in the overlapping region when there is large parallax between two images or moving objects, but the non-linear algorithm proposed in this paper, keeps the clarity of the main content of the scene, and greatly reduce the movement ghosting and fuzzy phenomenon.

3   The Image Stitching Method in Real-Time

The video surveillance system with multiple cameras needs some certain overlapping region between each camera. Under the circumstance of a few cameras, we usually use the method of frame-to-frame to calculate the transformation relationship between each two cameras and all the image sequences will be aligned

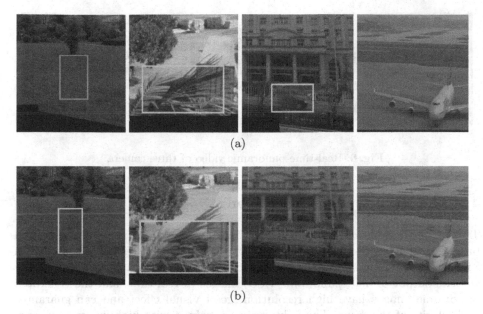

(a)

(b)

Fig. 5. (a) The results of Non-linear fusion (b) The results of Linear fusion

to one reference frame according to the transformations. But in the case of the system with large number of cameras, registering a large set of images introduces difficulties. In this paper, we adopt a method that combines the frame-to-mosaic and mosaic-to-mosaic methods to stitch video sequences of multiple cameras. Assume that there are some images C_i ($i = 1,..., 4$) captured by four cameras, we select one of the images (such as C_1) as a reference frame, and align C_2 to C_1, thereby generating a temporary stitching image M. Then align image C_3 to M, and update M using the C_3, and deal with C_4 the same way, in the end, we can get all the image alignment parameters.

In addition, an important element of a video surveillance system is to ensure its real-time performance, The SIFT features this paper choose has a good robustness of translation, rotation, scale change, illumination change, but the obvious disadvantage is its slow calculation speed, in order to overcome the shortcomings of slow calculation while maintaining precision of the SIFT features, this system learn to determine the homographic matrixes between each camera only using a few frames in the beginning, and once established, they will no longer change, then we project the video sequences onto global coordinate system using these alignment parameters, finally the small view video sequences can form a large view video sequence, so as to realize the real-time video processing.

Fig. 6. Real-time panoramic video of three camera

4   The Results and Conclusion

This paper designed and implemented a panoramic video surveillance system based on image stitching technology, the experimental results are shown in Fig. 6. By stitching and fusing the videos fixed in certain angle, we can finally get the output of 360° panoramic video images in real-time, and the generated panoramic images have high resolution, good visual effect and can guarantee high clarity of the scene. The light system is robust with high integration, easy to apply to financial systems, warehouses, prisons, mobile monitoring and many other occasions, especially suitable for indoor and outdoor monitoring system.

Acknowledgments. We acknowledged the support of the Natural Science Foundation of China, under Contracts 61272052 and 61473086, and the Program for New Century Excellent Talents of the University of Ministry of Education of China.

References

1. Brown, M., Lowe, D.G.: Recognizing panoramas. In: Proceedings of the 9th IEEE International Conference on Computer Vision, pp. 1218–1227. IEEE Press, Nice (2003)
2. Foote, J., Kimber, D.F.: Practical panoramic video and automatic camera control. In: Proceedings of the 1st IEEE International Conference on Multimedia and Expo., pp. 1419–1422. IEEE Press, New York (2000)
3. Rybski, P.E.: Camera assisted meeting event observer. In: Proceedings of the 21st IEEE International Conference on Robotics and Automation, pp. 1634–1639. IEEE Press, New Orleans (2004)
4. Xiangyang, Z., Limin, D.: An Automatic and Robust Image Mosaic Algorithm. Journal of Image and Graphics **9**, 417–422 (2004)
5. Dongmei, L., Yanjie, W.: Research of the Image Mosaic Method Based on Feature Point Match. Control and Automation **24**, 296–298 (2008)
6. Hsu, S., Sawhney, H.S., Kumar, R.: Automated Mosaics via Topology Inference. IEEE Computer Graphics and Applications **22**, 44–54 (2002)
7. Szeliski, R., Shum, H.Y.: Creating full view panoramic image mosaics and environment maps. In: Proceedings of the 24th Annual Conference on Computer Graphics and Interactive Techniques, pp. 251–258. ACM Press, Los Angeles (1997)

8. Lowe, D.G.: Distinctive Image Features from Scale-Invariant Keypoints. International Journal of Computer Vision **60**, 91–110 (2004)
9. Harris, C.G., Stephens, M.: A combined corner and edge detector. In: Proceedings of the 4th Alvey Vision Conference, pp. 147–151. Elsevier Academic Press, Manchester (1988)
10. Beis, J.S., Lowe, D.G.: Shape indexing using approximate nearest-neighbor search in high-dimensional spaces. In: Proceedings of the 10th IEEE Computer Society Conference on Computer Vision and Pattern Recognition, pp. 1000–1006. IEEE Press, Puerto Rico (1997)
11. Forsyth, D.A., Ponce, J.: Computer Vision: A Modern Approach. Pearson Education Limited, New York (2011)
12. Hartley, R.I., Zisserman, A.: Multiple View Geometry in Computer Vision. Cambridge University Press, Cambridge (2004)
13. Burt, P.J., Adelson, E.H.: A Multi-Resolution Spline with Application to Image Mosaics. ACM Transactions on Graphics **2**, 217–236 (1983)

Edge Multidirectional Binary Pattern Applies to High Resolution Thermal Infrared Face Database

Xiaoyuan Zhang, Jucheng Yang[✉], Na Liu, and Jianzheng Liu

College of Computer Science and Information Engineering,
Tianjin University of Science and Technology, Tianjin, China
jcyang@tust.edu.cn

Abstract. This paper introduces the establishment of a high resolution thermal infrared face database and presents a new thermal infrared face recognition method based on the Edge Multidirectional Binary Pattern. The high resolution thermal infrared face database is captured by Testo 890-1 High-end infrared digital camera with the image resolution 1280×960 pixels through the Super Resolution Technology. The database collects images from 60 persons, and each person has seven images with variations of poses. A new thermal infrared face recognition method based on Edge Multidirectional Binary Pattern (EMDBP) is also proposed, which fully considers the directional information of the image, and extracts more edge directional information. Experimental results show the new method achieved better performance compared with traditional methods.

Keywords: High resolution thermal infrared face database · Edge Multidirectional Binary Pattern · Thermal infrared face recognition

1   Introduction

Face recognition [1] is one of the most popular biometric recognition technologies because of its characteristics of intuitive, non-invasive and non-contact. And it is unsurprising that it continues to be one of the most active research areas due to its wide range of applications. The key issue of a face recognition system is adapting to the changes of face due to the environmental changes in practical applications. After decades of development, visible-spectrum face recognition has made great achievement, but it still faces enormous challenges in lighting conditions, face posture changes, facial expression, makeup, photo fraud and other influencing factors [2].Among various approaches which have been proposed in an attempt to overcome these limitations, the use of infrared imaging has emerged as a particularly promising research direction. Thanks to the price of thermal cameras has decreased significantly, and their technologies have improved, obtaining better resolution and quality infrared images became easier, the infrared face recognition has attracted increasing interest in recent years. Infrared Face Recognition [3] is independent of the light source, and not susceptible to camouflage, skin color, facial expression and posture of influence, which can effectively avoid the lack of visible-spectrum face recognition. So it has become an important research direction of biometrics recognition technology.

© Springer International Publishing Switzerland 2015
J. Yang et al. (Eds.): CCBR 2015, LNCS 9428, pp. 508–515, 2015.
DOI: 10.1007/978-3-319-25417-3_60

Face database is the basis for face recognition research and performance evaluation. Any proposed methods need the help of face database to evaluate their performance. Because of the long terms research of visible-spectrum face recognition, there are many international standard visible-spectrum face databases. Such as ORL, YALE, FERET [4], and AR [5].While infrared face recognition is still a new field, at present, there is no standard database for the research. One of the most famous infrared face databases is the "Human Identification at a Distance" database [6], collected by Equinox Corporation, which has been the most used data set for the evaluation of infrared based face recognition. However, it is not freely available for downloading now.

In the development of infrared face recognition, a lot of methods have been proposed with good performances. Ross [7] is the first researcher who applied Eigenface method for infrared face recognition, and the experimental results show that it achieved better performance on infrared face database than on visible-spectrum face database. Wu et al. [8] proposed a blood perfusion model based on thermodynamics and thermal physiology, which uses the more stable blood perfusion data for infrared face recognition. In order to extract the local features of the infrared face, Li [9] proposed an infrared face recognition method based on the local binary pattern (LBP), which can extract a wealth of local texture information efficiently. Buddharhaju [10] used the blood vessel information for infrared face recognition. His methods tried to extract the distribution information of face blood vessels to identify the infrared face image. In our previous research [11], we proposed a new method based on the modified blood perfusion model and the improved Weber Local Descriptor. However, all of the methods are based on the low resolution infrared face databases.

In order to improve the performance of the infrared face recognition, we try to use the high resolution infrared face databases for recognition, and our biometrics team purchased the thermal infrared face image capture device, the testo 890-1 High-end infrared camera with digital camera. This device is capable of capturing high-resolution thermal infrared face image with 1280×960 pixels through the super resolution technology. The database collects images from 60 persons, and each person has seven images with variations of poses. This is the four times of the resolution of the existing databases. Besides, due to the LBP operator simply describes the difference between the pixel and its neighboring pixels, but it does not take the edge directional information of image into account. This paper proposed a new thermal infrared face recognition method based on Edge Multidirectional Binary Pattern (EMDBP), which can describe the directional information of a thermal infrared face image better.

The structure of the paper is arranged as follows: The second section introduces the high-resolution thermal infrared face database; the third section describes a new edge multi-directional binary pattern method for thermal infrared face feature extraction; the fourth section shows the experimental results; and the fifth section gives the conclusion.

2   High Resolution Thermal Infrared Face Database

2.1   Thermal Infrared Face Image Acquisition Equipment

The acquisition equipment of our high resolution thermal infrared face image is the testo 890-1 High-end infrared digital camera, as show in Fig. 1, which can capture high quality thermal infrared images and visible-spectrum images at the same time.

Fig. 1. Testo 890-1

The technical data of infrared image output captured by testo 890-1 High-end infrared digital camera is shown in Table 1. The infrared images are captured with high quality Wide-angle lens 42° x 32°, and the resolution of the infrared images is 640 × 480 pixels, which can be upgraded to 1280 × 960 pixels with the Super Resolution Technology. Its Spectral range is 7.5 μm~14 μm, and thermal sensitivity is less than 40 mK at +30 °C.

Table 1. Technical data of infrared output image

Infrared resolution	640 x 480 pixels
Spectral range	7.5 μm~14 μm
SuperResolution (Pixel)	1280 x 960 pixels
Focus	auto / manual
Image refresh rate	33 Hz
Field of view	42° x 32°
Thermal sensitivity	< 40 mK at +30 °C

2.2   Establishment of Database

By using the testo 890-1 High-end infrared camera with digital camera introduced in Section 2.1, we collected a high resolution thermal infrared face database of 60 persons. In the process of collecting images, the volunteers are asked to sit half meter away in front of the camera, when the volunteers look straight at the camera, the front images of the volunteers were collected. Then, behind the camera, we set up several signs to tell the volunteers turn around to the direction of left 45°, left 30°, left 15°, right 15°, right 30° and right 45°.So it will help the camera to capture images of the side faces with seven directions of left 45°, left 30°, left 15°, right 15°, right 30° and right 45°. With the variation of poses, 7 infrared images of each person were collected finally. The collected high resolution thermal infrared face images for one person is as shown in Fig. 2.The High Resolution Thermal Infrared Face Database contains images from 60 person, each contributing 7 images of different poses, in total, 420 images were collected in the database. All the images of the database are captured in the same acquisition environment.

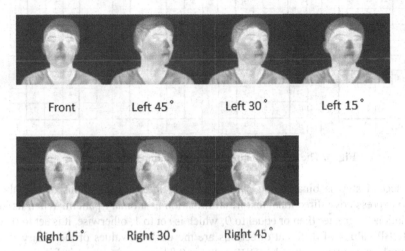

Fig. 2. Sample images of the high resolution thermal infrared face database with one person

3   Edge Multidirectional Binary Pattern (EMDBP)

LBP operator [9] describes the differences information between the center pixel and its surrounding pixels, but it does not take the edge directional information of image into account. Considering that the thermal infrared images is more blurred than the visible face image, and extracting the edge directional information of the infrared images, which can describes the local detail changes. So this paper presents a thermal infrared face recognition method based on Edge Multidirectional Binary Pattern (EMDBP).

Inspired by the edge direction detection operator Krisch [12], which contains eight templates to detect edge direction of the image, EMDBP describes the edge directional information of neighboring pixels in eight directions 0 degrees, 45 degrees, 90 degrees, 135 degrees, 180 degrees, 225 degrees, 270 degrees and 315 degrees. The specific steps of EMDBP are as follows:

The first step is to calculate the intensity variations between each pixel and its preceding pixel in the given eight directions as shown in the Fig. 3. The results reflect the edge gray value differences of the image in eight directions.

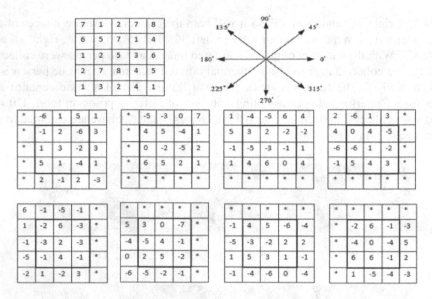

Fig. 3. The calculation of intensity variations in 8 directions

The second step is binarization, which utilizing intensity variations of neighboring pixels to express edge directional texture information as a binary pattern. When its intensity variations is greater than or equal to 0, which is set to 1, otherwise, it is set to 0. Then the EMDBP values of different directions are the decimal values of the binary strings. For example, the calculation of EMDBP value in 0 °direction is shown in Fig. 4.

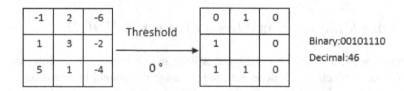

Fig. 4. The calculation of EMDBP in 0 °directions

The third step is to rank the eight EMDBP values of eight directions, and the final value of EMDBP is the median value of the eight EMDBP values of eight directions. Setting the median of eight EMDBP values as the final value of EMDBP is effective for noise suppression nonlinear processing technology, which is based on the theory of order statistics, the median filter can smooth noise well and protect the signal edge information not to be fuzzy.

Compared with LBP, more surrounding pixels are taken into consideration in calculating the image local detail changes of eight directions in EMDBP, so EMDBP can extract more spatial information than LBP. Meanwhile, EMDBP described edge directional information of pixels around the center pixel in different directions, which is very important to describe the local detail of a blurry thermal infrared face image.

The framework of thermal infrared face recognition method based on EMDBP is shown in Fig. 5. Firstly, we divide the face image into sub-regions for processing. In the second step, we do the feature extraction by the MDBP operator in each block sub-region. For each block, we get an EMDBP feature matrix, and then all of the sub-region feature matrix are connected together to get the whole feature matrix. In the third step, PCA [13] with the contribution rate of 95% is applied to reduce the dimension of features. For example, a sub-region of the images with 160 x 120 sizes has the dimension of 19200, after the dimension reduction by PCA, the dimension is reduced to 320, which effectively improve the efficiency of the recognition system. In the fourth step, face image is matched by ELM. We use the Extreme Learning Machine (ELM) [14] to classify the features and get the recognition result.

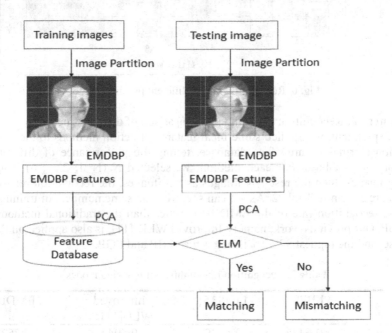

Fig. 5. The framework of face recognition system

4   Experiments

To test and evaluate the performance of this new method in infrared face recognition, we carried out experiments on our high resolution infrared face database. At the same time, we compared the proposed method with some traditional local feature extraction methods, and our previous method.

Experiment 1: Choice of the best image partition mode
In order to investigate the effect of blocking mode on the recognition performance, we tested the different blocking modes to find the optimal one. In this experiment, the partition modes are: 1x1 (non-partition), 2x2, 4x2, 4x4, 8x4 and 8x8. We selected 6 images as training images, the other 1 image as a test image. The experimental results

are shown in Fig. 5. From the figure, we can see that, the recognition rate is 96.77% without image partition, while the recognition rate is improved in different partition modes with image partition. When the partition mode is 4x2, 4x8 and 8x8, we obtained the highest recognition rate. For simplicity, we choose the partition mode 4x2 as the best one.

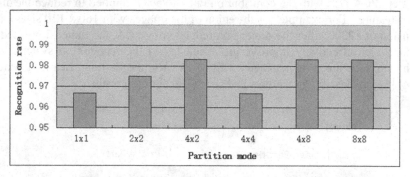

Fig. 6. Recognition rate of different partition mode

Experiment 2: Recognition performance comparison of different methods

In this experiment, we applied some local feature extraction methods to the new high resolution thermal infrared face database, testing the performance of different methods on this database, For each method, we selected N (N=1, 2,..., 6) images as training images, then the rest 7-N images as test images, the recognition rate of each method are shown in Table 2. As we can see, with the same numbers of training samples, the recognition rate of the EMDBP is better than the traditional methods LBP and LGP. Our previous work, namely Improved WLD [11], is also applied on the new database, and the highest 92.50% is better than LBP and LGP.

Table 2. Recognition rate of different blocking modes

	LBP[9]	LGP[15]	Improved WLD[11]	EMDBP
N=1	0.6426	0.6420	0.5944	0.7528
N=2	0.8056	0.7830	0.7267	0.8533
N=3	0.8792	0.8458	0.7625	0.9125
N=4	0.9056	0.8833	0.8333	0.9444
N=5	0.9083	0.9083	0.8750	0.9583
N=6	0.9167	0.9167	0.9250	0.9837

5   Conclusions

This paper introduces the establishment of a high resolution thermal infrared face database which contains totally 420 images from 60 persons, and each person has 7 images with variation of poses. It is the highest resolution thermal infrared face database so far. A new thermal infrared face recognition method based on EMDBP is also proposed, which fully considers the directional information of the image, and extracts more edge directional information. Experiment results shows that the new method is able to achieve better recognition performance than traditional methods on the high resolution thermal infrared face database.

Acknowledgments. This paper was supported by the 2015 key projects of Tianjin science and technology support program No.15ZCZDGX00200.

References

1. Ghiass, R.S., Arandjelovic, O., Bendada, H., et al.: Infrared face recognition: a comprehensive review of methodologies and databases. J. Eprint Arxiv **47**(9), 2807–2824 (2014)
2. Hermosilla, G., Javier, R.S., Verschae, R., Correa, M.: A comparative study of thermal face recognition methods in unconstrained environments. J. Pattern Recognition **45**, 2445–2459 (2012)
3. Li, J., Yu, W.X., Kuang, G.Y.: The research on face recognition approaches of infrared imagery. J. Journal of National University of Defense Technology **28**(2), 73–76 (2006)
4. Phillips, P.J., Moon, H., Rizvi, S.A., Rauss, P.J.: The FERET evaluation methodology for face-recognition algorithms. J. IEEE Trans. Pattern Anal. Machine Intell. **22**(10), 1090–1104 (2000)
5. Yang, W.K., Sun, C.Y., Zhang, L.: A multi-manifold discriminant analysis method for image feature extraction. J. Pattern Recognition **44**, 1649–1657 (2011)
6. Equinox human identification at a distance database. http://www.equinoxsensors.com/products/HID.html
7. Cutler, R.: Face Recognition Using Infrared Images and Eigenfaces. Computer Science Technical Report Series (1996)
8. Wu, S.Q., Zheng, H.G., Kia, A.C., Sim, H.O.: Infrared facial recognition using modified blood perfusion. In: Information and Communications Security 9th International Conference, China (2007)
9. Li, S.Z., Chu, R., Liao, S., et al.: Illumination invariant face Recognition using near-infrared images. J. IEEE Transactions on Pattern Analysis and Machine Intelligence **29**(4), 627–639 (2007)
10. Buddharhaju, P.: Physiology-based face Recognition in the thermal infrared spectrum. J. IEEE Transactions on PAML **29**(4), 613–626 (2007)
11. Zhang, X., Yang, J., Dong, S., Wang, C., Chen, Y., Wu, C.: Thermal infrared face recognition based on the modified blood perfusion model and improved weber local descriptor. In: Sun, Z., Shan, S., Sang, H., Zhou, J., Wang, Y., Yuan, W. (eds.) CCBR 2014. LNCS, vol. 8833, pp. 103–110. Springer, Heidelberg (2014)
12. Jabid, T., Kabir, M.H., Chae, O.: Gender classification using local directional pattern. In: 2010 International Conference on Pattern Recognition, Turkey (2010)
13. Lu, Y., Xie, Z.H., Fang, Z.J., Yang, J.C., Wu, S.Q., Li, F.: Time-lapse data oriented infrared face recognition method using block-PCA. In: The International Conference on Multimedia Technology (ICMT), China (2010)
14. Huang, G.B., Zhou, H., Ding, X., et al.: Extreme Learning Machine for Regression and Multiclass Classification. J. IEEE Transactions on Systems Man & Cybernetics Part B Cybernetics A Publication of the IEEE Systems Man & Cybernetics Society **42**(2), 513–529 (2012)
15. Jun, B.J., Kim, D.J.: Robust face detection using local gradient patterns and evidence accumulation. Pattern Recognition **45**(9), 3304–3316 (2012)

A Multi-model Biometric Image Acquisition System

Haoxiang Zhang[✉]

School of Electronic and Information Engineering, Ningbo University of Technology,
89 Cuibai Road, Ningbo 315010, Zhejiang, China
sean_public@qq.com

Abstract. Iris and face are two very popular biometrics features used for personal identification, and to acquire images of good quality is vital to assure the reliability of the recognition. It is especially challenging to acquire good-quality iris images in real time. We propose an innovative iris acquisition system to tackle some of the major difficulties in practice. The proposed multi-mode biometrics image acquisition (MMIA) system uses a single camera to capture the whole face image of the user, and then extracts the iris images. Thus it is able to provide images for both face and iris recognition. Meanwhile, in comparison to some commercial systems, MMIA system increased the working distance and capture volume, greatly reduces the user cooperation. Experiments show that MMIA provides satisfactory image quality and very quick corresponding speed.

Keywords: Biometrics · Iris recognition · Iris image acquisition · Face recognition · Eye detection

1 Introduction

With the ever growing requirements for reliable and stable security systems, various biometrics-based recognition and identification equipment receives more and more attention, and many commercial devices have been launched to the market. Among the biometric recognition techniques, human face and iris are especially popular in practice.

The uniqueness of iris patterns across humans makes it one of the most reliable and accurate biometrics methods[1,2,3], which is further favored due to its stability and the non-intrusiveness to acquire. It is now used in places such as custom clearance, airport boarding, congregation entrance etc.

However, there is one disadvantage of iris recognition system: the iris image acquisition is challenging. To ensure the patterns of an iris is sufficiently conveyed in a image, ISO iris image format standard noted that the accepted iris diameter is 150 pixels or more [4]. Considering the diameter of a typical iris is only around 11-12mm, taking an effective photo of the iris is not easy. In practice, many products on the market work at very close range, and they often require users to actively adjust the physical position of the eyes to suit the machine. It could take a long time to capture a good enough image. In comparison, the face recognition is much less demanding in image acquisition, and the device normally could response more quickly. Such inconvenience has become a

© Springer International Publishing Switzerland 2015
J. Yang et al. (Eds.): CCBR 2015, LNCS 9428, pp. 516–525, 2015.
DOI: 10.1007/978-3-319-25417-3_61

drawback for iris recognition system. To make iris recognition(IR) systems more convenient to use, an IR system should be able to work at a longer distance, and adjust itself automatically to suit the user. Many people have worked on it and some prototypes of IR systems at a distance have been developed.

In this paper, we present an innovative design of iris acquisition system, which consists a lot of new features to ensure a very user-friendly experience, while a very high recognition rate is still maintained.

The rest of the paper is organized as follows. In Section 2, we introduce the major research and development trend for iris image acquisition. In Section 3, some of the commercial IR devices and some of the difficulties we aim to tackle are listed. In Section 4 we introduce the system structure and its processing algorithm of the proposed system respectively. The experimental results of our system is presented in Section 5, and Section 6 concludes this paper.

2   The Evolution of Iris Image Acquisition Systems

Iris has been the focus of research interests for a long time. As early as in 1991, an iris recognition system has been implemented by Johnson[5]. Later, more prototypes of IR systems by Daugman [6] and Wildes [7] are documented. At this stage, the systems relies on the users to position themselves to put the eyes in the proper region in front of the cameras. More and more commercial iris image acquisition platforms are seen in the market later [8,9]. Their platforms could be based on PC, or embedded systems for others. Most of the systems have mechanism to guide the users to adjust their eyes so that a good iris mage could be taken. This often defects the user experience and sometimes it could take a long time for the user to adjust their position[10]. In general, these systems work in a short distance and needs the users' active cooperation.

An iris acquisition system is similar to a typical digital camera: it has optical lens, illuminator, and image sensor. A control unit is normally added to help detect and adjust the users' position to make sure the eyes are within the proper region. A signal processing unit makes use of the iris image to perform the recognition algorithm and make the pass/fail decision.

The lens choice is made based on the imaging geometry. The depth of field, field of view and focal length are the major factors to consider when building an iris acquisition system. The magnification of the iris image depends on the focal length of the lens [11]. Fixed focus lens is used in some iris acquisition products[12,13]. In such a design, the users have to locate their eyes within the very limited depth of field. Obviously, this defects the convenience of the usage. Some other devices choose to use fully automated lens[8,14,15] so it is quicker to finish the acquisition.

Near-infrared LED is a common choice of illumination for commercial IR products. Illumination helps to improve the iris image quality, and it is also vital for users with dark eyes. The intensity of the lighting should be kept within the limit to assure the safety of the users[16]. Researches on various wavelength of the illumination light have been seen[17]. It is showed that different iris textures could be revealed under different wavelength of light. Various lights other than NI LED are tested in researches, but not adopted in any commercial products[18].

Like in most digital cameras, image sensors used in IR systems are CCD or CMOS[19,20]. Together with the lens, an image sensor of proper resolution and size acquires the iris image at designed working distance. To ensure the quality of the iris is good enough for recognition, the resolution of the sensitivity must match the choices of the lens and illuminators.

Finally, we need some processor to run the recognition algorithm. With the development of the semi-conductor techniques, the processing unit tends to be implemented on a embedded system, or a very compact system. An ARM based IR system was proposed by Wang et al[21], and an iris biometric system based on DSP was presented by Zhao and Xie [22]. Processing units implemented on GPU [23] or FPGA[24] are also reported in literature. They have also been seen working on "mobile personal-computer" [25]. Commercial mobile phones with iris recognition system are also seen on the market [26].

A good iris acquisition unit is important for reliable iris recognition. Yet this is a challenging job due to the position and size of the iris. A lot of research has been performed in the past years, and a lot of new techniques are seen in labs and commercial devices.

3   Current Products for Iris Image Acquisition

As described in the above section, the main drawback of IR as a biometrics algorithm is the inconvenience for acquiring a good iris image. Such inconvenience comes in several ways. In this section, we go through the current development of the IR products, and show how such difficulties in acquiring iris image causes inconvenience, and what we need to do to improve it.

3.1   Typical Commercial Iris Imaging Systems

The iris recognition has been developed for many years and many commercial IR devices have been launched by companies such as Panasonic [8], OKI, LG[9], Sarnoff[12,13], Aoptix[29], etc.. Most of them are designed to be non-contacting and can acquire iris images at a distance. These systems vary substantially in design styles and demonstrate different performances. In Table 1, we list their performances.

In the table, the "Capture Volume" refers to the volume of space in front of the iris acquisition system within which the iris can be recorded by an image of accepted quality for recognition. For most of them, the "Operating range" of typical commercial iris acquisition systems are less than 1 meter, 2 of them are over 2 meters. Autofocus lenses are adopted by the few cameras with a long operating range. Embedded system is the main type of the signal processor to ensure a compact product. From the operating range, it can be seen that the depth of field is generally very small. NIR illumination is widely adopted by all of them.

3.2   Major Difficulties to Tackle for Improving Iris Imaging Systems

As can be seen from Table 1, because of the special features of human irises, the iris image acquisition systems tend to have some features that could cause inconvenience to the users, or could be improved[28],

- The acquisition volume is small and the working distance is short. This would require the users to cooperate with the device to position the eyes within a relatively small range, which could be time consuming or even cause the recognition to fail.
- 2 cameras are needed for recording 2 iris images. If this can be done using only 1 camera, then the corresponding speed could be greatly improved.
- The illumination mode can be improved.Using different wavelength of light could reveal different features of the iris, thus a more reliable recognition could be developed.

Some other issues, such as processing time, adaptive to different user height, system compactness etc, should be considered too.

Table 1. Performance comparison of typical commercial iris image cameras.

System type	Capture volume (cm3)	Operating Range (m)	Illumination	Iris camera	Processing Type
IrisAccess 3000	\	0.08-0.25	2 NIR LED	auto focus	PC
IrisAccess 4000	\	0.26-0.36	2 NIR LED	auto-focus, two cameras	Embedded system
IrisAccess 7000	\	0.31-0.35	2 NIR LED	auto-focus, two cameras	Embedded system
BM-ET300	\	0.30-0.40	NIR LED	fix-focus, two cameras	Embedded system
BM-ET200	\	0.30-0.40	NIR LED	fix-focus, two cameras	Embedded system
IOM PassPort™	50x50x20	3	NIR LED	Fix-focus,four cameras	PC
IOM RapID-Cam™ II	\	0.30-0.45	NIR LED	\	wireless Embedded system
IOM N-Glance™	13x10x28	0.53-0.80	NIR LED	\	Embedded system
InSight™ SD	100x75 at 2m	1.5-2.5	850nm LED	auto-focus	PC
InSight® Duo	100x75 at 2m	1.5-2.5	850nm LED	auto-focus, two cameras	PC
IKEMB-100	\	0.22-0.4	NIR LED	Fix-focus,two cameras	Embedded system

4   The Multi-Mode Image Acquisition (MMIA) System

Taking the above analysis into consideration, we propose an innovative design of a Multi-Mode Image Acquisition (MMIA) system. The MMIA system adopts a different design to reduce the user cooperation during the recognition process, and enables a much quicker response.

Furthermore, since MMIA records a series of pictures of the whole face and then relies on automatic eye detection to extract the iris images, it could then easily record the human face image for recognition purpose. This enables the device to be used for multi-mode recognition, in which the recognition accuracy could be substantially improved by cross checking different biometrics features.

4.1   The Structure of the MMIA System

The primary aim of MMIA system design is to increase the operating range of the IR system to be larger than 30cm, and the imaging range covers more than 30cm(vertical) × 40cm(horizontal).

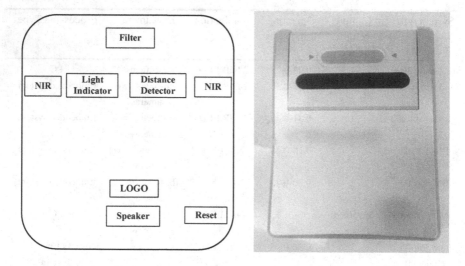

Fig. 1. The diagram and photo of Front Panel of the MMIA system.

For this purpose, the system provides an embedded iris recognition equipment, which consists front panel, optical lens, camera module, processor board, memory, power input and network interface. The processor board is connected to the camera module, memory, power supply. A set of automatic filter lenses are installed on the upper part of the front panel, between the user and the camera. The effective recording range of that camera is between 450mm and 600mm, with a tilt-flaw adjusting mechanism, which helps to adapt to users of different height.

Figure 1 shows the front panel of a MMIA system. A distance detecting module is installed in the front of the panel, together with distance light and a speaker. The distance detecting module feeds the detected results to the processor, which then controls the lights and speaker to feedback the instructions to the user for cooperation and recognition result information.

Two groups of NIR LED lights are installed on both sides of the camera, each giving NIR illumination of 700nm~980nm. They are both set to be installed at fixed angle to make sure that the users' both eyes are lit with evenly spread light, so that spectacles do not affect the iris image quality.

An output signal to the Access Control device is provided. Other features include LOGO light for power indication, data output interface, reset button, etc.

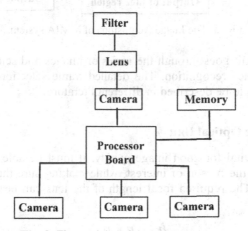

Fig. 2. The modules of the MMIA system.

Figure 2 shows the diagram of the components of a MMIA system, and illustrates the connecting relationship of the various modules. In practice, these modules are all installed underneath the front panel.

4.2   The Working Process of MMIA

When a person of interest stands in front of a MMIA system, the distance detection unit measures the distance between the person and the camera unit. Through the lights and speaker, instructions are given back to the user to make sure the person stays within the capture volume. Then the human-machine interface mechanism starts to automatically adjust the tilt-flaw unit to aim the camera at the subject person. In comparison to the previous systems, MMIA enables a longer working range, and a complete automatic targeting and focusing process, thus greatly reduced the user cooperation.

Unlike other IR systems described in earlier Sections, MMIA system only has a single camera unit, yet it aims at acquiring the iris images from both eyes of the person of interest simultaneously. The camera takes a series of successive images that records the whole face region, and then detects the eyes within the picture to extract the iris image.

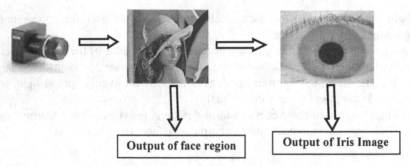

Fig. 3. The Image Acquisition of MMIA system.

The processing unit goes through the series of images and selects frames of good quality for Iris or face recognition. The detailed frame selection and iris extraction algorithms are going to be described in different literature.

4.3   Design of the Optical Unit

The optical part is vital for good image quality. It must be able to acquire both the face and the iris of the person of interest, while making sure the iris part is still of enough resolution. The required focal length of the lens can be calculated from the magnification M,

$$M = \frac{h_i}{h_o} = \frac{n \times p}{12} \ . \tag{1}$$

where h_i is the required image size, and h_o is the typical human iris; n is the number of pixels required for iris image, and p is the pixel size of the CMOS unit. Once the magnification is obtained, the focal length can be calculated with equation (2),

$$f = \frac{M \times D}{M + 1} . \tag{2}$$

where D is the distance from the front of lens to the subject person. Our target performance for MMIA system is to increase the operating range of the IR system to be larger than 30cm (45-60cm), and the capture volume is around 30cm(vertical) ×40cm (horizontal) ×15cm.

5   Experiments and Results

The proposed MMIA system is implemented and experiments have been run on it.

5.1   Image Quality

Image quality is a major performance to be tested for an iris acquisition system. We developed an iris image database of 86 subjects using the MMIA system, and a conventional close range device. Since MMIA records a series of images each time, and the quality of the images could vary substantially. We picked images only within stable time-slots, during which a subject faces the camera in a relatively stable manner. We then fed the images from both devices to the same iris recognition algorithm (the software is provided by Eyesmart Technology Ltd) to compare the difference in recognition results. According to the image quality, the series of images from MMIA is then classified into 3 sets, A(good), B(pass) and C(poor). Set A is good for effective and accurate recognition, while set C does not provide acceptable iris image for the recognition algorithm. Set B is in between, it indicates the right subject, but only with marginal difference.

Table 2. Recognition rates of different image sets.

System type	Close Range Good Images	MMIA Image Set A	MMIA Image Set B	MMIA Image Set C
Frame Set Percentage	93%	88-89%	9-10%	1-2.5%

As shown in Table 2, the results show that the difference between the good image rates from the two databases is below 5 percentage points. With nearly 90% of the frames to be of good quality, the IR system could perform the algorithm and make very reliable Pass/Fail results. This clearly shows the MMIA acquires enough good quality images for commercial IR devices.

5.2   System Performance

Another feature we are interested in is the system usage convenience. This mainly involves the capture volume and recognition time. We list our system with some other commercial systems in Table 2. Some of the values in the table are obtained from literatures.

Table 3. Comparisons of some IR systems' performance .

System type	Capture volume (W×H×D)(cm)	Standoff distance (m)	Average recognition time (s)
LG-3000	2 × 2 × 10	0.10	2
IG-H100	5 × 5 × 15	0.4	2
BM-ET300	10 × 5 × 10	0.35	4
IOM system	20 × 40 × 10	3.0	3
IrisPass-WG	18 × 55 × 30	0.45	7
MMIA	**40 × 50 × 15**	**0.45**	**≤1**

It can be seen the MMIA shows a reasonably good capture volume and process range. On the other hand, MMIA has a very compact design, and the all the processing algorithms are well optimized and they perform on a single DSP chip. Here MMIA shows a very quick corresponding tine.

6   Conclusion

Biometrics recognition has attracted a lot of interest in both industry and academic field. In this paper, we present a innovative multi-mode biometrics image acquisition system. The system uses a single camera to capture the whole face image, and two iris images, providing information for different biometrics recognition algorithms. It also greatly increases the capture volume, reduces the user cooperation, allowing outstanding user experience. Experiments show that the proposed system gives satisfactory recognition rate and an outstanding corresponding speed.

Acknowledgments. The authors would like to thank the Eyesmart Technology Ltd for providing the database and relevant software.

References

1. Mansfield, T., Kelly, et al.: Biometric Product Testing Final Report. CESG ContractX92A/ 4009309, Centre for Mathematics & Scientific Computing, National Physical Laboratory, Queen's Road, Teddington, Middlesex TW11 0LW
2. Tan, T., Ma, L.: Iris Recognition: Recent Progress and Remaining Challenges. Proceedings of SPIE - The International Society for Optical Engineering **5404**, 183–194 (2004)
3. Daugman, J.: The Importance of Being Random: Statistical Principles of Iris Recognition. Pattern Recognition **36**, 279–291 (2003)
4. http://www.biometrics.gov/Documents/irisrec.pdf
5. Johnson, R.G.: Can iris patterns be used to identify people? In: Los Alamos National Laboratory Chemical and Laser Sciences Division LA-12331-PR. Los Alamos, Calif. (1991)
6. Daugman, J.: High Confidence Visual Recognition of Persons by a Test of Statistical Independence. IEEE **15**, 1148–1161 (1993)
7. Wildes, R., et al.: Machine-vision System for Iris Recognition. Machine Vision and Applications **9**, 1–8 (1996)
8. http://catalog2.panasonic.com/webapp/wcs/stores/servlet/
9. http://www.irisid.com/
10. £9million iris recognition scheme introduced to slash queues at airports is scrapped. DAILY MAIL REPORTER. UPDATED: 10:51 GMT, 17 February 2012. http://www. dailymail.co.uk/travel/article-2102489/Iris-recognition-scheme-airports-scrapped-years.html
11. Yuqing, H.: Key techniques and methods for imaging iris in focus. In: International Conference on Pattern Recognition, vol. 4, pp. 557–561 (2006)
12. http://www.sri.com
13. Matey, J.R., Hanna, K., et al.: Iris on the move: Acquisition of Images for Iris Recognition in Less Constrained Environments. Proceedings of the IEEE Col. **94**(11), 1936–1947 (2006)
14. Jung, H.G., Jo, H.S., Park, K.R., Kim, J.: Coaxial optical structure for iris recognition from a distance. Optical Engineering **50**, 053201 (2011)
15. Yazhuo, G., David, Z., Pengfei, S., Jingqi, Y.: High-Speed Multispectral Iris Capture System Design. IEEE (2012)
16. Hugo, P.: On the feasibility of the visible wavelength, at-a-distance and on-the-move iris recognition. In: IEEE Workshop on Computational Intelligence in Biometrics, p. 7 (2009)

17. Vatsa, M., Singh, R., Ross, A., Noore, A.: Quality-based fusion for multichannel iris recognition. ICPR **2010**, 1314–1317 (2010)
18. James, R., et al.: Iris Recognition – Beyond One Meter. Part II (2009)
19. He, Y., Wang, Y., Tan, T.: Iris Image Capture System Design for Personal Identification. In: Li, S.Z., Lai, J.-H., Tan, T., Feng, G.-C., Wang, Y. (eds.) SINOBIOMETRICS 2004. LNCS, vol. 3338, pp. 539–545. Springer, Heidelberg (2004)
20. Chou, C.T., et al.: Non-Orthogonal View Iris Recognition System. IEEE Transactions on Circuits and Systems for Video Technology **20**, 417–430 (2010)
21. Yuanbo, W., et al.: Design method of ARM based embedded iris recognition system. In: The International Society for Optical Engineering, September 26, vol. 6625, pp. 66251G-1-9 (2007)
22. Xin, Z., Mei, X.: A practical design of iris recognition system based on DSP. In: IHMSC 2009, vol. 1, pp. 66–70 (2009)
23. Petr, G., Jan, P., Pavel, M.: Iris Recognition on GPU with the Usage of Non-Negative Matrix Factorization. In: Proceedings 10th International Conference on Intelligent Systems Design and Applications (ISDA 2010), pp. 894–899 (2010)
24. Rakvic, R.N., et al.: Parallelizing Iris Recognition. IEEE Transactions on Information Forensics and Security **4**, 812–823 (2009)
25. Jang, Y., et al.: A Novel Portable Iris Recognition System and Usability Evaluation. International Journal of Control, Automation, and Systems **8**, 91–98 (2010)
26. http://digi.tech.qq.com/a/20150104/036772.htm
27. Wenbo, D., Zhenan, S.T.: A design of iris recognition system at a distance. In: CJKPR, pp. 553–557 (2009)
28. Liu, Y., He, Y., Gan, C., Zhu, J., Li, L.: A Review of Advances in Iris Image Acquisition System. In: Zheng, W.-S., Sun, Z., Wang, Y., Chen, X., Yuen, P.C., Lai, J. (eds.) CCBR 2012. LNCS, vol. 7701, pp. 210–218. Springer, Heidelberg (2012)
29. A Review of Advances in Iris Image Acquisition System 217. http://www.aoptix.com/index.php

Multi-biometrics
and Information Fusion

Significance of Being Unique from Finger Patterns: Exploring Hybrid Near-infrared Finger Vein and Finger Dorsal Patterns in Verifying Human Identities

Wenming Yang, Wenyang Ji$^{(\boxtimes)}$, and Qingmin Liao

Shenzhen Key Laboratory of Information Sci&Tech, Graduate School at Shenzhen,
Tsinghua University, Beijing, China
jiwenyang666@163.com

Abstract. Automated biometrics identification using finger vein images has increasingly generated interests among researchers with emerging applications in human biometrics. Prior efforts in the biometrics literature have only investigated the near-infrared finger patterns which only consist of finger vein patterns. This paper investigates the possible usage of finger patterns to which finger dorsal texture information is added i.e. hybrid patterns. Including both the information of finger vein and finger dorsal textures, the hybrid patterns can be used as independent biometric patterns. A completely automated approach for the hybrid finger patterns is developed with key steps for region of interest segmentation, images normalization, feature extraction and robust matching. This paper also introduces an available hybrid finger pattern database from 126 different subjects. The efforts to develop automated hybrid finger pattern matching scheme achieve promising results and provide new insights on the finger pattern identification.

Keywords: Finger-vein identification · Hybrid infrared finger pattern · Vascular biometrics · Finger dorsal textures

1 Introduction

Automated identification of humans using biometrics has been increasingly investigated because of the tremendous growth in various security applications. Using the near-infrared biometrics recognition technology, the pattern recognition based on finger vein has emerged as a promising component of biometrics study, due to its higher security and recognition rate, friendly acquisition process, etc. Miura proposed two classical methods of person identification based on finger-vein patterns, i.e. repeated line tracking [1] and maximum curvature [2]. Finger dorsal texture images have also been researched widely using various patterns. Yang [3] presented a multi-modal personal identification system using finger vein and finger dorsal images with their fusion applied at the feature level.

As Fig. 1(a) shows, on account of the abundant textures of finger vein viewed from the inner side of the finger(Fig. 1(a)) and finger dorsal surface (Fig. 1(b)), great

© Springer International Publishing Switzerland 2015
J. Yang et al. (Eds.): CCBR 2015, LNCS 9428, pp. 529–535, 2015.
DOI: 10.1007/978-3-319-25417-3_62

efforts have been put into the research of personal identification using traits from either or both of the features extracted from them. However, to the best of our knowledge, there are no known efforts to exploit the finger image which consists of numerous finger vein and finger dorsal textures simultaneously, as (Fig. 1(c)) shows.

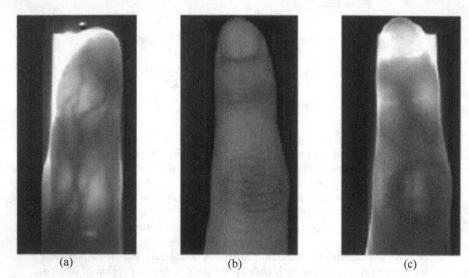

(a)   (b)   (c)

Fig. 1. (a) is the traditional inside near-infrared view of finger vein, (b) is the traditional finger dorsal texture, (c) is our new near-infrared view of finger vein

Key contributions from this paper can be summarized as in the following:

a) This paper investigates on the possibility of using image which contains hybrid finger vein and finger dorsal textures and this hybrid kind of patterns in one image prove effective in biometric identification, which provides a new perspective in the field of finger vein identification.

b) This paper provides a new database consisting of the mixture of finger vein and finger dorsal texture patterns in one image, from 126 different subjects. Accordingly, a new set of device using the infrared technique is designed. In the best of our knowledge, this will be the first finger vein database with hybrid finger patterns and help to advance further research in this area.

c) This paper uses 4 classical and improved algorithms to test the effectiveness of the new finger database, and contrasts it with the result of the traditional finger pattern database acquired in the same condition. The result shows that the patters in our new database are more unique and therefore it performs better in distinguishing different finger patterns.

The rest of this paper is organized as follows. Section 2 describes our acquired database with hybrid finger patterns using the infrared technique. Section 3 details the steps in constructing this database, including the image acquisition device and region of interest extraction method. Section 4 shows the experiments and results using the classical algorithms including local binary patterns (LBP) [4], gabor competitive coding (GCC)[5], local maximum curvature (LMC)[2] and vein location and direction coding (LDC)[10] on the database proposed in this paper. Finally, the key conclusion from this paper are summarized in section 5.

2   Database Description

In our newly established database, 21 people are invited in the experiment. The images of index, middle and third fingers of left and right hand are collected. Using the device detailed in section 3, we acquire a database containing 126 different outside finger images using the infrared technique, the purpose of which is to provide an in-depth experimental set of realistic finger vein and finger dorsal textures captured in one image simultaneously. Each of the infrared finger dorsal image is taken twice, one for train set and the other for test set. For comparison, a traditional database is established, which includes the near-infrared images as shown in Fig. 1(a). The two databases both contain 252 images, 126 for train set and the other 126 for test set respectively. The images in the databases show a range of variation, including finger rotation, translation, as well as the change of luminance etc. This variation makes the database closer to the application situation.

3   Database Acquisition Process

3.1   Image Acquisition Device

Fig. 2 (a) shows our newly designed finger vein and finger dorsal texture imaging device which consists of a black JAI camera based on CCD image sensor and one rectangular near infrared illuminant. The principle is that infrared light penetrates the finger and those passing through the veins will be absorbed by the hemoglobin in the blood to some extent, so the part of images where the vein is will be darker than other places. Fig. 2 (b) shows the transmission principle in detail.

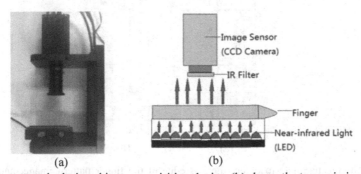

(a)   (b)

Fig. 2. (a) is our newly designed image acquisition device, (b) shows the transmission principle

3.2   Region of Interest Extraction

Since further experiments are done on the preprocessed images, region of interest finger extraction plays a really important part in the whole identification procedure. This procedure consists of 3 steps concretely as the following.

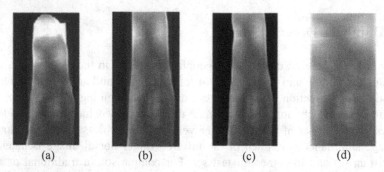

(a)   (b)   (c)   (d)

Fig. 3. (a) is the raw image, (b) is the vertically truncated image based on (a), (c) is the horizontally extracted image, (d) is the final ROI image

a) Fig. 3(a) shows the raw image we acquire with our device. It can be seen that the part of the finger nail is very bright, so we first consider to truncate the image in the vertical direction roughly by hand. In other words, 200th to 600th pixels in the vertical direction are extracted in this first step.

b) As we can see in Fig. 3(b), the vertical edges of the finger has a clear brightness jump, so here we use an extension of sobel gradient operator [10] to detect the boundary. The result is shown in Fig. 3(c), in which the region of uninterest is shown in complete black color and this gradient based operator is concretely described in Fig. 4. This template is convoluted with the original image to detect the edges. The convolution result of the pixel higher than the threshold is marked as the edge pixel.

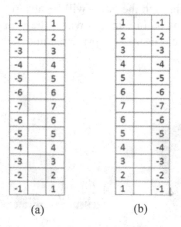

(a)   (b)

Fig. 4. (a) is the template to detect the left edge of the finger pattern image, and (b) is the template to detect the right edge of the finger pattern image

c) Last but not least, we expand the region of interest to a 200×100 rectangle using linear interpolation, and normalize the brightness as follows.

$$\hat{I}(i,j) = \hat{m} + \hat{\sigma}/\sigma * (I(i,j) - m)$$

(1)

In the above equation, I, m, σ and $\hat{I}$, $\hat{m}$, $\hat{\sigma}$ respectively represent the brightness, mean and deviation of the image before and after preprocessing. The final result after pre-processing is as Fig. 3 (d) shows.

4   Experiments and Results

In this section, experiments on our newly established database with hybrid finger patterns and the results are described. This database includes 126 finger samples from male and female volunteers. For comparison, corresponding 126 finger vein images (traditional database) are also acquired with the same device, which help to demonstrate the effectiveness of our newly established database of mixture of finger vein and finger dorsal images viewed from the outer side. 4 algorithms mentioned in the section 1 are respectively tested on each of them on matlab platform with 3.30 GHz CPU.

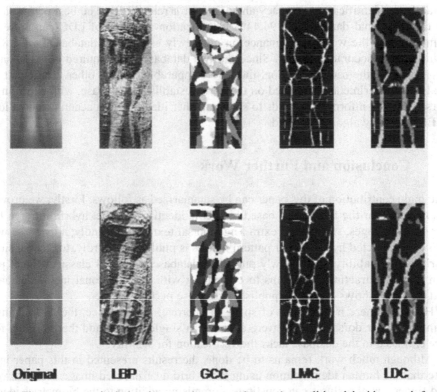

Original   LBP   GCC   LMC   LDC

Fig. 5. The upper row includes the experiment results on the traditional inside near-infrared finger vein view, the lower row includes the experiment results on the new established outside near-infrared finger pattern view

Fig. 5 shows the feature extraction results of different algorithms. The upper row is based on the traditional inside finger vein database, and the lower is based on our newly established hybrid finger pattern database. It can be seen that with the finger dorsal texture information added, there appears more horizontal textures in the final feature images and the features extracted become more complicated and therefore unique on the whole, which helps to improve the identification result.

Furthermore, experiments on the two whole databases are conducted and the results of different algorithms are shown in Table 1.

Table 1. The final experiment results of LBP, GCC, LMC and LDC on the two database

		LBP	GCC	LMC	LDC
Traditional	Accuracy(%)	90.48	91.27	93.65	94.44
Database	EER	0.079	0.064	0.055	0.063
Established	Accuracy(%)	96.83	96.83	99.21	100
Database	EER	0.032	0.030	0.008	0.008

As is shown in Table 1, every algorithm performs better on the newly established database in identification accuracy and equal error rate (EER). The best performance on the traditional database i.e. 94.44% identification accuracy of LDC can not even come up with the worst performance on our newly established database i.e. 96.83% identification accuracy of LBP. Since the two databases are acquired with the same device and in the same condition, they are comparable to each other. The result reveals that experiments conducted on the newly established database, with extra finger dorsal textures information, tends to show a higher identification accuracy and a lower EER in every algorithm tested.

5   Conclusion and Further Work

The main contribution of this paper can be summarized as follows. Firstly, we provide a novel way for the finger vein based biometric identification i.e. hybrid infrared finger pattern images, which adds extra finger dorsal textures. Secondly, a database with 126 ROI extracted hybrid finger pattern images is published. Thirdly, to test the superiority and reliability of the newly published database, we use 4 classical finger pattern texture extracting algorithms to compare it with the traditional inside database, and the result shows our newly published database performs better.

However, there is also a lot of space to improve. For instance, the hybrid finger vein and finger dorsal textures were acquired in single session and therefore the feature extracted in the database lacks the verification for stability.

Although much work remains to be done, the results presented in this paper indicate that the human identification using the hybrid near infrared image of finger vein and finger dorsal textures can constitute a promising addition to the biometrics identification.

References

1. Miura, N., Nagasaka, A., Miyatake, T.: Feature extraction of finger-vein patterns based on repeated line tracking and its application to personal identification. Machine Vision and Applications **15**(4), 194–203 (2004)
2. Miura, N., Nagasaka, A., Miyatake, T.: Extraction of finger-vein patterns using maximum curvature points in image profiles. IEICE TRANSACTIONS on Information and Systems **90**(8), 1185–1194 (2007)
3. Yang, W., Huang, X., Zhou, F., et al.: Comparative competitive coding for personal identification by using finger vein and finger dorsal texture fusion. Information Sciences **268**, 20–32 (2014)
4. Ojala, T., Pietikainen, M., Maenpaa, T.: Multiresolution gray-scale and rotation invariant texture classification with local binary patterns. Pattern Analysis and Machine Intelligence, IEEE Transactions on **24**(7), 971–987 (2002)
5. Kong, A.W.K, Zhang, D.: Competitive coding scheme for palmprint verification. In: Proceedings of the 17th International Conference on Pattern Recognition, ICPR 2004. IEEE, vol. 1, pp. 520–523 (2004)
6. Kumar, A., Zhou, Y.: Human identification using finger images. IEEE Transactions on Image Processing **21**(4), 2228–2244 (2012)
7. Kumar, A.: Importance of being unique from finger dorsal patterns: Exploring Minor Finger Knuckle Patterns in verifying Human Identities (2014)
8. Yang, W., Qin, C., Liao, Q.: A Database with ROI Extraction for Studying Fusion of Finger Vein and Finger Dorsal Texture. In: Sun, Z., Shan, S., Sang, H., Zhou, J., Wang, Y., Yuan, W. (eds.) CCBR 2014. LNCS, vol. 8833, pp. 266–270. Springer, Heidelberg (2014)
9. Chaudhuri, S., Chatterjee, S., Katz, N., et al.: Detection of blood vessels in retinal images using two-dimensional matched filters. IEEE Transactions on medical imaging **8**(3), 263–269 (1989)
10. Yang, W., Rao, Q., Liao, Q.: Personal identification for single sample using finger vein location and direction coding. In: 2011 International Conference on Hand-Based Biometrics (ICHB). IEEE, pp. 1–6 (2011)

Parallel Nonlinear Discriminant Feature Extraction for Face and Handwritten Digit Recognition

Qian Liu[1], Fei Wu[1(✉)], Xiaoyuan Jing[1,2(✉)], Xiwei Dong[1], Kun Xu[1], Xuejing Shi[1], and Xiaoyu Xi[1]

[1] School of Automation, Nanjing University of Posts and Telecommunications, Nanjing, China
{wufei_8888,jingxy_2000}@126.com
[2] State Key Laboratory of Software Engineering, School of Computer, Wuhan University, Wuhan, China

Abstract. For recognition tasks with large amounts of data, the nonlinear discriminant feature extraction technique often suffers from large computational burden. Although some nonlinear accelerating methods have been presented, how to greatly reduce computing time and simultaneously keep favorable recognition result is still challenging. In this paper, we introduce parallel computing into nonlinear subspace learning and build a parallel nonlinear discriminant feature extraction framework. We firstly design a random non-overlapping equal data division strategy to divide the whole training sample set into several subsets and assign each computational node a subset. Then we separately learn nonlinear discriminant subspaces from these subsets without mutual communications, and finally select the most appropriate subspace for classification. Under this framework, we propose a novel nonlinear subspace learning approach, i.e., parallel nonlinear discriminant analysis(PNDA). Experimental results on three public face and handwritten digit image databases demonstrate the efficiency and effectiveness of the proposed approach.

Keywords: Parallel nonlinear discriminant feature extraction framework · PNDA · Face and handwritten digit recognition

1 Introduction

Supervised subspace learning is an effective feature extraction technique for face and handwritten digit recognition application, since it utilizes class information to extract discriminative features. Linear discriminant analysis (LDA)[1] is a representative supervised subspace learning method, which calculates the projective subspace by maximizing the between-class scatter and simultaneously minimizing the within-class scatter. To improve the performance of LDA, many methods have been addressed, such as discriminative orthogonal neighborhood-preserving projection[2] and L_1-norm maximization based LDA[3].

Due to the non-linear nature of most real-world image data, many nonlinear discriminant subspace learning methods have been developed, such as kernel

© Springer International Publishing Switzerland 2015
J. Yang et al. (Eds.): CCBR 2015, LNCS 9428, pp. 536–543, 2015.
DOI: 10.1007/978-3-319-25417-3_63

discriminant analysis (KDA)[4], rank-one based kernel Foley-Sammon optimal discriminant vectors[5] and quasiconformal kernel common locality discriminant analysis[6].

However, these nonlinear methods usually suffer from huge computational burden when encountering the recognition tasks with large amounts of data. Thus, some non-linear accelerating methods have been presented, which can be roughly divided into four types:

(1) Some methods express nonlinear projective vectors using a part of mapped training samples that are selected by a designed criterion, such as accelerated kernel feature analysis (AKFA)[7] and fast kernel-based nonlinear discriminant analysis for multi-class problems[8].

(2) Some methods learn the nonlinear subspace by avoiding the eigen-decomposition of kernel matrix. For example, spectral regression KDA (SRKDA)[9] casts discriminant analysis into a regression framework by using spectral graph analysis, which can keep the classification accuracies of KDA.

(3) Some methods attempt to study large-scale nonlinear learning problem, such as random Fourier and Binning features based kernel learning[10] and sparse approximation and boosting learning based kernel machine[11].

(4) Some methods are not specifically designed for distributed computing or parallel computing, but they can be used in distributed or parallel cases. For instance, distributed kernel Fisher discriminant (DKFD)[12] is presented for multi-class discrimination problem, and also can be realized by distributed computing.

1.1 Motivation

The above accelerated or nonlinear accelerating methods have following drawbacks: (a) The first type of methods cost much time in selecting the appropriate mapping samples. And their classification accuracies are often worse than those of unaccelerated nonlinear methods like KDA. (b) The second and third types of methods often cannot hold favorable accelerating capabilities especially for recognition applications with large amounts of data. (c) The fourth type of methods also just holds limited accelerating capabilities when they are run by the way of distributed computing.

When we study the nonlinear discriminant feature extraction technique for face and handwritten digit recognition, an important problem is: how to greatly improve computational efficiency and simultaneously keep favorable recognition rates? In this paper, we try to design a parallel nonlinear discriminant subspace learning framework. Under this framework, we solve three concrete problems that are how to divide the sample set, design parallel nonlinear discriminant subspace learning algorithm and effectively combine multiple obtained nonlinear subspaces.

1.2 Contributions

We summarize the contributions of this paper as follows:

(1) We introduce the parallel computing into nonlinear subspace learning and build a parallel nonlinear discriminant feature extraction framework for face and handwritten digit recognition. We design a random non-overlapping equal data division strategy and perform the nonlinear feature extraction by using a nonlinear discriminant subspace selection strategy. This framework can not only improve computational efficiency, but also keep favorable recognition results for nonlinear learning methods.

(2) Under the built parallel framework, we propose a novel nonlinear approach that is parallel nonlinear discriminant analysis (PNDA), and analyze the time complexities of PNDA and related methods.

(3) In the experiments, we establish a parallel computing environment and employ two large-scale handwritten digit databases and a large-scale face database as the test data. Experimental results demonstrate PNDA can significantly improve the computational efficiency of nonlinear learning tasks and effectively keep the recognition rates of corresponding non-parallel KDA method.

2   Parallel Nonlinear Discriminant Subspace Learning Framework

In this section, we build a parallel nonlinear discriminant feature extraction framework, which contains three parts: random non-overlapping equal data division based on classes, communication-free parallel nonlinear feature extraction and nonlinear discriminant subspace selection.

2.1   Random Non-overlapping Equal Data Division Based on Classes

Given a parallel computing environment that contains U nodes (i.e., computers) with the same configuration, we need to divide the sample sets into U subsets with the same sample number, so that the computing time of all nodes is basically same. Suppose that $X=\{x_1, x_2,...,x_N\}$ denotes the original training sample set with the size of N, $x_i \in R^d$, c denotes the number of classes in X, and n^i denotes the sample number of class i. We randomly divide X into U non-overlapping subsets $X^1, X^2,..., X^U$, where X^j is assigned to the jth node, X^j contains N^j training samples, and $N^j=N/U$. Note that in order to guarantee the distribution of each subset is similar to that of the whole training sample set, there are n^i/U training samples from class i in X^j for $i=1,2,...,c$ and $j=1,2,....,U$.

2.2   Communication-Free Parallel Nonlinear Feature Extraction

Given a group of divided subsets from the original dataset, we separately map these subsets into nonlinear spaces, and independently extract nonlinear features on each node without communications with other nodes. Let $\varphi: R^d \rightarrow F$ denote a nonlinear mapping. X^j ($j=1,2,...,U$) is projected into F by $\varphi: x_{ji} \rightarrow \varphi(x_{ji})$, where x_{ji} denotes the ith training sample in X^j, and we obtain a set of mapped training samples $\Psi^j=\{\varphi(x_{j1}), \varphi(x_{j2}),..., \varphi(x_{jN^j})\}$. Then we construct a symmetric kernel matrix K^j with its element

$$K_{mn}^{j} = k\left(x_{jm}, x_{jn}\right), \quad m = 1, 2, \cdots, N^{j}, n = 1, 2, \cdots, N^{j} \tag{1}$$

where $k(.\,,.)$ is a kernel function. According to the kernel reproducing theory [13], the projective transformation $W^{j\psi}$ in F can be linearly expressed by using all mapped training samples in the jth subset:

$$W^{j^{*}} = \sum_{i=1}^{N^{j}} \alpha_{i}^{j} \varphi(x_{ji}) = \Psi^{j} \alpha^{j} \tag{2}$$

where $\alpha^{j} = [\alpha_{1}^{j}, \alpha_{2}^{j} \cdots \alpha_{Nj}^{j}]^{T}$ is a coefficient matrix. After we get the optimal solution $\alpha^{j^{*}}$ by using a specific feature extraction method (e.g. the following PNDA approach), we can extract nonlinear features Z^{j} as

$$Z^{j} = W^{j^{*T}} \Psi^{j} = \alpha^{j^{*T}} \Psi^{jT} \Psi^{j} = \alpha^{j^{*T}} K^{j} \tag{3}$$

2.3 Nonlinear Discriminant Subspace Selection

Now we obtain the optimal coefficient matrices $\alpha^{1^{*}}$, $\alpha^{2^{*}}$,..., $\alpha^{U^{*}}$ and the nonlinear feature sets Z^{1}, Z^{2},...,Z^{U}. As we know, these coefficient matrices or feature sets cannot be simply combined, since they may have different dimensionalities. For a testing sample y, how can we do recognition?

To solve the above problem, we design a nonlinear discriminant subspace selection strategy. Different nonlinear feature sets Z^{1}, Z^{2},..., Z^{U} are intrinsically laid in different nonlinear subspaces. We separately project y into U nonlinear subspaces, and extract nonlinear features according to Formula (3). For the jth nonlinear space, we achieve the nonlinear feature vector Z^{jy} of y as

$$Z^{jy} = W^{j^{*T}} \varphi(y) = \alpha^{j^{*T}} \Psi^{jT} \varphi(y) = \alpha^{j^{*T}} K^{jy} \tag{4}$$

where K^{jy} is a vector and its element $K_{m}^{jy} = k(x_{jm}, y)$. Then we calculate the cosine distance between Z^{jy} and each feature vector in Z^{j}.

We compute the cosine distances between the feature vector of y and each feature vector in Z^{j} in a parallel manner, where $j=1,2,...,U$. If the maximal distance appears in the subspace spanned by $\alpha^{k^{*}}$, we select the kth nonlinear discriminant subspace and feature set Z^{k}. Then, we determine the class label of y by using the nearest neighbor classifier with the cosine distance to classify Z^{ky} in Z^{k}.

2.4 Parallel Nonlinear Discriminant Analysis (PNDA) Approach

In this section, we propose parallel nonlinear discriminant analysis (PNDA) approach under the designed framework.

The original training sample set $X=\{x_{1}, x_{2},..., x_{N}\}$ is divided into U non-overlapping subsets X^{1}, X^{2},..., X^{U} by using the random equal data division strategy described in the designed framework. For the jth nonlinear mapped subset $\Psi^{j}=\{\varphi(x_{j1}), \varphi(x_{j2}),..., \varphi(x_{jN})\}$, PNDA defines the nonlinear Fisher criterion as

$$J\left(W^{J^{\varphi}}\right) = \max_{W^{J^{\varphi}}} \frac{trace\left(W^{J^{\varphi T}} S_b^{J^{\varphi}} W^{J^{\varphi}}\right)}{trace\left(W^{J^{\varphi T}} S_w^{J^{\varphi}} W^{J^{\varphi}}\right)} \tag{5}$$

where $S_b^{j\varphi}$ and $S_w^{j\varphi}$ are the between-class scatter matrix and within-class scatter matrix of Ψ^j, respectively. Substituting Formula (2) into Formula (5), we have

$$J\left(\alpha^j\right) = \max_{\alpha^j} \frac{trace\left(\alpha^{jT} K^j M K^j \alpha^j\right)}{trace\left(\alpha^{jT} K^j W K^j \alpha^j\right)} \tag{6}$$

where M and W are constant coefficient matrices. The optimal solution α^{j*} is constructed by the eigenvectors corresponding to nonzero eigenvalues of $(K^j W K^j)^{-1} K^j M K^j$.

After obtaining α^{1*}, α^{2*},..., α^{U*} in parallel, we can extract nonlinear features for all subsets and realize recognition.

3   Time Complexity Analysis

We use the term flam [14] to measure the time complexity, which is a compound operation consisting of one addition and one multiplication. Table 1 shows the time complexities of KDA [4], AKFA [7], SRKDA [9], global DKFD (G-DKFD)[12] and our approach, where l denotes the number of nonlinear projective vectors in AKFA. Due to Table 1, our approach can achieve lower time complexity than other methods, when U is not too small.

Table 1. Time complexities of all compared methods.

Method	Complexity	Method	Complexity	Method	Complexity
KDA	$\frac{1}{2} N^2 d + \frac{19}{3} N^3$	AKFA	$\frac{1}{2} N^2 d + \frac{7}{4} N^2 l$	SRKDA	$\frac{1}{2} N^2 d + \frac{1}{6} N^3$
G-DKFD	$\frac{N^2 d}{U} + \frac{76 N^3}{3Uc}$	PNDA	$\frac{N^2 d}{2U^2} + \frac{19 N^3}{3U^3}$		

4   Experiments

4.1   Database Introduction and Experimental Setting

To evaluate the recognition performance of our approach, we employ three public large-scale databases, including the USPS [15] and MNIST [16] handwritten digit databases and the extended Yale face database B [17] (abbreviated to ExYaleB). The USPS database contains 9298 image samples, each with the size of 16×16. Pictures represent digits from 0 to 9 collected from handwritten postcodes. The MNIST database contains 10000 handwritten digit image samples, each with the size of 28×28. The ExYaleB database contains 16128 face image samples of 28 people with pose and illumination variations. We crop the facial region from an original image and resize the cropped image to 32×32. Histogram equalization is used to preprocess the samples. In USPS, MINST and ExYaleB databases, we randomly select 700, 800 and 350 samples per class for training, and use the remainders for testing.

We establish a parallel computing environment, which contains 12 computers with the same configuration (CPU: 2.93GHz and RAM: 4GB). To construct the environment, we set up a local network by connecting all computers with a switch, and use the parallel computing toolbox of Matlab R2009b to realize our approach.

In the experiment, we take KDA[4], AKFA[7], SRKDA[9] and G-DKFD[12] as the compared methods. The Gaussian RBF kernel is employed for all nonlinear methods. For our approach, the subset number U is determined by using K-fold cross validation. To control the computational cost of parameter choice, we set $K=5$ and search U in the set $\{4,5,6,7,8,9,10,11,12\}$. $U=8$ is selected as the optimal number of subsets on three databases.

4.2   Evaluation of Recognition Performance

Fig. 1 shows the computing time of our approach on three databases when U varies from 1 to 12. Note that when $U=1$, PNDA is equivalent to KDA. We can see that when U changes from 1 to 4, PNDA dramatically lessens the computing time. We do not provide the comparison about testing time, since the testing time of all methods is similar.

Table 2 shows the average recognition rates and average training time of all compared methods across 20 random runs on three databases, where $U=8$. Here, G-DKFD randomly divides all cost-normalized KFD units into U groups with the same unit number, and assigns each computational node a group. Obviously, PNDA can greatly reduce the average computing time as compared with other methods. And it can keep and even improve the recognition rates of KDA.

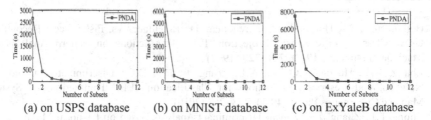

(a) on USPS database   (b) on MNIST database   (c) on ExYaleB database

Fig. 1. Computing time of our approach with different number of subsets.

Table 2. Average recognition rates (%, with standard derivations) and computing time (s) of all methods.

Method	USPS Recognition rate	Time	MNIST Recognition rate	Time	ExYaleB Recognition rate	Time
KDA	98.41±0.24	2663.54	97.34±0.37	5606.13	97.96±0.44	7463.82
AKFA	96.58±0.31	304.13	93.45±0.36	683.49	91.82±0.37	822.64
SRKDA	98.38±0.22	153.76	**97.53±0.30**	285.60	97.84±0.31	518.16
G-DKFD	97.99±0.27	173.27	96.93±0.35	282.91	98.31±0.35	477.70
PNDA	**98.42±0.19**	**9.41**	97.47±0.28	**11.30**	**99.50±0.24**	**23.59**

5   Conclusions

In this paper, we build a parallel nonlinear discriminant subspace learning framework for face and handwritten digit recognition. Under this framework, we propose a novel nonlinear learning approach called PNDA. By analyzing the time complexity, we show the superiority of our approach in comparison with several related methods. In the experiment, we establish a parallel computing environment to simulate the real-world applications, and evaluate the proposed approach on three public large-scale image databases. Experimental results demonstrate that our approach can greatly improve the computing speed and effectively keep or improve the recognition rates of KDA. And PNDA outperforms several related subspace learning methods.

It is noticed that besides the conventional KDA method, the built parallel nonlinear discriminant subspace learning framework can be used for other nonlinear discriminant subspace learning methods.

Acknowledgements. The work described in this paper was fully supported by the NSFC under Project No. 61272273, the Research Project of NJUPT under Project No. XJKY14016, and the Postgraduate Scientific Research and Innovation Plan of Jiangsu Province Universities under Project No. CXLX13_465.

References

1. Belhumeur, P.N., Hespanda, J., Kiregeman, D.: Eigenfaces vs. Fisherfaces: Recognition Using Class Specific Linear Projection. IEEE Transactions on Pattern Analysis and Machine Intelligence **19**(7), 711–720 (1997)
2. Zhang, T.H., Huang, K.Q., Li, X.L., Yang, J., Tao, D.C.: Discriminative Orthogonal Neighborhood-preserving Projections for Classification. IEEE Transactions on Systems Man and Cybernetics Part B **40**(1), 253–263 (2010)
3. Zhong, F.J., Zhang, J.S.: Linear Discriminant Analysis Based on L1-norm Maximization. IEEE Transactions on Image Processing **22**(8), 3018–3027 (2013)
4. Baudat, G., Anouar, F.: Generalized Discriminant Analysis Using A Kernel Approach. Neural Computation **12**(10), 2385–2404 (2000)
5. Zheng, W.M., Lin, Z.C., Tang, X.O.: A Rank-one Update Algorithm for Fast Solving Kernel Foley-Sammon Optimal Discriminant Vectors. IEEE Transactions on Neural Networks **21**(3), 393–403 (2010)
6. Li, J.B., Peng, Y., Liu, D.T.: Quasiconformal Kernel Common Locality Discriminant Analysis with Application to Breast Cancer Diagnosis. Information Sciences **223**, 256–269 (2013)
7. Jiang, X.H., Snapp, R.R., Motai, Y.C., Zhu, X.Q.: Accelerated kernel feature analysis. In: IEEE Conference on Computer Vision and Pattern Recognition, pp. 109–116 (2006)
8. Xu, Y., Zhang, D., Jin, Z., Li, M., Yang, J.Y.: A Fast Kernel-Based Nonlinear Discriminant Analysis for Multi-Class Problems. Pattern Recognition **39**(6), 1026–1033 (2006)
9. Cai, D., He, X.F., Han, J.W.: Speed Up Kernel Discriminant Analysis. International Journal on Very Large Data Bases **20**(1), 21–33 (2011)
10. Rahimi, A., Recht, B.: Random features for large-scale kernel machines. In: Advances in Neural Information Processing Systems, pp. 1–10 (2009)

11. Sun, P., Yao, X.: Sparse Approximation through Boosting for Learning Large Scale Kernel Machines. IEEE Transactions on Neural Networks **21**(6), 883–894 (2010)
12. Fu, J.S., Yang, W.L.: Distributed kernel fisher discriminant analysis for radar image recognition. In: International Conference on Mechanic Automation and Control Engineering, pp. 1241–1244 (2011)
13. Taylor, J.S., Cristianini, N.: Kernel Methods for Pattern Analysis. Cambridge University Press, Cambridge (2004)
14. Chawla, N.V., Karakoulas, G.I.: Learning from Labeled and Unlabeled Data: An Empirical Study across Techniques and Domains. Journal of Artificial Intelligence Research **23**, 331–366 (2005)
15. Ma, Z.Y., Leijion, A.: Bata mixture models and the application to image classification. In: International Conference on Image Processing, pp. 2045–2048 (2009)
16. Mizukami, Y., Tadamura, K., Warrell, J., Li, P., Prince, S.: CUDA implementation of deformable pattern recognition and its application to MNIST handwritten digit database. In: International Conference on Pattern Recognition, pp. 2001–2004 (2010)
17. Lee, K.C., Ho, J., Kriegman, D.: Acquiring Linear Subspaces for Face Recognition Under Variable Lighting. IEEE Transactions on Pattern Analysis and Machine Intelligence **27**(5), 684–698 (2005)

A Novel Feature Fusion Scheme for Human Recognition at a Distance

Xianglei Xing[✉], Kejun Wang[✉], Xiaofei Yang, and Tongchun Du

College of Automation, Harbin Engineering University, Harbin 150001, China
{xingxl,wangkejun}@hrbeu.edu.cn

Abstract. Human identification at a distance remains a challenging problem. Two biometric sources that are available in such situations are gait and face. In this paper, we present a new approach that utilizes and integrates information from frontal gait and face at the feature level. A novel kernel coupled mapping method is introduced to project both the gait features and the face features into a unified subspace where the heterogeneous modalities are transformed into the homologous features naturally. Moreover, the proposed feature level fusion scheme is compared with the match score level fusion schemes (Sum, Max and Product rules) and two feature level fusion schemes. The experimental results demonstrate that the proposed feature level fusion scheme outperforms the match score level and the other two feature level fusion schemes.

Keywords: Gait recognition · Multi-biometrics · Information fusion

1 Introduction

Biometrics is a fast developing field for human identification based upon intrinsic physical or behavioral traits. Vision-based human identification from a distance is a promising technology for access control and crime prevention in security-sensitive environments such as secret department, banks, and airports. At a distance, many typical physiologic features, such as iris, fingerprint and DNA, are obscured or cannot be obtained at all. By contrast, both gait and face can usually be obtained from most video surveillance systems.

In practice, the performance of the automatic face recognition system is limited by the factors like low resolution, varying illumination, multiple poses and blur or occlusion. Similarly, the performance of the automatic gait recognition system may be limited by the covariate factors such as variations of viewing angle, clothing, shoe types and carrying condition. In the task of human recognition at a distance, it is a potential approach to fuse face and gait which can be acquired from the same camera. As such, we combine physiologic and behavior based features together. Moreover, these two traits may be complemented for recognition since face is robust to covariates that affect gait recognition, such

© Springer International Publishing Switzerland 2015
J. Yang et al. (Eds.): CCBR 2015, LNCS 9428, pp. 544–552, 2015.
DOI: 10.1007/978-3-319-25417-3_64

as walking surface, clothing and carrying condition; while gait is less sensitive to the factors which affect face recognition, such as low resolution and varying illumination.

Compared with human identification based on the face or gait from a larger distance, study on the fusion of face and gait is still at its early stage. Most of the existing fusion schemes have focused on the fusion of gait and face at the match score level [1–7]. For example, Zhou et al. [5] proposed to perform a score-level fusion of gait silhouette and enhanced side face image (ESFI) from the video sequences taken by a single camera. Geng et al. [6] proposed an adaptive score-level fusion scheme by claiming that the reliability of face and gait varies with different subject-camera distances. In their scheme, the weights of the face score and gait score are distance-driven. Hofmann et al. [7] proposed to use the alpha matte preprocessing to segment gait and face images with improved qualities before score-level fusion. Experimental results have demonstrated improved performance after fusion.

Fusion of face and gait at the feature level is a relatively understudied problem because of the difficulties in practice. The modalities of gait and face have incompatible feature sets and the relationship between the feature spaces of gait and face are usually unknown. Moreover, the concatenated feature vectors may lead to the problem of curse of dimensionality which leads to a decrease in the performance of the classifier.

However, it is believed that pattern recognition systems integrate information at an early stage of processing are more effective than those systems that perform integration at a later stage. Thus, although it is not easy to achieve in practice, fusion of face and gait at the feature level has drawn more attention in recent years. For example, Zhou and Bhanu [8] conducted feature concatenation after dimensionality reduction by the PCA and LDA combined method to fuse face and gait information at the feature level. They further proposed a new feature level fusion scheme to fuse information from side face and gait, where LDA is applied after the concatenation of face and gait features [9]. They found that the new scheme allows the generation of better discriminating features and leads to the improved performance.

In this paper, we propose a novel feature level fusion scheme to fuse information related to the frontal face and gait for human recognition at a distance in a single camera scenario. We introduce a kernel coupled mapping method to project the heterogeneous modalities (e.g. face and gait) into a unified space. In this common space, the heterogeneous modalities are transformed into the homologous features naturally. Therefore, we can combine the face features and the gait features without normalization which must be performed before feature fusion in the traditional feature level fusion methods.

The rest of the paper is organized as follows. Section 2 presents the kernel coupled mapping algorithm and our feature level fusion scheme. Experimental results are compared and discussed in Section 3. Section 4 concludes the paper.

2   Kernel Coupled Mapping for Feature Fusion

2.1   Problem Statement

Given two sets of heterogeneous sample points $X = \{x_i \in \mathbb{R}^{D_x}, i = 1, \ldots, N\}$, $Y = \{y_i \in \mathbb{R}^{D_y}, i = 1, \ldots, N\}$ and a similarity constraint set $\mathcal{S}$ in the form of two-tuples for the data points having similarity relation across heterogeneous sets. Thus, if $x_i \in X$ has the same class label with $y_j \in Y$, then $(i, j) \in \mathcal{S}$. We consider the problem in the feature spaces $\mathcal{F}_1$ and $\mathcal{F}_2$ induced by some nonlinear mapping $\phi : \mathbb{R}^{D_x} \rightarrow \mathcal{F}_1; \mathbb{R}^{D_y} \rightarrow \mathcal{F}_2$. For a proper chosen ϕ, the inner product $\langle, \rangle$ can be defined on $\mathcal{F}_1$ and $\mathcal{F}_2$ which makes for a so-called reproducing kernel Hilbert space (RKHS). Specifically, $\langle \phi(x_i), \phi(x_j) \rangle = \mathcal{K}(x_i, x_j)$ and $\langle \phi(y_i), \phi(y_j) \rangle = \mathcal{K}(y_i, y_j)$ hold where $\mathcal{K}(\cdot, \cdot)$ is a positive semi-definite kernel function.

The objective of kernel coupled mapping is to learn a couple of mappings P_x and P_y in the feature spaces to projective the heterogeneous data sets into a unified space, where the point pairs in the similarity constraint set $\mathcal{S}$ are as close as possible. So that the corresponding face and gait features which have heterogeneous attributes (e.g. different dimensions and different physical meanings) of one subject turn into homogeneous features in such a common space. Kernel coupled mapping seeks the optimal projective matrices by solving the following optimization problem:

$$\underset{P_x, P_y}{\operatorname{argmin}} J(P_x, P_y) = \sum_i \sum_j \| P_x^T \phi(x_i) - P_y^T \phi(y_j) \|^2 S_{ij} \qquad (1)$$

where S is a $N \times N$ similarity matrix that denotes the similarity constraint set $\mathcal{S}$, defined as:

$$S_{i,j} = \begin{cases} 1 & if \ (i, j) \in \mathcal{S} \\ 0 & otherwise \end{cases}. \qquad (2)$$

2.2   Optimization Solution

Using some deductions of linear algebra, we can rewrite the objective function (1) into a new form as (3).

$$J(P_x, P_y) = Tr \left\{ \begin{bmatrix} P_x \\ P_y \end{bmatrix}^T \begin{bmatrix} \Phi(X) & \\ & \Phi(Y) \end{bmatrix} \left(D - \begin{bmatrix} 0 & S \\ S^T & 0 \end{bmatrix} \right) \begin{bmatrix} \Phi(X) & \\ & \Phi(Y) \end{bmatrix}^T \begin{bmatrix} P_x \\ P_y \end{bmatrix} \right\} \qquad (3)$$

where $\Phi(X) = [\phi(x_1), \phi(x_2), \cdots, \phi(x_N)]$, $\Phi(Y) = [\phi(y_1), \phi(y_2), \cdots, \phi(y_N)]$. Let $W = \begin{bmatrix} 0 & S \\ S^T & 0 \end{bmatrix}$, then D is a diagonal matrix whose entries are row sums of W. Let $P_x = [p_x^1, p_x^2, \cdots, p_x^m]$ and $P_y = [p_y^1, p_y^2, \cdots, p_y^m]$. By the representer theorem, we know that p_x^i can be linearly expanded by $p_x^i = \sum_{j=1}^N \alpha_j^i \phi(x_i)$.

Similarity, we have $p_y^i = \sum_{j=1}^{N} \beta_j^i \phi(y_i)$. Let $A = [\alpha^1, \alpha^2, \cdots, \alpha^m] \in \mathbb{R}^{N \times m}$, where $\alpha^i = [\alpha_1^i, \alpha_2^i, \cdots, \alpha_N^i]^T \in \mathbb{R}^{N \times 1}$ and $B = [\beta^1, \beta^2, \cdots, \beta^m] \in \mathbb{R}^{N \times m}$, where $\beta^i = [\beta_1^i, \beta_2^i, \cdots, \beta_N^i]^T$. It is easy to show:

$$P_x = \Phi(X)A \tag{4}$$

$$P_y = \Phi(Y)B \tag{5}$$

Substituting Eqs. (4) and (5) into Eq.(3), it can be proved that the objective function (3) is equivalent to:

$$J(A, B) = Tr\left\{ \begin{bmatrix} A \\ B \end{bmatrix}^T \begin{bmatrix} K_x & \\ & K_y \end{bmatrix} \left(D - \begin{bmatrix} 0 & S \\ S^T & 0 \end{bmatrix} \right) \begin{bmatrix} K_x & \\ & K_y \end{bmatrix}^T \begin{bmatrix} A \\ B \end{bmatrix} \right\} \tag{6}$$

where K_x and K_y are kernel matrices, $K_x(i, j) = \mathcal{K}(x_i, x_j)$ and $K_y(i, j) = \mathcal{K}(y_i, y_j)$. Let $P = \begin{bmatrix} A \\ B \end{bmatrix}$, $K = \begin{bmatrix} K_x & \\ & K_y \end{bmatrix}$, $W = \begin{bmatrix} 0 & S \\ S^T & 0 \end{bmatrix}$, and D is a diagonal matrix whose entries are row sums of W. Consequently, we obtain a concise form as

$$J(P) = Tr\left\{ P^T K (D - W) K^T P \right\} \tag{7}$$

Finally, we add a constraint $P^T K D K^T P = I$ to remove an arbitrary scaling factor in the embedding. It is easy to see that the above optimization problem has the following equivalent variation:

$$P^* = \underset{P^T K D K^T P = I}{\text{argmin}}\ Tr\left\{ P^T K (D - W) K^T P \right\} = \underset{P^T K D K^T P = I}{\text{argmax}}\ Tr\left\{ P^T K W K^T P \right\} \tag{8}$$

The optimal P can be obtained by solving the maximum eigenvalue eigenproblem:

$$(K W K^T)P = (K D K^T)P\Lambda \tag{9}$$

P is composed of the eigenvectors corresponding to the first m largest eigenvalues of Eq. (9). Clearly, $A = [\alpha^1, \alpha^2, \cdots, \alpha^m] \in \mathbb{R}^{N \times m}$ corresponds to the 1-st to N-th rows of the matrix P, and $B = [\beta^1, \beta^2, \cdots, \beta^m] \in \mathbb{R}^{N \times m}$ corresponds to the $(N + 1)$-th to $2N$-th rows of P.

2.3   Feature Fusion in the Kernel Coupled Space

To eliminate the heterogeneous attributes between the face and the gait features, we project them into the kernel coupled subspace. Suppose the training datasets of face and gait are denoted as $X \in \mathbb{R}^{D_x \times N}$ and $Y \in \mathbb{R}^{D_y \times N}$, respectively. The projective point sets $X^p \in \mathbb{R}^{m \times N}$ and $Y^p \in \mathbb{R}^{m \times N}$ in the unified kernel subspace can be computed as follows:

$$X^p = P_x^T \Phi(X) = A^T \Phi(X)^T \Phi(X) = A^T K_x \tag{10}$$

$$Y^p = P_y^T \Phi(Y) = B^T \Phi(Y)^T \Phi(Y) = B^T K_y \qquad (11)$$

where we have used Eqs. (4) and (5). The coefficient matrix $P = \begin{bmatrix} A \\ B \end{bmatrix}$ is computed by Eq. (9). Since the objective function of our kernel coupled mapping enforces the projective point pairs (e.g. face and gait features of one subject) to be as close as possible in the kernel coupled subspace, it is reasonable to fuse each point pair from the two training datasets together by simply computing the mean of two projective points. We can obtain the fusion training set $Z \in \mathbb{R}^{m \times N}$ by:

$$Z = \frac{1}{2}(X^p + Y^p) \qquad (12)$$

Suppose the test sets of face and gait are denoted as $X_t = \{x_i^t \in \mathbb{R}^{D_x}, i = 1, \cdots, N_t\}$ and $Y_t = \{y_i^t \in \mathbb{R}^{D_y}, i = 1, \cdots, N_t\}$, respectively. According to a similar process as in the training phase, X_t and Y_t can be coupled into the common kernel subspace by:

$$X_t^p = P_x^T \Phi(X_t) = A^T \Phi(X)^T \Phi(X_t) = A^T K_x^t \qquad (13)$$

$$Y_t^p = P_y^T \Phi(Y_t) = B^T \Phi(Y)^T \Phi(Y_t) = B^T K_y^t \qquad (14)$$

where K_x^t and K_y^t are kernel matrices, $K_x^t(i,j) = \mathcal{K}(x_i, x_j^t)$ and $K_y^t(i,j) = \mathcal{K}(y_i, y_j^t)$. The fusion test set $Z_t \in \mathbb{R}^{m \times N_t}$ can be calculated by:

$$Z_t = \frac{1}{2}(X_t^p + Y_t^p) \qquad (15)$$

Finally, we can use the fusion training set Z, class label l of the corresponding training set and any supervised learning algorithm to train a supervised classifier $\widehat{f}$. For test sets X_t and Y_t, we first compute the fusion test set Z_t using Eqs. (13)~(15), and then predict their class labels by $\widehat{f}(Z_t)$.

2.4   Computational Complexity Analysis

The complexity of our method is composed of three parts: learn the coefficient matrix $P = \begin{bmatrix} A \\ B \end{bmatrix}$, couple the heterogeneous sets X and Y into the same unified space: $X^p = A^T K_x$ and $Y^p = B^T K_y$, and compute the fusing training set: $Z = \frac{1}{2}(X^p + Y^p)$. The coefficient matrix P can be derived from Eq. (9). The computational complexity of the eigen-problem described in Eq. (9) is $O(N^3)$. In the second part, the complexity of coupling X and Y into the unified space is $O(mN^2)$. In the third part, the computational complexity of computing the fusing training set (Eq. (12))is $O(mN)$. Therefore, the total time complexity of the proposed feature-level fusion algorithm is: $O(N^3 + mN^2 + mN)$.

3   Experimental Results

In this section, we investigate the performance of our proposed feature fusion scheme in the application of access control at a distance. For non-intrusive access control systems, cameras are generally placed in narrow spaces such as corridors where people are in a frontal position. Information from frontal face and gait are utilized and integrated for human recognition at a distance. After feature fusion, the nearest neighbor classifier is used for all the methods.

3.1   Simulated Data

To verify the proposed approach, we construct an experimental database containing data from the CASIA gait database B [10] and the ORL face database [11]. The constructed experimental database includes 40 subjects from these two databases. Each subject consists of six gait sequences and six face images.

Gait Database. The normal walking sequences in frontal view from the first 40 subjects of CASIA gait database B are considered to test the algorithm. Under near frontal view (e.g. $0°$ or $18°$), each person contains six sequences in normal walking. For each individual, $Ntr(= 1, 2, 3)$ sequences from the $0°$ viewing angle are randomly selected as training samples, and the rest sequences from the $18°$ viewing angle are used for testing, since, in practice, the test view may not be equal to the training view exactly. The gait energy image (GEI) [12], which is used to characterize human walking properties, is generated as the gait feature representation. We normalize and crop each GEI to 64×64 pixels.

Face Database. The ORL (Olivetti Research Laboratory) face database is considered to test the proposed method. It has 40 persons and 10 images per person. The images were taken with a tolerance for some tilting and rotation of the face up to 20 degrees. To test the proposed algorithm, the first six images of each person are used in our experiments. For each individual, $Ntr(= 1, 2, 3)$ images are randomly selected as training samples. Each training image is normalized and cropped to 64×64 pixels. To simulate the low-resolution test face image at a distance, the rest $6 - Ntr$ images are first blurred and then down-sampled into 12×12 pixels.

3.2   Compared Algorithms

Ten algorithms are compared in our experiments. These algorithms belong to three schemes: single biometric scheme, match score level fusion scheme, and the feature level fusion scheme. Among the single biometric algorithms, 'Gait_Baseline' simply performs recognition in the original 4096-dimensional image space;

'Gait_PCA+LDA' applies LDA to the PCA features of the gait energy images. 'Face_Baseline' first restores the low-resolution test images by bicubic interpolation and then performs recognition in the original 4096-dimensional image space; Similarly, 'Face_PCA+LDA' first restores the low-resolution test images and then applies LDA to the PCA features of the face images. 'Match Score_Sum', 'Match Score_Max' and 'Match Score_Product' are the match score level fusion algorithms using Sum, Max and Product rules as explained in [5]. We also compare our proposed kernel coupled mapping based feature level fusion algorithm ('Feature level_Kcm') with the other two feature level fusion algorithms 'Feature level_1' and 'Feature level_2', which are proposed in [8] and [9], respectively. Gaussian RBF kernel is selected for building kernel representation in our algorithm. To determine proper parameters for kernels, we use the global-to-local search strategy [13]. After globally searching over a wide range of the parameter space, we find a candidate interval $\sigma \in [0.1, 20]$ where the optimal parameters might exist. Then, we find the optimal kernel parameters within these intervals and the best result is reported.

Table 1. Comparison of the average accuracy (followed by the corresponding standard derivations inside the parentheses) for the task of human identification at a distance. The highest recognition rate of different methods is boldfaced.

Methods	Ntr=1	Ntr=2	Ntr=3
Gait_Baseline:	68.65(9.04)	73.933(6.56)	76.78(3.47)
Gait_PCA+LDA:	68.65(9.04)	82.13(4.95)	88.00(4.33)
Face_Baseline	54.25(7.03)	69.50(5.96)	80.75(3.56)
Face_PCA+LDA	54.25(7.03)	76.81(3.53)	85.25(2.67)
Match Score_Sum	75.45(2.65)	89.75(2.54)	93.08(2.06)
Match Score_Max	69.60(8.36)	82.94(4.61)	88.33(3.93)
Match Score_Product	74.10(2.67)	89.25(2.55)	92.83(2.45)
Feature level_1	77.25(3.83)	88.31(3.52)	93.67(1.58)
Feature level_2	78.70(3.49)	90.19(3.33)	94.17(2.39)
Feature level_Kcm	**79.00(3.31)**	**92.06(1.95)**	**97.58(1.44)**

3.3   Results

The recognition accuracies of different algorithms are reported in the Table 1. For each Ntr, we average the results over 10 random splits and report the mean as well as the standard deviation. Fig. 1 shows the recognition rate with different feature dimensionalities of different algorithms. Table 1 and Fig. 1 reveal a number of interesting facts: (1) Generally speaking, the algorithms combine both gait and face features perform better than the single biometric algorithms ('Gait_Baseline', 'Gait_PCA+LDA', 'Face_Baseline' and 'Face_PCA+LDA'). (2) Feature level fusion scheme (e.g. 'Feature level_1', 'Feature level_2' and 'Feature level_Kcm') usually performs better than the match score level fusion scheme (e.g. 'Match Score_Sum', 'Match Score_Max' and 'Match Score_Product').

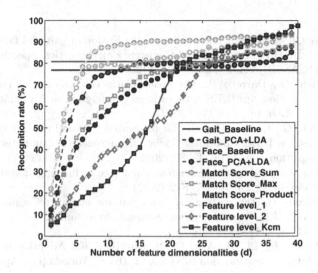

Fig. 1. Recognition results with different dimensionalities when the number of training samples $Ntr = 3$ for each subject.

(3) Among the match score level fusion algorithms, 'Match Score_Sum' performs better than the others. (4) Among the feature level fusion algorithms, our proposed 'Feature level_Kcm' performs the best of all.

4   Conclusion

In this study, we propose a novel feature level fusion scheme to integrate information from frontal gait and face for recognizing individuals at a distance in the video. Unlike the traditional feature level fusion algorithms which have to normalize the individual gait features and face features to have their values lie within similar ranges, we introduce a novel kernel coupled mapping method to project the heterogeneous features into a unified space. In this common space, the individual gait features and face features tend to be as close as possible. Therefore, we can fuse the mapping gait and face features using weighted averaging in this unified space. Experimental results show that our method outperforms previously published fusion schemes at the match score level [5] and the feature level [8,9]for face and gait-based human recognition at a distance in the video.

Acknowledgments. This work was supported by the Postdoctoral Sustentation Fund and Natural Science Fund of Heilongjiang Province of China under Grant LBH-Z14051 and 42400621-1-15114.

References

1. Kale, A., RoyChowdhury, A.K., Chellappa, R.: Fusion of gait and face for human identification. In: IEEE International Conference on Acoustics, Speech, and Signal Processing (ICASSP), vol. 5, pp. V-901-4 (2004)
2. Shakhnarovich, G., Darrell, T.: On probabilistic combination of face and gait cues for identification. In: IEEE International Conference on Automatic Face and Gesture Recognition, pp. 169-174 (2002)
3. Shakhnarovich, G., Lee, L., Darrell, T.: Integrated face and gait recognition from multiple views. In: IEEE Computer Society Conference on Computer Vision and Pattern Recognition, vol. 1, pp. I-439 (2001)
4. Liu, Z., Sarkar, S.: Outdoor recognition at a distance by fusing gait and face. Image and Vision Computing 25(6), 817-832 (2007)
5. Zhou, X., Bhanu, B.: Integrating face and gait for human recognition at a distance in video. IEEE Transactions on Systems, Man, and Cybernetics, Part B: Cybernetics 37(5), 1119-1137 (2007)
6. Geng, X., Wang, L., Li, M., Wu, Q., Smith-Miles, K.: Adaptive fusion of gait and face for human identification in video. In: IEEE Workshop on Applications of Computer Vision, pp. 1-6 (2008)
7. Hofmann, M., Schmidt, S.M., Rajagopalan, A., Rigoll, G.: Combined face and gait recognition using alpha matte preprocessing. In: 5th IAPR International Conference on Biometrics (ICB), pp. 390-395 (2012)
8. Zhou, X., Bhanu, B.: Feature fusion of face and gait for human recognition at a distance in video. In: IEEE 18th International Conference on Pattern Recognition, vol. 4, pp. 529-532 (2006)
9. Zhou, X., Bhanu, B.: Feature fusion of side face and gait for video-based human identification. Pattern Recognition 41(3), 778-795 (2008)
10. Yu, S., Tan, D., Tan, T.: A framework for evaluating the effect of view angle, clothing and carrying condition on gait recognition. In: 18th International Conference on Pattern Recognition, vol. 4, pp. 441-444 (2006)
11. Jain, A.K., Li, S.Z.: Handbook of face recognition, vol. 1. Springer (2005)
12. Lv, Z., Xing, X., Wang, K., Guan, D.: Class energy image analysis for video sensor-based gait recognition: A review. Sensors 15(1), 932-964 (2015)
13. Müller, K.R., Mika, S., Rätsch, G., Tsuda, K., Schölkopf, B.: An introduction to kernel-based learning algorithms. IEEE Transactions on Neural Networks 12(2), 181-201 (2001)

Multimodal Finger-feature Fusion and Recognition Based on Tolerance Granular Space

Ruimei Li, Guimin Jia, Yihua Shi, and Jinfeng Yang[(✉)]

Tianjin Key Lab for Advanced Signal Processing,
Civil Aviation University of China, Tianjin, China
jfyang@cauc.edu.cn

Abstract. A finger has three modalities, fingerprint (FP), finger-vein (FV) and finger-knuckle-print (FKP). Taking these finger traits as a whole for recognition is a very natural maneuver. Granular computing can effectively solve a fusion problem using knowledge from multiple levels of information granularity. Viewing finger-based recognition as a multi-granularity problem, a multimodal finger feature tolerance granular space model (MFTGSM) is proposed to implement feature fusion of FP, FV and FKP. Granular space is constructed in bottom-up manner, and a sliding window scheme is adopted for processing a multilevel granular partition with suitable overlapping. For saving computational cost, based on MFTGSM, the recognition process is implemented using a coarse-to-fine granular matching strategy. Experiments are performed on a self-built database with the three modalities. And the results demonstrate that the proposed method achieve good results in identification performance with higher reliability and accuracy.

Keywords: Multimodal feature fusion · Granular computing · Fingerprint (FP) · Finger-Vein (FV) · Finger-Knuckle-Print (FKP)

1   Introduction

With the increasing demand of accurate authentication, biometric-based technology has been proved to be an effective method in guaranteeing information security. In some real applications, compared with iris and face, finger has an inherent advantage in convenience. So finger-based recognition method, such as fingerprint (FP), finger vein (FV) and finger-knuckle-print (FKP), has been widely studied in the biometric community. Compared with FP, FV and FKP are two new biometric features that have been paid more attentions recently. A lots of researches demonstrates that mul-timodal biometrics are more effective than single modal [1-3]. Therefore, fusing these three traits together should be more robust in solving a person recognition problem. Importantly, these features can be captured simultaneously from one finger without difficulty. Moreover, the three modalities are all ridge texture images [4-7]. These characteristics show that fusing these modalities together for recognition is feasible both in theory and practice.

© Springer International Publishing Switzerland 2015
J. Yang et al. (Eds.): CCBR 2015, LNCS 9428, pp. 553–560, 2015.
DOI: 10.1007/978-3-319-25417-3_65

Traditionally, fusion of multimodal biometrics can be performed in four levels, that is pixel level, feature level, matching score level and decision level. Among these levels, feature level fusion has been expected to provide the best recognition results since the discrimination is directly determined by features. Unfortunately, many researches demonstrated that it is very difficult for implementing feature fusion effectively and reliably.

Granular computing (GrC) is a new information processing approach, which can deal with problems using knowledge from different levels of information granularity. Since Zadeh firstly proposed the notion and principle of information granulation in 1979 [8], GrC has rapidly permeated abundant information processing fields [9-12]. In recent years, Rizzi utilized GrC for image classification [13], Zheng proposed tolerance granular space model and applied it to image segmentation and recognition [14,15], Shi measured similarity between image regions based on GrC [16], Chan detect pedestrian by granulation method [17], Bhatt applied granular feature to face recognition [18]. These researches indicate that image analysis and recognition is a new stage for GrC in computer vision.

In this paper, a finger-based trait is composed of FP, FV and FKP. Based on traditional GrC theories, we propose a multimodal finger feature tolerance granular space model (MFTGSM) to solve finger feature fusion and recognition problem. First, the three modality images are respectively normalized for eliminating the scale variations. Then, the ordinal measure proposed in [19-20] is used for extracting ordinal features of three modalities. The obtained ordinal feature images are respectively partitioned into rectangle regions, which form the original-layer granules by fusing corresponding regions from three modalities. Third, by overlapping sliding a window, the original granules are combined level-wise to construct coarse-granules in bottom-up manner. For reducing computational cost, a top-down scheme is adopted for doing recognition process. Finally, experiments are implemented to validate that our method performs reliable and precise in feature fusion and personal identification.

2   Multimodal Finger Feature Granulation and Recognition

GrC can analyze features from different granularities as humans, so the multi-granularity analysis makes feature fusion more compatible and effective. Thus, in this paper, we introduce multimodal finger feature tolerance granular space model (MFTGSM) to fuse FP, FV and FKP images. The model is described by a triplet [21], Where OS denotes an object set system, and NTC denotes a nested tolerance covering system.

2.1   Original Object Set System Construction

OS is a kind of hierarchical structure, which has a strong capacity in knowledge representation. An object set system can be formalized as:

$$OS = \{\{\cup\{O_0\}\} \cup \{\cup\{O_i\}\} \cup ... \cup \{\cup\{O_n\}\}\} \tag{1}$$

where $\cup \{O_0\}$ denotes the original domain of the three finger modalities.

In order to improve the compatibility of the three modalities and prepare for subsequent granulation processing, the images of FP, FV and FKP are respectively normalized to165×165, 90×210 and 90×210. Feature extraction is very important for original domain construction. Ordinal feature [22,23], invariant feature for image under illumination variation, used here is shown in Fig. 1.

Fig. 1. Ordinal feature images.

A granule can be formalized as a 2-tuple $G=(IG,EG)$, IG is the intention of G, which denotes the general features of all the elements in a granule, and the extension of $G(EG)$ is a set of all the elements in a granules.

2.2   Feature Fusion and Granulation

In order to fuse the features of three image modalities and obtain basic granules effectively, the ordinal FP, FV and FKP images are respectively divided into blocks. The fusion process is shown in Fig. 2.

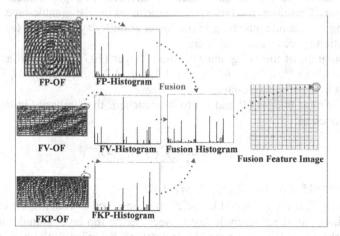

Fig. 2. Partition of three ordinal feature images and fusion of histogram feature.

Then, a predefined sliding window of 3×3 blocks is used to construct the second, third and fourth layer granules. The hierarchical granulation process is illustrated in Fig. 3. In each high-layer granules construction process, the window sliding has 1/3 overlapping, which can further conquer the rotation and translation of image to a certain extent. Thus, we can obtain 7×7 blocks after first window-sliding, 3×3 blocks after second window-sliding and one block after final window-sliding.

Accordingly, from the first layer to the fourth layer, their tolerance covering is sequentially defined as $G1$, $G2$, $G3$, $G4$, and we obtain the nested tolerance covering (NTC) as $NTC=\{G1, G2, G3, G4\}$. By this step, MFTGSM has been established.

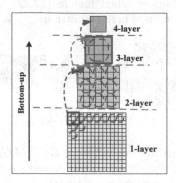

Fig. 3. The proposed bottom-up granulation process of finger ordinal feature image.

2.3   Recognition

From Fig. 3, we can see that dealing with problems in the coarse (up) granule-layer is able to narrow the scope of problem solving and accelerate calculating speed. However, much useful information may often be attenuated by granulation in the coarse granule-layer. Therefore, the unsolved problems in coarse granule-layer may be answered using the granule matching in the lower granule-layer. Thus, a top-down granular recognition process is adopted here.

The histogram of the mth granule in the zth layer (HG_z^m) is named as granular descriptor, $HG_z^m=(h_z^{m1}, h_z^{m2},..., h_z^{mH})$, $z=1,2,3,4$, $m=1,2,...,M_z$, where M_z is the number of granules in the zth granule-layer.

For two finger images (P and Q) to be matched, the similarity in the zth granule-layer is defined as:

$$Sim_z = \frac{1}{M_Z}\sum_{m=1}^{M_z}(\sum_{i=1}^{H}(h_{zP}^{mi} - h_{zQ}^{mi})^2)^{1/2} \tag{2}$$

where $M_1=15\times15$, $M_2=7\times7$, $M_3=3\times3$, $M_4=1\times1$.

If $Sim_z \leq T_z$ (T_z is the threshold in the zth granule-layer, $z=1,2,3,4$), the two finger images are similar in the zth granule-layer. Because the top layer granules are extremely coarse as shown in Fig. 3, a successful matching behavior in the high granule layer cannot ensure that the two finger images are from the same individual. Then, we need further conduct granule matching in the next granule-layer.

3   Experiments and Analysis

In this paper, a self-built database that contains 600 finger-vein images, 600 finger-print images and 600 finger-knuckle-print images from 60 individuals is used in the experiments.

The ROC curves are usually used as a standard evaluation of the biometric system performance. Hence, ROC curves are selected to make a comparison between different algorithms. To prove the feasibility and effectiveness of our algorithm, we conduct several experiments described as follows:

1) Different Fusion Method: As mentioned above, three modalities fusion is very important for finger feature recognition, here three fusion methods are used to fusion the feature of FP, FV and FKP. In the first fusion method, we concatenate the histogram feature IG_{IFP}^{kl}, IG_{IKV}^{kl} and IG_{IFKP}^{kl} to form multimodal granular feature IG_{l}^{kl} (l=1, 2, 3, 4) (MGF-C). In the second fusion method, we obtain IG_{l}^{kl} by viewing IG_{IFP}^{kl}, IG_{IKV}^{kl} and IG_{IFKP}^{kl} as a whole (MGF-W). The third fusion method is using the average value of IG_{IFP}^{kl}, IG_{IKV}^{kl} and IG_{IFKP}^{kl}, as multimodal granular feature (MGF-A). The recognition results of three methods in each layer are shown in Fig. 4. From Fig. 4, we can see that the first fusion method can reach a best recognition performance. One possible reason is that feature concatenation can more fully consider the resolution of each modal than the other two fusion methods. So MGF-C is selected as the fusion approach in the following experiments.

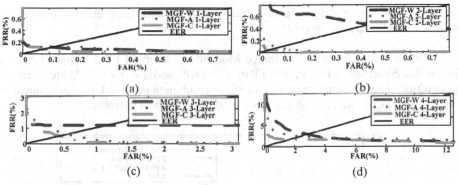

Fig. 4. Comparison of different fusion methods. (a)Results in first granule-layer, (b)Results in second granule-layer, (c)Results in third granule-layer, (d)Results in fourth granule-layer.

2) Window with No-Overlapping and overlapping: When we use window of 2×2 blocks with no-overlapping (WNO-2) and window of 3×3 blocks with no-overlapping (WNO-3) to construct the coarse granules, the recognition results in second granule-layer are shown in Fig. 5. Fig. 6 shows the comparative results of MGF-C in different granule-layer. We can see from Fig. 6 that the recognition performance of fine granule-layer is better than coarse granule-layer on the whole. However the second-layer granules have much better discrimination than first-layer granules. Fig. 4 illustrates that we can obtain a better recognition performance when we construct the granules using window with overlapping than that using window with no-overlapping. The reason is that the granules that construct by sliding-window with overlapping have more abundant information and more robust to image rotation and translation. So, in the following experiments, we just consider the granule matching in second-layer, third-layer and fourth-layer. That is, if $Sim_4 \leq T_4$, $Sim_3 \leq T_3$ and $Sim_2 \leq T_2$ are satisfied at the same time, we believe that the two finger images are from an identical individual.

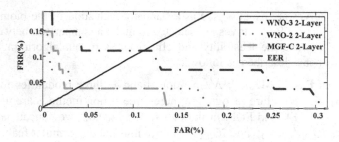

Fig. 5. Comparision of window with no overlapping and overlapping.

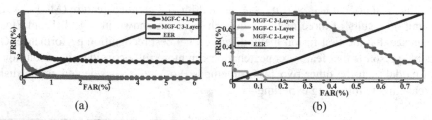

(a)   (b)

Fig. 6. Comparision of different granule-layer. (a)Results in different granule-layer (1), (b) Results in different granule-layer (2)

3) Different Combinations of Image Modalities: Based on FP, FV and FKP, four fusion combinations, FP+FV, FP+FKP, FV+FKP, and FP+FV+FKP, are used for recognition. The recognition results of these combinations in 2-Layer are shown in Fig. 7. From Fig.7, we can see that three-modal has the best performance.

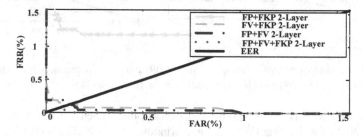

Fig. 7. Comparision of different combinations of image modalities

Table 1. Recognition perfomance

Recognition method	Performance	
	Time Cost (s)	EER (%)
MGF-C 4-layer	0.3319	1.67
MGF-C 3-layer	2.3183	0.481
MGF-C 4-layer and 3-layer	1.1205	0.481
MGF-C 2-layer	17.0983	0.037
MGF-C 4-layer, 3-layer and 2-layer	9.52	0.037

4) Multi-granularity Recognition: The experiments above all only use a single granule-layer for recognition, then experiments about the coarse-to-fine multi-granularity method as mentioned above are conducted. For some experiments, the matching time of a finger image is listed in Table 1. It shows that the recognition accuracy of multi-granule-layer and sole granule-layer is almost the same. However, multilayer-granular recognition can reduce the time cost since the non-matched granules in the high layer are neglected for granule matching in the low layer.

4   Conclusion and Future Work

In this paper, a new multimodal biological recognition method based on three finger traits is proposed. We use granular computing to address multimodal feature fusion problems, and construct a bottom-up granular model. Based on a self-built database we conduct several experiments, the results show that finger recognition based on granular computing can obtain a good identification performance with higher reliability and accuracy. However, the algorithm still has much room for improvement, such as, a proper size of sliding window to construct granules and a more appropriate feature extraction method. Nevertheless, as the database is not big enough, our method need further verification in large database and we also need to find a more effective recognition approach.

Acknowledgements. This work is jointly supported by National Natural Science Foundation of China (Nos.61379102, U1433120) and the Fundamental Research Funds for the Central Universities (No. 3122014C003).

References

1. Yang, J., Zhang, X.: Feature-level fusion of fingerprint and finger-vein for personal identification. J. Pattern Recognition Letters **33**, 623–628 (2012)
2. Meraoumia, A., Chitroub, S., Bouridane, A.: Multimodal biometric person recognition system based on fingerprint & finger-knuckle-print using correlation filter classifier. In: 2012 IEEE International Conference on Communications (ICC), pp. 820–824. IEEE Press, Ottawa (2012)
3. Yang, W., Li, Y., Liao, Q.: Fast and Robust Personal Identification by Fusion of Finger Vein and Finger-Knuckle-Print Images. J. Applied Mechanics and Materials. **556**, 5085–5088 (2014)
4. Dass, S.C., Jain, A.K.: Fingerprint-Based Recognition. J. Technometrics. **49**, 262–276 (2007)
5. Yang, J., Shi, Y.: Towards Finger-Vein Image Restoration and Enhancement for Finger-Vein Recognition. J. Inform. Sci. **268**, 33–52 (2014)
6. Zhang, L., Zhang, L.: Online Finger-Knuckle-Print Verification for Personal Authentication. J. Pattern Recognition. **43**, 2560–2571 (2010)
7. Hong, L., Jain, A.: Integrating faces and fingerprints for personal identification. J. Lecture Notes in Computer Science. **1351**, 1–16 (1998)

8. Zadeh, L.A.: Fuzzy Sets and Information Granulation Advances in Fuzzy Set Theory and Application. North Holland Publishing Press, Netherlands (1979)
9. Yao, Y.: Interpreting Concept Learning in Cognitive Informatics and Granular Computing. IEEE Transactions on Systems, Man, and Cybernetics, Part B: Cybernetics **39**, 855–866 (2009)
10. Butenkov, S. A.: Granular computing in image processing and understanding. In: Proceedings of the IASTED International Conference, pp. 811–816. Artificial Intelligence and Application, Innsbruck (2004)
11. Pedrycz, W.: Knowledge-based clustering - from data to information granules. J. Information Processing & Management **42**, 321–322 (2005)
12. Bargiela, A., Pedrycz, W.: Toward a Theory of Granular Computing for Human-Centered Information Processing. J. IEEE Transactions on Fuzzy Systems. **16**, 320–330 (2008)
13. Rizzi, A., Del Vescovo, G.: Automatic image classification by a granular computing approach. In: Proceedings of the 2006 16th IEEE Signal Processing Society Workshop on Machine Learning for Signal Processing, pp. 33–38. IEEE Press, Arlington (2006)
14. Shi, Z., Zheng, Z.: Image segmentation-oriented tolerance granular computing model. In: IEEE International Conference on Granular Computing, GrC 2008, pp. 566–571. IEEE Press, Hangzhou (2008)
15. Zheng, Z.: Image Texture Recognition Based on Tolerance Granular Space. J. Journal of Chongqing University of Posts and Telecommunications **24**, 484–489 (2009)
16. Shi, J., Du, G.: A similarity measuring method between image regions based on granular computing. In: IEEE International Conference on Granular Computing, pp. 755–758. IEEE Press, San Jose (2010)
17. Chan, Y., Fu, L., Hsiao, P., Lo, M.: Pedestrian detection using histograms of Oriented Gradients of granule feature. In: 2013 IEEE Intelligent Vehicles Symposium (IV), pp. 1410–1415. IEEE Press, Gold Coast, QLD (2013)
18. Bhatt, H.S., Bharadwaj, S., Singh, R., Vatsa, M.: Recognizing Surgically Altered Face Images Using Multiobjective Evolutionary Algorithm. J. IEEE Transactions on Information Forensics and Security **8**, 89–100 (2013)
19. Shu, L., Chung, A.C.S.: Multimodal image registration using ordinal feature and multi-dimensional mutual information. In: 4th IEEE International Symposium on Biomedical Imaging: From Nano to Macro, ISBI 2007, pp. 5–8. IEEE Press, Arlington, VA (2007)
20. Zhang, M., Sun, Z., Tan, T.: Deformed iris recognition using bandpass geometric features and lowpass ordinal features. In: 2013 International Conference on Biometrics (ICB), IEEE, pp. 1–6. IEEE Press, Madrid (2013)
21. Yang, J., Shi, Y.: Finger–vein ROI localization and vein ridge enhancement. Pattern Recognition Letters. **33**, 1569–1579 (2012)
22. Zhang, L., Zhang, L., Zhang, D.: Finger-knuckle-print: a new biometric identifier. In: 2009 16th IEEE International Conference on Image Processing (ICIP), pp. 1981–1984. IEEE Press, Cairo (2009)
23. Kekre, H.B., Bharadi, V.A.: Fingerprint's core point detection using orientation field. In: International Conference on Advances in Computing, Control, & Telecommunication Technologies, ACT 2009, pp. 150–152. IEEE Press, Trivandrum (2009)

A Finger-based Recognition Method
with Insensitivity to Pose Invariance

Zhen Zhong, Guimin Jia, Yihua Shi, and Jinfeng Yang[✉]

Tianjin Key Lab for Advanced Signal Processing,
Civil Aviation University of China, Tianjin, China
jfyang@cauc.edu.cn

Abstract. The robust-feature extraction has been an important problem in biometrics research. This issue is especially important for finger-based recognition method since the finger is prone to vary in pose during imaging. To reliably represent the multimodal finger-based biometric features, this paper proposes a novel feature extraction method based on the Gabor ordinal measure (GOM). Firstly, to obtain the illumination invariance feature of three modalities, finger print (FP), finger-vein (FV) and finger-knuckle-print (FKP), of a finger, the feature maps are respectively obtained using GOM. Secondly, the finger feature maps are granulated hierarchically in a bottom-up manner by varying granularity. The intension of each granulation is represented by Gabor-Ordinal-based Local-invariant Gray Features (GOLGFs). Finally, the experimental results show that the proposed method can achieve higher accuracy recognition in a large homemade database.

Keywords: Gabor ordinal measure · Fingerprint · Finger-vein · Finger knuckle print · Rotation invariance

1 Introduction

Nowadays, an uni-modal finger-based biometrics for personal identification usually is far from perfect in many real applications, so multimodal biometrics has become a research topic in personal identification[1,2]. In this paper, the used multimodal biometric trait contains fingerprint [3,4], finger-vein[5] and finger-knuckle-print[6,7]. The feature analysis has been a key step in the processing of fusing the multimodal feature together.

Recently, many feature analysis methods have been proposed. Daugman [5] proposed 2D Gabor filter which can exploit the image information in multi-scale and multi-orientation. Chai et al. [8] proposed a GOM descriptor which combined Gabor wavelets and ordinal filters. It has more robustness under the condition of illumination variation. However, the above two feature analysis methods are sensitive to the finger-pose variation. Fan.B et al.[9] proposed a multisupport region rotation and intensity monotonic invariant descriptor (MRRID) which is effective in rotation variation. However, it still has two drawbacks in the application of describing multimodal finger feature. First, due to the small number of interest points in finger images, extracting interest points is not suitable for finger feature analysis. This inevitably impairs the

J. Yang et al. (Eds.): CCBR 2015, LNCS 9428, pp. 561–568, 2015.
DOI: 10.1007/978-3-319-25417-3_66

accuracy of finger-based recognition. Second, the MRRID has rotation invariance only in describing local image feature.

In order to effectively overcome the above limitations and solve the issue of finger-pose variation, we present a new descriptor in finger-feature analysis which named Gabor-Ordinal-based Local-invariant Gray Feature(GOLGF). Firstly, a bank of even-symmetric Gabor filter with eight orientations is used to exploit the magnitude features in FP, FV, FKP , then they are encoded by ordinal measure. Secondly, we select the original feature object set on the basis of the GOM feature maps, each original feature object is granulated into non-overlapping rectangle granules in a bottom-up manner to construct the multilevel feature granules(FGs). Third, the intension of each FG is described by improved MRRID. The experimental results show that the proposed method has a good robustness to better effect in the issue of finger-pose variation and yields higher identification accuracy in finger-based recognition.

2   The Proposed Method

2.1   Multimodal Finger Image Acquisition

To obtain multimodal images of a finger, we have designed a homemade imaging system, which can capture three modality images automatically and simultaneously when a finger is available, as shown in Fig. 1(a). To acquire the reliable finger-feature, double spectral in different bands was used [10]. Due to the scale variation of uni-modal ROI images, FP, FV, FKP images are respectively resized in 160×160, 96×208, 96×208, as shown in Fig. 1(b).

2.2   GOM Feature Extraction

The GOM is a descriptor on ordinal coding derived from Gabor features of images, and it has a good robustness against illumination. Firstly, the magnitude information with eight orientations [11] is extracted by Gabor filter in the FP, FV, FKP images. Then, the ordinal measures of three modal are respectively conducted with the multi-channel Gabor magnitude features to get the ordinal feature-maps. In [9], the difference filter is defined as

$$MLDF = C_p \sum_{i=1}^{N_p} \frac{1}{\sqrt{2\pi}\delta_{pi}} \exp[\frac{-(X-\omega_{pi})^2}{2\delta_{pi}^2}] - C_n \sum_{j=1}^{N_n} \frac{1}{\sqrt{2\pi}\delta_{nj}} \exp[\frac{-(X-\omega_{nj})^2}{2\delta_{nj}^2}] \quad (1)$$

here ω is the central position, δ is the scale of ordinal filter. N_p is the number of positive lobes, and N_n is the number of negative lobes. Constant coefficients C_n and C_p are used to keep the balance between positive and negative lobes. To satisfy $C_pN_p = C_nN_n$, we assume $C_p=1$, $N_p=2$; $C_n=2$, $N_n=1$, since the difference filter with three lobes is more stable. The GOM feature maps of three modal are shown as Fig.1(c).

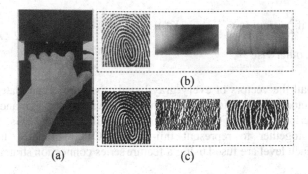

Fig. 1. A homemade imaging device and finger feature extraction results

2.3   Feature Granulation

In order to overcome the MRRID limitation which only has rotation invariance in local feature analysis, the GOM feature maps of three modal respectively are divided into rectangle blocks with different scales. Moreover, to effectively improve the matching rate, we adopt a bottom-up method to construct the multilevel blocks based on GOM, and each of these rectangle blocks represents a feature granule [12], as shown in Fig. 2.

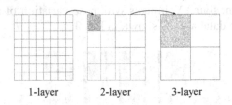

1-layer   2-layer   3-layer

Fig. 2. The 3-layer bottom-up granulation process

2.4   Feature Granule Intension Description

Due to the small number of interest points in GOM finger-feature images, we have a corresponding improvement on MRRID which viewed each pixel as an interest point.

Firstly, for each feature granule (FG), the local gray feature vectors are generated as the following procedure:

Step 1: gray-based grouping.

The intensities of pixel points are sorted in non-descending order. According to the number of the pixels, this sequence is divided into k groups [10]. The parameter k is determined by the scale of each FG.

Step 2: calculating the gray vector.

We extract its eight nearest neighboring points regularly for each pixel. By comparing the gray of opposite adjacent points, we get a 4-bin binary vector. A local gray feature vector can be obtained by mapping the 4-bin binary vector into 16-bin binar

$$f_j = \begin{cases} 1, \text{ if} \sum_{k=1}^{4} sign(I(X_i^{m+4}) - I(X_i^m)) \times 2^{m-1} = j - 1 \\ 0, \text{ otherwise} \end{cases}, j = 1, 2, \cdots, 2^4, m = 1, 2, 3, 4. \quad (2)$$

Secondly, all the vectors of every gray-based group are accumulated. Then, the accumulated vectors are concatenated together to represent each FG, and the constructed intension descriptor of each FG is called GOLGF. All uni-modal FGs of every level are concatenated together to represent uni-modal GOLGF. Finally, the three modal GOLGFs of each level are fused using a feature series connection strategy.

3   Experiments and Analysis

To evaluate the rotation invariance of GOLGF descriptor, a homemade database which totally contains 3000 sets of FP-FV-FKP images with pose variations is used in this experiment. This database has two characteristics, one is that the ROI images based on same finger are collected in different time, the other is that multimodal images of a finger are obtained at the same time.

3.1   GOLGF Poses Reliability Analysis

In order to verify that the proposed GOLGF descriptor can effectively deal with the issue of pose variation, four FV images with pose variation of a same individual are selected in homemade database, as shown in Fig. 3.

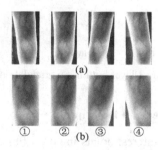

Fig. 3. The variable pose of FV images (a)the exacted images from a homemade imaging system(b)the extracted ROI images

Here, the method in [13] is used to measure the similarity of ROIs variable in pose.

$$D(m_1, m_2) = \frac{1}{M * N} \sqrt{\sum_{i=1}^{L} [H_{m_1}(i) - H_{m_2}(i)]^2} \quad (3)$$

where $D(m_1, m_2)$ denotes the histogram euclidean metric of two matching images, L is the dimension of histogram. M is the number of pixels in each row, N is the number of pixels in each column.

From Table 1, we can see that GOLGF descriptor has better rotation invariance. This shows that can effectively deal with the problem of finger-pose variation.

Table 1. The euclidean metric of histogram

Labeled matching image	GOLGF	GOM	Improved MRRID
①—②	0.4240	0.5944	0.5421
①—③	0.4991	0.7009	0.6445
①—④	0.4774	0.6909	0.6025
②—③	0.4735	0.6435	0.5857
②—④	0.4894	0.7370	0.6162
③—④	0.5432	0.7714	0.7129

3.2   GOLGF Parameter Selection

To determine the parameter k of gray groups, the Gabor-Ordinal-based images in three levels are tested by different k. In this experiment, we use the 1000 sets of three modals. Fig. 4 shows the comparison of different k in three levels. From Fig. 4 we can clearly see that the finger-feature recognition performs better in $k=5$, 8, 10 respectively in three levels.

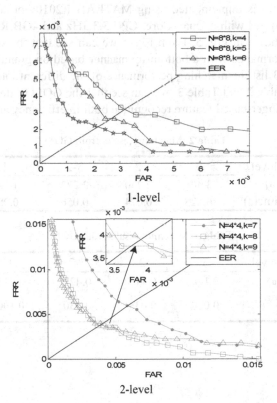

1-level

2-level

Fig. 4. The comparison of different k in three levels

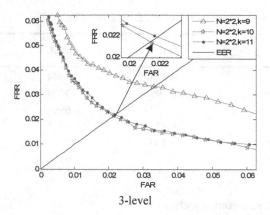

3-level

Fig. 4. *(Continued)*

3.3   Recognition Results

Here, we use the ROC curves to test the performance of the proposed method. The proposed algorithm is implemented using MATLAB R2010a on a standard desktop PC which is equipped with a Quad-Core, CPU 3.3GHz and 4GB RAM. The identification result is shown in Fig. 5. From Fig. 5 we can see that the GOLGF descriptor has the best performance with a bottom-up manner based on granulates. Further, Table 2 and Table 3 list the matching performance of the different intension description method. From Table 2 and Table 3, we can see that the GOLGF descriptor has better performance in finger-based feature recognition both in efficiency and accuracy.

Table 2. Matching results from GOM

Granular level	3	2	3-2	1	3-2-1
EER (%)	3.408	2.230	2.222	1.126	1.111
Matching time(s)	0.028	0.074	0.056	0.257	0.129

Table 3. Matching results from GOLGF

Granular level	3	2	3-2	1	3-2-1
EER(%)	2.148	0.415	0.422	0.215	0.207
Matching time(s)	0.020	0.038	0.030	0.100	0.060

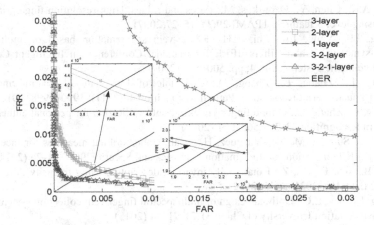

Fig. 5. The identification results

4   Conclusion

To deal with the problem that a finger is prone to vary in poses during imaging, a new intension description method of feature granules (FGs) is proposed in this paper. The obtained finger features are called Gabor-ordinal-based Local-invariant Gray Features (GOLGFs). First, the FP, FV, FKP images were respectively processed by Gabor filter with different parameters to obtain Gabor magnitude feature, and then they were respectively encoded by ordinal measure. Second, to describe the local gray feature of finger-based images, the three modal features were granulated at three levels of information granularity in a bottom-up manner based on granulates of scale variation. Then, the intension of each FG was described by improved MRRID. It could improve intension description robustness of finger-based FG. Finally, to describe a total finger feature, these three modal features were fused using a feature series connection strategy. The experimental results showed that the proposed method had a superior performance in improving the finger-feature recognition accuracy as well as efficiency.

Acknowledgements. This work is jointly supported by National Natural Science Foundation of China (Nos.61379102, U1433120) and the Fundamental Research Funds for the Central Universities(No. 3122014C003).

References

1. Ross, A., Jain, A.K.: Information fusion in biometrics. Pattern Recognition Letters **24**(13), 2115–2125 (2003)
2. Ross, A., Jain, A.K.: Multimodal biometrics: an overview. In: 12th European Signal Processing Conference, pp. 1221–1224. IEEE press (2004)
3. Jain, A.K., Hong, L., Bolle, R.: On-line fingerprint verification. TPAMI **19**(4), 302–314 (1997)

4. Jain, A.K., Chen, Y., Demirkus, M.: Pores and ridges: High-resolution fingerprint matching using level 3 features. TPAMI **29**(1), 15–27(2007)
5. Yang, J.F., Yang, J.L., Shi, Y.H.: Finger-vein segmentation based on multi-channel even-symmetric Gabor filters. IEEE International Conference on Intelligent Computing and Intelligent Systems, vol. 4, pp. 500–503 (2009)
6. Zhang, L., Zhang, L., Zhang, D.: Ensemble of local and global information for finger-knuckle-print recognition. Pattern Recognition **44**(2011), 1990–1998 (2010)
7. Zhang, L., Zhang, L.: Online finger-knuckle-print verification for personal authentication. Pattern Recognition **43**(7), 2560–571 (2010)
8. Chai, Z., Sun, Z., Mendez-Vazquez, H., et al.: Gabor ordinal measures for face recognition. IEEE Transactions on Information Forensics and Security. **9**(1), 14–26 (2014)
9. Fan, B., Wu, F., Hu, Z.: Rotationally invariant descriptors using intensity order pooling. TPAMI **34**(10), 2031–2045 (2012)
10. Yang, J.F., Lv, E.C.: Optimal design of multispectral finger vein collection system. Journal of Civil Aviation University of China **31**(2), 71–74 (2013)
11. Yang, J.F., Shi, Y.H.: Finger-Vein ROI Localization and Vein Ridge Enhancement. Pattern Recognition Letters **33**, 1569–1579 (2012)
12. Li, Y., Peng, J., Zhong, Z., Jia, G., Yang, J.: A Multimodal Finger-Based Recognition Method Based on Granular Computing. In: Sun, Z., Shan, S., Sang, H., Zhou, J., Wang, Y., Yuan, W. (eds.) CCBR 2014. LNCS, vol. 8833, pp. 458–464. Springer, Heidelberg (2014)
13. Zhao, C., Li, Z.: An improved measuring method of face histogram distance for face recognition based on shrinking factor. Journal of Xihua University **32**(5), 8–10 (2013)

Fusion of Face and Iris Biometrics on Mobile Devices Using Near-infrared Images

Qi Zhang[1,2]($\boxtimes$), Haiqing Li[1], Man Zhang[1], Zhaofeng He[1], Zhenan Sun[1], and Tieniu Tan[1,2]

[1] Center for Research on Intelligent Perception and Computing,
Institute of Automation, Chinese Academy of Sciences, Beijing, China
[2] College of Engineering and Information Technology,
University of Chinese Academy of Sciences, Beijing, China
qi.zhang@nlpr.ia.ac.cn

Abstract. With the wide use of cell phones and tablets, large amounts of private data are stored on mobile devices and personal information security has become a growing concern. Biometrics is able to provide encouraging personal recognition solutions to strengthen the security. This paper proposes a multimodal biometric system for mobile devices by fusing face and iris modalities. Face images are aligned according to eye centers and then represented by histograms of Gabor ordinal measures (GOM). Iris images are cropped from face images and represented by ordinal measures (OMs). Finally, the similarity scores produced by face and iris features are combined in the score level. Experiments are conducted on the CASIA-Mobile database which includes 1400 images of 70 Asians. The proposed system achieves impressive results and demonstrates a promising solution for personal recognition on mobile devices.

Keywords: Face recognition · Iris recognition · Multimodal biometric · Near-infrared · Mobile devices

1 Introduction

Mobile devices such as cell phones and tablets have been widely used for social communication, online shopping and banking. Unprecedented amounts of personal data are stored on mobile devices and facing serious security challenges. It is urgent to build reliable and friendly personal recognition systems for sensitive data protection. While traditional passwords and personal identification numbers (PINs) are easy to crack by guessing or by dictionary attacks, biometrics provides encouraging personal recognition solutions with benefits of its high universality and distinctiveness. Fingerprint recognition is currently available on many mobile devices such as Apple iPhone 6 and Huawei Ascend Mate 7. A number of face recognition applications have been released on line. However, fingerprints left on screens can be easily replicated for spoof attacks and the accuracy of visible light face recognition drops dramatically in complex illumination environment. Fusion of face and iris biometrics using near-infrared (NIR)

© Springer International Publishing Switzerland 2015
J. Yang et al. (Eds.): CCBR 2015, LNCS 9428, pp. 569–578, 2015.
DOI: 10.1007/978-3-319-25417-3_67

images will overcome these limitations. Firstly, iris imaging does not require contact so that irises are difficult to be replicated. Secondly, NIR illumination is robust to visible light variations and reduces intra-class differences. Finally, face and iris images can be captured simultaneously and possess complementary identity information that will improve the accuracy of a single modality after fusion.

Table 1 summaries recent work on face and iris recognition on mobile devices. Most existing work is based on visible light imagery [1–5]. Marsico et al. [1] implement an embedded biometrics application by fusing face and iris modalities at the score level. After that they build a visible wavelength iris image database named MICHE-I using three different mobile devices under uncontrolled settings [2]. The database collects 3732 images from 92 subjects and has been tested by several algorithms, including spatial histograms [3] and deep sparse filtering [4]. In [4], Raja et al. release a small iris images dataset which consists of 560 images from 28 subjects. Santos et al. [5] build an iris and periocular dataset using four different mobile devices for cross-sensor recognition. All the subjects in the above datasets are Caucasians whose iris texture is clearly displayed under visible light. But as shown in Fig. 1, Asian irises reveal rich texture features only in NIR light due to high density of melanin pigment. Park et al. [6] use a NIR illuminator and a NIR pass filter for iris imaging on mobile phones. 400 face images of 100 subjects are captured in the experiment but not released to the public. In addition, the face information is ignored during recognition.

Table 1. Related work and the corresponding databases.

Contributors	Database	Devices	Illumination	Subjects	Year
BIPLab [2]	MICHE	iPhone5; SamsungGalaxyS4; SamsungGalaxyTab2	visible light	92 Caucasians 3732 images	2015
NISlab [4]	VSSIRIS	iPhone 5S; Nokia Lumia 1020	visible light	28 Caucasians 560 images	2015
Santos et al. [5]	CSIP	Sony Ericsson Xperia Arc S; iPhone 4; ThL W200; Huawei U8510	visible light	50 Caucasians 2004 images	2015
Park et al. [6]	Not released	Samsung SPH-S2300	NIR light	70 Asians 30 Caucasians 400 images	2008

In this paper, we fuse face and iris biometrics on mobile devices for higher security and ease of use. A portable NIR iris imaging module is connected to mobile devices via micro USB to capture rich texture features of Asian irises. The module can capture face and iris images simultaneously and enable us to fuse these two modalities. Face and iris images are first aligned and normalized, and then represented by histograms of Gabor ordinal measures (GOM) [7] and ordinal measures (OMs) [8] respectively. Their similarity scores are added

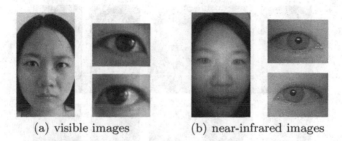

(a) visible images   (b) near-infrared images

Fig. 1. Comparison of visible and near-infrared light iris images. The texture of NIR images is much richer than that of visible images.

together to make the final decision. In order to test our algorithm, the CASIA-Mobile database which consists of 1400 images from 70 Asians is constructed and will be released to the public in the near future. The remainder of this paper is organized as follows. In Section 2, the technical details are described. The experimental results are presented in Section 3. Finally, Section 4 concludes this paper and outlines the future work.

2   Technical Details

2.1   The NIR Iris Imaging Module

The NIR iris imaging module we employed composes of a NIR camera and several NIR illuminators. It is small (about 5cm × 2cm × 1cm in Width × Height × Thickness) and therefore can be conveniently attached to a mobile phone through micro USB. The module captures valid images at about 25cm standoff distance. The resolution of the whole image is 1080×1920 while the diameter of an iris is about 110 pixels. A face image and two iris images cropped from the face image have been shown in Fig. 1(b).

2.2   Image Preprocessing

In order to reduce the intra-class differences caused by pose variations, face images are cropped and downsampled to 128 × 128 pixels by transforming eye centers to (22, 36) and (108, 36) with similarity warp. The eye centers of face images are determined by eye detection and iris segmentation. First, the coarse eye regions are detected by Adaboost eye detectors [9]. Then the eye centers and iris boundaries are accurately localized by our previous method [10]. Fig. 2 shows some examples of face alignment. The NIR illuminators are mainly used for iris imaging so that mouths are darker than noses. Only the eye and nose regions are retained to reduce the effects of uniform illumination and barrel distortion. Afterwards, the circular iris is unfolded from polar coordinates into a 70 × 540 rectangle using the rubber sheet model [11].

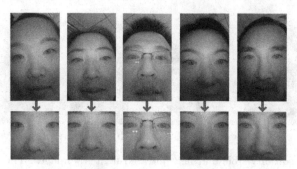

Fig. 2. Examples of face alignment.

2.3 Face Feature Analysis

The method we use for face feature extraction is local feature descriptor, which can extract the detailed information that facilitates the recognition. Two most popular local image descriptors: Gabor filters [12] and OMs are used. The definition of Gabor filter is shown in Eq. (1). The OMs can be expressed as Multi-Lobe Differential Filters (MLDF), which is shown in Eq. (2).

$$G(x,y) = exp(-\frac{1}{2}(\frac{x^2}{\sigma_x^2} + \frac{y^2}{\sigma_y^2})) \cdot exp(-2\pi J(\mu_0 x + \nu_0 y)) \tag{1}$$

where (μ_0, ν_0) is the center frequency and σ_x, σ_y is the standard deviation of x and y direction.

$$MLDF = C_m \sum_{i=1}^{N_m} \frac{1}{\sqrt{2\pi}\delta_{mi}} exp[\frac{-(X - \mu_{mi}^2)}{2\delta_{mi}^2}] - C_n \sum_{j=1}^{N_n} \frac{1}{\sqrt{2\pi}\delta_{ni}} exp[\frac{-(X - \mu_{nj}^2)}{2\delta_{nj}^2}]$$

$$\tag{2}$$

where μ and δ are used to describe the size of each lobe. N_m and N_n is the number of positive and negative lobe, respectively.

The Gabor filter has the advantage in distinctiveness and the ordinal measures have the merit of robustness. Therefore, we integrate these two filters together to achieve a better recognition result. Face images are represented by GOM. Firstly, multi-channel Gabor filters are applied on the normalized face images. Five frequencies and eight orientations Gabor filters are used. Therefore, forty Gabor feature images are generated. Subsequently, four di-lobe and four tri-lobe ordinal measures, whose orientation values are 0°, 45°, 90°, 135°, are used on the phase, magnitude, real and imaginary parts of the Gabor images, respectively. There are totally 5760 dimensional GOM for each feature map block. It is necessary to reduce the feature dimensionality. The widely used linear discriminant analysis (LDA) approach is applied in our paper. LDA is a supervised method aims to find a linear combination of features that best explains the data and can be used for dimensionality reduction. The main idea of LDA is finding a line to project the data that maximizes the between class distance and minimizes the within class variance. The optimal objection function of LDA is shown in Eq. (3).

$$J(\omega) = \frac{\omega^T S_B \omega}{\omega^T S_w \omega} \tag{3}$$

where S_B is between class scatter matrix and S_w is within class scatter matrix. The goal is to maximize the $J(\omega)$.

2.4 Iris Feature Analysis

The robust local image descriptor OMs are used for iris feature extraction, which are widely used in iris recognition [13]. The OMs have many parameters, which differ in scale, orientation, location, lobe numbers, distance, etc. After comprehensive consideration, the di-lobe and tri-lobe ordinal filters are jointly used. Totally, there are 830 various OMs.

In order to get more texture information, the normalized iris image is divided into multiple regions. Usually, the regions adjacent to pupil contain more texture information than other regions. Therefore, various regions of the iris image should be treated differently. In our study, feature extraction is implemented on different regions with various filters. In total, 47,089 regional OMs are extracted to form a huge feature pool.

Taking the time cost into consideration, feature selection is necessary. The number of selected features is usually much smaller than the huge number of candidates, which can speed up the recognition processes. Choosing the distinctive features manually is time-consuming and usually is not the optimal option for a certain database. AdaBoost is used in this paper. Compared with other feature selection methods, AdaBoost has the advantages in high speed, simplicity, classification and feature selection at the same time, etc. AdaBoost algorithm chooses a complementary ensemble of weak learners in a greedy way. It selects a new feature on the reweighted samples. The reweighting strategies are that gain weight of the misclassified examples and lose weight of the correctly classified ones. In this way, future weak learners pay more attention to the examples that are misclassified by previous weak learners. In training process, AdaBoost selects only those features known to improve the predictive power of the model. Thus, it can reduce feature dimensionality. Among the AdaBoost algorithms, GentleBoost outperforms others in that it is more robust to noisy data and less emphasis on the outliers [14]. GentleBoost is used in this paper.

The most distinctive features are obtained on the training dataset using the GentleBoost algorithm. Based on our previous study [15], the recognition performance increases as the number of features increases from zero. However, when the feature number reaches 15, the performance achieves stability. Therefore, in our study, 15 regional features are selected from 47,089 OMs candidates. Subsequently, only the selected 15 regional features are extracted and evaluated on the testing dataset. Thus it can save time and improve the recognition performance.

2.5   Score Level Fusion by the Sum Rule

The cosine similarity is computed to generate matching scores of two face templates (x_1 and x_2). The equation is shown in Eq. (4).

$$cos\theta = \frac{\sum_{k=1}^{n} x_{1k} \cdot x_{2k}}{\sqrt{\sum x_{1k}^2} \cdot \sqrt{\sum x_{2k}^2}} \tag{4}$$

The matching score of two iris codes is calculated by hamming distance (HD). The HD is transformed to similarity at first and then fused with the cosine similarity using the sum rule. Finally, the matching score is normalized to [0,1]. The score level fusion by the sum rule is shown in Eq. (5).

$$FS = (cos\theta + 1 - HD)/2 \tag{5}$$

where FS denotes fusion score. HD is the matching score of two iris codes.

3   Experimental Results

We verify our method on the new built CASIA-Mobile database. At first, face recognition and iris recognition experiments are performed separately. Subsequently, score level fusion of the two modalities is performed.

3.1   CASIA-Mobile Database

In order to promote the face and iris recognition research on mobile phones, we build the CASIA-Mobile database, which will be provided freely for the public. The CASIA-Mobile database includes 1400 face images and 2800 iris images from 70 Asians. There are 40 males and 30 females. The age of the subjects ranges from 22 to 64, among which less than 30 account for 67% proportion. The gender and age distributions can be seen in Fig. 3. For each subject, 20 face images are captured. The left and right irises can be detected and segmented from one face image.

The features of the CASIA-Mobile database are as follows: it is the first public near-infrared mobile database as far as we know. Besides, all the subjects are Asians. Furthermore, the acquisitions of face and iris images are at the same time, which are convenient and beneficial to use more information and perform a bimodal recognition. The challenges of this database include specular reflection of wearing glasses, low resolution images, illumination variation, occlusions of eyelashes and eyelids, etc.

3.2   Face Recognition

The face images of the first 25 subjects are used for training. Each subject has 20 face images. Therefore, there are altogether 500 images for training. 900 face images from the rest 45 subjects are used for testing. There are totally

8550 intra-class matching and 396000 interclass matching. Receiver operating characteristic (ROC) curve and equal error rate (EER) are used for performance measurements. The smaller EER is, the better the performance is. The ROC curve of the face recognition of the CASIA-Mobile database is shown in Fig. 4. The vertical axis is false reject rate (FRR) and the horizontal axis is false accept rate (FAR). The EER is 0.0313.

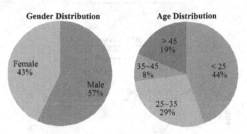

Fig. 3. The gender and age distributions of the subjects in the CASIA-Mobile database.

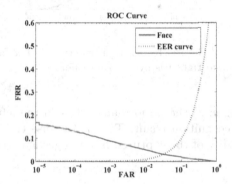

Fig. 4. The ROC curve of the face recognition.

3.3 Iris Recognition

The iris images of the first 25 subjects are used for training. 10 images are chosen for each iris. Therefore, there are altogether 500 images in the training phase. 1800 iris images from the rest 45 subjects (20 images for each iris) are used for testing. In the GentleBoost based feature selection part, there are 2250 intra-class matching scores as positive samples and 4900 inter-class matching scores as negative samples.

The experiments are performed on left and right iris separately. Afterwards, the left and right matching scores are fused by sum rule for better recognition. The EER results are listed in Table 2. The ROC curves of the three experiments are drawn in the same figure, as is shown in Fig. 5.

From the EER results and the ROC curves, it can be concluded that: 1) after score level fusion of the left and right iris, the EER decrease about 50% of the

Table 2. The EER of the iris recognition, where 'Iris LR fusion' represents the score level fusion of left and right iris by the sum rule.

Method	EER
Right iris	0.0757
Left iris	0.0536
Iris LR fusion	0.0389

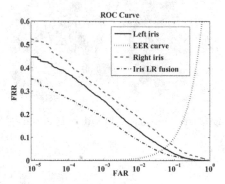

Fig. 5. The ROC curve of the iris recognition, where 'Iris LR fusion' represents the score level fusion of left and right iris by the sum rule.

EER of right iris images; 2) the performance of both the left and right iris are worse than the face recognition result. That is because the iris images are low in resolution. The quality of the captured face images is better than that of the iris images.

3.4   Score Level Fusion

The iris LR fusion experiment is performed at the previous study and achieved better result than the separate iris. In order to further improve the performance, score level fusion of face and iris biometrics experiment is conducted and the sum rule is applied. The EER results are listed in Table 3. The ROC curves of the iris LR fusion, the face and the score level fusion of face and iris biometrics are drawn in the same figure, as is shown in Fig. 6.

Table 3. The EER of the iris and face fusion, where 'Face and iris fusion' represents the score level fusion of face and iris biometrics by the sum rule.

Method	EER
Iris LR fusion	0.0389
Face	0.0313
Face and Iris fusion	0.0076

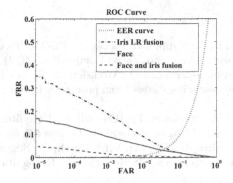

Fig. 6. The ROC curve of iris and face fusion, where 'Face and iris fusion' represents the score level fusion of face and iris biometrics by the sum rule.

From the EER results and the ROC curves, we can draw conclusions that: 1) the EER of the left and right iris fusion is similar to the face recognition result, but the ROC curve is still worse than that of the face recognition; 2) after score level fusion of face and iris biometrics, both the ROC curve and the EER are improved dramatically. It can be inferred that the face and iris modalities have some complementary information and via simple fusion better result can be achieved.

4   Conclusions

In this paper, we have proposed a multimodal biometric system for mobile devices by fusing face and iris modalities. There are three major contributions. First, a portable module has been employed to capture NIR face and iris images simultaneously. Second, an efficient and effective recognition algorithm has been presented. Taking the limited source of mobile devices into consideration, feature dimensionality reduction and feature selection approach are applied to find a small number of features. Face recognition and iris recognition are performed separately and then fused at the score level. Third, a near-infrared database named CASIA-Mobile has been built to promote face and iris recognition algorithm development on mobile devices. After fusion of face and iris modalities, an impressive EER of 0.76% is achieved on the CASIA-Mobile database, which proves the feasibility of our system.

The proposed system can be improved further. The accuracy of iris recognition in our experiments is far from satisfactory due to the low resolution of iris images. The quality of iris images will be improved by better imaging modules and image enhancement algorithms. Apart from the score level fusion, we will also consider other levels of fusion in our future work.

Acknowledgments. This work is supported by the National Natural Science Foundation of China (Grant No.61403389) and the Beijing Nova Programme (Number Z14110-1001814090), China.

References

1. De Marsico, M., Galdi, C., Nappi, M., Riccio, D.: FIRME: face and iris recognition for mobile engagement. Image and Vision Computing **32**(12), 1161–1172 (2014)
2. De Marsico, M., Nappi, M., Riccio, D., Wechsler, H.: Mobile iris challenge evaluation (MICHE)-I, biometric iris dataset and protocols. Pattern Recognition Letters **57**, 17–23 (2015)
3. Barra, S., Casanova, A., Narducci, F., Ricciardi, S.: Ubiquitous iris recognition by means of mobile devices. Pattern Recognition Letters **57**, 66–73 (2015)
4. Raja, K.B., Raghavendra, R., Vemuri, V.K., Busch, C.: Smartphone based visible iris recognition using deep sparse filtering. Pattern Recognition Letters **57**, 33–42 (2015)
5. Santos, G., Grancho, E., Bernardo, M.V., Fiadeiro, P.T.: Fusing iris and periocular information for cross-sensor recognition. Pattern Recognition Letters **57**, 52–59 (2015)
6. Park, K.R., Park, H.A., Kang, B.J., Lee, E.C., Jeong, D.S.: A study on iris localization and recognition on mobile phones. EURASIP J. Adv. Sig. Proc. (2008)
7. Chai, Z., Sun, Z., Mendez-Vazquez, H., He, R., Tan, T.: Gabor ordinal measures for face recognition. IEEE Transactions on Information Forensics and Security **9**(1), 14–26 (2014)
8. Sun, Z., Tan, T.: Ordinal measures for iris recognition. IEEE Transactions on Pattern Analysis and Machine Intelligence **31**(12), 2211–2226 (2009)
9. Viola, P., Jones, M.J.: Robust real-time face detection. International Journal of Computer Vision **57**(2), 137–154 (2004)
10. He, Z., Tan, T., Sun, Z., Qiu, X.: Toward accurate and fast iris segmentation for iris biometrics. IEEE Transactions on Pattern Analysis and Machine Intelligence **31**(9), 1670–1684 (2009)
11. Daugman, J.G.: How iris recognition works. IEEE Transactions on Circuits and Systems for Video Technology **14**(1), 21–30 (2004)
12. Daugman, J.G.: High confidence visual recognition of persons by a test of statistical independence. IEEE Transactions on Pattern Analysis and Machine Intelligence **15**(11), 1148–1161 (1993)
13. Wang, L., Sun, Z., Tan, T.: Robust regularized feature selection for iris recognition via linear programming. In: International Conference on Pattern Recognition, pp. 3358–3361 (2012)
14. Friedman, J., Hastie, T., Tibshirani, R.: Additive logistic regression: a statistical view of boosting. The Annals of Statistics **28**(2), 337–407 (2000)
15. Sun, Z., Wang, L., Tan, T.: Ordinal feature selection for iris and palmprint recognition. IEEE Transactions on Image Processing **23**(9), 3922–3934 (2014)

Other Biometric Recognition
and Processing

Boosting-Like Deep Convolutional Network
for Pedestrian Detection

Lei Wang[1], Baochang Zhang[1(✉)], and Wankou Yang[2]

[1] School of Automation Science and Electrical Engineering,
Beihang University, Beijing 100191, China
wtiffanyl@163.com, bczhang@buaa.edu.cn
[2] School of Automation, Southeast University, Nanjing 210096, China
wkyang@seu.edu.cn

Abstract. This paper proposes a boosting-like deep learning (BDL) framework for pedestrian detection. The fusion of handcrafted and deep learned features is considered to extract more effective representations. Due to overtraining on the limited training samples, over-fitting and convergence stability are two major problems of deep learning. We propose the boosting-like algorithm to enhance the system convergence stability through adjusting the updating rate according to the classification condition of samples in the training process. We theoretically give the derivation of our algorithm. Our approach achieves 15.85% and 3.81% reduction in the average miss rate compared with ACF and JointDeep on the largest Caltech dataset, respectively.

Keywords: Pedestrian detection · Boosting-like · Feature learning · Feedback propagation

1   Introduction

Pedestrian detection has an important significance in real life, which has been widely used in intelligent control systems, traffic safety assist systems, robotics research and other fields. It attracts more and more attention, and a variety of feature extraction and classification methods have been proposed. Two major strategies are hand crafted extraction and automatic learning. The commonly used handcrafted methods are HOG [1], Haar-like [2], 3D geometric characteristic [3], and so on. With the computer development and data scale increasing, automatic learning methods are gradually put forward. Sermanet et al. [4] propose the ConvNet combining unsupervised and supervised methods to train multi-stage automatic sparse convolution encoder. UDN [5] is a joint deep neural network model combined with deformation and occlusion model, which achieves a lower miss rate on ETH [6] and Caltech [7] datasets. The manual extraction has a superior description of pedestrian, but it can't learn the essential characteristics and shows poor adaptability. The latter can automatically extract pedestrian features by methods such as feedback propagation. But it requires abundant training samples and takes a lot of time. What's more, it has a higher hardware requirement.

J. Yang et al. (Eds.): CCBR 2015, LNCS 9428, pp. 581–588, 2015.
DOI: 10.1007/978-3-319-25417-3_68

Based on the characteristics, we propose a novel pedestrian detection framework. It combines manual method with deep learning model to extract more rich features. We introduce the boosting idea into deep framework by gradually adjusting sample weights in feedback propagation. Our method can not only improve detection performance, but also strengthen the stability of the network. In addition, our input features are inspired by [8], but we regularize them in order to improve the detection rate. Our deep structure adopts a concise convolutional neural network (CNN) [9] including two convolutional layers to access to higher level feature representations. The final classifier we adopt is a simple single neural network. The main contributions of this paper are as follows: firstly, the fusion of handcrafted features and learning-based features improves the system performance; secondly, the proposed boosting-like algorithm enhances the convergence stability.

The remainder of this paper is arranged as follows: in section 2, our pedestrian detection structure is described, including the input channel features and deep learning structure. In section 3, the boosting-like algorithm that we propose is elaborated. In section 4, experimental results are presented and analyzed. In section 5, we conclude the paper.

2   Pedestrian Detection Framework

2.1   Input Channel Features

In this paper, we extract the low-level channel features inspired by [8] including three color channels LUV, one gradient magnitude channel $|G|$, and six gradient oriented channels $G_1 \sim G_6$. Then, each channel is processed to be zero mean and unit variance. The gradient magnitude $G(x,y)$ multiply with indication function $I[x,y]$ of θ, we get the gradient oriented channels $G_\theta(x,y)$

$$G_\theta(x, y) = G(x, y) \cdot I[\vartheta(x, y) = \theta] \tag{1}$$

Fig.1 shows the visualizations of *ACF* and normalization. The results demonstrate that normalization not only significantly enhances the image resolution, but also highlights pedestrian details.

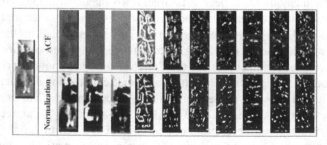

Fig. 1. Comparison of channel features

2.2   CNN Structure

CNN is the neural network including multilayer, whose depth and width should be designed in views of different recognition tasks and dataset scales. The fundamental CNN structure we use is shown in Fig.2.

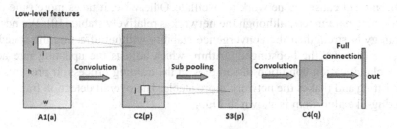

Fig. 2. Deep convolutional structure

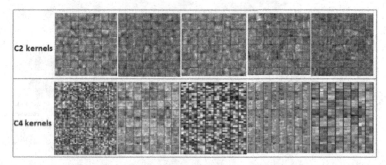

Fig. 3. The first row is the visual maps of C2 kernels, and the second row is the visual maps of C4 kernels. It can be seen that the filter kernels of the second layer mostly contain edges, lines features, while the fourth layer mainly consists of corner information. Deep network extracts more and more essential features of pedestrian with layers increasing.

A1 contains a low-level feature maps with size $w \times h$. C2 includes p convolution maps, where kernel size is set to $i \times i$. In this paper, we randomly initialize the kernel parameters ω_{nk}. The convolutional feature maps can be calculated as:

$$C_k^l = F\left(\sum_{n \in I_k} \omega_{nk} * M_n^{l-1} + b_n^l\right) \qquad (2)$$

here I_k represents the feature maps of the kth channel. $F(\cdot)$ is the activation function. In this paper, C2 layer uses sigmoid function and C4 layer employs hyperbolic tangent function. S3 is the sub-sampling layer, and β is scalar parameter. This paper uses mean-pooling $\beta = 1/m$. The operation of the sub-sampling can be expressed as :

$$S_k^l = F\left(\beta \sum_{n \in I_k} M_n^{l-1} + b_n^l\right) \qquad (3)$$

Through cascading feature maps in C4 layer we obtain the convolutional features. CNN classifier used in this paper is a single fully connected neural network. When we use Caltech to train our network, the visualization of the partial kernels in C2 and C4 layer are shown in Fig.3.

3   Boosting-Like Deep Learning

As we all know, the training method of CNN primarily uses back propagation. The network convergence stability and speed are common problems in training process. If the learning rate is too large to gain a fast convergence speed, it is easy to fall into local minimum and cause the network to oscillate. Otherwise, it takes more time to update the learning parameters, although the network is relatively stable [10]. We need to find a strategy to strengthen the convergence stability without affecting the speed. Therefore, we consider the boosting algorithm, which adjusts the updating rate according to the classification condition of samples in the training process. It prevents network over-fitting and makes the network more stable. The overall detection framework with boosting-like algorithm is shown in Fig.4.

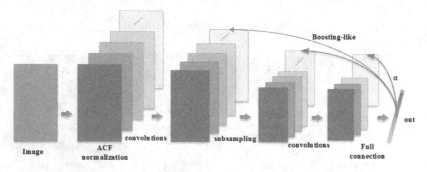

Fig. 4. Our pedestrian detection framework

If the squared-error is the loss function, we consider the nth sample error E with c classes. It is expressed as

$$E = \frac{1}{2}\sum_{k=1}^{c}(t_k^n - y_k^n)^2 \tag{4}$$

here t_k^n denotes the kth dimension of the nth sample label, and y_k^n is similarly the kth output layer unit in response to the nth sample. The input u^j of the j layer and output x^{j-1} of j-1 layer have the following linear relationship.

$$u^j = \alpha w^j x^{j-1} + b^j , \quad x^j = f(u^j) \tag{5}$$

where w^j denotes output layer weight and b^j denotes the bias, α is the penalty weight, and f is the excitation function. Then the output layer sensitivity is

$$\delta^j = f'(u^j) * (y^n - t^n) \tag{6}$$

The derivative of error E against weight w^j is expressed as

$$\frac{\partial E}{\partial w^j} = \delta^j \frac{\partial u}{\partial w} = x^{j-1} f'(u^j) * (y^n - t^n)\alpha \tag{7}$$

Finally, the delta updating rule is applied to each neuron to gain the new weights. The equation is given by

$$w^{j+1} = w^j - \eta x^{j-1} f'(u^j) * (y^n - t^n)\alpha \tag{8}$$

here η is the learning rate, thus we can obtain the weight w updating method. Actually, the convolution neural network itself can be seen as several cascaded feature extractors. The features extracted are from low-level to high-level, and the results have a mutual suppression, that is to say that a classifier output not only has a relationship with the previous layer but also the next one. According to equation (8), we distribute the feedback weights of right and wrong classification samples, which is feedback propagated from the last layer to the beginning layer.

$$Od_{t+1} = \begin{cases} (O_t - Y_t)\alpha_r, & Od_t < 0.5 \\ (O_t - Y_t)\alpha_w, & Od_t \geq 0.5 \end{cases} \tag{9}$$

where Od_t is the output error, O_t is the actual detection value of the network, and Y_t is the sample target value. Meanwhile Od_t is the output layer sensitivity δ in our network. α_r and α_w represent the penalty coefficients of right and wrong classified samples, respectively. When the sample output is different with its label, the penalty weight should be increased. On the contrary, it should be decreased when it is the same.

The solving process of α_r and α_w is very important. In this paper, the adaptive parameter selection method is employed. According to samples' new classification results, there will be a new redistribution W_i of sample weights. The concrete solving process is as follows.

If the initial sample weight distribution is $W_1 = (w_{11}, \cdots, w_{1i}, \cdots, w_{1N})$ where $w_{1i} = 1/N$, $i=1,2,\cdots,N$, and training iterations $m=1,2,\cdots,M$, we use samples with weight distribution W_m to train the classifier $F_m(x)$. The classifier error rate on the training data set is

$$e_m = P(F_m(x_i) \neq y_i) = \sum_{i=1}^{N} \omega_{mi} I(F_m(x_i) \neq y_i) \tag{10}$$

where $I(x,y)$ is the indicative function, w_{mi} is the weight of the current sample. The classification performance β_m is calculated as

$$\beta_m = \frac{1}{2} In \frac{1-e_m}{e_m} \tag{11}$$

here α_m is a factor which indicates the classification performance. The new distribution $W_{m+1} = (w_{m+1,1}, \cdots, w_{m+1,i}, \cdots, w_{m+1,N})$. It can be expressed as

$$\omega_{m+1,i} = \frac{\omega_{mi}}{N_m} exp(-\beta_m y_i F_m(x_i)), i = 1,2,\cdots,N \tag{12}$$

$$N_m = \sum_{i=1}^{N} \omega_{mi} exp(-\beta_m y_i F_m(x_i)) \tag{13}$$

here N_m is a normalized factor. During the training process, we use the sample weight distribution W_{m+1} to update the parameters α_r and α_w of our network.

4   Experiment

Our pedestrian detection framework is evaluated on the challenging Caltech test, which is the largest among commonly used. It covers diverse complicated scenes including occlusion, illumination, deformation, and so on. In the experiment, we use set00~set05 to train our model. There are about 60000 training samples, which include about 4000 positive ones. Set06~set10 are adopted as test sets. Usually sliding windows are used to traverse the pedestrian image in the detection stage. It is well known that the feedback process in the deep learning network structure takes a lot of time. Therefore, we use the strategy similar to UDN [5] to prune candidate detection windows to save computation. These candidate windows have a high recall rate, and certainly contain a lot of false positive windows.

4.1   Illustration of Stability

Fig.5 shows the comparison of whether using boosting-like algorithm on Caltech. The curve is relatively stable and volatility is smaller when using the algorithm. While it is poor in stability and volatility is large. The proposed algorithm achieves 0.48% performance gain. This algorithm can not only enhance the convergence stability, but also slightly improve detection accuracy without reducing the convergence speed.

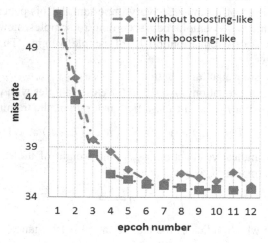

Fig. 5. The abscissa represents *epoch numbers*, and the ordinate denotes the *miss rate* which is tested by every trained model on Caltech-test dataset. This log-average miss rate is evaluated by the unified criteria proposed in [7].

4.2   Results

The evaluation method proposed in [7] is used to check detection performance of our framework. We evaluate the detection performance in the reasonable subset which is a commonly used pedestrian set. It includes pedestrians more than 49 pixels in height, and the occluded portions are less than 35%. We compared with the popular public approaches related to our method: ConvNet [11], ACF [8], JointDeep [5], HOGCSS [5]. The ACF is our low-level handcrafted channel features, and this paper uses HOGCSS prune candidate windows. Jointdeep also adopts low-lever channel features and CNN structure. Our experimental method is denoted by BDL.

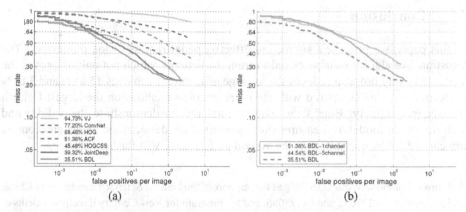

(a)   (b)

Fig. 6. (a) Comparison of *log-average miss rate* vs. *false positives per image* (FPPI) between our approach BDL and related methods on Caltech dataset. (b) Result of input channels design.

Fig. 7. Samples of pedestrian detection results on Caltech dataset

Fig.6 (a) shows the miss rate of BDL is 35.51%. It can be seen that our approach gets 15.85% and 3.81% performance gains compared with ACF and Joint Deep on Caltech test, respectively. Fig.6 (b) the experiment results of the influence of input channels in Section 2.1. When the input channel only has first L-channel, the miss rate is 51.36%. The introduction of $|G|$ and $G_1{\sim}G_3$ reduces the miss rate by 6.82%. Our method (BDL) uses 10 channels. It should be noted that complicated operations such as deformation, occlusion and context information are not employed in our framework. Fig.7 shows some detection results of pedestrian on Caltech.

5   Conclusion

In this paper, we propose a simple but effective pedestrian detection framework. The boosting-like algorithm is proposed to train the network which not only improves the system stability but also reduces the average miss rate. It achieves 15.85% and 3.81% performance gains compared with the corresponding methods on the largest Caltech dataset, respectively. Finally the experimental results demonstrate the validity and stability of our model. If measures such as multi-scale, deformation model and context are carried out by our structure, the system performance will further enhance.

Acknowledgments. We acknowledged the support of the Natural Science Foundation of China, under Contracts 61272052 and 61473086, and the Program for New Century Excellent Talents of the University of Ministry of Education of China.

References

1. Dalal, N., Triggs, B.: Histograms of oriented gradients for human detection. In: IEEE Conference on Computer Vision and Pattern Recognition, pp. 886–893. IEEE Press, San Diego (2005)
2. Viola, P., Jones, M.J., Snow, D.: Detecting pedestrians using patterns of motion and appearance. In: Proceedings of Ninth IEEE International Conference on the Computer Vision, pp. 53–161. IEEE Press, Nice (2003)
3. Hoiem, D., Efros, A.A., Hebert, M.: Putting objects in perspective. J. International Journal of Computer Vision **80**, 2137–2144 (2006)
4. Sermanet, P., Kavukcuoglu, K., Chintala, S., Lecun, Y.: Pedestrian detection with unsupervised multi-stage feature learning. In: IEEE Conference on Computer Vision and Pattern Recognition, pp. 3626–3633. IEEE Press, Rhode Island (2012)
5. Wanli, O.Y., Xiaogang, W.: Joint deep learning for pedestrian detection. In: 14th IEEE International Conference on the Computer Vision, pp. 266–274. IEEE Press, Sydney (2013)
6. Ess, A., Leibe, B., Gool, L.V.: Depth and appearance for mobile scene analysis. In: Proceedings of 11th IEEE International Conference on the Computer Vision, pp. 1–8. IEEE Press, Rio de Janeiro (2007)
7. Dollár, P., Wojek, C., Schiele, B., Perona, P.: Pedestrian detection: An Evaluation of The State of The Art. J. IEEE Transactions on Pattern Analysis and Machine Intelligence **34**, 743–761 (2012)
8. Dollar, P., Appel, R., Belongie, S., et al.: Fast Feature Pyramids for Object Detection. J. IEEE Transactions on Pattern Analysis and Machine Intelligence **36**, 1532–1545 (2014)
9. LeCun, Y., Bottou, L., Bengio, Y., et al.: Gradient-based Learning Applied to Document Recognition. J. Proceeding of the IEEE **86**, 2278–2324 (1998)
10. Chen, Y.N., Han, C.C., Wang, C.T., et al.: The application of a convolution neural network on face and license plate detection. In: Proc. 18th Int. Conf. Pattern Recognition, pp. 552–555. IEEE Computer Society Press, Hong Kong (2006)
11. Sermanet, P., Kavukcuoglu, K., Chintala, S., et al.: Pedestrian detection with unsupervised multi-stage feature learning. In: IEEE Conference on Computer Vision and Pattern Recognition, pp. 3626–3633. IEEE Press, Rhode Island (2012)

Human Behavior Recognition Based on Velocity Distribution and Temporal Information

Manyi Wang, Yaling Song[✉], Xiuxiang Hu, and Liang Zhang

Tianjin Key Lab for Advanced Signal and Image Processing of Civil Aviation,
University of China, Tianjin, China
songyaling1990@163.com

Abstract. Traditional temporal template method can recognize actions which have different speed, because of loss of speed information. On the other hand, this method will mix up the action which has the similar shape and different force. To solve this problem, a temporal template representation method is proposed to perfect the description of the motion which combines the MOFI(maximal optical flow image) and MHI(motion history image). In this paper, MOFI represents the distribution of the maximal optical flow. The optical flow is calculated by Farnebäck algorithm. The direction of movement is represented by different colors. The value of the speed is indicated by shades of color. Then, the maximal optical flow image is obtained. After calculating the wavelet moments of the maximal optical flow image and motion history image, we get feature vectors which are rotation, translation and scale invariant. Experiments based on UT-interaction dataset verify the effectiveness of the proposed method. Our method can distinguish similar actions, for example "hitting" and "patting" or "handclapping" and "handwaving".

Keywords: Human behavior recognition · The Maximal Optical Flow Image · Motion History Image · Wavelet moments · SVM(Support Vector Machine)

1 Introduction

In recent years, human behavior recognition remains a serious concern which is widely used in intelligent monitoring, human-computer interaction, motion analysis and virtual reality. The human body is non-rigid so that motion has a certain degree of freedom. Different people do the same action also has a big difference, therefore the recognition of human behavior is full of challenge.

So far, temporal template method based on vision is one of the commonly used methods to describe the body movement. This method is both simple and robust. A series of video frames are represented by a two-dimensional image. Behavior recognition based on temporal templates has many excellent researches, and has been used in many fields. LanChao [2] et al and Timotius [7] et al apply motion history images to gesture recognition. In [2], motion history image and pyramid histogram of oriented gradients are combined to identify hidden dangers during driving, such as smoking and calling. Timotius [7] et al use motion history image to recognize gestures on a simple human-computer interaction system. Chen [3] et al apply the temporal template method to facial expression recognition by combining the MHI-HOG (motion history

© Springer International Publishing Switzerland 2015
J. Yang et al. (Eds.): CCBR 2015, LNCS 9428, pp. 589–596, 2015.
DOI: 10.1007/978-3-319-25417-3_69

image- histogram of oriented gradient) and the Image-HOG of the face and body movements. In [5], temporal template method is applied to a kind of biological recognition technology--gait recognition. After single frame gait silhouettes are extracted and colored, the spatio-temporal gait images are obtained. The main task of intelligent monitoring is finding the abnormal behavior and eliminating hidden safety trouble promptly. This method is used for the detection of abnormal behavior by [11]. For the number of old people who live alone increasing, Julia[6] et al put forward using motion history image to observe the old people who live alone in order to find out whether they need help or not. In [14], 3VMHI (3 views motion history image) is proposed to identify the body posture. First they project depth images onto three orthogonal planes. Then they calculate motion history image of each orthogonal planes. Pyramid Histogram of Oriented Gradients is used to extract the features of the 3VMHI. In order to solve the self-occlusion problem, multi-direction motion history image (Directional Motion History Image) is proposed by Ahad [8,9] et al. For the repetitive action, Gupta[13] et al proposed RGB-motion history image. Dan [10] et al proposed multi-decay motion history image. This action representation method can make the decay parameter adaptive and make a series of continuous movement from some motion history images. In this paper, we propose an improved temporal template motion representation method combines the representation of speed and movement patterns to make up for the motion history image and motion energy image lack of speed information.

In 1962, M.K.Hu constructed 7 invariant moments with translation, rotation and scaling invariant. Bobick and Davis extract temporal templates' features by HU moment. According to this, they develop a virtual sport device to observe person's motion and react. In recent decades, with the development of wavelet, wavelet moments achieved more research and be widely used in image description. In this paper, the clustering result is compared to choose which should be used for feature extraction in color images. The article is divided into 4 parts: Section 2 forms motion history images and motion energy images. Section 3 calculates their HU moments and wavelet moment to compare the distance between them and clustering centers in order to know which one describe the motion better. Section 4 proposes the definition of maximal optical flow image(MOFI). Section 5 uses the SVM(support vector machine) method to train classifier and estimate MOFI' classification result.

2   Temporal Templates

2.1   Motion History Image

MHI convert image sequences to a 2-dimantional static image. The brightness of pixel and its appearance time are in proportion. The pixel which comes first is 255(white). The pixel which comes last is 0(black). The update function $\psi(x, y)$ shows whether there is a movement in current frame or not. Fig. 1. is the MHI in different time.

$$H_\tau(x,y,t) = \begin{cases} \tau & \text{if } \psi(x,y,t) = 1 \\ \max(0, H_\tau(x,y,t-1) - \delta) & \text{otherwise} \end{cases} \tag{1}$$

where (x, y) and t show the pixel' position and time, τ is duration, δ is the decay parameter.

Fig. 1. MHI of two actions in different time

2.2 Motion Energy Image

The MEI is the cumulative binary motion image, which can describe where a motion is in the video sequence, computed from the start frame to the final frame. Let $I(x, y, t)$ be an image sequence. Then the binary MEI $E_\tau(x, y, t)$ is defined as follows

$$E_\tau(x,y,t) = \begin{cases} 1 & if\, H_\tau(x,y,t) \geq 0 \\ 0 & otherwise \end{cases} \tag{2}$$

Fig. 2. MEI of two actions in different time

Corresponding to the Fig.1, Fig.2 shows the MEIs in different time.

3 Clustering Result Estimation

3.1 HU Moments

The regular moment m_{pq} is defined as follows:

$$m_{pq} = \iint x^p y^q f(x,y) dx dy \tag{3}$$

$$\mu_{p+q} = \iint (x - \bar{x})^p (y - \bar{y})^q f(x,y) dx dy \, \backslash eta. \tag{4}$$

The symbols $\bar{x}$ and $\bar{y}$ are the centroid of the original image, where $x = m_{10}/m_{00}, y = m_{01}/m_{00}$. μ_{p+q} is the central moments, and η_{p+q} is defined as the normalized central moments for μ_{p+q}. When $p+q \leq 3$, 7 invariant moments are obtained by η_{p+q}, the 7 moments are called HU moments. HU moments are rotation, scaling, translation invariants.

3.2   Wavelet Moments

Although wavelet moment invariants are rotation invariant naturally, translation invariant and scaling invariant are achieved by using a normalization base on regular moments. Translation invariant is achieved by transforming the original image into a new one whose first order regular moments, m_{01} and m_{10} are both equal to zero. This is done by transforming the original image to a new one $f(x+\bar{x}, y+\bar{y})$.

Scaling invariant can be achieved by transforming the original image $f(x, y)$ to a new function $f(x/a, y/a)$, where $a = \sqrt{s/m_{00}}$, S is the expected size of the image. Therefore, the original images can be normalized according to the following transformation:

$$\begin{pmatrix} x \\ y \end{pmatrix} \to \begin{pmatrix} (x-\bar{x})/a \\ (y-\bar{y})/a \end{pmatrix} \tag{5}$$

After normalization, wavelet moment has not only rotation, shift, scale invariants, but also has multi-resolution characteristic of wavelet. It is not sensitive to noise. It can extract image local features and global features so that it can describe the image comprehensively. In this paper, the wavelet moments of MHI and MEI are used as the templates.

After polar coordinating, the regular moment m_{pq} changes to

$$F_{pq} = \iint f(r,\theta) g_p(r) e^{jq\theta} r\,dr\,d\theta \tag{6}$$

where F_{pq} is the order moment, $p+q$ is the kernel function of radial variable r, p and q are integer parameters, $e^{jq\theta}$ is the kernel function of angle variable. Equation (6) can be rewritten as $F_{pq}=\int S_q(r)g_p(r)dr$, where $S_q(r)=\int f(r,\theta) e^{jq\theta}d\theta$.

We use wavelet basis function $\psi^{a,b} = \frac{1}{\sqrt{a}}\psi(\frac{r-b}{a})$ instead of $g_p(r)$, where $a=0.5^m$, $b=n*a$, $m=0,1,2,3$, $n=0,1,2,\ldots,2^m-1$, and $\psi_{m,n}=2^{m/2}\psi(2^m r-n)$. The expression of wavelet moment is $\|F_{m,n,q}\| = \| \int S_q(r) \psi_{m,n}(r)dr \|$. The discrete wavelet moment is

$$\|F_{m,n,q}\| = \sum_{r=0}^{1}\sum_{\theta=0}^{2\pi} f(r,\theta)\psi_{m,n}(r) e^{jq\theta} r \tag{7}$$

We choose the cubic B-spline wavelet as wavelet basis function

$$\psi(r) = \frac{4\alpha^{n+1}}{\sqrt{2\pi(n+1)}} \sigma_w \cos(2\pi f_0(2r-1))*\exp(-\frac{(2r-1)^2}{2\sigma_w^2(n+1)}) \tag{8}$$

where $n=3$, $a=0.697066$, $f_0=0.409177$, $\sigma_w^2=0.561145$.

3.3   Clustering Result Estimation

In this paper, HU moments and wavelet moments are used as classified examples in the K-means algorithm [15] respectively. Then the clustering centers are obtained. Euclidean distance is the estimation standard of distance between samples and centers.

Firstly, we define k categories (in this section, we use Weizmann Dataset, so $k=10$). The samples are classified into k categories, then the clustering centers can be obtained.

The average distance between the same kind samples and the clustering center is calculated by Euclidean distance and normalized. Finally, the degree of clustering of two kinds of moments can help us to find which one should be used to describe the motion.

Table 1. The Degree of the Clustering

Action No.	HU moments	Wavelet moments
bend	0.23242	0.10287
jack	0.13912	0.19495
jump	0.70881	0.52795
pjump	0.61104	1.00000
run	0.82492	0.45455
side	1.00000	0.66772
skip	0.32846	0.19229
walk	0.60740	0.17050
Wave1	0.22562	0.16524
Wave2	0.28407	0.11153
Average	0.49618	0.34898

The smaller the distance, the better clustering result. As Table 1 shows, the clustering result of wavelet moments is better than HU's. So, in the next study stage, we will use wavelet moments as the features of the motions.

4   A New Descriptor of Motion

To some similar actions, it's difficult to recognize by MHI only. Adding the speed information to the motion descriptor will make the descriptor more comprehensive. Optical flow has excellent spatial-temporal characteristic which includes instantaneous moving velocity and direction of pixels. The maximal optical flow image (MOFI) is obtained by calculating the maximal optical flow in the video and coloring. We use the Musell color system to represent color [16]. Different colors represent the moving direction, and its different intensity represent the speed. I_t shows the image at time t.

$$F_{max} = \begin{cases} F_{(x,y)t} & \text{if } F_{(x,y)t} > F_{(x,y)(t-1)} \\ F_{(x,y)(t-1)} & \text{otherwise} \end{cases} \qquad (9)$$

where $F_{(x,y)t}$ is the optical flow in (x, y) at time t. After comparing the optical flow at every moment, we get the maximal optical flow.

The optical flow can be used to represent the spatial-temporal characteristics of actions, but it is susceptible to environmental disturbances. We should extract foreground before computing the optical flow. In this paper, Gaussian Mixture Model is used to extract foreground. Moving region usually account for about 40 percent of the whole picture. Calculating optical flow of foreground can accelerate the operation.

We calculate optical flow by Farnebäck Algorithm. The size of feature window is $m \times m$. In this paper m is set to 5. Assuming that the optical flow of pixels in the window is roughly the same. Polynomial expansion is used to approximate the neighboring pixels. Every feature window is approximated by $f(x)=x^TAx+b^Tx+c$, $A_1(x)$, $b_1(x)$ and $c_1(x)$ are the first image's polynomial parameters, $A_2(x)$, $b_2(x)$ and $c_2(x)$ are the second image's polynomial parameters.

$$A(x) = \frac{A_1(x) + A_2(x)}{2}, \Delta b = -\frac{1}{2}(b_2(x) - b_1(x)) \tag{10}$$

Then the equation is obtained.

$$A(x)d(x) = \Delta b(x) \tag{11}$$

Supposing that the shift of pixels between two frames is slow.

$$\sum_{\Delta x \in I} w(\Delta x)\|A(x + \Delta x)d(x) - \Delta b(x + \Delta x)\|^2 \tag{12}$$

where $w(\Delta x)$ is the weight function of points around the pixel. We give the most weight to the center point and let the weights decrease radially. The minimum is obtained by $d(x)=(\sum wA^TA)^{-1}\sum wA^T\Delta b$.

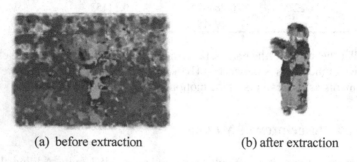

(a) before extraction   (b) after extraction

Fig. 3. The maximal optical flow image before and after extracting the foreground

5   Experiment

The MOFI is a RGB-image. For R-channel、G-channel and B-channel image, wavelet moments are calculated.UT-interaction dataset is used to evaluate the effectiveness of the method. UN-interaction dataset includes 6 interaction actions.

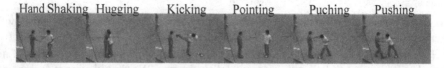

Fig. 4. UT-interaction dataset

Fig.4 shows every action in the UT-interaction dataset, these are handshaking, hugging, kicking, pointing, punching and pushing. Every action is done by different people in different scene. The gender, clothing and age of the person who does these actions are different. The MHIs and the MOFIs of theseactions are shown in Fig.5, and the first column and the third column represent theMHIs of actions, the second column and the forth column represent the MOFIs of actions.

It can be seen that the MHI of the two actions are very similar in Fig. 6. But their MOFIs are different because of the different force.

SVM is utilized to classify the actions. The leave-one-out method is used as the evaluation method. Assuming that there are K samples in the dataset. Cycle test is conducted for K samples to ensure that each sample is tested at least once and, simultaneously, other K-1 samples are considered as training samples. The average of the recognition accuracy shows the classifier's performance.

The recognition rate of this method is represented by confusion matrix. The elements in the main diagonal are the correct recognition rate. The other elements are the wrong recognition rate. UT-interaction dataset's average recognition rate is 89%.

Fig. 5. The MHIs and MOFIs of UT-interaction   Fig. 6. The MHI and the MOFI of patting and punching

Table 2. The confusion matrix of UT-interaction dataset

Action	A1	A2	A3	A4	A5	A6
A1	0.8	0.1	0.1			
A2	0.05	0.9	0.05			
A3	0.1	0.1	0.8			
A4				1		
A5					0.9	0.1
A6					0.1	0.9

6   Conclusion

A temporal template representation method is proposed to perfect the description of the motion which combines the MOFI and MHI. MHI show how the motion move. MOFI include the whole moving region and emphasize the speed information. To get a feature vectors as the motion's feature, we calculate and compare the spatial-temporal descriptors' wavelet moments and HU moments. Finally the wavelet moments are chosen to represent the motion. We train a SVM to do classification. The experimental results prove this method's effectiveness and robustness both on the single behavior and interaction behavior.

Acknowledgements. This work is jointly supported by National Natural Science Foundation of China (No.61179045).

References

1. Bobick, A., Davis, J.: The recognition of human movement using temporal templates. IEEE Transactions on Pattern Analysis and Machine Intelligence **23**(3), 257–267 (2001)
2. Lan, C., Coenen, F., Zhang, B.L.: Driving posture recognition by joint application of motion history image and pyramid histogram of oriented gradients. International Journal of Vehicular Technology (2014)
3. Chen, S.Z., Tian, Y.L., Liu, Q.S., et al.: Recognizing expressions from face and body gesture by temporal normalized motion and appearance features. Image and Vision Computing **31**(2), 175–185 (2013)
4. Lee, J., Park, J.-S., Seo, Y.H.: Emergency detection based on motion history image and adaboost for an intelligent surveillance system. In: Park, J.J., Barolli, L., Xhafa, F., Jeong, H.-Y. (eds.) Information Technology Convergence. LNEE, vol. 253, pp. 881–888. Springer, Heidelberg (2013)
5. Liu, J.Y., Zhang, N.N.: Gait history image: a novel temporal template for gait recognition. In: Proceedings of IEEE International Conference on Multimedia and Expo, pp. 663–666 (2007)
6. Julia, R., Gangolf, H.: Novel methods for feature extraction based on motion history images and evaluation with regard to altering viewing angles. In: Proceeding of IEEE third Conference on Consumer Electronics, pp. 1–5 (2013)
7. Timotius, I., Setyawan, I.: Hand gesture recognition based on motion history images for a simple human-computer interaction system. In: Proceedings of International Conference on Graphic and Image Processing, Singapore, pp. 87684M-1-87684M-5 (2013)
8. Ahad, M., Tan, J., Kim, H.: Motion history image: its variants and applications. Machine Vision and Applications **23**(2), 255–281 (2012)
9. Ahad, M., Tan, J., Kim, H., et al.: Action recognition by employing combined directional motion history and energy images. In: Proceedings of IEEE Computer Society Conference on Computer Vision and Pattern Recognition Workshops, San Francisco, pp. 73–78 (2010)
10. Dan, M., Toshitaka, M., Koji, K., et al.: Human motion analysis under actual sports game situations: sequential multi-decay motion history image matching. In: Proceedings of International Conference on Computer Vision Theory and Applications, pp. 229–236 (2013)
11. Hiba, H., Sreela, S.: Detection of abnormal behavior in dynamic crowded gatherings. In: Proceedings of Applied Imagery Pattern Recognition Workshop: Sensing for Control and Augmentation, Washington, DC, pp. 1–6 (2013)
12. Tian, Y.L., Cao, L.L., Liu, Z.C., et al.: Hierarchical filtered motion for action recognition in crowded videos. IEEE Transactions on Systems, Man, and Cybernetics **42**(3), 313–323 (2012)
13. Gupta, R., Jain, A., Rana, S.: A novel method to represent repetitive and overwriting activities in motion history images. In: Proceedings of International Conference on Communications and Signal Processing, Melmaruvathur, pp. 556–560 (2013)
14. Qin, S.X., Yang,Y.P., Jiang, Y.S.: Gesture recognition from depth images using motion and shape features. In: 2013 2nd International Symposium on Instrumentation and Measurement, Sensor Network and Automation, pp. 172–175 (2013)
15. Wang, D.L., Lu, Z.H., Li, S.B., et al.: Clustering analysis of complex energy formulation based on k-means. In: 2012 International Conference on Computer Science and Information Processing, pp. 1349– 1352 (2012)
16. Fred, W., Anna, K.: Interrelation of the natural color system and the munsell color order system. Color Research & Application **12**(5), 243–255 (2007)

Gesture Detection and Recognition Fused with Multi-feature Based on Kinect

Haifeng Sang and Wei Li[✉]

School of Information Science and Engineering,
Shenyang University of Technology, Shenyang, China
785349306@qq.com

Abstract. Aiming at the high demand of the background environment and the user, this paper designs a real-time human static gesture recognition algorithm based on the depth information of Kinect. The localization of the joint points of the hand is realized by using the Kinect skeleton. The depth image is acquired by the depth sensor, and the joint points of the hand are tracked continuously; After locating the position of the hand, the region of interest is intercepted, and the depth threshold is set up to segment the hand from the depth image; The segmentation image is processed by morphology, and the circular rate, filling rate, perimeter rate, convex hull, convex defect, Hu moments of the hand contour are 9 kinds of features; Six kinds (0 to 5) of gesture are recognized using SVM method. Recognition rate and robustness of gesture recognition experiments are conducted in static and dynamic environment respectively. The experimental results show that the proposed algorithm can achieve better recognition result in a variety of environments.

Keywords: Kinect · Depth data · Multi-feature · SVM

1 Introduction

Gesture recognition is a kind of human-computer interaction technology. Compared with the traditional keyboard and mouse, it's more natural, intuitive and easy to learn.

The limit method is limited by wearing the logo with color or using the background with fixed color, so that we can segment the gesture from the special color. [1] This method reduces the freedom of the gesture. The color detection method based on the color space distributes the color of the image to the corresponding color space for the threshold separation. Using skin detection method can isolated skin color regions directly from the image, but current technology mainly gets following problems: easy to influenced by complex background and light conditions; can not overlap with the face and other position that are similar with skin color, can not wear non skin gloves etc.

Aiming at the high demand of the background environment and the user, the system locates the hand joint by using Kinect skeleton. Segmenting the hand area combined with the depth image. Then extracting the features of hand contour, recognizing the gesture by using SVM classifier. This method overcomes the influence of complex background and light changing efficiently. The user doesn't need to wear any

© Springer International Publishing Switzerland 2015
J. Yang et al. (Eds.): CCBR 2015, LNCS 9428, pp. 597–606, 2015.
DOI: 10.1007/978-3-319-25417-3_70

device to operate system. In this way, the system reflects the convenience of human-computer interaction. The experimental results show that the proposed algorithm can achieve better recognition result in a variety of environments.

2   Human Static Gesture Recognition System

2.1   Whole System

This paper proposes a hand gesture recognition system based on Kinect depth data. It's more efficient to take advantage of depth data for overcoming the influence of complex background and light changing. It's more convenient for user to operate the system because there is no need to wear any device. First the localization of the joint points of the hand is realized by using the Kinect skeleton. The depth image is acquired by the depth sensor, and the joint points of the hand are tracked continuously. After getting the three-dimensional coordinate of hand, the ROI is intercepted and the depth threshold is set up to segment the hand from the depth image; Extracting feature of the segmented gesture and recognizing the gestures by using the SVM classifier. Fig. 1 is the process of gesture recognition system.

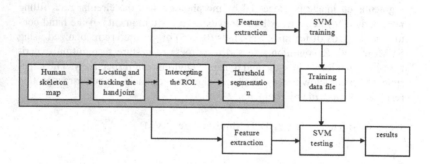

Fig. 1. Process of gesture recognition system.

2.2   Gesture Contour Acquisition Based on Depth Data

In this paper, we obtain the human skeleton map with Kinect. After hand location, we intercept a ROI of 140×140 pixels that contains the hand image. Then double threshold is set to segment the hand. In this way we can remove the influence of foreground and background efficiently. Fig. 2 is process of gesture acquisition.

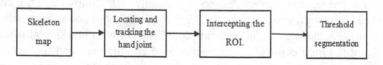

Fig. 2. Process of gesture acquisition.

2.2.1   Human Skeleton Map and Hand Locating and Tracking

Kinect can provide depth image using the depth camera. [2][3] Pixel of the image records the calibration depth. This depth camera can eliminate the background noise and extract the information of the people. Shotton labeled various parts of the characters' body in the picture. [4] Using large, rich and varied training data, he ensures the decision tree classifier assessing the various parts of the body is not misclassified no matter different individuals, clothing and posture. After the division of the body parts, the 3 dimensional position of the body joints can be predicted. [5] In the process of recognition, a depth map is required to identify the 3 dimensional positions of the individual joints, as shown in Fig. 3.

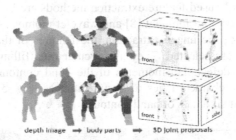

depth image ➡ body parts ➡ 3D Joint proposals

Fig. 3. Process of human body joints recognition.

After the human skeleton recognition, we map the three-dimensional coordinate on the depth image. Then obtaining the real-time 3D gesture information to achieve the gesture tracking.

2.2.2   Intercepting the ROI and Hand Segmentation

1)   Intercepting the ROI

According to the coordinate X and Y of the hand, intercepting a 140×140 pixels (according to the experience) ROI which includes the hand image part. In this way we can prevent the influence of the object in the same depth plane.

2)   Hand segmentation

①   depth theory

The Z coordinates of the hand position represent the relative distance between the hand and the Kinect. The general depth value is represented by 12bit, that is, the maximum is 4095. If the depth data we collected need to be expanded to a gray-scale figure, it should multiplied by a factor 255/4095.

②   threshold segmentation

The threshold range is T:

$$[Z \times (255/4095) - 5] < T < [Z \times (255/4095) + 5] \qquad (1)$$

The contour of the hand is determined according to the depth information of the hand. Then binaryzation and filtering of the contour are processed. In Fig. 4, A is gesture segmentation sketch map and B is a gesture contour segmentation graph.

A   B

Fig. 4. A) gesture segmentation sketch map   B) gesture contour segmentation graph.

2.3   Feature Extraction

After preprocessing, the binary image, edge image and contour matrix of gesture can be obtained. Commonly used feature extraction methods are Hu moment [6], Zernike moment [7], Fourier contour moment [8] and wavelet moment [9] and so on. In view of the characteristic of the image extraction, the features of the translation, rotation and scale invariance are selected. They are circular rate, filling rate, perimeter rate, convex hull, convex defect, Hu moments of the hand contour. These features can effectively reflect the characteristics of gesture images. Fig. 5 is the calculation of rectangle and circle of six kinds of hand contour.

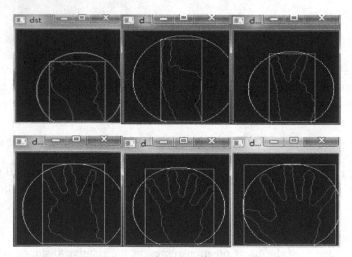

Fig. 5. Rectangle and circle of six kinds of hand contour.

2.3.1   Circular Rate, Filling Rate, Perimeter Rate

In this paper, we take the circular rate, the filling rate, the perimeter ratio of contour as features. Collecting 100 frames of each gesture with the method in 2.2 to analysis the feature. Table 1 is the average value of the circular ratio, filling ratio and perimeter ratio of 6 kinds of gestures.

Table 1. Circular ratio, filling ratio, perimeter ratio of 6 kinds of gestures.

	Zero	One	Two	Three	Four	Five
Circular ratio	1.66	2.75	3.49	4.25	5.33	5.94
Filling ratio	0.70	0.50	0.62	0.52	0.48	0.44
Perimeter ratio	0.73	0.83	1.09	1.17	1.45	1.61

1) Circular ratio

The circular ratio is the degree of the similarity between the contour and the circle. The ratio is close to 1, and the contour is close to the circle. L is the circumference of the contour and A is the area of the contour.

$$circularra\ tio = \frac{l^2}{4\pi A} \tag{2}$$

2) Filling ratio

The filling ratio is the ratio of the contour area to the rectangular area of the gesture. The larger the ratio, the more square the contour is. A is the contour area and R is the outer positive rectangular area.

$$fillingrat\ io = \frac{A}{R} \tag{3}$$

3) Perimeter ratio

The perimeter ratio is the ratio of hand contour and perimeter of minimum circumscribed circle. The larger the ratio, the more open the gesture is. L is perimeter of the contour and C is the perimeter of the minimum circumscribed circle.

$$perimeterratio = \frac{l}{C} \tag{4}$$

2.3.2 Convex Hull and Convex Defect

The convex hull and the convex defect of contour are used to describe the shape of the object. The convex hull and the convex defect of the gesture can better reflect the characteristics and status of the the gesture. The main idea of gesture convex hull points and convex defect points extraction is using Douglas Peucker algorithm to simplify the contour. Draw the outline of the simplified contour after the treatment, and then calculate and draw out the convex hull and convex defect points of the contour. Fig. 6 is convex hull points and convex defect points of six kinds of hand contour.

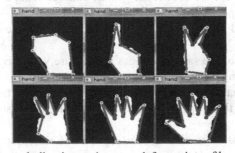

Fig. 6. Convex hull points and convex defect points of hand contour.

2.3.3 Hu Moment

In this paper, the Hu moment is chosen as the feature of gesture. The Hu matrix is a set of moment invariant which is composed of the nonlinear combination of moments. They well resolved the scale changing, image shifting, coordinate conversion and rotation changing during the process of feature matching.

7 invariant moments of Hu are composed of two order and three order central moment. The most useful information of the gesture image is contained in the low order moment. High order moments are complicated and noisy. In order to overcome the effects of noise and reduce the amount of computation, we choose the top four feature vector as the feature parameters of gesture image.

$$\phi_1 = \mu_{20} + \mu_{02} \tag{5}$$

$$\phi_2 = (\mu_{20} - \mu_{02})^2 + 4\mu_{11} \tag{6}$$

Using 2.2 method, gesture images of 100 frames are obtained. The average Hu moment parameter of each gesture is calculated. Table 2 is the average value of the first four invariant moments of the six gestures.

Table 2. The average value of the first four invariant moments.

	Zero	One	Two	Three	Four	Five
ϕ_1	0.1876	0.2683	0.2621	0.2376	0.2297	0.2207
ϕ_2	0.0076	0.0343	0.0256	0.0171	0.0098	0.0022
ϕ_3	0.0003	0.0056	0.0010	0.0007	0.0009	0.0008
ϕ_4	0.0001	0.0038	0.0021	0.0005	0.0002	0.0003

2.4 SVM Classifier

The SVM classifier is based on the theory of VC dimension and the least structural risk of statistical learning. In order to obtain the best generalization ability, SVM Seeks the best compromise between the complexity of the model and the ability to learn according to the limited sample information.

Considering the limitation of the sample and the accuracy of the recognition, this paper uses the SVM classifier to recognize the gesture.

1) In the training phase we extract the gesture contour using 2.2 method, and extract 100 frame images respectively for six different gestures.

2) Filter out the bad sample in the image and save the sample contains the complete gesture contour.

3) Extract features of the sample images and feature vector is sent to SVM training to construct the training parameters file.

4) In the testing phase we obtain real-time gesture contour and extract features by using the method in this paper. SVM classifier is used to test and then returns the recognition results.

Fig. 7 is the process of training and testing of SVM classifier.

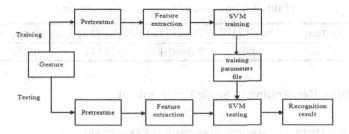

Fig. 7. Training and testing of SVM classifier

3 Experiment and Analysis

3.1 Gesture Recognition in Dynamic Environment

3.1.1 System Robustness Experiment

In addition to the normal environment, the system can still achieve good recognition results in a complex environment. According to the algorithm proposed in this paper, a series of experiments are carried out in the dynamic environment: the condition of complex background; the changing of environmental light conditions; gestures for rotation; the condition of multiple human interference. From Fig. 8 the correspondence of recognition results five and color image gesture, we can be see that the performance of the proposed algorithm is good in dynamic environment, and it shows strong robustness.

Fig. 8. Gesture recognition effect in dynamic environment.

3.1.2 Running Time Experiment

The recognition time of the system in this paper is tested in a complex background. The test set is 100 frames each gesture in SVM training stage. From the gesture detection to recognition, the average time of the system is 0.05s. Compared with other hand gesture recognition system [10][11][12], ours has a large advantage and is more suitable for online real-time gesture recognition applications.

Table 3. Comparison of system recognition time.

System	Paper [10]	Paper [11]	Paper [12]	This paper
Time	0.4s	0.09-0.11s	0.1333s	0.05s

3.2   Gesture Recognition in Static Environment

3.2.1   Fixed Distance Gesture Recognition Experiment

In the static environment, gesture recognition experiment is carried out in a complex background with same light condition. The official recommended distance of Kinect camera is between 1.2 meters to 3.8 meters. Experiments were conducted by 10 operators at a fixed distance of 1.5 m. The operator makes 0-5 six gestures 10 times respectively (guaranteed gestures are within the range) to calculate the recognition rate of gestures by using the proposed algorithm. Table 4 is the average recognition rate for each gesture in a static environment.

Table 4. The average recognition rate for each gesture.

Gesture	Zero	One	Two	Three	Four	Five
Recognition rate	97%	93%	96%	94%	94%	98%

From the table 4, the recognition rate of gesture zero and gesture five is higher and other hand gesture recognition rate is relatively low. The analysis is:

1) Human gesture is a flexible object and there is not a standard for gestures. The recognition error is caused by the randomness of the operator's finger.

2) The features of gesture zero and gesture five are more obvious than other gestures and the recognition rate is higher than other gestures.

3) Gesture recognition is carried out by using depth image. The operator need to locate the palm facing the camera in order to acquire a completed gesture image. When the operator's gestures have bias, the recognition rate will be affected.

3.2.2   Changing Distance Gesture Recognition Experiment

Gesture recognition experiments are conducted at different distances. From 0.5 meters, 10 operators test 5 times every 0.25 meters for the same gesture. Experimental results are shown in Fig. 9. The results show that when the distance between the camera and operator is 1.2-1.5 meters, recognition rate is the highest. When the distance is less than 0.5 meters, the system cannot obtain complete gesture image to recognize. When the distance is larger than 2 meters. The depth resolution is lower so that some information of the hand is lost and the recognition rate drops.

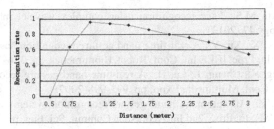

Fig. 9. Recognition results of different distance.

4   Conclusion

This method overcomes the influence of complex background and light changing efficiently. The experimental results show that the proposed algorithm can achieve better recognition result in a variety of environments.

At the same time, this system has some disadvantages, and it is also the research direction in the future.

1) Enrich the static gesture library by defining more gestures to improve the type of static gestures;

2) Try other feature extraction methods and classification. Different features, classification and recognition methods will get different recognition effect. Try new combination to improve the recognition rate;

3) Add gesture control function. Using the static gesture to control picture zoom, the start and stop of program and the game control. Enhance the practicality.

References

1. Yang, B., Sun, X.N., Fang, Z.Q.: Gesture Recognition in Complex Background Based on Distribution Features of Hand. Journal of Computer-Aided Design & Computer Graphics **22**, 1841–1848 (2010)
2. Sungil, K., Annah, R., Hyunki, H.: Using depth and skin color for hand gesture classification. In: IEEE International Conference, Las Vegas, pp. 155–156 (2011)
3. He, J.G., Shao, L., Xiao, D., Jamie, S.: Enhanced Computer Vision with Microsoft Kinect Sensor: A Review. IEEE Transactions on Cybernetics **43**(5) (2013)
4. Jamie, S., Andrew, F., Mat, C.: Real-time human pose recognition in parts from single depth images. In: 2011 IEEE Conference on Computer Vision and Pattern Recognition, Colorado Springs, pp. 1297–1304 (2011)
5. Georg, H., Rod, M., Wolfgang, B.: Lightweight palm and finger tracking for real-time 3D gesture control. In: IEEE Virtual Reality, Singapore, pp. 19–23 (2011)
6. Guo, J.Y., Zhang, Y.W.: Face Recognition Based on Moment Invariants and Neural Networks. Computer Engineering and Applications **7**(2008)
7. Teague, M.R.: Image analysis via the general theory of moments. Optical Society of America. **70**(8), 920–930 (2010)
8. Li, Y., Tong, X.L., Liang, C.Q.: Hand Gesture Recognition Based on Fourier Descriptors with Complex Backgrounds. Computer Simulation **22**(12), 158–161 (2005)

9. Song, C.D., Ali, M.S.: Face recognition using complex wavelet moments. Optics and Laser Technology **47** (2013)

10. Chung, W., Wu, X., Xu, Y.: A real-time hand gesture recognition based on Haar wavelet representation. In: Proc. IEEE Int. Conf. Robot. Biomimetics, pp. 336–341 (2009)

11. Fang, Y., Wang, K., Cheng, J., Lu, H.: A real-time hand gesture recognition method. In: Proc. IEEE Int. Conf. Multimedia Expo, pp. 995–998(2007)

12. Yun, L., Peng, Z.: An automatic hand gesture recognition system based on viola-Jones method and SVMs. In: Proc. 2nd Int. Workshop Comput. Sci. Eng, pp. 72–76(2009)

An Interactive Method Based on Random Walk for Segmentation of Facial Nerve in NMR Images

Zewei Zhang, Yue Ma, and Li Guo[✉]

School of Medical Imaging, Tianjin Medical University, Tianjin, China
gl6290@126.com

Abstract. In this paper, a nerves segmentation algorithm is presented based on the combination of hessian matrix and random walk techniques. We used hessian matrix to enhance the nerve area, then used morphological operations for nerve skeleton extraction and got the seed for random walk. Our algorithm has three phases, enhancement of nerve area on hessian matrix, extraction of skeleton points on enhanced area, finally segmentation of nerves. The experimental results show that the proposed method works well in segmentation of the nerve in NMR images with high accuracy.

Keywords: Nerve segmentation · Hessian matrix · Random walk

1 Introduction

Reliable and efficient facial nerve localization and segmentation are essential for diagnosis of maxillofacial diseases, treatment planning, and image-guide interventions. Tumors of the salivary glands represent 3%-10% of all head and neck neoplasms [1]. Among these neoplasms, 75%-85% occur in the parotid gland, from which 70%-80% are benign [2]. They include various lesions, the most common being pleomorphic adenoma, followed by adenolymphoma [3]. Today, surgery resection for benign parotid tumors has emerged as a procedure describable as both practical and safe.

Customarily, benign parotid tumors were often treated by total conservative paratidectomy (TCP), decreasing the risk of recurrence. Nevertheless, the main disadvantage of TCP is that the branches of the facial nerve may be injured, which is as a result of the contiguous adjacent relationship between the parotid gland and the facial nerve. Hence, partial superficial paratidectomy (PSP) combining with facial nerve dissection is considered as the standard method of choice. Most authors have drawn the conclusion that the cervical branch causes less damage than other branches from the study on facial nerves contrary dissection in parotid gland surgery [4,5].

During the facial nerve contrary dissection, the apriority distance from cervical branch to mandible angle is purposed to guide doctors to locate the facial nerve. However, as a result of the complexity adjacent relationship mentioned before, part of the tumor tissues constantly shoving the facial nerve, cause facial nerves displacement, which generates the inaccurate localization during the surgery. In the case of tumor tissues clinging to facial nerves, doctors attempt to avoid the planted recurrence

© Springer International Publishing Switzerland 2015
J. Yang et al. (Eds.): CCBR 2015, LNCS 9428, pp. 607–614, 2015.
DOI: 10.1007/978-3-319-25417-3_71

caused by tumor rupture, as well as protect the facial nerve from damaging. Consequently, accurate localization and segmentation of cervical branch preoperatively are of significance on decreasing the incidence of facial nerves dysfunction. The application based on the proposed method is widely used ranging from the image guide of parotid tumor resection to other maxillofacial surgery, including the SMAS rhytidectomy and platysma myocutaneous flap separation. The methodology proposed herein is of extreme help in increasing the successful rate and improving the prognosis of submandibular disease.

Hessian-based methods have been widely used in vessel enhancement, because Hessian matrix is able to retrieve directional and dimensional information of vessels from images [6-9]. Koller et al. presented the eigenvectors of Hessian matrix for vessel direction estimation and applied a matching filter along the vessel direction to detect vessel presence [10]. Sato et al. described a multi-scale line enhancement filter for the segmentation of curvilinear structures in medical images, which is based on the directional second derivatives of smoothed images using Gaussian kernel using multi scales with adaptive orientation selection using the Hessian matrix [11]. Compared to other famous Sato filter and Lorenz filter, a method developed by Frangi in is a representative method and produces much better results in practice [12,13]. In this paper, we used hessian matrix to enhance the nerve area, because the nerves have similar directional and dimensional information to vessels. The result shows that Hessian based nerve enhancement methods have been successful in segmentation of cervical branch of facial nerve.

2   Algorithm

2.1   Hessian Matrix

For an image I, we can regard the image $I(x,y)$ as the three-dimensional surface which is composed of the two-dimensional coordinates of pixels, as well as grayscale value corresponding to the pixel. Coordinates of the three-dimensional surface can be expressed as:

$$\{(x, y, z) \mid z = I(x, y)\}, \tag{1}$$

where (x,y) is the pixel location coordinates, $I(x,y)$ is the image gray value. Hessian matrix can be used to represent the curvature of the surface, which is defined as follows:

$$H(x, y) = \begin{bmatrix} I_{xx}(x,y) & I_{xy}(x,y) \\ I_{yx}(x,y) & I_{yy}(x,y) \end{bmatrix} \tag{2}$$

where $I_{xx}(x,y)$, $I_{xy}(x,y)$, $I_{yx}(x,y)$, $I_{yy}(x,y)$ denote the four second-order partial derivative of two-dimensional images $I(x,y)$

There are two eigenvalues λ_1, $\lambda_2(|\lambda_1| \leq |\lambda_2|)$ of Hessian matrix, which can be used to construct the enhancement filter.

Table 1. Possible patterns in 2D images, depending on the value of eigenvalues

Object shape	λ_1	λ_2
Tubular structure (bright)	L	H-
Tubular structure (dark)	L	H+
Circular structure (bright)	H-	H-
Circular structure (dark)	H+	H+

Because of the facial nerve has a higher intensity than background, the Hessian-based enhancement filter which was defined by Frangi for 2D vessel detection is:

$$f(x,y) = \begin{cases} 0, & \text{if } \lambda_2 > 0 \\ e^{-\frac{R_B^2}{2\beta^2}}(1 - e^{-\frac{s^2}{2c^2}}), & \text{elsewhere} \end{cases} \tag{3}$$

$$R_B = \frac{|\lambda_1|}{|\lambda_2|} \tag{4}$$

$$S = \sqrt{\lambda_1^2 + \lambda_2^2}, \tag{5}$$

where β and c are thresholds which control the sensitivity of the line filter to the measures R_B, S. The details about the hessian matrix based method are illustrated in Table 1. According to equation (3), the filter output will be the best when the width of facial nerves matches to a suitable scale factor σ. In the multi-scale vessel enhancement algorithm, $f(x,y)$ is calculated in different scale factor σ at each pixel, then take the maximum as the final filter output.

$$F(x) = \max_{\sigma} f(x,\sigma). \tag{6}$$

Frangi filter alone is not capable of completely segmenting the facial nerves from complex background. Hence, we need to further process the output of Frangi filter.

2.2   Random Walk

Grady [14] proposed an interactive algorithm for image segmentation based on the use of random walk. The main idea is as follows: a set of seed pixels are first specified by the user. For all the other pixels, using an efficient process, we determine the probability that a random walk starting at that pixel first reaches each particular seed, given some definition of the probability of stepping from a given pixel to each neighbour. The segmentation is formed by assigning the label of the seed first reached to the non-seed pixel.

The segmentation is formulated on a weighted graph [15, 16], where each node represents a pixel or voxel. A graph is a pair $G=(V, e, W)$. An edge e spanning two vertices, v_i and v_j, is denoted by e_{ij}. A weighted graph has a value (typically nonnegative and real) assigned to each edge called a weight graph. The weight of edge e_{ij}, is denoted by $W(e_{ij})$ or W_{ij}. The degree of a vertex is $d_i = \sum W_{ij}$ for all edges e_{ij} incident on v_i.

Given a weighted graph, a set of marked nodes V_M, and a set of unmarked nodes V_U, such that $V_M \cup V_U = V$ and $V_M \cap V_U = \emptyset$, we would like to label each node $v_i \in V_U$. With a label from the set $G = \{g^1, g^2, ..., g^k\}$ having cardinality $k = |G|$, we term a node $v_i \in V_U$, as free because its label is not initially known. Assume that each node $v_j \in V_M$ has also been assigned a label $y_i \in G$.

The random walk approach to this problem given in [15] is to assign to each node $v_i \in V_U$, the probability x_i^s that the random walk starting from that node first reaches a marked node $v_j \in V_M$ assigned to label g^s. The segmentation is then completed by assigning each free node to the label for which it has the highest probability, i.e. $V_i = max_s v_i^s$. Note that the values for y_i, if $v_j \in V_M$, are given by user-interaction.

It is known that the minimization of

$$E_{spatial} = x^{sT} L x^s \tag{7}$$

For a $n \times 1$, real-valued, vector x^s, defined over the set of nodes yields the probability x_i^s, that a random walk starting from node v_i, first reaches a node $v_j \in V_M$ with label g^s (set to $x_j^s = 1$), as opposed to first reaching a node $v_j \in V_M$, with label $g^{q \neq s}$ (set to $x_j = 0$), where L represents the combinatorial Laplacian matrix defined as

$$L_{v_i v_j} = \begin{cases} d_{v_i} & \text{if } i = j \\ -w_{ij} & \text{if } v_i \text{ and } v_j \text{ are adjacent nodes} \\ 0 & \text{otherwise} \end{cases} \tag{8}$$

The notation Lv_iv_j is used to indicate that the matrix Lv_iv_j is indexed by vertices v_i and v_j. By partitioning the Laplacian matrix into marked (i.e. pre-labeled) and unmarked (i.e. free) blocks

$$L = \begin{bmatrix} L_M & B \\ B^T & L_U \end{bmatrix} \tag{9}$$

And denoting an $|VM| \times 1$ indicator vector f^s, as

$$f_j^s = \begin{cases} 1 & \text{if } y_j = g^s \\ 0 & \text{if } y_j \neq g^s \end{cases}$$

The minimization of equation (7) with respect to x_U^s is given by

$$L_U x_U^s = -B f^s \tag{10}$$

This is a sparse, symmetric, positive-definite, system of linear equations.

3   Experimental Results and Analysis

3.1   Experimental Data

In order to verify the effectiveness of the algorithm, we applied the algorithm on the data including 16 cases which are provided by First Affiliated Hospital of Tianjin University of Traditional Chinese Medicine Radiology Department. The images are clear and voxels of each image are isotropous, which ensure the accuracy of the segmentation.

3.2   Extraction the Seeds

Skeleton extraction has been an indispensable and important part of medical image processing for a very wide range of applications, first proposed by Blum et al. We use skeleton extraction to get the skeleton of facial nerves and other tubular structures which are filtered by Frangi filter.

According to our analysis, we found that the skeleton extracted from the facial nerve is longitudinal in coronal or sagittal MR images. Therefore, using the longitudinal direction filter for filtering skeleton, we can remove the tubular structures in other directions from the image.

After the longitudinal direction filter, there are still some other tissues around the facial nerves not being removed. The manually marked point is the only one interactive action by a radiologist. Radiologists select a point P manually around the facial nerve. Some ray casting lines are used to extract the skeleton of facial nerves which is the nearest to the point P.

Then we extract skeleton of facial nerves spaced points as target points, and two points by the two sides of each target point as background points. These points are used for the random walk segmentation.

3.3   The Segmentation results

The original images on three different facial nerves are shown in Fig. 1. We can see that the facial nerves' shape is very like the vessels. So this paper presents the hessian matrix to enhance the nerves.

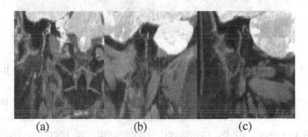

(a)   (b)   (c)

Fig. 1. The original images.

Fig. 2. The process of the segmentation for Fig.2 (b).

From the figure we can see that the seeds are the endpoint and bifurcation.

3.4   Discussion

In order to put the quality of our method into perspective, we compared the method proposed herein to ACM and Level Set for segmenting the facial nerves, which used the same set of NMR images to make the comparison fair and comparable. Fig.3. shows the segmentation results of these methods. Image (a) presents the original image. In image (b), we show the result of ACM. It is obviously to discover that the segmentation of facial nerve is incomplete, that only parts of the object region can be marked. The segmented image (c) corresponds to the result conducted after Level Set. The result points out a low astringency, which reduces the accuracy of the segmentation. We notice that our method result, presented in image (d), does better in both continuity and astringency. The high accuracy makes our method more competitive. Furthermore, the initial value affects the result seriously both in ACM and Level Set, while our method shows better.

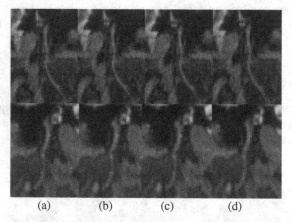

(a)   (b)   (c)   (d)

Fig. 3. The segmentation results of facial nerves in different algorithms.

Due to the highly accurate segmentation result, this method can be useful as an image-guide intervention tool for maxillofacial surgery, indicating the location of facial nerves that always need to be protected. Regarding the medical field, we hold the view that our works lie in developing a method which improves the treatment and prognosis of the submandibular surgery. In the field of engineering, we develop a methodology which is easy, convenient to apply and promising with techniques that have been described above. Furthermore, the proposed method is able to run on simple computers, which is available in hospital as a financially attractive solution.

4   Conclusions

In this work, we have proposed an automatic segmentation algorithm based on random walk to extract the facial nerve. Our design with the hessian matrix enhances the facial nerve from the other organizations. In the proposed facial nerves detection method, the seed information is extracted by using the skeleton extraction method, which is obtained by using hessian matrix enhancing the facial nerves area. And then, we improved the accuracy of facial nerves segmentation. The detected results have shown the superiority of the proposed method, which improve the correct rate of facial nerves segmentation. This methodology contributes to diagnosis of maxillofacial diseases and is able to be an essential component in image-guide intervention for specialist who is attempting to detect facial nerves.

Acknowledgments. This work was supported by National Natural Science Foundation of China (Project No.81000639) and China Postdoctoral Science Foundation (Project No.20100470791, Project No.201104307) and Tianjin Medical University's Undergraduate Research Opportunities Program (TMUUROP).

References

1. Foresta, E., Torroni, A., Di-Nardo, F., De-Waure, C., Poscia, A., Gasparini, G., Matteo-Marianetti, T., Pelo, S.: Pleomorphic Adenoma and Benign Parotid Tumors: Extracapsular Dissection vs Superficial Parotidectomy-Review of Literature and Meta-analysis. Or. Surg. Or. Med. Or. Pa. **117**, 663–676 (2014)
2. Woods, J.E., Chong, G.C., Beahrs, O.H.: Experience with 1,360 Primary Parotid Tumors. Am. J. Surg. **130**, 460–462 (1975)
3. Arshad, A.R.: Benign Parotid Lesions: Is near total Parotidectromy Justified? Ann. Acad. Med. Singap. **35**, 889–891 (2006)
4. Yi-Fan, L., Ye-Hai, L., Wen-Wen, C., Yi, Z., Jing, W.: Research Advancement on the Clinical Anatomy of Cervical Branch and Marginal Mandibular Branch of the Facial Nerve. Anat. Clin. **16**, 75–77 (2011)
5. Li-Min, L., Jing-Qiu, B., Chun-Ming, L., Xiao, M., Zhong-Hong, Y.: A Comparative Study of Three Methods of Facial Nerve Contrary Dissection in Parotid Gland Surgery. Chin. J. Oral. Maxil. Surg. **15**, 67–68 (2005)
6. Yuan, Y., Yi-shan, L., Albert, C.S.C.: VE-LLI-VO: Vessel Enhancement Using Local Line Integrals and Variational Optimization. IEEE T. Med. Imaging **20**, 1912–1924 (2011)
7. Wink, O., Niessen, W.J., Viergever, M.A.: Multiscale Vessel Tracking. IEEE T. Med. Imaging **23**, 130–133 (2004)
8. Sofka, M., Stewart, C.V.: Retinal Vessel Centerline Extraction using Multiscale Matched Filters, Confidence and Edge Measures. IEEE T. Med. Imaging **25**, 1531–1546 (2006)
9. Martinez-Perez, M.E., Hughes, A.D., Thom, S.A., Bharath, A.A., Parker, K.H.: Segmentation of Blood Vessels from Red-free and Fluorescein Retinal Images. Med. Imag. Anal. **11**, 47–61 (2007)
10. Koller, T.M., Gerig, G., Székely, G., Dettwiler, D.: Multiscale detection of curvilinear structures in 2-D and 3-D image data. In: 5th IEEE International Conference on Computer Vision, pp. 864–869. IEEE Press, Cambridge (1995)
11. Frangi, A.F., Niessen, W.J., Vincken, K.L., Viergever, M.A.: Multiscale vessel enhancement filtering. In: Wells, W.M., Colchester, A.C., Delp, S.L. (eds.) MICCAI 1998. LNCS, vol. 1496, pp. 130–137. Springer, Heidelberg (1998)
12. Sato, Y., Nakajima, S., Shiraga, N., Atsumi, H., Yoshida, S., Koller, T., Gerig, G., Kikinis, R.: Three Dimensional multi-scale line filter for segmentation and visualization of curvilinear structures in medical images. Med. Imag. Anal. **2**, 143–168 (1998)

13. Frangi, A.F., Niessen, W.J., Hoogeveen, R.M., Van Walsum, T., Viergever, M.A.: Quantitation of vessel morphology from 3D MRI. In: 2nd International Conference on Medical Image Computing and Computer-Assisted Intervention, pp. 358–367. Springer, Cambridge (1998)

14. Leo, G.: Random Walks for Image Segmentation. IEEE T. Pattern Anal. **28**, 1768–1783 (2006)

15. Meila, M., Shi, J.: Learning segmentation by random walk. In: 15th International Conference on Neural Information Processing Systems, Vancouver, pp. 873–879 (2001)

16. Meila, M., Shi, J.: A random walks view of spectral segmentation. In: the 8th International Workshop On Artificial Intelligence And Statistics, Florida, pp. 575–583 (2001)

Learning 3D Compact Binary Descriptor for Human Action Recognition in Video

Dongcheng Huang[✉], Xiang Li, Hongwei Li, and Weishi Zheng

School of Information Science and Technology,
Sun Yat-sen University, Guangzhou 510006, China
orangehdc@outlook.com, {lixiang651,hungway.lee}@gmail.com,
wszheng@ieee.org

Abstract. Hand-crafted descriptors are widely used for human action recognition in video at present. However, they are not optimized and may lack discriminative information. To compensate this drawback, this paper presents a learning-based 3D compact binary descriptor (3D-CBD) for human action video representation. The proposed descriptor is a 3D extension of the compact binary face descriptor (CBFD). Given a video sequence, we first extract pixel difference vectors (PDVs) in local volumes and then learn a feature mapping to project these PDVs into low-dimensional binary vectors. Finally, we cluster and pool these binary codes into histogram feature as the representation of the video sequence. Experimental results on two action datasets (KTH and WEIZMANN) demonstrate the effectiveness of the proposed descriptor.

Keywords: Action recognition · Binary descriptor · Feature learning

1 Introduction

Human action recognition in videos is one of the most active research areas in the past few years. It is essential for several applications including video indexing/browsing, video summarization, human-computer interfacing and smart home. However, it remains a challenging problem due to background clutter, occlusion, viewpoint changes and illumination changes.

Currently, hand-crafted features have shown excellent results for action recognition[1]. Calculation of these local features involves two steps: 1) interest point detection, which aims to find the informative regions for action understanding; 2) local feature representation, whose goal is to describe the patterns of extracted regions. Recently, many interest point detectors and descriptors have been proposed. Interest point detectors include detectors based on Gabor filters [2,3], Harris detector[4] and dense trajectories[5]. Feature descriptors range from optical flow, gradient information to spatio-temporal extensions of image descriptors such as 3D-SIFT[6] and HOG3D[7].

However, hand-crafted features usually require strong priors to engineer them by hand[8], which are simple but not discriminative enough. For example, HOG[9] descriptor quantizes gradient vectors into only 8 orientations and

© Springer International Publishing Switzerland 2015
J. Yang et al. (Eds.): CCBR 2015, LNCS 9428, pp. 615–623, 2015.
DOI: 10.1007/978-3-319-25417-3_72

HOG3D descriptor quantizes them into 20 orientations. Large amounts of contextual information may be lost in the quantization step in hand-crafted descriptors. In order to compensate the drawback of hand-crafted descriptors, we attempt to obtain video descriptors by a learning process for human action recognition.

In this work, we present a new learning-based descriptor to address the human action recognition problem in video. This new descriptor is inspired by the compact binary face descriptor (CBFD)[8] which is a learning method for still face image representation. We explore the idea of CBFD and extend it into 3D space to learn our descriptor which is termed as *3D Compact Binary Descriptor* (3D-CBD). More specifically, for each human action video sequence, we first extract pixel difference vectors (PDVs) in local volumes and then learn a feature mapping to project these PDVs into low-dimensional binary vectors. Finally, we cluster and pool the binary codes into histogram feature as the representation of the video sequence. Our 3D-CBD contains much compact and discriminative information by an effective learning process and could provide more reliability for action recognition compared with existing hand-crafted descriptors.

Extensive experiments are conducted on two human action datasets, including KTH [10] and WEIZMANN [11]. The results show that our learning-based 3D-CBD descriptor is more effective for video sequence representation in human action recognition.

2   Proposed Descriptor

2.1   Compact Binary Face Descriptor

In this work, the idea of compact binary face descriptor (CBFD) [8] is employed to learn our descriptor in 3D space. In this section, we first briefly review the CBFD learning method.

The CBFD is utilized to describe still images and its overall learning framework is shown intuitively in Figure 1. In this framework, for each pixel in an image, its neighbors in a $(2R+1) \times (2R+1)$ space are identified first. Then we compute the difference between the center point and neighboring pixels as the pixel difference vector (PDV). For each training image, we extract all the PDVs and learns a feature mapping to project each PDV into low-dimensional binary codes.

Specifically, given a training set containing N samples denoted by $X = \{x_1, ..., x_N\}$, where $x_n \in \mathbb{R}^d$ is the nth PDV. K hash functions are learned to map each training sample into a binary vector $b_n = [b_{n1}, ...b_{nK}] \in \{0, 1\}^{1 \times K}$. We denote $w_k \in \mathbb{R}^d$ as the projection vector of the kth hash function, b_{nk} as the kth binary code of x_n, and we can map each sample x_n into a binary code as follows:

$$b_{nk} = 0.5 \times (sgn(w_k^T x_n) + 1) \tag{1}$$

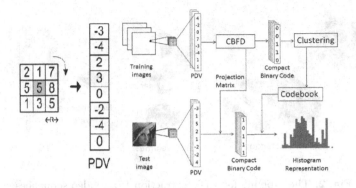

Fig. 1. The CBFD learning framework.

CBFD formulates the following optimization objective function in order to make b_n discriminative and compact:

$$\min_{w_k} J(w_k) = J_1(w_k) + \lambda_1 J_2(w_k) + \lambda_2 J_3(w_k)$$

$$= -\sum_{n=1}^{N} \|(b_{nk} - \mu_k)\|^2 + \lambda_1 \sum_{n=1}^{N} \|(b_{nk} - 0.5) - w_k^T x_n\|^2 \qquad (2)$$

$$+ \lambda_2 \| \sum_{n=1}^{N} (b_{nk} - 0.5)\|^2$$

where μ_k is the mean of the kth binary code of all the PDVs, λ_1 and λ_2 are parameters to balance the effects of J_1, J_2 and J_3. The first term J_1 in Eq.(2) is to maximize the variance of the learned binary codes. The second term J_2 in Eq.(2) is to minimize the quantization loss. The third term J_3 in Eq.(2) is to ensure that feature bins in the learned binary codes distribute evenly, so that they are more compact and discriminative.

After obtaining the projection matrix, we can map each training sample x_n into binary codes, then a codebook is learned from the binary codes by clustering. Therefore, for a test image, the PDVs could be first extracted and encoded into binary codes by the learned feature mapping. Then the histogram of the binary codes is calculated as the representation of the image under the learned codebook.

2.2   3D Compact Binary Descriptor

CBFD is a learning-based binary feature descriptor, which is more discriminative and more compact than the hand-crafted descriptors. However, it is designed for still images and cannot be directly applied to describe video sequence. Therefore, we extend it into 3D space and propose a 3D compact binary descriptor (3D-CBD).

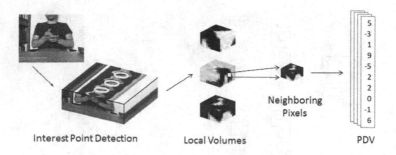

Fig. 2. The pipeline for PDV extraction from video sequences.

PDV Extraction. The proposed 3D-CBD is used to describe a local region in a video. Commonly, local regions are determined by using an interest point detector or by dense sampling of the video [7]. In this work, we use the Harris3D detector [4]. Because the interest points detected by Harris3D detector are sparsely distributed so that the selected local volumes will not be highly overlapped, which can reduce the redundancy of the training data.

In [9], the size of the selected local volumes$(\Delta_x, \Delta_y, \Delta_t)$ is given by $\Delta_x, \Delta_y = 2k\sigma, \Delta_t = 2k\tau$. But we use a fixed size in our work for simplicity. For each pixel in the local volumes, we identify its neighbor in a $(2R+1)\times(2R+1)\times(2T+1)$ space, then we compute the difference between the center point and the neighboring pixels as the PDV, which is similar to the CBFD. Finally, we combined the PDVs in each local volumes as an unoptimized representation of the video. The overall process is shown in Figure 2.

The Training Process. After all the PDVs are extracted, we can get a training set $X = \{x_1, x_2, ..., x_N\}$, where $x_n \in \mathbb{R}^d$ is the nth pixel difference vector (PDV). Then we follow the step in CBFD[8] to learn the projection matrix W and codebook D. We denote the projection matrix as $W = [w_1, w_2, ...w_K] \in \mathbb{R}^{d \times K}$. For each sample x_n, we can obtain a binary vector:

$$b_n = 0.5 \times (sgn(W^T x_n) + 1) \tag{3}$$

Then Eq.(2) can be re-written as

$$\min_{w_k} J(w_k) = J_1(w_k) + \lambda_1 J_2(w_k) + \lambda_2 J_3(w_k)$$

$$= -\frac{1}{N} \times tr((B - U)^T (B - U)) + \lambda_1 \|(B - 0.5) - W^T X\|_F^2 \tag{4}$$

$$+ \lambda_2 \|(B - 0.5) \times \mathbf{1}^{N \times 1}\|_F^2$$

where $B = 0.5 \times (sgn(W^T X) + 1) \in \{0, 1\}^{K \times N}$ is the matrix of all the binary codes and $U \in \mathbb{R}^{N \times K}$ is the mean matrix of the binary vectors obtained from the training samples. According to the mathematical derivation in [8], the objective function in Eq.(4) can be re-written as

$$\min_{W} J(W) = tr(W^T Q W) + \lambda_1 \|(B - 0.5) - W^T X\|_2^2$$
$$- \lambda_2 \times N \times tr(\mathbf{1}^{1 \times K} W^T X \mathbf{1}^{N \times 1}) \qquad (5)$$
$$\text{subject to:} \qquad W^T W = I$$

where

$$Q \triangleq -\frac{1}{N} \times (X X^T - 2 X M^T + M M^T) + \lambda_2 X \mathbf{1}^{N \times 1} \mathbf{1}^{1 \times N} X^T \qquad (6)$$

The constraints, $W^T W = I$ are used to make W to be orthogonal projections, and $M \in \mathbb{R}^{N \times d}$ is the mean matrix of all the PDVs.

We follow the step in [8] to update B with a fixed W and update W with a fixed B iteratively. The process is repeated until convergence and we can get the solution of W. Then we project each PDV into a binary feature vector and apply K-means method to learn a codebook from the training set.

3D-CBD Representation. After the projection matrix W and codebook D are learned in the training process, given a set of video sequences, we first follow the PDV extraction step as mentioned above to get the unoptimized representation $X_i = \{x_{i_1}, ..., x_{i_n}\}$, where X_i denotes the extracted PDVs of the ith video. Then the PDVs are mapped into binary code by the learned projection matrix. Finally, we calculate their distribution according to the learned codebook as a histogram feature descriptor of the video sequences. The proposed descriptor is availably utilized to represent the video sequences, which is more discriminative and compact than the hand-crafted video descriptors.

3   Experiments

3.1   Datasets

KTH Dataset. The KTH dataset[10] contains six human action classes (see Figure 3) performed by 25 subjects in 4 different scenarios (outdoors, outdoors with scale variation, outdoors with different clothes and indoors). In total, the data consists of 599 video clips (160×120 pixels).

WEIZMANN Dataset. The WEIZMANN dataset was provided by Blank et al.[11] in 2005. It contains 93 low-resolution (180×144 pixels) video clips of 9 different people. WEIZMANN dataset contains 10 different actions (see Figure 3). The length of each video clips is about 2 seconds and the camera setting is fixed.

Fig. 3. Example frames from KTH dataset (top), WEIZMANN dataset (middle and button).

3.2 Experimental Settings

For the KTH dataset, we followed the setting of Laptev et al.[12] and divided the video sequences into test set (9 people) and training set (the remaining 16 people). For the WEIZMANN dataset, we choose Leave-One-Out-Cross-Validation (LOOCV) as suggested by Scovanner et al.[6].

For the proposed 3D-CBD, in the PDV extraction step, we empirically set $\Delta_x, \Delta_y = 18, \Delta_t = 14, R = T = 3$. The parameters λ_1 and λ_2 was simply set as 0.001 and 0.0001 as suggested by Lu et al.[8]. We optimized binary code length L and the codebook size S and observed that the best result was obtained when $L = 15$ and $S = 1500$.

For classification, we use a linear support vector machine in the publicly available machine learning library LIBLINEAR[13].

3.3 Results and Analysis

In this section, we compare our 3D compact binary descriptor (3D-CBD) with other widely used hand-crafted video descriptors on KTH and WEIZMANN datasets. The confusion matrices of the proposed 3D-CBD are shown in Figure 4 and the results of different descriptors are all reported in Table 1.

For the KTH dataset, it is evident that the proposed 3D-CBD performs much better than most of the other hand-crafted descriptors in Table 1, e.g. 3D-CBD achieves 3.1% improvement over HOG3D, 10.5% improvement over HOG, 5.5% over Cuboid, and 1.7% over 3DGrad, respectively. These results highlight the effectiveness of the proposed descriptor. Furthermore, Table 1 also shows that our descriptor has a competitive performance with HOF descriptor. The result of [2] on KTH is not reported in Table 1, since this method uses more training data and is not comparable to ours.

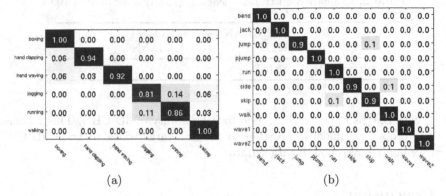

(a)   (b)

Fig. 4. Recognition performance of our 3D-CBD method using confusion matrices: (a) KTH dataset, accuracy: 92.1% (b) WEIZMANN dataset, accuracy: 96.8%

Table 1. Comparison with other hand-crafted descriptors on the KTH and WEIZMANN datasets.

Methods	KTH	WEIZMANN
3D-CBD	**92.1%**	**96.8%**
HOG3D[7]	89.0%	84.3%
Cuboid[3]	86.6%	87.3%
3DGrad[14]	90.4%	92.3%
IIOG[9]	81.6%	-
HOF[9]	92.1%	-
Local Jets[10]	71.7%	-
Gradients+PCA[15]	86.7%	-
3D SIFT[6]	-	82.6%
Spin Images[16]	-	74.2%
ST Features[16]	-	68.4%
Clouds of STIP[2]	-	96.7%

For the WEIZMANN dataset, it is clear that the 3D-CBD gives a significant improvement over the vast majority of other descriptor in Table 1. More specifically, the precision rate is 96.8% for 3D-CBD, versus 84.3% for HOG3D, 87.3% for Cuboid, 92.3% for 3DGrad, 82.6% for 3D SIFT .The advantage of 3D-CBD for human action recognition is demonstrated once again. From the Table 1, we can see that the performance of Clouds of STIP is closed to our descriptor. This is because the descriptor uses a feature selection method after feature extraction, it has a superior performance as well.

Moreover, we evaluate the transfer learning performance of 3D-CBD. Table 2 shows that our 3D-CBD learned from KTH gives a comparable result with the default 3D-CBD setting on WEIZMANN. But the performance of the 3D-CBD learned from WEIZMANN falls by 6.5% on KTH. That's because KTH (599 video clips) contains a greater variety of data than WEIZMANN (93 video

Table 2. Evaluation on transfer learning performance of 3D-CBD

	WEIZMANN→ KTH	KTH→ MANN	WEIZ-
Recognition Rate	85.6%	96.8%	

clips), which helps improve the generalization ability of 3D-CBD. This transfer learning properties make it possible to use non-target data to train 3D-CBD when we don't have enough target data.

4   Conclusion

In this paper, we have proposed a learning-based 3D compact binary descriptor (3D-CBD) for human action recognition in video which is a 3D extension of compact binary face descriptor (CBFD). Given a video sequence, we first use a Harris3D detector and extract PDVs from the local volumes of interest points, then we follow the step of CBFD method to quantize PDVs into compact binary code and calculate the histogram feature. Experimental results on the KTH and WEIZMANN datasets show that our 3D compact binary descriptor is more discriminative than other hand-crafted video descriptors.

Acknowledgments. This work was supported partially by the National Natural Science of Foundation of China (Nos. 61472456) and Guangzhou Pearl River Science and Technology Rising Star Project under Grant 2013J2200068 and the authors would like to thank Xiaozhong Chen's valuable advice on paper writing.

References

1. Wang, L., Qiao, Y., Tang, X.: Action recognition with trajectory-pooled deep-convolutional descriptors. arXiv preprint arXiv:1505.04868 (2015)
2. Bregonzio, M., Gong, S., Xiang, T.: Recognising action as clouds of space-time interest points. In: 2009 IEEE Conference on Computer Vision and Pattern Recognition (CVPR), pp. 1948–1955. IEEE (2009)
3. Dollár, P., Rabaud, V., Cottrell, G., Belongie, S.: Behavior recognition via sparse spatio-temporal features. In: VS-PETS, pp. 65–72 (2005)
4. Laptev, I.: On space-time interest points. International Journal of Computer Vision **64**(2–3), 107–123 (2005)
5. Wang, H., Kläser, A., Schmid, C., Liu, C.L.: Action recognition by dense trajectories. In: 2011 IEEE Conference on Computer Vision and Pattern Recognition (CVPR), pp. 3169–3176. IEEE (2011)
6. Scovanner, P., Ali, S., Shah, M.: A 3-dimensional sift descriptor and its application to action recognition. In: ACM International Conference on Multimedia, pp. 357–360. ACM (2007)

7. Klaser, A., Marszałek, M., Schmid, C.: A spatio-temporal descriptor based on 3d-gradients. In: BMVC 2008-19th British Machine Vision Conference, pp. 275:1–275:10. BMVA (2008)

8. Lu, J., Liong, V.E., Zhou, X., Zhou, J.: Learning compact binary face descriptor for face recognition. IEEE TPAMI (2015)

9. Laptev, I., Marszałek, M., Schmid, C., Rozenfeld, B.: Learning realistic human actions from movies. In: 2008 IEEE Conference on Computer Vision and Pattern Recognition (CVPR), pp. 1–8. IEEE (2008)

10. Schüldt, C., Laptev, I., Caputo, B.: Recognizing human actions: a local SVM approach. In: 2004 Proceedings of the 17th International Conference on Pattern Recognition, ICPR 2004, vol. 3, pp. 32–36. IEEE (2004)

11. Blank, M., Gorelick, L., Shechtman, E., Irani, M., Basri, R.: Actions as space-time shapes. In: 2005 Tenth IEEE International Conference on Computer Vision, ICCV 2005, vol. 2, pp. 1395–1402. IEEE (2005)

12. Wang, H., Ullah, M.M., Klaser, A., Laptev, I., Schmid, C.: Evaluation of local spatio-temporal features for action recognition. In: BMVC 2009-British Machine Vision Conference, pp. 124–1. BMVA (2009)

13. Fan, R.E., Chang, K.W., Hsieh, C.J., Wang, X.R., Lin, C.J.: Liblinear: A library for large linear classification. The Journal of Machine Learning Research, 1871–1874 (2008)

14. Ballan, L., Bertini, M., Del Bimbo, A., Seidenari, L., Serra, G.: Effective codebooks for human action categorization. In: ICCV Workshops (2009)

15. Wong, S.F., Cipolla, R.: Extracting spatiotemporal interest points using global information. In: 2007 IEEE 11th International Conference on Computer Vision, ICCV 2007, pp. 1 8. IEEE (2007)

16. Liu, J., Ali, S., Shah, M.: Recognizing human actions using multiple features. In: 2008 IEEE Conference on Computer Vision and Pattern Recognition (CVPR), pp. 1–8. IEEE (2008)

Multi-scale Medical Image Segmentation Based on Salient Region Detection

Yingxue Wu[1], Xi Zhao[2], Guiyang Xie[1], Yangkexin Liang[1], Wei Wang[1], and Yue Li[1(✉)]

[1] College of Software, Nankai University, Tianjin 300071, China
liyue80@nankai.edu.cn
[2] School of Computer Science and Information Engineering,
Tianjin University of Science and Technology, Tianjin 300222, China

Abstract. In this paper, we introduce an adaptive medical image segmentation algorithm based on salient region detection. By implementing Gaussian Mixture Models and classifying the output in correlation comparison, our method is capable to localize the Region of Interest in multi-scales without adjusting any parameters. Two different types of medical image datasets, containing different scales of medical images are used for evaluate the method, comparing the other six general segmentation algorithms. Experiments prove that our method can self-adapt for different images, and outperform the other algorithms in all of the global, regional and vessel scales.

Keywords: Medical image segmentation · Salient region detection · Gaussian mixture models

1 Introduction

In bio-medical image processing, precise image segmentation would aid doctors greatly in providing visual means for inspection of anatomic structures, identification of disease and tracking of its progress, and even in surgical planning and simulation. In medical image analysis, low contrast and resolution greatly increase the difficulty in designing an effective segmentation algorithm. Moreover, background noises, instrumental limitations of reconstruction algorithms and body movements of the patient increase to the complexity of the task. Although there have been quite a lot of research on medical image segmentation [1][2][3][4], few algorithm can deal with general kinds of medical image with a precise segmentation at the same time. In general, most of the current medical image segmentation methods share a high strong pertinence and can be divided into two categories: one is based on prior knowledge of pathology, the other is taking advantage of the strong features of the image processing without the prior knowledge.

Medical image segmentation based on prior knowledge mainly utilizes the organ anatomical and morphological information, as well as the geometry and topology relation, to construct a model for rough image segmentation. This kind of method is

© Springer International Publishing Switzerland 2015
J. Yang et al. (Eds.): CCBR 2015, LNCS 9428, pp. 624–632, 2015.
DOI: 10.1007/978-3-319-25417-3_73

particularly suitable for segmenting the organs with certain shapes, such as the left and right atria. [1] presents an improvement to the watershed transform that enables the introduction of prior information in its calculation, then applies this algorithm to knee cartilage and gray matter/white matter segmentation in MR images. [2] models with organ shape exhibiting better performance than other existing methods on 2D prostate localization and 3D prostate segmentation in MRI scans.

Algorithms, without using prior information but depending on the strong image features, require the image containing obvious boundary or strong color contrast. The traditional edge detection methods such as gradient based operators like Sobel, Prewitt, Robert, cannot output precise edges in medical image with strong noise. Considering these difficulties, [3] proposes a method called as Active Contour method capturing edge for brain MRI images. For the image with strong color contrast, the segmentation based on threshold is usually taken into consideration to extract the region of interest from background. [4] proposed a threshold segmentation method to extract the cerebral vessels in MRA images.

Once medical images neither contain strong feature nor clear prior information, designing a feasible method turns to a process of guessing out the parameters in the existing methods. Such guessing is a time-consuming and blind process. A potential solution is to find a segmentation method which simulates human vision to extract the salient regions, which is the region of interest in an image and determined by visual attention mechanism. The main contribution of the paper is to introduce a self-adapted segmentation method to extract salient region and prove the feasibility of the employed method in segmenting medical image at multi-scales. Comparing with the other six general methods for segmentation, the method we present proves to be more effective to variety medical images in multi-scales.

2   Algorithm Presentation

This paper presents a self-adaptive image segmentation method based on salient region extraction inspired by [10]. This emerging topic on visual attention mechanism has been widely studied since the concept on salient region is proposed.

Our method can effectively discover the global salient regions by considering the appearance similarity and spatial distribution of each image pixel. In order to get an abstract global representation, we cluster image colors and represent them using Gaussian Mixture Models (GMM). Each pixel color C_i is represented as a weighted combination of several GMM components, and the probability of each pixel belong to a component m as following:

$$p(\mathrm{m}\,|\,C_k) = \frac{\omega_m N(C_k\,|\,\mu_m,\Sigma_m)}{\sum_m \omega_m N(C_k\,|\,\mu_m,\Sigma_m)} \tag{1}$$

where ω_m, μ_m and Σ_m, represent respectively the weight, mean color, and covariance matrix of the mth component. We run color quantization in RGB color space with each color channel in to 12 uniform parts and choose the most frequently occurring color.

Generally speaking, the regions with high contrast compared to other region, is attached to great importance. So the contrast of GMM component m_i is defined as:

$$T(\mathrm{m}_i) = \sum_{m_i \neq m_j} \exp(\frac{D(\mathrm{m}_i, \mathrm{m}_j)}{-\sigma^2}) \cdot \omega_{m_j} \cdot \| \mu_{m_i} - \mu_{m_j} \| \tag{2}$$

where $D(m_i, m_j)$ is the spatial distance between the two GMM components m_i and m_j, and we use $\sigma^2 = 0.4$ in the experiment.

While direct GMM will ignore the valuable spatial correlations in images, we plan building the correlation between each two GMM components to discover the spatial correlations. The correlation of two GMM components m_i and m_j is defined below:

$$C(\mathrm{m}_i, \mathrm{m}_j) = \frac{\sum_{C_k} \min(p(\mathrm{m}_i \mid C_k), p(\mathrm{m}_j \mid C_k))}{\min\left(\sum_{C_k} p(m_i \mid C_k), \sum_{C_k} p(\mathrm{m}_j \mid C_k)\right)} \tag{3}$$

By computing the correlation of each pair GMM components, the correlation matrix is obtained, which can be considered as the similarity measurement for the components. Then we cluster the GMM components based on the matrix using method[13], thus the probability of each pixel color C_k belonging to each cluster S is the sum of its probabilities for belonging to all GMM components m in the cluster:

$$p(S \mid C_k) = \sum_{m \in S} p(\mathrm{m} \mid C_k) \tag{4}$$

We adopt the method suggested in [11] to compute the color spatial distribution. Referring to[11], the distribution of each cluster component can be compute by combining the horizontal and vertical spatial variances together. The horizontal variance of each cluster S is defined as:

$$V_h(S) = \frac{1}{|K|_S} \sum_k p(S \mid C_k) \cdot | \mathrm{x}_h - M_h(S) |^2 \tag{5}$$

$$M_h(S) = \frac{1}{|K|_S} \sum_k p(S \mid C_K) \cdot x_h \tag{6}$$

where x_h is the x-coordinate of the pixel k, and $|K|_S = \Sigma_k P(S|C_k)$. The vertical spatial variance $V_v(S)$ can be computed similarly. So the spatial variance of a cluster S is

$$V(S) = V_h(S) + V_v(S) \tag{7}$$

The appearance similarity and spatial distribution are the two saliency detectors, and each of them is a complementary to each other. Combing the two saliency detector through the measure[14], we can achieve the final saliency map.

3   Experiments

In this section, we evaluates our method on two different types of medical image datasets, and compared it with 6 alternate methods, which are Otsu[5], Cell segmentation(Cellseg), Graph based image segmentation(Graseg)[8], Fuzzy logic edge detection(IFDedge)[6], K-means[7] and segmentation using Particle Swarm Optimization(PSO)[9]. In the experiments, the breast image dataset was obtained from the BI-RADs[12], and tested in global scale. The cervical spine dataset is gathered by the clinic doctors. Three groups of experiments are respectively employed in global scale, the regional scale and the vessel scale. We compute the average IoU and the image precision with a given IoU for each methods in every image dataset for measurement. The IoU, intersection-over-union, is determined as $N_{seg \cap gt} / N_{seg \cup gt}$, where $N_{seg \cup gt}$ and $N_{seg \cap gt}$ are the pixel numbers of the intersection and union of the segmentation result and the ground truth segmentation, respectively. The image precision is defined as the ratio of number of the images that are above the given IoU and the number of the whole image dataset.

3.1 Evaluation on Breast Image Dataset

In the breast image dataset, the salient regions, which is the part been highlighted, are defined as the breast regions after removing the fat and ectopectoralis. The images in the dataset are captured in different shapes, sizes, and brightness, and are difficult to segment accurately. Figure 1 gives a visual comparison of different methods. Our result shows a more accurate region than others. Table 1 and Figure 2 are average IoU and image precision results

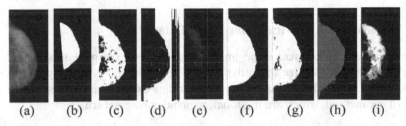

(a)   (b)   (c)   (d)   (e)   (f)   (g)   (h)   (i)

Fig. 1. Visual comparison for the segmentation result. (a) Original image,(b) ground truth ,(c) Cell segmentation, (d) Graph based segmentation, (e) Fuzzy logic edge detection, (f) K-means, (g) Otsu, (h) PSO and (i) Ours.

As the result in Table 1 shown, our method generally outperforms the other 6 methods on the breast dataset with the average IoU 0.638.

Table 1. Comparison of average IoU for different segmentation methods in breast image dataset

Method	Ours	Cellseg	Graseg	IFDedge	K-means	PSO	Otsu
Average IoU	0.638	0.588	0.349	0.196	0.611	0.140	0.634

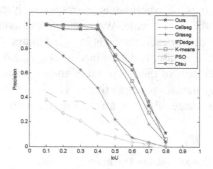

Fig. 2. The precision comparison based on the given IoU in breast image dataset

In the experiments, the salient and non salient regions are adhered to each other, resulting in the fact that K-means and Otsu also perform better. Figure 2 can illustrate the result intuitively. For Graseg, PSO, and IFDedge methods, the three methods show poor performance with low accuracy for any given IoU. While for the other four methods, including the proposed one, the performances are generally the same.

3.2   Evaluation on Cervical Spine Image Dataset

The experiments on cervical spine image dataset proves the method we employ not only can accurately localize the salient regions but also self-adaptively suit in multi-scales. In this image dataset, we make three groups experiment to illustrate the adaptivety of our method, which are in global, regional and vessel scales.

3.2.1   Evaluation on Cervical Spine Image Dataset in Global Scale.

The global scale cervical spine images are the transaction cervical spine images with complex background which includes the blood vessels and anocelia. Such complex background greatly increases the difficulty to extract the salient regions. Figure 3 gives an presentation for the original image and results of all methods. The salient regions here are defined as many non-adhesion blood vessels, which are distributed in the center and at the edge of the image. For Graseg, it tends to consider the anocelia as the target region. For Cellseg, K-means and Otsu, they add too much environment in the vessels. Only our method can accurately extract the blood vessels.

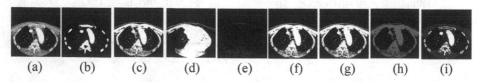

(a)   (b)   (c)   (d)   (e)   (f)   (g)   (h)   (i)

Fig. 3. Visual comparison for the segmentation result. (a) Original image,(b) ground truth ,(c) Cell segmentation, (d) Graph based segmentation, (e) Fuzzy logic edge detection, (f) K-means, (g) Otsu, (h) PSO and (i) Ours.

Table 2. Comparison of average IoU for different segmentation methods in global scale

Method	Ours	Cellseg	Graseg	IFDedge	K-means	PSO	Otsu
Average IoU	0.719	0.292	0.160	0.027	0.216	0.393	0.278

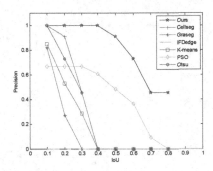

Fig. 4. The Precision comparison based on the given IOU in global scale

Table 2 and Figure 4 illustrate the method performance measured by IoU. Corresponding to the visual observation, our method is far superior to other methods. In table 2, the behavior of our algorithm perform excellent with the average IoU 0.719, which is generally higher than others at least thirty percentage points. The reason why others performs poor may be that they take the whole anocelia as the salient regions. In Figure 4, it is clear to see that the line of our method is much higher than another six. For a given IoU of 0.8, the precision can achieve more than forty percent, while the result of others is nearly zero. It is noticed that for some methods, with a proper parameter determination aiding algorithm, other algorithm may also achieve higher accuracy. However, such aiding algorithm has to be developed based on the individual segmentation scene and, compared to our self-adaptive segmentation algorithm, this extra designing is with high time and computation cost.

3.2.2 Evaluation on Cervical Spine Image Dataset in Regional Scale.

The regional scale cervical spine images are the transaction cervical spine images removing the complex background of anocelia, basically only containing about the blood vessels. Different images have diversity in number, size and shape of blood vessels. The main purpose is to extract the highlighted blood vessels from the images. Figure 5 demonstrates an example been segmented. For the given image, there are two blood vessels as the target regions.

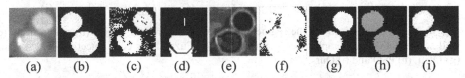

(a)	(b)	(c)	(d)	(e)	(f)	(g)	(h)	(i)

Fig. 5. Visual comparison for the segmentation result. (a) Original image,(b) ground truth ,(c) Cell segmentation, (d) Graph based segmentation, (e) Fuzzy logic edge detection, (f) K-means, (g) Otsu, (h) PSO and (i) Ours.

Table 3. Comparison of average IoU for different segmentation methods in regional scale

Method	Ours	Cellseg	Graseg	IFDedge	K-means	PSO	Otsu
Average IoU	0.837	0.719	0.379	0.195	0.433	0.840	0.879

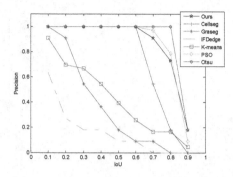

Fig. 6. The precision comparison based on given IoU in regional scale

Table 3 and Figure 6 are the statistical results, from which we can observe that most methods have good performance especially the Otsu, PSO and our methods with more than eighty percent IoU value, while the results of the other four are inferior to the three mentioned above. Figure 6 show the result visually for each given IoU value. The values of Otsu, PSO and ours, are competitive with image precision more than seventy percent with the IoU value of 0.8.

3.2.3 Evaluation on Cervical Spine Image Dataset in Vessel Scale.

The vessel scale cervical spine images refer to generally only one blood vessel in the image, and the blood vessel contains the calcification part, which is also the highlighted region for diagnosis. The calcification region attached to the blood vessel, which may be inside or outside of the blood vessel. Therefore, the salient region in the small scale image should be the calcification part. Figure 7 gives a visual illustration of different methods. It is obvious that our method can give an accurate segmentation results compared to other vague and coarse results.

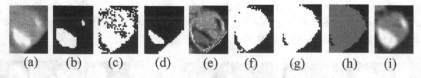

(a)   (b)   (c)   (d)   (e)   (f)   (g)   (h)   (i)

Fig. 7. Visual comparison for the segmentation result. (a)Original image, (b)ground truth, (c) Cell segmentation, (d) Graph based segmentation, (e) Fuzzy logic edge detection, (f) K-means, (g) Otsu, (h) PSO and (i) Ours.

Table 4. Comparison of average IoU for different segmentation methods in vessel scale

Method	Ours	Cellseg	Graseg	IFDedge	K-means	PSO	Otsu
Average IoU	0.770	0.254	0.167	0.123	0.142	0.558	0.334

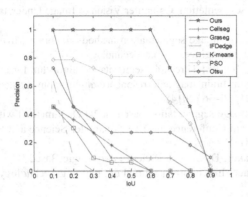

Fig. 8. The Precision comparison based on given IoU for in vessel scale

As the result in Table 4, the performance of our algorithm is still better than other methods. Our method obtains the average IoU value with 0.770, which is much superior to the results of others. Except our method, only the PSO algorithm can get better result compared to others. After careful observation, we discover that they are very weak in detecting the calcification region, and always take the whole blood vessel as the salient region. Thus, even the calcification part in the salient region, the IoU value will be influenced enormously. In Figure 8, the same situation appears with the set experiment in global scale. Given the IoU value of 0.7, our method can have the accurate rate of more than seventy percent, while the best result of others only achieve less than fifty percent. When the IoU value is 0.8, it is amazing that our result can still obtain more than forty percent.

4   Conclusion

In this work, we have introduced a new method for image segmentation by considering both appearance similarity and spatial variance. We extensively evaluated our method on two different types of medical image datasets which are breast image and cervical spine image datasets, and compared it against 6 alternate methods.It is proved that our algorithm outperforms the other 6 methods and can always find the salient regions, no matter how complex the environment was, or how minute the region is.

Acknowledgments. The authors are grateful to the anonymous referees for their valuable comments. This work has been supported by the NSFC (61202415), the NSF of Tianjin (15ICQ-NJC00700).

References

1. Grau, V., Mewes, A.U.: Improved watershed transform for medical image segmentation using prior information. IEEE Transactions on Medical Imaging **23**, 447–458 (2004)
2. Yan, P., Zhang, W., Turkbey, B.: Global structure constrained local shape prior estimation for medical image segmentation. Computer Vision & Image Understanding **117**, 101–1026 (2013)
3. Matkar, S., Borse, M.: Image segmentation methods for brain MRI images. International Journal of Research in Engineering and Technology (2015)
4. Rui, W., Chao, L., Jie, W.: Threshold segmentation algorithm for automatic extraction of cerebral vessels from brain magnetic resonance angiography images. Journal of Neuroscience Methods **241**, 30–36 (2014)
5. Zhang, J., Hu, J.: Image segmentation based on 2D Otsu method with histogram analysis. In: 2008 International Conference on IEEE. Computer Science and Software Engineering, pp. 105–108 (2008)
6. Khan, A.U.R., Thakur, D.K.: An Efficient Fuzzy Logic Based Edge Detection Algorithm for Gray Scale Image. International Journal of Emerging Technology and Advanced Engineering (2002)
7. Ng, H.P.: Medical image segmentation using k-means clustering and improved watershed algorithm. In: 2006 IEEE Southwest Symposium on IEEE. Image Analysis and Interpretation, pp. 61–65 (2006)
8. Felzenszwalb, P.F., Huttenlocher, D.P.: Efficient graph-based image segmentation. International Journal of Computer Vision **59**, 167–181 (2004)
9. Ghamisi, P., Couceiro, M.S., Benediktsson, J.A., et al.: An efficient method for segmentation of images based on fractional calculus and natural selection. Expert Systems with Applications **39**, 12407–12417 (2012)
10. Cheng, M.M.: Efficient salient region detection with soft image abstraction. In: 2013 IEEE International Conference on Computer Vision (ICCV). IEEE (2013)
11. Borji, A., Itti, L.: State-of-the-art in visual attention modeling. IEEE Transactions on Pattern Analysis and Machine Intelligence **35**(1), 185–207 (2013)
12. American College of Radiology (ACR). Breast Imaging Reporting and Data System (BI-RADS). 3rd edn. Reston, VA: American College of Radiology (2003)
13. Frey, B.D.: Dueck. Clustering by passing messages between datapoints. Science **315**(5814), 972–976 (2007)
14. Gopalakrishnan, V., Hu, Y., Rajan, D.: Salient region detection by modeling distributions of color and orientation. IEEE Trans. Multimedia **11**(5), 892–905 (2009)

A Method of ECG Identification
Based on Weighted Correlation Coefficient

Min Dai[1(✉)], Baowen Zhu[1], Gang Zheng[2], and Yisha Wang[1]

[1] Tianjin Key Laboratory of Intelligence Computing and Novel Software Technology,
Tianjin University of Technology, Tianjin 300384, People's Republic of China
daimin@tjut.edu.cn, baowen080808@163.com
[2] Key Laboratory of Computer Vision and System, Ministry of Education,
Tianjin University of Technology, Tianjin 300384, People's Republic of China
kenneth_zheng@vip.163.com

Abstract. When the correlation coefficient (CC) method is used in electrocardiograph (ECG) identification, the accuracy of identification can be affected by the number of templates and different representative templates. In this paper, a template selection method is proposed based on contribution rate of each ECG waveform in the data set, and the second-order differential threshold value is used to determine the number of templates and select representative ECG templates for each individual. The weighted correlation coefficient method is proposed for ECG identification, and weights are calculated by the sorted sequence of contribution rate. The performance of the presented method is tested on the MIT-BIH ECG data set and the hand ECG data collected in real scenery. Comparing with the traditional correlation coefficient method, experimental results show that the average identification accuracies are increased 10.52% and 3.85% respectively when using the presented method.

Keywords: Weighted correlation coefficient · ECG template · ECG identification

1 Introduction

Identification is of great importance and necessity in the field of security. Compared with traditional identification technologies, some are based on items (including key, smart card, etc.), some are based on knowledge (including password, etc.), biometric identification technology is more and more recognized by people because of its convenience, accuracy, security, and difficulty of forge [1-2]. Currently, many biological characteristics have been used for identification, such as facial features, fingerprint [3] and iris [4].These technologies have been used in some areas, but they might face the possibility of fraud. One advantage of ECG signal as biological characteristics is that it requires individual involved in recognition process, and the individual must be alive. Moreover, ECG signal is a continuous electrical signal, and it is not easy to be stolen or copied. So ECG identification can improve the security in application.

At present, identification methods based on ECG can be roughly divided into two categories: one is based on feature (calculated by characteristic point), the other is

© Springer International Publishing Switzerland 2015
J. Yang et al. (Eds.): CCBR 2015, LNCS 9428, pp. 633–640, 2015.
DOI: 10.1007/978-3-319-25417-3_74

based on waveform morph (every point value in the waveform). Some similarity measurement methods are often used for ECG identification, such as Euclidean distance [5], correlation coefficient [6], cosine distance [7]. Hausdorff distance [8] and template matching [9] etc.

In this paper, we proposed a weighted correlation coefficient method for ECG identification and optimized the template selection method. According to the contribution rate of each ECG waveform in data set, the most representative ECG waveform was selected as template. Then the contribution rate sequence are transferred to different weights and assigned to each sample for selected template. ECG identification is processed by the weighted correlation coefficient.

2   Application of Correlation Coefficient in ECG Identification

The correlation coefficient method is widely used in ECG identification. It is the statistical indicators which can reflect the linear relationship between two variables. Calculating the correlation between two ECG waveforms, we can determine whether the two ECG waveforms belong to the same class.

Let $T= (t_1, t_2, ..., t_p)$ is ECG template set, and $t_i = (t_{i1}, t_{i2}, ..., t_{im})$ is one individual ECG template set. Where p is label of every individual, that is to say, we have p individuals in the whole data; m is the number of templates for one individual; $t_{ij}=(t_{ij}^1, t_{ij}^2, ..., t_{ij}^q)$ is one ECG waveform template for one individual. Let $S=(s^1, s^2, ..., s^q)$ is one unknown ECG signal, and q is dimension of a ECG waveform. Then the correlation coefficient r_{ij} between S and the j-th ECG template from the i-th individual, can be calculated as formula (1):

$$r_{ij} = \frac{q\sum_{k=1}^{q} s^k t_{ij}^k - \sum_{k=1}^{q} s^k \sum_{k=1}^{q} t_{ij}^k}{\sqrt{q\sum_{k=1}^{q} (s^k)^2 - (\sum_{k=1}^{q} s^k)^2}\sqrt{q\sum_{k=1}^{q} (t_{ij}^k)^2 - (\sum_{k=1}^{q} t_{ij}^k)^2}} \tag{1}$$

For the traditional correlation coefficient method, ECG templates are usually selected at random. Due to the individual difference of ECG signal, the number of templates and different representative templates will affect the accuracy of ECG identification. We will discuss the problem in next section.

3   ECG Identification Based on Template Contribution Rate

In order to solve the problem of template selecting, we proposed a weighted correlation coefficient strategy for ECG identification. The main idea is that the most representative ECG waveforms were selected as templates relying on sequence of contribution rate, and the contribution rate sequence are transferred to different weights and assigned to each sample for selected template. The correlation coefficient is calculated on the basis of weight.

3.1 ECG Template Selection Based on Waveform Contribution Rate

Supposed we choose m ECG waveforms as initial ECG template set of a person. We randomly choose an ECG waveform and calculate the cosine similarity between it and the other m-1 ECG waveforms respectively. The contribution of this ECG template can be calculated as formula (2):

$$fsc_i = \sum_{j=1}^{m} \cos_{ij} \tag{2}$$

In formula (2), cos_{ij} is cosine distance between the i-th template and the j-th template of the same individual, and fsc_i is the contribution of the i-th template. All templates are sorted according to the contribution from big to small, and a decline curve can be derived from the contribution sequence. To selecting the most representative ECG templates, we used an automatic threshold selection algorithm based on second-order difference [10].

We used the template selection method on MIT-BIH ECG data set. Table 1 lists the number of ECG templates for part of data set.

Table 1. Number of ECG templates on MIT-BIH ECG data.

No.	Number of ECG templates	No.	Number of ECG templates	No.	Number of ECG templates
1	5	8	6	15	8
2	9	9	7	16	7
3	7	10	5	17	4
4	9	11	10	18	6
5	8	12	9	19	13
6	11	13	8	20	5
7	6	14	7	21	8

3.2 ECG Identification Based on Weighted Template

With contribution rate sequence of templates, we can calculate the weight of each template as formula (3):

$$W_{ij} = \frac{fsc_{ij}}{\sum_{j=1}^{m'} fsc_{ij}} \tag{3}$$

In formula (3), w_{ij} is the weight of the j-th ECG template from the i-th individual in the data set. Where m' is the number of templates for one individual, and fsc_{ij} is the contribution of the j–th template from the i-th individual.

To improve the accuracy of ECG identification, correlation coefficient was calculated by adding weighted on each ECG template. The weighted correlation coefficient is described by formula (4):

$$rm_i = \sum_{j=1}^{m'} r_{ij} \times w_{ij} \tag{4}$$

According to the contribution of the ECG template, each r_{ij} was assigned a weight, which reflected the importance of the ECG template. Where rm_i is the sum of weighted coefficient of correlation between the unknown single S and all ECG templates of the *i-th* individual.

The steps of ECG identification based on weighted template are as follows:

(1). If the *i-th* individual ECG template set is consist of m waveforms in initial ECG template set T. Calculating the contribution *fsc* of each ECG template using cosine similarity distance measurement method as formula (2) .

(2). Sorting m ECG templates by their contribution *fsc* in descending order. Selecting the most representative ECG template set (including m' ECG waveforms, $m' <= m$) relying on automatic threshold selection algorithm of second-order difference.

(3). Calculating each weight of m' ECG templates by formula (3).

(4). Input the unknown ECG signal S.

(5). Calculating correlation coefficient between S and m' ECG templates from the *i-th* individual respectively.

(6). Calculating rm_i between S and the *i-th* individual by formula (4).

(7). Calculating rm_1, rm_2, ..., rm_p by repeating the above steps.

(8). Finding the maximal value of rm_1, rm_2, ..., rm_p to identify the corresponding individual.

4   Experiments and Results Analysis

4.1   Experimental Data and Method

Two types of ECG data are used in our experiment. One comes from MIT-BIH ECG data set, and the other is the hand ECG data collected in real scenery. The sampling frequency of MIT-BIH data is 360Hz. We selected 21 individuals from MIT-BIH and extract 600 continue cardiac cycle samples for each individual. Our own ECG data is collected by a hand-held ECG device designed by our lab (figure 1). Its sampling frequency is 250Hz. We collected the hand ECG data from 14 healthy testers which age is from 22 to 25 and 7 males and 7 females. Similarly, 600 continue cardiac cycle samples are extracted for each individual. In our experiment, we chose 10% ECG data as the training samples, and the remaining 90% as the test samples.

In order to validate the presented method, we perform three groups of experiments on above two different data sets respectively.

Experiment 1: Selecting template randomly from all 600 ECG waveform and ECG identification based on traditional correlation coefficient (CC) method.

Experiment 2: Firstly, selecting 60 waveforms from 600 ECG samples randomly. Then determine the most representative ECG template set based on their contribution rate using method in section 3.1. Finally, ECG identifying based on traditional correlation coefficient method.

Experiment 3: On the basis of ECG template selected in experiment 2, the weighted correlation coefficient (WCC) method is used for ECG identification.

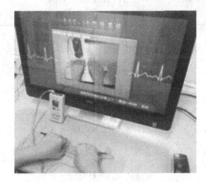

Fig. 1. A hand-held ECG collection device

4.2   Experimental Result

The accuracy of ECG identification for each experiment is shown in table 2 and table 3 respectively.

Table 2. The identification accuracy for hand ECG data set

No.	ID accuracy of CC	ID accuracy of representative templates	ID accuracy of WCC
1	76.46%	78.98%	82.28%
2	70.26%	72.09%	81.88%
3	80.32%	88.48%	91.9%
4	86.03%	88.62%	90.02%
5	81.68%	81.95%	84.49%
6	67.53%	82.67%	87.25%
7	63.01%	85.15%	88.94%
8	81.23%	84.38%	89.78%
9	88.15%	90.43%	94.77%
10	73.79%	77.08%	82.1%
11	83.53%	87.76%	91.33%
12	86.08%	86.71%	88.97%
13	72.11%	80.49%	87.86%
14	69.98%	78.15%	85.76%

Table 3. The identification accuracy for MIT-BIH data set

No.	ID accuracy of CC	ID accuracy of representative templates	ID accuracy of WCC
1	99.58%	99.96%	100%
2	100%	100%	100%
3	99.51%	99.54%	99.57%
4	85.41%	98.9%	98.8%
5	96.71%	97.12%	98.13%
6	85.25%	88.65%	90.26%
7	99.8%	100%	100%
8	98.78%	99.01%	99.45%
9	99.9%	100%	100%
10	97.08%	99.8%	99.8%
11	82.13%	87.54%	92.65%
12	88.75%	97.89%	98.9%
13	100%	100%	100%
14	97.8%	98.65%	98.96%
15	89.04%	94.98%	97.65%
16	96.73%	97.09%	97.99%
17	99.4%	100%	100%
18	91.23%	95.07%	97.88%
19	84.9%	88.08%	91.22%
20	99.1%	99.38%	99.7%
21	86.07%	90.11%	95.02%

From table 2, we can see that the identification accuracies of 14 individuals are all improved in experiment 3. But only the sample 3, 4, 9 and 11 are above 90% when using hand ECG data. Since our hand ECG data is collected in real scenery, it is easy to interfere with the noise, and the data are distributed unevenly, resulting in a decrease of their identification accuracy. From table 3, we can see that all accuracies are above 90% when using the presented method, and even 18 of them are reaching 95%.

In addition, we calculated the average accuracy of all samples in three experiments, and the result is shown in table 4.

Table 4. The average identification accuracy of all samples for MIT-BIH and hand ECG data set in three experiments.

Data set	Average accuracy of CC	Average accuracy of representative templates	Average accuracy of WCC
MIT-BIH	94.15%	96.75%	98%
Hand ECG	77.15%	83.07%	87.67%

We can see form table 4, comparing with the traditional correlation coefficient method, experimental results show that the average identification accuracies of ECG ID are increased 10.52% and 3.85% respectively when using the presented method.

5   Conclusion

When the correlation coefficient method is used for ECG identification, the template selection will affect the accuracy of identification. In this paper, we proposed a weighted correlation coefficient method for ECG identification and optimized the template selection method. According to the contribution rate of each ECG waveform in data set, the most representative ECG waveform was selected as template. Then the contribution rate sequence are transferred to different weights and assigned to each sample for selected template. ECG identification is processed by the weighted correlation coefficient. Experiment results show that the presented method can improve the identification accuracy.

Acknowledgment. This paper is supported by Tianjin Natural Science Foundation under Grant No. 15JCYBJC15800, and Tianjin Key Foundation on Science Supporting Plan (10ZCKFSF-00800).

References

1. Zhang, Y.M.: Analysis of Authentication technology based on biometric feature information. Information Technology, 153–154 (2014)
2. Wang, F.: Research and development of Authentication technology based on biometric feature information. Scientific Information, 433–434 (2013)
3. Kumar, A., Zhou, Y.B.: Human Identification Using Finger Images. IEEE Transactions on Image Processing **21**, 2228–2244 (2012)
4. Li, H.L., Guo, L.H., Chen, T., Yang, L.M., Wang, X.Z.: Based on PCHIP-LMD method in iris identification. Optics and Precision Engineering, 197–206(2013)
5. Javed, J., Yasin, H., Ali, S.F.: Human movement recognition using euclidean distance: a tricky approach. In: 2010 3rd International Congress on Image and Signal Processing (CISP), vol. 1, pp. 317–321 (2010)
6. Yan, L.W., Ren, X.K.: Wavelet transform image fusion algorithm based on correlation coefficient. Computer Engineering And Science **33**, 103–107 (2011)

7. Xia, P.P., Zhang, L., Li, F.Z.: Learning similarity with cosine similarity ensemble, 39–52 (2015). Elsevier Inc.
8. Chen, L.Z., Wang, B.B., Dong, J.G.: An improved Hausdorff distance template matching algorithm. Computer Technology and Development, 82–85 (2009)
9. Winchell, S.D., Rakvic, R.N.: Feasibility of iris identification algorithm optimization by fractional template matching. In: IET Conference on Image Processing (IPR 2012), pp. 1–5 (2012)
10. Liu, T.T.: Research on Similarity Analysis for Biomedical Signal. Tianjin University of Technology (2013)

Discriminative Feature Fusion with Spectral Method for Human Action Recognition

Xiang Xiao[1,2], Le Liu[3], and Haifeng Hu[1,2(✉)]

[1] School of Information Science and Technology, Sun Yat-sen University, Guangzhou, China
1154598146@qq.com, huhaif@mail.sysu.edu.cn
[2] SYSU-CMU Shunde International Joint Research Institute, Shunde, China
[3] Supercomputer Office, Sun Yat-sen University, Guangzhou, China
liule2@mail.sysu.edu.cn

Abstract. In this paper, we propose an effective action recognition approach which differs significantly from previous interest points based approaches in that spectral information of video data is exploited. Firstly, we extract the motion interchange patterns feature and the HOG/HOF features of videos, respectively. We concatenate them into single feature representation. Secondly, Laplacian Eigenmaps is performed on the feature space to achieve the goal of dimensionality reduction. Spectral clustering is used to cluster the training set. Finally, SVM is taken for multi-class classification. Experiments using the UCF50 dataset and the YouTube dataset demonstrate that our approach achieve state-of-the-art performance.

Keywords: Action recognition · Laplacian Eigenmaps · Dimensionality reduction · Spectral clustering · SVM

1 Introduction

Human action recognition still remains a challenging problem due to substantial variations in the video data that are caused by varying factors which include personal style, action length, background clutter, subject's appearance, multiple video objects and so on. To overcome the above challenges, many previous works can be roughly categorized into appearance-based methods and motion-based methods. Appearance-based approaches mainly employ local [1, 2] or global [3, 4] visual features from video data. For example, Dollar *et al.* [1] model human action as bags of orderless and independent visual words by clustering local features. Motion-based methods generally depend upon human pose estimation or human body tracking and view the action recognition as a problem of temporal classification. For example, Yamato *et al.* [3] model a sequence of grid-based silhouette features as outputs of class-specific HMMs [5].

Graph-based methods are an effective way which applied to exploit the structure of data space by adopting spectral information of data matrix so that they are useful for enhancing the performance of machine learning tasks, such as dimensionality reduction or clustering. Using spectral methods for clustering have emerged in a number of fields. The top eigenvectors of a matrix derived from the distance between points are

© Springer International Publishing Switzerland 2015
J. Yang et al. (Eds.): CCBR 2015, LNCS 9428, pp. 641–648, 2015.
DOI: 10.1007/978-3-319-25417-3_75

considered to construct the feature vector space, which could avoid the situation of having many local minimal. Such algorithms have been successfully used in many applications including text categorization and action recognition.

To improve the identification accuracy of human action from videos, in this work, we present an effective method for action recognition that builds upon several recent ideas including space-time features and graph-based methods. We first detect interest points and describe them by employing two types of features. The first type of feature is global visual feature that encodes the motion information of actions, which is called motion interchange patterns (MIP) feature [8]. The second is local feature, e.g. HOG and HOF descriptors [13] that encode the appearance information of action videos. Laplacian Eigenmaps [7] are exploited to reduce the dimension of features and spectral clustering instead of k-means is applied on clustering, each type of feature in a video is represented by a histogram. Then a final single feature representation is a concatenation of two types of features. Finally, the linear Support Vector Machine (SVM) is learned on visual features to recognition.

In summary, the main contributions of this paper are mainly twofold.

1. Several discriminative features which include the global MIP feature and the local HOG/HOF features are combined so that the compound features could achieve better recognition performance.
2. We employ the spectral methods that include Laplacian Eigenmaps and spectral clustering instead of the original PCA and k-means methods so that to obtain a higher accuracy rate.

The rest of the paper is organized as follows. In section 2, we review the related work. In section 3, we introduce the Laplacian Eigenmaps and spectral clustering, which utilize spectral information of feature matrix to achieve dimensionality reduction and clustering, respectively. The experiments and results of the UCF50 dataset and the YouTube dataset with discussions are provided in section 4. Finally, a conclusion is given in section 5.

2   Related Work

Earlier works in human action recognition mainly adopt holistic features such as body model, shape and silhouette. However, these methods highly rely on the results of segmentation and tracking, which may not achieve optimal performance in realistic videos due to cluttered and occlusion background. These years, there are two popular trends which could be identified in the action recognition literature. First, a considerable amount of research has been focused on extracting local visual features from video data [1, 2]. Second, computing visual representations according to nearby frames has attracted keen attentions, such methods usually depends upon appearance and optical flow.

The local self-similarity method [9], computes the histogram of similarity between a central cuboid and nearby cuboids, forms a vector to describe the central cuboid. Yeffet et al. [10] improve the self-similarity method by extending Local Binary

Patterns (LBP) [11] to Local Trinary Patterns (LTP). Gross *et al.* [8] propose a Motion Interchange Patterns (MIP) method to capture local changes in motion directions by using local pattern encoding and a patch-based method.

Graph-based methods are a powerful way of exploiting the underlying structure of data space to improve the performance of unsupervised and semi-supervised tasks. The most successful graph-based approaches include manifold ranking, Laplacian Eigenmaps [7], spectral clustering [12]. The latent structure of a high-dimensional data space might be obtained through using graph-based methods.

In this work, we propose a simple and effective multi-feature representation, which combines the discriminative global MIP feature with the local HOG/HOF features to achieve rich description of human actions. Unlike [8], rather than the original PCA and k-means methods, we take two graph-based methods Laplacian Eigenmaps and spectral clustering to yield the histogram of word occurrences, which lead to improved results.

3   Effective Feature Extraction and Spectral-Based Methods

In the task of human action recognition, extracting local or global visual features from video have shown many encouraging results. In this work, we intend to describe an action video by several global and local features. In subsection 3.1, we introduce the discriminative MIP feature [8], which has been proofed via a large-scale experiment; in subsection 3.2, we introduce the HOG and HOF features [13]. A combination of the MIP and HOG/HOF is taken to achieve rich description of human actions; in subsection 3.3, Laplacian Eigenmaps and spectral clustering are used to realize the dimensionality reduction and data clustering, respectively.

3.1   MIP Feature

Given an input video, MIP method [8] encodes every patch on three consecutive frames (i.e., previous, current, and next frame) from the video by eight strings of eight trinary digits. Each digit denotes the compatibility of two motions by the sum of squared differences (SSD) patch-comparison operator: one motion in a specific direction from the previous frame to the current frame, and one motion in another direction from the current frame to the next frame. Thus two SSD values could be obtained according to corresponding two motions. There are eight directions, which numbered from 0 to 7, locate around the patch in the current frame. This is depicted in Fig. 1(a). Eight directions in the previous frames and the next frames are denoted i and j, respectively. For considering all combinations of i and j, each pixel $p=(x, y, t)$ can be encoded by a 64-trinary digit denoted by $E(p)$. Each trinary digit $E_{i,j}(p)$ corresponds to one kind of combination of i and j. Through the comparison of two SSD values, $E_{i,j}(p)$ could be denoted as follows:

$$E_{i,j}(p) = \begin{cases} 1, & \text{if } SSD2 < SSD1 - T \\ 0, & \text{if } |SSD1 - SSD2| \leq T \\ -1, & \text{if } SSD1 < SSD2 - T \end{cases} \tag{1}$$

A value of 1 indicates that the latter motion is more likely and -1 indicates that the former motion is more likely. A value of 0 means that both are compatible in the same degree. The encoding scheme can be illustrated by Fig. 1 [8].

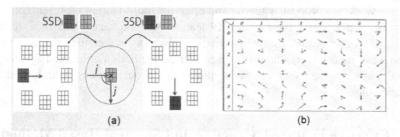

Fig. 1. (a) By computing two SSD scores from every triplet frames and comparing them, each central patch in the current frame can be encoded by a trinary digit. (b) Considering all combinations of i and j. Red arrows represent the motion from the current frame to the next frame, and blue arrows represent the motion from the previous frame to the current frame.

3.2   HOG/HOF Features

To improve the ability of recognizing actions, we characterize motion and appearance of local features simultaneously by computing histogram descriptors of space-time volumes in the neighborhood of detected points. Here we detect interest points using a space-time extension of the Harris operator [1]. Each 3D volume is subdivided into several grids of cuboids. Then histograms of oriented gradient (HOG) and histogram of optic flow (HOF) are computed to describe a cuboid. Normalized histograms are concatenated into HOG and HOF descriptor vectors [13].

3.3   Spectral-Based Methods for Dimensionality Reduction and Clustering

One of the central problems in action recognition is to develop appropriate representations for complex data. Dimensionality reduction is an essential step to process the higher dimensional data. Principal components analysis (PCA) is the most versatile method in machine learning due to its simplicity and validity. However, PCA does not explicitly consider the structure of the manifold on which the data may possibly reside. In this work, Laplacian Eigenmaps [7] is used to construct a representation for data sampled from a low dimensional manifold embedded in a higher dimensional space.

Finding good clusters and achieving good cluster performance have been the focus of considerable research in pattern recognition and machine learning. EM and k-means are two commonly used methods for clustering. However, they may have many local minima so that multiple restarts are required to find a good solution using iterative algorithms [12]. Using spectral methods for clustering become increasingly prevalent, which use the top eigenvectors of an affinity matrix W derived from the distance between data points. A heat kernel applied to the χ^2 distance between two points x_i and x_j: $W_{ij} = exp(-\chi^2(x_i, y_j)/\sigma^2)$. The Laplacian matrix L can be calculated using the following: $L=D^{-1/2}WD^{-1/2}$, Where D is the diagonal matrix and D_{ii} denotes the sum of the i-th row of W [14]. Then k highest eigenvectors of L are found and concatenated columnwise to form the matrix $X=[e_1, ..., e_k]$. Renormalizing each row of X and clustering them into k clusters via k-means method.

4   Experiments

4.1   Dataset and Experimental Setup

Our experiments are conducted on UCF50 dataset [15] and YouTube dataset [6].

The UCF50 dataset is composed by 6681 video sequences distributed in 50 different human actions. Videos composing the dataset are subject to large camera motion, viewpoint change and cluttered backgrounds. All the sequences are split into 25 groups, such that each group consists of at least four clips. The clips in the same group share similar background and subject. Fig. 2 shows some key frames of videos in the dataset.

Fig. 2. Examples of the key frames in the UCF50 dataset.

YouTube dataset contains 11 action categories collected under large variations in scale, illumination and camera motion. This dataset has 1168 video sequences of human activities in total. Fig. 3 shows some key frames of videos in the dataset.

Fig. 3. Examples of the key frames in the YouTube dataset

The publicly available code for MIP feature and HOG/HOF features are used as presented in Gross *et al.* [8] and Laptev *et al.* [13]. We take the default settings. The dimension of MIP feature is reduced to 50 by Laplacian Eigenmaps. We apply spectral clustering to generate the codebooks of both features with k equal to 5000. For HOG/HOF, each volume(Δ_x, Δ_y, Δ_z) is set that $\Delta_x = \Delta_y = \Delta_z$, the parameter value $m=9$. A volume is subdivided into (n_x, n_y, n_z) cuboids. We made all the experiments on Tianhe-2A platform, which is ranked as the world's fastest supercomputer and can be used to speed up the computation largely. We evaluate the performance by using the leave-one-out cross validation scheme which involves employing one group of clips in a dataset as the testing data and the remaining groups of clips as the training data. Then we report average accuracy over all classes.

4.2   Experimental Results

Two approaches are designed in order to evaluate and contrast with the performance of our algorithm in UCF50 dataset. The first method only extracts the MIP feature while the second method only extracts the HOG/HOF features. These methods use bag-of-words model which includes k-means to represent the local features. The above methods are referred to as 'MIP+BOW', 'HOG/HOF+BOW', respectively. We randomly select 11 actions from UCF50, and it contains 20 groups per action category. Each method is run for 20 trials and the mean accuracy overall results is shown in Table 1. It shows that our approach achieves a higher performance on the UCF50 dataset. Moreover, we can observe the following conclusions:

(1) MIP+BOW approach, reaching the accuracies of 60.2%, is 12.3% higher than that of the HOG/HOF+BOW approach. It demonstrates that extracting motion interchange pattern feature from consecutive frames is more discriminative than the HOG/HOF feature.

(2) Our approach achieves the best accuracy value of 61.8%. It indicates that the combination of global and local features as well as spectral methods will lead a sufficiently informative and discriminative representation for human actions.

Table 1. The performance of three approaches on the UCF50 dataset.

Method	MIP+BOW	HOG/HOF+BOW	Our approach
Accuracy	60.2%	47.9%	61.8%

Table 2. The comparison of our approach with the state-of-the-art approaches on the YouTube dataset.

Method	FGSM	LE	Our approach
Accuracy	89%	74.6%	86.5%

Table 2 shows the comparison of our approach with the state-of-the-art approaches on the YouTube dataset.

FGSM algorithm [14] takes a multigraph representation to fully capture the relationship between multiple separate components; LE [7] applies Laplacian Eigenmaps to the histogram and uses RBF kernel SVM for classification. The comparison between the proposed approach and two other approaches is shown in Table 2. As can be seen, FGSM achieves the best results on YouTube dataset. Our approach outperforms Laplacian Eigenmaps, and it performs similarity to the FGSM algorithm. However, the FGSM method is time consuming because it needs to compute the eigenvectors of all Laplacian matrixes. Our method is close to the best reported in an effective manner.

5   Conclusion

This paper has presented an approach for action recognition, which includes a combination of multi-feature that consists of global and local features. Spectral-based methods such as spectral clustering and LE algorithms are considered to improve the recognition performance. Experimental results demonstrate that our approach could achieve promising recognition results and surpass the state-of-the art recognition accuracy on two public datasets.

Acknowledgments. This work is supported by the National Science Foundation of China (60802069 and 61273270), the Fundamental Research Funds for the Central Universities of China, the Natural Science Foundation of Guangdong Province (2014A030313173), the Science and Technology Program of Guangzhou (2014Y2-00165, 2014J4100114 and 2014J4100095).

References

1. Laptev, I.: On space-time interest points. Int. J. Comput. Vis., 107–123 (2005)
2. Niebles, J., Wang, H., Fei-Fei, L.: Unsupervised learning of human action categories using spatial temporal words. Int. J. Comput. Vis., 299–318 (2008)
3. Yamato, J., Ohya, J., Ishii, K.: Recognizing human actions in time-sequential images using hidden Markov model. In: Proc. IEEE Conf. Comput. Vis. Pattern Recognit., pp. 379–385 (1992)
4. Wang, H., Klaser, A., Schmid, C., Liu, C.L.: Dense trajectories and motion boundary descriptors for action recognition. Int. J. Comput. Vis., 60–79 (2013)
5. Luo, G., Yang, S., and Tian, G. D., Yuan, C.F., Hu, W.M.: Learning Human Actions by Combining Global Dynamics and Local Appearance. IEEE Trans. Pattern Anal. Mach. Intell., 2466–2482 (2014)
6. Liu, J., Luo, J., Shah, M.: Recognizing realistic actions from videos "in the Wild". In: Proc. IEEE Conf. Comput. Vis. Pattern Recognit., pp. 1996–2003 (2009)
7. Belkin, M., Niyogi, P.: Laplacian eigenmaps for dimensionality reduction and data representation. Neural Computation, 1373–1396 (2002)

8. Kliper-Gross, O., Gurovich, Y., Hassner, T., Wolf, L.: Motion interchange patterns for action recognition in unconstrained videos. In: European Conf. on Computer Vision, pp. 256–269 (2012)
9. Veeraraghavan, A., Chowdhury, A.R., Chellappa, R.: Matching shape sequences in video with application in human movement analysis. IEEE Trans. Pattern Anal. Mach. Intell., 1896–1909 (2005)
10. Yeffet, L., Wolf, L.: Local trinary patterns for human action recognition. In: Proc. IEEE Int. Conf. Comput. Vis., pp. 492–497 (2009)
11. Ojala, T., Pietikainen, M., Maenpaa, T.: Multiresolution gray-scale and rotation invariant texture classification with local binary patterns. IEEE Trans. Pattern Anal. Mach. Intell., 971–987 (2002)
12. Ng, A.Y., Jordan, M., Weiss, Y.: On Spectral Clustering: Analysis and an algorithm. Advances in Neural Information Proc. Syst., 849–856 (2001)
13. Laptev, I., Marszalek, M., Schmid, C., Rozenfeld, B.: Learning realistic human actions from movies. In: Proc. IEEE Conf. Comput. Vis. Pattern Recognit., pp. 1-8 (2008)
14. Jones, S., Ling, S.: A multigraph representation for improved unsupervised/semi-supervised learning of human actions. In: Proc. IEEE Conf. Comput. Vis. Pattern Recognit., pp. 23–28 (2014)
15. Reddy, K.K., Shah, M.: Recognizing 50 human action categories of web videos. Machine Vision and Applications, 971–981 (2013)

DFDnet: Discriminant Face Descriptor Network for Facial Age Estimation

Ting Liu, Zhen Lei, Jun Wan, and Stan Z. Li[✉]

Center for Biometrics and Security Research & National Laboratory of Pattern
Recognition, Institute of Automation, Chinese Academy of Sciences, Beijing, China
{ting.liu,zlei,jun.wan,szli}@nlpr.ia.ac.cn

Abstract. Age estimation is an important part of biometric recognition.
In this paper, we propose to use Discriminant Face Descriptor (DFD)
which learns the most discriminative and related features to age variation in a data-driven way. We use it, for the first time, for facial age Age
estimation is an important part of biometric recognition. In this paper,
we propose a stacked structure called Discriminant Face Descriptor network (DFDnet) to learn the most discriminative and related features
to age variation. We extract the multi-stage Discriminant Face Descriptor (DFD) features which are age sensitive. We first introduce DFD for
facial age estimation instead of original face recognition. Then the bag-
of-features method is used so that each image can be represented by
the histogram of visual words. Finally, age estimation is achieved via
simple linear regression algorithm. Experiments on the publicly available MORPH and FG-NET databases validate the effectiveness of our
proposed DFDnet method. To further illuminate the usefulness of our
approach in unconstrained environments, we also conduct the experiment on Cross-Age Celebrity Dataset (CACD) which is collected from
Internet movie database (IMDB).

Keywords: Age estimation · Discriminant Face Description (DFD) ·
Bag of features · DFD network

1 Introduction

Automatic human age estimation is an important research trend in facial analysis
for its real-world applications, such as security control and surveillance monitoring, commercial user management, harmonious human-computer interaction,
criminal investigation, image and video retrieval, and biometrics. In real life,
one can use a wealth of information to estimate age, like the human body, clothing, hair, appearance which all reflect the age information. Among them, the
face plays the biggest role. Facial age estimation means that a face image is
automatically labeled with the exact age (year) or the age group (year range).

Age estimation shares many issues encountered in other face-related tasks
such as face detection and face recognition. Facial feature deformations caused
by pose, illumination and expression (PIE) variation have a negative effect on the

© Springer International Publishing Switzerland 2015
J. Yang et al. (Eds.): CCBR 2015, LNCS 9428, pp. 649–658, 2015.
DOI: 10.1007/978-3-319-25417-3_76

performance of facial age estimation. In addition, age estimation has some unique challenges. For example, the aging process of human face is uncontrollable and personalized. It is affected by various intrinsic and extrinsic factors like identity, gender, ethnicity, living style and health condition. As a result, it is necessary and critical to extract appropriate features to represent the face images.

Typical age estimation methods mainly involve two concatenated modules: age feature representation and age estimation techniques. For the age feature representation, at the early stage, the main methods were based on geometric features to estimate the age group (baby, adult and senior) of face image. Later, studies focus on obtaining the exact age instead of coarse age range. AAM (Active Appearance Model) [1], AGES (AGing pattErn Subspace) [2,3], and age manifold [4–6] are used to extract shape and appearance features. However the above methods cannot represent the local textures which cause some loss of effective information. In recent years, local features continue to spring up such as LBP [7], Gabor features [8], SFP (Spatially Flexible Patch) [9], graphical facial features [10], and BIF (Biologically Inspired Features) [11]. Based on these features, the performance of age estimation has been greatly improved. Nevertheless, basically these features are originally proposed for face recognition and not designed for age estimation. Their effectiveness on age estimation may not be optimal. With the development of deep learning, the CNN (Convolutional Neural Network) [12] has also been used for age estimation. For age estimation, it can be treated as classification or regression problems, or the combination of the two. SVM and SVR [13] are two common used methods. Partial Least Squares (PLS) and Canonical Correlation Analysis (CCA) are also introduced for joint estimation of age, gender and race. Among existing methods, BIF features with CCA [14] was almost the best method in terms of accuracy. LARR [6] that Guo et al. proposed is an example of the hybrid method.

In this paper, we focus on effective age-sensitive feature extraction for age estimation. Intuitively, the methods that aim to deal with the unique characteristics of aging can yield better results compared with general approaches. Recently, Lei et al. proposes Discriminant Face Descriptor (DFD) [15] for face representation, which achieves competitive face recognition performances. In this work, we introduce DFD to estimate age. As far as we know, it is the first time to use DFD in this research area. Furthermore, we propose a stacked structure called Discriminant Face Descriptor network (DFDnet) to obtain more powerful and discriminative features. The DFDnet architecture incorporates multi-stage DFD and Bag-of-Features (BOF). Experiments on the widely used databases MORPH [16] and FG-NET [17] validate the effectiveness of our proposed method. The highlights and main contributions of the paper are summarized as follow.

(1) DFD is introduced to extract age-sensitive features. With the descriptor, we learn the most discriminative and related features to age variation.
(2) To obtain more powerful and discriminative features, we propose a new representation—DFDnet for age estimation.

(3) To study the performance of our proposed algorithm under unconstrained settings, we first perform an experiment on the publicly available dataset— Cross-Age Celebrity Dataset (CACD) [18].

The rest of this paper is organized as follows. Section 2 proposes our algorithm based on DFD and BOF model. Section 3 gives the experiments. Section 4 concludes this paper.

2 Discriminant Face Descriptor Network (DFDnet)

2.1 DFD

Original DFD [15] is designed for face recognition. The method learns the most discriminative features to distinguish different people and has achieved excellent performance. In this work, we propose to apply DFD for age estimation. Age-sensitive features are extracted instead of initial person-related features. In this method, each age is regarded as a class. Assume that images of the same age people are similar and can be considered as the same class while images of different ages are regarded as different classes. So our aim is to shrink the intra-class differences and enlarge the inter-class differences. To describe the image precisely, we learn the local DFDs. First, we evenly divide the image into several non-overlapping regions and learn the DFD of each part, respectively. The discriminant learning procedure includes two steps: image filters learning and optimal neighborhood sampling.

Given an image, we perform the LBP-like operator. For each pixel in the image, the pixel difference vector (PDV) is calculated based on its neighbor pixels. Taking the example of the pth pixel, the corresponding PDV is represented as $dI^p = [I^p - I^{p_1}, I^p - I^{p_2}, ..., I^p - I^{p_d}]^T$ where I^p is the pixel value at the center p, and I^{p_i} is the neighbor pixel value. d is the number of the pixels in the neighborhood. Two 8-Neighbor circles ($d = 16$) are considered as the neighborhood of the center pixel in this paper.

Image filter learning is to find a discriminant filter f so that the PDVs of filtered images of the same age are consistent and those of different ages are distinct. The optimal neighborhood sampling is to learn a weighting matrix corresponding to each PDV because different neighboring pixels could be of different effects on age estimation. The image filter size is set to $l1 \times l2$. We combine all the PDVs in the same patch together to form pixel different matrix (PDM) DI^p. After the discriminant learning, the pth pixel is encoded as $w^T * DI^p * v$, where w and v are image filters and neighborhood sampling matrix, $v = [v_1, v_2, ..., v_d]^T$.

Following Fisher criterion, the purpose of DFD learning can be denoted as minimizing the between-class scatter S_b and maximizing within-class scatter S_w. That is computed as follows

$$\min_{w,v} \quad S_w/S_b \tag{1}$$

$$S_w = \sum_{i=1}^{L} \sum_{j=1}^{C_i} \sum_{p=1}^{N} w^T (DI_{ij}^p - Dm_i^p) vv^T (DI_{ij}^p - Dm_i^p)^T w$$

$$S_b = \sum_{i=1}^{L} \sum_{p=1}^{N} C_i w^T (Dm_i^p - Dm^p) vv^T (Dm_i^p - Dm^p)^T w$$

where DI_{ij}^p is the PDM of the jth image in class i at position p and Dm_i^p is the mean PDM for the ith class. We preserve $k1$ image filters and $k2$ sampling vectors—$\{w_i\}_{i=1}^{k1}$ and $\{v_j\}_{j=1}^{k2}$. After encoded with w and v, the PDM is projected into a $k1 \times k2$ matrix. The matrix is reshaped to a $k1k2$-dimensions discriminant pattern vector (DPV). The obtained DPVs of the images at the same age are alike, and the differences of DPVs of different ages people are enlarged. Whereafter, the K-means clustering method is used to learn the dominant patterns which constitute the codebook. The pixel is labeled with the ID of dominant pattern which is most similar with the extract discriminant pattern vector. Then, we compute the histogram feature of each region and concatenate them into the final features. We reduce the high dimensions features by principal component analysis (PCA). And the simplest linear regression are used to estimate the age based on an image.

2.2 DFD Network

To explore more discriminative information, we propose to construct a stacked structure—DFDnet for age estimation. The DFDnet process is composed of two-stage DFD learning and BOF extraction. Suppose that we are given a set of N images $\{I_k\}_{k=1}^{N}$ of size $m \times n$ and their corresponding age labels. The entire process of DFDnet is illustrated in Fig. 1.

The First Stage: DFD. The discriminant learning procedure includes two steps: image filters learning and optimal neighborhood sampling. Based on the previous DFD model, we learn $k1$ image filters $W_1 = [w_1, w_2, ..., w_{k1}] \in R^{l1l2 \times k1}$ and $k2$ sampling strategies $V_1 = [v_1, v_2, ..., v_{k2}] \in R^{d \times k2}$. Each pixel of an input image I_k is projected into a matrix $M = W_1^T * DI^p * V_1 \in R^{k1 \times k2}$ and then the matrix is reshaped to a $k1k2$-dimension discriminant pattern vector f. Let the $k1k2$-dimensions vector f as the pixel value of a $k1k2$-channel image $\widehat{I}_k$. We regard the $k1k2$-channel image $\widehat{I}_k$ as a group of $k1k2$ images $\{X_{k,l}\}_{l=1}^{k1k2}$. Then, similar to the PCAnet [19], we carry out stacked DFDs to extract higher level and powerful features.

The Second Stage: DFD. The input images of this stage are the results of the previous stage. All the images of the second stage can be denoted as $\{X_{k,l}\}_{k=1}^{N}, l = 1, 2, ..., k1k2$. For each l, we treat $\{X_{k,l}\}_{k=1}^{N}$ as a group of input images. Repeat the learning process at the first stage. The learning result of the lth group input images are obtained as $S^l = \{w_i^2\}_{i=1}^{k1}$ and $T^l = \{v_j^2\}_{j=1}^{k2}$. Encoding $X_{k,l}$ with S^l and T^l, we get output images $O_{k,l} = \{Y_{k,l,h}\}_{h=1}^{k1k1}$.

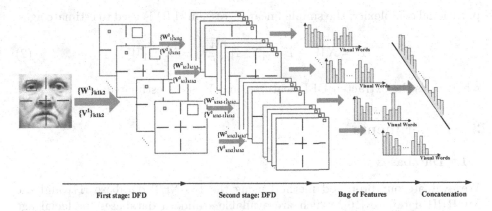

Fig. 1. The pipeline of the proposed 2-stage DFDnet. In the DFD learning stage, the discriminant image filters and the optimal nationhood sampling strategy are obtained. An image generates a group of images though different filters and sampling strategy. In the BOF stage, images in a group are treated as an image whose pixels are discriminant pattern vectors. K-means method is used to build the codebook. For each pixel, the corresponding vector is labeled with the ID of the similar visual word. Histogram features of each group are extracted and finally concatenated together.

The final learned image filters and sampling strategies of the whole second stage are represented as $W_2 = \{S^l\}_{l=1}^{k1k2}$ and $V_2 = \{T^l\}_{l=1}^{k1k2}$. We concatenate $O_{k,l}$ for all N images as the final output

$$O_l = \{O_{k,l}\}_{k=1}^N, \ l = 1, 2, \dots k1k2.$$

The total images number of output of this stage is $k1k2 \times k1k2$.

Output Stage: BOF. For each l, the output of the second DFD stage O_l is the input of the BOF as a whole group. $O_{k,l}$ is treated as an $k1k2$-channel image, and each channel corresponds to $Y_{k,l,h}$ at a certain h. That is to say, each pixel of the image is represented with a $k1k2$-dimensions vector. We intend to convert vector represented pixels to visual words, which also produces a codebook. A visual word can be considered as a representative of several similar pixels. K-means clustering method is used to construct the codebook and visual words are defined as the centers of clusters. By matching the pixels with the visual words, each pixel is labeled with the ID of the matched visual word. The $k1k2$-channel image $O_{k,l}$ can be represented by the histogram of the visual words. $\{O_{k,l}\}_{l=1}^{k1k2}$ are derived from the same image, so we concatenate all groups together into the final feature descriptors to represent the image I_k.

Estimation Stage: LR. In our experiments, we treat age estimation as a regression problem, where ages are taken as regression values. To decrease computational complexity, the simple linear regression (LR) is used to estimate ages.

$$Y = X\overline{W} + E = [X \quad 1] \begin{bmatrix} \overline{W} \\ E \end{bmatrix} = [X \quad 1] W \tag{2}$$

where X is the extracted DFD features, and Y is the estimated age.

3   Experiments

3.1   Databases

We evaluate our proposed method using the FG-NET database [17] and the MORPH database [16], which are available standard databases for facial age estimation. Moreover, CACD [18] are used to evaluate the performance of our proposed algorithm in practice.

FG-NET database contains 1,002 color or gray scale face images of 82 subjects. Images are from multiple races with large variation of lighting, pose, and expression. In the database, each subject has $6 \sim 18$ images attached with exact corresponding ages. The age ranges from 0 to 69 years but the age distribution is highly uneven.

MORPH consists of two albums. MORPH-I is so small that we only use MORPH-II for our study. The total number of MORPH-II is about 55,000 and MORPH-II provides the personal information, such as age, gender, and ethnicity. Compared with FG-NET, MORPH database is more abundant in the age information, but the faces in the set are under uneven illumination i.e., the forehead is in a strong light.

CACD (Cross-Age Celebrity Dataset) is collected from Internet movie database (IMDB) which is the largest public cross-age database. The database includes more than 160 thousands images of 2000 celebrities taken from 2004 to 2013 (10 years in total). The age ranges from 16 to 62. Compared with MORPH and FG-NET, CACD has the biggest total quantity and average number of each subject.

3.2   Comparison Between DFD and DFDnet

In the FG-NET database, images in the age range of 31 to 69 account for the minority. So we carry out our experiment on images with age from 0 to 30. For each specific age, half of the images are randomly selected as training set, and the other half are used as test set. For the MORPH database, we follow the standard evaluation protocol. The complete database is partitioned into two disjoint sets. One set is used for training and the other is used for testing. The number of test images is the overwhelming majority (about 80%). To reduce the effect of scale, rotation, and translation variations, we align the face regions based on the pupils and cropped them to 60×60 pixels.

For the two databases, the parameters of the learners are adjusted from a tuning data set (part of the training set) which covers images of all ages and are applied to the training and test set. We implement three groups of experiments with different parameters. In each group, both DFD method and the DFDnet method are used for age estimation. For the sake of contrastive analysis, their parameter settings are consistent. Only in this way can the effectiveness of DFDnet be proved. The filter size, the number of optimal filters, and the number of sampling strategies are empirically set to $l1 = l2 = 5, k1 = 5, k2 = 4$ as [15]. The face images are evenly divided into 2×2 or 3×3 local regions. The number of visual words in the codebook are set to 512 or 1024.

Table 1 shows the MAEs and CSs [11] in the two methods (DFD and DFDnet) with three groups of parameter settings. From the point of view of the horizontal comparison, applying the same method, the larger the image size, the more the local regions and the bigger the codebook size, the better the performance is. At the same time, through the vertical comparison, with the same parameter settings, our proposed DFDnet algorithm is more powerful in comparison with original DFD algorithm. On average, the MAEs reduce at least one year and the CSs have a rise of ten percent.

Table 1. The improvement of DFDnet

Methods	Setting		MAE		CS(5-year)	
	regions num & codebook size		MORPH	FG-NET	MORPH	FG-NET
DFD	2×2	512	6.45	4.93	0.46	0.60
DFDnet	2×2	512	5.47	3.48	0.53	0.77
DFD	3×3	1024	5.80	3.79	0.51	0.72
DFDnet	3×3	1024	4.65	**3.30**	0.60	0.77

The CS curves are shown in Fig. 2. The smaller the MAE is, the higher the cumulative score. This illustrates that the performance has a great improvement on both MAE and CS by DFDnet method.

3.3   Comparison with Other Age Estimators

Table 2 lists the age estimation results from various age estimators on MORPH and FG-NET. The BIF+LR method adopts the same training and test sets as our proposed DFDnet method. On the MORPH database, our method achieves an MAE of 4.65 years. As far as feature representation is concerned, our proposed method is pretty close to the BIF. In FG-NET, the MAE of our method is 3.3 years, which is far smaller than the 4.73 of the BIF+LR method. It follows that DFDnet overperforms the BIF method in terms of age estimation.

3.4   Age Estimation in Unconstrained Environment

Age estimation is necessary to operate on unconstrained face images in order to support the use of this technology in real life applications. So we use CACD to

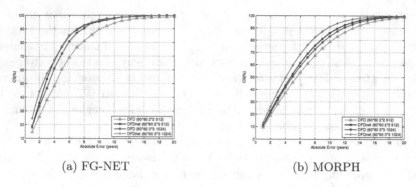

(a) FG-NET   (b) MORPH

Fig. 2. Cumulative scores on FG-NET and MORPH.

Table 2. The MAEs and CSs on the FG-NET and MORPH

Methods	MAE		CS(5-year)	
	MORPH	FG-NET	MORPH	FG-NET
AAM+BIF(2013)[20]	4.8	4.8	–	–
BIF+LR	4.48	4.73	0.63	0.60
DFDnet+LR(Ours)	4.65	3.30	0.60	0.77

evaluate the performance of our proposed algorithm in practice. It is the first time to estimate the ages on this dataset. We select a subset of 200 celebrities. They are manually checked and the noisy images are removed. The total number of the selected images is 7600. One half images are the training set, and the other are the test set. We crop and resize the facial images into 60×60 pixels, and divide the images into 3×3 parts. The codebook size are set to 2048.

Table 3 shows the results of DFDnet, DFD and BIF methods. The MAE of DFD is 8.50 years. The MAE of DFDnet is reduced to 5.57, which is also better than BIF method. It is shown that DFDnet based method has good robustness to variations in practice for age estimation.

Table 3. The MAEs and CSs on the CACD

Methods	MAE	CS(5-year)
BIF+LR	6.54	0.49
DFD+LR	8.50	0.44
DFDnet+LR(Ours)	**5.57**	**0.53**

4   Conclusions

We employ the DFD for age estimation. In order to enhance the performance of DFD, we construct a simple DFD network to explore more useful and discriminative information. The DFDnet architecture consists of two-stage DFDs and BOF. The network parameters like the size and number of filters, the number of sampling patterns and the size of codebook are pre-defined. The results on MORPH, FG-NET as well as the real-world CACD validate the performance improvement on account of our proposed algorithm.

Acknowledgments. This work was supported by the Chinese National Natural Science Foundation Projects ♮61203267, ♮61375037, ♮61473291, ♮61175034, National Science and Technology Support Program Project ♮2013BAK02B01, Chinese Academy of Sciences Project *No.* KGZD-EW-102-2, and AuthenMetric R&D Funds.

References

1. Lanitis, A., Taylor, C.J., Cootes, T.F.: Toward automatic simulation of aging effects on face images. Pattern Analysis and Machine Intelligence (2002)
2. Geng, X., Zhou, Z.H., Zhang, Y., Li, G., Dai, H.: Learning from facial aging patterns for automatic age estimation. In: Multimedia. ACM (2006)
3. Geng, X., Zhou, Z.H., Smith-Miles, K.: Automatic age estimation based on facial aging patterns. Pattern Analysis and Machine Intelligence (2007)
4. Fu, Y., Xu, Y., Huang, T.S.: Estimating human age by manifold analysis of face pictures and regression on aging features. In: Multimedia and Expo. IEEE (2007)
5. Fu, Y., Huang, T.S.: Human age estimation with regression on discriminative aging manifold. Multimedia (2008)
6. Guo, G., Fu, Y., Dyer, C.R., Huang, T.S.: Image-based human age estimation by manifold learning and locally adjusted robust regression. Image Processing (2008)
7. Gunay, A., Nabiyev, V.V.: Automatic age classification with LBP. In: Computer and Information Sciences. IEEE (2008)
8. Takimoto, H., Mitsukura, Y., Fukumi, M., Akamatsu, N.: Robust gender and age estimation under varying facial pose. Electronics and Communications in Japan (2008)
9. Yan, S., Liu, M., Huang, T.S.: Extracting age information from local spatially flexible patches. In: Acoustics, Speech and Signal Processing. IEEE (2008)
10. Suo, J., Wu, T., Zhu, S., Shan, S., Chen, X., Gao, W.: Design sparse features for age estimation using hierarchical face model. In: Automatic Face & Gesture Recognition. IEEE (2008)
11. Guo, G., Mu, G., Fu, Y., Huang, T.S.: Human age estimation using bio-inspired features. In: Computer Vision and Pattern Recognition. IEEE (2009)
12. Yi, D., Lei, Z., Li, S.Z.: Age estimation by multi-scale convolutional network. In: Cremers, D., Reid, I., Saito, H., Yang, M.-H. (eds.) ACCV 2014. LNCS, vol. 9005, pp. 144–158. Springer, Heidelberg (2015)
13. Fernández, C., Huerta, I., Prati, A.: A comparative evaluation of regression learning algorithms for facial age estimation. In: FFER in conjunction with ICPR. IEEE (2014) (in press)
14. Guo, G., Mu, G.: Joint estimation of age, gender and ethnicity: CCA vs. PLS. In: Automatic Face and Gesture Recognition. IEEE (2013)
15. Lei, Z., Pietikainen, M., Li, S.Z.: Learning discriminant face descriptor. Pattern Analysis and Machine Intelligence (2014)

16. Ricanek, K., Tesafaye, T.: Morph: a longitudinal image database of normal adult age-progression. In: Automatic Face and Gesture Recognition. IEEE (2006)
17. The FG-NET aging database. http://www.fgnet.rsunit.com/
18. Chen, B.-C., Chen, C.-S., Hsu, W.H.: Cross-age reference coding for age-invariant face recognition and retrieval. In: Fleet, D., Pajdla, T., Schiele, B., Tuytelaars, T. (eds.) ECCV 2014, Part VI. LNCS, vol. 8694, pp. 768–783. Springer, Heidelberg (2014)
19. Chan, T.H., Jia, K., Gao, S., Lu, J., Zeng, Z., Ma, Y.: Pcanet: A simple deep learning baseline for image classification? arXiv preprint arXiv:1404.3606 (2014)
20. Geng, X., Yin, C., Zhou, Z.H.: Facial age estimation by learning from label distributions. Pattern Analysis and Machine Intelligence (2013)

Action Detection Based on Latent Key Frame

Xiaoqiang Li[(⊠)] and Qian Yao

School of Computer Engineer and Science, Shanghai University, Shanghai, China
xqli@shu.edu.cn

Abstract. Human action detection in videos is a challenging problem in the field of Computer Vision and it has become an active researching field in recent years. For most published methods, which analyses entire video and assign a single action label; by contrast, in our research, it has been proved that most of actions could be detected within only a few frames. Based on this hypothesis, a temporal structure based model named Latent Key Frames Model (LKFM) is proposed, in which the action was represented as a sequence of Key Frames. LKFM is able to find the optimal Key Frames sequences with the help of latent support vector machine (Latent SVM); and for each Key Frame in the Key Frames sequence, a 2d model is built with the help of Deformable Part-based Model (DPM). The proposed method has been evaluated on Weizmann dataset and UCF sports dataset, and the experimental results demonstrate that this model is able to achieve competitive performance.

Keywords: Action detection · Latent Support Vector Machine · DPM

1 Introduction

The detection and recognition of human actions in videos is a topic of active researches in computer vision, and significant progress has been made in recent years, particularly with the invention of local invariant features and the bag-of-features framework [1]. Past researches can be roughly classified into two approaches: one is extracting global features from videos [2, 3], and aiming to assign a single label to the entire video with these features. The other approach is extracting features locally for each frame (or a small set of frames), and assigning one individual action label to each frame [4-6]. However, these approaches discard temporal information inherent in actions and are, thus, not be well adapted to distinguish actions with several motion or posture changes.

As described in paper [7], depending on the time scale of movements, actions are traditionally grouped into: short but punctual actions (e.g. drink, hug), simple but periodic actions (e.g. walking, boxing), and more complex activities that are considered as a composition of shorter or simpler actions (e.g. a long jump, cooking). According to our observations, no matter how simple or complex the motion is, an action can be naturally divided into a sequence of postures (Fig.1). Each posture in the sequence should be only performed in the particular frames. When them once be found, it's easy to recognize the action by us. Therefore, temporal information helps action detection at all time scales. Nevertheless, obtaining most discriminative frame

© Springer International Publishing Switzerland 2015
J. Yang et al. (Eds.): CCBR 2015, LNCS 9428, pp. 659–668, 2015.
DOI: 10.1007/978-3-319-25417-3_77

sequence of actions is challenging, especially in action video with great intra-class variation and complex environment. In fact, many success approaches ignore this, model an action as a spatio-temporal cuboid represented by a global Bag-of-words (BoW) [16-18].

In this paper, a simple discriminative framework is proposed for classifying human actions by introducing a new temporal structure based model, named Latent Key Frames Model (LKFM). In LKFM, Key Frames are defined as the most representative frame sequence of the action. Then LKFM will find the optimal Key Frames with the help of Latent SVM and build Deformable Part-based Model (DPM) [8] for each posture performed in the Key Frames. Since this proposed approach takes temporal information of Key Frames into DPM, so it could be regarded as temporally structured extension of DPM in spatio-temporal.

Fig. 1. Actions can be recognized easily with only a few postures. Making phone call (Top) and playing golf (bottom).

The rest of this paper is structured as following. Related works are discussed in section 2; and proposed approaches are elaborated in section 3 including the definition of Key Frames and finding optimal Key Frames with latent support vector machine (Latent SVM); then extensive experimental results is shown in section 4; lastly section 5 is for conclusion.

2   Related Work

Recently, a few researches describe the methods of detecting actions with temporal information mining from only parts of a video instead of the entire video.

K. Schindler et al. [10] discussed the number of frames that required in human action recognition by presenting an action recognition system which using very short sequences called "snippets" including 1 to 10 frames; And prove that even information in a single frame is enough to achieve the correct recognitions for some sample actions, such as walking or jumping.

Nowozin et al. [21] introduced Discriminative Subsequence Mining, which is used to find optimal discriminative subsequence patterns and represent video as a sequence of discretized spatio-temporal words sets.

Niebles and et al. [7] proposed a simple discriminative framework for classifying human activities by aggregating information from motion segments that are considered both for their visual features as well as their temporal composition. Unfortunately, motion segmentation is a difficult task. The method used by us is similar to [8], which proposed a model that based on a sequence of atomic action units, termed actom; following by representing the temporal structure of actions as a sequence of histograms constituted by actom-anchored visual features, which can be seen as a temporally structured extension of the bag-of-feature.

The approach proposed by us could be regarded as temporally structured extension of DPM [11] in spatio-temporal. There are already exist some researches focusing on this field, such as T. YiCong et al. [9] generalized the DPM by changing HOG [15] to HOG3D [14]. In our approach, Actions are represented as discriminative Key Frames sequences, which are found through Latent SVM [11] automatically, and the postures performed in each Key Frame will be represented by DPM.

3   Latent Key Frames Model

3.1   Key Frames Definition

According to our observations, actions can be easily detected within only a few frames. Based on this hypothesis, first of all, Key Frames are defined as a sequence of frames with which actions could be detected easily; and then for each Key Frame i in Key Frames, it will be represented in three parts: 1. A 2d model $d_i(x)$ which represents the posture performed in this Key Frame. For here we choose DPM as the 2d model, the "parts" in DPM contain detailed information of the posture, so that it is helpful to discriminate different postures; 2. The temporal position p_i and the offset o_i. Key Frame i is most likely to be appeared in the neighborhood of P_i (Fig. 2), and o_i is used to handle the intra-class temporal variation; 3. The weight of 2d model w_{di} and the weight of temporal position w_{pi}. The structure of LFKM shows in Fig. 2.

Given a video with m frames $X=\{x_1, ..., x_m\}$, where x_i is the i th frame of the video. Then the score of a LKFM with n Key Frames is :

$$f(X) = \max_{t \in T^n} \sum_{i=1}^{n} (w_{d_i} \times d(x_{t_i}) + w_{p_i} \times \Delta t_i)$$ (1)

T^n is the Key Frame space. $T^n = \{t \mid t=(t1, ..., tn), 1 \leq ti \leq m\}$.   And

$$\Delta t_i = \frac{1}{2\pi o_i} \exp(\frac{-(t_i - t_0 - p_i)^2}{2o_i^2})$$ (2)

where t_0 is the beginning frame of the action in the video. Δt_i is a gaussian function and will reach maximum when $t_i - t_0 = p_i$. t_0 has been manually labeled on the training set. The method of finding t_0 in a real video will be discussed in section 3.3.

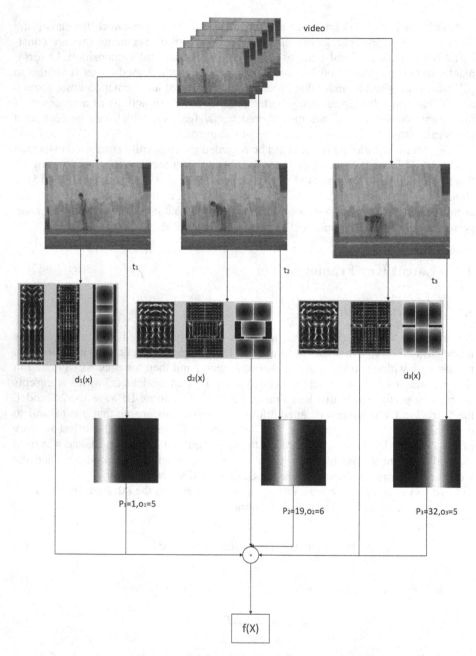

Fig. 2. The matching process on $t \in T^n$. Top layer is the video X. Second layer is the t_i th frame of X. Third layer contain the DPM $d_i(x)$ of each Key Frame. Last layer is the visualize of temporal position p_i and offset o_i.

3.2   Latent Information Mining

It is hard to decide which frames are the optimal Key Frames, since Key Frames space T^n is so big that it is impossible to enumerate all the possible Key Frames. However, enlightened by [11], the position of Key Frames could be regarded as latent variable ,thus a similar approach is able to used for solving our problem. Rewrite (1):

$$f(X) = \max_{t \in T^n} \sum W \cdot \Phi(X,t)$$

$$W = (w_d, w_p) \tag{3}$$

$$\Phi(X,t) = (d(x_t), \Delta t)$$

t is treated as latent value. Then given a labeled training set $D=\{<X_1,Y_1>, \ldots, <X_i,Y_i>,\ldots\}$ where $X_i=\{x_1,\ldots,x_m\}$ and $Y_i \in \{-1, 1\}$, the goal is to minimizing the objective function:

$$L_D(W) = \tfrac{1}{2}\|W\|^2 + C \sum_{i=1}^{n} \max(0, 1 - Y_i f_W(X_i)) \tag{4}$$

Following [11], first initializing the model:

Divide D into positive set D_p and negative set D_n , initialize the model with N Key Frames. See Algorithm below for detail.

```
Algorithm 1
Input: D_p , D_n , N
Output: Initialized  d_i(x) , p_i , o_i , w_{d_i} , w_{p_i}
Initialize: pos = 1 , M = min({m | m = length(X), X ∈ D_p}),
S =[], S.length = M

 1. pSet = {x_i | i = pos, x_i ∈ X, X ∈ D_p}
 2. nSet = {x_i | i = random(), x_i ∈ X, X ∈ D_n}
 3. for i = 1...N
 4.     d_i(x) = BUILD_DPM(pSet, nSet)
 5.     pSet = {}, nearList = {}
 6.     for each X in D_p
 7.         nearList = nearList + {NEAREST_MAXIMA(X, pos, d_i(x))}
 8.         for j=1...M
 9.             S[j] = S[j] + d_i(x_j)
10.         endfor
11.     endfor
12.     p_i = average(nearList)
13.     o_i = (max(nearList) - min(nearList)) / 2
14.     pos = arg min(S[pos])
                pos
```

15. $pSet = \{x_i \mid i = pos, x_i \in X, X \in D_p\}$

16. **endfor**

17. compute w_{d_i} , w_{p_i} with a Linear SVM

The function *BUILD_DPM* (*pSet*, *nSet*) builds DPM with positive frame set *pSet* and negative frame set *nSet*; and the function *NEAREST_MAXIMA*(*X*, *pos*, $d_i(x)$) looks for all maxima of $d_i(x)$, returns the one that nearest to *pos* (Fig.3).

In Algorithm 1, *pSet* and *nSet* are the positive and negative frame set used to train DPM model, and *S* is the DPM score of each frames. Such that in main loop (3 to 16), first, a new DPM $d_i(x)$ is trained with *pSet* and *nSet* and p_i and o_i are initialized according to the score of $d_i(x)$ on each frame in D_p; then *pSet* is renewed for the next loop; finally, after the loop, w_{di}, w_{pi} are trained with SVM.

Once the model has been initialized, the algorithm iteratively train it as follow:

1. Find the optimal $t_{opt} \in T^n$ where $t_{opt}=argmax_t \in {}_{Tn} W \cdot \Phi(X, t)$ update p to the average of all t_{opt} and update o to the radius of all t_{opt}. Training new DPM $d(x)$ with t_{opt} frames.
2. Optimize $L_D(W)$ over W where $f(X)=\sum \Phi(X, t_{opt})$ with stochastic gradient descent. Read [11] for more detail. Thus, the models are updated to better capture action characteristics.

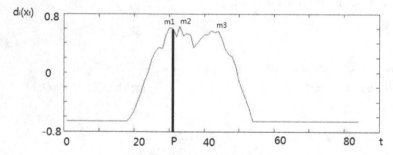

Fig. 3. Example of *NEAREST_MAXIMA*(*X*, *P*, $d_i(x)$). m1, m2, m3 are maxima of $d_i(x)$. m1 is the maxima nearest to *P*. So we will return the position of m1.

3.3   Action Detect with LKFM

When a test video is given, the first thing is to determine the beginning frame t_0 of the action. In the training set, t_0 has been manually labeled, but in test video, action might begin at any frames, such that searching all possible t_0 is required. Read algorithm 2 for detail.

```
Algorithm 2
Input: X
Output: finalScore , startTime
Initialize: M = LENGTH(X), N =Key Frames number
```

1. $S = \{s_{i,j} \mid s_{i,j} = d_i(x_j)\}$
2. $finalScore = \{\}, startTime = \{\}$
3. **for** $t_0 = 1 \ldots M$
4. $score = 0$
5.   **for** $i = 1 \ldots N$
6. $score = score + \max\limits_{t_0 \le t \le M}(w_{d_i} \times s_{i,t} + w_{p_i} \times \Delta t)$
7.   **endfor**
8.   **if** $(score > threshold)$
9. $finalScore = finalScore + \{score\}$
10. $startTime = startTime + \{t_0\}$
11. **endif**
12. **endfor**

In Algorithm 2, $d_i(x)$ is computed on every frames in advance so that it can be reused later. The next step is searching the whole video; for line 5 to 7, the score of each Key Frames is computed, following by picking up and sending the maximum one into *score*; for line 8 to 11, the ones exsiting in *score* as well as larger than the threshold will be added to the *finalScore*.

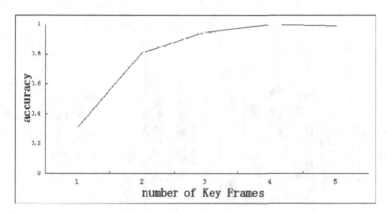

Fig. 4. Accuracy on weizmann dataset reaches peak when there are 4 Key Frames in our model

4   Experimental Evaluation

4.1   Experiment on Weizmann Dataset

Weizmann dataset [13] collected a database of 90 low-resolution (180 × 144, de-interlaced 50 fps) video sequences showing nine different people, each one performed 10 natural actions. The main advantage of Weizmann dataset is that the controlled conditions of those performed actions and the availability of pixel-level actor masks given us the ability to training DPM.

This dataset has been proved for easily use and great recognition performance through other approaches, thus it's the primarily tool to find out how the number of Key Frames affect detection result (Fig. 4).

In Fig. 4, It is easy to find that the number of Key Frames will greatly affect result, and the peak of accuracy occurred when Key Frames number is 4, therefore 4 Key Frames are enough to recognize and detect actions in controlled conditions like Weizmann dataset.

4.2   Experiment on UCF Sports Dataset

The UCF Sports Dataset [19] consists of videos, which are captured in realistic scenarios with complex and cluttered background from sports broadcasts with a total of 150 videos in 10 action classes, which exhibit significant intra-class variation. Frame-level annotations are provided to ease the training of DPM. In our experiment, bad videos are fixed, and dataset has been splited into disjoint training and testing sets, in order to build models with 4 Key Frames and test the models. In action recognition, The result is 76.4% , over 73.1% from [9], and 75.1% from [12] (Fig. 5). Furthermore, [9] treats human location as latent variable and uses figure-centric model to represent actions; [12] is another temporally structured extension of DPM.

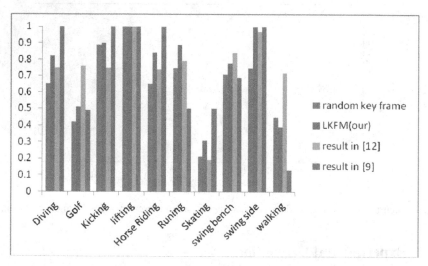

Fig. 5. Comparisons on UCF sports with [9] and [12] and random key frame

Another model is trained with random chosen Key Frames(without using LSVM) for comparison, see Fig.5.. when it is trained by the random key frames(without LSVM), the accuracy drops a lot, which supports the hypothesis that optimal Key Frames is helpful to the action Detection. Fig. 6 is the visualize of one of such model.

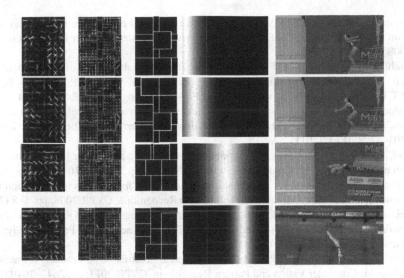

Fig. 6. Model of action Diving with 4 Key Frame 3,10,35,49. Left is the visualize of the DPM of each Key Frame, middle is the visualize of Key Frame position p and offset o, right is the key frame find in one positive video.

5   Conclusion

This paper present a temporal structure method for human action recognition which extension Deformable Part-based Models with Latent Key Frames, and such method was employed to prove the hypothesis that action can be recognized with a few discriminative frames instead of the whole video. Then in a detailed experimental evaluation, it's confirmed that Latent Key Frames are critical to improve the result of action detection, and Intra-class variation in real world actions can be handled easily with DPM and offset o. Finally, the speed of our model is the bottleneck, but some recent researches like [20] might be helpful for the speeding up of our model.

References

1. Laptev, I., Lindeberg, T.: On space-time interest points. In: ICCV, vol. 1, pp. 432–439 (2003)
2. Laptev, I., Lindeberg, T.: Local descriptors for spatio-temporal recognition. In: MacLean, W. (ed.) SCVMA 2004. LNCS, vol. 3667, pp. 91–103. Springer, Heidelberg (2006)
3. Ali, S., Basharat, A., Shah, M.: Chaotic invariants for human action recognition. In: IEEE 11th International Conference, pp. 1–8 (2007)
4. Niebles, J. C., Fei-Fei, L.: A hierarchical model of shape and appearance for human action classification. In: IEEE Conference on Computer Vision and Pattern Recognition, CVPR 2007, pp. 1–8 (2007)
5. Duchenne, O., Laptev, I., Sivic, J., Bach, F., Ponce, J.: Automatic annotation of human actions in video. In: IEEE 12th International Conference, pp. 1491–1498 (2009)

6. Laptev, I., Marszałek, M., Schmid, C., Rozenfeld, B.: Learning realistic human actions from movies. In: IEEE Conference on Computer Vision and Pattern Recognition, CVPR 2008, pp. 1–8 (2008)
7. Niebles, J.C., Chen, C.-W., Fei-Fei, L.: Modeling temporal structure of decomposable motion segments for activity classification. In: Daniilidis, K., Maragos, P., Paragios, N. (eds.) ECCV 2010, Part II. LNCS, vol. 6312, pp. 392–405. Springer, Heidelberg (2010)
8. Gaidon, A., Harchaoui, Z., Schmid, C.: Actom sequence models for efficient action detection. In: IEEE Conference on Computer Vision and Pattern Recognition, CVPR 2011, pp. 3201–3208. IEEE (2011)
9. Lan, T., Wang, Y., Mori, G.: Discriminative figure-centric models for joint action localization and recognition. In: Computer Vision, ICCV 2011, pp. 2003–2010 (2011)
10. Schindler, K., Van Gool, L.: Action snippets: how many frames does human action recognition require? In: Computer Vision and Pattern Recognition, CVPR 2008, pp. 1–8 (2008)
11. Felzenszwalb, P.F., Girshick, R.B., McAllester, D., Ramanan, D.: Object detection with discriminatively trained part-based models. IEEE Transactions on Pattern Analysis and Machine Intelligence 32(9), 1627–1645 (2010)
12. Tian, Y., Sukthankar, R., Shah, M.: Spatiotemporal deformable part models for action detection. In: Computer Vision and Pattern Recognition, CVPR 2013, pp. 2642–2649 (2013)
13. Oneata, D., Verbeek, J., Schmid, C.: Action and event recognition with Fisher vectors on a compact feature set. In: Computer Vision, ICCV 2013, pp. 1817–1824 (2013)
14. Russell, B.C., Freeman, W.T., Efros, A., Sivic, J., Zisserman, A.: Using multiple segmentations to discover objects and their extent in image collections. In: 2006 IEEE Computer Society Conference, vol. 2, pp. 1605–1614 (2006)
15. Laptev, I.: On space-time interest points. International Journal of Computer Vision 64 (2–3), 107–123 (2005)
16. Niebles, J.C., Wang, H., Fei-Fei, L.: Unsupervised learning of human action categories using spatial-temporal words. International Journal of Computer Vision, 299–318 (2008)
17. Klaser, A., Marszałek, M., Schmid, C.: A spatio-temporal descriptor based on 3D-gradients. In: BMVC 2008-19th British Machine Vision Conference, p. 275–1. British Machine Vision Association (2008)
18. Dalal, N., Triggs, B.: Histograms of oriented gradients for human detection. In: Computer Vision and Pattern Recognition, CVPR 2005, pp. 886–893 (2005)
19. Li, W., Zhang, Z., Liu, Z., Ogunbona, P.: Human action recognition with expandable graphical models. In: Machine Learning for Human Motion Analysis: Theory and Practice, pp. 187–212 (2010)
20. Sadeghi, M.A., Forsyth, D.: 30Hz object detection with DPM V5. In: Fleet, D., Pajdla, T., Schiele, B., Tuytelaars, T. (eds.) ECCV 2014, Part I. LNCS, vol. 8689, pp. 65–79. Springer, Heidelberg (2014)
21. Nowozin, S., Bakir, G., Tsuda, K.: Discriminative subsequence mining for action classification. In: Computer Vision, ICCV 2007, pp. 1–8. IEEE (2007)

A Facial Pose Estimation Algorithm Using Deep Learning

Xiao xu, Lifang Wu$^{(\boxtimes)}$, Ke Wang, Yukun Ma, and Wei Qi

School of Electronic Information and Control Engineering,
Beijing University of Technology, Beijing 100124, China
{xuxiao2013,wangke_0729,yukuner,
qw10020012}@emails.bjut.edu.cn, lfwu@bjut.edu.cn

Abstract. Pose estimation is one of key issues in face recognition in complex background and human-computer interaction. In this paper, we propose a novel algorithm to estimating facial pose using deep learning. We design a convolutional neural network with four convolutional layers, and a fully-connected layer. The experimental results on CMU-PIE database show that the proposed method outperforms previous traditional methods facial pose.

Keywords: Facial pose estimation · Convolutional Neural Network · Deep learning

1 Introduction

Facial pose estimation is important in many computer vision systems such as human-computer interaction, face recognition in complex background, video conference, driver monitoring and so on. In face recognition, facial pose variation has significantly influenced the performance of face recognition. Some researchers focus on estimating the facial pose and normalize facial pose before face recognition. However, facial pose estimation is a challenging problem since the estimation results usually are influenced by variant factors such as identity, facial expression, illumination and so on.

Many facial pose estimation methods have been proposed over decades. These methods can be classified into three categories: model-based [1], geometric [2], and image-based [3-4]. Model-based approaches usually use 2D or 3D statistical models to simulate the shape of human head. A. Dahmane et al. [5] proposed an approach to selecting a set of features from the symmetrical parts of the face, and they trained a Decision Tree model to recognize facial pose with regard to the areas of symmetry. The approach does not need the location of interest points on face and is robust to partial occlusion. X. Zhu et al. [6] employed tree-structured model to locate facial landmarks and used view-based models to describe the topological changes caused by facial pose variations. However, it is time-consuming to solve the optimization problem for landmarks localization.

Geometric methods detect the significant facial features, such as corners of eyes, nose tip and corners of mouth, to estimate facial pose from their relative configurations. A. Younesi et al. [2] proposed an algorithm to estimating facial pose by considering the locations of facial components such as eyes and mouth. They used two

© Springer International Publishing Switzerland 2015
J. Yang et al. (Eds.): CCBR 2015, LNCS 9428, pp. 669–676, 2015.
DOI: 10.1007/978-3-319-25417-3_78

algorithms to develop a new image in which the eyes and mouth are emphasized in face image, and then computed the sum of pixels in each column of new image to extract proper features. J. G. Wang et al. [7] estimated the facial pose using the automatic corners detection of each eye and mouth. The method was fast and simple without training process, and an acceptable result of facial pose could be got with only a few features. Geometric methods are usually straightforward and fast. However, they need detect the facial features accurately, which is usually difficult due to occlusion and facial expressions variability.

Image-based approaches considered the whole face region as a feature vector. Meydanipour et al. [8] proposed a method to facial pose estimation using Histogram of SIFT descriptors. Meydanipour G et al. [9] proposed a method, which applied contourlet SD transform on images, and then create feature vector by computing gray-level co-occurrence matrix (GLCM) from each contourlet sub-band. It used LDA to reduce the dimension of feature vector and used SVM for classification. X. Liu et al. [10] proposed a discriminative representation method of head images to perform facial pose estimation. In this method head images were preprocessed to improve facial features and to remove redundant information by skin color model and Laplacian of Gaussian transform. Then the eigen pose subspace is constructed by a matrix factorization method. Xin Geng et al. [11] proposed to give soft labels (a multivariate label distribution (MLD)) rather than hard labels to each image, and the feature they applied is Histogram of Oriented Gradients (HOG).

In this paper, we propose a novel method for facial pose estimation based on deep learning. We introduce a convolutional neural network with four convolutional layers, two pooling layers and a fully-connected layer. The output of the last fully-connected layer is fed to a 9-way soft-max which produces a distribution over the 9 poses ($-90°$, $-67.5°$, $-45°$, $-22.5°$, $0°$, $+22.5°$, $+45°$, $+67.5°$, $+90°$). Without relying on the hand-crafted features, the proposed framework automatically learns an effective discriminant representation of the face images and estimates the facial pose.

The rest of the paper is organized as follows. In section 2, the proposed facial pose estimation algorithm is introduced in details. In section 3, the compared experiments on CMU-PIE database are conducted, the experimental results confirm efficiency of the proposed approach. Finally, the paper is concluded in section 4.

2   The Proposed Algorithm

2.1   Overview of the Proposed Algorithm

We estimate the facial pose using the convolutional neural network (CNN) on Cuda-convnet. CNN is an end-to-end system. It does not need hand crafted feature. Therefore, what we should do is to design the network structure and to obtain the parameters from the training set.

First, the structure of the convolutional neural network is designed. In our work, a network with 4 convolution layers, 2 pooling layers and 1 fully-connected layer is designed. The last fully-connected layer can extract global features about facial pose.

The database is split into 5 groups. The first four groups are training set. And the fifth group is the test set. The training set is used to train the parameters in CNNs. For a face image, preprocessing is first implemented, in which face region is detected and it is split into ten different patches. Then all of the processed images are input into the CNNs, in the training stage, it is used for parameters training from the labeled pose classes. In the testing stage, the output shows the probability of each pose. The pose with the maximum probability is thought as the estimated pose.

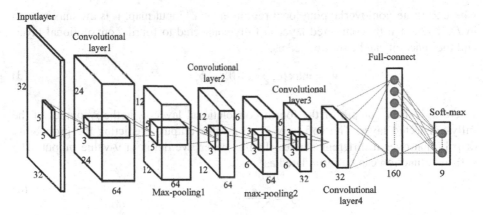

Fig. 1. The structure of convolutional neural network in our system

2.2 The Network Architecture

The architecture of CNN is shown in Figure 1. Four convolutional layers are stacked after the input layer. The first two convolutional layers are weight-sharing, and followed by max-pooling layer. The last two convolutional layers are Locally- connected, and without any weight-sharing. The last fully-connected layer is fully-connected to the fourth convolutional layer. The soft max output layer includes 9 classes, the pose with the maximum probability is thought the estimated pose.

The input layer is 32×32×3 image patches. The first convolutional layer and the following max-pooling layer have 64 convolution kernels respectively, and the size of every kernel is 5×5. The second convolutional layer and the following max-pooling layer also have 64 convolution kernels respectively, and the size of every kernel is 3×3. The last two convolutional layers are locally-connected layer with unshared weights, and every layer has 32 convolution kernels of size 3×3. The last fully-connected layer has 160 neurons, and it is fully-connected to the fourth convolutional layers. Soft-max output layer has 9 neurons, predicts 9 pose classes in our work.

The convolution function of forward propagation can be expressed as follows:

$$y_j = \max\{0, \sum_i W_{i,j} * x_i + b_j\} \tag{1}$$

where x_i is the ith input, y_j is the jth output. W^{ij} is the convolution kernel between the i-th input x_i and the jth output y_j. $*$ denotes convolution operation. b_j is the bias of the j-th output. The hidden neuron that we use is ReLU nonlinearity, $f(x)=max(0, x)$ which is proven to have better fitting abilities than the standard function $f(x)=tanh(x)$ and $f(x)=(1+e^{-x})^{-1}$ [12]. The max-pooling function can be formulated as:

$$y_j = \max_{k \in D}\{x_i^K\} \tag{2}$$

where D is the non-overlapping local region in the ith input map. y_j is the max neuron in D. The last fully-connected layer is fully-connected to fourth convolutional layer, and the function can be formulated as:

$$y_j = \max\{0, \sum_i x_i \cdot W_{i,j} + b_j\} \tag{3}$$

where x_i is the ith output of the fourth convolutional layer, y_j is the jth output of the fully-connected layer. The soft-max is an n-value output, predicting the probability distribution over n different classes. In this paper, we define a 9-value output. The soft-max function can be formulated as:

$$y_i = \frac{e^{x_i}}{\sum_j e^{x_j}} \tag{4}$$

where x_i is the vector of the 160 output of fully-connected layer. y_j is the ith output of soft-max layer.

2.3   Preprocessing

We get the image including face region for training or testing, before it is input into the CNNs, the image preprocessing is needed. In the paper, we use two image preprocessing methods. Firstly, we get the face region using face detection algorithm[18]. Secondly, the face region is normalized to size of 32×32, and 10 patches of 24 × 24 are cropped out from the 32 × 32 input images. These patches are overlapped. They correspond to the four corners and central region in the original image. Thirdly, the five patches are flipped horizontally and we get total 10 patches. Finally, 10 samples are generated from a face image.

In training stage, the total ten image patches are used. While in the testing stage, only the central patch of the test image is used for pose estimation.

2.4   The Training Stage

We trained the model using stochastic gradient descent. As known in section 2.1, the training set includes 4 groups of face images. The following two steps would be included:

1) The first 3 groups are utilized for training, the forth group are used for validation. The network with a learning rate of 10^{-3} is obtained by the 300 epochs.
2) The total 4 groups are used for training, the forth group is still used for validation. The network with still a learning rate of 10^{-4} is obtained by the 100 epochs.

3 Experimental Results

Our algorithm is tested in CMU PIE database. We compared our algorithm with state-of-the-art algorithms including LAG[14], Ba (PF+GMM)[15], Brown (NN)[16], Brown (Probabilistic)[16], Tian[17]. They are publicly available and challenging benchmarks. The experimental results are shown in two evaluation measures. One is the regression measures, in which the mean absolute error (MAE) between the predicted pose and the "ground truth" pose is obtained. It is a statistical measure of how far the estimated values are from actual values, and it is computed by averaging the difference between ground truth pose and estimated pose for all test images. The other one is the classification measures, in which the accuracy of the predicted pose with respect to the "ground truth" pose is obtained.

3.1 The Database

The CMU Pose, Illumination, and Expression (PIE) database (CMU PIE)[13] contains 41,368 images of 68 people under 13 poses, 43 different illumination conditions, and with 4 different expressions. 9 pose angles of the 13 poses are ranging from -90° to +90° at approximately 22.5° intervals across yaw with neutral expressions and natural room lighting, which is usually estimated in existing methods. In order to compare to existing state-of-the-art methods, we also only use these 9 poses in our experiment. Of the total 68 subjects, the first 34 persons are selected and the features of their facial poses used to train the network. The face images of other 34 persons are used for testing. Therefore, no subject appears in both training and testing sets. The 9 facial poses we use in this paper are show in Figure 2.

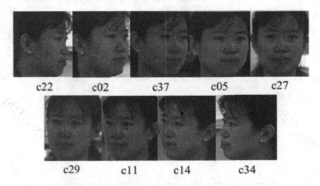

Fig. 2. The 9 example pose images in CMU PIE database

3.2   Comparison with State-of-the-Art

We compares our algorithm with LAG[14], Ba (PF+GMM)[15], Brown (NN)[16], Brown (Probabilistic)[16], Tian[17].

Figure 3 and figure 4 show the compared accuracy rate and MAE respectively. From the Figures, we can observe that our algorithm gets the highest accuracy of 99.4% with minimum MAE of 0.135 degree. The Lie Algebrized Gaussians (LAG)

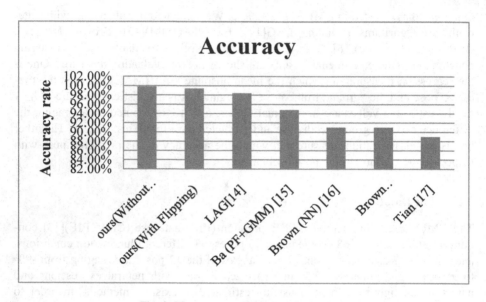

Fig. 3. The accuracy on CMU PIE database

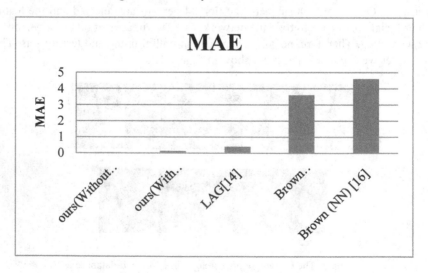

Fig. 4. The compared MAE on CMU PIE database

approach gets the accuracy of 98.4% with MAE of 0.4 degree, which is the best result in the compared algorithms. And it has a little worse performance than ours. Furthermore, it includes three steps to extract LAG features, and it is not an end to end algorithm. But in our work, the convolutional neuron network is end to end, it can get the features by only one step.

When training the dataset, the images are flipped horizontally. However, the images before and after flipping are very similar. So we do not flip the images when training. From the Figures, we can observe that our algorithm without flipping gets the accuracy of 99.8% with MAE of 0.045 degree. The result is best compared with other algorithms.

4   Conclusion

In this paper, we propose a facial pose estimation algorithm using convolutional neuron network. Compared with the traditional algorithms, the convolutional neuron network does not need hand crafted feature, and it is an end to end system. By learning the network layer by layer, the network is effective for pose estimation. The experimental results on CMU PIE Database show that the proposed algorithm outperforms previous traditional pose estimation algorithms.

References

1. Zhu, X., Ramanan, D.: Face detection, pose estimation, and landmark localization in the wild. In: CVPR, pp. 2879–2886 (2012)
2. Younesi, A., Kalbkhani, H., Shayesteh, G.: Robust head pose estimation using locations of facial components. In: Proc. of 16th CSI IEEE Intl Symposium on Artificial Intelligence and Signal Processing, pp. 1–5 (2012)
3. Jiang, M., Deng, L., Zhang, L., Tang, J., Fan,C.: Head pose estimation based on active shape model. In: Proc. of 2012 IEEE Int'l Conf. on Systems, Man and Cybernetics, pp. 1–4 (2012)
4. Raytchev, B., Yoda, I., Sakaue, K.: Head pose estimation by nonlinear manifold learning. In: Proc. of 2004 IEEE 17th Int'l Conf. on Pattern Recognition, pp. 462–466 (2004)
5. Dahmane, A., Larabi, S., Djeraba .C., Bilasco, I. M.: Learning symmetrical model for head pose estimation. In: Proc. of 21 th Int. Conf. on Pattern Recognition, pp. 1–4 (2012)
6. Zhu, X., Ramanan, D.: Face detection, pose estimation, and landmark localization in the wild. In: CVPR, pp. 2879–2886 (2012)
7. Wang, J.G., Sung, E.: Em enhancement of 3d head pose estimated by point at infinity. Image and Vision Computing 25(12), 1864–1874 (2007)
8. Meydanipour, G., Faez, K.: Head pose estimation using histogram of SIFT descriptors. In: 2014 22nd Iranian Conference on Electrical Engineering (ICEE), pp. 976–979. IEEE (2014)
9. Meydanipour, G., Faez, K.: Robust head pose estimation using contourletSD transform and GLCM. In: 2013 8th Iranian Conference on Machine Vision and Image Processing (MVIP), pp. 375–380. IEEE (2013)

10. Liu, X., Lu, H., Luo, H.: A new representation method of head images for head pose estimation. In: Proc. of 2009 IEEE 16th Int'l Conf. on Image Processing (ICIP), pp. 3585–3588 (2009)
11. Xin, G., Yu, X.: Head pose estimation based on multivariate label distribution. In: 2014 IEEE Conference on Computer Vision and Pattern Recognition (CVPR), pp. 1837–1842. IEEE (2014)
12. Krizhevsky, A., Sutskever, I., Hinton, G.: Imagenet classification with deep convolutional neural networks. In: Proc. NIPS (2012)
13. Sim, T., Baker, S., Bsat, M.: The CMU pose, illumination, and expression database. IEEE Transactions on Pattern Analysis and Machine Intelligence (PAMI) **25**(12), 1615–1618 (2003)
14. Hu, C., Gong, L., Wang, T.: Effective head pose estimation using Lie Algebrized Gaussians. In: 2013 IEEE International Conference on Multimedia and Expo (ICME), pp. 1–6. IEEE (2013)
15. Ba, S.O., Odobez, J.M.: A probabilistic framework for joint head tracking and pose estimation. In: IEEE International Conference on Pattern Recognition, ICPR (2004)
16. Brown, L.M., Tian, Y.-L.: Comparative study of coarse head pose estimation. In: IEEE Workshop on Motion and Video Computing, pp. 125–130 (2002)
17. Tian, Y.-L., Brown, L., Connell, J., Pankanti, S., Hampapur, A., Senior, A., Bolle, R.: Absolute head pose estimation from overhead wide-angle cameras. In: Proc. IEEE Int'l Workshop Analysis and Modeling of Faces and Gestures, pp. 92–99 (2003)
18. Viola, P., Jones, M.: Rapid object detection using a boosted cascade of simple features. In: IEEE Conference on Computer Vision and Pattern Recognition, CVPR 2001, vol. 1, pp. I-511–I-518 (2001)

Age Estimation Based on Canonical Correlation Analysis and Extreme Learning Machine

Jie Si[1], Jun Feng[1(✉)], Qirong Bu[1], Xiaohu Sun[1], Xiaowei He[1], and Shi Qiu[2]

[1] School of Information Science and Technology, Northwest University, Xi'an 710127, China
359251149@qq.com, fengjun@nwu.edu.cn
[2] Xi'an Institute of Optics and Precision Mechanics of CAS, Xi'an 710119, China

Abstract. We proposed a novel age estimation scheme based on feature fusion according to Canonical Correlation analysis. Specifically, the shape and texture attributes of feature points in human faces are characterized by both Active Appearance Model (AAM) and Local Binary Pattern (LBP). Then, the canonical projective vectors are built via canonical correlation analysis for feature fusion. To improve computational efficiency, we first introduce Extreme Learning Machine (ELM) to the field of age estimation, and uncover the relation of the fused features and ground-truth age values for age prediction. The experimental results conducted on FG-NET age database show that the proposed method achieves better estimation accuracy while requires less computation time than the state of art algorithms such as BIF.

Keywords: Age estimation · Canonical Correlation Analysis · Feature fusion · Extreme Learning Machine

1 Introduction

As a crucial part of human biological feature, human face reveals many facts about a person, such as, mood, truthfulness, gender, and age to name a few. In recent years, face-based age estimation has become a prominent topic in the field of computer vision, due to many possible applications, such as security control, electronic customer relationship management and surveillance monitoring. For example, Age Specific Human Computer Interaction (ASHCI) system [1] help prevent young kids from surfing harmful web pages, or control underage drinkers or smokers. More recently, Microsoft has also developed an interesting web application "How Old Do I Look?" to determine gender and age from uploaded facial images [2].

However, human face aging is a complicated process since people usually age in different ways [3, 4]. At present, most of age estimation systems have been casted into the framework of machine learning, which are typically divided into age factors extraction and age estimation.

Since the true age of human is usually hidden in intrinsic factors such as gender, ethnicity, heredity and extrinsic factors including environment, living styles, or smoking, accurate determination of a person's age from the face is very difficult. One of the main challenges is to find out "true" aging factors and characteristics from human

© Springer International Publishing Switzerland 2015
J. Yang et al. (Eds.): CCBR 2015, LNCS 9428, pp. 677–685, 2015.
DOI: 10.1007/978-3-319-25417-3_79

of age changing. Many researchers proposed different models for factors extraction. For example, Kwon et.al proposed body measurement factors called anthropometric model [5, 6].To classify the age of faces, the facial images are firstly divided into three categories roughly, i.e. babies, young and old. Head-heart shaped outline development theory are employed for facial texture analysis. However, the method are not able to complete fine age estimation.

Geng et.al proposed to treat a known face image as a subspace of the whole age range images, and then the image position in the subspace is indicated for age estimation [7]. However, the algorithm needs collect face images in all the different age stages which is very hard in practice.

Manifold Learning Model is also investigated for feature space optimization. High dimensional factors are expressed by a set of low dimensional age features, in order to capture the potential of the age structure of the face [8]. However, the method is only suitable for large age database and is required for each age data distribution.

In age estimation, regression analysis is the most common method. The age estimation is considered as a multi-linear regression problem, and the age estimation is achieved by establishing a functional model of the age variation of human face [9]. This method is simple and efficient, and it is the most widely used method currently.

Most existing facial age estimation method, usually unitize only the single features of facial images for age estimation. We believe that the shape information and texture information fusion, which is more able to express the face age information. Motivated by this reason, in this paper, we propose to combine the shape features with AAM [10] and the texture features with LBP [11] by canonical correlation analysis (CCA) [12]. Furthermore, in order to improve the computational efficiency, we propose to estimate the age by Extreme Learning Machine (ELM) [13]. Experimental results show that, compare to the state-of-art algorithms, our method achieve better performance both in accuracy and time efficiency.

2   Feature Extraction Based on Canonical Correlation Analysis

We first extract the shape and texture features of each face sample, respectively, and then fuse then by the canonical correlation analysis (CCA) method to further exploit their correlation.

For the shape feature, each face image was manually labeled with landmark points, and the positions of which define the face shape were used for face modeling. Fig. 1 shows a face with landmark points. Having acquired the points, each face shape was described by a vector: $s_i = (x_i^1, y_i^1, \ldots, x_i^m, y_i^m)^{\mathrm{T}}$. The Active Appearance Model (AAM) unified modeling of the shape and gray scale of deformable objects by principal component analysis, and obtain the changed features using the minimum norm strategy of an unknown target matching. Then AAM is used to extract the feature vector x_i for the image I_i.

Fig. 1. A face with landmark points.

For the texture feature, the LBP is a powerful method for describing the image texture by thresholding the surrounding pixels with its center pixel. According to the basic characteristics of face images, this paper we choose Rotation-invariant uniform pattern $LBP_{P,R}^{riu2}$ and circular neighborhood (16, 2) to extract the texture feature of facial image. Then LBP is used to extract the feature vector y_i for the image I_i.

    (a)original image   (b)gray-scale   (c)texture map

Fig. 2. Comparison of original image, gray-scale and texture map, as can be seen, the texture map can reflect the texture information of the face clearly.

From the Fig.1-2 we can see that the shape and texture information of each face sample is intrinsically different as they represent each face from two different aspects. Hence, our goal is to find two aspects of mutual benefit from the shape and texture. Canonical correlation analysis (CCA) is one of the statistical methods dealing with the mutual relationships between two random vectors. In multivariate statistical analysis, the correlation problem of two random vectors often needs to be studied, and that is to convert the correlation research of two random vectors into that of a few pairs of variable. Based on this idea, we find the feature of age information by combining the features of shape and texture. We extract two groups of feature vectors with same facial image-AAM method for shape feature and LBP method for texture feature, then to establish the correlation criterion function between the two groups of feature vectors, to extract their canonical correlation features according to this criterion, and to form effective discriminant vectors for age estimation.

Concretely, suppose $\vartheta=\{\ \xi\ |\ \xi \in R^N\}$ is a training faces space. Given $P=\{x|x\in R^p\}$ and $Q=\{y|y\in R^q\}$, where x and y are the two feature vectors of the same face ξ extracted by AAM method and LBP method. We will discuss the feature fusion in the transformed training sample feature space P and Q. We will find a pair of directions α and β that maximize the correlation between the projections $p_1= \alpha^T P$ and $q_1=\beta^T Q$.

The projections p_1 and q_1 are called the first pair of canonical variates. Then finding the second pair of canonical variates p_2 and q_2, which is uncorrelated with canonical variates p_1 and q_1 each other and also maximize the correlation between them. Just do like this until all the correlation features of P and Q are extracted. In order to study the correlation of P and Q, we only need analyze the correlation of a few pairs of canonical variates.

We can give the criterion function as the following:

$$J(\alpha,\beta) = \frac{\alpha^T S_{xy}\beta}{\sqrt{(\alpha^T S_{xx}\alpha\beta^T S_{yy}\beta)}} \tag{1}$$

Suppose that S_{xx} and S_{yy} denote the covariance matrices of P and Q respectively, while S_{xy} denotes their between-set covariance matrix. Our idea is to extract the canonical correlation features between x and y based on the idea of CCA; we denote them as $\alpha_1^T x$ and $\beta_1^T y$ (the first pair), $\alpha_2^T x$ and $\beta_2^T y$ (the second pair), ..., $\alpha_d^T x$ and $\beta_d^T y$ (the dth pair). Given the following:

$$P' = (\alpha_1^T x, \alpha_2^T x, \cdots, \alpha_d^T x)^T = (\alpha_1, \alpha_2, \cdots \alpha_d)^T x = W_p^T x \tag{2}$$

$$Q' = (\beta_1^T y, \beta_2^T y, \cdots, \beta_d^T y)^T = (\beta_1, \beta_2, \cdots \beta_d)^T y = W_q^T y \tag{3}$$

where $Wp=(\alpha_1, \alpha_2, ..., \alpha_d)$, $Wp=(\beta_1, \beta_2, ..., \beta_d)$. The following linear transformation (4):

$$Z = \begin{pmatrix} W_p \\ W_q \end{pmatrix}^T \begin{pmatrix} x \\ y \end{pmatrix} \tag{4}$$

as the combinatorial feature projected, is used for age estimation, while the transformation matrix is

$$W = \begin{pmatrix} W_p \\ W_q \end{pmatrix} \tag{5}$$

We call W the canonical projective matrix (CPM), Z the canonical correlation discriminant feature (CCDF).

3   Human Age Estimation By Extreme Learning Machine

It is important to select and design a better classifier in pattern recognition. Because of the characteristic of the age, we employ the regression theory to estimate the age. In the regression analysis, the most common method is the support vector machine regression (SVR)[14]. In 2009, Guo-dong Guo et.al investigated the biologically inspired features (BIF) for human age estimation from faces[15], they also use SVR for age estimation. However, the computation time of SVR is very long. In this paper, we introduce Extreme Learning Machine (ELM) method to the field of age estimation. ELM is a simple and effective single hidden layer feed-forward neural network (SLFNs) learning algorithm put forward by Guang-Bin Huang [13]. The traditional neural network learning algorithm (such as BP algorithm) needs to set up a large number of network training parameters, and it is easy to produce local optimal solution. ELM network only need to set the number of hidden nodes, and the algorithm implementation process does not require the network to adjust the input weights and hidden element of bias and uniqueness of the optimal solution, so it has the advantages of speed and good generalization performance. For these advantages, we propose to use ELM to estimate the age, it can achieve the same effect by using the SVR, and has a significant improvement in time consumption.

ELM is a supervised learning method. Given N training samples (z_1, y_1), (z_2, y_2), (z_3, y_3) with $z_i \in R^m$ and $y_i \in R$, where z_i is the CCDF vectors of m dimensions using Canonical Correlation Analysis and y_i is the corresponding regression value, which is the age value. The output function of SLFNs is:

$$f_L(z) = \sum_{i=1}^{L} \beta_i G(a_i, b_i, Z) \tag{6}$$

In (6), $f_L(z)$ is the estimate value, β_i is the output weight vector connecting the ith hidden node and the output nodes. L is the number of the hidden nodes. The hidden node output function is:

$$G(a_i, b_i, Z) = g(a_i \times Z + b_i) \tag{7}$$

In (7), a_i and b_i ($i=1,\ldots,L$) are the assign randomly hidden node parameters, which are generated by the dimension of the CCDF and the number of hidden nodes.

The nonlinear regression can be realized by using kernel function, according to different needs, we can choose different kernel function. In this paper, we use Gauss radial basis function RBF(8)through trial-and-error.

$$K(z, z') = \exp\left(-\frac{\|z - z'\|^2}{2\sigma^2}\right) \tag{8}$$

Here, the face aging functions are built by using Extreme Learning Machine (ELM).Given an input image, the shape feature is extracted using AAM and the texture feature is extracted with the use of LBP. The combined features are first extracted using CCA as described (CCDF) in section 2. We then use Extreme Learning Machine (ELM) with a Gaussian (RBF) kernel to determine the age of the face.

4   Experimental Results

For our experiments, we used the FG-NET[16] face aging dataset to test our method. The FG-NET database contains 1002 face images of 82 subjects with ages ranging from 0 to 69. Sample images from the databases are shown in Figure 3.

The Mean Absolute Error (MAE), defined as the average of the absolute error between the estimated ages and the ground truths, is computed using (9) and is used as our performance metric to compare the different age estimation techniques.

$$MAE = \frac{1}{N} \sum_{k=1}^{N} |a_k - \overline{a_k}| \tag{9}$$

In (9), $\overline{a_k}$ is the estimated age for the kth testing sample, a_k is the corresponding ground truth age (the true age), and N is the total number of testing samples.

Fig. 3. Sample images from the FG-NET face aging database showing the quality of images in them. As can be seen, the images are non-ideal in that they contain slight pose and illumination effects.

In our experiment, the Leave-one-person-out (LOPO) scheme is set up to experimentally evaluate the different methods on the FG-NET database. In this scheme, all facial images of one subject are used as the testing set and the remaining images are used as the training set. This process is applied in turn to all 82 subjects in the FG-NET database. Finally, the overall MAE is computed. Table 1 lists the MAE values obtained by several age estimation methods when the LOPO scheme was used on the FG-NET database. Table 2 lists the MAE values based on two single features and the fusion feature method when the LOPO scheme was used on the FG-NET database.

Some previously published results used the Cumulative Score (CS) rather than MAE to evaluate their estimation results. It is computed using (10), in which $N_{e \leqslant L}$ is the number of testing samples with MAE values less than or equal to L. Figure 2 compares the cumulative scores obtained by our method against such single features when tested on the FG-NET database.

$$CumScore_L = \frac{N_{e \leqslant L}}{N} \times 100\% \tag{10}$$

Table 1. Comparison of estimation results on FG-NET database with ages from 0 to 69 years.

Methods	MAE/years	year
WAS[17]	8.06	1999
AGES[7]	6.77	2007
RUN[18]	5.78	2008
Rank[19]	5.79	2010
AO graph[20]	5.97	2010
IIS-LLD[21]	5.77	2013
BIF [15]	4.77	2009
HC-SVR[22]	5.28	2014
AAM+2D-DCT[23]	5.39	2015
How-Old.net[2]	6.01	2015
CCA-ELM(our method)	5.55	/

From Table 1 and 2 and Figure 4 it is clear that our method obtains more accurate age estimates than several existing methods. In addition, through the experimental statistical, we know using ELM method for age estimation, each time we get estimation results only need about three seconds. Compared with other regression methods, the time consumption has been greatly improved.

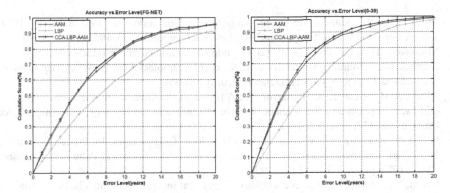

Fig. 4. Comparison of cumulative scores of age estimation methods, use the single feature (AAM, LBP) and the fusion feature (CCA-LBP-AAM) by ELM. Because of the lack of high age samples in FG-NET, we also have a statistical analysis of the range of 0-39, as shown on the right. As can be seen, the results were better more.

Table 2. Comparison of estimation results use the single feature(AAM,LBP) and the fusion feature(CCA-LBP-AAM) on FG-NET database with ages from 0 to 69 yesrs/0 to 39 years employ ELM.

Methods	MAE/(0-69)years	MAE/(0-39)years
AAM(only)	6.52	4.91
LBP(only)	7.95	6.03
CCA-LBP-AAM(our method)	5.55	4.45

5   Conclusion

In this paper, a combined age estimation scheme based on feature fusion has been proposed. To characterized aging features more completely, shape descriptors extracted by AAM and the texture descriptors extracted by LBP are combined and fused via Canonical correlation analysis (CCA). Additionally, we firstly propose to estimate the age based on Extreme Learning Machine (ELM), which can significantly reduce the computation cost during the process of regression. Experimental results showed that the proposed method outperforms the state-of-art methods such as on the FG-NET database. In the future work, the system would be enhanced by considering the effect of gender, facial expression, and race etc.

Acknowledgments. This work is supported by the grant from National Natural Science Foundation of China (No.61372046) and Shaanxi Province Natural Science Foundation (No.2014JM8338).

References

1. Fu, Y., Guo, G., Huang, T.S.: Age synthesis and estimation via faces: A survey. IEEE Transactions on Pattern Analysis and Machine Intelligence **32**(11), 1955–1976 (2010)
2. Microsoft. "How Old do I Look?" (2015). http://how-old.net/?ref=product-hunt
3. Ricanek, K., Sethuram, A., Patterson, E.K., et al.: Craniofacial aging. Wiley Handbook of Science and Technology for Homeland Security (2008)
4. Albert, A.M., Ricanek, K., Patterson, E.: A review of the literature on the aging adult skull and face: Implications for forensic science research and applications. Forensic Science International **172**(1), 1–9 (2007)
5. Kwon, Y.H., Lobo, N.D.V.: Age classification from facial images. In: Proceedings of the 1994 IEEE Computer Society Conference on Computer Vision and Pattern Recognition, CVPR 1994, pp. 762–767. IEEE (1994)
6. Kwon, Y.H., Lobo, N.: Age classification from facial images. Comput. Vis. Image Underst **74**(1), 1–21 (1999)
7. Geng, X., Zhou, Z.H., Smith-Miles, K.: Automatic age estimation based on facial aging patterns. IEEE Transactions on Pattern Analysis and Machine Intelligence **29**(12), 2234–2240 (2007)
8. Fu, Y.: Huang, T, S.: Human age estimation with regression on discriminative aging manifold. IEEE Transactions on Multimedia **10**(4), 578–584 (2008)
9. Yan, S., Wang, H., Tang, X., et al.: Regression from uncertain labels and its applications to soft biometrics. IEEE Transactions on Information Forensics and Security **3**(4), 698–708 (2008)
10. Cootes, T.F., Edwards, G.J., Taylor, C.J.: Active appearance models. IEEE Transactions on Pattern Analysis & Machine Intelligence **2001**(6), 681–685 (2001)
11. Günay, A., Nabiyev, V.V.: Automatic age classification with LBP. In: 23rd International Symposium on Computer and Information Sciences, ISCIS 2008, pp. 1–4. IEEE (2008)
12. Hardoon, D.R., Szedmak, S., Shawe-Taylor, J.: Canonical correlation analysis: An overview with application to learning methods. Neural Computation **16**(12), 2639–2664 (2004)
13. Huang, G.B., Zhu, Q.Y., Siew, C.K.: Extreme learning machine: theory and applications. Neurocomputing **70**(1), 489–501 (2006)
14. Smola, A.J., Schölkopf, B.A.: tutorial on support vector regression. Statistics and Computing **14**(3), 199–222 (2004)
15. Guo, G., Mu, G., Fu, Y., et al.: Human age estimation using bio-inspired features. In: IEEE Conference on Computer Vision and Pattern Recognition, CVPR 2009, pp. 112–119. IEEE (2009)
16. The FG-NET Aging Database [DB/OL] (2011). http://www-prima.inrialpes.fr/FGnet/html/benchmarks.html
17. Lanitis, A., Taylor, C.J., Cootes, T.F.: Modeling the process of ageing in face images. In: The Proceedings of the Seventh IEEE International Conference on Computer Vision, vol. 1, pp. 131–136. IEEE (1999)
18. Yan, S., Zhou, X., Liu, M., et al.: Regression from patch-kernel. In: IEEE Conference on Computer Vision and Pattern Recognition, CVPR 2008, pp. 1–8. IEEE (2008)

19. Chang, K.Y, Chen, C.S., Hung Y.P.: A ranking approach for human ages estimation based on face images. In: 20th International Conference on Pattern Recognition (ICPR), pp. 3396–3399. IEEE (2010)
20. Suo, J., Zhu, S.C., Shan, S., et al.: A compositional and dynamic model for face aging. IEEE Transactions on Pattern Analysis and Machine Intelligence **32**(3), 385–401 (2010)
21. Geng, X., Yin, C., Zhou, Z.H.: Facial age estimation by learning from label distributions. IEEE Transactions on Pattern Analysis and Machine Intelligence **35**(10), 2401–2412 (2013)
22. Liu, J., Ma, Y., Duan, L., et al.: Hybrid constraint SVR for facial age estimation. Signal Processing **94**, 576–582 (2014)
23. Günay, A., Nabiyev, V.V.: Age estimation based on AAM and 2D-DCT features of facial images. International Journal of Computer Science and Applications, 6(2) (2015)

Research on the Intelligent Public Transportation System

Yingkun Huang, Shaoshu Huang, Changdong Wang$^{(\boxtimes)}$,
Dekai Kang, and Wenkai Huang

School of Mobile Information Engineering, Sun Yat-sen University,
Tangjia Wan, Xiangzhou District, Zhuhai, China
ykhuang147@126.com,
{shaoshuhuang,kangdekai,huang.wenkai}@foxmail.com,
wangchd3@mail.sysu.edu.cn

Abstract. Nowadays, most traditional industries are facing great challenges, and so is the traditional bus industry. To design or renew a route in a metropolis cost our government a considerable amount of money, and human resource as well. Effective as it might be when being put into use, an increasing volume of data is still being neglected. In our research, we apply multi-source data analysis technique to the traditional bus system. By analyzing the orient-destination flow, routes can be designed or changed based on our algorithm, thus reducing the expenses.

Keywords: Intelligent city · Pattern recognition · Transportation system

1 Introduction

The transportation system is one of the closest linked industries to our daily lives. The past decade has witnessed a dramatic development of metropolises. The excessive demands for transportation lead to problems like traffic congestion and road blocking.

The bus company would like to make best use of these resource to satisfied citizens while the citizens' demand for a better service from the bus system. Also, the bus company like to have a system flexible enough to schedule base on real time scenario.

Under the circumstance of this occasion, we build a Route Design System (RDS) and a Decision Making System (DMS). To form the best combination of the routes based on certain constrains and help meet the requirements of real-time schedule. We propose Route Combination Algorithm (RCA) to evaluate the performance of different route combination and find out the best performing one.

There are, certainly, some approaches to address these issues, three of which are listed here: (1) accelerate the building of the transportation infrastructure to catch up with the booming traffic; (2) Strengthen the control of urban city traffic system so as to effectively regulate the traffic flow; (3) Introducing the intelligent transportation technique into the original system to ease the burden of the current system. The former two approaches are to be dealt with by the government while the third one is the one we are capable of making changes.

© Springer International Publishing Switzerland 2015
J. Yang et al. (Eds.): CCBR 2015, LNCS 9428, pp. 686–693, 2015.
DOI: 10.1007/978-3-319-25417-3_80

Regarding problems of public transportation, most of them occurs in the following aspects: (1) Citizens consider it inconvenient to take a bus because they need to take several transfers before they reach their destinations; (2) Passengers are not likely to take bus unless they are allowed for uncertain factors and punctual arrival can still be guarantee.

Here, we focus on the idea of applying various data sources to obtain the best route combination for the enhancement of bus system's efficiency. In the pre-processing step, we input data into Origination-Destination flow (OD flow), a simple format with the row showing the destination and the column represents for the origin station. Then, by adopting the theory in linear algebra, qualified routes between every two stops are chosen. Finally, with the objected function we need to maximize, the best combination under certain constrains can be found.

2   Related Work

The idea of Intelligent Public Transportation System (IPTS) has been brought out since the very beginning of this century. But it has not developed much until recent years. One of the most inspiring works is done by taking the taxi traces as evidence for the design of night bus routes. [1] They use the Taxi GPS traces to design the routes for night buses. This idea works for night routes because the taxi system serves as the only mean of transportation during night but during day time the taxi trace is not as representative. Sabeur Elkosantini and Saber Darmoul [2] show us the architecture of the IPTS. S.A Mulay [3] makes contributions in the traffic management to schedule the traffic to avoid traffic jam. Bartlomiej Placzek [4] performs a way to evaluate the traffic by applying a fuzzy cellular model. Others [5-10] give me an overlook of the IPTS.

2.1   Our Contributions

Our contributions are: (1) Never before had someone applied techniques in multi-view clustering into IPTS; (2) Most researches available focus on the scheduling instead of redesigning route. (3) We find a shortcoming of current system that can be improved, as the problem and brief solution stated here:

-As we can observe from our daily lives, during the rash hours, running buses are always crowded with citizens. However, in the opposite direction, empty buses are running just to balance the two-way system. Inefficient as it seen, but how to refine this situation?

We proposed a solution for it. Instead of making changes inside the two-terminal system. Another terminal is brought in to the system. We calculate the cost and profit of running straight back and running to the third terminal to ease the burden of other heavy lines before getting back.

3   The Proposed BRC Model

This section presents the ideas of the Best Route Combination in the IPTS. There are three steps necessary for our model: "Pre-processing", "Candidates selection", "Route combination". Each step will be detailed in the following sections.

3.1   Notations

The basic constrains are shown in table 1. The model is based on the following assumptions, constrains and definitions. The assumptions are normally obeyed when the bus company is designing the route combination.

Assumption 1. The length of a route shouldn't be longer than the maximum route constrain. It's also for the convenience of management. If the length of a route is too long, the arrival of the bus cannot be estimated accurately. Also, too long a route has proven to be not finance friendly.

Assumption 2. Buses run in a fixed speed.

Table 1. Font sizes of headings. Table captions should always be positioned *above* the tables.

Definition	Explanation
length of a route	aiming at metropolises, the length of a route should between 5km and 15km
circuit quotient	circuit quotient means the actual distance between two terminals divided by the length of the route. This constrain mainly enhance the efficiency of the system. The smaller the value, the faster citizens get where they want.
maximum capacity	every bus has a maximum capacity to carry passengers.

3.2   Data Pre-Processing

The later processing of the algorithm needs data in a structure of Orientation-to-Destination flow (OD-flow). To form the data-set like this, we need to find out where the citizens take a bus and where they take off. Then, transform the data set into a x-y (orientation-destination) coordinate system. Here, the data from three public transport systems (Bus system, Subway system and Taxi system) is taken into usage. After that, we perform the Sub-space Projection, which project only the OD space that we need, neglecting the irrelevant data.

3.3   Candidates Selection

The second step is to choose the qualified routes based on the graph theory. With the od-flow, we are trying to get the qualified routes between every two terminals for the combination step's usage. The purpose of this process is to get rid of routes that are inefficient and cumbersome.

There are some rules we need to follow during designing:

-rule 1.A one-way line should not entry the same bus station twice or more.

-rule 2.The later stop should be farther away from the origin station than the former stop

-rule 3.The later stop should be closer from the terminal station Some of situations that need to be eliminated are shown in Figure 1

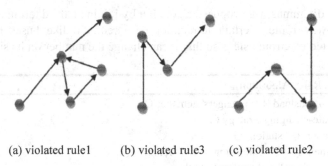

(a) violated rule1   (b) violated rule3   (c) violated rule2

Fig. 1. Several situations that violate the rules

3.4   Route Combination

Here is the most significant step in this research.

In the previous steps, we manage to find the qualified routes between every two terminals. Now, with pre-knowledge and other constrains, we try to get the best performed combination of routes.

The objected function we need to maximize is the directed arrive flow.

The idea is like this. We could find out where the "hot-lines" are base on the od flow. Ranking the hot-lines, the biggest flow stays the highest priority, so on and so forth. The hot-line is different from route as it is not from the start stations to the terminals.

We performed an algorithm with the idea of greedy algorithm. We find the qualified routes that contains the most hot-lines and put it into the lines combination.

Then, we renew the od- flow. We create a parameter named "potential od-flow". We consider the routes which cover the same line split the passenger flow averagely. When the first route is chosen, the od-flows that it covers change to potential od- flow that only have 50% of the original value, as a potential passenger flow.

We perform this idea until the remains passengers is not satisfy the minimum constrain to build a new route.

4   The Proposed Solution for Peek Dilemma

The Peek Dilemma (PD) refers to a situation that occurs during rush hours. Bus company has to send buses picking up seldom passenger mainly in purpose to balance the buses between two terminals.

Other than this, another dilemma need to be brought out here. We all know that buses spend more time on the road than usual during rush hours. Limited by the amount of buses equipped for a certain line, bus company is forced to expand the break time between buses as to maintain its continuing service, to be noticed, it's during the period of most demands but sending relatively less buses.

4.1   RH-S Algorithm

To solve these dilemmas, we proposed a solution by joining a third terminal to form a ring like one-way route. Certain foundations are required like buses need to be equipped with led electronic signs so that it can change the number on its sign.

Algorithm 1. RH-S Algorithm
1: Input: rate of busload R, passengers' demands Q
2: Output: route-changing strategy C_t
3: for all car enter the station do
4: Calculate the Payoffs of choosing action "return"
5: if the Payoff is smaller than threshold then
6: Calculate the Maximum Payoff of choosing action "change" and change the bus's strategy $C_{t \cdot i_1}$ to corresponding $C_{t \cdot i_1}$
7: else
8: The bus take the same route back
9: end if
10: end for

Table 2. Font sizes of headings. Table captions should always be positioned *above* the tables.

Definition	Explanation
B	The busload, defined as the number of passengers on the bus.
S	The number of seats on the bus, a fixed number, set as a reference compound. In this experiment, the value of S is set to 30 because the buses running around are mostly equipped with around 30 seats or so.
R	The rate of busload, an significant indicator to show the condition of passengers load. Defined as R = B:S. The range of the rate is from 0 to 200% as the max capacity we set is precisely a double of the amount of seats.
D	The square deviation of the R, revealing the general passenger distribution.
X	The mixture indicator of the comfort degree and effectiveness of the bus system. We consider the empty bus as inefficient and overcrowded as uncomfortable. It a function peek around the R equals 130%
P	The total amount of passengers we have served, it's distinguishing from the B and the R because citizens travel varying length.

This algorithm is named Rush-Hour Schedule Algorithm (RH-S). Let's assume that a bus start from terminal A to terminal B in a rush hour. After the arrival of the bus in terminal B, we evaluate the passengers it will carry if it goes back to terminal A with the same line and when the amount of passengers is low than threshold, actions are taken. Instead of inefficiently going back to the same line, we check if any route starting at this terminal is under heavy burden. If so, we estimate the time and the profit it take to detour to the terminal C and then serve as another route from C to A comparing to the normal strategy in busload rate. Other than this, the change of this bus should not cause the route A-B to a overburden line on the absence of this bus.

4.2   Performance Evaluation

The performance of our system is evaluated by calculating the rate of the busload. Here, the value is set by contrasting to the seats on the bus. The indicator is generated to show the effectiveness of the design system.

The indicators are listed in Table 2, using as an evaluation of the system's performance. The performance of each line is set by the objected function here:

$$F(P, Q, T, R, D) = \frac{P}{R} \times (1 - \frac{T}{\beta}) \times y(R) \times (1 - D)$$ (1)

where β is the tolerance of the citizens, in our case set as 20.

$$y(R) = \begin{cases} \dfrac{x}{a} & x \leq a \\ 1 - \dfrac{x-a}{1-a} & x > a \end{cases}$$ (2)

where a is the optimal busload. As soon as the bus arrived at the terminal, scheduling method is performed to analysis the best strategy that can be taken. The amount of passengers who can be taken is calculated if the bus leave on its own route. If the expecting pick-up amount is lower that the threshold (set 2/5 of the average busload), it is considered as inefficient and transform to a spare bus that can be scheduled the ease the other route's burden.

Then, every possible route combination that can eventually return to the other terminal is considered as an option. Using equation 4.1, every possible route is compared and the busload is considered most important here.

5   Experiments

The experiment is based on a simulating data set objectively generated to test the solution we give in Peek Dilemma. The passengers flow is represented as OD-flow, a two dimensional coordinate system as the x stands for the originate station while the y is on behalf of the destination station. The value indicates the number of citizens travel from x to y. Buses can only started and ended at the terminals, along with many stops.

Each terminal and each stop is tagged with a category (e.g living area, working area, business area...) to illustrate a specified passengers flow distribution, which is set as the pre-knowledge.

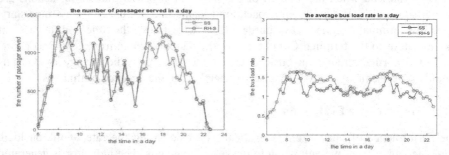

Fig. 2. The left graph shows the comparison between the standard algorithm and the RH-S we proposed, X-axis represents the time (from 6:00a.m to 23:00p.m) while the Y-axis indicates the amount of served passengers. The red line show the performance of standard schedule (SS) and the blue line is the performance of the RH-S algorithm. The right graph shows the comparison between the standard algorithm and the RH-S we proposed, X-axis represents the time (from 6:00a.m to 23:00p.m) while the Y-axis indicates the rate of the busload. The red line show the performance of standard schedule (SS) and the blue line is the performance of the RH-S.

5.1   Data-Set Generation

Under the guidance received from Zhu-hai Bus Culture Media Company (ZHBCMC), we generate the experiment data-set. Properties existing in the real system are followed in our data-set. Again, thanks to the participation of the ZHBCMC. Here we listed some of the many properties we follow in our data generation in order to guarantee the validity of our data-set. The scheme we referring to shows the recent (2015/05/01) statistics information of the bus system.

The range of each route's length is set with clear evidence. The service time is set from 6:00 to 23:00, also referencing to their scheme. The amount of car input for usage is determined by the length and the interval. Rush Mode is triggered during rush hour. The corresponding properties of the Rush Mode are also set in comparison to the ordinary hour. In the experiment, the regularized routing system is set under supervision and guided under the real time schedule. Also, constraints are set during the set up for regularized system as the average rate of busload should not be under 120%. Citizens are set to have a tolerance of 20 minutes before they alter to other means.

5.2   Result Display

As we can observe from the Figure 2, the RH-S algorithm outperforms standard algorithm by about 30% mainly during the rush hour.

In regular hour, the RH-S shows little evidence of advantages, may even be outperformed by the routine schedule. The reason is that based on the previous records the algorithm predict and trade-off between leave the terminal now or sometime later, also scheduling the spare buses on the other less burden route to this line. This scheduling method may seemed surprising to some paleo conservatism as they think buses just can running on its fixed routes. But what we have done is actually aim at equipping in intelligent city public transportation system where the changing of the route number wouldn't be an issue for the buses.

In Figure 2, the rate of the busload separate at around the rush hour, it shows that we are making the spare bus picking up more citizens and have more citizens served.

In reality, the steady schedule have its advantages as for the convenience of the management. But, as the managing system rapidly developed, the management is gradually out of an issue, what really matter is the efficiency of the scheduling system because the profit is produced here, not at administration.

Appendix

Thanks for the support from Google, who is kind enough to have the financial and technical guidance for this research.

References

1. Chao, C., Daqing, Z., Zhi-Hua, Z., Nan, I..: B-planner night bus route planning using large scale taxi GPS traces. In: IEEE International Conference on Pervasive Computing and Communication, pp. 225–233. IEEE Press, San Diego (2013)
2. Elkosantini, S., Darmoul, S.: Intelligent public transportation systems a review of architectures and enabling technologies. In IEEE International Conference on Advanced Logistics and Transport, pp. 233–238. IEEE Press, Sousse (2013)
3. Mulay, S. and Gadgil, S.: Intelligent city traffic management and public transportation system. In: International Journal of Computer Science Issues, pp. 126–131, Beijing (2013)
4. Płaczek, B.: Performance evaluation of road traffic control using a fuzzy cellular model. In: Corchado, E., Kurzyński, K., Woźniak, M. (eds.) HAIS 2011. LNCS, vol. 6679, pp. 59–66. Springer, Heidelberg (2011)
5. Urli., T.: Balancing bike sharing systems (bbss) instance generation from the city bike NYC data. In: ARXIV (2013)
6. Akai, Y., Hiromori, T.: Mitigating location and speed errors in floating car data using context-based accuracy estimation. In: 13th International Conference on ITS Telecommunications, pp. 104–110. IEEE Press, Tampere (2013)
7. Mnasser, H.: Towards an intelligent information system of public transportation. In: 2013 International Conference on Advanced Logistics and Transport, pp. 75–81. IEEE Press, Sousse (2013)
8. Pepper, J., W., Golden, B., L.: Solving the traveling salesman problem with annealing-based heuristics: a computational study. In: IEEE transactions on Systems, Man and Cybernetics, pp. 72–77. (2002)
9. Al-Jumailey, S.I.: Planning of operation policies for fixed bus routes in Baghdad City. In: 2011 International Conference on Remote Sensing, Environment and Transportation Engineering, pp. 8395–8398. IEEE Press, Nanjing (2011)
10. Elleuch, W.: Mining road map from bug database of GPS data. In: 14th International Conference on Hybrid Intelligent Systems, pp. 193–198. IEEE Press, Kuwait (2014)

Discriminative Scatter Regularized CCA for Multiview Image Feature Learning and Recognition

Yunhao Yuan[1,2(✉)], Jinlong Yang[1], Xiaobo Shen[3],
Chaofeng Li[1], and Xiaojun Wu[1]

[1] Department of Computer Science and Technology, Jiangnan University, Wuxi, China
yyhzbh@163.com
[2] Key Laboratory of Advanced Process Control for Light Industry of Ministry of Education,
School of IoT Engineering, Jiangnan University, Wuxi, China
[3] School of Information Technology and Electrical Engineering,
The University of Queensland, Brisbane, Australia

Abstract. In this paper, we propose a novel supervised canonical correlation analysis approach based on discriminative scatter regularization for multiview image feature learning. This method at the same time considers the between-view correlations and within-view class label information of training samples. The proposed method is applied to handwritten digit image recognition. The experimental results on multiple feature dataset demonstrate the superior performance of our approach compared with the existing multiview feature learning methods.

Keywords: Image recognition · Canonical Correlation Analysis · Regularization · Multiview feature extraction · Discriminative learning

1 Introduction

In many real-world applications, the images are usually represented by multiple different types of high-dimensional features. This kind of data is referred to as multiview data [1]. A typical example is a color image, which naturally has three kinds of visual features, i.e., red, green, and blue components. Since different views usually have different physical meanings and statistical properties, how to effectively and efficiently use the complementary nature of different views to learn meaningful low-dimensional features for classification tasks is a challenging problem.

Proposed by Hotelling [2], canonical correlation analysis (CCA) is a powerful technique for finding the linear correlations between two different views. CCA seeks a pair of linear transformations associated with the two views such that the projected data in the low-dimensional subspace are maximally correlated. CCA has found many applications in, for example, feature fusion [3], image super-resolution reconstruction [4], machine learning [5], and detection of neural activity in fMRI [6], etc. Since different views come from the same image data, there are, naturally, the correlation relationships between them. In this case, CCA is very suitable for feature extraction of multiview image data.

© Springer International Publishing Switzerland 2015
J. Yang et al. (Eds.): CCBR 2015, LNCS 9428, pp. 694–701, 2015.
DOI: 10.1007/978-3-319-25417-3_81

However, CCA is essentially an unsupervised subspace learning method. Thus, it is not effective to preserve discriminative information in canonical subspaces for image classification tasks. To improve the performance of CCA in multiview data learning, researchers have developed some supervised CCA methods [7-11] by introducing the class label information of training samples. For instance, Sun et al. [7] proposed a generalized CCA method by using the within-class information of training data. Kim et al. [8] presented a discriminative CCA approach for image set classification, which maximizes the canonical correlations of within-class image sets and minimizes the canonical correlations of between-class image sets. Peng et al. [11] proposed a local discriminative CCA (LDCCA) that considers a combination of local properties and discrimination between different classes. Moreover, some other variants of CCA have also been proposed; see, for example, [12-16].

The foregoing supervised CCA methods have been proved to be effective for feature extraction and classification tasks. Motivated by recent progress in canonical correlations, in this paper we propose a novel CCA approach based on discriminative scatter information regularization for multiview image feature learning. This method simultaneously considers the between-view correlations and within-view class label information of training samples under a regularization framework. The proposed method is applied to handwritten digit image recognition. The experimental results demonstrate the superior performance of our approach compared with existing multi-view feature learning methods.

2   CCA

Given two zero-mean random vectors $x \in \mathfrak{R}^p$ and $y \in \mathfrak{R}^q$, CCA aims at finding a pair of projection directions, $\alpha \in \mathfrak{R}^p$ and $\beta \in \mathfrak{R}^q$, such that the correlation between the projected variables $\alpha^T x$ and $\beta^T y$ is maximized as

$$\max_{\alpha,\beta} \frac{\alpha^T S_{xy} \beta}{\sqrt{\alpha^T S_{xx} \alpha} \cdot \sqrt{\beta^T S_{yy} \beta}}, \tag{1}$$

where S_{xx} and S_{yy} are, respectively, within-set covariance matrices of vectors x and y, and S_{xy} is the between-set covariance matrix between x and y. Since the objective function of the optimization problem in (1) is invariant with respect to scaling of α and β, the problem in (1) can be reformulated as follows:

$$\max_{\alpha,\beta} \alpha^T S_{xy} \beta$$
$$s.t. \quad \alpha^T S_{xx} \alpha = 1, \ \beta^T S_{yy} \beta = 1. \tag{2}$$

The optimal solution α and β of (2) can be obtained by computing the following generalized eigenvalue problem:

$$\begin{pmatrix} & S_{xy} \\ S_{yx} & \end{pmatrix} \begin{pmatrix} \alpha \\ \beta \end{pmatrix} = \lambda \begin{pmatrix} S_{xx} & \\ & S_{yy} \end{pmatrix} \begin{pmatrix} \alpha \\ \beta \end{pmatrix}, \tag{3}$$

where $S_{yx} = S_{xy}^T$. Taking the top d eigenvectors of (3), we can obtain d pairs of projection directions $\{(\alpha_i, \beta_i)\}_{i=1}^d$ of CCA, where $d \le \min(p, q)$.

3   Approach

In this section, we define the data scatter with class information for each view. Then, we build a discriminative scatter regularized CCA for multiview feature learning.

3.1   Characterize the Scatter with Class Information

Assume two feature representations (views) from the same n images are given as $\{X^{(i)} \in \Re^{p_i \times n}\}_{i=1}^2$, where $X^{(i)} = (x_1^{(i)}, x_2^{(i)}, \cdots, x_n^{(i)})$ is a feature matrix of view i containing p_i-dimensional sample vectors in its columns, and the paired samples $(x_j^{(1)}, x_j^{(2)})$ are labeled by $l_j \in \{1, 2, \cdots, c\}$ for a total of c classes, $j = 1, 2, \cdots, n$. Also, we assume $\{x_j^{(i)}\}_{j=1}^n$ have been centered, i.e., $\sum_{j=1}^n x_j^{(i)} = 0$, $i = 1, 2$.

Specifically, for n samples $x_1^{(i)}, x_2^{(i)}, \cdots, x_n^{(i)}$ in view $X^{(i)}$, we get their images $y_1^{(i)}, y_2^{(i)}, \cdots, y_n^{(i)}$ after the projection onto the projection axis $\alpha^{(i)}$, $i = 1, 2$. The scatter with intraclass information is then characterized by

$$J_w^{(i)} = \sum_{j=1}^n \sum_{k=1}^n s_{jk}^{(i)} \left(y_j^{(i)} - y_k^{(i)} \right)^2 = \sum_{j=1}^n \sum_{k=1}^n s_{jk}^{(i)} \left(\alpha^{(i)T} x_j^{(i)} - \alpha^{(i)T} x_k^{(i)} \right)^2$$

$$= \alpha^{(i)T} \left[\sum_{j=1}^n \sum_{k=1}^n s_{jk}^{(i)} \left(x_j^{(i)} - x_k^{(i)} \right) \left(x_j^{(i)} - x_k^{(i)} \right)^T \right] \alpha^{(i)} = \alpha^{(i)T} S_w^{(i)} \alpha^{(i)} \tag{4}$$

where $S_w^{(i)} = \sum_{j=1}^n \sum_{k=1}^n s_{jk}^{(i)} \left(x_j^{(i)} - x_k^{(i)} \right) \left(x_j^{(i)} - x_k^{(i)} \right)^T$, $s_{jk}^{(i)} \in \Re$ is the weighting of the jth and kth samples in the ith view, and defined by

$$s_{jk}^{(i)} = \begin{cases} 1, & \text{if } l_j = l_k, \\ 0, & \text{otherwise.} \end{cases} \tag{5}$$

Similarly, the scatter with interclass information can be characterized by

$$J_b^{(i)} = \sum_{j=1}^n \sum_{k=1}^n \tilde{s}_{jk}^{(i)} \left(y_j^{(i)} - y_k^{(i)} \right)^2$$

$$= \alpha^{(i)T} \left[\sum_{j=1}^n \sum_{k=1}^n \tilde{s}_{jk}^{(i)} \left(x_j^{(i)} - x_k^{(i)} \right) \left(x_j^{(i)} - x_k^{(i)} \right)^T \right] \alpha^{(i)} \tag{6}$$

$$= \alpha^{(i)T} S_b^{(i)} \alpha^{(i)}$$

where $S_b^{(i)} = \sum_{j=1}^{n}\sum_{k=1}^{n} \tilde{s}_{jk}^{(i)}\left(x_j^{(i)}-x_k^{(i)}\right)\left(x_j^{(i)}-x_k^{(i)}\right)^T$, $\tilde{s}_{jk}^{(i)} \in \Re$ has the same meaning as $s_{jk}^{(i)}$, and is defined by

$$\tilde{s}_{jk}^{(i)} = \begin{cases} 1, & \text{if } l_j \neq l_k, \\ 0, & \text{otherwise.} \end{cases} \tag{7}$$

It is easy to show that minimizing (4) makes the intraclass sample points in each view as compact as possible and maximizing (6) makes the interclass samples in each view as far apart as possible.

3.2   CCA with Discriminative Scatter Regularization

On the basis of (4) and (6), now let us build a new supervised CCA model for multi-view feature learning of images, as follows:

$$\max_{\alpha^{(1)},\alpha^{(2)}} J(\alpha^{(1)},\alpha^{(2)}) = \tau_1\alpha^{(1)T}X^{(1)}X^{(2)T}\alpha^{(2)} + (1-\tau_1)\left(J_b^{(1)}+J_b^{(2)}\right)$$

$$s.t. \begin{cases} \tau_2\alpha^{(1)T}X^{(1)}X^{(1)T}\alpha^{(1)} + (1-\tau_2)J_w^{(1)} = 1, \\ \tau_2\alpha^{(2)T}X^{(2)}X^{(2)T}\alpha^{(2)} + (1-\tau_2)J_w^{(2)} = 1, \end{cases} \tag{8}$$

where τ_1 and τ_2 are two regularization parameters, and $0 < \tau_1 \leq 1$, $0 < \tau_2 \leq 1$. As we can see in (8), the first term in the objective function ensures the maximal correlation between two-view samples; and the second term guarantees the interclass separability of samples in each view. Moreover, our proposed method reduces to CCA when $\tau_1 = \tau_2 = 1$, that is, CCA can be regarded as a special case of our method. More specifically, the optimization problem can be written as

$$\max_{\alpha^{(1)},\alpha^{(2)}} J(\alpha^{(1)},\alpha^{(2)}) = \tau_1\alpha^{(1)T}X^{(1)}X^{(2)T}\alpha^{(2)} + (1-\tau_1)\sum_{i=1}^{2}\alpha^{(i)T}S_b^{(i)}\alpha^{(i)}$$

$$s.t. \quad \alpha^{(1)T}A^{(1)}\alpha^{(1)} = 1, \quad \alpha^{(2)T}A^{(2)}\alpha^{(2)} = 1, \tag{9}$$

where $A^{(1)} = \tau_2 X^{(1)}X^{(1)T} + (1-\tau_2)S_w^{(1)}$ and $A^{(2)} = \tau_2 X^{(2)}X^{(2)T} + (1-\tau_2)S_w^{(2)}$.

Using the Lagrange multipliers technique, we can obtain the following Lagrangian function:

$$L = J(\alpha^{(1)},\alpha^{(2)}) - \frac{\lambda_1}{2}\left(\alpha^{(1)T}A^{(1)}\alpha^{(1)}-1\right) - \frac{\lambda_2}{2}\left(\alpha^{(2)T}A^{(2)}\alpha^{(2)}-1\right) \tag{10}$$

with λ_1 and λ_2 as Lagrange multipliers. Let $\partial L/\partial\alpha^{(1)} = 0$ and $\partial L/\partial\alpha^{(2)} = 0$, we get:

$$\begin{pmatrix} 2(1-\tau_1)S_b^{(1)} & \tau_1 X^{(1)}X^{(2)T} \\ \tau_1 X^{(2)}X^{(1)T} & 2(1-\tau_1)S_b^{(2)} \end{pmatrix}\begin{pmatrix} \alpha^{(1)} \\ \alpha^{(2)} \end{pmatrix} = \begin{pmatrix} \lambda_1 A^{(1)}\alpha^{(1)} \\ \lambda_2 A^{(2)}\alpha^{(2)} \end{pmatrix}, \tag{11}$$

Since the following equation

$$\begin{pmatrix} \lambda_1 A^{(1)} \alpha^{(1)} \\ \lambda_2 A^{(2)} \alpha^{(2)} \end{pmatrix} = \begin{pmatrix} \lambda_1 I_{p_1} & \\ & \lambda_2 I_{p_2} \end{pmatrix} \begin{pmatrix} A^{(1)} & \\ & A^{(2)} \end{pmatrix} \begin{pmatrix} \alpha^{(1)} \\ \alpha^{(2)} \end{pmatrix}, \tag{12}$$

holds, (11) can be rewritten as

$$\begin{pmatrix} 2(1-\tau_1)S_b^{(1)} & \tau_1 X^{(1)} X^{(2)T} \\ \tau_1 X^{(2)} X^{(1)T} & 2(1-\tau_1)S_b^{(2)} \end{pmatrix} \begin{pmatrix} \alpha^{(1)} \\ \alpha^{(2)} \end{pmatrix} = \begin{pmatrix} \lambda_1 I_{p_1} & \\ & \lambda_2 I_{p_2} \end{pmatrix} \begin{pmatrix} A^{(1)} & \\ & A^{(2)} \end{pmatrix} \begin{pmatrix} \alpha^{(1)} \\ \alpha^{(2)} \end{pmatrix} \tag{13}$$

with $I_{p_i} \in \mathfrak{R}^{P_i \times P_i}$ as the identity matrix, $i = 1, 2$.

It is obvious that (13) is an unusual generalized eigenvalue problem, which is actually referred to as multivariate eigenvalue problem (MEP) [18]. It is very difficult for MEP to be solved exactly. Up to now, there are no analytical solutions to MEP. This means that we are merely able to obtain the approximate solutions to MEP using, for example, dedicated numerical iterations or relaxation techniques. Consequently, in this paper we solve a relaxed version of (13) by setting $\lambda = \lambda_1 = \lambda_2$, as follows:

$$\begin{pmatrix} 2(1-\tau_1)S_b^{(1)} & \tau_1 X^{(1)} X^{(2)T} \\ \tau_1 X^{(2)} X^{(1)T} & 2(1-\tau_1)S_b^{(2)} \end{pmatrix} \begin{pmatrix} \alpha^{(1)} \\ \alpha^{(2)} \end{pmatrix} = \lambda \begin{pmatrix} A^{(1)} & \\ & A^{(2)} \end{pmatrix} \begin{pmatrix} \alpha^{(1)} \\ \alpha^{(2)} \end{pmatrix}. \tag{14}$$

Solving the generalized eigenvalue problem in (14), we can obtain d pairs of projection directions $\{(\alpha_i^{(1)}, \alpha_i^{(2)})\}_{i=1}^d$ which consist of the first d eigenvectors corresponding to the first d largest eigenvalues, where $d \le \min(p_1, p_2)$.

Once d projection direction pairs are obtained, the projection matrix for each view can be formed by letting $W_i = (\alpha_1^{(i)}, \alpha_2^{(i)}, \cdots, \alpha_d^{(i)})$, $i = 1, 2$. As a result, for any given pairwise observation $x^T = (x^{(1)T}, x^{(2)T})$ with $x^{(i)} \in \mathfrak{R}^{P_i}$, multiview feature extraction can be performed by the form of $W_1^T x^{(1)}$ and $W_2^T x^{(2)}$. After feature extraction, we use the following fusion strategy [3] to combine the low-dimensional features for classification tasks:

$$Z = W_1^T x^{(1)} + W_2^T x^{(2)} = W^T x, \tag{15}$$

where $W^T = \left(W^{(1)T}, W^{(2)T} \right)$.

4   Experiment

In this section, we evaluate the performance of our proposed method on the popular handwritten numeral data set and compare it with related multiview feature learning methods, including generalized multiview linear discriminant analysis (GMLDA) [17]. Note that, in all the experiments, the nearest neighbor (NN) classifier is used for recognition tasks.

4.1   Data Set

The multiple feature dataset (MFD)[1], which is widely used to test multiview feature learning algorithms, is adopted in our experiment. The digit dataset consists of 10 classes of handwritten numerals (i.e., "0"-"9") extracted from a collection of Dutch utility maps. Two hundred samples per class (for a total of 2,000 samples) are available in the form of 30×48 binary images. These numerals are represented in terms of six feature sets, as shown in Table 1.

Table 1. Six feature sets of handwritten numerals in MFD.

Pix: 240-dimension pixel averages feature in 2×3 windows;
Fac: 216-dimension profile correlations feature;
Fou: 76-dimension Fourier coefficients of the character shapes feature;
Kar: 64-dimension Karhunen-Loève coefficients feature;
Zer: 47-dimension Zernike moments feature;
Mor: 6-dimension morphological feature.

4.2   Compared Algorithms

To demonstrate how the performance can be improved by our proposed method, we compare the following five popular multiview feature learning algorithms:

- LDCCA [11], which is a locality-based supervised CCA method and considers the local correlations of within-class and between-class samples.
- Discriminative CCA (DCCA) [8], which is a supervised variant of CCA and maximizes within-class correlations, while minimizes between-class correlations between two views.
- Random correlation ensemble (RCE) [16], which uses partial random cross-view correlations between within-class samples.
- Generalized multiview linear discriminant analysis (GMLDA) [17], which is a multiview generalization of classical linear discriminant analysis. This method has three parameters for two view data. In our experiment, the three parameters involved in GMLDA are set as the same as those used in [17], which have been proven to be effective for recognition purpose.
- Discriminative scatter regularized CCA, which is the new proposed algorithm in this paper. Our method has two regularization parameters, i.e., τ_1 and τ_2. As in GMLDA, how to find the optimal parameters is still an open problem. Thus, we empirically set $\tau_2 = \tau_1$ for avoiding the exhaustive search and select the parameter value with the best performance from $\{0.1, 0.2, \cdots, 1\}$.

4.3   Experimental Results

On MFD, we can choose any two feature sets as $X^{(1)}$ and $X^{(2)}$ views. As a result, there are 15 pairs of different feature combinations in total. For each combination, 100

---

[1] http://archive.ics.uci.edu/ml/datasets/Multiple+Features

samples per class are randomly chosen for training, while the rest are used for testing. Thus, the number of training samples and testing samples is, respectively, 1000 and 1000. We report the averaged results in Table 2 under NN classifier after 10 random test experiments. From Table 2, we can see that our proposed method outperforms RCE and DCCA on all cases, and LDCCA only except the combination Mor and Zer. Compared with the state-of-the-art algorithm GMLDA, our method performs better on 11 feature combinations, while GMLDA achieves better results than ours only on four cases. These results show the superiority of our proposed approach for multiview image feature learning.

Table 2. Ten-run average recognition accuracy of LDCCA, RCE, DCCA, GMLDA, and our proposed method under the nearest neighbor classifier on MFD.

$X^{(1)}$	$X^{(2)}$	LDCCA[11]	RCE[16]	DCCA	GMLDA	Ours
Fac	Pix	0.9760	0.9464	0.9691	0.9527	**0.9821**
Fou	Fac	0.9629	0.9508	0.9501	0.9679	**0.9866**
Fou	Pix	0.9469	0.9199	0.9335	0.9697	**0.9713**
Kar	Fac	0.9803	0.9777	0.9701	0.9561	**0.9837**
Kar	Fou	0.9578	0.9575	0.9356	0.9699	**0.9757**
Kar	Pix	0.9654	0.9567	0.9474	0.9572	**0.9698**
Mor	Fac	0.9074	0.8784	0.8733	0.9488	**0.9772**
Mor	Fou	0.8124	0.8021	0.7933	0.8103	**0.8146**
Mor	Kar	0.8923	0.8634	0.8634	**0.9593**	0.9359
Mor	Pix	0.8773	0.8399	0.8449	**0.9639**	0.9483
Mor	Zer	0.7972	0.7744	0.7825	**0.8007**	0.7905
Zer	Fac	0.9679	0.9679	0.9588	0.9752	**0.9842**
Zer	Fou	0.8525	0.8478	0.8341	**0.8629**	0.8577
Zer	Kar	0.9571	0.9642	0.9312	0.9571	**0.9687**
Zer	Pix	0.9445	0.9426	0.9296	0.9544	**0.9623**

5   Conclusions

In this paper, we have proposed a novel supervised CCA approach for multiview image feature learning and classification, called discriminative scatter regularized CCA, which simultaneously considers the between-view correlations and within-view class label information of training samples under the regularization framework. Moreover, our method can reduce to CCA, while other variants of CCA (e.g., DCCA and LDCCA) can not. The proposed method is applied to handwritten digit image recognition. The experimental results demonstrate the superior performance of our approach, in contrast with algorithms LDCCA, RCE, DCCA, and GMLDA. A future study direction is how to theoretically determine the best parameters of our algorithm.

Acknowledgments. This work is supported by the National Science Foundation of China under Grant Nos. 61402203, 61273251, 61305017, 61170120, and the Fundamental Research Funds for the Central Universities under Grant No. JUSRP11458. Moreover, it is also supported by the Program for New Century Excellent Talents in University under Grant No. NCET-12-0881.

References

1. Long, B., Yu, P.S., Zhang, Z.: A General Model for Multiple View Unsupervised Learning. In: Proceedings of the 2008 SIAM International Conference on Data Mining (SDM), pp. 822–833 (2008)
2. Hotelling, H.: Relations between Two Sets of Variates. Biometrika **28**, 321–377 (1936)
3. Sun, Q.-S., Zeng, S.-G., Liu, Y., Heng, P.-A., Xia, D.-S.: A New Method of Feature Fusion and Its Application in Image Recognition. Pattern Recognition **38**, 2437–2448 (2005)
4. Huang, H., He, H., Fan, X., Zhang, J.: Super-resolution of Human Face Image Using Canonical Correlation Analysis. Pattern Recognition **43**, 2532–2543 (2010)
5. Hardoon, D.R., Szedmak, S.R., Shawe-Taylor, J.R.: Canonical Correlation Analysis: An Overview with Application to Learning Methods. Neural Computation **16**, 2639–2664 (2004)
6. Worsley, K.J., Poline, J.B., Friston, K.J., Evans, A.C.: Characterizing the Response of PET and fMRI Data Using Multi-variate Linear Models. NeuroImage **6**, 305–319 (1997)
7. Sun, Q.-S., Liu, Z.-D., Heng, P.-A., Xia, D.-S.: A Theorem on the Generalized Canonical Projective Vectors. Pattern Recognition **38**, 449–452 (2005)
8. Kim, T.-K., Kittler, J., Cipolla, R.: Discriminative Learning and Recognition of Image Set Class Using Canonical Correlations. IEEE Trans. on PAMI **29**, 1005–1018 (2007)
9. Sun, T.K., Chen, S.C., Yang, J.Y., Shi, P.F.: A novel method of combined feature extraction for recognition. In: Proceedings of the 8th IEEE Conference on Data Mining, pp. 1043–1048 (2008)
10. Sun, T.K., Chen, S.C., Jin, Z., Yang, J.Y.: Kernelized discriminative canonical correlation analysis. In: Proceedings of the International Conference on Wavelet Analysis and Pattern Recognition, pp. 1283–1287 (2007)
11. Peng, Y., Zhang, D., Zhang, J.: A New Canonical Correlation Analysis Algorithm with Local Discrimination. Neural Processing Letters **31**, 1–15 (2010)
12. Hardoon, D.R., Shawe-Taylor, J.R.: Sparse Canonical Correlation Analysis. Machine Learning **83**, 331–353 (2011)
13. Kim, T.K., Cipolla, R.: Canonical Correlation Analysis of Video Volume Tensors for Action Categorization and Detection. IEEE Trans. on PAMI **31**, 1415–1428 (2009)
14. Yuan, Y.-H., Sun, Q.-S., Zhou, Q., Xia, D.-S.: A Novel Multiset Integrated Canonical Correlation Analysis Framework and Its Application in Feature Fusion. Pattern Recognition **44**, 1031–1040 (2011)
15. Yuan, Y.-H., Sun, Q.-S., Ge, H.-W.: Fractional-order Embedding Canonical Correlation Analysis and Its Applications to Multi-view Dimensionality Reduction and Recognition. Pattern Recognition **47**, 1411–1424 (2014)
16. Zhang, J., Zhang, D.: A Novel Ensemble Construction Method for Multi-view Data Using Random Cross-view Correlation between Within-class Examples. Pattern Recognition **44**, 1162–1171 (2011)
17. Sharma, A., Kumar, A., Daume III, H., Jacobs, D.W.: Generalized multiview analysis: a discriminative latent Space. In Proc. IEEE Conf. on CVPR, pp. 2160–2167 (2012)
18. Chu, M.T., Watterson, J.L.: On A Multivariate Eigenvalue Problem: I. Algebraic Theory and Power Method. SIAM J. Sci. Comput. **14**, 1089–1106 (1993)

A Novel Supervised CCA Algorithm for Multiview Data Representation and Recognition

Yunhao Yuan[1,2(✉)], Peng Lu[1], Zhiyong Xiao[1],
Jianjun Liu[1], and Xiaojun Wu[1]

[1] Department of Computer Science and Technology, Jiangnan University, Wuxi, China
yyhzbh@163.com
[2] Key Laboratory of Advanced Process Control for Light Industry of Ministry of Education,
School of IoT Engineering, Jiangnan University, Wuxi, China

Abstract. In this paper, we propose a novel supervised CCA method for multiview dimensionality reduction and classification, which simultaneously considers the class information of within-view and between-view training samples. The proposed method is applied to face and general object image recognition. The experimental results on the AT&T and Yale-B face image databases and the COIL-20 object image database show our proposed algorithm provides better recognition results on the whole than existing multiview feature extraction methods.

Keywords: Image recognition · Canonical Correlation Analysis · Dimensionality reduction · Supervised learning

1 Introduction

In pattern recognition, the same objects are often described by different views. For example, an image can be expressed by different types of features; a speaker can be represented by audio and video information features; a webpage on the internet can be described by text information and its hyperlink. This kind of data is referred to as multiple view data. Since different views can reflect different statistical information of the same objects and the information is complementary each other, learning from multiview data is very meaningful in real-world classification tasks.

Proposed by Hotelling, canonical correlation analysis (CCA) [1] is a classical but still powerful tool for analyzing multiple view data, which can reveal the linear correlations between two view data. Currently, CCA has been widely used in the areas of pattern recognition and computer vision. Sun et al. [2] used CCA to fuse multiple sets of features for the first time. Specifically, this method first extracts the low-dimensional features from two groups of high-dimensional features, and then forms the discriminative feature vectors based on given fusion strategies for classification tasks. When training samples are limited or disturbed by noise, the sample covariance matrices in CCA usually deviate from the real covariance matrices. To solve this issue, Yuan et al. [3] proposed a fractional-order embedding CCA (FECCA), which

© Springer International Publishing Switzerland 2015
J. Yang et al. (Eds.): CCBR 2015, LNCS 9428, pp. 702–709, 2015.
DOI: 10.1007/978-3-319-25417-3_82

reduces the deviation of sample covariance matrices. Experimental results show that the extracted features are more discriminative than CCA.

Since CCA is a linear learning method, it can not effectively reveal the nonlinear correlations between two sets of features (views). To this end, Melzer et al. [4] proposed a kernel CCA (KCCA) approach for pose estimation, which implicitly maps the input data into potentially much higher dimensional feature vectors by using two nonlinear mappings determined by kernels. Based on the locality idea, a locality preserving CCA (LPCCA) [5] was developed, which obtains better results than CCA and KCCA in pose estimation. In essence, CCA is an unsupervised learning method. To improve the performance of CCA, Sun et al. [6] presented a generalized CCA (GCCA) method using the class information of within-set (within-view) samples. Later, Kim et al. [7] presented a discriminative learning approach of CCA for image set classification, which maximizes the canonical correlations of within-class image sets and minimizes the canonical correlations of between-class image sets. Peng et al. [8] proposed a local discriminative CCA (LDCCA) method that considers a combination of local properties and discrimination between different classes. In addition, some other supervised CCA methods [9, 10] have also been proposed.

Motivated by recent progress above, in this paper we propose a new supervised CCA method for multiview dimensionality reduction and classification. Different from GCCA and discriminative CCA (DCCA) [10] where the class information of only within-view or between-view samples is considered, our method simultaneously takes the above two kinds of information into account. The proposed method is applied to face and general object image recognition. The experimental results on the AT&T, Yale-B, and COIL-20 databases show our proposed algorithm provides better recognition results on the whole than existing multiview feature extraction methods.

2   Review of CCA

Assume n pairs of samples are given as $\{(x_i, y_i)\}_{i=1}^n$, where $x_i \in \Re^p$ and $y_i \in \Re^q$. Let $X = [x_1, x_2, \cdots, x_n]$ and $Y = [y_1, y_2, \cdots, y_n]$ be two data matrices. Assume both $\{x_i\}_{i=1}^n$ and $\{y_i\}_{i=1}^n$ are centered, i.e., $\sum_{i=1}^n x_i = 0$ and $\sum_{i=1}^n y_i = 0$. CCA aims at finding two projection vectors, $w_x \in \Re^p$ and $w_y \in \Re^q$, such that the correlation

$$\rho = \frac{w_x^T XY^T w_y}{\sqrt{w_x^T XX^T w_x} \cdot \sqrt{w_y^T YY^T w_y}}, \tag{1}$$

is maximized. Since ρ is invariant with respect to scaling of w_x and w_y, (1) can be reformulated as

$$\max_{w_x, w_y} w_x^T XY^T w_y$$
$$s.t. \quad w_x^T XX^T w_x = 1, \ w_y^T YY^T w_y = 1. \tag{2}$$

With the Lagrange multipliers technique, the solution w_x and w_y to the problem in (2) can be obtained by computing the following generalized eigenvalue problem:

$$\begin{bmatrix} & XY^T \\ YX^T & \end{bmatrix}\begin{bmatrix} w_x \\ w_y \end{bmatrix} = \lambda \begin{bmatrix} XX^T & \\ & YY^T \end{bmatrix}\begin{bmatrix} w_x \\ w_y \end{bmatrix} \tag{3}$$

where the eigenvalue λ is precisely equal to ρ. Taking the top d eigenvectors of the generalized eigenvalue problem in (3), we are able to obtain d pairs of projection directions $\{(w_{xi}, w_{yi})\}_{i=1}^{d}$, where $d \leq \min(p, q)$.

3   Approach

3.1   Motivation

As discussed in Section 1, GCCA only considers the class label information of within-view data, and DCCA merely employs the class information of between-view data. This suggests that the above two methods do not fully make use of the supervised information hidden in multiple view data. In addition, GCCA, DCCA, and some other improved CCA have actually been far away from the *original meaning of correlation*. That is, they are only the improvements of CCA and their criteria actually do not depict the correlation between two views. Motivated by the above issues, in this paper we not only simultaneously employ the class label information hidden in within-view and between-view data, but also our proposed criterion can reflect the original meaning of correlation.

3.2   Formulation

Assume n pairs of samples for c classes in all are given as $\{(x_j^{(i)}, y_j^{(i)})\}_{j=1}^{n_i} \in \Re^p \times \Re^q$, $i = 1, 2, \cdots, c$, where n_i denotes the number of pairwise training samples in class i, and $\sum_{i=1}^{c} n_i = n$, $\{x_j^{(i)}\}_{j=1}^{n_i}$ and $\{y_j^{(i)}\}_{j=1}^{n_i}$ in class i have been centered, i.e., $\sum_{j=1}^{n_i} x_j^{(i)} = 0$ and $\sum_{j=1}^{n_i} y_j^{(i)} = 0$. Let $X^{(i)} = [x_1^{(i)}, x_2^{(i)}, \cdots, x_{n_i}^{(i)}]$ and $Y^{(i)} = [y_1^{(i)}, y_2^{(i)}, \cdots, y_{n_i}^{(i)}]$, we get their images $\tilde{x}^{(i)}$ and $\tilde{y}^{(i)}$ after the projections onto projective axes $w_x \in \Re^p$ and $w_y \in \Re^q$. The intraclass correlation between $\tilde{x}^{(i)}$ and $\tilde{y}^{(i)}$ can thus be defined as

$$\rho^{(i)}(w_x, w_y) = \frac{\tilde{x}^{(i)} \tilde{y}_y^{(i)T}}{\sqrt{\tilde{x}^{(i)} \tilde{x}^{(i)T}} \cdot \sqrt{\tilde{y}^{(i)} \tilde{y}^{(i)T}}} = \frac{w_x^T X^{(i)} Y^{(i)T} w_y}{\sqrt{w_x^T X^{(i)} X^{(i)T} w_x} \cdot \sqrt{w_y^T Y^{(i)} Y^{(i)T} w_y}} \tag{4}$$

From (4), we can see that the criterion not only reveals the intraclass correlation of between-view samples, but also utilizes the intraclass scatter information (i.e., $\tilde{x}^{(i)} \tilde{x}^{(i)T}$, $\tilde{y}^{(i)} \tilde{y}^{(i)T}$, and $\tilde{x}^{(i)} \tilde{y}^{(i)T}$) of within-view and between-view samples.

Our proposed method aims at finding the pairwise projection directions, w_x and w_y, such that all the intraclass correlations between two views are simultaneously maximized. To this end, we combine all the intraclass correlations in a summing way, which leads to our optimization model as follows:

$$\max_{w_x, w_y} \sum_{i=1}^{c} \frac{w_x^T X^{(i)} Y^{(i)T} w_y}{\sqrt{w_x^T X^{(i)} X^{(i)T} w_x} \cdot \sqrt{w_y^T Y^{(i)} Y^{(i)T} w_y}} \tag{5}$$

Since the objective function of the optimization problem in (5) is invariant with respect to the scaling of w_x and w_y, (5) can be reformulated as follows:

$$\max_{w_x, w_y} \quad w_x^T \left(\sum_{i=1}^{c} X^{(i)} Y^{(i)T} \right) w_y$$

$$s.t. \quad \begin{cases} w_x^T X^{(i)} X^{(i)T} w_x = 1, \; w_y^T Y^{(i)} Y^{(i)T} w_y = 1 \\ i = 1, 2, \cdots, c. \end{cases} \tag{6}$$

3.3   Solution

To maximize the objective function of (6) under constraints, we use the Lagrange multiplier technique. The Lagrangian of the optimization problem in (6) is

$$L = w_x^T \left(\sum_{i=1}^{c} X^{(i)} Y^{(i)T} \right) w_y - \frac{1}{2} \sum_{i=1}^{c} \lambda_x^{(i)} (w_x^T X^{(i)} X^{(i)T} w_x - 1)$$

$$- \frac{1}{2} \sum_{i=1}^{c} \lambda_y^{(i)} (w_y^T Y^{(i)} Y^{(i)T} w_y - 1) \tag{7}$$

with $\lambda_x^{(i)}$ and $\lambda_y^{(i)}$ as the Lagrange multipliers, $i = 1, 2, \cdots, c$. Setting $\partial L / \partial w_x = 0$ and $\partial L / \partial w_y = 0$, we have

$$\begin{bmatrix} & S_{xy}^{(c)} \\ S_{yx}^{(c)} & \end{bmatrix} \begin{bmatrix} w_x \\ w_y \end{bmatrix} = \begin{bmatrix} \sum_{i=1}^{c} \lambda_x^{(i)} X^{(i)} X^{(i)T} & \\ & \sum_{i=1}^{c} \lambda_y^{(i)} Y^{(i)} Y^{(i)T} \end{bmatrix} \begin{bmatrix} w_x \\ w_y \end{bmatrix}, \tag{8}$$

where $S_{xy}^{(c)} = \sum_{i=1}^{c} X^{(i)} Y^{(i)T}$, $S_{yx}^{(c)} = \sum_{i=1}^{c} Y^{(i)} X^{(i)T}$, and $S_{yx}^{(c)} = S_{xy}^{(c)T}$.

Unfortunately, the problem in (8) is not a generalized eigen-equation, which is very hard and has no analytical solutions (i.e., exact solutions). This means that the optimization problem in (6) has no closed form solution in the current form. Borrowing the relaxation idea in [11], we thus couple the $2c$ constraints in (6) to obtain a relaxed version of the optimization problem with two constraints as

$$\max_{w_x, w_y} \quad w_x^T \left(\sum_{i=1}^{c} X^{(i)} Y^{(i)T} \right) w_y$$

$$s.t. \quad \sum_{i=1}^{c} \left(w_x^T X^{(i)} X^{(i)T} w_x \right) = 1, \; \sum_{i=1}^{c} \left(w_y^T Y^{(i)} Y^{(i)T} w_y \right) = 1. \tag{9}$$

Following the same approach as in (7) and (8), we obtain the following:

$$\begin{bmatrix} & S_{xy}^{(c)} \\ S_{yx}^{(c)} & \end{bmatrix}\begin{bmatrix} w_x \\ w_y \end{bmatrix} = \lambda \begin{bmatrix} S_{xx}^{(c)} & \\ & S_{yy}^{(c)} \end{bmatrix}\begin{bmatrix} w_x \\ w_y \end{bmatrix}, \tag{10}$$

where $S_{xx}^{(c)} = \sum_{i=1}^{c} X^{(i)} X^{(i)T}$ and $S_{yy}^{(c)} = \sum_{i=1}^{c} Y^{(i)} Y^{(i)T}$.

Like CCA, we select the top d eigenvectors of (10) to form two projection matrices $W_x = [w_{x1}, w_{x2}, \cdots, w_{xd}]$ and $W_y = [w_{y1}, w_{y2}, \cdots, w_{yd}]$, where $d \leq \min(p,q)$. For any given pairwise samples (x, y) with $x \in \Re^p$ and $y \in \Re^q$, we can obtain their low-dimensional embeddings by the form of $W_x^T x$ and $W_y^T y$. After feature extraction, the following strategy [2] which has been proven to be effective is adopted to combine the low-dimensional features for recognition tasks:

$$Z = \begin{bmatrix} W_x^T x \\ W_y^T y \end{bmatrix}. \tag{11}$$

3.4   Discussion

Difference with CCA. Both CCA and our method obtain two lower-dimensional spaces for multiple high-dimensional views. CCA only obtain a lower-dimensional space where the class label information is not considered, while our proposed method tries to obtain a discriminative lower-dimensional space for classification purpose, in which we simultaneously take into account the class label information hidden in within-in-view and between-view samples.

Difference with GCCA and DCCA. As mentioned before, the within-view and between-view class information is employed in our proposed algorithm, while GCCA only takes advantage of the within-view class information, and DCCA only the between-view class information. In addition, note, particularly, that our method needs to solve an abnormal generalized eigen-equation before relaxation, while both GCCA and DCCA solve a generalized eigenvalue problem, as shown in [6] and [10].

Difference with LPCCA. LPCCA is a local, unsupervised subspace learning method. Generally, its discriminant power is weak for recognition tasks, while our proposed method is a non-local, supervised subspace learning approach which can obtain more discriminative low-dimensional projections as demonstrated in Section 4.

Difference with LDCCA. Like DCCA, LDCCA only considers the class information of between-view samples in a certain local field. Also, it has two parameters and is thus time-consuming for searching for the proper parameters in practical applications, while ours has no parameter.

4   Experiments

In this section, three experiments have been performed on the popular face and object image databases. We compare the effectiveness of the proposed method with related multiview feature extraction algorithms, i.e., CCA-s [9], DCCA [10], and multi-view discriminant analysis[1] (MvDA) [12]. In all the experiments, we use two kinds of different features from original images, i.e., histogram of oriented gradient (HOG) [13] descriptor and local binary pattern (LBP) [14], and respectively reduce their dimensions to 100 using PCA for avoiding the small sample size problem.

4.1   Experiment Using the AT&T Database

The AT&T database[2] contains 400 face images from 40 persons. There are 10 grayscale images per person with a resolution of 92×112. In some persons, the images are taken at different times. The lighting, facial expressions and facial details are also varied. The images are taken with a tolerance for some tilting and rotation of the face up to $20°$, and have some variation in the scale up to about 10%.

In this experiment, N images (N = 6, 7, and 8) per person are randomly chosen for training, while the rest are used for testing. For each given N, we perform 10 independent recognition tests to evaluate the performances of CCA-s, DCCA, MvDA, and our proposed method. Table 1 shows the average recognition accuracy of each method under the nearest neighbor (NN) classifier. As we can see, our proposed method and MvDA achieve better results than CCA-s and DCCA, no matter how many training samples are used in each class. Also, our method outperforms the state-of-the-art algorithm MvDA on all cases.

Table 1. Ten-run average recognition accuracy of CCA-s, DCCA, MvDA, and our proposed method with different training sample sizes on the AT&T database.

# / class	CCA-s	DCCA	MvDA	Ours
6	0.8713	0.9631	0.9744	**0.9806**
7	0.9433	0.9767	0.9817	**0.9900**
8	0.9650	0.9875	0.9912	**1.0000**

4.2   Experiment Using the Yale-B Database

The Yale-B database [15] contains 5,760 single-light-source images of 10 individuals, each under 576 viewing conditions (9 poses × 64 illumination conditions). The extended Yale-B database [16] contains 16,128 images of 28 individuals with the same condition and data format as in the Yale-B database. In our experiment, we adopt a combinatorial subset[3] (still called Yale-B) from these two databases, which contains 2,414 images with size 32 × 32 of 38 individuals and each has around 64 near frontal images under different illuminations.

---

[1] Matlab code available at http://vipl.ict.ac.cn/resources/codes
[2] http://www.cl.cam.ac.uk/research/dtg/attarchive/facedatabase.html
[3] http://www.cad.zju.edu.cn/home/dengcai/Data/FaceData.html

In this experiment, N images (N = 6, 8, and 10) per individual are randomly selected to form the training set, and the rest are taken for the testing set. For each N, 10 test runs are performed using the NN classifier. Table 2 summarizes the average recognition results of each method. From Table 2, we can find that the proposed method outperforms CCA-s, DCCA, and MvDA. This result demonstrates again that our method is more powerful in contrast with other methods.

Table 2. Ten-run average recognition accuracy of CCA-s, DCCA, MvDA, and our proposed method with different training sample sizes on the Yale-B database.

# / class	CCA-s	DCCA	MvDA	Ours
6	0.8221	0.9410	0.9635	**0.9833**
8	0.9691	0.9646	0.9854	**0.9906**
10	0.9906	0.9788	0.9934	**0.9937**

4.3   Experiment Using the COIL-20 Database

The COIL-20 database [17] contains 1440 grayscale images of 20 objects (72 images per object) under various poses. These objects have a wide variety of complex geometric, appearance and reflectance characteristics. They are rotated through 360 degrees against a black background and taken at the intervals of 5 degrees. The size of each object image is 128 × 128 pixels.

In this experiment, N images (N = 15, 20, and 25) per class are randomly chosen for training, and the rest for testing. For each N, 10 independent classification tests are carried out using the NN classifier. Table 3 lists the average recognition results of each method. From Table 3, we can find that our method and MvDA perform better than CCA-s and DCCA. Also, our method only performs slightly worse than MvDA with 20 training samples per class, and better in other two cases.

Table 3. Ten-run average recognition accuracy of CCA-s, DCCA, MvDA, and our proposed method with different training sample sizes on the COIL-20 database.

# / class	CCA-s	DCCA	MvDA	Ours
15	0.9346	0.9504	0.9616	**0.9660**
20	0.9664	0.9680	**0.9754**	0.9753
25	0.9772	0.9764	0.9836	**0.9850**

5   Conclusions

In this paper, we propose a new supervised CCA method for multiview dimensionality reduction and classification tasks. Different from GCCA and DCCA where the class information of only within-view or between-view samples is considered, our method simultaneously takes the above two kinds of information into account. The experimental results on the AT&T, Yale-B, and COIL-20 databases show our proposed algorithm provides better results on the whole than CCA-s, DCCA, and MvDA.

Acknowledgments. This work is supported by the National Science Foundation of China under Grant Nos. 61402203, 61273251, 61305017, 61170120, and the Fundamental Research Funds for the Central Universities under Grant No. JUSRP11458. Moreover, it is also supported by the Program for New Century Excellent Talents in University under Grant No. NCET-12-0881.

References

1. Hotelling, H.: Relations between Two Sets of Variates. Biometrika **28**, 321–377 (1936)
2. Sun, Q.-S., Zeng, S.-G., Liu, Y., Heng, P.-A., Xia, D.-S.: A New Method of Feature Fusion and Its Application in Image Recognition. Pattern Recognition **38**, 2437–2448 (2005)
3. Yuan, Y.-H., Sun, Q.-S., Ge, H.-W.: Fractional-order Embedding Canonical Correlation Analysis and Its Applications to Multi-view Dimensionality Reduction and Recognition. Pattern Recognition **47**, 1411–1424 (2014)
4. Melzer, T., Reiter, M., Bischof, H.: Appearance Models Based on Kernel Canonical Correlation Analysis. Pattern Recognition **36**, 1961–1971 (2003)
5. Sun, T.K., Chen, S.C.: Locality Preserving CCA with Applications to Data Visualization and Pose Estimation. Image and Vision Computing **25**(5), 531–543 (2007)
6. Sun, Q.-S., Liu, Z.-D., Heng, P.-A., Xia, D.-S.: A Theorem on the Generalized Canonical Projective Vectors. Pattern Recognition **38**, 449–452 (2005)
7. Kim, T.-K., Kittler, J., Cipolla, R.: Discriminative Learning and Recognition of Image Set Class Using Canonical Correlations. IEEE Trans. on PAMI **29**, 1005–1018 (2007)
8. Peng, Y., Zhang, D., Zhang, J.: A New Canonical Correlation Analysis Algorithm with Local Discrimination. Neural Processing Letters **31**, 1–15 (2010)
9. Sun, T.K., Chen, S.C.: Class Label versus Sample Label-based CCA. Applied Mathematics and Computation **185**, 272–283 (2007)
10. Sun, T.K., Chen, S.C., Yang, J.Y., Shi, P.F.: A novel method of combined feature extraction for recognition. In: Proceedings of IEEE International Conference on Data Mining, pp. 1043–1048 (2008)
11. Sharma, A., Kumar, A., Daume III, H., Jacobs, D.W.: Generalized multiview analysis: a discriminative latent space. In: Proc. IEEE Conf. on CVPR, pp. 2160–2167 (2012)
12. Kan, M., Shan, S., Zhang, H., Lao, S., Chen, X.: Multi-view discriminant analysis. In: Fitzgibbon, A., Lazebnik, S., Perona, P., Sato, Y., Schmid, C. (eds.) ECCV 2012, Part I. LNCS, vol. 7572, pp. 808–821. Springer, Heidelberg (2012)
13. Dalal, N., Triggs, B.: Histograms of oriented gradients for human detection. In: Proc. IEEE Conf. on CVPR, pp. 886–893 (2005)
14. Ojala, T., Pietikainen, M., Maenpaa, T.: Multiresolution Gray-scale and Rotation Invariant Texture Classification with Local Binary Patterns. IEEE Trans. on PAMI **24**, 971–987 (2002)
15. Georghiades, A., Belhumeur, P., Kriegman, D.: From Few to Many: Illumination Cone Models for Face Recognition under Variable Lighting and Pose. IEEE Trans. on PAMI **23**, 643–660 (2001)
16. Lee, K.-C., Ho, J., Kriegman, D.: Acquiring Linear Subspaces for Face Recognition under Variable Lighting. IEEE Trans. on PAMI **27**, 684–698 (2005)
17. Nene, S.A., Nayar, S.K., Murase, H.: Columbia Object Image Library (COIL-20), Technical Report CUCS-005-96, February 1996

Facial Aging Simulation via Tensor Completion

Heng Wang, Di Huang$^{(\boxtimes)}$, Yunhong Wang, and Hongyu Yang

Laboratory of Intelligent Recognition and Image Processing,
Beijing Key Laboratory of Digital Media, School of Computer Science
and Engineering, Beihang University, Beijing 100191, China
{hengwang,dhuang,yhwang,hongyuyang}@buaa.edu.cn

Abstract. In aging simulation, the most essential requirements are (1) human identity should remain stable in texture synthesis; and (2) the texture synthesized is expected to accord with human cognitive perception in aging. In this paper, we address the problem of face aging simulation by using a tensor completion based method. The proposed method is composed of two steps. In the first stage, Active Appearance Models (AAM) is applied to facial images to normalize pose variations. In the second stage, the tensor completion based aging simulation method is adopted to synthesize aging effects on facial images. By introducing age and identity prior information in the tensor space, human identity is mostly protected during the aging procedure and proper textures are generated to simulate the aged appearance. Experimental results achieved on the FG-NET database are not only in the age as subjective expectation, but also reserve the person specific cues, which demonstrates the effectiveness of the proposed method.

Keywords: Face · Aging simulation · Tensor completion

1 Introduction

Human face aging simulation (also namely aging synthesis or aging progression) is one of the most interesting topics in computer vision and pattern recognition, and it has received increasing attention within the community in recent years. On the one hand, facial aging is a very complex process, in which facial appearance changes gradually, affected by a number of factors, such as gender, ethnicity, living environment, and so on, thereby making it a quite difficult problem that contains challenging scientific issues [1] [2]. On the other hand, it can be widely applied to many real world applications, such as forensic art, electronic customer relationship management, security control and surveillance monitoring, biometrics, entertainment, cosmetology, *etc.* [1]. For instance, it is crucial to robust face recognition systems. During human aging, facial appearance variations make negative influence on identification which can be largely improved by facial image aging simulation technologies. Additionally, it offers direct or indirect cues and substantially contributes to seeking missing children, whose photos are more likely to be recognized as progressed after years.

© Springer International Publishing Switzerland 2015
J. Yang et al. (Eds.): CCBR 2015, LNCS 9428, pp. 710–719, 2015.
DOI: 10.1007/978-3-319-25417-3_83

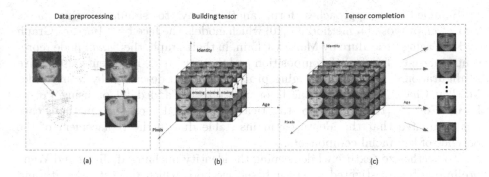

Fig. 1. Approach framework: the proposed method is composed of two steps, *i.e.*, face normalization and aging. In the first step, all the facial images are transformed to gray-scale, and then normalized to the mean template using AAM. In the second step, the tensor completion based method is adopted to simulate aging effects on the given image. (a) Image preprossing by using AAM, (b) building tensor according to age, identity, and pixel information, and (c) simulation through tensor completion.

To address the problem of simulating aging effects on human facial images, two essential requirements should be emphasized. One lies in that the simulated image is desired to be in the right age according to the perception of human beings. Another is that the identity information should be protected in the synthesized image so that they look similar, both of which decide the success of aging simulation. In the literature, various approaches have been proposed for such an issue. Early studies mainly focus on statistical model based aging simulation techniques. In [3] [4], Lanitis *et al.* presented the fundamental work, providing the basic concept and a specific solution to the problem of aging simulation. They extended the well-known Active Appearance Models (AAM) to simulate the aging effects of human faces, and designed an aging function using the AAM coefficients. This work also showed an alternative to age-invariant face recognition. Another statistical model was introduced by Ramanathan and Chellappa [5], where they analyzed shape variations when people are young and proposed an aging simulation method to handle young faces. Their method modeled the aging process according to face anthropometry, and the 'revised' cardioidal strain transformation was applied on the face profile. After that, texture clues were attempted in [6] and an improved version which considered texture and shape simultaneously was proposed. A more general shape model and the application of Poison Image Edit based texture transformation were presented in their later work [7]. 3D information proved very important to aging simulation as well. Park *et al.* [8] converted 2D images to 3D models by using simplified deformable model, and a 3D aging model composed by shape and texture aging patterns was built to model the aging process of human faces. Their simulation process was decided by specific aging function, making use of advantages both from 3D geometry and 2D texture. However, these statistical model based techniques process identity and texture cues in a single channel, and the identity component is changed in texture synthesis.

Sample-based approaches form another way to simulate aging faces. Suo *et al.* proposed a method [9] [10] which models the face by *"And/or"* Graph and the aging procedure by Markov Chain. In their graph, the *"and"* node represents coarse-to-fine face decomposition and the *"or"* node represents alternative configurations. The dynamic aging process was then described by a first-order Markov Chain. The wrinkle addition was directly added [9] or using Poison Image Edit [7] [10]. Similar to statistical model based ones, such methods cannot guarantee that the identity remains stable due to the replacement of the patches of key facial components.

To synthesize texture while keeping the identity unchanged, Jiang and Wang preliminarily investigated a tensor based method, which projects identity and age (*i.e.* texture clues) into individual directions. They claimed that facial images of high resolution and the ones of low resolution share intrinsic identity information (*i.e.* holistic configuration). Besides, high resolution images convey more details in facial appearance. As a result, they proposed an approach based on super-resolution in the tenor space. Intrinsic identity information was extracted from low resolution images, based on which aging texture was added in super-resolution. They further extended this approach by embedding AAM to reduce the blurring of the results caused by head pose variations [11]. Even though the identity is protected as illustrated by their face recognition experiment, the texture synthesized is not good enough as expected, since the mappings learned between textures of different ages are not robust.

Motivated by these facts, in this paper we propose a tensor completion based aging simulation method which synthesizes the proper texture while preserving human identity information during aging process. Tensor analysis has been applied to several application, such as face recognition [12] and texture analysis [13]. As mentioned above, in aging simulation, identity and texture can be modeled in separate components in the tensor space; therefore, we formulate a 3 order tensor to simulate aging effects on face images. Similar to [11], AAM based head pose normalization of facial images is first adopted to reduce the influence of blurring. In contrast to [11] where downsampled face images are super-resolved to the ones of higher resolution in which age related features learned from unstructured samples are added, the proposed method emphasizes the importance of the samples that possess high similarity with the test face image, to better synthesize the texture corresponding to the given age.

The remainder of the paper is organized as follows: Section 2 provides a detailed description of the proposed tensor-completion based face simulation method, and Section 3 displays and discusses the experimental results achieved on the FG-NET database [4]. Section 4 concludes the paper.

2   Tensor Completion Based Aging Simulation

In this paper, we address the problem of simulating aging effects in human face using the tensor completion method. Tensor analysis based methods have been applied to several applications due to its powerful ability of data organizing and analysing. The advantage of tensor lies in data representation and processing through multimodalities [11]. In the problem of aging simulation process, the tensor completion method considers both identity and age information at same time but in different channels. In the following section, we introduce the proposed method in detail.

2.1 Face Normalization by Using AAM

As stated in [11], the blurring in result is mainly caused by pose variations. This means that a face normalization step before aging simulation is required. Following the way in [11], all facial images in our study are normalized by using AAM [14]. The Delaunay triangulation and piecewise linear affine transformation method are adopted to warp the textures to a mean shape. After that, all face images are aligned to the same shape. This step removes spurious texture variations caused by shape differences, so that the blurring influence caused by head pose changes is reduced. The face normalization process is shown in Figure 2.

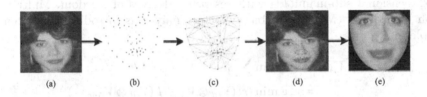

(a)   (b)   (c)   (d)   (e)

Fig. 2. Face normalization: Facial images are normalized before building tensor aging model. (a) is the original image, (b) and (c) are samples of landmarks and Delaunay triangulation respectively, (d) is visualization of Delaunay triangulation on the facial image, and (e) is face normalization result.

2.2 Tensor Completion based Aging Simulation

There are many factors which influence the human facial appearance simulation, and the major ones contributing to such a problem are identity and age. We analyze them by tensor analysis, and the tensor is constructed following the way as in [11]. Tensor structure X is used to represent the training image set. According to the fact that identity and age are major factors in aging simulation. The 3 order tensor X is constructed by using information of identity, age, and pixels:

$$X = Z \times_1 V_{Id} \times_2 V_{Ages} \times_3 V_{Pix} \tag{1}$$

where Z is the core tensor, and V_{Id}, V_{Ages}, and V_{Pix} are identity, age and pixel respectively. When the face image is modeled as a tensor, the texture is then synthesized through tensor completion. Tensor completion is a powerful tool, and its original aim is to fulfill the missing data in matrix. The completion method has been successfully applied to several scenarios, such as video image completion [13] [15], texture completion [16] and facial expression analysis [17]. However, to the best of our knowledge, it has not been investigated for the issue of aging simulation. The goal of aging simulation is to synthesize images after years. We assume that all images but one of a person are missing, and this problem can thus be transformed to a standard missing data completion work. According to the definition in [13], the tensor completion problem is formulated as follows:

Given a tensor $X_0 \in R^{I_{Id} \times I_{Age} \times I_{Pix}}$, Tensor completion tries to find a tensor X with its components $Z, V_{Id}, V_{Age}, V_{Pix}$ so that X_0 and X have the same observed entries:

$$X = Z \times V_{Id}^T \times V_{Age}^T \times V_{Pix}^T$$
$$s.t. \quad \Omega(X_0) = \Omega(X) \tag{2}$$

where Z is an nth-order tensor of the same size as X_0, and each V denotes an $I \times I$ matrix. As mentioned in [13], if we do not include any prior in the model components, the solutions of this object function are infinite. On the other hand, auxiliary relations are encoded by factor priors that lie in multiple low-dimensional sub-manifolds with restricted degrees of freedom. Multilinear graph embedding (MGE) [18] based factor analysis is introduced into tensor completion.

$$\hat{V_{Id}}, \hat{V_{Age}} = \arg \min \sum \|v^{i_{Id}, i_{Age}} - v^{j_{Id}, j_{Age}}\|_2^2 \omega_{ij}$$
$$= \arg \min tr((V_{Id} \otimes V_{Age})L(V_{Id} \otimes V_{Age})^T) \tag{3}$$

where L is Laplacian matrix, and $L = D - W$. The element of W is ω_{ij} which describes the weight of age or identity. D is diagonal matrix whose (i, i)th element is equal to $\sum_j \omega_{ij}$. After introducing factor priors into tensor completion, the problem is further transformed to the following form:

$$\hat{X}, \hat{Z}, \hat{V_{Id}}, \hat{V_{Age}}, \hat{V_{Pix}} = \arg \min \gamma \|Z\|_F^2$$
$$+ \alpha_{Id} \|V_{Id}\|_* + \alpha_{Age} \|V_{Age}\|_* + \alpha_{Pix} \|V_{Pix}\|_* \tag{4}$$
$$+ \beta tr((V_{Id} \otimes V_{Age})L(V_{Id} \otimes V_{Age})^T)$$
$$s.t. X = Z \times_1 V_{ID}^T \times_2 V_{Age}^T \times_3 V_{Pix}^T \text{ and } \Omega(X) = \Omega(X_0)$$

The algorithm can be finally optimized by inexact Augmented Lagrange Multiplier Method (IALM) [19], and more details can be found in [13].

Given a new young face image, it is used to construct a tensor without the images of other ages belonging to this identity. The tensor completion results are the simulated aged images of this person. The key problem in aging simulation is to deal with age variations for different subjects. As a result, there are two joint sub-manifolds in aging simulation. The edge of the identity sub-model between the ith face and jth face is defined as:

$$\omega_{Id}^{i,j} = \begin{cases} exp(\dfrac{-\|x_i - x_j\|_2^2}{\sigma^2}), & if\ i_k \in N(j_k)\ or\ j_k \in N(i_k), \\ 0, & otherwise \end{cases} \tag{5}$$

where ID_i is the identity index. To better synthesize the aged texture, different from the straightforward manner used in [11], we propose to emphasize the importance of the subject who has higher similarity to that of the given face image. In our case, the similarities between identity are measured by Euclidean distance. If the identity similarity is not within the first N nearest neighbor (N is found experimentally), its weight is set at 0. As age information is known as prior, the edge of age sub-model is defined as:

$$\omega_{Age}^{i,j} = \begin{cases} exp(-|i - j|), & if\ |i - j| < 2 \\ 0, & otherwise \end{cases} \tag{6}$$

where i, j is age labels. Due to the fact that age information are ordered, we can directly use such information as the priority of tensor.

3 Experimental Results

In order to evaluate the performance of the proposed aging simulation method, several experiments are carried out on the FG-NET database. The details of database, experiment setting, and results are described subsequently in this section.

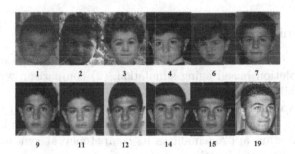

Fig. 3. Image samples of a subject from the FG-NET database [4] (The numbers below the pictures are the ages of the subject when the pictures were captured).

3.1 Database

The aging simulation experiment in this paper is conducted on the FG-NET database [4] which is the most popular database for age estimation and aging simulation. Figure 3 shows some samples of one person in the FG-NET database. It contains 1002 face images from 82 different subjects, and the age of individuals ranges from 0 to 69. The major part of the pictures are from teenagers. The image size is about 400×500. Figure 4 shows the age group distribution of the samples in the FG-NET database.

Age Range	FG-NET (%)
0-9	37.03
10-19	33.83
20-29	14.37
30-39	7.88
40-49	4.59
50-59	1.50
60-69	0.80

Fig. 4. Age distribution of images in the FG-NET database.

3.2 Experiment Setting

First, all images are divided into 5 groups according to their age labels, *i.e.* [0, 10], (10, 20], (20, 30], (30, 40], and 40+. As shown in Figure 1, each facial image is transformed to gray-scale. Then, following the way in [11], facial images are normalized by using AAM for pose correction. Finally, the images are resized to 82×82 in pixels.

Some parameters are tuned during the tensor building and tensor completion stages. To reduce the influence caused by gender, we build two individual tensors for male and female respectively. There are 48 men and 34 women in the FG-NET database, and for each person, we select the proper model to simulate aging effects. The leave one person out strategy is adopted in the aging simulation process. Any image of the test identity is excluded in the training set, and the youngest image is used as the test sample.

3.3 Aging Simulation

We analyze our experimental results in three aspects: (1) the effectiveness of the tensor completion based aging simulation, (2) comparison with the ground truth, and (3) failure analysis.

Firstly, we evaluate the effectiveness of tensor completion based aging simulation. Regarding the aging simulation as the missing data completion problem, the tensor completion approach shows its competency at synthesizing faces in different ages while reserving the person specific cues.

Secondly, the results are compared with the corresponding ground truth. From Figure 5, 6, 7, 8, we can see that aging effects appear in the synthesized images that are close to the ground truth.

Thirdly, the synthesized images are definitely not the same as their ground truth images. This phenomenon is caused by many factors, such as gene, environment, and disguise. Additionally, the quality of the synthesized images is decided by the amount of training images. The more images are used in the training set, the higher quality the synthesized images have. The uneven distribution of age groups even incurs the unsuccessful synthesis in certain ages, e.g. for the ages above 40.

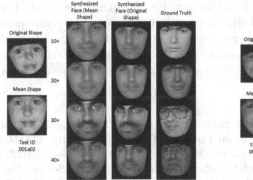

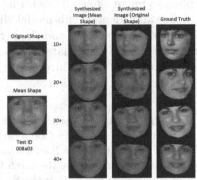

Fig. 5. Comparison between synthesized images (of mean shape and of the pose in ground truth) and ground truth images of the subject (ID 001) in the FG-NET database.

Fig. 6. Comparison between synthesized images (of mean shape and of the pose in ground truth) and ground truth images of the subject (ID 008) in the FG-NET database.

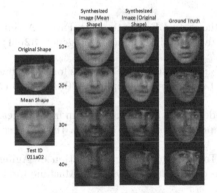

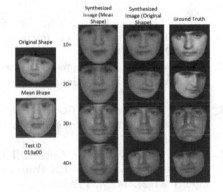

Fig. 7. Comparison between synthesized images (of mean shape and of the pose in ground truth) and ground truth images of the subject (ID 011) in the FG-NET database.

Fig. 8. Comparison between synthesized images (of mean shape and of the pose in ground truth) and ground truth images of the subject (ID 013) in the FG-NET database.

4   Conclusion

In this paper, we propose a tensor completion based method to address the aging simulation problem. In order to protect human identity during simulating aging effects on human faces, both identity and age information is considered in our framework. The proposed method is composed of two steps. In the first step, the blurring effect caused by head pose variations is reduced by AAM based preprocessing. In the second stage, tensor completion based aging simulation method is applied to make aging effects on facial images. By optimizing the object function at age and identity sub-model simultaneously but in separate components, human identity is retained and the proper texture is added. Experimental results achieved on the FG-NET database demonstrate the effectiveness of our method. In our future work, we will investigate the use of depth information, to ameliorate the result in aging simulation.

Acknowledgement. This work was supported in part by the HongKong, Macao and Taiwan Science & Technology Cooperation Program of China (No. L2015TGA9004); the National Natural Science Foundation of China (No. 61273263 and No. 61202237), the Foundation for Innovative Research Groups of the National Natural Science Foundation of China (No. 61421003); the Specialized Research Fund for the Doctoral Program of Higher Education (No. 20121102120016); the joint project by the LIA 2MCSI lab between the group of Ecoles Centrales and Beihang University; and the Fundamental Research Funds for the Central Universities.

References

1. Fu, Y., Guo, G., Huang, T.S.: Age Synthesis and Estimation via Faces: A Survey. IEEE Transactions on Pattern Analysis and Machine Intelligence **32**(11), 1955–1976 (2010)
2. Ramanathan, N., Chellappa, R., Biswas, S.: Computational Methods for Modeling Facial Aging: A Survey. Journal of Visual Languages & Computing **20**(3), 131–144 (2009)
3. Lanitis, A., Taylor, C.J., Cootes, T.F.: Modeling the process of aging in face images. In: 7th International Conference on Computer Vision, pp. 131–136. IEEE Press, Kerkyra (1999)
4. Lanitis, A., Taylor, C.J., Cootes, T.F.: Toward Automatic Simulation of Aging Effects on Face Images. IEEE Transactions on Pattern Analysis and Machine Intelligence **24**(2), 442–455 (2002)
5. Ramanathan, N., Chellappa, R.: Modeling age progression in young faces. In: IEEE Computer Society Conference on Computer Vision and Pattern Recognition, pp. 387–394. IEEE Press, New York (2006)
6. Ramanathan, N., Chellappa, R.: Modeling shape and textural variations in aging faces. In: 8th IEEE International Conference on Automatic Face & Gesture Recognition, pp. 1–8. IEEE Press, Amsterdam (2008)
7. Perez, P., Gangnet, M., Blake, A.: Poisson Image Editing. ACM Transaction on Graphics **22**(3), 313–318 (2002)
8. Park, U., Tong, Y., Jain, A.K.: Age-Invariant Face Recognition. IEEE Transactions on Pattern Analysis and Machine Intelligence **32**(5), 947–954 (2010)
9. Suo, J., Min, F., Zhou, S., Shan, S., Chen, X.: A multi-resolution dynamic model for face aging simulation. In: IEEE Computer Society Conference on Computer Vision and Pattern Recognition, pp. 1–8. IEEE Press, Minneapolis (2007)
10. Suo, J., Zhu, S., Shan, S., Chen, X.: A Compositional and Dynamic Model for Face Aging. IEEE Transactions on Pattern Analysis and Machine Intelligence **32**(3), 385–401 (2010)

11. Wang, Y., Zhang, Z., Li, W., Jiang, F.: Combining Tensor Space Analysis and Active Appearance Models for Aging Effect Simulation on Face Images. IEEE Transactions on Systems, Man, and Cybernetics, Part B: Cybernetics **42**(4), 1107–1118 (2012)
12. Vasilescu, M.A.O., Terzopoulos, D.: Multilinear analysis of image ensembles: tensorfaces. In: Heyden, A., Sparr, G., Nielsen, M., Johansen, P. (eds.) ECCV 2002, Part I. LNCS, vol. 2350, pp. 447–460. Springer, Heidelberg (2002)
13. Chen, Y., Hsu, C., Liao, H.Y.M.: Simultaneous Tensor Decomposition and Completion using Factor Priors. IEEE Transactions on Pattern Analysis and Machine Intelligence **36**(3), 577–591 (2014)
14. Cootes, T.F., Edwards, G.J., Taylor, C.J.: Active Appearance Models. IEEE Transactions on Pattern Analysis and Machine Intelligence **23**(6), 681–685 (2001)
15. Liu, J., Musialski, P., Wonka, P., Ye, J.: Tensor Completion for Estimating Missing Values in Visual Data. IEEE Transactions on Pattern Analysis and Machine Intelligence **35**(1), 208–220 (2013)
16. Liu, J., Musialski, P., Wonka, P., Ye, J.: Tensor completion for estimating missing values in visual data. In: 12th International Conference on Computer Vision, pp. 2114–2121. IEEE Press, Kyoto (2009)
17. Wang, H., Ahuja, N.: Facial expression decomposition. In: 9th International Conference on Computer Vision, pp. 958–965. IEEE Press, Nice (2003)
18. Chen, Y., Hsu, C.: Multilinear Graph Embedding: Representation and Regularization for Images. IEEE Transactions on Image Processing **23**(2), 741–754 (2014)
19. Lin, Z., Chen, M., Wu, L., Ma, Y.: The Augmented Lagrange Multiplier Method for Exact Recovery of Corrupted Low-Rank Matrices. Technical Report UILU-ENG-09-2215, Univ. of Illinois at Urbana-Champaign (2009)

Single-image Motion Deblurring Using Charbonnier Term Regularization

Zhaojing Diao, Guodong Wang$^{(\boxtimes)}$, and Zhenkuan Pan

Department of Information Engineering, Qingdao University, Qingdao, China
diaozj1223@126.com, doctorwgd@gmail.com, zkpan@qdu.edu.cn

Abstract. The blind deconvolution algorithm of motion blur image is one of very hot research in the image processing field currently. In order to get the sharp image and point spread function (PSF), variational method is used. In this paper, we select TVL2 term as data term and propose the Charbonnier term as smooth term. Normalized Charbonnier term can lead the energy decrease while solving the equation and make the energy equation get its convergence much faster. In order to reduce the complexity of the solving the equation, a fast method called Split method is introduced. Not only Charbonnier term has the strong local adaptability which can select large gradient information of the image, exclude small disturbance on the boundary and enhance the selected edges, but also it have a faster convergence speed get the sharp image and point spread function quickly. Experiments demonstrate the validity of the proposed method.

Keywords: Blind deconvolution · Variational method · Normalized charbonnier term

1 Introduction

In the 21 century, with the rapid development of the technology and the improvement of the people life, more and more digital camera appeared. Many people trend to go on a trip and take pictures for memory. However, owing to a long exposure time or hand shaking when camera shooting, most of the pictures are blur. In order to deblur these pictures, many scholars take a series of researches. Beause the kernel is uncertain previously, the procedure is called blind deconvolution. Single-image blind deconvolution is an ill-posed problem and it is one of very hot research in the image processing field currently.

There are many papers about the blind deconvolution algorithm of motion blur image at home and abroad. Chan [1] was the first one who proposed motion deblurring method using variational method. Despite the method has some generality, it does not using any priors and fitting for any real case. Fergus [2] proposed the heavy-tailed distribution of gradients as deblurring priors and the distribution of gradients in natural scenes obeys heavy-tailed distribution. On the contrary, the blurred image does not obey this rule. He also used multi-scale

© Springer International Publishing Switzerland 2015
J. Yang et al. (Eds.): CCBR 2015, LNCS 9428, pp. 720–727, 2015.
DOI: 10.1007/978-3-319-25417-3_84

framework for searching the solver which was used by the later deblurring methods. Shan [3] proposed piece-wise function to fit heavy-tailed function. Then the data terms of first derivative and second derivative were introduced into the model for ring effect reducing. Hui [4] estimated point spread function (PSF) by gradients information in frequency domain. The result only fit for motion deblurring caused by straight line. Xu [5] proposed two phase method for motion deblurring. Firstly, shock filter was used for enhancing the edges of large objects. Considering that tiny edge information may weaken the PSF, he proposed the rule of selecting useful information. If only large gradient information was used for kernel estimation, the estimated kernel has certain errors. Then he proposed a modified method for the estimated kernel. Hong [6] proposed single-image motion deblurring method using adaptive anisotropic regularization. He modified the estimated PSF by assumption of single pixel width of the motion path. Cho [7] proposed a fast motion deblurring method. Firstly the noise was removed by bilateral filtering. And then shock filter was used for enhancing the edges. Gradient selection rule was proposed for the PSF estimation and keep the gradient information which was greater than a certain threshold. Levin [8] did not propose any new algorithm but analyzed that in the procedure of deblurring the total energy is not always decreased because of the interference of tiny objects. All the methods mentioned above need auxiliary method for getting real images from blurred images. Krishnan [9] conformed that using normalized total variational term can facilitate blurring image turn into clear image. But the priors of gradients do not fit for heavy-tailed distribution. Hurley [10] compared the normalized total variational term with the other smooth term and pointed that it is superior with others. Xu [11] proposed L0 sparse expression as regularization, L0 sparse regularization is more than L1 norm in the aspects of sparsity. So the solved natural image used the method was much more clear than others. Sung [12] proposed to substitute piece-wise linear model for heavy-tailed function. The kernel function was two-dimensional parametric curve, but the piecewise-linear model was found to be an effective trade-off between flexibility and robustness. Although the kernel estimation that was solved by this method can fit the reliable blur kernel function well, it does not apply to the condition which motion blur and out-of-focus blur were co-existed. Ashwini [13] proposed the method of single image motion deblurring is new one. The method not only can estimate kernel function precisely, but also can reduce the ringing effect of edge. However, the method only fit for motion deblurring caused by straight line. Hu [14] proposed a new method that utilizes light streaks to help deblur low-light images, which can automatically detect useful light streaks in the input images and pose them as constraints for estimating the blur kernel. Both low-light images and other images can be deal with the method well. Mai [15] proposed various kernel fusion model and found that kernel fusion using Gaussian Conditional Random Fields performs better than others. The proposed method can significantly improve image deblurring by combining kernels from multiple methods into a better one. Su [16] proposed an approach that can obtain sharp and undistorted output when the input is a single rolling shutter motion blurred image. The key to the proposed method is a global modeling of the camera motion trajectory, which enables each scanline of the image to be deblurred with the corresponding motion segment.

Based on the other scholars research, we propose the Charbonnier [17] term as a new regularization term in this paper. The Charbonnier term has the strong local adaptability in selecting large gradients of the image, excluding small disturbance on the boundary and enhancing the selected edges, but also it can reduce the complexity of the algorithm and then get the sharp image and point spread function quickly. In this paper, the nonlinear diffusion term is normalized to ensure that the total energy is decreased, so that the energy equation can converge to a clear image. The algorithm avoids the disadvantages of other models, and then integrates the advantages of other models.

2   Proposed Method

Mathematical model of motion blurred image can be expressed as follows:

$$f = k * u + n \tag{1}$$

where f, k, u and n denote the observed motion blurred image, the blur kernel, the original sharp image and the noise respectively. $*$ is the convolution operation. The blur kernel function k also can be known as point spread function (PSF). Indeed, most of elements of kernel functionare zero and only the point that be on the path of movement is not zero. So it is a sparse matrix.

2.1   The Blind Deconvolution Model

In this paper, the high frequency information of the image is used to estimate the convolution kernel function and the normalized Charbonnier term is selected as the smooth term. The proposed cost function for spatially invariant blurring is:

$$E(u, k) = \int_\Omega (k * \nabla u - \nabla f)^2 \, dx + \lambda_1 \frac{\int_\Omega ch(|\nabla u|) \, dx}{\int_\Omega |\nabla u|^2 \, dx} + \lambda_2 \int_\Omega |k| \, dx \tag{2}$$

where $ch(|\nabla u|) = 2\lambda^2(\sqrt{1 + \frac{|\nabla u|^2}{\lambda^2}} - 1)$, λ is a parameter of the Charbonnier term. λ_1 is the penalty parameter of the Charbonnier term. λ_1 will be smaller when the Charbonnier term becomes larger. λ_2 is the penalty parameter of blur kernel function. The curve of estimated blur kernel function will be thinner when λ_2 becomes larger. Blur kernel function is subjected to the constrains that $k(x, y) \geqslant 0$, $\sum_{x,y} k(x, y) = 1$. The Charbonnier term is normalized to ensure that the total energy is decreased, so that the energy equation can converge to a clear image.

2.2   The Solver of the Proposed Model

Because that the equation (2) has two variables, alternating optimization method was proposed in this paper. For convenience, let $w = \nabla u$ and $v = \nabla f$, so the energy equation can be written as:

$$E(w, k) = \int_\Omega (k * w - v)^2 \, dx + \lambda_1 \frac{\int_\Omega ch(|w|) \, dx}{\int_\Omega |w|^2 \, dx} + \lambda_2 \int_\Omega |k| \, dx \qquad (3)$$

The variable w is separated and then the relative energy function becomes as follows:

$$E(w) = \int_\Omega (k * w - v)^2 \, dx + \lambda_1 \frac{\int_\Omega ch(|w|) \, dx}{\int_\Omega |w|^2 \, dx} \qquad (4)$$

Because the denominator of the above equation contains the variable, the energy equation is non convex and difficult to solve directly. But the term $\int_\Omega |w|^2 \, dx$ of the current step is approximated by using the value of last step on the iteration, so it can be deemed as a constant. The derivation of w of the equation (4) can be obtained as follows:

$$2k' * (k * w - v) + \lambda_1 \frac{ch'(|w|)}{\int_\Omega |w|^2 \, dx} \frac{w}{|w|} = 0 \qquad (5)$$

where $k'(x, y) = k(-x, -y)$, in other word k' is the centrosymmetric matrix of k. The smooth term $ch(|w|) = 2\lambda^2(\sqrt{1 + \frac{|w|^2}{\lambda^2}} - 1)$ was replaced by of the equation (5) and then the equation (6) can be obtained:

$$k' * (k * w - v) + \lambda_1 \frac{|w|}{(\sqrt{1 + \frac{|w|^2}{\lambda^2}}) \int_\Omega |w|^2 \, dx} \frac{w}{|w|} - 0 \qquad (6)$$

Using gradient-descent equation to solve the step $k + 1$ of w:

$$w^{k+1} = w^k - \Delta t(k' * (k * w^k - v) + \lambda_1 \frac{|w^k|}{(\sqrt{1 + \frac{|w^k|^2}{\lambda^2}}) \int_\Omega |w^k|^2 \, dx} \frac{w^{k+1}}{|w^{k+1}|}) \qquad (7)$$

The aboved formula use the semi-implicit scheme. So there are two items on the right side of the equation. Using soft shrinkage-thresholding, the w can be solved as follows:

$$w^{k+1} = max(abs(w^k - \Delta t \cdot k' * (k * w^k - v)) - \lambda_1 \frac{\Delta t \cdot |w^k|}{(\sqrt{1 + \frac{|w^k|^2}{\lambda^2}}) \int_\Omega |w^k|^2})$$

$$\cdot \, sign(w^k - \Delta t \cdot k' * (k * w^k - v)) \qquad (8)$$

For k, because the dimension size of w is bigger than k, it can not be solved by the Euler-Lagrange equation. The relative energy function of k is:

$$E(k) = \int_\Omega (k * w - v)^2 \, dx + \lambda_2 \int_\Omega |k| \, dx \qquad (9)$$

Subject to the constraints that $k(x,y) \geqslant 0$, $\sum_{x,y} k(x,y) = 1$. We use unconstrained iterative re-weighted least squares (IRLS) [18] followed by a projection of the resulting k onto the contraints which is setting negative elements to 0 and renormalizing. During the iterations we run IRLS for only 1 iteration, with the weights being computed from the kernel of the previous calculated k. We solve the inner IRLS system to a low level of accuracy, using a few (about 5) conjugate gradient (CG) iterations. After recovering the kernel from finest level, we threshold small elements of the kernel to zero as most blind deconvolution methods does, thereby increasing robustness to noise.

For large kernels, our method may fail because of an excessive number of w and k updates needed. To mitigate this problem, we perform multiscale estimation of the kernel using a coarse-to-fine pyramid of image resolutions as the method used in [2]. Firstly we deblur the image in coarsest level, and then the calculated kernel and latent image are upsampled as the initial value for the next finer level. The kernel size at the coarsest level is 3*3, and the number of levels is determined by the size of the kernel k using levels with a size ratio of 1.414 in each dimension between the adjacent scales. All of the resizing operations are done using bilinear interpolation.

Once the kernel k for the finest level has been estimated, we can use it to recover the latent image. We choose to use the TV model as non-blind deconvolution method, since it is fast and robust to small kernel errors. The energy function of the TV method is:

$$E(u) = \frac{1}{2} \int_{\Omega} (k * u - f)^2 \, dx + \lambda \int_{\Omega} |\nabla u| \, dx \tag{10}$$

In order to accelerate the proceeding of the sloving equation, the split Bregman is use.

3   The Experimental Results and Performance Analysis

In order to verify the validity of the proposed algorithm, we select six images with the parameters provided by the authors from the papers and compare the results of our algorithm with the algorithms mentioned in the [2], [3], [5], [7] and [9]. We select the Peak-Signal-to-Noise Ratio (PSNR) as a quality metrics of the images that are widely used in image processing to measure the image reconstruction quality. That the value of PSNR is large illustrate the quality of the restored images is good.

We compare the deblurred results of our method with results using the online code of Fergus [2] in figure 1 and 2. Figure 3 and 4 compare with the result by running code provided to us by Shan [3] and Krishnan [9]. We also compare with the result by running code provided to us by Shan [3], Xu [5], Cho [7] in figure 5. The PSNR of our method is larger than others. the above figures also show that our algorithm can obtain clearer images than others. The estimated kernel function can fit the motion path of camera shooting well. So experiments demonstrate the validity of our method.

(a)   (b)   (c)

Fig. 1. Comparison with previous deblurring methods. (a)Original blurry image. (b) Deblurred with Fergus [2]. (c) Deblurred image and recovered kernel.

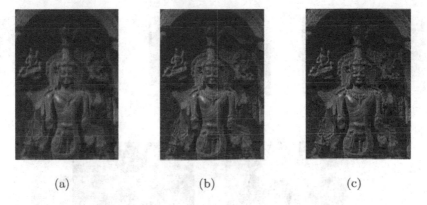

(a)   (b)   (c)

Fig. 2. Comparison with previous deblurring methods. (a)Original blurry image. (b) Deblurred with Fergus [2]. (c) Deblurred image and recovered kernel.

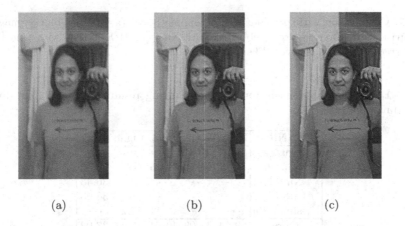

(a)   (b)   (c)

Fig. 3. Comparison with previous deblurring methods. (a)Original blurry image. (b) Deblurred with Shan [3]. (c) Deblurred image and recovered kernel.

(a)   (b)   (c)

Fig. 4. Comparison with previous deblurring methods. (a)Original blurry image. (b) Deblurred with Krishnan [9]. (c) Deblurred image and recovered kernel.

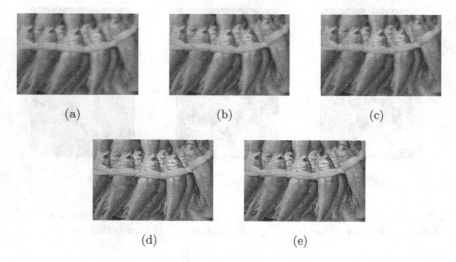

(a)   (b)   (c)

(d)   (e)

Fig. 5. Comparison with previous deblurring methods. (a)Original blurry image. (b) Deblurred with Shan [3]. (c) Deblurred with Xu [5]. (d)Deblurred with Cho [7]. (e) Deblurred image and recovered kernel.

Table 1. Visual quality measurement of deblurring results generated from different algorithms.

PSNR	Fig.1.	Fig.2.	Fig.3.	Fig.4.	Fig.5.
Fergus [2]	36.24	39.87	⋯	⋯	⋯
Shan [3]	⋯	⋯	39.26	⋯	36.02
Xu [5]	⋯	⋯	⋯	⋯	36.43
Cho [7]	⋯	⋯	⋯	⋯	36.03
Krishnan [9]	⋯	⋯	⋯	42.23	⋯
Ours	39.14	41.09	40.84	45.62	37.02

4   Conclusions

A new blind deconvolution algorithm of motion blur image was proposed in this paper. The proposed method select the Charbonnier term as the smooth term. The proposed method can restore the image and get the blur kernel well.

References

1. Chan, T.F., Wong, C.K.: Total variation blind deconvolution. IEEE Transactions on Image Processing **7**(3), 370–375 (1998)
2. Fergus, R., Singh, B., Hertzmann, A., Roweis, S.T., Freeman, W.T.: Removing camera shake from a single photograph. ACM Transaction on Graphics **25**(3), 787–794 (2006)
3. Shan, Q., Jia, J.Y., Agarwala, A.: High-quality motion deblurring from a single image. ACM Transaction on Graphics **27**(3), 731–740 (2008)
4. Hui, J., Chao, Q.L.: Motion blur identification from image gradients. In: Proc. of IEEE CVPR, vol. 1, pp. 1–8 (2008)
5. Xu, L., Jia, J.: Two-phase kernel estimation for robust motion deblurring. In: Daniilidis, K., Maragos, P., Paragios, N. (eds.) ECCV 2010, Part I. LNCS, vol. 6311, pp. 157–170. Springer, Heidelberg (2010)
6. Hong, H.Y., Park, K.: Single-image motion deblurring using adaptive anisotropic regularization. Optical Engineering **49**(9), 097008-1-13 (2010)
7. Cho, S., Lee, S.: Fast motion deblurring. ACM Transaction on Graphics **28**(5), 1451–1450 (2009)
8. Levin, A., Weiss, Y., Durand, F., Freeman, W.T.: Understanding and evaluating blind deconvolution algorithms. In: Proc. of IEEE CVPR, pp. 1964–1971 (2009)
9. Krishnan, D., Tay, T., Fergus, R.: Blind deconvolution using a normalized sparsity measure. In: Proc. of IEEE CVPR, pp. 233–240 (2011)
10. Hurley, N., Rickard, S.: Comparing measures of sparsity. IEEE Trans. Information Theory **55**(10), 4723–4741 (2009)
11. Xu, L., Zheng, S.C., Jia, J.Y.: Unnatural L0 sparse representation for natural image deblurring. In: Proc. of IEEE CVPR, pp. 1107–1114 (2013)
12. Oh, S., Kim, G.: Robust Estimation of Motion Blur Kernel Using a Piecewise-Linear Model. IEEE Transactions on Image Processing **23**(3), 1394–1407 (2014)
13. Deshpande, A.M., Patnaik, S.: Single image motion deblurring: An accurate PSF estimation and ringing reduction. Optik **125**, 3612–3618 (2014)
14. Hu, Z., Cho, S., Wang, J.: Deblurring low-light images with light streaks. In: Proc. of IEEE Conference on Computer Vision and Pattern Recognition (2014)
15. Mai, L., Liu, F.: Kernel fusion for better image deblurring. In: Proc. of IEEE CVPR, pp. 371–380 (2015)
16. Su, S.C., Heidrich, W.: Rolling shutter motion deblurring. In: Proc. of IEEE CVPR, pp. 1529–1537 (2015)
17. Charbonnier, P., Blanc-Feraud, L., Aubert, G., Barlaud, M.: Deterministic edge-preserving regularization in computed imaging. IEEE Transactions on Image Processing **6**(2), 298–311 (1997)
18. Levin, A., Fergus, R., Durand, F., Freeman, W.: Image and depth from a conventional camera with a coded aperture. ACM Transaction on Graphics **26**(3), 701–709 (2007)

Using GrCC for Color Image Segmentation
Based on the Combination of Color and Texture

Yaqiong Wang, Guimin Jia, Yihua Shi, and Jinfeng Yang[✉]

Tianjin Key Lab for Advanced Signal Processing,
Civil Aviation University of China, Tianjin, China
jfyang@cauc.edu.cn

Abstract. Color image segmentation has been a significant and challenging topic in the field of digital image processing. Due to the complexity of color images, the results of traditional segmentation based on granular computing clustering (GrCC) are often undesirable. In this paper, a new improvement approach based on granular computing (GrC) for color image segmentation is proposed. First, to increase the discriminability of pixels, a simple but effective filtering method is proposed. Then, to increase the discriminability of the content of an image, Gabor filter is used to analyze the texture information of the image. Thus, combining color and texture information, we use GrCC to process pixel clustering. Moreover, to obtain the segmentation result, an image is reconstructed by pixel cluster information. Finally, to evaluate the segmentation method objectively, the results of the proposed segmentation method are compared with the ground truth images. Extensive experiments performed on Microsoft Research (MSR) image data base have been conducted to validate the proposed method.

Keywords: Color image segmentation · Granular Computing · Texture information · Granular Computing Clustering

1   Introduction

Image segmentation is a process of affixing different labels for each pixel of an image, so that pixels with the same label are nearly homogeneous. For now, with increasing attention drawn from researchers, there have been varieties of techniques for image segmentation, such as K-means, mean shift [1], the traditional GrCC [2] and so on. However, these methods are mostly performed in color or texture space independently [3]. Segmentation methods combining color and texture are relatively new and still leave many problems to be further investigated [4]. In this paper, a new method of combing color and texture feature for color image segmentation based on GrC is proposed.

Since Zadeh first introduced the concept of GrC in 1979 [5], the basic idea of GrC is the using of information granules during complex problem solving [5,6]. Many related applications have been proposed [7-9], such as face recognition [8], image

© Springer International Publishing Switzerland 2015
J. Yang et al. (Eds.): CCBR 2015, LNCS 9428, pp. 728–735, 2015.
DOI: 10.1007/978-3-319-25417-3_85

fusion [9] and so on. These works imply that GrC is an effective way to deal with image processing, for example, color image segmentation.

Hence, in this paper, a granule represents a point corresponding to a pixel in a feature space [15]. Firstly, as the objective of segmentation is to partition an image into multiple regions [3], a simple but effective filtering method is proposed to reduce noise and increase the discriminability of pixels. Secondly, in order to improve the discriminability between pixel classes, Gabor filter is used to analyze the texture information [11,12]. Thus, combining color and orientation features, granules represent the points corresponding to pixels in the feature space. Thirdly, GrCC is used to realize pixel clustering and to obtain the final segmentation result, an image can be reconstructed by pixel cluster information. Finally, to evaluate the segmentation result of the proposed method objectively [13], images from MSR image database are used in this experiment [13]. Compare the results of segmentation with ground truth images [14], segmentation accuracy of each result is calculated. Extensive images have been tested to conduct the experiment and the results show that the proposed method yields high segmentation accuracy.

2   The Proposed Method

Segmentation based on GrC is a feature-space [17,18] based clustering. Since a hyperspherical granule represents a point corresponding to a pixel in a feature space, the granule is expressed as $G_i=(C_i, r_i)$ [15], where $C_i=(x_1, x_2, ..., x_t)$ (t is the number of features) is the center of G_i, r_i is the user-defined initial radius of G_i. Therefore, it is an important task to acquire an effective and desirable feature vector for segmentation based on GrC. In this section, we want to find some appropriate feature vectors for implementing color image segmentation effectively.

2.1   Image Filtering

Since the objective of clustering is partitioning an image into multiple regions, in order to cluster the pixels into different regions, the proposed filtering method aims at increasing the discriminability of pixels. Suppose the size of image is $M \times N$, the initial hyperspherical granule set is $GS=\{G_1, G_2,..., G_{M \times N}\}$. The detailed steps are described as follows:

Firstly, in RGB color space, each pixel has a corresponding color vector. Calculating the similarities of each pixel with its four neighboring ones using

$$sim(\vec{A_0}, \vec{A_i}) = \cos(\theta) = \frac{\vec{A_0} \cdot \vec{A_i}}{\left\|\vec{A_0}\right\|\left\|\vec{A_i}\right\|} \tag{1}$$

where $i=1,2,3,4$, $\vec{A_0}$ is the color vector of the central pixel, we can obtain the weights of the four neighboring pixels with the central one, which is expressed as w_i ($i=1,2,3,4$).

Secondly, the color vector of the central pixel is updated by Eq. (2). So, the color feature of each pixel is changed, and the center of each hyperspherical granule in GS is expressed as $C_i=(x_1, x_2, x_3)$. The filtering image is shown in Fig. 1. Moreover, the filtering image is used for the following feature extraction.

$$\vec{A_0} = \sum_{i=1}^{4} w_i \vec{A_i} \tag{2}$$

(a)Original image   (b)Filtering image

Fig. 1. The result of image filtering

2.2   Texture Feature Extraction

Since the traditional segmentation method based on GrCC is performed in RGB space [2,10], it is undesirable for the task of color image segmentation in practice. In this paper, texture feature is added to the feature vector to increase the discriminability between classes. Due to Gabor filters have been widely used to extract texture information of images, and have been verified effectively [4,11,12,16]. Orientation features are extracted using Gabor filter.

However, the value of orientation plays an important role in making Gabor filter suitable for color image segmentation [12]. To select a proper value for the orientation of Gabor filter, experiments are conducted with the Gabor filter of 4,6,8 orientations respectively, which is demonstrated in part 5. Moreover, the amplitude of each pixel is used to exploit the underlying orientation feature from the filtering image [11,12].

Thus, the feature vector is the combination of color and texture. The center of each hyperspherical granule in GS becomes $C_i=(x_1, x_2, x_3, x_4, ..., x_t)$, where $(x_4 ...x_t)$ are orientation features.

2.3   GrCC and Reconstruction

According to the initial hyperspherical granule set we have obtained from the above steps, the process of segmentation includes clustering and reconstruction.

Firstly, clustering is developed by the union operator [15] and the user-defined threshold th.

Step 1: For the initial granule set $GS=\{G_1, G_2, ..., G_{M\times N}\}$,compute the similarities between $G_1$and the rest elements in GS, which is expressed as s_{1j} $(j=2, 3, ..., M\times N)$.The fuzzy infusion measure function is used to get the similarities [2,15].

Step 2: Find the maximal similarity s_{1k}, which means G_k has the most in common with G_1. The union of G_1 and G_k is demonstrated in [15]. If the radius of the union of G_1 and G_k is less than or equal to the user-defined threshold th, the granule G_k is replaced by the union and G_1 in GS turns to zero, otherwise, G_1 is the new member of $GS1$.

Step 3: For the rest granules in GS, repeat the steps above, then $GS2=GS \cup GS1$, the non-zero elements in $GS2$ form the clustering results, which can be expressed as $ES=\{E_1, E_2, ..., E_m\}$ (m is the number of clusters).

Secondly, when every pixel finds its corresponding cluster [2], we can obtain the final segmentation result.

For the original image, each pixel is represented by a granule, which is corresponded to the point the pixel mapped in RGB space. So the granule set of an original image can be expressed as $G=\{g_1, g_2, ..., g_{M \times N}\}$. For each granule in G, we can compute its similarity with each cluster in ES, the cluster that has the maximal similarity with the granule denotes the cluster is corresponded to the pixel [2]. Therefore, the pixel color of an original image can be rendered using the number of color clusters. Thus, different clusters of the segmented image can be represented by different colors.

3   Evaluation of Segmentation

To evaluate the performance of the proposed method objectively, ground truth segmentation is used as a standard to compare with the segmentation result. Take Fig. 2(a) for example, the detailed steps are demonstrated as follows:

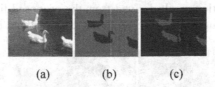

(a)   (b)   (c)

Fig. 2. Segmentation result based on the proposed method (a) Original image (b) Ground truth segmentation (c) Segmentation result based on the proposed method

Step 1: Different clusters of ground truth image and segmentation result are shown in Fig. 3.

(a)   (b)

Fig. 3. Results of different clusters (a) Different clusters of Ground truth image (b) Different clusters of segmentation result

Step 2: According to Fig. 3, we can find the images with the same label. For example, the first cluster in Fig. 3(a) and Fig. 3(b), matching the two images, the number of pixels which are wrong classified can be computed. As to the last cluster in Fig. 3(a), the number of 1 in the matrix of its corresponding binary image is the number of the wrong classified pixels.

Step 3: Until all the clusters are involved in calculating the number of wrong classi-fied pixels, which are expressed as n_i (i=1, 2, ..., m, m is the number of clusters), the total number of the wrong classified pixels is computed by Eq. 3. The accuracy is achieved by Eq. 4.

$$F = \frac{1}{2} \times \sum_{i=1}^{m} n_i \qquad (3)$$

$$E = 1 - \frac{F}{M \times N} \qquad (4)$$

4   Experiments and Analysis

To evaluate the performance of the proposed segmentation method based on GrC, images from MSR image database is used in this experiment.

4.1   Filtering Analysis

To illustrate the effectiveness of the proposed filtering method, we select an image to compare the segmentation result derived from the proposed filtering method with the classical median filtering and the segmentation result without filtering.

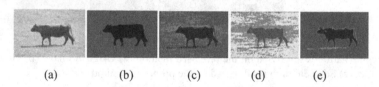

(a)   (b)   (c)   (d)   (e)

Fig. 4. Segmentation Results of different filtering methods (a) Original image (b) Ground truth image (c) Segmentation result without filtering (d) Segmentation result of median filtering (e) Segmentation result of the proposed filtering method

Table 1. Performance of different filtering method

Filtering method	Without filtering	Median filtering	The proposed filtering
Accuracy (%)	79.52	59.31	92.51

It can be seen from Fig. 4 that the segmentation result of the proposed filtering me-thod distinguishes the object and the background obviously, however, the other two segmentations only identify part of the grasses, including many noises. Because the proposed filtering method reduces the discriminative of pixels which belong to one cluster and increases the discriminative of pixels between clusters. The accuracy shown in Table1 proves the superiority of the proposed filtering method.

4.2   The Value of Orientation Selection

To select the most appropriate value of orientation for Gabor filter, an color-texture image from Microsoft Research Database is selected to perform the experiment on Gabor filter with 4,6,8 orientations respectively.

(a)   (b)   (c)   (d)   (e)   (f)

Fig. 5. Segmentation results of different values of orientation (a) Original image (b)Ground truth segmentation (c) The traditional segmentation based on GrC (d-f) The segmentation results of the proposed method with Gabor filter of 4,6,8 orientations respectively

Table 2. Performance of different values of orientation

Orientation	0	4	6	8
Accuracy (%)	70.52	93.24	87.14	65.41

In Table 2, when the Gabor orientation is 0, the result corresponds to the traditional GrCC. Comparing (c) with (b,d-f) in Fig. 5, we can conclude that the segmentation without considering texture information performs the worst, because it is difficult to distinguish sky and grass in this image only using color information, this illustrates adding orientation features is helpful for color image segmentation. Moreover, as is shown in Table 2, when the Gabor orientation is 4, the performance of segmentation is much better than the other two. Because the more orientations, the more meticulous the image is segmented. Thus, there are many pixels which should share the same label clustered into different classes, such as the image Fig. 5(f), which leads to low segmentation accuracy.

4.3   Segmentation Results Analysis

To verify the superiority of our method, we compare the proposed segmentation method with the traditional GrCC, K-means and Mean-shift. The results are demonstrated as follows:

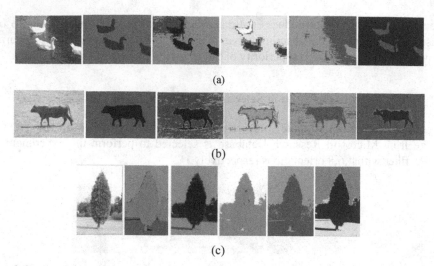

(a)

(b)

(c)

Fig. 6. Segmentation results. (From left to right: Original image, Ground truth image, Segmentation results of tradition GrCC, mean shift, k-means, and the proposed GrCC) (a) Img1. (b) Img2. (c) Img3.

Table 3. Performance of different segmentation methods

Image	Traditional GrCC(%)	Mean-shift(%)	K-means(%)	The proposed GrCC(%)
Img1	82.48	84.99	56.41	95.81
Img2	79.67	83.82	90.95	92.51
Img3	70.52	67.74	70.93	93.24

From Fig. 6, we can see that the proposed method is more accurate in segmentation. Moreover, for all these images, the proposed method distinguishes the objects and background completely. The final segmentation results of the proposed method are the closest to ground truth segmentations. In Table 3, we present the performance of different segmentation method, which shows that compared to segmentation of K-means, Mean-shift and the traditional GrCC for each image, the proposed method achieves the best accuracy.

5   Conclusion and Future Work

A novel approach using GrCC for color image segmentation based on the combination of color and texture was proposed in this paper. First, to increase the discriminative of pixels, a new filtering method was proposed. Secondly, to increase the discriminative of the content of an image, Gabor filter was used to analyze the texture information. The feature vector was composed by the combination of color and four-orientation feature. Thirdly, the process of clustering was based on GrCC. Finally, Ground truth image was used as a standard to evaluate the performance of segmentation. The experimental results showed that the proposed method yielded high accuracy in color image segmentation. However, there still left many problems to be solved, such as the threshold was different for each image, it will be more convenient and effective if the threshold is self-adaptive.

Acknowledgements. This work is jointly supported by National Natural Science Foundation of China (Nos.61379102, U1433120) and the Fundamental Research Funds for the Central Universities (No. 3122014C003).

References

1. Liu, L.X., Tan, G.Z., Soliman, M.S.: Color image segmentation using mean shift and improved ant clustering. Springer **19**, 1040–1048 (2012)
2. Liu, H.B., Li, L., Wu, C.A.: Color Image Segmentation Algorithms based on Granular Computing Clustering. International Journal of Signal Processing and Pattern Recognition **7**(1), 155–168 (2014)
3. Yan, Y.X., Shen, Y.B., Li, S.M.: Unsupervised color-texture image segmentation based on a new clustering. In: International Conference on New Trends in Information and Service Science (2009)
4. Tao, W., Canagarajah,.N.: Multiscale color-texture image segmentation with adaptive region merging. In: IEEE ICASSP (2007)
5. Yao, J.T., Vasilakos, A.V., Pedrycz, W.: Granular Computing: Perspectives and Chal-lenges. IEEE Transactions on Cybernetics **43**(6), 1977–1989 (2013)
6. Miao, D.Q., Wang, G.Y., Liu, Q.: Granular computing: past, present and prospect (in Chinese). Science Publishing House, Beijing (2007)
7. Zheng, Z., Hu, H., Shi, Z.Z.: Tolerance granular space and its applications. In: IEEE International Conference on Granular Computing, pp. 367–372 (2005)
8. Bhatt, H.S., Bharadwaj, S., Singh, R., Vatsa, M.: Recognizing Surgically Altered Face Images using Multi-objective Evolutionary Algorithm. IEEE Transactions on Information Forensics and Security **8**, 89–100 (2013)
9. Li, Z.G., Meng, Z.Q.: Technique of medical image fusion based on tolerance granular space (in Chinese). Application Research of Computers **27**(3), 1192–1194 (2010)
10. Li, W.H.: Color Image Segmentation Algorithm Based on Spherical Granular Computing. Journal of Xinyang Normal University Natural Science Edition **27**(2) (2014)
11. Yang, J., Shi, Y., Yang, J.: Finger-vein recognition based on a bank of gabor filters. In: Zha, H., Taniguchi, R.-I., Maybank, S. (eds.) ACCV 2009, Part I. LNCS, vol. 5994, pp. 374–383. Springer, Heidelberg (2010)
12. Yang, J.F., Shi, Y.H., Wu, R.B.: Finger-Vein Recognition Based on Gabor Features. Biometric Systems, Design and Applications, 17–33 (2011). In Tech, ISBN 978-953-307-542-6
13. Ranjith, U., Croline, P.: Toward Objective Evaluation of Image Segmentation Algorithms. IEEE Transactions on Pattern Analysis and Machine Intelligence **29**(6) (2007)
14. Meila, M.: Comparing clustering—an information based distance. Journal of Multivariate Analysis **98**, 873–895 (2007)
15. Liu, H.B.: Research on Multi-objective Granular vector machines and their applications. Wuhan University of Technology (2011)
16. Jesmin, F.K., Reza, R.A., Sharif, M.A.B.: Color image segmentation utilizing a customized gabor filter. IEEE (2008)
17. Farmer, M.E., Jain, A.K.: A wrapper-based approach to image segmentation and classification. IEEE Transaction on System, Man, and Cybernetice-Part b: Cybernetics **35**(1), 44–53 (2005)
18. Makrogiannis, S., Economou, G., Fotopoulos, S.: A region dissimilarity relation that combines feature-space and spatial information for color image segmentation. IEEE Transactions on Systems, Man, and Cybernetixs-Part b: Cybernetics **35**(1), 44–53 (2005)

Author Index

Printed in the United States
By Bookmasters